THE ARCHAEOLOGY OF JAPAN

This is the first book-length study of the Yayoi and Kofun periods of Japan (c. 600 BC–AD 700), in which the introduction of rice paddy field farming from the Korean peninsula ignited the rapid development of social complexity and hierarchy that culminated with the formation of the ancient Japanese state. The author traces the historical trajectory of the Yayoi and Kofun periods by employing cutting-edge sociological, anthropological, and archaeological theories and methods. The book reveals a fascinating process through which sophisticated hunting-gathering communities in an archipelago on the eastern fringe of the Eurasian continent were transformed materially and symbolically into a state.

Dr. Koji Mizoguchi is Professor of Social Archaeology, Graduate School of Social and Cultural Studies, Kyushu University, Japan. He is the author of *An Archaeological History of Japan: 30,000 BC to AD 700* (2002) and *Archaeology, Society and Identity in Modern Japan* (2006). Dr. Mizoguchi is regarded as a leading Japanese archaeologist, particularly in the study of the Yayoi period and mortuary archaeology. His many contributions to scholarly journals focus on the postcolonial archaeologies of East Asia with special emphasis on Japan, the relationship between modernisation and the disciplinisation of archaeology, mortuary practices and the constitution of social identities, and the study of the centralisation and hierarchisation of social relations by using formal network analysis methods. He was elected the sixth president of the World Archaeological Congress in January 2013.

CAMBRIDGE WORLD ARCHAEOLOGY

SERIES EDITOR
NORMAN YOFFEE, *University of Nevada, Las Vegas*

EDITORIAL BOARD
SUSAN ALCOCK, *Brown University*
TOM DILLEHAY, *Vanderbilt University*
TIM PAUKETAT, *University of Illinois*
STEPHEN SHENNAN, *University College London*
CARLA SINOPOLI, *University of Michigan*
DAVID WENGROW, *University College London*

The Cambridge World Archaeology series is addressed to students and professional archaeologists, and to academics in related disciplines. Most volumes present a survey of the archaeology of a region of the world, providing an up-to-date account of research and integrating recent findings with new concerns of interpretation. While the focus is on a specific region, broader cultural trends are discussed and the implications of regional findings for cross-cultural interpretations considered. The authors also bring anthropological and historical expertise to bear on archaeological problems and show how both new data and changing intellectual trends in archaeology shape inferences about the past. More recently, the series has expanded to include thematic volumes.

RECENT BOOKS IN THE SERIES

MIKE SMITH, *The Archaeology of Australia's Deserts*
LI LIU AND XINGCAN CHEN, *The Archaeology of China*
STEPHEN D. HOUSTON and TAKESHI INOMATA, *The Classic Maya*
PHILIP L. KOHL, *The Making of Bronze Age Eurasia*
LAWRENCE BARHAM AND PETER MITCHELL, *The First Africans*
ROBIN DENNELL, *The Palaeolithic Settlement of Asia*
CHRISTOPHER POOL, *Olmec Archaeology and Early Mesoamerica*
SAMUEL M. WILSON, *The Archaeology of the Caribbean*
RICHARD BRADLEY, *The Prehistory of Britain*
LUDMILA KORYAKOVA AND ANDREJ EPIMAKHOV, *The Urals and Western Siberia in the Bronze and Iron Ages*
DAVID WENGROW, *The Archaeology of Early Egypt*
PAUL RAINBIRD, *The Archaeology of Micronesia*
PETER M. M. G. AKKERMANSA AND GLENN M. SCHWARTZ, *The Archaeology of Syria*
TIMOTHY INSOLL, *The Archaeology of Islam in Sub-Saharan Africa*

CAMBRIDGE WORLD ARCHAEOLOGY

THE ARCHAEOLOGY OF JAPAN: FROM THE EARLIEST RICE FARMING VILLAGES TO THE RISE OF THE STATE

KOJI MIZOGUCHI

CAMBRIDGE
UNIVERSITY PRESS

CAMBRIDGE
UNIVERSITY PRESS

University Printing House, Cambridge CB2 8BS, United Kingdom

One Liberty Plaza, 20th Floor, New York, NY 10006, USA

477 Williamstown Road, Port Melbourne, VIC 3207, Australia

314-321, 3rd Floor, Plot 3, Splendor Forum, Jasola District Centre, New Delhi-110025, India

79 Anson Road, #06-04/06, Singapore 079906

Cambridge University Press is part of the University of Cambridge.

It furthers the University's mission by disseminating knowledge in the pursuit of education, learning and research at the highest international levels of excellence.

www.cambridge.org
Information on this title: www.cambridge.org/9780521711883

First published 2013
First paperback edition 2017

A catalogue record for this publication is available from the British Library

Library of Congress Cataloging in Publication data
Mizoguchi, Koji, 1963– author.
The archaeology of Japan : from the earliest rice farming villages to the rise of the state/Koji Mizoguchi.
    pages   cm. – (Cambridge world archaeology)
Includes bibliographical references and index.
ISBN 978-0-521-88490-7 (hardback)
1. Yayoi culture – Japan.   2. Neolithic period – Japan.   3. Japan – Antiquities.   I. Title.
GN776.2.Y3M59   2013
952′.01–dc23   2012037616

ISBN 978-0-521-88490-7 Hardback
ISBN 978-0-521-71188-3 Paperback

for Hiromi,

and

everyone and every thing I loved/love

.

CONTENTS

FIGURES

TABLES

PREFACE AND ACKNOWLEDGEMENTS

Writing about what was going on in a temporal segment of the past of a modern nation-state is an impossible task. Or one might say that it is only made possible by accepting artificiality and arbitrariness creeping in. A modern nation-state is a created entity, and its boundaries have been drawn, redrawn, taken for granted, and disputed in order to hold those who live within them together, or at times to split them apart. The boundaries work as filters to choose who and what can come inside, and they are there to be referred to when those who dwell inside the nation-state identify who they are and who they are *not*. And writing about what has been going on in the inside, in any manner and intension, is bound to "reproduce" the boundaries; if one accepts them as taken for granted, so it would; and if one tries to dispute their validity, authenticity, significance, and so on, still so it would, because it would evoke claims for and against, and as a result reinforce their presence in the mind of those who become aware of the problems concerning them.

However, such history still has to be written, or so I believe, because we all were born into a nation-state, fully 'functioning' or otherwise, which is meant to protect and further our rights, and constitute and determine, to a significant degree, how we live, die, and are remembered/forgotten. Therefore, the nation-state matters a great deal, thinking about it matters a great deal, imagining how it can be otherwise matters a great deal, and therefore, to think about how 'it' has come about, despite this 'it' being an artificial, arbitrary, and specific-value-committed entity, matters a great deal to us.

In that sense, books like this have to be written in the manner which illustrates the range of ways in which a nation-state's history has been investigated and written, and which explicitly reveals how the author thinks about it, engages with it, and imagines how it can be otherwise. That is the intension which I have been keeping with myself throughout my writing of this book about the supposed 'critical phases' of the history of Japan: the Yayoi and Kofun periods.

The Yayoi period witnessed the introduction and establishment of rice paddy field agriculture, and the Kofun period saw the construction of a large number of keyhole- and variously shaped tumuli, some of which are truly gigantic. Naturally, the periods have attracted significant scholastic interest and evoked popular imagination concerning how the ancient Japanese 'state' emerged. The mythological origin of the imperial family, depicted in the two oldest imperial chronicles, namely, the *Kojiki* and the *Nihonshoki*, is 'regarded' by many Japanese people, albeit ambiguously but firmly, to have marked not only the origin of the Japanese 'race' but also the beginning of the basic traits of the uniquely Japanese lifeways and customs, and, those constitutive components of 'Japaneseness' are regarded to be traced back to those periods. As we will see later in the volume in detail, the legal status of the emperor in the current constitution, that is, the Constitution of Japan, is the symbol of the integration of the nation, and in the previous one, that is, the Constitution of the Empire of Japan, was a sort of absolute sovereign. It is well known that the emperor's legal status was abused during World War II and the Asian-Pacific War, which brought immense devastation and suffering to the neighbouring countries such as China and Korea as well as Japan itself. Because of that, the basic elements of the 'Japaneseness', both positive and negative, are also regarded to have their origins traced back to those periods. That implies that the origins and sources of the failures and successes of the Japanese nation can be found in those periods, and, accordingly, the study of the periods has been the arena of both scholastic and popular debates concerning the (good and bad) origin(s) of the Japaneseness.

Naturally, the study of the periods has confined itself to the investigation of such issues, and has not necessarily been aware of or had its wider potential recognised, such as the possibility of making contributions to the deepening of the study of the emergence and development of social complexity and state formation. Consequently, the periods have not attracted as much international interest as the Jomon period, the era of 'affluent foragers', does.

This volume is meant to change the situation by illustrating for the international audience the potential and excitement of the study of the Yayoi and Kofun periods. I shall not pretend to be thorough in the coverage of the available evidence, the topics previously covered, and the models and interpretations previously proposed; the richness of the scholarship and the amount of the evidence accumulated are simply staggering. I also admit that the evidence analysed is considerably biased to western Japan, where a larger number of the phenomena that are related to causes of the changes took place. (I have to admit that it is also significantly due to my familiarity with the data from western Japan.) Admitting these shortcomings, I shall focus on being as explicit as possible about the framework with which I choose the evidence, the methods to analyse them, and the theory to make sense of/interpret the outcomes. I shall also avoid reproducing established Japaneseness narratives by focussing on the unique contextuality in which the individual was situated when she or he was engaged in communications with the others and the contingency generated by it. By drawing upon the theory of social systems and communication proposed by the late Niklas Luhmann, the German sociologist, I shall recognise communication as the basic unit of social phenomena and the basic arena in which sociality is reproduced, and I shall try to describe the historical trajectory of the periods as the trajectory through which the material media and structure of communication were transformed in order to react to changes generated within and outside a given field of communication/a communication system. By doing so, I shall ensure that the picture I present can be compared with preexisting general models on the emergence and development of social complexity and state formation and with cases from various parts of the world.

I learnt archaeology in Japan and the United Kingdom, and I have been made to see what I am doing as a form of 'mimicry': in order to communicate about and do archaeology with my colleagues in Japan, I tacitly but strongly feel that I have to conform to the expectations my colleagues have of me; and the same happens with my colleagues abroad. This makes my attitude to Japan, and the ways in which I see that archaeology is done in this country, chronically oscillate, at times violently. That, I think, is a cause of my being obsessed with theorisation, which at least allows me to pin down the framework through which I observe how I oscillate.

I have been extremely fortunate to have many colleagues and friends, in Japan and abroad, who have tolerated my oscillation and obsession, and who have provided me with various kinds of support when I felt lost. I would particularly like to thank my colleagues in Kyushu University, Yoshiyuki Tanaka, Shozo Iwanaga, Kazuo Miyamoto, Jun'ichiro Tsujita, Takahiro Nakahashi, Ren'ya Sato, Yoshinori Tajiri, and Kyoko Funahashi for providing me with an excellent research and teaching environment; Sander van der Leeuw, Gina Barnes, Ian Hodder, Colin Renfrew, Simon Kaner, and Julian Thomas for their academic and personal mentorship and friendship; and Norman Yoffee for understanding, supporting, and encouraging me throughout the process of the writing of this volume and being extremely patient. My wife, Hiromi, has always been with me and shared with me all good and bad times.

For various influences on the way I do archaeology and stimulations to the way in which I wrote the volume, I would like to thank the late Koichi Yokoyama, the late Takato Kojima, the late Takashi Okazaki, the late Yoshiro Kondo, the late Peter Ucko, the late Bruce Trigger, the late Yukio Matsunaga, Tadashi Nishitani, Hitoshi Fujita, Fujio Oda, Nobuyuki Shimojo, Hiroaki

Takakura, Jun'ichi Takesue, Hiroshi Tsude, Tatsuo Kobayashi, Hideji Harunari, Seigo Wada, Takao Uno, Takanobu Sawashita, Koichi Sugimura, Kenji Tsutsumi, Kenji Takaku, Kim Jaehyun, Takeshi Ishikawa, Yudai Itakura, Shimpei Hashino, Yoshinori Ozawa, Yoshinori Hira, Tomoko Ishida, Ari Tanizawa, Yoshitaka Hojo, Yasuyuki Murakami, Hisao Kuwabara, Shoji Morishita, Yoshiro Watanabe, Yoshiro Miyai, Motoji Doi, Motoki Yamada, Kazuaki Yoshimura, Yoshiki Fukasawa, Hideto Morioka, Kaoru Terasawa, Hideshi Ishikawa, Hiromi Shitara, Shin'ya Fukunaga, Takehiko Matsugi, Yasunobu Ikeda, Yukio Sato, Eitaro Suga, Kunihiko Wakabayashi, Hiromichi Ando, Yoichi Kawakami, Katsunori Takase, Hiroshi Yoshida, Takeo Kusumi, Hitoshi Fujii, Koji Araki, Hitoshi Shimogaki, Ken'ichi Yano, Katsuyuki Okamura, Yumiko Ogawa, Ikuko Toyonaga, Nobiru Notomi, Katsuhiro Nishinari, Mark Edmonds, Michael Shanks, Marie Louise Sorensen, John Barrett, Mike Parker-Pearson, Ian Bapty, J.D. Hill, John Carman, Jonathan Last, Gavin Lucas, Brian Boyd, Joe Kovacik, Sarah Tarlow, Lesley MacFadyen, Mark Lake, Joshua Pollard, Claire Smith, Robert Preucel, Cornelius Hortolf, Stephaney Koerner, Stephen Shennan, Kristian Kristiansen, Anthony Harding, Timothy Dervil, Greham Barker, Richard Bradley, John Bintliff, Martin Carver, Paul Garwood, and Keith Ray.

Last but not least, I would also like to thank everyone who excavated and published the traces of human lives from the periods that this volume covers; without their toil, the past cannot materially prove its existence.

Parts of Chapter 8 were based upon my article 'Nodes and edges: A network approach to hierarchisation and state formation in Japan' *Journal of Anthropological Archaeology*, 28(1) 1:14–26.

What I feel with particular poignancy now is that what you are is what you have loved, that is, people, their works, and their ways to live their lives, and all sorts of things, smells, touches, goods, buildings, landscapes, and so on. This work is composed of what I have loved, and particularly of the memories I have of them. I dedicate the book to those who have been and things and matters that have been with me and dwelled and/or been etched in my ever-changing and, in a way, growing, memory, that enabled me to endure and finish writing this book.

Koji Mizoguchi
Fukuoka, Japan
March 2012

PART I

FRAMEWORKS

CHAPTER 1

INTRODUCTION: THE BEGINNING
OF EVERYTHING?

Paddy fields, shining golden under the crisp early autumn sunshine, extend as far as the plains stretch, finally meeting the surrounding mountain range. The terrain is dotted with hamlets of thatched houses, with dragonflies hovering. Although there are few human figures in sight, the air is filled with signs of life. At one time, such a scene could be seen almost everywhere in the Japanese archipelago, except for its northern- and southernmost regions. Today, however, such scenes are things of the past. For the majority of the Japanese, these scenes only live on in their nostalgic memories. For the young, the image described earlier may well be one which can only be accessed virtually, through photographs they might encounter in magazines and on websites or experience in the form of tailor-made digital presentations in museums. Rice paddies used to be a constituent element of the lifeworld of the Japanese until only four or five decades ago. Back then, approximately 43 per cent of the Japanese population was still involved in farming.[1] In addition, in the case of those who either chose to or were compelled to work in commercial or industrial towns – many of which were on the road to recovery from the devastation caused by the U.S. bombings during the final phase of World War II – most regularly returned to their own agricultural villages and towns, which enjoyed an island-like existence in a sea of paddy fields, in order to celebrate annual festivities (the *Bon*, 盆, a period in the month of August, and the *Shogatsu*, 正月, in the beginning

of the year) and reconfirm their bonding with their extended families.

Rice paddies were not merely places where people performed the laborious task of farming. They were also a habitat wherein people mingled with nature; in early summer, when the paddies were irrigated for the planting and initial cultivation of rice, fishes and insects came to lay eggs in these paddies. Herons and other birds came to the paddy fields in order to feed on these creatures (see Kaku 1997). In summer and early autumn, dragonflies gathered and flew over them, while even deer and wild boar occasionally came down from surrounding hills, sometimes doing some damage to the growing rice plants as well as paddies. Rice paddy field farming during summer is all about battling weeds, and farmers have to toil very hard to get rid of them under the scorching rays of the harsh summer sun. Farmers spend long hours working in the paddies during the rice plant's period of growth, that is, between June and September, and therefore, they also end up spending a considerable amount of time with the previously mentioned animals, small creatures and weeds.[2]

Rice itself is a living being: it is born in spring, grows throughout summer and ripens and is reaped (i.e. dies) in autumn. Rice grains, however, preserve the source of life somehow, and with the coming of the next spring, they are resurrected again. Hence, rice repeats the cycle of life and death every year – a cycle experienced by the majority of the population in the past. In this

---

[1] According to the 1946 census, the farming population was 34,137,272, and according to the 1947 census, the population of Japan was 78,101,473. Statistical Bureau of the Ministry of Internal Affairs and Communications, http://www.stat.go.jp.

[2] Some of these creatures constituted the core of the pictorial representations of the Yayoi period, appearing on *Dotaku* bronze bells, bronze daggers, burial jars, pots and so on. I will return to them in Chapter 6.7.2.

way, rice was an important medium through which people in the past could seek to comprehend and cope with life and mortality (e.g. Ohnuki-Tierney 1993).

All these little dramatic scenes were played out in locales created by the collaborative work of people, and the collaboration itself involved human drama, competition, conflict, sacrifice, anger and reconciliation. Many social relations were generated and reproduced in these locales.

In short, rice paddies, until the 1960s or 1970s, constituted an essential feature of the land of Japan.[3] In other words, their presence was powerful enough to make the majority of Japanese people believe that rice paddies were the chief symbol of Japan. In fact, Japan was even described as *Toyoashihara-mizuho-no-kuni* (豊芦原瑞穂国, the land of fertile marshes yielding abundant rice grains).[4] Considering this description, it is not very surprising to note that the feeling of unique attachment to rice paddy field agriculture persists in the minds of Japanese people long after they have actually stopped working on the rice paddies themselves.

Systematic rice paddy field agriculture, which means the *socio-technological complex* consisting of (a) the technique of constructing and maintaining paddies and their irrigation systems; (b) the materials required for cultivating, harvesting, processing, preserving and consuming rice; and (c) the various norms and symbolic devices that enable and maintain a rice-agriculture-based lifestyle, was introduced to the archipelago at some point during the first millennium BC.[5] Japanese archaeologists

refer to the period between its introduction and the emergence and spread of the custom of burying the elite in keyhole-shaped mounds as the 'Yayoi' (弥生) period.

The name is derived from the place in Tokyo where the first acknowledged example of pottery from the period was excavated (Figure 1.1).[6] The word *Yayoi* also represents the month of March in Old Japanese. March, in Japan, is widely regarded as the first month of spring. The Yayoi period ushered in many things that have become an integral part of Japan's historical identity. This peculiar coincidence only contributes to the widespread belief that the Yayoi period marks an important stage or, in fact, represents the beginning of the history of Japan.[7]

The Kofun (古墳, which means 'mounded tomb') period that followed the Yayoi period is also regarded as a period of new beginnings – in this case, the beginning of the imperial reign. The imperial system (*Ten'no* [天皇, emperor] *sei* [制, system]) and its allegedly uninterrupted longevity (*bansei* [万世, ten thousand generations] *ikkei* [一系, single inheritance line]) are widely regarded as another decisive trait of Japan. As discussed subsequently, the emperor and the imperial genealogy played a vital role in the formation of the modern nation-state of Japan in the nineteenth century. Critics of the imperial system have regarded it as the root cause of the inherent ills in modern Japan; they also hold it responsible for its self-destruction as well as the suffering inflicted on the people of neighbouring nations (most notably China and Korea) in World War II (e.g. Mizoguchi 2010b). In addition, the current Japanese Constitution (The Constitution of the State of Japan, 日本国憲法), drawn up after the end of World War II,[8] defines the emperor as the 'symbol of the integration of the nation'.[9] This is a downgrading of the emperor's status from that of the constitutional absolute sovereign in the pre-war Constitution

3 Of course, we must neither dismiss nor ignore minority views and their histories, particularly in areas where rice farming was never the principal subsistence activity or was not even adopted (see e.g. Amino 2000). I shall return to this point, that is, how to deal with the 'other' *Japans*, later in this volume.

4 This description is to be found in *Kojiki*, 古事記, one of the two earliest imperial chronicles in the history of Japan, the compilation of which was completed in AD 712 (the other is *Nihonshoki*, 日本書紀, completed in 720). I will also return to these chronicles in subsequent chapters. The significant Japanese terms, place names, site names, book names and generic artefact names, such as *Kojiki*, are given Chinese character descriptions at their first mention.

5 Ongoing debate concerning the dating of the beginning of systematic rice paddy field agriculture at some spots in the coastal area of the northern Kyushu region, as well as that of other important episodes of the

historical process covered in the volume, are described in Chapter 3.3.2.

6 The exact location of the discovery is disputed; see Ishikawa (2008).

7 The positionality of the Yayoi period in the discursive space concerning the Japaneseness in relation to the Jomon and the Kofun periods; see Mizoguchi (2002, 29–42).

8 Enacted on 3 May 1947.

9 Chapter 1, Article 1 of the Constitution.

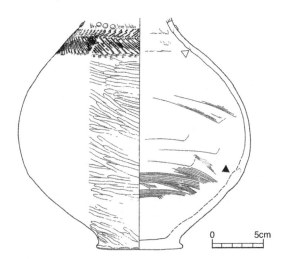

Figure 1.1. The first-ever "Yayoi" pottery excavated and so recognised, allegedly in March (the month of Yayoi) 1884, from present-day Yayoi, Bunkyo Ward, Tokyo (after Sameshima 1996, fig. 5).

(The Constitution of the Empire of Japan, 大日本帝国憲法, or the 'Meiji' Constitution);[10] in that Constitution, the emperor's status and (the limitations of) his power were clearly defined, but the definition also described that the emperor's status and power were 'sacred and inviolable' (Chapter 1, Article 3 of the Constitution) (e.g. Yasuda 1998).[11] In the current Constitution, the emperor no longer possesses any executive or political power, but his symbolic presence is still strongly felt at times.

Most of the gigantic keyhole-shaped tumuli (hereafter abbreviated as 'keyhole tumuli') are designated as 'imperial mausolea'[12] (Figure 1.2), representing the final resting place of the souls (*mitama*, 御霊) of the ancient emperors and their kin (Nihonshi-kenkyu-kai and Kyoto-minka-rekishi-bukai 1995). Aerial photographs of the

tumulus designated as the mausoleum of Emperor Nintoku (仁徳) are still prominently featured in school textbooks; at times, these are accompanied by the somewhat misleading caption that describes the mausoleum as 'the world's largest tomb'. These ancient emperors, according to the oldest remaining imperial chronicles in existence, the *Kojiki* (古事記, consisting of three volumes, the compilation of which was completed in AD 712) and the *Nihonshoki* (日本書紀, consisting of thirty volumes, the compilation of which was completed in AD 720), were the direct descendants of the gods residing in heaven. They were sent down to earth by the gods, who entrusted the emperors with the reign *Ashihara-no-nakatsu-kuni* (芦原中国; also described earlier as *Toyoashihara-mizuho-no-kuni*), and Emperor Nintoku, especially, was lauded as the 'sacred emperor' in the chronicles – particularly in the latter[13] – for his good governance, exemplified by the episode wherein he stopped taxation and the mobilisation of the commoners to perform public works for three years in order to ease their suffering from food (rice) shortage. The emperors who were buried in the great tumuli governed a land that depended on rice cultivation; they were responsible for the well-being of the land and its people.[14]

In that sense, the Kofun period marked another decisive 'beginning' for Japan and the Japanese people; the emperor, as the 'symbol of the integration of the nation', has an uninterrupted genealogy that can be traced back to this era.

This volume covers those eras of *Japanese beginnings*, or eras that are widely perceived as such in the popular imagination – the Yayoi and Kofun periods.[15] With regard to the three-age system, the periods span the time from the Neolithic to the

10 Enacted from 29 November 1890 until 2 May 1947.

11 The Constitution also described the basic human rights of citizens as *being granted and guaranteed* by the emperor: see Chapter 1, Articles 5 and 6, and Chapter 2 of the Constitution.

12 There are a number of large keyhole tumuli which the Imperial Household Agency (宮内庁) has difficulty designating to any recorded emperors as their tombs. Those tombs are designated as 'likely imperial mausolea', and like the designated imperial mausolea, public access is basically prohibited, except for a limited number of scholars representing learned societies on designated occasions (cf. Takagi 2010, see esp. 100–105). Figure 1.2 is a detailed contour map of the Haji-Nisanzai tumulus produced by the agency (from Suenaga 1975).

13 For a standard English translation, see Aston (2008).

14 This shared inference is based on what has been 'recorded' in the imperial chronicles: in Chapter 3.2.4 of this volume, I will return to some matters concerning the nature of those chronicles, the background against which they were compiled and the accuracy of their descriptions as historical sources.

15 This volume does not uncritically endorse the view that those eras marked the beginnings of some significant attributes of the 'Japaneseness' and institutions of the nation-state of Japan. Rather, it critically relativises and problematises such conceptions by investigating historical contingencies surrounding their roots and subsequent genealogies. For an earlier attempt from the same author, see Mizoguchi (2002).

Iron Age. Referring to a conventional social evolutionary terminology (cf. Service 1962), the periods cover the segmentary/tribal, the chiefdom and the ancient state stages. As mentioned previously, a significant number of features that have contributed to Japan's identity originated during those periods: the introduction of systematic rice paddy field agriculture is widely, albeit tacitly, regarded as marking the beginning of *Japanese history*, and the Kofun period is considered to mark the beginning of the *imperial reign*. In addition, between 1999 and 2009, primary school textbooks stopped featuring the Palaeolithic and the Jomon hunter-gatherer periods, which preceded the Yayoi and Kofun periods (Social Studies/History Textbooks Discussion Committee 2008). Even though this change lasted for a relatively short time, it resulted from a tacit and somewhat disturbing governmental policy to represent Japanese history, as it was taught to primary school pupils, as having begun in the Yayoi period, not the beginning of the human occupation of the land that was later to be known as the domain of Japan.[16]

The problematic nature of this perception immediately becomes clear. For instance, this view assumes the continuous existence of a clearly marked and internally homogeneous entity called Japan. *The Japanese*, in this perception, are equated with a rice-cultivating population that was ruled (and taken care of) by a succession of emperors (and their ancestral predecessors). This concept, interestingly, is identical to the one formalised during the period of establishment of the ancient state, between the mid-seventh and early eighth centuries AD (we should keep in mind that the earliest imperial chronicles, mentioned previously, were compiled exactly during this period; e.g. Yonetani 2001). Moreover, the formative phase of the modern nation-state of Japan, spanning the late

nineteenth to the early twentieth century (the 'Meiji restoration', which is widely regarded as marking the beginning of the establishment of the modern nation-state, dating back to 1867), saw the conscious revitalisation/resurrection of the concept, engineered by the executive elite of the newborn modern nation-state.[17]

It is well established that the construction of a nation-state, in many cases, requires the invention of 'ethno-national traditions' and a common history (e.g. Smith 2001). It is important to cultivate the belief that such traditions originated with the emergence of the very same group of people who were later to form the nation, and that these traditions were continuously nurtured and protected, at times with immense difficulty, by these people, who were often led by heroic figures who serve to embody the traditions (cf. Smith 2001, esp. chap. 2). According to Anthony Smith, such an ethnic grouping, called an 'ethnie', is not entirely groundless and fictitious; in many cases, there exist some sociocultural elements, items and memories that, having survived over a long period, form the core of an ethnic culture and its unity, and the case of Japan is no exception (Nishikawa and Matsumiya 1995). Nevertheless, the way in which these core elements of an ethnic culture are recognised, appreciated and examined is bound to be strongly influenced by the way in which the state, ancient and modern, looks back on its own past. In other words, we are unwittingly compelled, or even forced, to see the past in the way the state would like us to see it. Needless to say, such an approach to history confines and hence impoverishes our imagination rather than liberating and enriching it.[18]

The study of human history before the emergence of writing is covered by the discipline of

16 In 2006, the Japanese Archaeological Association set up a subcommittee (Social Studies/History Textbooks Discussion Committee, 社会科・歴史教科書等検討委員会) to analyse the issues concerning the coverage of Japan's pre- and proto-history, along with the outcomes of the archaeological study of Japanese past in school textbooks, and issued a statement against the education ministry's policy of projecting the Yayoi period as the beginning of Japanese history. Consequently, the education ministry was compelled to change its policy, and in 2009, primary school textbooks went back to featuring 'the hunter-gatherer way of life' that had prevailed before the Yayoi period.

17 During the Edo feudal period that preceded the Meiji restoration, commoners vaguely knew about the emperor's existence, but they did not really grasp who or what he (or very occasionally, she) was, let alone his or her genealogical roots. Instead, the emperor's image was that of a magical figure who could work miracles, such as making prophesies and curing various diseases (Fujitani 1994, 13–15). The early Meiji period saw the foundation (claimed by the executive as the resurrection) of pageantries representing the emperor as the embodiment of the nation (Fujitani 1994).

18 We also have to be aware, however, that, in this age of globalisation, increasing difficulty in identifying oneself with something stable leads some to become dependent

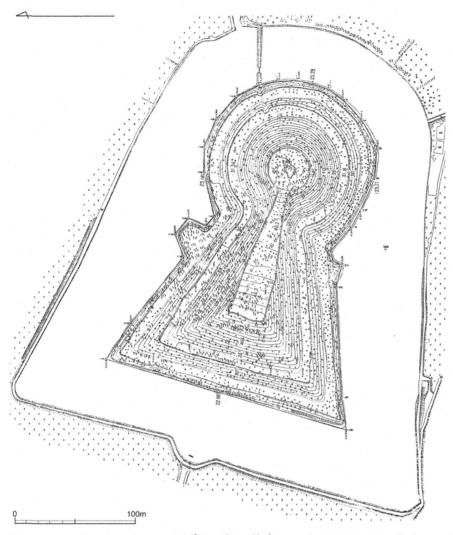

0   100m

Figure 1.2. The Haji-Nisanzai [土師ニサンザイ] tumulus, Sakai City, Osaka prefecture. Designated by the Imperial Household Agency as a 'probable mausoleum'. The length of the mound is about 290 metres (after Suenaga 1975). The trace of an outer moat has been confirmed. With kind permission from the Imperial Household Agency and Gakuseisha Publishing Co.

archaeology, although that is not necessarily the exclusive domain of archaeology. The desire to trace the roots of the core elements of an ethnic culture as far back as possible is strong and universally shared. In that sense, archaeology cannot be entirely uninfluenced by the way in which the nation-state regards its own past. In fact, the relationship between archaeology and the modern nation-state is symbiotic; as a number of recent studies have revealed, archaeology was established as an academic discipline only as a consequence

of modernity and the formation of the modern nation-state (e.g. Mizoguchi 2006a; Díaz-Andreu 2007). In addition, this fateful nature of archaeology has projected, and continues to project, the image of the past that it generates in the contemporary world in terms of our own likeness. Admittedly, we can only speak about and describe the past in our own languages and manners. However, we should also be able to discuss it in terms of what and how it is different from ourselves and from the world in which we live.

The unique context in which the construction of the modern nation-state of Japan took place significantly influenced the subsequent trajectory of the development of Japanese archaeology (cf. Mizoguchi 2006a). Moreover, the events

on extremist ideologies such as religious fundamentalism. Concerning that fact, it would be counterproductive just to criticise the state as a referential point for self-identification and for the recognition and learning of history.

that occurred in Japan since then, leading up to the catastrophe of World War II, still cast a long and dark shadow over the study of those periods today. Since 1945, when the war ended with Japan's unconditional surrender to the allied nations, Japan experienced a rapid economic recovery, an unprecedented prosperity and then a prolonged period of recession. In fact, the transformations and problems which are being experienced by the Japanese today can only be properly characterised as 'post-industrial' or even 'postmodern' (Mizoguchi 2006a).

Naturally, the history of modern Japan can be divided into several phases, punctuated by the sociopolitical, economic and cultural changes it has undergone. These, in turn, have generated distinct themes and modes of *doing archaeology*. I wish to begin this study by examining at length the different themes and modes of doing archaeology that have been adopted and discarded over the years. The reason is threefold. First, this exercise will illustrate the changing theoretical and methodological trends in archaeology and allow us to situate the study of the Yayoi and Kofun periods, covering the period from the emergence of the earliest rice farming villages to the rise of the ancient state, in a properly focused manner. Second, it will enable us to critically assess the respective achievements of those changing trends and recognise the problems generated by them. Third, recognising these achievements and problems will allow us to devise a proper, and hopefully better, framework for the volume, that is, a framework not for only tracing and writing about the history of the Yayoi and Kofun periods but also for revealing the meanings and contemporary implications of doing so. Through this exercise, it is hoped that this volume itself will act as an active and meaningful intervention in the current situation in terms of the way in which the periods are studied, appreciated and 'used' inside and outside the nation-state of Japan. Most of all, it is hoped that this work will enable us to see the past as something unique and different, to see it as something we have to make an effort to understand and sympathise with, rather than as something on which we can project our own favourite image of ourselves.

CHAPTER 2

A TALE OF CO-TRANSFORMATION: THE HISTORY OF MODERN JAPAN AND THE ARCHAEOLOGY OF THE YAYOI AND KOFUN PERIODS

1. INTRODUCTION

As mentioned in the previous chapter, the history of the modern nation-state of Japan can be divided into several phases, and the unique conditions that characterised those phases led to the articulation of distinct themes and approaches in archaeology. At first glance, those paradigmatic traits appear to have come and gone. However, in actuality, some of them have survived and still form significant characteristics of Japanese archaeology today.

The period between the Meiji (明治) restoration (1867) and the end of World War II (1945) saw the construction of the modern nation-state of Japan, its rapid rise to the status of one of the (economically and militarily) strongest nations in the world, its colonial expansion to mainland Asia and its subsequent catastrophic defeat. In other words, the period witnessed the rise and fall of imperial Japan. In order to integrate this new, artificially and hastily created nation, the authorities needed to promote the image of Japan as a unique nation (the *only one* in the world, according to the official narrative) that had been continually ruled by a succession of emperors from a single bloodline, whose uninterrupted genealogy could be traced back to the deepest past.[1] In order to ensure the working of this strategy, the executive had to check any findings or discourses that contradicted it. The birth and initial development of modern archaeology in Japan took place in such circumstances. Thus, the theoretical and methodological trends[2] generated in this period can best be described under (a) the 'imperial-ancestral' approach.

The prevalent trends during the phase between the end of World War II and the 1950s are characterised by a great emphasis upon the autonomous development of ancient communities in the archipelago. The war had caused immense devastation, and Japan's militaristic-imperialistic attempt to colonise its neighbouring nations was strongly denounced internationally. As a gesture of remorse, it seemed necessary for Japan to attribute the cause of its mistakes and their resulting devastation to internal and indigenous historical factors. Accordingly, the role played by external factors such as Japan's interactions with mainland Asia in shaping the historical trajectory of Japanese state formation tended to be neglected, albeit heuristically. Hence, the trends characterising this period can be described under (b) the 'independent-autonomous' approach.

The period between the 1950s and the 1970s saw Japan's reintegration into global politics and economics and its subsequent rise to the status of an economic giant. International relations steadily increased in importance in Japanese people's perception as well as living reality, which led to trends in archaeology which can be described under (c) the 'international' approach. In contrast to the previous phases, this approach emphasises the importance of external factors in the process of formation

---

1 The notion and belief widely known as *Bansei* (ten thousand generations) – *ikkei* (one uninterrupted genealogical line, 万世一系). The word, for instance, can be found in Chapter 1, Article 1 of the Constitution of the Empire of Japan that defines the sovereignty of the emperor (see Chapter 1 of this volume).

2 Such trends formed a kind of disciplinary norm which can be described as a paradigm. However, it has to be emphasised that its elements had different currencies from one another, and some of them survived and continued to be drawn upon long after the paradigm which they constituted had been replaced by the next.

of the ancient Japanese state, for example, the role played by migrant groups (*Kika-jin*, 帰化人) from the Korean peninsula.

The period between the 1970s and 1980s was one in which Japan was confronted by many negative consequences of its post–World War II success and prosperity. Rapid industrialisation resulted in severe pollution and environmental degradation. People also became aware of the fact that their prosperity had resulted from the Cold War and its brutal geo-political and politico-economic realities. These realisations led to trends in archaeology which emphasised the role played by violence in the transformation of ancient communities in the archipelago. This phase, thus, can be characterised by the term (d) *violence*, the role of which was emphasised in archaeological explanations.[3]

Between the 1990s and the present, Japan has entered the 'post-industrial' or the 'postmodern' era.[4] The preexisting value systems based on various hierarchical dichotomies and crystallised through the experience of the realities of the Cold War, for example, pro- and anti-imperial family sentiments, pro- and anti-socialism, and so on, have disintegrated in recent times. Such a situation has led to the proliferation of a number of trends that coexist and do not necessarily compete for dominance; the situation is aptly described by the word (e) *fragmentation*.

In the following sections, we examine in detail the way in which archaeology and the contemporary society became intertwined and shared certain characteristics of the era during the previously mentioned phases. The investigation emphasises

not only the transformation of the society and archaeology but also the enduring characteristics of Japanese archaeology, including the study of the Yayoi and Kofun periods, which have been the outcome of that process. The coverage cannot be thorough; an exhaustive investigation of the whole picture demands another book. Instead, topics exemplifying the way archaeology and the contemporary society are entangled have been chosen.[5] It is hoped that this exercise will prepare us to construct a better framework for the undertaking of the current volume.

2. JAPANESE MODERNITY AND ARCHAEOLOGY: A TALE OF CO-TRANSFORMATION

2.1. The Modernisation of Japan and Its 'Imperial-Ancestral' Past

As mentioned earlier, the intrinsic connection between the formation of the nation-state and the disciplinisation of archaeology has received significant attention in recent times (Kohl and Fawcett 1996; Díaz-Andreu and Champion 1996; Mizoguchi 2006a; Díaz-Andreu 2007). This connection can also be discerned in Japan. In fact, the unique socio-historical conditions that existed at the time of the formation of the modern nation-state of Japan made the connection quite intense – probably much more intense, and in a way more exemplary, than that in many other countries or parts of the world (Mizoguchi 2006a, 55–81).

As an entity functioning as a unit that internally guarantees its members basic human rights while it externally competes against and negotiates with other equivalents over politico-economic matters, a modern nation-state has to be equipped with the following characteristics: (a) it should be industrialised; (b) its operation, rationalized; (c) its contents, that is, human labour and so on, commodified; and its organisation should be (d) bureaucratised, (e) constituted by the citizens, (f) deconstructed of kinship/local ties, (g) secularised and (h) institutionally segmented and specialised (Waters 1999, xii–xiii; Mizoguchi 2006a, 19).

---

3 Before this phase, the Yayoi period was perceived to mark the beginning of 'good' and proud constitutive traditions of Japan and *Japaneseness*. After this phase, however, negative consequences of the beginning of systematic rice paddy field agriculture became emphasised (cf. Mizoguchi 2002, 13–42). Makoto Sahara (1987), for instance, argued that the introduction of systematic rice paddy field agriculture, the definitional attribute of the Yayoi culture and period according to him, also marked the origin of warfare, one of the ills suffering the contemporary world, in the archipelago.

4 According to some social scientists, most notably the late Niklas Luhmann (1994), the 'postmodern' era is a misconception in that its characteristics are the consequence of the development and/or intensification of the constitutive characteristics of modernity, and there is no fundamental structural difference between them. The present author agrees with this opinion, and uses the term *postmodern* as a heuristic terminology.

5 In that sense, this exercise is my own interpretative intervention to the way the history of Japanese archaeology can be written.

This implies that its citizens' common beliefs, religious and otherwise, and agrarian way of life that is based on 'traditions' would no longer suffice as the means for reproducing order within and between the communities constituting the state. In fact, these common beliefs and traditions, generated through a people's communal sharing of a lifeworld, including a common set of rites of passage and other daily experiences, would necessarily have to be replaced with something else. It was possible to replace such traditions with a common vernacular language and a common culture, which would serve as a point of identity with which the members of the newly created entity, the nation, could identify themselves (Smith 2001). Moreover, in many cases, such languages and cultures were invented to meet the national demand (Anderson 2006; Gellner 2006). The land as well as the landscape of the supposed mother- or fatherland also served as media that were as effective as, or possibly more effective than, shared languages and cultures, because the former aspects would have remained unchanged from the beginning of the history of the people who occupied the land, whereas the latter aspects would certainly have undergone some changes through time. It should be noted that archaeological monuments and artefacts constitute parts of the land and the landscape.[6]

In the case of Japan, however, the circumstances surrounding its transformation into a modern nation-state were quite different from those which existed during the modernisation of many of the Western countries. First of all, Japan's transformation into a modern nation-state was an enforced one. The circumstances surrounding the Chinese Ching (清, also described as 'Qing') dynasty's defeat by Britain in the Opium Wars and its consequent acceptance of a hugely unfair treaty that compelled it to hand over a part of its territory, that is, Hong Kong, to Britain also rang the death knell of the extremely stable and successful Tokugawa (徳川) feudal regime in Japan (Jansen 1989). These events prompted powerful feudal clans such as the Shimazu (島津) and the Mohri (毛利), which had long been strategically oppressed by the Tokugawa

clan, to call on the almost dormant imperial system (e.g. Fujitani 1994, 9–15) in an effort to stir up sentiment against the expanding western colonial powers as well as the Tokugawa regime. The movement, however, was subsequently modified to unify and modernise the country in order to prevent its being colonised (Jansen 1989).

However, many of the eight constitutive attributes of modernity had not been sufficiently developed in Japan. Inter-feudal clan competition had, by that time, laid a foundation on which some of those attributes of modernity, such as industrialisation, rationalisation and bureaucratisation, could develop quickly. However, it was impossible to establish the concept of citizenship – a vital, constitutive characteristic of modernity – virtually overnight. Japan's manufacturing and commercial sectors had not developed to such an extent as to dis-embed the people from their kinship- and agrarian-tradition-based social ties and re-embed them in a common concept of nationhood (Mizoguchi 2006a, 60–65). Instead of striving to establish the citizenship, the Meiji administration and its newly established ruling class devised a unique conceptual tool to achieve a functionally compatible effect: the concept of the 'national body', the *Koku* (national)-*tai* (body, 国体). According to this concept, the nation was perceived as similar to the human body, and its people corresponded with the organs. It is important to note that the emperor was regarded as and was embodied as the head of this conceptualized body. If a part or organ of the body fails, the body dies, and if the head dies, so does the body. In this way, the concept also managed to depict the relationship between the people and the emperor as one of reciprocity: the people cannot exist without the emperor, and the emperor cannot exist without the people (Mizoguchi 2006a, 60–65). By internalising this concept in the Japanese people's conception of the mind and body, it became possible to dis-embed, re-embed and integrate the people into one unified nation without establishing a unified citizenship (ibid.).

The internalisation of the national body concept required the use of various devices and tools. Pageants and related pseudo-traditional rituals, significant among these being the rites of passage of the members of the imperial family, were invented for this purpose by putting together references

---

6 Archaeological monuments are often depicted as landscape features in paintings from the early modern era. Some of them depict overtly patriotic themes such as the departure of conscripted soldiers to the front line (cf. Sorensen 1996).

to old imperial documents and certain elements of ceremonies organised for European monarchs on equivalent occasions (Fujitani 1994). The myth of the origin of the imperial genealogy as having descended from the gods residing in heaven ('recorded' in the two oldest imperial chronicles, *Kojiki* and *Nihonshoki* mentioned in Chapter 1) and that of the uninterrupted continuation of this genealogy until the present time (the *Bansei-ikkei* concept, see Footnote 1 of this chapter) were intensively mobilised for the purpose. The origin of the imperial genealogy came to be equated with the origin of the 'Japanese nation' through the effective mediating strategy of the national body concept; through this strategy, the national body came to be perceived as having existed since prehistoric times in Japan, and this perception inculcated the feeling in people that they owed their very existence to the national body. Therefore, the people felt that it was their obligation to give back to the national body, to the extent of sacrificing their lives, if necessary.

It did not matter whether or not people believed the myth; it was always surrounded by a discourse in which people were supposed to communicate and act *as if* they genuinely believed it (Teshigawara 1995, 78–79), and it was only the maintenance of the discourse that mattered. After all, the authenticity of the myth, which was *supposed* to authenticate the existence of the national body before everything else in Japan, was the only basis on which the validity of the notion of the national body depended.

Because of its inherent artificiality, the discourse constantly needed supportive inputs from the intellectuals, and for that very reason, their activities came under the nation-state's surveillance and strict, at times even fanatic, regulation (Tsude 2005, 663–664; Teshigawara 1995, 2005, 40–42). Any thesis, utterance or activities which could potentially cast doubt on the authenticity of the mythical origin of the imperial family, the Japanese nation, and the national body, was subjected to severe and often violent crackdowns (ibid.). Michiyo Naka (1888), for example, was purged for his groundbreaking investigation into the authenticity of the dates of the reigns of early emperors and related events recorded in *Kojiki* and *Nihonshoki*. Naka (1888, 108) meticulously enumerated internal discrepancies and contradictions between

those dates, such as a record in *Kojiki* which indicates that two princes and sons of Emperor Nintoku were born after their mother, the queen Iwanohime (磐之媛), had passed away, and claimed that the peculiar longevity of the early emperors, the unrealistic length of their reigns and all the contradictions relating to those figures derived from the fictitious date ascribed to the beginning of the first emperor Jin'mu's (神武) reign. Naka (1888) revealed that most of the discrepancies and contradictions could be explained by hypothetically assuming that the authors and editors of those chronicles divided the years between the arbitrary dates ascribed to the beginning of Emperor Jin'mu's reign and the reigns of Seinei (清寧; AD 480~485) and Kenzo (顕宗; AD 485~488), by the number of emperors believed to have reigned in between; it appears that the official recording of the date of an emperor's reign began only around the time of Seinei and Kenzo. Naka was careful enough to state that he did not have any doubt about the authenticity of the deeds of the emperors, which were also described in the chronicles. He argued, however, that the recalculation of those dates would enable their comparison with the history of other nations in the world (Naka 1888, 107). However, his work was severely criticised for being disrespectful (*fu* [not]-*kei* [respectful], 不敬) to the emperor and to the national body (Teshigawara 2005, 40–42).

Kunitake Kume was even forced to resign from the professorship of Tokyo Imperial University for claiming that Shintoism originated with the worship of the sun and heaven (Kume 1891a, 1891b, 1891c). Kume carefully stated that Shintoism and its core principle of worshipping the sun and heaven not only laid the foundation but also provided a source of stability for the uninterrupted imperial genealogy. However, he also argued that the natural evolution which came with the progression of the imperial genealogy also necessitated transformations in its accompanying religious belief, that is, Shintoism, and the introduction of Confucianism and Buddhism. He concluded his thesis by stating that in order to secure the continuous prosperity of the imperial genealogy and the nation, it was necessary to discard the outdated elements and superstitions which derived from Shintoism. This was surely a modernist's statement.[7] Kume's plea for the modernisation of Japan was made by highlighting Japan's unique potential that was rooted in the 'uninterrupted reign of the successive emperors' (Kume 1891c, 22–24). However, right-wing Shintoists claimed that his statements were disrespectful to not only the sacred unity and immaculateness of the imperial genealogy but also the Shintoistic beliefs that formed the basis of the national body. His forced resignation was later followed by the closure of the government-founded institute for the study of Japanese history, which was attached to Tokyo Imperial University and to which Kume belonged. Such incidents ensured that scholars would avoid making *any* remark which might cast the slightest doubt on the authenticity of the imperial-national-body myth and its ideological foundation.

The effect of this 'climate of fear' on the study of archaeology (Tsude 2005, 663–664), still in its infancy in terms of theoretical and methodological development, was wide-ranging and serious. The fear was most acutely manifest in the study of the Kofun period, because this period was believed to coincide with the era of the foundation and establishment of the imperial genealogy and the Japanese nation. The imperial ancestors, descending from heaven (*Takamagahara*, 高天原), were *supposed* to have brought with them metal tools and other advanced technologies, conquered the land and established the imperial reign; the assemblages excavated from the Kofun tumuli were *supposed* to coincide with the picture.[8]

---

7 Kume was a member of the delegation, led by Tomomi Iwakura, which was dispatched by the Meiji government to learn about various modern technologies of the Western world. The tour lasted from 1871 to 1873.

8 There is a peculiar contradiction in the mythological beginning of the imperial reign of the land, as depicted in the *Kojiki* and the *Nihonshoki*, in that the land itself was created by the gods, but when the imperial ancestors descended on the land, it had already been occupied by barbaric tribes (*Kunitsukami*, 国津神) which the imperial ancestors had conquered (Teshigawara 2005, 94–95). There also exist a number of discrepancies between the entries of the *Kojiki* and that of the *Nihonshoki*: as the former takes a unilinear, episodic narrative form, the latter adopts the style of pseudo-objective historiography with its main narrative line accompanied by numerous quotations from a number of related (or 'certain') documents (described as *arufumi* 一書). The official narrative of the imperial ancestry was created by cherry-picking the depictions that fit to the notion of

Let us see how the development of archaeology was actually hindered because of such beliefs. The differential development of chronological systems between the Kofun and the preceding Jomon and Yayoi periods aptly exemplify the situation. As we can see from the incident involving the recalculation of the dates of reigns of the early emperors and related events as recorded in *Kojiki* and *Nihonshoki* by Naka, the dates ascribed to the origin and development of the early imperial genealogy provided a foundation for the engineered authenticity of the imperial mythology and the notion of the national body. For instance, the 2,600th anniversary of the foundation of the first court in Yamato by Emperor Jin'mu was celebrated as a national festivity in 1940, during which the Kofun-related archaeological images were utilised as historical evidence (cf. Edwards 1998). In other words, the mythical origins of the imperial genealogy and the unity of the Japanese nation had to be made *real* by situating them in a concrete quantitative-temporal framework. The Kofun tumuli, supposedly the most prominent attestation of the greatness of the early emperors and their vassals, however, were curiously exempted from close study.

During this phase, there was an increasing enthusiasm for conducting chronological studies into the Jomon and, to a lesser extent, the Yayoi periods (e.g. Yamanouchi 1937). The establishment of a detailed and reliable relative chronological system came to be recognised as the vital foundation of sociocultural analyses, and there was even a lively debate concerning how to balance chronological and sociocultural studies (the so-called Hidabito debate exchanged on the journal *Hidabito*, ひだびと, around 1938; cf. Teshigawara 1995, 171–176). In stark contrast, there were few attempts to construct a pottery typo-chronology-based relative chronological system for the Kofun period. Instead, the study of the period almost solely consisted of attempting to infer the meaning of cultural items, that is, artefacts, tumuli and their features, by comparing them with similar descriptions in *Kojiki* and *Nihonshoki* in an uncritical manner. Apparently, it was not necessary to apply an archaeological relative chronological scheme for

Bansei-ikkei (Teshigawara 2005, and see Footnote 1 of the current chapter).

the period, because those early imperial chronicles were officially regarded as the exact records
of what had happened and when, with regard to
the successive reigns of the early imperial ancestors and their deeds. The archaeologist only had
to undertake the task of comparing the available
archaeological materials with the descriptions of
those *accurate and faultless historical records*.[9]

In addition, there were hardly any attempts to
investigate the *society* of the period. For instance,
Shogoro Tsuboi, one of the founding fathers of
Japanese archaeology and anthropology, excavated
the tumuli of the Ashikaga park (足利公園) in
Tochigi prefecture in 1886. He not only made
careful recordings of the artefacts discovered in
the stone chambers but also provided a highly
insightful interpretation, for that time, about social
stratification and hierarchy: he inferred the existence of division between labourers, artisans and
those who were buried in the chambers (Tsuboi
1888). However, this was one of very few academic remarks made on the social organisation of
the Kofun period before the end of World War
II. Tsuboi himself neither developed the idea nor
continued to study the Kofun period. Instead, he
concentrated his energies on the issue of who
were the original inhabitants of the archipelago.
Because these people were believed to have been
either replaced by or assimilated into the ancestral population of the imperial family, the study of
the aboriginal population(s) of the archipelago had
no connection with the imperial past and hence
was relatively safe from the danger of persecution
(Mizoguchi 2006a, 63–65).

Without a sufficiently detailed chronological
framework, however, the outcomes of the cultural study of the Kofun artefacts were inevitably descriptive and often erroneous.[10] An exception to this norm was the study of the temporal
changes in mortuary facilities by Sadakichi Kita,
the history professor of Kyoto Imperial University. By examining the existing mortuary facilities of the 'imperial mausolea' and their dates (i.e.

the dates of death of the *O-kimi*s, 大君) recorded in *Kojiki* and *Nihonshoki*, Kita claimed that
cists had later been replaced by stone-built chambers (Kita 1979). However, his thesis – proved
by subsequent research to be basically correct –
was disputed on the grounds that the descriptions
of the netherworld (*Yomi-no-kuni*, 黄泉国) in the
Kojiki and the *Nihonshoki* resembled the inside of
the stone chambers. The critics of Kita's thesis,
drawing on this line of inference, argued that
stone chambers were the older type of mortuary
facility. However, as both theses drew their arguments from these chronicles and its different interpretations, their validity could not be examined
objectively without an independent chronological
framework, and the debate naturally ended up
inconclusive.

It must be added, in this context, that the
first systematic typo-chronology of the keyhole
tumulus, somewhat ironically, was also constructed by accepting as facts or almost-facts the dates of
deaths of the early emperors that were 'recorded' in
those chronicles as well as the designation awarded
to their 'mausolea' by the then-imperial household ministry (*kunai-sho*, 宮内省). Yukio Kobayashi, who had the opportunity to study the then-
undisclosed maps of the mausolea made by the
forestry section of the ministry (Anazawa 1994,
190), arranged them in the temporal order suggested by the chronicles and examined them in order
to see if he could trace any trend in terms of continuous changes in their mound shape (Kobayashi
1937). The outcome was that the changes in the
mound shape of the keyhole tumuli indicated a
steady and progressive increase in the dimensions
(length and width) of the square part in relation
to the diameter of the round part (ibid.). This
has since been proved to be fairly accurate (which
also suggests that the chronicles and the designation of the mausolea actually *reflect* reality, to
some extent). Meanwhile, rigorous textual critiques conducted after the end of World War II
have revealed that the descriptions in the *Kojiki*
and the *Nihonshoki* of the reigns of certain emperors – especially the first eight emperors and the
emperors Chuai (仲哀), Seimu (成務) and Keiko
(景行) – were either almost completely fabric-
ated, in some cases by borrowing the deeds and
achievements of much later emperors (e.g. Inoue
1960, 19–122), or their authenticity cannot be

9 It has to be noted that some detailed typo-chronological
studies of artefacts such as iron arrowheads (Goto 1939),
whose nomenclature was derived from historical documents, were conducted. However, they were rare
exceptions. They were not used as chronological frameworks for culture-historical descriptions, either.
10 Rare exceptions for the trend, see Footnote 9 to this
chapter.

confirmed by any external evidence (e.g. Inoue 1965, 29–34). Despite this, the scheme persisted until as late as the 1950s, when a major summary volume was published that featured a slightly modified scheme with a table outlining the dates of the deaths of those emperors recorded in the chronicles (Kobayashi 1959, 8–9, fig. 12). This can be understood as a pragmatic approach to an archaeological issue, and the fact that it worked means that the approach was worth taking. However, this also exemplifies the potential danger that is inherent in the archaeology of state formation; the state-formation phase is often the earliest historical period in the history of a region/nation, and the document(s), while reflecting what actually occurred to various degrees, are invariably compiled to connect the emergent ruling class with the transcendental (Smith 2001). More often than not, this constructed connection between the elite at the time of the origin of a region/nation and the transcendental is later rediscovered, often by the 'intellectuals' (Díaz-Andreu 2007, 282), and given new meanings in the formation period of a modern nation-state and/or during its times of crisis (Smith 2001; Díaz-Andreu 2007). In that sense, archaeological pragmatism regarding the use of the earliest historical document available of a region should always be guarded by critical attitudes and perspectives.

In summary, the study of the Kofun period, from the modernisation phase of Japan to the end of World War II, constituted a unique domain: within it, archaeologists and historians had to behave *as if* they genuinely believed the authenticity of the *Kojiki* and *Nihonshoki* imperial chronicles. It is important to add that references, albeit very cautious ones, to the chronicles in the archaeological study of the Kofun period continued well into the post–World War II years. However, these studies were lacking in that they failed to critically examine the authenticity of the depictions of the chronicles by comparing them with the outcomes of the archaeological studies of the period. Since then, scholars have gradually realised the importance of a more critical academic stance (e.g. Tsude 2005). Historians are particularly keen on incorporating the outcomes of archaeological studies into their critical readings of the chronicles (e.g. Yamao 2003). However, archaeologists tend to be satisfied with examining the 'goodness of fit' between the results of their studies and the relevant depictions in the chronicles.[11] This can be treated as predominantly a methodological problem, but it can also be interpreted as reflecting the deep-rootedness and resilience of the imperial ideology that was nurtured in the previously mentioned domain.

2.2. The Post–World War II Reformation and the 'Independent-Autonomous' Past

Japan's defeat in World War II and the devastation caused by the war not only in Japan but also in the neighbouring countries inevitably led to some introspection regarding the factors which allowed these events to occur across a wide range of sectors. Consequently, there were high expectations placed on the general discipline of history, including archaeology. During World War II and the process leading up to it, the ideological control imposed by the military-led executive permeated into every corner of social life and made for a dysfunctional democracy, and it was apparent that the image of the emperor as a living god and the only embodiment of Japan's history as well as destiny sustained this grotesque state of affairs. The academia was widely convinced of the absolute necessity of deconstructing the ideology and the entire system that was based on it, which entailed getting down to the very root of the problem, that is, the origin of the imperial genealogy. The memory of prominent historians (such as Sokichi Tsuda, whose books were officially banned in 1940) persecuted for their objective investigation into issues related to this matter (e.g. Tsuda 1924) further raised expectations.

Amidst such a heated atmosphere, Marxism came to be recognised as an important guiding framework for the historical deconstruction of the imperial ideology. Marxism was introduced in Japan under the liberal atmosphere and economic prosperity of the 1920s, and it quickly established itself as an influential universal theory covering a wide range of sociocultural, economic and political issues. However, as the depression and increasingly harsher treatments (or so it was interpreted)

11 As of 2011. The current state of the affair can be characterised by the coexistence of Marxist-influenced interpretations and references to descriptions in the *Kojiki* and the *Nihonshoki* in individual scholarly works.

meted out to Japan by the Western powers led to the rise of militarism, Marxism and Marxist political parties were subjected to severe persecution. The very few scholars who continued to explicitly oppose the imperial ideology, some of whom were imprisoned, tortured and even killed, drew upon Marxist doctrines as their guiding theory (e.g. Watabe [1936] 1947). Naturally, Marxism became the driving force of the historical disciplines, including archaeology, which had been liberated from the iron cage of the national body (e.g. Oguma 2002, chap. 8). The imperial system, the most significant pillar of the ideological control imposed by the military-led executive, was recognised as the determinant ill of Japan, and an important objective of the study was to reveal the process through which the imperial ancestors came to achieve their dominance.

A prominent Marxist explanatory model of the social development during the Yayoi and Kofun periods focused on the processes through which kin-based communities unknowingly destroyed themselves and cleared the way for hierachisation due to their very attempts to preserve themselves. The model, originally devised by Seiichi Wajima (1966)[12] and developed by Yoshiro Kondo (1983), is an innovative one and deserves discussion. It proceeds as follows. The introduction of rice paddy field agriculture to the archipelago led to a significant development in the force of production. Ever-increasing harvests, even though hampered by bad years at times, encouraged individual kin-based communities to break away from the larger corporate organisation that they formed with other communities and become autonomous and independent. Meanwhile, because the means of production only developed gradually, the occasional cooperation of the larger corporate group was still necessary for work which required input on a larger scale. For instance, the members of each individual kin-based community could

perform their daily agricultural activities in their own paddies. However, when new paddies needed to be constructed, or when the irrigation systems needed some repairs, the tasks could not be solely undertaken by such a community; they required the participation and cooperation of communities constituting a larger corporate group. This generated a contradiction in the form of conflicting interests among individual communities and between them and the larger corporate group which they constituted. Because such situations gave rise to the need for mediating between the increasing tensions and conflicts, the people chose mediators who were entrusted with the task of easing the tensions and conflicts, which would allow for the larger corporate-group-scale co-operation. It is possible that these mediator figures carried out their task by organising communal-agricultural rituals which stressed the necessity of communal co-operation and the importance of rice harvests, and these two facets of the rituals probably led to the gradual convergence of the images of ancestral and rice spirits. However, as mentioned above, as long as harvests continued to be increasingly plentiful, individual communities continued to aspire for autonomy and independence from the larger corporate group. Nevertheless, as long as the development of the means of production remained at such a level as to necessitate a larger scale of co-operation, the larger corporate group had to be maintained. The tensions and conflicts must have increased with time, and easing them must have become increasingly difficult. In other words, the contradiction between the force and relations of production increased. In order for the large-scale cooperation to survive under the increasing pressure, the rituals would have had to be intensified. Accordingly, the authority entrusted to the mediator-ritual-leader had to be enhanced. In this manner, when the force of production developed to the level at which individual communities could become autonomous and independent from the larger corporate group, and their positions began to be hierarchised, the mediator figures were transformed into the ruler figures. However, the ruler figures continued to pretend to be mediator figures representing communal interests by organising and presiding over the community's rituals. This crucial transformation from the mediator to the ruler figure took place at the

12 Seiichi Wajima was a member of a circle of historians (Yuibutsu-ron kenkyukai [Historical materialism study group]) compiling *Nihon rekishi kyotei* (The seminar in Japanese history) (Watabe et al. 1936) led by Yoshimichi Watabe. Wajima was tasked to write about prehistoric social organisation and production by incorporating the latest archaeological findings (under the name Akira Misawa), and he was strongly influenced by the Marxist theory of historical developmental stages which the books drew on.

beginning of the Kofun period and marked the emergence of the ancestral figure(s) of the imperial genealogy.

Three points can be made in relation to the argument presented here. First, the image of the ancestral figure(s) of the imperial genealogy as the pseudo-communal ritual-conducting mediator-ruler figure(s) almost exactly replicated the image attached to and symbolic function fulfilled by the modern emperors, the Meiji (on the throne between 1867–1912), the Taisho (1912–1926) and the Showa (1926–1989). Second, the closed nature of the model – in terms of the tightly connected, coherent causal interrelationships between the factors – enabled the explanation of the functioning of and changes in almost any type of archaeological item, as long as the item could fit into one of the factors. Third, because of the previous point, the archaeological study of the Yayoi and Kofun periods became insular, because it was assumed that any change could be, and ought to be, explained internally.

All of those points fit into the atmosphere of the time very well. First, the post-war reconstruction of the Japanese economy, although it occurred with the help of foreign aides and was engineered by the United States (which needed a militarily and economically strong Japan in order to counter the expansion of Soviet- and Chinese-led communism in the region), was perceived as a self-recovering endeavour (cf. Komori 2001). The Japanese people shared the sentiment that Japan had lost everything it had strived to achieve through its own fault, and because of that, it was necessary for Japan to identify the mistakes and root out the problems by itself, without outside help (ibid.). A new framework for international politico-economic coordination was still being devised. These conditions made the closed framework of Marxism, which explained social change as an autonomous process, appear persuasive as well as attractive. In addition, the heavy industry–based economic recovery initiated at the time allowed for a causal linkage between the force of production and other social constitutive elements, with the former being considered the determinant factor. Under these circumstances, the Marxist explanation of social change as a process of chain reactions to technological developments was convincing as well as persuasive.

2.3. The Post–World War II Economic Success and the 'International' Past

The feverish enthusiasm for Marxist approaches was assuaged with the passing of the 1950s and 1960s, as the previously mentioned high expectations of implementing drastic reforms in Japan by drawing on critical reflections of the ills of the pre–World War II era gradually faded out of the consciousness of the general public. Gone with it was the public's enthusiasm for painting the bigger picture based on the thesis of developmental stages and the Marxist theory of social change. The popular academic trends of the time shifted to reconstructing individual events and attempting to determine their direct, concrete causes and consequences. In the discipline of history, such trends were driven by case studies drawing on rigorous textual critiques of the *Kojiki* and the *Nihonshoki* (e.g. Inoue 1960, 1965). Many of these studies revealed the importance of Japan's contact with the Korean peninsula in the process of the rise of the state.

Academic interest in the impact of contacts with mainland Asia on early Japanese history was rooted in the movement of denouncing the notion of an uninterrupted imperial genealogy, and the horse-rider-conquest dynasty theory (*Kiba-minzoku-ocho-setsu*, 騎馬民族王朝説) was one of the most prominent. Scholars such as Namio Egami and Yu Mizuno claimed that there were discontinuities (in their opinion) that were concealed and/or overlooked in the early imperial genealogy as depicted in the official chronicles and the relevant archaeological evidence. They argued that these discontinuities resulted from events wherein groups of people, some of which came from the mainland through the Korean peninsula, replaced the previous, indigenous elite groups and established their new 'dynasties' (Mizuno 1954; Egami 1967). Many elements of their theses have failed to withstand the test of time and have been disproved by the findings of subsequent research (e.g. Onoyama 1975a, 1975b). However, the enduring legacy of scholars such as Egami and Mizuno has been the recognition of discontinuities in the process previously recognised as continuous and evolutionary and the importance of contact with the continent in understanding Japanese history, particularly its early periods.

Subsequent studies emphasised the role played by the *Kika-jin* (帰化人) clans, which came from the Korean peninsula, in the development of culture and technology in the state-formation process of Japan (e.g. Seki 1956). These studies also investigated cultural-historical issues such as how the immigrant groups were incorporated into the indigenous social organisation, how they effectively changed it, the new and advanced technologies that they brought with them and so on.

The advent of the new academic trend was driven by a sense of fatigue and disillusionment with the Marxism-based movement to reform the discipline of history (including archaeology) in an intellectual-political endeavour to construct a better society, that is, a socialist Japan (Oguma 2002, 307–353). The movement, which called itself the 'national history movement (based on historical science)' (国民的歴史学運動; in this context, *science* represents the Marxist version of historical materialism), produced a number of important works which had long-lasting impacts, including the theorisation of the social hierarchisation of prehistoric and proto-historic Japan, as we saw in the previous section. However, the movement increasingly confined itself to political activities rather than pursuing its objectives through sober academic research, which undeniably resulted in the lowering of the academic standard of the discipline (ibid.).

However, the trend was also associated with Japan's re-incorporation into the global politico-economic arena and factors deriving from this. The peace treaty (Treaty of Peace with Japan), signed in 1951, was ratified by all the Allied nations, with the exception of the Soviet Union and its allies. Japan's mutual security treaty with the United States firmly incorporated Japan into the Western bloc in the intensifying Cold War. This determined the position and status of Japan in the politico-economic landscape of the Cold War era and consequently ensured its economic success and prosperity. Meanwhile, its relations with the United States prevented Japan from fully compensating for the damage it had caused to China and the now two Koreas and from re-engaging with them politically, culturally and economically.[13] This was

13 In terms of international legal framework, the obligation of the compensation for individual victims was cancelled out in the treaty (based upon its Clause 16).

also perceived as a huge setback by those who advocated the broad movement of constructing a socialist-democratic Japan. It was a mixture of these factors that gave rise to the trend emphasising the roles played by Japan's contact with Korea and China in the early history of Japan.

Although Egami's horse-rider-conquest dynasty theory was subjected to a number of detailed critiques based on archaeological evidence, it served to highlight the importance of the emergent, inchoate state's contact with the successive Chinese dynasties and Korean polities. The *Kojiki* and the *Nihonshoki* chronicles were also subjected to critical rereadings. Many of the critical works attempted to examine the authenticity of individual entries by checking whether they were also recorded in Chinese and Korean documents. Since the latter were written by those who did not share political interests and/or motives with the authors of the Japanese chronicles, instances where the entries agreed with one another could, at least, be treated as reflecting real occurrences, to a great extent (Inoue 1960, 1965). Such works inevitably involved careful readings of Chinese and Korean documents, which enabled scholars to reconstruct, to a certain extent, the sequences of events in the archipelago, the peninsula, and China and compare them from cause-and-effect perspectives (ibid.).

In the study of the Kofun period, this established the research tradition of comparing Korean and Japanese artefacts in terms of their production technology as well as their appearance. If occurrences of a certain artefact were found to be distributed across both the peninsula and the archipelago, if the specimens appeared to be produced with the same technology and artisanship and if their typo-technological genealogy could only be traced back to one of those regions, the distribution of the specimens across both areas was most likely the consequence of either the spread of the specimens from the production centres or the movement of the artisans from the production centres of one region to the other. Furthermore, by examining the way in which the initially common technology was modified and localised, scholars hoped to reconstruct the way in which artisans moved from their original production centres and were incorporated into the production system of the other region. By comparing the outcomes of such researches with those of the critical readings and authenticating the entries of the Japanese and Korean chronicles and documents of the period, we can determine what type of contacts and interactions existed between which polities, and how they changed through time.[14]

In the study of the Yayoi period, the academic trend gave rise to a debate concerning the 'beginnings' of the Yayoi period. An important focal feature of the debate was whether these beginnings resulted from a sizeable wave of migration or from the active and selective introduction of elements of the rice-agriculture-based way of life by the indigenous population. Due to the paucity of available evidence both in the peninsula and the archipelago, the debate remained inconclusive for some time. Since then, as explained in Chapter 5 of the current volume, the accumulated evidence has enabled scholars to trace the trajectory of change through a range of elements constituting both the society and the culture of the peninsula as well as the archipelago just before and after the beginning of this period. The emerging picture points to a combination of both internal and external factors that led to the formation of a new type of sociocultural and socioeconomic organisation. It would be a truism to state that in order to fully explain and/or understand a change, both the internal and the external factors of the change need to be taken into account. However, the dichotomous notions that were crystallised during this period persist even today, particularly in the form of debates over the *scale* of the migration and the manner in which the migrants settled down in the Japanese archipelago (cf. Tanaka 2002), and whether the Jomon (indigenous) or the Yayoi (incoming) population played a more determinant role in the transition is treated as the ultimate question.[15]

14 A classic example of such endeavour is Takashi Onoyama's (1975a, 1975b) work.
15 The exercise of archaeological periodisation itself implies an intrinsic tendency of promoting the dichotomous attitude rigidifying differences between what came before and after the dividing line. In the present volume the trajectory of individual material items is traced across period boundaries to avoid this tendency. See Chapter 3.2.1 and Chapter 3.4 of the present volume for a theoretical explication.

2.4. Consequences of Economic Success and the 'Violent' Past

During the late 1960s and the 1970s, Japan began to suffer from the negative consequences of its post–World War II economic success. The environmental degradation and pollution which had resulted from the unchecked industrialisation caused human suffering of previously unimaginable scales. The illusion of unlimited growth was also crushed by the Middle East oil crisis, which hit the world in 1973. The Cold War reached its climax when the Reagan administration (1981~1989) undertook a series of confrontational approaches towards the USSR. It was the Cold War and the politico-economic system generated by it that had ensured the economic growth of Japan, and this had given rise to severe ambivalence in Japan: without the nuclear umbrella provided by the United States, Japan's security was under threat, but that would also make Japan a primary target of nuclear attacks by the USSR. Moreover, secession from the security treaty with the United States, which was demanded by left-wingers and progressives, would jeopardise Japan's politico-economic prospects.

During this period, Japan's economic base also shifted from heavy industry to light industry, commerce and service. This weakened the link between people's occupations and their political inclination and blurred the division between value systems based on social-class affiliation (Mizoguchi 1997a). Hence, it became increasingly difficult for the Japanese people to share a unified image of a better society and form a united front in order to achieve this vision (ibid.).

In such an atmosphere of despair and anxiety, the idea of the Yayoi period as the origin of large-scale violence became widespread. On one hand, Japan was seized by ambivalence and fear due to the Cold War, while on the other, there was a growing sense of impossibility in its people's ability to share common values and strive for the construction of a better society. The ultimate violence, that is, a nuclear strike, perpetrated upon Japan had its roots in the Neolithic age, in the Yayoi period in Japan, claimed scholars such as Makoto Sahara (1987, 283–298). Scholars also argued that the widespread destruction of nature and the environment began during the Yayoi period (ibid.). No one can escape a nuclear holocaust and environmental pollution.

These factors, I would like to argue, added the weight of reality to the issue as well as the thesis, as a potential unifier of the fragmented discursive domain of archaeology and, in fact, that of Japan.

In the study of the Yayoi period, an emerging trend was to attribute the causes of changes to the evolution of organised violence. For instance, skeletal remains with a tip or tips of stone or bronze weapons lodged in them were assumed to belong to victims of 'warfare', without sufficiently considering the possibility that the victims could have been the casualties of chronic feuds, typical of small-scale societies (e.g. Johnson and Earle 2000). In reality, however, the manner in which the victims met their death – they were mostly either stabbed/pierced from the back or injured by a large number of arrowheads (Fujiwara 2004) – point to their being the victims of skirmishes rather than those of 'wars' (Mizoguchi 2001, 145). More importantly, the cause of population convergences, which took place several times through the period – from the Middle Yayoi onwards, in particular – was attributed to an increase in inter-communal tension and frequency of violent confrontation. This trend culminated in the following explanatory paradigm derived from the study of the Yayoi and Kofun periods: the scale, organisation and intensity of violence continued to increase; the necessity of an institution for mediating conflicts and restoring/creating order became permanent; the organisational sophistication of such an institution and the scale of social integration maintained by the institution continued to increase and the process eventually led to the formation of the ancient state (see e.g. Matsugi 1998).

This model can be compared with the Marxist model explained earlier. The model draws upon the premise that the ever-intensifying contradiction between the force and relations of production, and the continual sophistication of the means to conceal/naturalise this contradiction, led to the formation of the ancient state. However, it is obvious that the Marxist model can accommodate many more variables than the violence model: while the latter reduces the number of factors involved in social change to a single variable, the former can accommodate not only the three significant variables, that is, the force of production, the relations of production and ideology, but also the

ways in which they are interconnected as further variables.

To sum up, I would like to argue that the popularity of the model positing violence as the ultimate cause of the changes that led to the formation of the Japanese ancient state lay in its simplicity. The model was simple not only as an explanatory model but also in its appeal; as mentioned previously, the whole of Japan was faced with the threat of the ultimate, inescapable violence – namely, the nuclear holocaust. In such a situation, the bare simplicity of the model was welcomed by the audience, including archaeologists and the public, who had begun to suffer from a sense of loss of purpose, resulting from the changing socioeconomic and sociopolitical environment, as described earlier.[16]

2.5. Globalisation in the Postmodern and 'Fragmented' Past

The cycle which began during the formative phase of the modern nation-state of Japan appears to have come to an end during the 1970s. This cycle, which we divided into stages based on the unique historical episodes of modern Japan and analysed here, also shows a number of similarities with the histories of other 'developed' countries since the beginning of their modernisation. The enthusiasm during early modernisation for seeking the origins and highlighting the longevity of the nation was replaced, once the developing nation had faced the negative consequences of the previous era, by the desire – scientific, political or otherwise – to explain and theorise about historical changes as inevitable in the long-term process of the nation's evolution.[17] Then the economy shifted from a production-industry-based to a service-industry-based mode, and the earlier enthusiasm for developing the bigger picture (in the form of 'Grand Narratives'), such as tracing the history of a nation to the deepest past or the evolution of human societies, gradually diminished (e.g. Mizoguchi 1997a). Now the focus is on the details of history

16 Takehiko Matsugi's seminal work organically synthesises the explanatory framework of the paradigm and that of the Marxist tradition, embodying a positive culmination of the trend (Matsugi 2007).

17 The trend was embodied in the United States and the United Kingdom by the rise of variously neo-evolutionism-inspired archaeologies described as the processual archaeology.

and history-telling: we are obsessed with investigating the micro-causes of individual episodes and events, and we are increasingly concerned with how to talk and/or write about history differently (Mizoguchi 2006a, chap. 5).[18] This trend has been accelerated by an increasing demand for respecting the autonomy of various ethno-religious cultures which had been suppressed in the process of modernisation in order to secure the internal homogenisation of individual nation-states (ibid.).

In Japan, as well as elsewhere in the developed countries, the construction of a better society is no longer the foremost issue facing the nation. Instead, ensuring better living conditions for each individual appears to be the goal of policy making, and various social, cultural and scientific academic activities seem to be geared up to support this goal. After all, the most important objective of the labour movement of Japan since the 1970s has been to demand pay hikes rather than seek improvements in working conditions or protect the rights of the labour force (Mizoguchi 1997a).

The disappearance of the 'grand narratives' and/or shared singular objectives have given rise to a number of problems in Japan. For instance, the loss, or the slow forgetting, of the Marxist approach resulted in the loss of shared media for exchanging opinions and established channels through which the achievements of previous studies could be properly inherited and assessed (ibid.).[19] In archaeology, the number of specialised topics is ever-increasing. Each of these topics is pursued enthusiastically, sometimes even fanatically,[20] with certain results. Meanwhile, attempts to synthesise the outcomes of such studies

in order to arrive at a coherent explanatory picture are becoming increasingly rare. Even when archaeologists make such an attempt, they tend to be uncertain about how to compare the picture with the pre-existing ones (Mizoguchi 1997a, 2004). On the whole, it appears that the fear of engaging with *others* – ranging from fellow scholars to themes that differ from one's own to the preexisting theses concerning one's own topic – seems to have gripped us all. As academicians, we are increasingly confining our research interests to topics with ever-narrowing coverage/dimensions in order to avoid engaging with others.

My acknowledgement of this state of affairs does not imply that I advocate the revitalisation of a grand narrative. We have come a long way to reach the state where we *feel* that the data we now have are so rich in quality as well as quantity that *any* attempt to reduce their meanings to any singular cause or fact might do more harm than good. Besides, as illustrated previously, the reality of the contemporary society in which we live itself discredits the meaningfulness and usefulness of theorising, that is, imposing order on things and phenomena by drawing on the smallest possible number of principles. However, the widely shared feeling of uselessness attached to *theorisation*, in general – which has contributed to the disappearance of the grand narratives in Japanese archaeology – seems to blur the very aims and objectives of doing archaeology. This, in turn, might actually be contributing to lowering the quality of the critical data handling that we undertake. This very feeling appears to be behind the increasing sense of purposelessness among archaeologists, as explained earlier, and it even seems to be prompting some of them to indulge in a kind of sensationalism. For example, the outcome of a new accelerator mass spectrometry (AMS) dating programme, which, if peer-reviewed and proved to be valid, would put back the beginning of the Yayoi period by about five or six hundred years, from 300/400 BC to 900/1000 BC, was initially publicised in newspapers under leads such as 'the text book entry has to be altered', even before it went through the peer-review process.[21] (We will return to this issue later, in Chapter 3.3: 'Chronology'.) Moreover, when

18 The parallel phenomenon in the United Kingdom and the United States is widely described as the rise of post-processual archaeologies. I argued elsewhere that this was an academic/sociocultural expression of globalisation and post/late-modern social formation, and that parallel phenomena can be recognised across the world (Mizoguchi 2006a, chap. 5).

19 As mentioned, the Marxist framework had been working as a paradigm for archaeological practice as a whole in that its nomenclature and its differentiation of analytical components enabled archaeologists to arrange archaeological data and the methods used for analysing them into an organically structured system which can be shared, debated about, taught and learnt.

20 Competition over describing ever-minute details of artefacts and archaeological phenomena sometimes appears to be taken as a goal of archaeology.

21 I do not mean to deny some important contributions that the AMS dating project initiated by the National

this sensationalising tendency meets the undercurrent of the history of modern Japan and Japanese archaeology, that is, the trend of tracing the roots of the national character back to the deepest past, it is inevitable that the consequences would be of the sort exemplified by the infamous Palaeolithic forgery scandal (Japanese Archaeological Association 2003).

Let us now situate the Yayoi and Kofun archaeologies in terms of the above-described framework.

3. SITUATING THE YAYOI AND KOFUN ARCHAEOLOGIES

The Yayoi period, although it was first recognised as an independent archaeological period, was actually treated as a sort of an *intermediary* period. In the early years of its study, the period was described as the *Chukan* (中間, intermediary)-*jidai* (時代, period); it was situated between the *Sekki* (石器, lithic)-*jidai* (時代, period) and the Kofun period – the former being the period wherein Japan was mainly inhabited by aboriginal populations (i.e. the Jomon period; it was not until 1949 that archaeologists discovered the existence of the Palaeolithic age in the archipelago; Sugihara 1956) and the latter being the period characterised by the emergence of the early imperial ancestors and the beginning of the Japanese nation (Nakayama 1917a, 1917b, 1918a, 1918b). The intermediary character of the period is also captured by the term *Kin* (金, metal) – *seki* (石, lithic) – *ryoki-heiyou* (両器併用, parallel use) – *no* – *jidai* (時代, period; cf. Nakayama 1918b); the period occurred between the Lithic period, characterised by the use of stone tools, and the Kofun period, by which time metal tools were abundantly being used as well as produced.

The initial characterisation, retrospectively speaking, was extremely foresighted; the period was generally studied as the prelude to the Kofun period. As archaeologists found evidence of rice agriculture (e.g. Nakayama 1920, 24–27, Yamanouchi 1925) – in the form of impressions of rice ears and grains on potsherds, distribution of sites in low-lying areas which were well suited for paddy

field farming, and carbonised rice grains – in their excavations, the period came to be recognised as the first era of systematic rice farming in Japanese history. Since the evidence also indicated that the rice farming culture was first established in the northern Kyushu region, from which it subsequently diffused eastward, the onset of the period as well as the people who supposedly brought it to Japan came to be associated with the imperial ancestors.[22] Some scholars even tried to connect the culture's eastward diffusion with the Nihonshoki's description of the first emperor, Emperor Jin'mu – who initially resided in Hyuga, located in the present-day Miyazaki prefecture in southern Kyushu – and his moving to the present-day Nara Basin of the Kinki region, conquering tribes along the way in his quest to reign over the archipelago (the so-called Jin'mu Tosei, 神武東征, campaign; e.g. Goto 1947). However, the introduction of rice farming could not be directly connected with the gigantic keyhole tumuli designated as the resting places of the early emperors; the onset of both rice farming and the use of metal tools occurred *long before* the construction of the imperial mausolea. Because the archaeologists and historians left this discrepancy untouched, the study of the Yayoi period occupied an ambiguous status in the imperial ideology; the culture was supposedly brought to the archipelago by the imperial ancestors but could not be directly connected with the deeds of the early emperors. This ambiguity, however, allowed more freedom for the study of the Yayoi period than that enjoyed by the study of the Kofun period during the difficult years before and during World War II (see Section 2.1 in this chapter).

Even today, so many years after the end of the war, the study of the Yayoi period still retains this sense of ambiguity and intermediateness. For instance, the onset of the period is still passionately debated in terms of 'Which played the more important role, the indigenous Jomon population or the immigrant Yayoi population?'[23] This manner of framing a question discourages anyone

Museum of Japanese History has made to the re-examination of the absolute dates of important stages and events in the Yayoi and Kofun periods.

22 *Ten* (天, heaven)-*son* (孫, offspring)-*zoku* (族, tribe); however, the actual whereabouts of Takamagahara (高天原) itself (where the ancestral deities of the imperial genealogy were said to reside) were variously interpreted (see Mizoguchi 2006a, 60–71).

23 For a comprehensive and insightful review, see Y. Tanaka (1991, 2002).

who seeks to investigate the beginning of the Yayoi period as a process and attempts to give a nuanced causal explanation to it. Rather than investigating the historical process of the period itself, the question of *the origin*, that is, 'who started or who was responsible for the formation of the culture of the imperial ancestors and the Japanese', is prioritised albeit unwittingly. The development of social complexity in the Yayoi period is also often debated in terms of which region of western Japan managed to develop a more complex social organisation than the others and played a key role in the onset of the Kofun period (Tanabe and Sahara 1966). Concerning the logic behind this approach, it is similar to seeking the origin of the imperial ancestors who established their first court in Yamato in the present-day Nara Basin (as described in the *Kojiki* and the *Nihonshoki*). In addition, those who believe that the Kofun society was complex enough to be described as a state from its very beginning likewise tend to characterise the complexity of the Yayoi society highly. Some proponents of this viewpoint, for instance, argue that some of the large-scale settlements of the Middle and Late Yayoi periods could be described as 'towns' (Hirose 2003, 28–56), despite the fact that they lack many constitutive attributes of the 'town' as a socioeconomic/historical category (cf. Childe 1950); for instance, their principal source of sustenance was rice paddy field agriculture, and they do not show any signs of having clearly segregated quarters for full-time artisans (see Chapters 6 and 7 in the current volume). Through this contention, the proponents imply that the Yayoi period, at least in its later phases, achieved the social complexity of the early/proto-state level (e.g. Terasawa 2000). In short, there is an abiding tendency to treat the Yayoi period as the *prelude* to the Kofun period.

Traditionally, the onset of the Kofun period is marked by the emergence of the Kofun tumulus (e.g. Kondo 1983). This might sound tautological, which is indeed the case. A person's understanding of the Kofun tumulus is determined by how that person understands the nature and character of the society of the period, and that understanding, in turn, is determined by the person's understanding as to how the Kofun tumulus represents/embodies the structure and organisation of the society of the period (ibid.). Moreover,

archaeologists tacitly agree that the largest and the most exemplary Kofun tumuli – the gigantic keyhole tumuli of the Kinki region – were the tombs of the early emperors and their close relatives, as indicated by the historical records (e.g. Hishida 2007, 28–36). Hence, their study is the study of the early imperial history itself.

The tradition of burying a chosen few in clearly marked compounds or mounds began in the Yayoi period, and these mounds are sometimes quite large in size. Towards the end of the Yayoi period, such large mounds came to be constructed in some areas of western Japan, particularly in the San'in, Okayama and Kinki regions (see Chapter 7.3.2 and Chapter 8.3.2 of the present volume). The fact that some of these burial mounds also form the characteristic keyhole shape further complicates the problem. If the Kofun tumulus is defined by its most characteristic attribute, i.e. its keyhole shape, the keyhole-shaped mounds of the Yayoi period have to be recognised as the Kofun tumuli. However, the Kofun tumuli function as *the* defining attribute of the Kofun period, which is also considered to have certain characteristics that were absent during the Yayoi period, such as a network of interactions and exchanges covering much larger areas than any of their equivalents in the Yayoi period. Therefore, the presence of a *keyhole-shaped* tumulus belonging to the Yayoi period does appear to complicate matters.

The problem derives from the following tautological assumptions: (a) the Kofun period is distinguished from the Yayoi period in that the former shows some characteristics which the latter does not possess; (b) those characteristics are *embodied* by the Kofun tumulus and are *reflected* by its attributes; (c) in order to verify (b), it is essential to know the distinct characteristics of the Kofun period; and (d) the distinct characteristics of the Kofun period are identified through the study of the Kofun tumuli. In actuality, however, many of the constitutive attributes of the Kofun society evolved from those of the Yayoi society, and it is difficult to impose a dividing line between their trajectories. A tacitly accepted solution is to reverse the procedure, that is, to find the constitutive characteristics of the Kofun tumulus by *assuming* that they *reflected* the characteristics of the society and by defining the beginning of the Kofun period as marked by the construction of the oldest examples of the

Kofun tumuli.[24] There is an obvious fatal flaw in this logic, however; the validity of the entire procedure depends upon the validity of the recognition of what constitutes the Kofun tumuli and what does not, and on the recognition of their constitutive characteristics. As illustrated earlier, a definitive identification of the constitutive characteristics of the Kofun tumuli is bound to be subjected to endless disputes.

This conundrum aptly exemplifies the nature and character of the archaeology of the Kofun period. The keyhole tumulus is a prominent feature of this period in terms of its intriguing shape and the incredible scale of some of its examples. These tumuli also dominate the available archaeological material of the period in terms of their number, allegedly some 30,000 or more, and because of the relatively well-preserved states of many of them. In addition, many of the largest keyhole tumuli in the present-day Kinki region, most of which are also the largest in the archipelago during each of the phases of the period, are widely accepted to be the resting places of the imperial ancestors whose reign and exploits are recorded in the oldest imperial chronicles, the *Kojiki* and the *Nihonshoki*. In that sense, the range of information which can be extracted from the largest tumuli, one might comfortably assume with due caution, can be compared with the corresponding descriptions in those chronicles and can be treated as representing the early history of the imperial household and its genealogy.

These factors are responsible for the fact that the archaeology of the period has excessively focused on the study of keyhole tumuli, which has somewhat overburdened their study. The study of keyhole tumuli was expected not only to provide historians with a clear definition of the Kofun period and its accurate characterisation but also to enable them to trace the early imperial history. Moreover, this perception allowed scholars to feel covertly comfortable with equating the study of the early imperial history with that of the early

state formation of Japan (e.g. Kishimoto 2005, 54–55).

Thanks to this paradigm, however, the study of the keyhole tumuli has developed along unique lines. The three-dimensional morphological study of the mound and the typo-chronology of its features and grave goods have advanced to such an extent that now we can firmly relative-date the specimens to ten or so distinct phases (e.g. Wada 1987). Such a scheme allows us to not only reconstruct the regional sequences of tumuli but also synchronize them and compare their respective dynamics (the increase and decrease in the mound size, changes in the grave good assemblage and so on). It has also been revealed that the three-dimensional plan of the largest tumulus of each phase, most of which are situated in the present-day Nara Basin and the Osaka (Kawachi and Izumi) Plain (hereafter described as the Kinki-core region [KCR]), is shared by much smaller tumuli in certain regions (see Chapter 9). It has been pointed out that many of the latter are half, one-third, one-fourth, and so on the size of the largest, in terms of scale (Hojo 1986). This sharing of identical mound shapes is interpreted as reflecting close political ties between the paramount rulers and local chieftains (Hojo 1986). By combining the finding of all these studies, we hope to trace the changing relations of various sorts, including political alliances, between the KCR and other regions in the archipelago.

I do not deny the fact that this research paradigm works very well as long as its objective remains the reconstruction of the *political processes* of the period. However, this paradigm undeniably implies that the archaeological study of the Kofun period is disproportionately restricted to the life of the elite. Moreover, the information which the imperial chronicles and related documents offer us for comparison with the outcomes of such researches almost exclusively depict the lifestyles and record the deeds of only a select few, including the paramount rulers, the lesser chieftains, their family members and immediate followers.

In short, the restrictive undercurrents that define the archaeological study of the Yayoi and Kofun periods, shaped by remnants of the imperial ideology, have prevented the studies from realising their full potential. Instead, these undercurrents have compelled archaeological studies of the

---

24 The most commonly adopted characteristics are (a) the deposition of a large number of bronze mirrors as grave goods; (b) the use of a large, dugout log coffin; and (c) the adoption of a large, 'formalised' keyhole-shaped mound (Kondo 1983, 188–196). The sociocultural and political implications of each of these characteristics is examined in Chapter 9 of the present volume.

Yayoi period to concentrate on the emergence of the elite as imperial ancestors, which in turn has prompted archaeological studies of the Kofun period to concentrate on the history of the early imperial rule.

4. CONCLUSION

Japanese archaeology has been deeply rooted in and interconnected with the history of the modern nation-state of Japan. The above observations show that the study of the Yayoi and Kofun periods constitutes an important node in the intertwined nature of the relationship. The study of those periods has been deeply influenced by its engagement with the imperial ideology; during the period from the foundation of the modern nation-state of Japan to the end of World War II, the study of these periods was not only constrained by the imperial ideology but also mobilised for its glorification. Until recently, the course taken by the study can be described as a process of reflecting on that 'dark age', with scholars making successive attempts to deconstruct the imperial ideology. Marxism has played a critical role in this deconstructive attempt, and by devising the notion of contradictions and conflicts as the core explanatory concept, archaeologists posited a grand model to explain the process through which early agrarian communities evolved into a hierarchical society ruled by the imperial ancestors. This model enabled archaeologists to systematise their researches and situate the researches in the history of study of the periods.

The transformation of the economic structure, the end of the Cold War and the coming of globalisation systematically demolished the mental and material conditions which formed the basis for the shared desire to construct a better society through a shared scheme. This resulted not only in the disappearance of the Marxist model but also in the fragmentation of the archaeological discursive space itself. These developments made it even more difficult for scholars to properly engage with the legacies of the history of Japanese archaeology and study the Yayoi and Kofun periods by systematically exchanging information, ideas, and opinions and proposing sharable, coherent models.

Drawing on these observations, I would like to contend that archaeologists need a coherent theoretical framework based on which they can handle the available data and draw their interpretations. Needless to say, this framework would include an explicit explanation of the content and implications of the theory. This would enable us to not only engage with the outcomes and consequences of previous studies but also synthesise the outcomes of fragmented, highly specialised studies into a sufficiently broad and coherent picture for fruitful future scrutiny and critical appreciation. That would be the only way for archaeologists to confront and engage with the negative as well as positive legacies of Japanese archaeology and contribute something novel and meaningful to the contemporary world. For this reason, the final section of the next chapter is devoted to describing an appropriate theoretical framework for the investigation presented in the current volume.

CHAPTER 3

FRAMEWORKS

1. INTRODUCTION

Human history can be seen as a bundle of innumerable sequences of 'becoming': individual lives began and ended, and the deeds, thoughts, feelings and memories of people changed over time – gradually, at times, and rapidly and abruptly at other times. Some changes were desired and/or planned, whereas others either were made to happen un-/subconsciously or simply took place. While attempting to write a book like this one, it becomes necessary to decide beforehand the scope of the work – that is, where to begin, where to end, what to examine from among all of history's continuous and interconnected processes, and how to accomplish this task.

This chapter elaborates on (1) the temporal and spatial scope of the present volume, (2) the relative and absolute chronological framework used for the research and descriptions presented in the volume and (3) the theoretical framework needed for the investigations and discussions contained in the volume. What follows might, at times, come across as a theory-heavy undertaking, but such a theoretical base is essential for accurately following the previously mentioned frameworks, due to the complexities anticipated in the undertaking.

2. SCOPE

2.1. Temporal Scope

As mentioned earlier, the Yayoi period was the first fully agrarian phase in Japanese history.[1] The

Kofun period is commonly regarded as the state-formation phase.[2]

In that sense, the problem of where to begin the investigation is relatively uncontroversial: it has to begin with the period preceding the onset of the Yayoi period, that is, the Final Jomon period,[3] and even the years before it, if necessary (for an outline of the Jomon period, see Habu 2004). In order to understand the causes and consequences of the introduction of a complex of new social, cultural and economic traits (hereafter referred to as the Yayoi package), we need to understand the conditions that existed before the period. As I explain in

---

1 People during the Jomon period might have kept and/or tended some plants (e.g. *Perilla frutescens var. frutescens* [エゴマ], *Lagenaria siceraria var. gourdo* [ヒョウ タン]; soybeans, *Glycine max [L.] Merr.* [ダイズ]) and animals (e.g. boar), and carried out small-scale cereal farming, possibly the slash-and-burn type of farming (e.g. Miyamoto 2009). However, archaeologists have not yet discovered clear, direct evidence of the latter practice, such as carbonised grains of rice, barley (*Hordeum vulgare*), foxtail millet (*Steria italica*) and Japanese barnyard millet (*Echinochloa esculenta*), and their certain imprints on potsherds dating from the Late Jomon and before (Nakazawa 2009).

2 The issue of how to define this entity called the state deserves a book-length treatment (see e.g. Feinman 1998, Yoffee 2005). Some scholars define the Kofun period as the inchoate-state stage (e.g. Tsude 1996), while others argue that the inchoate-state stage began towards the end of the Middle Kofun period (e.g. Wada 2004). The majority of archaeologists and historians, however, accept the interpretation that the ancient state had been established by the beginning of the eighth century AD, when the Taiho-ritsuryo (大宝律令) law-code was implemented (in the year 701), thus firmly imposing a system of residence-based registration of people, taxation, conscription and so on.

3 The Jomon period is divided into the following subphases: the Incipient (c. 12,000~9,500 bp [uncalibrated]), the Initial (c. 9,500~6,000 bp) the Early (c. 6,000~5,000 bp), the Middle (c. 5,000~4,000 bp), the Late (c. 4,000~3,000 bp), and the Final (c. 3,000~2,300 bp) (Habu 2004, 39, fig. 2.5).

the next section, the absolute dating of the onset of the Yayoi period is the subject of ongoing controversy, with 900 BC being proposed as the oldest possible date and 400/300 BC being offered as the most recent one.

It is much more difficult, however, to decide where and how to conclude the volume. This problem is mainly caused by the difficulty, or rather impossibility, of defining the concept of the 'state' in a manner which is acceptable to everyone. Hence, in order to resolve this problem, I had to make a choice. I decided to end the coverage of this volume at the time when *the bureaucratic management of the flow, mobilisation and accumulation of material and human resources, supported by the registration of people by their place of residence, not by their kin affiliation, and enforced by institutionalised means and organisation of violence, came into place.* It is always problematic to impose an artificial cut-off point on a continuous process. There is often a gap between the time when the representative attributes of an organisation such as the state begin operation and the time by which they become firmly established across the domain controlled by the organisation. It is also often the case that the functional significance of kin grouping and kin affiliation do not completely cease, long after the establishment of a residence-based registration of people. Having said that, the combined effect of those attributes is not only clearly evident in the relevant historical documents (see Section 2.4, 'Written Sources', later in this chapter) but also known to have given rise to a number of highly visible changes in archaeological evidence. In other words, the scheme works fairly well as a heuristic device.

In this regard, the period between the late sixth and mid-seventh centuries is crucial. Historical studies have revealed that infrastructural developments and external tensions together accelerated the process of formation of the previously mentioned institutions and their increasing sophistication during the period (e.g. Inoue 1974; Yamao 1977, 85–222).[4]

In archaeological terms, the custom of burying the elite in keyhole tumuli ceased by the end of the sixth century AD, except in parts of the Kanto region.[5] During this period (i.e. between the late sixth and late seventh centuries AD), tumulus groups comprised a large number of round tumuli, which were mostly small in size (*Gunshu-fun*, 群集墳, meaning 'packed tumuli clusters' [PTC]; see Chapter 10.2) were formed throughout the archipelago, except in areas to the south of the southern Kyushu region and north of the northern Tohoku region.[6] In some regions, there was a proliferation of local industries, such as iron- and salt-producing industries, which were run on a substantial scale; notable among these regions were the Tsukushi (筑紫) province (roughly corresponding to the present-day Fukuoka prefecture) of northern Kyushu and the Kibi (吉備) province (centreing around the present-day Okayama prefecture) of the Setouchi region, both of which

---

4 The relationship between the confederacy of polities in the archipelago, called Wa (倭) by the successive Chinese dynasties, and those in the Korean peninsula, later to be integrated into the 'kingdoms' of Koguryo (高句麗), Paekche (百済) and Shilla (新羅), had always been tense – particularly between the late fourth century AD and the late sixth century AD – when the

Wa's foothold in the peninsula, called Mimana (任那) by the Wa, for politico-militaristic interventions into the ongoing conflicts between them was subjugated by the Shilla (this event occurred in AD 562, as recorded in the *Nihonshoki* chronicle). From then on, the re-establishment of a politico-militaristic bridgehead in the southern coast of the peninsula became one of the most important objectives of the emerging ancient state (e.g. Yamao 1977). The maintenance of (an ever-shifting) alliance with those polities – in the form of reciprocal exchanges of militaristic aides, prestigious goods, resources and artisans with sophisticated manufacturing and engineering technology – continued to be vital for the maintenance of the confederacy of powerful clans and their internal hierarchy during the Early and Middle Kofun periods, circa between the late third and the late fifth centuries AD (see Chapter 9). As the three previously mentioned Korean polities became stronger, and their internal conflicts made it increasingly difficult to control Mimana (particularly from about the beginning of the sixth century AD), the Wa's interventions in these conflicts became increasingly substantial and organised.

5 One of the last keyhole tumuli built in the Kinki region, the Mise-Maruyama (見瀬丸山) tumulus, is 318 metres long (the sixth largest of all the keyhole tumuli) and dates back to the late sixth century AD. We will learn more about the implications of its construction in Chapter 11.2.1.

6 However, there exist some large clusters of small round tumuli with mortuary facilities that copied (though much modified) the gallery mortuary chambers of the Late Kofun period, dated to about seventh and eighth century AD, in the northern Tohoku region. The Ezuriko (江釣子) tumuli cluster in Kitakami city, Iwate prefecture, is an example (cf. Takahashi 1991).

were remote from the centre, that is, the present-day central Kinki region (the region around the Nara and Osaka prefectures, or the 'Kinki-core' region [KCR]). Archaeologists have unearthed palatial elite residential compounds in the KCR (notably the Oharida [小墾田] palace, built in AD 603; see Chapter 11). The construction of Buddhist temples was widespread towards the end of the period.

All these findings suggest that during these centuries, there occurred some highly significant changes in the organisation of the work, life, death and worldview of both the elite and the commoners and the structure of their relations. Therefore, I end my analysis at the period around the late seventh century AD.

2.2. *Spatial Scope*

The process which has been summarised earlier unfolded within the area roughly corresponding to the Kyushu, Shikoku and Honshu islands. Its boundaries were very fluid and changed constantly (it is a problematic exercise to define them with any certainty; see Fujisawa 2004a, for instance).

The Yayoi package was initially introduced in certain *spots* of the northern Kyushu region; it gradually spread to the south until it reached the borders of Kyushu Island and to the northeast until it reached the borders of Honshu Island, although many of its elements were either dropped or heavily modified along the way. Interestingly, some elements of the package, including certain pottery shape-types and the technique of constructing rice paddies, diffused quickly along the coastal regions of the Japan Sea and the Pacific Ocean to reach the northern part of Tohoku region in Honshu Island by the end of the Early Yayoi period (the periodisation scheme is introduced later), which also meant that many areas between the southern Tohoku and Tokai regions were left behind, in terms of 'becoming the Yayoi', until the Middle Yayoi period (Takase 2004).

The northern part of the Tohoku region in Honshu, however, abandoned rice paddy field agriculture during the Late Yayoi period. During the Kofun period, a fluid boundary, archaeologically recognised by the use of different material culture items, house types, mortuary practices and so on, emerged around the northern borders

of the present-day Miyagi and Nigata prefectures (Fujisawa 2004a), and various types of exchanges and interactions took place between the communities, which appear to have identified themselves as mutually distinct groups (ibid.). The inhabitants of the area north of this boundary later came to be defined as a distinct ethnic group (variously referred to as 'Emishi' and 'Ezo', both described in Chinese characters 蝦夷; ibid.) and were targeted by militaristic expeditions undertaken by the emerging ancient state.[7]

The islands dotting the East China Sea in the area between the islands of Kyushu and Taiwan never fully adopted the Yayoi package, though various types of contacts continued between these islands throughout the time periods covered by the present volume (e.g. Fujimoto 1988, 76–102). During the Kofun period, southern Kyushu had very few elements in common with the Kofun *culture*, although the eastern part of the region was firmly located in the Kofun sociocultural horizon during the Early and Middle Kofun periods. As the ancient state emerged, the inhabitants of these non-conformist regions became defined as distinct ethnic groups, subject to various oppressions (Tanaka 2004).[8]

The history of these regions located *outside* the area – which consistently remained 'inside' the Yayoi and Kofun *sociocultural horizons* – deserve separate treatments, and their studies have to be assessed by taking firmly into account the fact that they have been conducted by the 'insiders' and hence may be biased to various degrees. In other words, these regions, which have been treated as the 'others' in the mainstream imperial history and therefore subjected to biased views, deserve separate book-length studies (see Fujimoto 1988). The current volume's spatial scope is confined to the areas 'inside' Japan, that is, the regions extending from southern Kyushu, excluding the Okinawa

7 The earliest recorded example of such a militaristic expedition was that conducted by Abe no Hirafu (阿部比羅夫), who has been mentioned in the *Nihonshoki* chronicle as having conducted military-emissary expeditions to the coastal regions of northern Japan that extended as far north as the southern part of Hokkaido Island between AD 658 and 660.

8 Their position can be understood as an artificial creation by an ancient state seeking to establish itself in the midst of 'barbaric peripheries' (Tanaka 2004). I return to the issue later on in the volume.

(i.e. the south-western section of the Ryukyu) islands, up to the Tohoku region, excluding its northern part, that is the present-day Iwate, Akita and Aomori prefectures. We can refer to this spatial entity as 'Middle Japan'.

This does not imply, however, that the volume does not mention the other regions. The regions 'inside' need the presence of those 'outside' in order to identify themselves and sustain their internal organisational coherence and operation. The 'inside', meanwhile, was the outside to the 'outside' regions. Such 'outsides' include the polities, states and empires that rose and fell in the Korean peninsula and mainland China. In this volume, such 'outsides' are referred to in terms of the ways in which Middle Japan interacted with them in order to identify and sustain itself.

2.3. *Regional Division and Names*

The regions on the 'inside', that is, the Japanese archipelago minus Hokkaido Island, the surrounding islets to the north and the Okinawa (i.e. the south-western section of the Ryukyu) islands to the south, can be divided into a number of regions, albeit in different ways based on different criteria. It is widely known and recognised that different material culture items and traits are often distributed differently, and even variables of individual attributes comprising a distinct artefact type show different spatio-temporal distributions (see Clarke 1978). In that sense, it is virtually impossible to propose a scheme of regional divisions that would exactly reflect the entirety of material, sociocultural, economic and political realities.

The sevenfold division of regions (*Chiho*, 地方)[9] aptly serves the purpose of practicality. The seven regions, from the north to the south, include the Tohoku, Kanto, Chubu, Kinki, Chugoku, Shikoku and Kyushu regions (Figure 3.1.A); of these, the Tohoku and Kanto regions are often subdivided into northern and southern parts. The northern Tohoku region consists of Aomori, Akita and Iwate prefectures, while the southern Tohoku region consists of Yamagata, Miyagi

and Fukushima prefectures. The northern Kanto region consists of Gunma, Tochigi and Ibaraki prefectures, while the southern Kanto region consists of Saitama, Tokyo, Kanagawa and Chiba prefectures. The Chubu region is subdivided into the Koshin'etsu (consisting of Yamanashi, Nagano and Nigata prefectures), the Hokuriku (Toyama, Ishikawa and Fukui prefectures) and the Tokai regions (Gifu, Aichi and Shizuoka prefectures), whereas the Kinki region consists of Shiga, Kyoto, Nara, Osaka, Hyogo, Wakayama and Mie prefectures. (Mie prefecture is at times treated as a part of the Tokai region.) The Chugoku region is subdivided into the San'yo (consisting of Okayama, Hiroshima and Yamaguchi prefectures) and San'in (Shimane and Tottori prefectures) regions, and the Kyushu region consists of Fukuoka, Oita, Saga, Nagasaki, Kumamoto, Miyazaki, Kagoshima and Okinawa prefectures (Figure 3.1.A). The regions are sometimes lumped together into two larger units, that is, *western* and *eastern Japan*; the former extends from the Kyushu region to the Kinki region, while the latter extends from the Chubu region to the Tohoku region (Figure 3.1.B). During the periods covered in the current volume, the Kyushu region, because of its proximity to the Korean peninsula, and hence to the mainland of Asia, occupied a unique and distinct position. For that reason, Kyushu is often treated as a distinct regional unit, separate from western Japan.

The regions in Japan are, as already indicated, currently subdivided into 'prefectures' (first designated in the Meiji era) (Figure 3.1.B). Many of their present boundaries roughly correspond to those of the ancient administrative provinces (*Kuni*, 国) that were officially designated in the early eighth century AD. The basic framework of the *region-wise* division also derives from that of ancient administrative districts called *Do* (道), which date back to the seventh century AD.[10] Their ancient origins suggest that the divisions reflect wider environmental-historical trajectories to a certain extent. In the following text, I refer the prefectures as indicators for the locations of the

---

9 The word *district* can also be considered as a candidate. However, in this case, administrative implications, the presence of which differentiates the word *district* from *region*, are weak or almost none. Therefore, the word *region* is used.

10 The proto-entities of the *Kuni* and *Do* would have certainly existed before the implementation of the Taiho-ritsuryo (大宝律令) law code (AD 801), which officially designated them as the basic administrative districts.

sites and refer to those ancient schemes, if needed, for further contextual clarity.

2.4. *Written Sources*

The oldest written record of the *activities* of people living in the land of Japan can be found in the Chinese imperial chronicle of *He Han-sue* (後漢書, *The Book of Late Han*), which was compiled by Fan Ye (范曄; AD 398–455), in the fifth century AD. The chronicle depicts the existence of a group called 'Wo' or 'Wa' (倭; the current volume follows the widely accepted convention and therefore uses Wa throughout), which inhabited the land across the ocean from the Han commandery of Lelang (楽浪郡; established in 108 BC).[11] The *He Han-sue* records that the Wa used to send an annual tributary delegation to the imperial authorities. The early Han empire's establishment of the four commanderies of Lelang (楽浪), Xuantu (玄菟), Zhenfan (真番) and Lintun (臨屯) around the north-eastern regions of China and northern part of the Korean peninsula incorporated the Japanese archipelago in terms of direct contact with and influence from the empire.[12] Since then, the chronicles of the successive Chinese dynasties, namely, the Wei (魏, AD 220–265), Liu Song (劉宋, AD 420–479) and Shui (隋, AD 581–611) have recorded the arrival of envoys and delegations sent by successive chiefs and paramount figures of the archipelago and have described the political situation as well as the visitors' customs that were found to be either interesting or relevant to their political strategy concerning interventions in communities residing along the empire's north-eastern periphery.

11 This commandery was a sort of colony set up for political, cultural and militaristic purposes. It was managed by a governor sent by the highest authority and was administered by bureaucrats either sent by the authority or locally recruited. Such commanderies were responsible for monitoring the military activities of polities on the periphery of the empire and controlling them by receiving tributes from these polities and granting them prestigious gifts and authorised statuses in exchange (e.g. Takakura 1995, 103–109).

12 The commanderies of Zhenfan and Lintun were abolished in 82 BC, Xuantu was moved to the Liaotong region in 75 BC and Lelang became the sole commandery in charge of dealing with the polities located along the north-eastern periphery of the empire (e.g. Takakura 1995, 103–109).

As already mentioned, the chronicles' depictions of the archipelago reflect the extent to which the empires valued contact with the archipelago and utilised it for furthering their interests. For instance, the *Wei-zhi* (魏志) chronicle, famous for its entry about the Yamatai-koku (邪馬台国) polity and its legendary Queen Himiko (卑弥呼), includes highly detailed – and at times even anthropological – descriptions of the political system and customs of the land. The chronicle's special treatment of the Wa is interpreted to have been related to the Wei's politico-militaristic rivalry with their neighbours to the south, the Wu (呉) (Yamao 1986). It appears that the archipelago at this time was mistakenly believed to stretch southward rather than north-westward and was believed to be located to the east of the present-day Fujian (福建) province across the East China Sea (ibid.). For the Wei, it was important to maintain tributary relations with the Wa in order to politically pressurise the Wu, and the special treatments meted out to the Wa, as revealed by the chronicle, in addition to the diplomatic dealings with them are interpreted by historians to be related to this ongoing tension in mainland China (Nishijima 1985).[13] The depictions, in that sense, might be biased in terms of exaggerating the politico-militaristic potential of Wa and its cultural sophistication. Hence, these descriptions should not be regarded as a definitive factual framework in which we should fit the patterns revealed by the relevant archaeological evidence. In a subsequent section, I return to the issue of possible biases caused by the interests and strategic concerns of the authors of written sources and the authority that ordered their compilation later.

Despite this inherent problem, it would be unwise to be totally dismissive about the importance of written sources. Careful readings of the chronicles would enable us not only to understand the role played by the Wa as seen from the Chinese perspective but also to get a glimpse of the political strategies followed by the period's dominant polities and their elite. For instance, the aforementioned Queen Himiko appears to have tactfully

13 In addition to the golden seal (*Kin* [金] – *in* [印]), which granted rulership under the Wei emperor's authority, and other symbolic items showing the emperor's authorisation, a hundred bronze mirrors were presented to Queen Himiko as her 'favourite items' (好物).

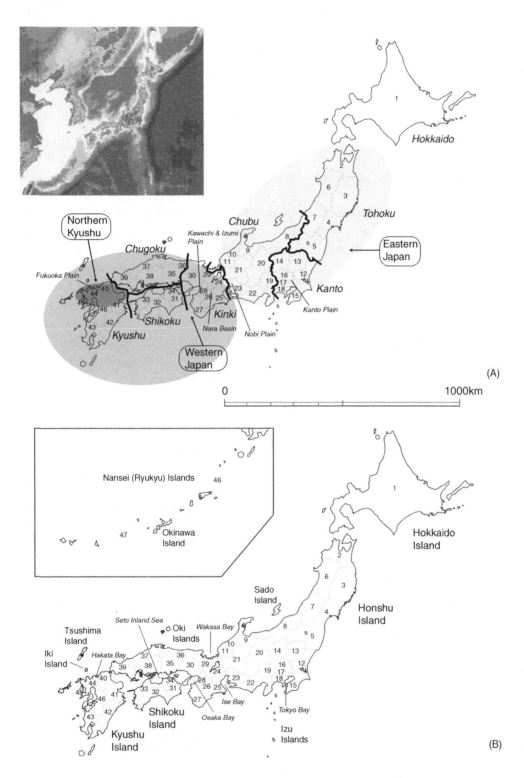

Figure 3.1. Regional divisions and names: prefectures, regions, and larger regional divisions (northern Kyushu, western Japan and eastern Japan, to be used in this volume). (**A**) Regions and larger regional divisions with major plains, and (**B**) prefectures. Inset for the location of the archipelago on the eastern fringe of the Asian mainland. The names of major islands and bays are also mentioned in (**B**). Prefectural names: 1 Hokkaido, 2 Aomori, 3 Iwate, 4 Miyagi, 5 Fukushima, 6 Akita, 7 Yamagata, 8 Niigata, 9 Toyama, 10 Ishikawa, 11 Fukui, 12 Ibaraki, 13 Tochigi, 14 Gunma, 15 Chiba, 16 Saitama, 17 Tokyo, 18 Kanagawa, 19 Yamanashi, 20 Nagano, 21 Gifu, 22 Shizuoka, 23 Aichi, 24 Shiga, 25 Mie, 26 Nara, 27 Wakayama, 28 Osaka, 29 Kyoto, 30 Hyogo, 31 Tokushima, 32 Kochi, 33 Ehime, 34 Kagawa, 35 Okayama, 36 Tottori, 37 Shimane, 38 Hiroshima, 39 Yamaguchi, 40 Fukuoka, 41 Oita, 42 Miyazaki, 43 Kagoshima, 44 Saga, 45 Nagasaki, 46 Kumamoto, 47 Okinawa.

shifted Yamatai's political alliance and utilised the Wei's authorisation of her as the ruler of the Wa in a conflict against a polity called Kuna or Kunu (狗奴). The chronicle of Liu Song, *Song-shu* (宋書), records the arrival of at least nine delegations sent by five successive paramount Wa chieftains between AD 421 and 478 (Nishijima 1985, chap. 2). *Song-shu* also records the contents of the letters handed to the emperors, in which the paramount chiefs, called O (大, great and supreme) – *kimi* (君, master), pleaded to be granted titles authorising them to act as the military rulers of not only the Wa but also the polities of the Korean peninsula.[14] Their pleas were partially granted.

The earliest Japanese imperial chronicles, that is, the *Kojiki* (古事記) and the *Nihonshoki* (日本書紀), were completed in AD 712 and 720, respectively, and included compilations of various historical records as well as ancestral legends dating back to ancient times, inherited by powerful aristocratic clans (which were later to form the ruling class of the ancient state) (Yamao 1977). In the process of their compilation, it has already been mentioned that the preexisting records and legends were selectively eliminated and/or modified, while some new fictitious episodes were created and added to the chronicles (e.g. Inoue 1960, 70–131). The episodes and events which do not fit into the official narrative line, such as those portraying the emperor Ten'mu (天武; who ordered the compilation of the *Nihonshoki* chronicle), his genealogy and his descendants as the legitimate and most worthy successors of the imperial genealogy, whose ancestry can be traced back to the supreme goddess Amaterasu (天照大神), are thought to have been either expunged or modified (e.g. Yamao 1977), and the gaps between the recorded and memorised events were often filled with newly invented episodes and events, such as heroic deeds by fictional figures (often depicted as the founding ancestors of the powerful clans forming the ruling class of the ancient state) and the founding of institutions which, in reality, were established much later (e.g. Inoue 1960, 1965). The *Nihonshoki* chronicle also refers to and cites other records, such as the Chinese imperial chronicles and the chronicles of the history

of the three dominant polities (recorded as the 'kingdoms' of Koguryo [高句麗], Paekche [百済] and Shilla [新羅] of the peninsula).[15] This means that those chronicles reflect a number of different (and, in some cases, mutually conflicting) political interests of different groups.

The textual critique undertaken by historians to remove biases generated by such conflicting interests involves a careful comparison between the texts and their different versions, which are then further compared with various Chinese and Korean sources that also recorded events which occurred during the time periods covered by the chronicles (e.g. works by Mitsusada Inoue and Yukihisa Yamao, cited in the present volume). Historians hope that this comparison between sources covering the same events but written by authors with differing political interests and strategic intentions will enable them to recognise contradictions, detect hints of exaggeration and reconstruct what really happened. Such comparative efforts not only have exposed the fictitious elements and those that have been modified in order to adapt them to the purpose of the compilation but also have revealed certain elements which can be treated as facts or reflections of real events. In addition, this work has also provided us with some insights into people's concrete opinions and perceptions regarding certain events and the ways in which they made sense of and coped with issues pertaining to the daily as well as special/political domain.

The initial entries in both the *Kojiki* and the *Nihonshoki* trace the mythical beginning of the reign of the imperial ancestors, described as the descendants of gods, and chronicle the deeds of successive emperors (and empresses) and events by the reign of each emperor. It is now widely agreed that the entries which either can be authenticated as to their factuality by referring to other sources or have sufficient feasibility which is confirmed by their content and context tend to increase from the reign of the emperor Ojin (応神), who reigned during the late fourth and early fifth centuries AD (Inoue 1960). Moreover, it is widely accepted that the five 'kings' who, as recorded in *Song-shu*, sent their envoys to the Liu Song court, requesting to be granted the official status of the commander of

14 See Footnote 4 to this chapter for the situation in the Korean peninsula at the time.

15 The *Chronicle/Records of Paekche* (*Baekje bongi*, 百済本記) is one of the most often referred and cited.

the peninsula as well as the archipelago, must be from among the emperors Nintoku (仁徳), Richu (履中), Hanzei (反正), Ingyo (允恭), Anko (安康) and Yuryaku (雄略). The chronicles record an increasing number of entries from the reigns of the emperors Keitai (継体), Ankan (安閑), Senka (宣化) and Kinmei (欽明) onwards, which can be compared to entries in many other sources.

It is essential to conduct careful comparisons between the outcomes of archaeological and historical studies. If we can determine any *correlates* and/or *co-transformations* between archaeological and historical/written evidences, we might be able to avoid being totally deceived by the intentional distortions and biases perpetrated by the authors of the chronicles and eventually extract some unique information and additional insights into the changing realities of the lives and world of these ancient people, filled with their own intentions, strategies and meanings. I have used the word *additional*, in this respect, because the available material culture items also mediate the execution of intentional, strategic and meaningful acts. In that sense, material culture studies can also reveal the nature and character of these aspects of the past, albeit from a different perspective. However, written information undoubtedly enriches our 'understanding' of those things; the word *understanding*, in this context, implies that we can incorporate something *outside of our own paradigm of making sense of things* into our study.

Our study of the Kofun period and its subsequent times will reveal the presence of any correlates and/or co-transformations between the archaeological and historical/written evidences. However, it has to be emphasised that useful comparisons can only be achieved if the archaeological investigations conducted are independent of the outcomes of historical studies. Otherwise, the comparisons would end up following a typical circular argumentation: the written source said so-and-so; therefore, the archaeological evidence can be interpreted in such-and-such manner, and because the same archaeological evidence revealed so-and-so patterns, the same written source can be understood in such-and-such manner. In that sense, I would not entirely concur with the position that the outcome of archaeological studies can be used to either authenticate or falsify the entries in written sources (cf. Tsude 2005). My study of the Kofun period and its subsequent times is expected to reveal the presence of any correlates and/or co-transformations between archaeological and historical/written evidences, and if it is indeed possible to determine such correlates and/or co-transformations, we carefully examine the historical/written sources in an appropriate manner for references that would make our interpretations more meaningful and 'thicker' (Geertz 1973).

3. CHRONOLOGY

3.1. Relative Chronology

The study of the periods covered in this volume can be characterised according to well-organised and detailed relative chronological systems (Table 3.1). The study of the Yayoi period, for instance, is basically based on the typo-chronology of its pottery (see Figure 6.1.A–D), whereas that of the Kofun period is based on the combined typo-chronology of its pottery (including the *Haji* and *Sue* wares and *Haniwa* vessels[16]), the typo-chronology of the mound shapes of the keyhole tumuli and the seriation of the grave good assemblages.

Their validity is repeatedly checked by the seriation of successive temporal type-artefacts and their co-presence in individual assemblages/contexts. They are also double-checked, whenever possible, by means of stratigraphy and by examining the overlap between features. At times, the importance of endlessly refining the systems is overemphasised, and there are cases in which the judicious application of relevant methods and caution is sacrificed for the sake of differentiating the artefacts into an ever-increasing list of subphases. However, this volume utilises the commonly used five-phase scheme for study of the Yayoi period (Table 3.1). Phases I, II, III, IV and V of the Yayoi period are commonly arranged

16 The *Haji* wares (土師器) are the direct descendant of the technological and stylistic tradition of the Yayoi pottery, fired in an oxidised atmosphere and characterised by their reddish-brown appearance. The *Sue* wares (須恵器) are a type of stoneware developed from the Korean stoneware tradition, fired in a deoxidised atmosphere (in sloped-tunnel kilns) and characterised by a greyish appearance. For more information on the *Haniwa* vessels, see Chapter 9.2.3.

TABLE 3.1. *Relative chronological chart*

Phase description (1)	(2)	(3)	Absolute dates	AMS dates
Final Jomon/Initial Yayoi (N. Kyushu)*	*Initial/Incipient*		c. 800 BC; TPQ (Cross-dating)	****
Yayoi I	*Early*			*****
Yayoi II	*Middle*			
Yayoi III	*Middle*			
Yayoi IV	*Middle*		c. 75–50 BC; TPQ (datable artefacts imported from China)	
Yayoi V**	*Late*			
Yayoi VI/Shonai	*Y-K transitional*		c. AD 200–250; TPQ (datable artefacts imported from China)	******
Kofun I	*Early*	*1st half EK***		
Kofun II	*Early*	*1st half EK*		
Kofun III	*Early*	*2nd half EK*		
Kofun IV	*Early*	*2nd half EK*		
Kofun V	*Middle*	*1st half MK*	c. AD 400	
Kofun VI	*Middle*	*1st half MK*		
Kofun VII	*Middle*	*2nd half MK*		
Kofun VIII	*Middle*	*2nd half MK*		
Kofun IX	*Late*	*1st half LK*	c. AD 500	
Kofun X	*Late*	*2nd half LK*		
Kofun XI/Final/Terminal Kofun			c. AD 600	
Asuka			AD 645 TAQ	

* See Footnote 18. ** Some gap between northern Kyushu and western Japan concerning beginning of the Yayoi V, see Footnote 17. *** Further explanations on the description in this volume of the phases of the Kofun period, see Note 1, Chapter 9. **** c. 900 cal BC according to the AMS dating of soot adhering to potsherds by the National Museum of Japanese History (2004), and c. 600 cal BC according to the AMS dating of human and animal bones further calibrated by taking oceanic reservoir effect into account (see Tanaka et al. 2004). ***** Dated to c. 600 cal BC according to the soot dating by the National Museum of Japanese History (2004). ****** Dated to c. 240–260 cal AD TAQ by the National Museum of Japanese History (2011). EK = Early Kofun; MK = Middle Kofun; LK = Late Kofun; TPQ = terminus post quem; TAQ = terminus ante quem.

into a three-period scheme in which the Yayoi I constitutes the Early Yayoi period, the Yayoi II–IV constitute the Middle Yayoi period and the Yayoi V constitutes the Late Yayoi period. Each phase can be further subdivided on the basis of temporal changes in individual pottery shape-types, but the five-phase scheme[17] is detailed enough for the investigation in the current volume

(Table 3.1).[18] The debate continues over when to mark the beginning of the Kofun period. The argument is focused on the phase characterised by the widespread use of the so-called Shonai (庄内) style pottery assemblage. This volume calls the period the Yayoi VI/Shonai phase. Moreover, this volume uses the eleven-phase scheme for the study of the Kofun period (Wada 1987). They are

17 It is important to subdivide the Yayoi IV period, however, in that there are some discrepancies between the first and second zones with regard to this phase. In western Japan, the Yayoi IV is commonly divided into four sub-stages, simply called the Yayoi IV-1~4. The Yayoi IV-3~4 corresponds with the earlier part of the first half of the Yayoi V in northern Kyushu and is commonly called the Takamizuma (高三潴)-style pottery phase. To be more precise, the Takamizuma style can be divided into two micro-phases, and the end of the Yayoi IV-4 in western Japan is contemporaneous with

the beginning of the later Takamizuma-style micro-phase. This situation has arisen from some confusion in the nomenclature, and I carefully synchronize the respective phenomena pertaining to these regions when we need to chart their temporal changes and compare them subsequently in the volume.

18 The 'incipient' phase is added to before the Yayoi I in the northern Kyushu region where a number of settlements adopted lifeways based on rice paddy field agriculture in the second half of the Final Jomon period (e.g. Sahara 1983, 4–5).

commonly divided into the Early (phases I–IV), Middle (phases V–VIII) and Late (phases IX–XI) Kofun periods. The Early and Middle Kofun periods are sometimes lumped together under the title of the *Earlier* Kofun period. Phase XI of the Kofun period extends from the end of the sixth century AD to the seventh century AD, when the construction of the keyhole tumuli ceased and the process towards the establishment of the ancient state accelerated. Scholars nowadays increasingly tend to separate phase XI of the Kofun period from the Late Kofun period, calling it the *Final* Kofun period. For this study's purposes, the five-phase scheme of the Yayoi period and the eleven-phase scheme of the Kofun period are highly reliable temporal frameworks for investigating the long-term processes that occurred during these periods (Table 3.1). The divisions between the phases are generally defined by the emergence of new and characteristic artefacts and other material items, ranging from the portable to the monumental. This volume elaborates on a selection of these items as 'time markers' in order to make the shift from one phase to the next one reflect significant cultural, social, economic, political changes and/or developments. In that sense, the systems can be used to trace the meaningful changes and developments in the long-term processes that are covered and investigated by the present volume.

3.2. Absolute Chronology

The aforementioned phases and sub-phases have long been absolute-dated by artefacts brought in from mainland China and the Korean peninsula. We also have an increasing number of calibrated carbon-14 (C-14) dates measured by the accelerator mass spectrometry (AMS) method.

The practices of writing, making calendars and recording matters of significance for the rulers of the domain began very early in China.[19] Accordingly, China has played the same role in the building of absolute chronology for the Korean peninsula and the Japanese archipelago as Egypt did for Europe; as various items from China made their way into the Korean peninsula, Korean artefacts can be cross-dated (i.e. their synchronicity can

be confirmed by finding the same combination of imported and domestic time-marker artefacts both in China and Korea) with the Chinese absolute chronological system, and the same process has been attempted for cross-dating the Korean and Japanese systems. However, the problems in this scheme are twofold. First, unless the year of production is inscribed on the item, the date of the item's production can only be determined in terms of the duration of years, which can be long at times. Second, the length of time elapsed between the production and deposition of an item can vary significantly, and this can only be inferred based on circumstantial evidences. The latter problem becomes increasingly worse as the chain of cross-dating is stretched. In short, by using datable artefact-based absolute chronology, we can only obtain the *termini post quem* (TPQ) of the items, with the elapse of an uncertain length of time between their production and the actual time of their deposition.

It is hoped that the rapid development and increasing use of the AMS method will solve these problems. However, there remain some issues that need to be resolved, the most serious of which concerns the calibration curve.

The amount of C-14 (the previous method is based upon the assumption that this amount is consistent in the Earth's atmosphere) has fluctuated considerably due to fluctuations in solar activity.[20] Therefore, the dates have to be calibrated with the measurement of the actual amount of carbon in the atmosphere at that time, taken from individual tree rings whose absolute dates have been determined by dendrochronology. The curve obtained by these measurements shows a number of plateaus marking the times of weak solar activity, when the amount of carbon in the atmosphere is larger than usual, thus making the uncalibrated dates appear older than the true dates (see Chapter 4.2, p. 45). The beginning of the Yayoi period, unfortunately for the archaeologists, exactly coincides with one of the longest plateaus of that kind in the calibration curve, which makes the accurate determination of the true date extremely difficult.

---

19 The so-called oracle bone script, used for the purpose of divination, dates from the late Shang dynasty (c. 1200–1050 BC).

20 Innumerable introductory texts on the method are available. For a concise and approachable description (also covering other radiometric dating methods), see Renfrew and Bahn (2008, chap. 4).

Some published AMS dates are also considerably older than the artefact TPQ dates (contra National Museum of Japanese History [NMJH] 2004; hereafter, the NMJH dates)[21]: as argued earlier, the latter are the oldest possible dates, and the true dates are likely to be later than them, naturally giving rise to a degree of caution for deciding the former. A potential cause of this discrepancy might be related to the nature of the material used for the dating, that is, soot adhering to the outer surface of potsherds; it has been claimed that the dates measured from collagen extracted from skeletal remains are consistently more recent than those measured from soot adhering to the outside of cooking vessels (Tanaka, Mizoguchi and Iwanaga 2004). The influence of the marine reservoir effect is also expected to make the skeletal remains appear considerably older than their true age. This means that the NMJH AMS dates are even older than the bone dates biased (i.e. made older than the true date) by the marine reservoir effect. In that sense, factors other than the 'old wood problem' (i.e. an older date than the true date of the time period from which the given artefact/feature used and abandoned/deposited is produced by the gap between the time when the tree was cut down and when it was used) are likely to be involved (ibid.).

We have no definite items with reliable TPQ dating back before the Yayoi IV, when we begin to find Early Han bronze mirrors of a certain type, dating back to the second quarter of the first century BC (Okamura 1984), deposited in relative-datable burial jars in the northern Kyushu region (Okazaki 1977). It has been suggested that some of these mirrors were presented as funeral offerings by the Chinese authorities (Yanagida 1983), and the time gap between their production and

deposition would have not been very long.[22] From then onwards, through the beginning of the Kofun period, there is a constant flow of fairly accurately absolute-datable bronze mirrors from the domain of the successive Chinese dynasties, which enables us to determine the TPQ of individual phases with some degree of certainty.

From the Early Kofun period onwards, however, this flow of absolute-datable Chinese mirrors and similar other artefacts reduces. However, increasing contact between the local communities and those in the Korean peninsula allows the cross-dating of the artefacts, which become increasingly connectable with the events that are recorded in the relevant written sources (e.g. Kawano and Nishikawa 2003). However, while using this method, it is obviously essential to be aware of the previously mentioned problems pertaining to the method.

In the following sections, the absolute dates accorded to the phases from the onset of the Yayoi period to the time immediately preceding the Yayoi IV include both the oldest and the most recent AMS dates; for instance, the onset of the Yayoi period and Yayoi I are indicated as 900/600 BC and 600/400 BC, respectively. In addition, the Chinese-bronze-mirror-based TPQ dates have been used for the years extending from the Yayoi IV to the beginning of the Kofun period. After the Early Kofun period, this volume adopts dates obtained through cross-dating, which are connected with recorded historical events (Table 3.1).

4. THEORETICAL FRAMEWORK AND STRUCTURE OF THE VOLUME

4.1. Theory

As illustrated in Chapter 2, the Japanese Marxist tradition has produced some innovative examples of studies in archaeological history writing (e.g. Kondo 1983). These studies are characterised by

21 Some potsherds typo-chronologically dated to the Incipient Yayoi were dated by soot adhering to them to around 900 BC. The soot is thought to have mostly been generated from heating for cooking. The beginning of the Yayoi period has been inferred by some circumstantial evidences, including imported iron implements dating from the Warring Nations period of China (c. 480–221 BC), to date from 400–300 BC. The publication of the initial outcome of the NMJH AMS dating project ignited a debate covering from the validity of the NMJH dates to the significance of the application of radiometric dating methods to archaeology, which is still ongoing.

22 Takashi Okazaki showed that the imported bronze mirrors were deposited in relative-chronologically datable burial jars with no inconsistency with their typo-chronological positions. He argued that this showed that the mirrors were not past on across generations as heirlooms and buried with the dead not long after they were imported (Okazaki 1977).

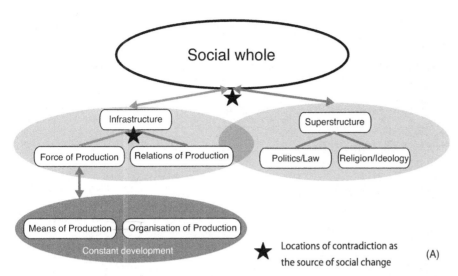

Figure 3.2. Marxist thesis of the structure of social totality (**A**), compared with the social systemic model adopted in the present volume (**B**). Note that the Marxist model comprises the components configured in a dendritic order with potential locations of contradiction as the source of social change at each of the junctures/interfaces of the hierarchically-situated components, whereas the Luhmannian social systemic model (e.g. Luhmann 1994) comprises a number of systems each of which self-reproduces/transforms itself by selectively reacting to its environment which is constituted by all the other systems and natural environment.

their emphasis on the significance of 'contradictions' for the explanation of *social change and stratification* (Figure 3.2.A). According to this approach, *contradictions* emerge between *the force of production* and *the relations of production* in the *infrastructure* of society. These are inevitably intensified by the ever-increasing imbalance and discontent generated between *the force of production* and *the relations of production* due to constant development in the force of production. Such imbalance and discontent have to be contained by the working of *ideology*, which, together with politico-judicial organisations, constitutes the *superstructure* of society, in order for the social organisation to maintain its stability. While ideology can hide or naturalise the emerging contradictions, it also has its limits. When an ideology can no longer contain the destabilisation generated by the contradictions, the composition and contents of the entire society have to change.[23]

This theoretical framework is extremely appealing because it allows us, if we wish, to attribute virtually every single archaeological object to one (or possibly more) of those categories as the material residue of their functional workings. This also implies that virtually every single material item can be explained in terms of the role it played in *social stability* and *change*.

However, the realities of social life are constituted of something more concrete than merely *the force of production* and *the relations of production*. Social reality is maintained and transformed through various *communications* between individuals which form distinct spheres or *fields*, such as the way of life in a certain area (Figure 3.2.B); burying the dead and commemorating the ancestors; producing, exchanging and distributing foodstuffs and material items; constructing architectural structures; praying for the well-being of individuals and groups; and so on. Each of these spheres, described as a 'field of discourse' by John Barrett (1993), or a 'communication system' according to the social systems theory (Figure 3.2.B; Luhmann 1994), is differentiated and marked by various media, both material and immaterial, and reproduced by drawing upon its own structure.[24] 'Structure', in this particular case of theorisation, would most appropriately be understood as the set of *expectations* which are generated through the continuation of communication and which enable future communications to take place and continue, if necessary, after an interval. This structure would involve a

23 For a good example of the application of the Marxist notion of 'contradiction' in the explanation of social reproduction and social change, see pp. 16–17 in Chapter 2.

24 The complex of such fields and their material and immaterial media constitute the 'lifeworld' of people.

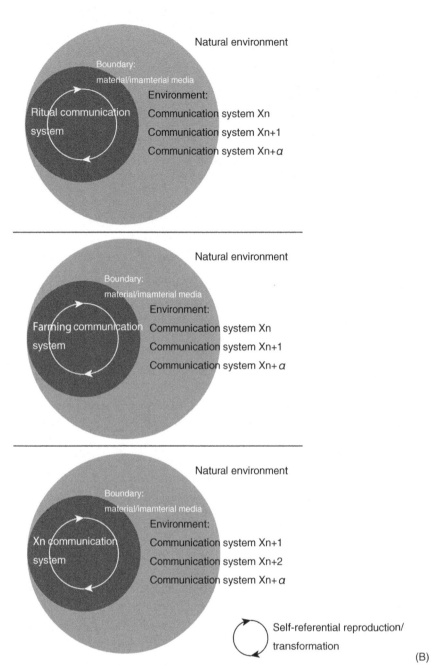

Figure 3.2 *(continued)*

combination of (1) one's expectations regarding others' behaviour in a certain circumstance or setting and (2) one's expectations regarding others' behavioural expectations from him or her in a certain circumstance or setting. In that sense, the *structure of expectations* can be described as *that of self-identities*, and such a structure is often associated with tangible and durable media of various scales, ranging from portable items to architectural structures to landscape features, in order for it to be mediated by their presence and reactivated after an interval. Therefore, to the above set

of expectations constituting the structure we can add a third category, that is, (3) one's expectations regarding how a certain circumstance or setting should be marked by and equipped with what media or items.

Changes in such a structure would naturally result from an increasing number of difficulties in continuing communication by drawing upon the pre-existing set of expectations, that is, the preexisting structure. Such difficulties would be generated by changes occurring (1) in other fields of communication (or communication systems),

(2) in the way a given field and other fields are connected or networked and (3) in the environment wherein a given field and other fields are situated.

A given field can only adjust or react to those changes by drawing upon its own history and the memory of its past operations. The process of such adjustment would involve the following stages: (1) trying out a range of new ways of functioning in order to cope with the new conditions, (2) narrowing the range and (3) establishing the best way of functioning in order to cope with the new conditions and then stabilising the set of expectations reproducing it (see e.g. Luhmann 1994, 432–436).

This volume studies the history of the Yayoi and Kofun periods by tracing the trajectories of such fields of communication/communication systems, and hence of *self-identification*. This study includes determining *what changes/contradictions* arose within/between those fields and examining *how the respective fields dealt with those changes/contradictions and in what way*.

The following study does not try to overemphasise the importance of any one of these fields, because doing so would reduce the complexity of the matter down to a limited number of factors, as the Marxist approach did. However, the reader may notice that the description of the trajectories of some fields such as way of life in a certain area and burial practices for the dead are 'thicker' (cf. Geertz 1973) than those of others. For instance, the village, as a constructed environment, itself works as a cluster of powerful material media that reproduce a wide range of fields of social reproduction. In other words, the village is a *node*, or *container*, or 'dominant locale' (Giddens 1981), of a vast range of human activities: it is the place where people are born, live and die; it is where they eat and excrete; produce things and reproduce themselves; store, use and consume things; and meet, communicate, and exchange things, people, and ideas. In addition, it is important to note that people categorise themselves and renew their mutual obligations through doing the above activities. Hence, our canvas of the archaeological village, in that sense, is a bundle of the remaining traces of those human acts, thoughts and feelings; the orders generated through them; and their changes. Some of them do not leave any tangible material trace,

while others leave their traces only in the form of their absence; dancing, for instance, would only leave its trace as an empty space between the traces of the other activities which leave something tangible and durable enough to be archaeologically recognised. Some activities might involve, either physically or mentally, those who do not usually live in a given village; some activities would be performed to create, confirm and/or renew and at times even sever people's ties with the inhabitants of other villages. Such activities are a part of wider fields of social reproduction whose spatio-temporal coverage exceeds the boundary of a village and extends across a number of villages. It is such fields – the famous exchange ring of kula being a good example in this regard (Malinowski [1922] 1984) – that play a crucial role in collecting people together; coordinating their acts, thoughts and feelings; and connecting various fields of social reproduction to form a larger community.

The act of burying the dead constitutes a significant rite from among the rites of passage-related discourses. The use of the term *burying* might present a very simplistic picture of all the cares, concerns, acts, emotions and their material media involved in the transformation of a person from the state of living to that of the dead, and in some cases, cultures, societies or periods, to the state of the ancestor. The process begins from the acknowledgement of death, involving various stages of treatment of the body, and ends with the disposal of the remains. The transformation of the dead person into an ancestor may involve a prolonged period of further rites/rituals. The rites of commemoration may also continue for a long time after the death. In that sense, to be precise, the discourse of burying the dead consists of, and crosscut, a number of distinct fields of social reproduction. In each of them, different sets of people gather together in order to fulfil different sets of mutual obligations and create, confirm and change different sets of social bonds. Again, the spatio-temporal extension of the social ties reproduced in them far exceeds the limited canvas of individual villages.

In such fields, we can observe the tangible expression of contradictions arising between various fields of social reproduction, and also the way in which people react to these contradictions and deal with them in an intensive manner; those *contradictions*, together with the *expansion* in scale of each field of social reproduction,[25] make difficult and improbable/unsustainable their reproduction themselves, and they have to be reacted to and dealt with. Accordingly, we can investigate both the character of the contradictions and the changes that occur in the fields of social reproduction during the process of people's reacting to and dealing with them.

Therefore, in this volume the topic of settlements and cemeteries is examined and discussed at length in the following chapters, although the other fields will certainly not be neglected.

5. STRUCTURE OF THE VOLUME

Based on the framework described above, Part II of the volume, titled 'Trajectories', first traces the trajectories of the environment and the East Asian context (Chapter 4). Virtually every field of social reproduction is required to react to a change in the natural environment in one way or the other (including the option of not reacting at all!) (Figure 3.2.B). The importance of ancient Japan's interactions with mainland Asia, and its people's concerns of how to react to the changes taking place there, must also have constituted the environment requiring *selective* reactions from the fields of social reproduction.

This chapter is followed by individual chapters describing the changes that simultaneously occurred across a number of fields of social repro-

duction. These changes can be assumed to result from discrepant rhythms of changes, expansion in scale,[26] and/or contradictions between the fields and the fields' reaction to the contradictions. In each of these individual chapters the contents and workings of the fields mentioned earlier are described and analysed and an attempt to interpret the changes in terms of the reactions to the expansion in scale of individual fields, and in terms of the contradictions generated between the fields, is made. Chapter 5 investigates the phase between the Initial Yayoi period and the Yayoi I; Chapter 6, between the final stage of Yayoi I to Yayoi IV; Chapter 7, between the final stage of Yayoi IV to Yayoi V; Chapter 8, the transitional phase between the Yayoi and the Kofun periods; Chapter 9, the Earlier Kofun period; Chapter 10, the Later Kofun period; and Chapter 11 investigates the Final Kofun period and the establishment of the ancient state.

Chapter 12 concludes the volume by succinctly retracing the trajectory of the individual fields of social communication, re-examining the correlations between them and reiterating the factors that are seen to have punctuated the trajectories. This final summing up, it is hoped, reveals the commonalities and uniqueness of the history of early agrarian communities of the Japanese archipelago; the recognition and appreciation of this aspect of history has significantly influenced, and will continue to influence, the way in which the Japanese recognise and identify themselves as a people.

---

25 The expansion, in spatio-temporal scale, of a given field of social reproduction (1) reduces the frequency of the communication responsible for the reproduction of the field to take place and, hence, (2) makes it difficult to re-ignite such communication. In order for these difficulties to be overcome, the structure of the communication needs to be institutionalised and/or the durable material media of the communication need to be invented (cf. Mizoguchi 2009). See Chapter 8.4 in this volume. It is a truism to say that communicative acts are executed by active agents (see e.g. Dobres and Robb 2000). However, in this volume, the fields of social reproduction are treated as constituting autonomous fields/systems, the work/operation of which cannot be reduced to the acts of agents; it is influenced and constituted as significantly by the nature and character of its material and immaterial media as by that of the acts executed by the agents.

26 Of course, some fields would have lost their significance, have shrunk in spatio-temporal scale, and have eventually disappeared. Some fields might have regained their significance after the decline, as a field that embodied (the memory of) the past deeds of the ancestors, for instance (e.g. Bradley 2002).

PART II

TRAJECTORIES

CHAPTER 4

ENVIRONMENT AND THE EAST ASIAN CONTEXT

1. INTRODUCTION

In academic circles, it is being increasingly recognised that seemingly minor climatic changes in the environmental record often have had significant, and at times devastating, effects on human as well as animal and plant communities in the past. A slight fluctuation in the precipitation and annual temperature pattern not only leads to a corresponding change in the faunal and floral populations but also can be connected with a topographic change; long-term trends in temperature fluctuation are often tightly correlated to trends in the fluctuation of the volume of ice in the polar regions, which in turn causes fluctuation in the sea level. Changes in sea level affect the rates of erosion and sedimentation of coastlines and riverine plains (e.g. Iseki 1983). The long-lasting influence of the Marxist approach (see Chapter 2.2.2, 'Post–World War II Reformation and the "Independent-Autonomous" Past'), which explains social reproduction and social change in terms of the management of internal contradictions and its failure, has resulted in keeping the majority of Japanese archaeologists (except the Palaeolithic specialists) away from palaeo-environmental information, in general, and palaeo-climatic data, in particular. However, the generally increasing interest in the application of natural scientific techniques is changing the situation.[1] The following sections summarise the recent and relevant outcomes of this change.

This chapter also reviews the historical trajectories of the areas surrounding the Japanese archipelago. The Yayoi and Kofun periods correspond to the time period extending from the Late Zhou (周) period (c. from the eighth to the third centuries BC) to the Sui (隋; c. AD 581–618) and the Tang (唐; c. AD 618–907) dynasties of China, and from the Bronze Age/the Mumun pottery (無文土器) period through the three-kingdom (三国) period to the unified Silla (新羅) period in Korea.

We can observe a remarkable parallelism between the Korean peninsula and the Japanese archipelago in their historical trajectories, especially from the Middle Yayoi period onwards in the case of the latter, and from the Late Mumun pottery period onwards in the case of the former. This parallelism resulted from increasingly intensifying interactions, including hostile ones, between those regions, both of which were situated on the periphery of the sphere of indirect, and occasionally direct, interventions of the Chinese empires.

Because a considerable number of historical studies have already examined the deepening tension and interdependence between the peninsula and archipelago polities, this chapter attempts to present only a very brief summary of the outcomes

---

1 For the development of the trend, the introduction of the AMS dating technique to the absolute dating of Japanese pre- and proto-history (see Chapter 3.3.2) has been instrumental in that the relationship between the calibration curve of raw C-14 data and the fluctuation of the amount of C-14 in the atmosphere of the earth resulting from the fluctuation of the amount

of solar black spots has made archaeologists realise the importance and possibility of collaboration with natural scientists for not only the dating but also environmental reconstruction (cf. Shitara 2006; Komoto 2007).

(e.g. Inoue 1960, 1965, 1974 Yamao 1977, 1986, 2003).

2. ENVIRONMENT

The Yayoi and Kofun periods coincided with a phase of gradual cooling in global temperature. The temperature rise which began at the end of the Younger Dryas event (c. 10,000 BC), following the sudden and sharp decline in temperature after the Bolling warm stage (c. 12,000 BC), marked the beginning of the post-glacial (Holocene) period and continued until about 4000 BC, when it is believed that the annual average temperature was about two degrees higher during summer than it is today (Burroughs 2005). After this point of time, called the Holocene climatic optimum, the dominant trend has been continuous cooling, with some global episodes of limited but rapid climate change (ibid.).

In northern Europe, scholars have investigated changes in the Holocene climate by studying pollen data gathered from peat bogs, based on which they have identified the following general climate periods: the Preboreal and the Boreal (c. 9500–7000 cal BC), the Atlantic (c. 7000–4000 cal BC), the Sub-Boreal (c. 4000–500 cal BC) and the Sub-Atlantic (c. 500 cal BC to the present). The Boreal period is generally characterised as a cool, dry period with rising temperature, and the Atlantic period, as a warm and wet period, towards the end of which the Holocene warming trend reached its peak (e.g. Burroughs 2005, 175–179). The sub-Boreal period, during which the Yayoi period began, is characterised as a warm and dry period, and the sub-Atlantic period, which substantially overlaps with the Yayoi and Kofun periods, is characterised as a cool and wet period (ibid.). During those periods, however, it is believed that there were some sharp and devastating climatic disturbances. For instance, three notable cooling events have been found to have occurred in the North Atlantic – around 2500–2200 cal BC, around 800 cal BC and around 1,400 cal AD (ibid., 251).

In Japan, the detailed analysis of pollen data by Yutaka Sakaguchi (1982, 1983), who uses the increase and decrease in the percentage of *Pinus* (pine) pollen as an indicator of temperature fluctuations, has revealed that the period between

circa the twenty-first century BC and the mid-ninth century BC was an 'unstable warm stage',[2] that between circa the mid-ninth century BC and the beginning of the fourth century BC was a 'cold stage', that between the beginning of the fourth century BC and the early first century BC was a 'warm stage' and that between the early first century BC and the mid-eighth century AD was an 'unstable cold stage, in which the cold, mild and warm spells frequently alternated' (Sakaguchi 1982, 16).

The preceding picture reasonably coincides with the episodes of 'black band' formation in oceanic sand dunes (Komoto 2007). A black layer in an oceanic sand dune indicates an episode of the slowing down or virtual stoppage of formation of the dune, which allowed vegetation, including grasses and low trees, to invade and form leaf mould (e.g. Iseki 1983). The growing of dunes indicates a cold spell, which in turn causes a lowering of the sea level and an increase in the supply of sediments that contribute to their growth (ibid.). In contrast, an episode of black band formation reflects a warm spell, in which the sea level rises, the supply of sediments ceases and dunes stabilise (Komoto 2007). During the Yayoi and Kofun periods, findings reveal that two major, widespread episodes of black band formation occurred in the archipelago (ibid.). The lack of purpose-specific excavations makes it difficult to specify the terminus post quem (TPQ) and terminus ante quem (TAQ) for the dunes, but it has been confirmed that the greyish layer that lies immediately underneath the sandy layer, which in turn is located below the lower black band, includes potsherds from the middle phase of the Final Jomon period (called the Kurokawa [黒川]-style assemblage; ibid.). The lower black band itself formed a stable base on which cemeteries, such as the Shinmachi (新町; Shima TBE 1987), were situated during the Incipient Yayoi and first half of the Yayoi I. The sandy layer sandwiched between the lower black band and the layer containing the Kurokawa potsherds indicates that the dune underwent a rapid formation episode.

---

2 Although Sakaguchi calibrated C-14 dates using his own method, the calibrated dates coincide fairly well with the calibrations of international conventions such as Intcal98 (Shitara 2006).

With regard to the mechanism of sand dune formation, this sandwiching of the sandy layer between the greyish layer and the lower black band indicates a cold spell and a lowering of the sea level. If we refer to Sakaguchi's findings based on his pollen analysis, the episode can be attributed to the period of cooling between circa the mid-ninth century BC and the beginning of the fourth century BC. It suggests that the beginning of the Yayoi period, that is, the Incipient Yayoi[3] (the Yusu [夜臼]-style assemblage phase; see Chapter 5.3.1–3), dates back to the time during this cold period, and that a part of the Incipient Yayoi and the first half of the Yayoi I date back to the period when it was warm, the sea level rose and the formation of the dunes ceased, that is, after the beginning of the fourth century BC.

Concerning the cooling and warming events illustrated earlier, it is particularly interesting that they appear to coincide with the famous plateau around 2400 uncal BP and the steep drop before that in the calibration curve for radiocarbon dating (IntCal09 2009). Carbon-14 (C-14) is produced by collisions between the nitrogen nuclei and cosmic rays in the upper atmosphere. The amount of cosmic rays reaching the upper atmosphere is influenced by the strength of the sunrays, which prevent cosmic rays to enter the solar system and reach the atmosphere. Therefore, when sunrays are strong, the amount of cosmic rays reaching the upper atmosphere decreases, and the production of C-14 is reduced accordingly.

The strength of sunrays correlates with the activity of sunspots, and the former is weak when the latter is low. These observations suggest that the amount of C-14 in the atmosphere is greater than usual when the sunrays are weaker than usual and vice versa. This means that the phase of steep drop in the calibration curve was a warmer-than-usual period, because a drop implies that there was less C-14 than usual in the atmosphere, which made the dates of the tree rings formed during the phase appear *younger*.[4] Based on a similar mechanism, we

can say that the plateau – resulting from the presence of more C-14 than usual in the atmosphere, which made the dates of the tree rings during the phase appear *older* – was a colder-than-usual period (Figure 4.1.A–C).

The steep drop before the plateau spans roughly the period between 800 and 700 BC, while the plateau roughly extends from 700 to 450 BC. The latter period appears to coincide with Sakaguchi's findings of the cooling episode between circa the mid-ninth century BC and the beginning of the fourth century BC.

If we focus on the calibration curve, however, we observe another steep drop immediately after the plateau. The drop spans roughly the period between 450 BC and 300 BC, and it indicates a warming episode based on the above-mentioned correlations between the strength of sunrays, amount of cosmic rays reaching the upper atmosphere and temperature of the atmosphere. The onset of this warming also reasonably coincides with the *onset* of Sakaguchi's warm stage, that is, circa the beginning of the fourth century BC; however, its end does not correspond with that of Sakaguchi's warm stage, that is, c. the early first century BC. After this drop, there is another plateau, much shorter than the previous one, which spans the time period from circa 300 to 100 cal BC. Since this 200-year period would have been a cooler-than-usual period, it is believed that Sakaguchi's pollen analysis might have missed the abrupt change from a warm to a cold spell.

Nevertheless, the pollen data collected from the site of Hie (比恵) in Fukuoka prefecture, might reflect this colder spell. Hideaki Noi, who examined column samples from the site, suggests that there might have been a drop of one degree centigrade in temperature at some point of time between the final phase of the Yayoi I and Yayoi III/IV. Noi's (1991, 231–233) analysis has revealed that the layers whose TAQ is the final phase of Yayoi I contain a significant amount of hackberry (*Celtis-Aphananthe*) pollen, whereas the amount of

---

3 Or also regarded as the later phase of the Latest Jomon period.

4 The relationship between the strength of sunrays, the amount of cosmic rays reaching the upper atmosphere, and the temperature of the atmosphere is thought to be highly complicated. For instance, it is argued that the amount of cosmic rays reaching the upper atmosphere

correlates with the rate of ionisation which correlates with the amount of cloud (e.g. Marsh and Svensmark 2003). Hence, it can be deduced that when the activity of the sun is weaker than usual, more cosmic rays can reach the upper atmosphere, which causes more cloud cover in the lower atmosphere, resulting in the cooling of the temperature.

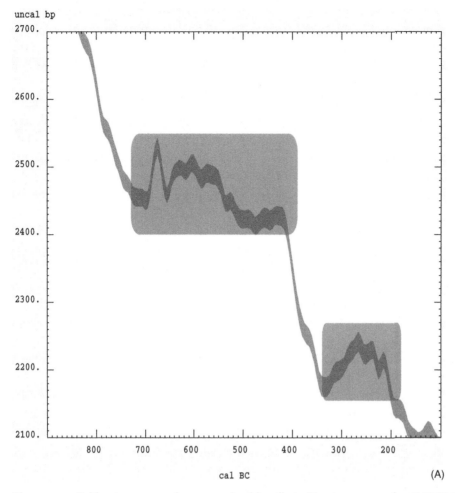

Figure 4.1. Calibration curve, plateaus, and cold spells (calibration curve after CALIB Radiocarbon Calibration, Executive Version 6.0, http://calib.qub.ac.uk/calib/). A: 900 BC to 100 BC; B: 400 BC to 400 AD; C: 100 AD to 700 AD. Possible cold spells are shaded.

oak (*Cyclobalanopsis*) pollen is significantly higher in the layers above this. Noi argues that the increase in the latter indicates a drop in temperature of about one degree centigrade (ibid., 233) and that the former plants tend to flourish during transitional phases between the appearance of warm- and cold-adapted flora (ibid.). This might suggest that the latter established itself in the flora during the above-mentioned cold spell, which probably began some time before the end of the Yayoi I. These observations suggest that the cooling episode which is indicated in the calibration curve began some time before the final phase of the Yayoi I and that the cold spell continued until around the Yayoi III period (and possibly the beginning of the Yayoi IV period), based on the TPQ for the latter, as determined by the imported Early Han Chinese bronze mirrors, dating from the second half of the first century BC (see Chapter 3.3.2, 'Absolute Chronology'). The

Yayoi III, IV and the beginning of the Yayoi V would have experienced climatic fluctuations (Figure 4.1.B).

This nicely corresponds with Noi's (1991) Hie data, which reveal that oak (*Cyclobalanopsis*) pollen remained significant in quantity throughout the Middle Yayoi period (i.e. the Yayoi II–IV).[5]

To sum up, the combination of the formation process of the sand dunes and the black bands in them, Sakaguchi's and Noi's pollen analyses, and the two significant drops and the plateau in the calibration curve suggest that the Yayoi period began during the cold period immediately following the warm period between circa the ninth and eighth centuries BC and that it generally continued to be cold until the early first century BC, except for a possible warm spell between circa the

5 If the data were found to reflect a prolonged colder spell, they would contradict Sakaguchi's pollen analysis, which suggests that the same period was a warm one.

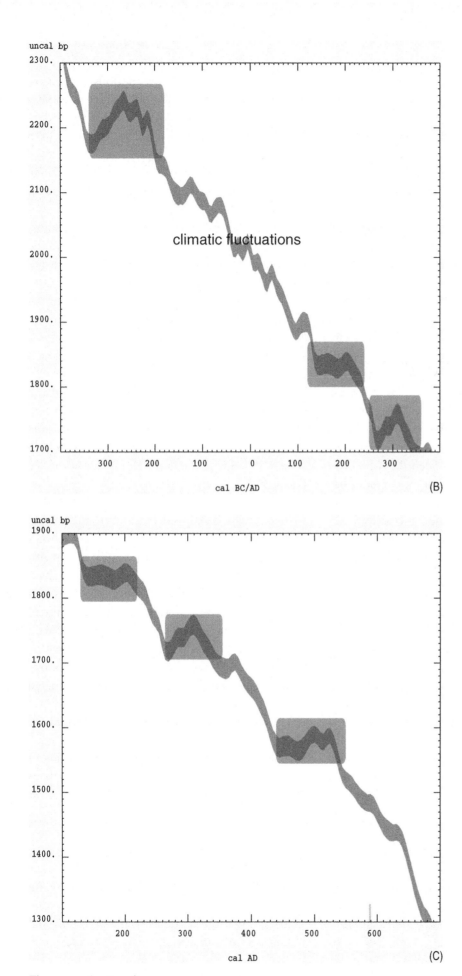

Figure 4.1 (*continued*)

mid-fifth and late fourth centuries BC – the end of which probably overlaps with the final phase of the Yayoi I.

The formation of the previously mentioned black band, based on the archaeological evidence, appears to have continued until at least the beginning of the Kofun period, indicated by the potsherds of the early *Haji* ware collected from the upper layers of the black band in the Doigahama site (Iseki 1983). However, Sakaguchi's (1982, 16) pollen analysis indicates that the period between circa the early first century BC and the late eighth century AD was 'an unstable cold stage, in which the cold, mild and warm spells frequently alternated'. The calibration curve shows a series of small steep drops and short plateaus during the same period, suggesting that there were alternate cold and warm spells (IntCal09 2009). Among them, there is a significant drop in the curve around 200 cal AD, and another one between 350 and 450 cal AD (Figure 4.1.C), indicating short, warm spells, with a fairly cold period between them (ibid.). It is interesting to note that the southern hemisphere experienced a cold spell between 250 and 550 cal AD (Burroughs 2005). These observations suggest that the Later Yayoi V and the earlier half (i.e. Early and Middle parts) of the Kofun period experienced a period of unstable cold weather. The upper sandy layer of the sand dune of Shibushi Bay in Kagoshima prefecture, on which the large keyhole tumulus of Yokose (横瀬) was built around the late fifth century AD, may have been formed during this cold spell (cf. Hashimoto, et al. 2008).

It appears that from the middle part of the Kofun period onwards, the sea level rose by a couple of metres. This is indicated by the complete burial of the shallow valleys originally created by the severe cooling episode before the beginning of the Yayoi, and it also suggests a warming episode (Tsuji 1997, 168–170). In Europe, the next cooling episode occurred between c. AD 950 and AD 1150.

In brief, the Incipient Yayoi began during a cold spell, while the Yayoi I might have corresponded with the onset of a warm spell. The late Yayoi I–III periods were generally cold periods with probable temperature fluctuations, and there was a cold spell during the second half of the Yayoi V; it again may have been quite cold around the Yayoi-Kofun transition and the Early Kofun.

The Early and Middle Kofun periods might have experienced a warm spell, but there is a possibility that cold spells momentarily emerged again during the late Middle and the Late Kofun (c. sixth century AD) period.

From the preceding discussion, we can conclude that the phases of climatic and topographic changes appear to coincide with the phases of change in the archaeological evidence fairly well: the transition from the warm to the cold spell around the seventh to fifth centuries BC coincided with the introduction of the Yayoi package (see Chapter 5); the subsequent warming might have corresponded with the spread of agrarian communities (see Chapter 5.3.4). The cold spells following this (i.e. between the late Yayoi I and Yayoi III) coincided with the periods of budding off of smaller hamlets from preexisting settlements and the rapid formation of regional structures consisting of central place–satellite settlement relations (see Chapter 6.4). The next cold spell appears to have corresponded with the Yayoi-Kofun transition (see Chapter 8).

Climate and topography constitute the physical settings in which people decide how to make sense of the environment and deal with it. These settings change, giving rise to changes in various domains of their world, to which the people have to react. In that sense, the above observation is not surprising. In that context, however, it is important to specify how the environmental changes affected the way in which individual fields of social reproduction worked, whether they generated contradictions between them and how they culminated in social change. Needless to say, in such specification we should avoid the fallacy of simplistic environmental determinism. Instead, let us consider environmental factors as one of the ranges of complexity which people and communities have to make sense of and deal with.

3. THE EAST ASIAN CONTEXT

China had already developed a complex sociopolitical organisation by the time of the Shang (商) period (c. the sixteenth to eleventh centuries BC), when the residents of the peninsula and archipelago still pursued the hunter-gatherer/early agricultural way of life. From the Zhou (周) period (late eleventh century BC to 256 BC) onwards, Chinese polities rapidly acquired state-like characteristics,[6] and the weakening of the Zhou authority (from the Late Zhou period [771 BC] onwards) led to a prolonged period of turmoil, which saw the rise and fall of polities competing over lands, resources and labour force (during the Spring and Autumn, 春秋, period [722–481 BC] and the Warring States, 戦国, period [476–221 BC]), which in turn accelerated developments in the systems of governance, production, transportation, military technology and diplomacy techniques. The exact nature of the effects of this dynamic process on the social transformation of its eastern periphery and beyond is unclear, but the period saw the development of a unique bronzeworking tradition represented by the Liaoning (遼寧) type of dagger and a general increase in social complexity across the peninsula, suggesting that various types of technologies, both material and immaterial, must have emanated from the competing polities through many channels including small-scale migrations. As mentioned earlier, the Yayoi package was also introduced in the northern Kyushu region of the archipelago at this time (see Chapter 5).[7]

After the unification by the Qin (秦; 221–206 BC), the relationship between the successive dynasties with all the fluctuating frontiers, and polities surrounding them, became one of asymmetrical co-dependency. The Han (漢) dynasty's two phases – the Early Han (206 BC–AD 8) and the Late Han (AD 25–220), with the short-lived Xin (新) dynasty (AD 8–23) between – certainly had an empire-like character from the very beginning; they tried to secure their boundaries by ever-expanding them, which took the form of incorporating polities on the frontiers into their economic-cosmological sphere. For

instance, according to the Confucian ideology which became particularly influential among the governing class from the middle Early Han period onwards, the lands beyond the frontiers were perceived to be occupied by barbarians (Nishijima 1983, 1985), unto which the god-given virtue of the emperors permeated (ibid.). The barbarians were then attracted to that virtue and naturally came to pay their respects and send their tributes to the emperor (ibid.). This implied that those areas and the communities occupying them were supposed to be incorporated, in one way or another, into the sphere over which the emperors reigned as representatives of the will of the god, who was cosmologically perceived as the emperor of heaven (ibid.).

In actuality, in cases where such communities were integrated under leaders whose status was stable enough for politico-diplomatic negotiations, they were either encouraged to or coerced into bringing tributes to the emperors, and in return, they were guaranteed the status of the emperor's faithful subordinates, with the presentation of titles and official seals. In contrast, outposts ('commanderies') were established in places where such communities were small, simple and unintegrated. Such expansion was accelerated from the Early Han period onwards, and the hierarchical relationship was symbolically represented by the imperial issuance of official seals made from different materials and with handles of different shapes for indicating status differences. When sending tributes, the accompanying official letters had to be clay-sealed with a stamp of the issued seal (ibid.). In Japan, this system of pseudo-king-vassal relationship was widely known as the Sakuho (冊封) system (Nishijima 1985).

In many cases, the expansion itself ignited the development of social complexity in and integration of the communities situated along the frontiers. Some polities which had prospered because of their contact with the dynasties became strong and internally unified enough to launch organised, large-scale attacks on the dynasties, even causing the eventual downfall of some of the dynasties (ibid.). For the polities of the peninsula and the archipelago, the Early Han empire's establishment of the four commanderies of Lelang (楽浪), Xuantu (玄菟), Zhenfan (真番) and Lintun (臨屯) in 108 BC along the north-eastern regions of

---

6 The definition of the state adopted in the present volume, see Chapter 3.2.1, 'Temporal Scope'.

7 The trajectory described here has been revealed and described in an innumerable numbers of works, among which (Nishijima 1983, 1985) are most respected and frequently cited. (Yamao 2003) is a concise summary of what he revealed throughout his long carrier specialised in Japanese ancient history and the history of interaction between polities in the peninsula and the archipelago, and well cited by Japanese Kofun specialists. The overall picture can be situated in a broad centre-and-periphery perspective (see e.g. Rowlands and Larsen 1987), although this volume does not draw on it.

China and the northern part of the Korean peninsula was significant (see Chapter 6).[8]

From the Late Han period onwards, nomadic and semi-nomadic tribal polities of the northern and north-eastern frontiers became strong enough to be a constant threat to the stability of the empires. Groups surrounding those polities became the subject of militaristic-diplomatic interventions by the successive dynasties in their attempts to check the growing power of those polities (e.g. Xiongnu [匈奴] and Koguryo [高句麗]).[9] The tribal groups of the southern part of the Korean peninsula and the western part of the Japanese archipelago became entangled in this dynamic system of asymmetrical co-dependency. In AD 57, the chief of Na (奴), a polity widely accepted to have been located in the Fukuoka plain of northern Kyushu, sent a delegation to Emperor Guangwu (光武), who granted its chief a kingship. In AD 107, records indicate that the king of Wa, called Suisho (帥升), and others sent a delegation to the court of Emperor An (安). The fact that the emperor had been enthroned in AD 106 might suggest that they knew of the event and tried to take advantage of it. Those events took place during the period covered in Chapter 7.

The downfall of the Late Han dynasty (AD 220) marked the end of the unified Chinese domain, and it remained divided until its reunification by the Sui (隋) dynasty in AD 581. The dynastic states within the Chinese domain competed against one another ideologically, cosmologically and militaristically by claiming sole legitimacy as the ruling dynasty. By this time, the Korean peninsula and the western part of the Japanese archipelago became integrated into a small number of complex polities, and they began to compete against one another by tactically forging ties with the competing Chinese dynasties.

The turmoil in the dying years of the Late Han dynasty saw the semi-independence of the commanderies of Liaotong (遼東), Xuantu, Lelang and Daifeng (帶方) under the rule of the Gongsun (公孫), who was originally appointed as the governor of the region by the Han authority but who later become an independent local ruler (AD 190–238). The Wa, who were now represented by Queen Himiko (卑弥呼) of Yamatai (邪馬台), as recorded in the book of Wei (魏) in the *Records of Three Kingdoms* (三国志), were described in the same record – together with some polities in the southern Korean peninsula – as 'belonging to' this Gongsun polity around the year AD 210. The Gongsun polity tried to maintain its independence by contacting and negotiating its status with the Three Kingdoms (三国) who were contesting for the legitimate emperorship of China – the Wei (魏), the Wu (呉) and the Shu (蜀); although the Wei and Wu kingdoms were the main contenders for this position, it was eventually achieved by the Wei in AD 238. Again, at this juncture, co-dependency appeared in the form of a delegation sent by Himiko through the commandery of Daifeng to Luoyang (洛陽), the capital of Wei, in AD 239; in return, the queen was appointed the king of Wa, issued the famous golden seal (金印) and presented with a range of items, including bronze mirrors, as her 'favourite items' (好物). For the Wei, it was profitable to retain Wa as a tributary state because the archipelago was believed to stretch not to the north-east but to the south and therefore extend towards the domain of Wu, that is, the region off the coast of the present-day Fujian province (Yamao 1986, 135–150), which would enable the Wei to keep an eye on Wu's manoeuvres. For the queen, the Wei emperor's authorisation as the legitimate chief of the Wa, along with the presentation of items which would raise her prestige far and wide, must have been advantageous in the ongoing hierarchisation and centralisation of inter-regional relations (the archaeological evidence of what was going on and its interpretation during this period are covered in Chapter 8).

The Wei defeated the Shu in AD 263, and the Wei emperor Cao Huan (曹奐) (posthumously called Emperor Yuan, 元) handed over the emperorship to Sima Yan (司馬炎; posthumously called Emperor Wu, 武), who founded the Jin (晋) dynasty in AD 265. In AD 266, Queen Toyo (台与,

---

8 For those commanderies' subsequent demises and reorganisation, see Footnotes 11 and 12 to Chapter 3.

9 Xiongnu launched an attack against the Xin in AD 10 for its being downgraded from the king to the load. The authorities ordered the lord of Koguryo, whose status was also downgraded, to lend his army to the Xin for its campaign to suppress Xiongnu, but Koguryo not only refused but also launched a counter-attack against the Xin (Nishijima 1985, 26–27).

possibly Iyo, 壱与) of Wa again sent a delegation to Jin. The Jin dynasty's defeat of the Wu in AD 280 marked the reunification of China after the demise of the Late Han dynasty, but the death of Emperor Wu ignited the War of the Eight Princes (八王之乱), which in turn caused the demise of the Jin dynasty in AD 316. Following this, other polities, many of them nomadic, successively came to power and then declined in northern China (the Sixteen Kingdoms, 五胡十六国) until the area's unification under the Northern Wei (北魏) in AD 439. The Eastern Jin dynasty, claiming to be the legitimate successor of the Jin dynasty, was founded in the south and lasted until AD 420, when the emperorship was handed over to another ruler, also called Emperor Wu, who founded the Song dynasty (Liu Song, 劉宋). The turmoil in the north only further strengthened the Koguryo kingdom of northern Korea and led to the development of the polities that were later to become the Paekche (百済) and Shilla (新羅) kingdoms. During this period, while northern China experienced a power vacuum, the Wa stopped maintaining official contacts with Chinese polities and appear to have begun exchanges with the increasingly integrated and complex communities of the peninsula, while intervening in their internal and external conflicts. The stele of King Gwanggaeto (好太王; reigning from AD 391 to 412) of Koguryo, erected in AD 414 by his son Jangsu (長寿王; AD 413–491), records that the Wa had begun military interventions in the Paekche and Shilla kingdoms (records indicate that they basically backed the former while trying to subjugate the latter) since AD 391 until King Gwanggaeto defeated the Wa in AD 400 and 404 and chased them out of the domain. This detail may have been exaggerated in order to glorify the king's achievement, but it is generally accepted that the descriptions reflect a real occurrence. Those events took place during the period covered in Chapter 9.

Since the foundation of Liu Song in AD 420, five successive kings of Wa – probably the paramount chieftains – sent a total of ten delegations (in AD 421, 425, 430, 438, 443, 451, 460, 462, 477 and 478) to the Liu Song court, requesting that they be granted the military rulership (i.e. be made the 'generals', 将軍) of not only Wa but also Paekche, Shilla and other smaller polities along the southern coastal region of the Korean peninsula. Their pleas were partially addressed but never fully granted. In addition, records indicate that after AD 478, the Wa did not send any official delegation to China until AD 600.

The period from the end of the fifth to the end of the sixth centuries AD was one of intense interactions and confrontations between the Wa and the Koguryo, Paekche, Shilla and other small polities of the Korean southern coast. During this period, goods, people and information were exchanged through a complex process of negotiations, forging of alliances and militaristic confrontations, thus developing the mechanisms of efficient governance and control in those polities. Against this background, it is but natural that the reunification of the Chinese domain under the Sui (AD 581–618) coincided with the final phase of inter-polity competition in the peninsula and the archipelago, while the establishment of the Tang (AD 618) coincided with the final formative phase of the ancient state of Japan, as well as that of Shilla, who unified the peninsula under their rule in AD 663 by annihilating the Paekche kingdom. Those events took place during the periods are covered in Chapters 10 and 11.

As in the case of environmental factors, we should avoid attributing the causes of the changes that occurred in the regions situated on the periphery of the Chinese imperial domain solely to their relationships with each other. While it appears that these relationships gained increasing importance as the process of early state formation progressed, what needs to be investigated is how these relationships led to changes and developments (i.e. increasing complexity) in the functioning of each field of social reproduction (see Chapter 3.4.1, 'Theory'). We need to study whether the relationships generated any contradictions between those fields and whether they subsequently led to any significant social changes. In that sense, again, contacts between those regions and political entities should be treated as a complex domain; the people and the communities in this domain had to make sense of and deal with such complexities as time progressed. We can infer that the experience of dealing with not only people who had different ways of thinking, feeling and acting but also events which became increasingly political – and later on even politico-militaristic – must have generated very different sets of contingencies from those generated by the erstwhile rice-agriculture-based daily life of the inhabitants of the archipelago. In that context, at least, we can safely assume that the deeper their commitments to matters concerning their relations with the Chinese dynasties and the polities of the peninsula, the greater were the changes effected in the inhabitants' ways of thinking, feeling and acting.

CHAPTER 5

BEGINNINGS: FROM THE INCIPIENT YAYOI (900/600 BC) TO THE LATE YAYOI I PERIODS (400/200 BC)

I. INTRODUCTION

As we have seen earlier, the beginning of paddy field rice farming has traditionally been connected with an imagined substance which can be described as 'Japaneseness'. The understanding that there was a singular 'beginning' implies that there was a clear-cut demarcation between the period before and after it. This preoccupation with finding the demarcation has also resulted in attempts to identify well-defined units in the material evidence, assuming that they represent the Jomon and Yayoi *identities*. However, as we all instinctively know, life was not, and has never been, as simple as that.[1]

This beginning was, as we will see in the following, not the result of a population or sociocultural *replacement*. Rather, it involved the processes of *hybridisation*, *acculturation* and *continuation*, wherein the original inhabitants of the land, the new immigrants to the area, and the things and ideas already possessed by the former and the new ones brought in by the latter were all intermingled, due to which some were transformed and some remained the same.[2] This newly emerged nexus of things and ideas are embodied both continuations and departures from the previous norms in terms of the way people did things; communicated with one another; and marked and categorised time, space, places, plants, animals and human individuals. The adoption of rice paddy field agriculture surely transformed the way in which people planned and did things on an annual basis and would have strongly influenced the character of the nexus. The construction, maintenance and use of paddy fields, along with the work involved in farming them, would have marked a significant departure from the people's previous way of life.

To put it in a drastically simplified manner, during the Jomon period, communities of people spent various lengths of time in various places within, near and far away from settlements of various scales and functions (e.g. Mizoguchi 2002, 66–115; Taniguchi 2005); they would have spent longer periods of time in larger settlements, which were often circular in shape (Taniguchi 2005), and might have spent some time away from them in order to procure particular types of resources only available in a particular season/seasons of the year (also see Habu 2004, esp. chap. 4). This general picture is more applicable to the eastern than to the western portion of the archipelago, where the mobility of populations appears to have remained fairly high until the end of the Jomon period (Hayashi 1986).[3] However, even in eastern Japan, it appears that communities organised both long- and short-term forays in order to acquire various resources only available in certain spots and territories, which were, at times, far away from the larger settlements. In that sense, these settlements were not 'central places'.

Moreover, from the Late Jomon period onwards, the large, circular settlements of eastern

---

1 See Section 3.4.1, 'Theory'. Different fields of social reproduction comprising a society have different structures and rhythms of transformation from one another.
2 See Footnote 1 to this chapter.

3 An exception to this norm was the central Kyushu region, especially the region around the present-day Kumamoto prefecture, where the scale of sites increased, thus revealing prominent traces of a largely sedentary way of life during the Late Jomon period (e.g. Hayashi 1986).

Japan were dissolved and replaced by smaller settlements built on a similar scale (Taniguchi 2005). This process is understood to have been a response to long-term environmental deterioration, thought to have occurred during a period of cooling (e.g. Imamura 1996; 1999, 100–118), due to which residential communities became smaller and more mobile in order to fully utilise the small, unevenly distributed ecological patches in the territory of individual communities.[4,5] It can be said that throughout the latter half of the Jomon period, there was no fixed, year-round focus on the management of time and the organisation and mobilisation of labour (Mizoguchi 2002, chap. 4, 230–232). In fact, the possibilities of diversification and flexibility would have been the main concerns

in the scheduling and organising of labour activities (e.g. Hirose 1997a, 43–45).

With the onset of paddy field rice farming, however, a considerable part of the year had to be spent at or near the paddy fields. For the farming communities, this inevitably transformed various elements of their social life and structure of their lifeworld:[6] previously unknown problems and necessities arising from these changes must have affected people's ideas regarding issues such as who did what, when, where, how often and how long; who did something better than whom and so on. From the preceding changes, we can infer that due to rice cultivation, there was now a *fixed focus* on the scheduling and organising of labour activities, which occupied a considerable part of the year. In addition, this focus gave rise to permanent features in the landscape and was firmly situated in them, that is, in the construction of paddies and related facilities.

In this context, however, it is important not to be overwhelmed by the seemingly drastic material consequences of the changes. It is true, for instance, that many of the Jomon material items that were apparently imbued with unique symbolic connotations either entirely disappeared or underwent significant modifications in their appearance. A notable example of this is the clay figurine. This famous material category witnessed fairly dramatic ups and downs in the quantities of its production and use and underwent significant changes in its appearance, but it continued to be used as a significant ritual item throughout the Jomon period (e.g. Kosugi 2002; Kaner 2009). With the onset of the Yayoi period, however, the category almost disappeared entirely; it had gone through a process of drastic transformation in its appearance and use: apart from a tiny number of exceptions in western Japan, it only survived in eastern Japan either as a container for human remains or in a drastically modified appearance (see Kaner 2009, 131). Since the general source of its metaphorical reference was basically

4 Some scholars argue that the introduction of *dry* rice cultivation and the cultivation of other domesticated plants such as barley and millet in dry fields took place as early as during the final phase of the Middle Jomon period. Although this thesis has not yet been fully accepted, its proponents argue that the lithic assemblage from the Late Jomon period onwards comprises tools used for maintaining dry fields and for reaping (e.g. Itakura 2006). Sumio Yamasaki recently reported that imprints of rice and millet were found on potsherds dated to the late Middle Jomon and the final Late Jomon, respectively, by examining them with the SEM (scanning electron microscopy; e.g. Yamasaki 2007). Its opponents, however, point out the most prominent reason for their objection: the fact that neither a sizeable amount of carbonised grains nor archaeologically tangible facilities for the storage of grains have yet been found (Yoshiyuki Tanaka, pers. comm.). The accuracy of the latter has also been disputed in terms of the morphological characteristics of the imprints themselves and the dating of the potsherds (Nakazawa 2009). Also see Chapter 3, Footnote 1.

5 The practice of cultivating rice and other crops in dry fields began in the Korean peninsula as early as c. 3000 BC (roughly contemporaneous with the Middle Jomon), and it is argued that the custom was introduced to the archipelago by fishing communities inhabiting the northern coastline of Kyushu Island (Hirose 1997a, 47–48, 71). The fact that the local communities maintained ties with the fishing communities inhabiting the southern coastline of the Korean peninsula (ibid.) is reflected by the characteristic composite fishhooks that were commonly used among those communities and the obsidians transported from their source in Kyushu Island to the peninsula (Watanabe 1985). In any case, the sufficiently clear, direct evidence of the dry-field farming of rice, wheat, barley, foxtail millet has not been found yet, and we have to be cautious in incorporating the thesis into the characterisation of the subsistence pattern of the Middle Jomon period and thereafter up to the early Final Jomon.

6 By the term 'lifeworld,' the world comprised of a certain set of communication fields in each of which the sense(s) of reality/realities possessed by individuals is/are reproduced through the repetitive enactment of certain acts upon certain rhythms mediated by certain material material/immaterial media is meant. See Footnote 24 to Chapter 3 and related descriptions.

associated with the reproductive power of the female body (Kosugi 2002; Mizoguchi 2007), the figurine's disappearance and/or modification suggests a change in the way of reference to the notion of *regeneration* and its mobilisation. This change might have resulted from a significant change in gender perception. Some other characteristically 'Jomon items', such as stone artefacts variously depicting male and female sexual organs, followed the same path (Kosugi et al. 2007a). The modifications also suggest a transformation in perceptions of the male and female reproductive roles. Meanwhile, other items and attributes, such as stone rods, survived well into the Early Yayoi period. Stone rods are thought to have symbolised the phallus, and their survival suggests that although symbolic references to the human regenerative power did not completely disappear, there was some change in their form and media (Y. Nakamura 2007). One possible explanation is that the perceived male role in regeneration became more significant, due to which the 'phallic' stone rods continued into the Yayoi period. (I return to this change in gender relations later on.)

Cord mark decorations, which gave the Jomon period its name (i.e. *Jo*, 縄, means 'cord' and *mon*, 文/紋, means 'mark' in Japanese), survived throughout the Yayoi period in areas across eastern Japan; the famous discovery of the first-ever Yayoi pot, which, rather ironically, is now known to date from the Yayoi-Kofun transitional phase,[7] has a cord mark band on it, made by rolling a twisted cord on its shoulder (see Figure 1.1 in this volume). As we will see subsequently in further detail, most of the Korean-originated items adopted by the northern Kyushu communities at the beginning of the Yayoi period (i.e. the Incipient Yayoi) did not have their functional equivalents in the preexisting Final Jomon assemblage; further, those items which did have functional equivalents in the preexisting assemblage were not adopted and used for those purposes. Moreover, the appearance of many of the adopted items was quickly modified from that of their Korean originals.

Human life, after all, is a patchwork of customs, copies and improvisations (some of which become customs themselves as others are quickly discarded or forgotten). The meaning ascribed to an item may change, but the (appearance of the) item itself may remain unchanged, and vice versa. In that sense, the investigation of which traits were replaced, which traits were modified and how, and which traits continued unchanged (see e.g. Yamanouhi 1967 [original published in 1932], 25) in the fields of social reproduction would be one way to gain fruitful and realistic insights into the changing *reality* of the *lifeworld* of the people and the ways in which they coped with their world, with the help of unchanged and changing material and immaterial media.

Let us begin our investigation by examining one of the oldest of the rice farming villages, where people lived, died and coped with the world with the help of things, customs and beliefs – old and new.

2. WHAT HAPPENED IN A VILLAGE: ETSUJI, ONE OF THE OLDEST RICE FARMING VILLAGES

There was a village, which might be better described as a hamlet, situated on a slightly higher terrain at the bottom of a floodplain at some point of time in the Incipient Yayoi period (Figure 5.1; Shintaku 1994, Kasuya Town Board of Education[8] 2002).[9] The place is now called Etsuji (江辻), Kasuya township, in the Fukuoka prefecture of northern Kyushu. Several rivers flowing west into the Hakata Bay met at a point not far away to the west of the village. Due to flooding, watercourses must have made the land around the village a patchwork of pools, marshes and sandbanks. The presence of reaping knives made of polished stone suggests there were rice paddies nearby, but neither have these been discovered as yet nor have their structures been identified. (We will see actual examples of paddies dated to the period later.) The village was not situated very far from the

7 The Shonai [庄内]-style phase, which is treated by some to be the final phase (or the Yayoi VI) of the Yayoi period. However, the phase also witnessed the spread of prototypic Keyhole-shaped tumuli across western Japan and parts of eastern Japan. The phase is covered in Chapter 8 of the present volume.

8 Town Board of Education will be abbreviated TBE in the following. In the case of Municipal Board of Education, MBE is used, and for Prefectural Board of Education, PBE is used.

9 The detailed (i.e. sub-phase-level) typo-chronological position is still being debated.

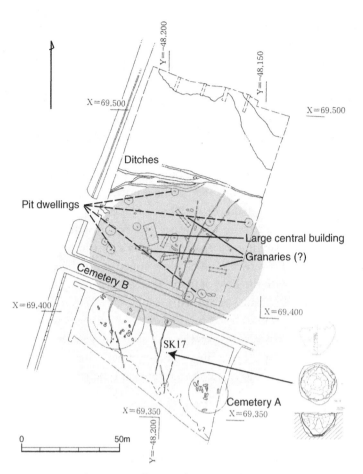

Figure 5.1. The Etsuji village, Fukuoka prefecture. Note the multiple concentric circular structure occupied by the large rectangular house-like building at the centre, encircled by probable granaries, further surrounded by pit dwellings (after Kasuya TBE 2002, fig. 2, with alterations).

foothills of the mountain range surrounding the floodplain. A number of obsidian arrowheads have been excavated from the site, suggesting that the inhabitants hunted, and probably foraged, across the surrounding terrain, which consisted of a diverse range of ecological zones. The area had been thickly populated by the Jomon people before the early rice farming community was established; approximately 300 metres to the north, archaeologists have excavated a large pit dwelling dating back to the Late Jomon period (Kasuya TBE 2009, 4–6); approximately 500 metres to the east, they have excavated artefacts dating back to the time between the Early to the Late Jomon period (ibid.); finally, six pit dwellings – two dating back to the mid-Late Jomon period, three dating back to the late-Late Jomon period and one dating back to the Final Jomon period – have been excavated approximately 600 metres to the south-east of the village site (ibid.). The prominent presence of obsidian arrowheads and scrapers

shows that the village inhabitants often hunted in the hills, but the location of these settlements strongly suggests that the inhabitants also utilised a wide range of terrestrial and freshwater resources that were abundantly available in the vicinity.[10] In any case, the findings reveal that the density of Jomon occupation in this area is unusually high in comparison with other areas of northern Kyushu, suggesting that its surrounding areas were well suited for the hunting-foraging way of life. The circular spatial layout of the village, which we will see in detail in the following, was one of the basic principles with which many of the Jomon villages and cemeteries were organised (see Figure 5.2). That the Etsuji village took a circular form may have been related to the fact that the village 'emerged' in an area densely occupied by those

10 Such as *Lycoris radiata* (ヒガンバナ), Kudzu (*Pueraria lobata*, クズ), and *Arisaema serratum* (テンナンショウ).

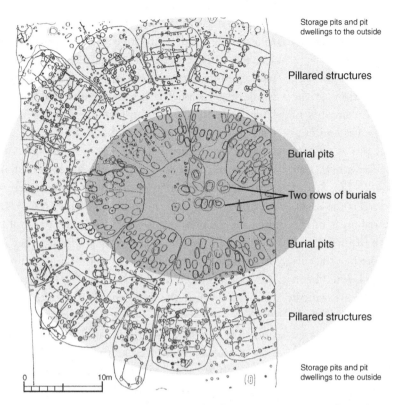

Storage pits and pit dwellings to the outside

Pillared structures

Burial pits

Two rows of burials

Burial pits

Pillared structures

Storage pits and pit dwellings to the outside

0   10m

Figure 5.2. The Nishida village, Iwate prefecture. Note structural similarities with the Etsuji (Figure 5.1). The presence of two rows of burials at the centre, and a number of segments in both the burials and pillared structures of unknown functions (and storage pits and pit dwellings distributed encircling them), are interpreted to have represented 'moieties' (see Footnotes 18 and 19) and distinct kin-groupings, respectively (e.g. Taniguchi 2005; after Aihara 1985, fig. 3 [original in Iwate PBE 1980], with alterations).

who were pursuing the Jomon way of life. We shall come back to the issue later.

In this village site, archaeologists excavated eleven round pit dwellings, five (actually six, but two of them intersect one another) longhouse-like structures, possibly with raised floors, and a large, rectangular house-like structure measuring approximately 5.5 metres by 10.3 metres (Figure 5.1; Shintaku 1994). There were two clusters of burials to the south and south-east. Ditches measuring approx. 0.7 metres in depth currently, and which would not have been more than 2 metres deep originally, had been dug to the north of the cluster of buildings, as if to mark the perimeter of the residential area. These intersect and must have been re-dug at least a couple of times, but it is uncertain whether they enclosed the living area like in some other settlements, such as the Naka (那珂) village (Fukuoka Municipal Board of Education 1994),[11] which were contemporaries

of the Etsuji. The presence of another, possibly contemporaneous settlement has been confirmed some 500 metres to the east of Etsuji, where two round pit dwellings, three longhouse-like structures and a large building have been unearthed in a small-scale rescue dig (Shintaku 1994, 118). The composition of the buildings suggests that this particular village had a fairly similar structure to that of Etsuji.

The intersection between the longhouse-like structures and between the ditches suggests that the village was occupied for some length of time. It also means that all the buildings were not necessarily contemporaneous. For instance, some of the pit dwellings are situated very close to one another (Figure 5.1), and this might have resulted from rebuilding. However, there is no way to confirm this surmise. With regard to the longhouse-like structures, some scholars believe that they had raised floors and hence could have been granaries. Similarly, the intersection between structures 3 and 4 suggest that not all of the five buildings

11 Abbreviated 'MBE' in the following.

were contemporaneous; their overlapping suggests that when they were rebuilt, the new building was built on the site of the old one.

In fact, it is quite possible that the longhouse-like structures were granaries. Excavations at the Maeda (前田) site in Dazaifu city, also situated in Fukuoka prefecture, are roughly dated as contemporaneous to the Etsuji; the storage pits at this site are situated in and around rectangular houses that are laid out in a circle (Ozawa 2006).[12] This layout suggests that storage facilities were, in some cases, situated in and around the residential areas of the settlements in the region during the Initial Yayoi period. It is difficult to confirm whether the village of Etsuji took a complete circular layout like in the Maeda site, because the residential areas most likely extend to the unexcavated east. However, we can certainly confirm the fact that the large rectangular building was most probably surrounded by granaries, which were further surrounded by the round pit dwellings (Figure 5.1).

2.1. *The 'Meaning Content' of the Village-Scape*[13]

In order to make sense of the previously mentioned spatial arrangements, we need to investigate the function of the enigmatic large, rectangular building situated in the centre (Figure 5.1). The building, building no. 6, appears to have been rebuilt at exactly the same location and in exactly the same size at least a couple of times, because some of the postholes intersect while others are situated quite close to one another. There are two large postholes on the long axis of the building, approximately 0.7 metres deep and 0.7 metres across, which would have supported the substantial roof ridge. Whereas the probable granaries may have had raised floors, the large central building did not, suggesting that the function of this building

included allowing a fairly large number of people to assemble inside it in order to carry out certain activities. Interestingly, its structure – particularly its intriguing arrangement of posts – shows some similarities to other large, rectangular buildings of later dates, such as a structure at the Yubihon'mura (柚比本村) site (e.g. Ozawa 2006, 17–18; see also Chapter 6, Figure 6.2.A). These buildings, and those dating from the Late Middle Yayoi period, in particular, are often associated with elite cemeteries (to be illustrated in detail in Chapter 6.6.1). In the case of the Yubihon'mura structure, the building was also rebuilt at the same spot a number of times, just like the Etsuji structure, and a number of the graves in the elite burial ground date back from before the first construction of the large building. These findings suggest that activities conducted inside those buildings had something to do with the *ancestors* as well as the dead. However, the possibility that buildings of much later dates, and having similar characteristics, are likely to have been related to rituals concerning the dead as well as the ancestors does not directly imply that the Etsuji building was also used for the same purpose. However, this theory is supported by some other pieces of evidence, albeit circumstantial. We shall study them in detail in a subsequent section. Let us first elaborate on the building under consideration. The location of the building suggests that the building was used for gatherings. The size of the building, approximately 5.5 metres by 10.3 metres, suggests that these gatherings were of communal nature, and the building's construction and reconstruction, in itself, would have been a major communal activity. It is also possible that those who were allowed to enter the building participated in a *secluded* discourse.

The fact that the central building was surrounded by structures that were most probably granaries may provide us with further clues regarding its function. If those longhouse-like buildings were indeed granaries, it is very likely that rice grains were stored in them. These buildings were, in turn, surrounded by the round pit dwellings, which means that for the inhabitants of the village, the central building was located beyond the granaries. In other words, whenever they went to do something inside the central building, they walked through between the granaries. If, indeed, the central building was associated with the dead and

---

12 The coexistence of round and rectangular houses in the same region itself is an interesting phenomenon for the Initial Yayoi period, which I discuss subsequently in the chapter.

13 The concept of village-'scape' is the one inspired by 'phenomenological' approaches to landscape developed by scholars such as Chris Tilley (1994). They emphasise that dwelling in a certain landscape and recursive encounters with its features constitute and transform both the way people make sense of them and the way people make sense of and identify themselves by referring to them in a dialectical manner.

the ancestors in some way, the images of rice grains and those of the dead and the ancestors would have been intermingled in the perception of the people.

The internal structure of the round pit dwellings of the Etsuji is quite characteristic, with two posts situated on the longitudinal edges of an oval central pit (Figures 5.1 and 5.9.C); the structure is derived from the contemporaneous pit dwellings in the Korean peninsula. These are known as the 'Songguk'ni' (松菊里) type of dwellings, a characteristic house style during the Middle Mumun period of the peninsula. At the settlement of Lgeum-dong (梨琴洞) (cf. Gyeongnam Archaeological Research Institute 2003; Hashino et al. 2006, fig. 9), dating back to the same period, Songguk'ni-type dwellings and structures resembling the Etsuji granaries coexisted with two extremely large longhouse-like structures (ibid.). These are much larger than the granary-like structures, suggesting that they had a special function. More importantly, they were situated right next to a burial ground containing linearly arranged graves including dolmen-like ones with fairly large capping stones (ibid.), which might hint at the possible purpose of the Etsuji central building. Those buildings are not planned like the Etsuji central building. However, their coexistence with and contrast to the granary-like structures leads us to infer that they functioned in a similar manner to the Etsuji central building.

Returning to the connection between rice grains and the dead, we can also identify this association in the portable material domain of the Initial Yayoi period: the pottery of the period. The emergence of the globular jar shape-type (called *Tsubo*, 壷, in Japanese), as we will see later in this chapter, marked the beginning of the Yayoi pottery assemblage (see Figures 5.4.2 and 5.4.3).[14] One of the main functions of these jars was to store rice grains. However, the globular jar shape-type also came to play an important role in burials of the dead: globular jars came to be used as coffins (see Figure 5.3.B; also see Section 5.1 in this chapter). As mentioned earlier, the main function of the globular jar shape-type was to store rice grains, and the grains were intended either to be eaten or to be sown as seeds.

If they were eaten, the grains 'died' in order to sustain the life of the consumer. If they were sown, however, they regenerated by reproducing themselves. Either way, as a container, the globular jar was seen as closely connected with the process of *transformation* of the grains, from death to life. When larger variants of the jar came to be used as coffins, they mostly contained infant bodies during the Incipient Yayoi period. Hence, I would like to argue that the death of the grains and their regeneration became metaphorically connected with the death of people (infants) and their regeneration (Mizoguchi 2002, 130–131) (see Figure 5.4), mainly due to the widespread use of the globular jar shape-type both to store grains and to contain the bodies of deceased individuals. Further, I would like to point out that some of these globular jars, regardless of their size, were painted red or, occasionally, black. In many ethnographic examples, the former represents life and the latter, death (Needham 1979).

The spatial structure of the Etsuji village increasingly appears to have been *meaningfully constituted*: its inhabitants experienced a connection between the images of rice grains and the dead, and this connection may have further been metaphorically linked to the death and regeneration of not only the life of rice grains but also those of the people. This structure, intriguingly, is reminiscent of the spatial structure of the circular settlements of the Jomon period. An enduring characteristic of these settlements, and those in eastern Japan, in particular − dating from the Early to the Final Jomon period − is their segmentary structure.[15] In many of the larger territorial-centre-type settlements, such as Nishida (西田) in Iwate prefecture, Tohoku region (Iwate PBE 1980; also see Taniguchi 2005), we find round pit dwellings with many postholes encircling the central hearth, storage facilities, other buildings used for unknown functions − as revealed by the presence of postholes − and burial sites, all of which are laid out in a multi-zoned concentric circular structure; each of these circular structures is further divided into

---

14 To be exact, the shape-type emerged in the Yusu [夜臼]-style assemblage, the temporal marker of the Incipient Yayoi, and became its stable component.

15 The Jomon period is commonly divided into six periods, that is, the Incipient (c. 12,000–9500 bp), Earliest (c. 9500–6000 bp), Early (c. 6000–5000 bp), Middle (c. 5000–4000 bp), Late (c. 4000–3000 bp) and Final (c. 3000– ; the end date is under debate, see Chapter 3.3.2 of the current volume). See Habu (2004, chap. 2).

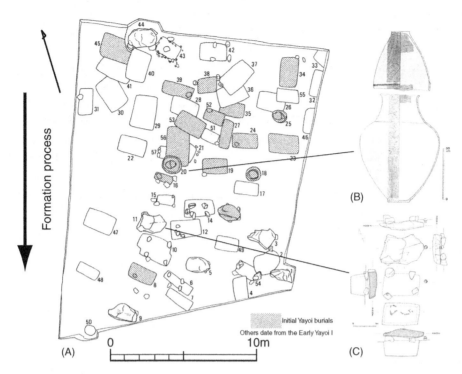

Figure 5.3. The Shinmachi cemetery, Fukuoka prefecture. **A:** General plan. **B:** Burial jars of no. 20 burial. **C:** The 'dolmen' of No. 11 burial. As seen from the distributional shift of burials from the Initial Yayoi to the Early Yayoi I, the cemetery expanded from the north to the south. Note the random placement of burials in the northern sector of the cemetery and the linear alignment-oriented placement in the southern sector (after Shima TBE 1987, with alterations: A: fig. 77; B: fig. 61, C: fig. 23).

segments, often in a symmetrical manner (Figure 5.2). At many of them, the burials are located in the centre, surrounded by a number of pillared buildings with unknown functions,[16] which are then further surrounded by pit dwellings and storage pits. The burials are placed close together but rarely intersect, suggesting that they were marked and probably topped with small heaps of soil; it is possible that they were even marked by perishable grave markers. This indicates, again, that the inhabitants marked the presence of the dead and the ancestors at the very centre of the residential area (Figure 5.2). In addition, it might be the case that the inhabitants had to wend their way through a number of storage facilities in order to gain access to the graves of the dead and the ancestors.

It is widely accepted that a range of Jomon ritual acts were associated with the reproduction and regeneration of natural beings, including people (e.g. Mizoguchi 2002, 105–111). As mentioned earlier, these functions were popularly represen-

ted by clay figurines depicting pregnant women, lithics depicting sexual organs and so on. Such figurines were used not only in rituals but also in mundane settings such as inside the pit dwellings. Often, these were accompanied by other clay figurines representing animals, plants and shells. This implies that the spatial materialisation of the metaphorical-transformative connection between death, regeneration of life, significance of food, the dead and the ancestors was a common feature not only in the village of Etsuji but also in many other villages during the Jomon period.

2.2. The Hybridisation of Discourses: Continuity and Change

As mentioned earlier, the Middle Mumum (無文) pottery period in Korea is roughly contemporaneous with the Initial Yayoi period (see Takesue 2004). Settlements at that time tended to be either unenclosed or enclosed by V-sectioned ditches dug around the inhabited areas (see Figure 5.10.A). These areas consisted of Songguk'ni-type pit dwellings, storage pits, raised-floor granaries – including longhouse-like ones – and occasionally

---

16 In the case of the Nishida, they are interpreted to have been facilities for excarnation, the drying of salmon fish for preservation, and the storage of nuts and other foodstuffs.

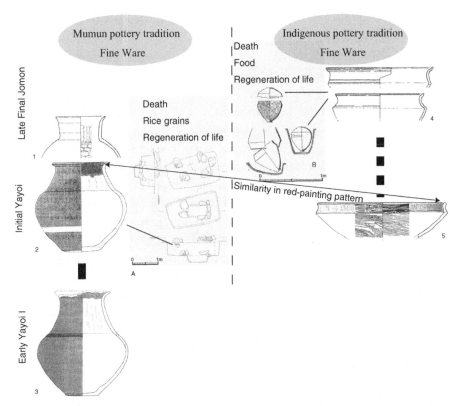

Figure 5.4. The globular jar originated from the Mumun pottery tradition and shallow bowl originated from the indigenous pottery tradition. Both constitute the finer ware category of their respective assemblages, and have a strong metaphorical connection to food, death and regeneration of life. 1 Hyuam-ri (Korea; after National Museum of Korea 1990); 2, 3, and A Shinmachi (Fukuoka; after Shima TBE 1987); 4 Hirota (Fukuoka; after Fukuoka PBE 1985a, fig. 6); 5 Sasai (Fukuoka; after Fukuoka MBE 2003a); B Negino (Oita; after Sakamoto 1994, fig. 3).

some large buildings with unknown functions, such as what we saw at the Lgeum-dong (梨琴洞) (Hashino et al. 2006). The Songguk'ni-type dwellings have round and square subtypes (see Figure 5.9), and as mentioned earlier, the era is contemporaneous with the Initial Yayoi period of the northern Kyushu region. In other words, as far as the buildings are concerned, Initial Yayoi settlements must have looked fairly similar to their Korean counterparts. However, these buildings were rarely laid out in a concentric circular structure in the peninsula.

The preceding findings suggest that what constituted the material embodiment and medium of the daily life of the Etsuji inhabitants was the *hybridisation* of the two traditions. For instance, although the buildings were mostly constructed according to the tradition that had originated in the peninsula, their layout was derived from the 'indigenous' tradition. According to Yoshinori Ozawa (2006), there were two types of villagescapes in the Initial Yayoi and Yayoi I periods in northern Kyushu: (a) those where pit dwell-

ings and storage facilities were mixed together and (b) those where the two were separated. Ozawa has also established that while the latter tended to be enclosed by V-sectioned ditches, the former tended to be unenclosed. The custom of digging a V-sectioned ditch to enclose a village originated in the peninsula (ibid.). Unfortunately, the two best-preserved V-sectioned ditch-enclosed villages in this region, the villages of Itazuke (板付; see Figure 5.10.B; e.g. Mori and Okazaki 1961) and Naka (那珂) (Fukuoka MBE 1994) – the former dating back to the beginning of the Yayoi I and the latter, to the Initial Yayoi period – had already lost their habitation layers when excavated, and it is impossible to confirm the layout of the pit dwellings. However, there is a V-sectioned ditch-bounded sector within the Itazuke enclosure in which we can find a cluster of storage pits but no dwelling (Mori and Okazaki 1961).[17] In any case,

17 The cluster appears to be further subdivided into a number of groups. What type of groupings were behind their formation is an important question. They may

it is evident that the circular villages of the Initial Yayoi and Yayoi I periods of northern Kyushu tended not to be enclosed by a V-sectioned ditch. This means they lacked the significant trait of contemporary settlements of the peninsula, though their architectural components derived from the peninsula.

In that case, how does the circular layout reflect the meaning content of the village-scape? In other words, how does it indicate the metaphorical connection between death, the regeneration of life, the significance of food, the dead and the ancestors? Did such connections derive from the peninsular tradition or from the indigenous Jomon tradition? In order to address this issue, let us now focus on the burial ground of the Etsuji. As mentioned previously, there were two burial clusters to the south of the residential area (Figures 5.1 and 5.15.A). Cluster A, the eastern cluster, consisted of thirteen composite wooden coffin burials, one pit burial (also possibly a wooden coffin burial) and two jar burials (in one, a large globular jar was used as a coffin, while the other's shape-type could not be determined). The graves were generally laid out to form several linear alignments. Burial cluster B, the western cluster, consisted of nine composite wooden coffin burials and fifteen pit burials. The latter might have included some composite wooden coffin burials, but it is impossible to identify them exactly due to the severe disturbance of the upper layers. The graves appear to have been situated in a circular layout.

Although the contemporaneity of those clusters cannot be confirmed with absolute certainty, the presence of SK17 is interesting in that regard (Figure 5.1). In this case, the globular jar was situated almost exactly halfway between the two clusters. The jar was placed vertically in the pit, with its mouth facing upwards, which is quite unusual for a burial container of the period. This might indicate that the jar was deposited at this spot for ritualistic purposes. It is also possible that the transitory nature of the location might have been intended to indicate connections between the burial of an infant and the transitory nature/liminality of its social being. Either way,

the jar marks a division between those buried in clusters A and B.

We have examples of burial grounds laid out in a circular pattern during the Jomon period. For instance, at Mukode (向出) in Osaka prefecture (Watanabe 2001, 45–48), the graves, dating back to the late Middle Jomon, were laid out in a circular pattern; burnt phallic stones were excavated from the vicinity of the circles (ibid., fig. 3). This indicates that placing graves in a circular pattern, as in cluster B of Etsuji, was a Jomon custom, and the use of lithics representing sexual organs in such burial grounds suggests that the dead and the ancestors were commemorated in connection with the notion of reproduction, and probably also with the notions of death and the regeneration of life. In addition, it is interesting to note the presence of two rectangular pits, probably graves, situated at the centre of some of the circles of the Mukode, parallel to one another. These are reminiscent of the two rows of burials in the middle of the burial ground situated at the centre of the previously mentioned Nishida (Figure 5.2). Yasuhiro Taniguchi pointed out some striking similarities between a typical village of the Bororo people interpreted by Claude Lévi-Strauss (1963, chap. 8) and some villages of the Early and Middle Jomon (Taniguchi 2005, 110–111), and proposed the thesis that the two rows of burials at the centre of the Nishida site and the presence of dual divisions in many other Jomon circular settlements represented dual organisations (Taniguchi 2005).[18] It should be noted at this point that the concept of a dual organisation arranges various social relations in a *symmetrical* order by drawing upon the principle of *reciprocity*: the groups involved in a dual organisation have to reciprocate through the exchange of people, goods and labour on various occasions relating to the rites of passage in order to firmly maintain mutual ties and an egalitarian relationship.

In contrast to cluster B, cluster A's linear alignments may have derived from a tradition that originated in the peninsula; in many Korean

have been either 'households' or 'lineage'-like kin-based groupings. I come back to issues concerning what groupings formed individual hamlets throughout the present and next chapter.

18 'Dual organisations' cross-cut sodalities and divide them into two larger corporate groupings that are supposed to reciprocate social obligations, often related to rite-of-passage ceremonies (cf. Tuzin 2001). The half of such organisations is called a 'moiety'. The possible continued presence of dual organisation into the Incipient Yayoi from the Jomon might have played an important role not only in social reproduction but in the spread of the Yayoi package. I come back to the point later on.

cemeteries of the Middle Mumun period, graves, including stone-capped ones called 'dolmens' were laid out in long, linear alignments. Even though it only shows a 'tendency' to form linear alignments, it is possible that cluster A was built according to this custom (see Figure 5.15.A). Moreover, if the globular jar SK17 were deposited to mark the symbolic dividing line between the clusters, the clusters might have been the burial grounds of two moiety-type groupings,[19] indicated by the central graves situated parallel to each other at Mukode and by the two rows of graves situated at the centre of the central burial ground of settlements such as Nishida. If this is true, intriguingly, we find that the burial layout of one of the two cemeteries of a settlement was based on the Jomon, and hence indigenous, tradition, whereas that of the other was based on a tradition that originated in the peninsula, from where the Yayoi package itself originated. In addition, there is an interesting possibility that the circular burial grounds of the Jomon period, including the central burial ground at Nishida, as mentioned earlier, suggest the presence of moieties.

Another possible explanation for this is that the cemetery in cluster B, which shows the Jomon influence, was formed first, after which the burial ground shifted to cluster A, or vice versa. However, this is quite an unlikely supposition: the duration of the settlement, one or two pottery stylistic sub-phases, was too short for the relocation of a burial ground, and both clusters A and B could have naturally grown in their respective locations, without any shift between locations. The presence of SK17, too, cannot be incorporated into this relocation theory. In any case, it would not be possible to *definitely* determine the actual circumstances. Nevertheless, we can confirm that the inhabitants were influenced by traditions originating from both the Jomon period and from the peninsula in terms of spatially structuring the village cemeteries. In another interesting observation, we find that the burial ground at the Shinmachi (新町) site, in the Itoshima peninsula of northern Kyushu, originally showed a seemingly random placement of burials in the earlier phase of the formation, which gradually shifted to the

formation of linear rows (Figure 5.3) (Shima TBE 1987; Mizoguchi 2001, 138–141). The graves dating from the beginning of this linear-formation process show the influence of the peninsular tradition and include types like the stone-capped dolmens (see Figure 5.12), but the inhabitants initially chose to position the burials in the indigenous traditional manner. This indicates that even the mode of spatially structuring the burial ground was a matter of choice. When various conditions contributed to making the peninsular manner of positioning graves more suitable, the inhabitants adopted that mode.

All in all, the picture concerning the burial of the dead points to continuation and choice. It suggests the following:

(1) The metaphorical-transformative connection between death and the regeneration of life, including its connection with food, continued from the Jomon to the Yayoi period.

(2) The nature of this connection, however, changed with the passage of time: the focus shifted from various foods with different seasonal availability to a single food that demanded a prolonged period of tending over the year, i.e., rice. This shift in focus was symbolically reflected by the use of globular jars as coffins.

(3) With the beginning of the Yayoi period, the death and regeneration of life in the life cycle of rice grains came to be connected with that of human beings. In other words, the beginning of a metaphorical-transformative connection between the death and regeneration of rice grains and the corresponding processes in the human life cycle marked the beginning of the Yayoi way of life.

2.3. Beginning as Becoming

The first inhabitants of Etsuji already possessed a considerable amount of knowledge that had originated in the peninsula, including various customs and their material media, which comprised a package, referred to as the Yayoi package in this volume. The package can also be described as a set of *discourses/communication systems* (see Chapter 3.4.1), or a set of ways of thinking, doing

---

19 'Moiety' is a component of *dual organisations*. The definition of this and other relevant terms and concepts concerning actual and fictive kin- and communal groupings; see pp. 70–71 in this chapter.

things and communicating with one another that involved the use of certain material media. A significant element of the package would have been the presence of rice itself, along with a set of technologies for cultivating, storing, exchanging and consuming it. Those who followed this way of life would also have had certain ways of organising labour and classifying people into categories that would ensure the smooth functioning of such labour. However, there were subtle additions to the discourse, such as the practice of following the Jomon-style spatial layout for peninsula-style buildings in the construction of the earliest rice farming villages in the archipelago, such as Etsuji.

One of the most important elements of Jomon life was the structuring principle (embodied by various material items including clay figurines, various stone implements shaped as sexual organs, the settlement-scape and so on) which involves organising things around the conceptual connection between death and the regeneration of the life of natural beings, including human beings. In the typical Jomon village-scape, this metaphorical-transformative connection was manifested in the form of a circular layout of facilities for burying the dead, commemorating them, storing foodstuffs and dwelling, for example, the spatial structure of Nishida village as described earlier (Figure 5.2). The village of Etsuji (Figure 5.1) was built according to a similar spatial structure, which appears to have represented a similar kind of metaphorical-transformative connection. However, the contents of the components in these two villages were different. According to the Jomon tradition, foodstuffs with different seasonal availability were stored in storage pits (and possibly in pillared buildings) surrounding the central burial ground of the typical Jomon village; these foodstuffs were replaced by rice grains, probably stored in the granary-like buildings with raised floors at Etsuji (Figure 5.1). In addition, graves and the facilities for commemorating the dead in the Jomon village were replaced by a large, rectangular, cult-house-like building located at the centre of the village-scape, which was further surrounded by the granary-like buildings with raised floors. The architectural style of the Etsuji dwellings and storage buildings originated from the Korean peninsula, where the Yayoi package itself originated. The

material media of communication, i.e., the dwellings and storage buildings, that were associated with the meaning and ideal order of social life would have been tightly connected to their concrete meaning contents and would have influenced the way in which the meaning and ideal order of social life was communicated and understood. However, the principle of *connecting* the meaning contents to one another appears to have remained intact: these connections were drawn with reference to the metaphorical-transformative connection between death and the regeneration of the life of natural beings, including human beings.

I would like to argue that the inhabitants of Etsuji village and/or their ancestors only *interpreted* the *Yayoi package/set of discourses* by referring to the pre-existing framework, that is, the *Jomon set of discourses/communication systems*, for making sense of the world and its order. While they embraced the new set of discourses, they embraced it in their own way, which ensured continuity in their own way of making sense of the world and its order: according to their conception, life was an endless cycle of death and regeneration of natural beings, including human beings. Although many material things were changed, there still remained a sense of continuity at the heart of the structuring principle, or the world view, of everyday life. In that sense, the beginning of the Yayoi was a kind of *becoming* rather than a *beginning*. It was not an event marking a break from the past but a process through which people, including the inhabitants of Etsuji and their ancestors, transformed themselves by maintaining continuity in their everyday life.

To put it in a rather simplistic manner, there was only one thing which changed fundamentally at the onset of the Yayoi period: the emergence of rice as the potential single major food, instead of various seasonal edible plants and animals. People were attracted to rice as a staple diet and accepted it, along with the discourses which came with it. They initially tried to embrace these lifestyle changes while retaining continuity with the past, but as we will see in the rest of this volume, their world would never be the same again.

This volume explains the fundamental significance attached to rice and the discourse accompanying its cultivation, storage, exchange and consumption which represented the metaphorical-transformative association between the death and regeneration of life of rice grains as well as of human beings – an association that repeatedly appeared throughout the Yayoi and Kofun periods. Pictorial representations on *Dotaku* bronze bells (Chapter 6.7.2, 'Understanding the Basic Structure of the Yayoi "Myth"; see Figures 6.26, 6.27 and 6.28) and the traits of the oldest type of *Haniwa* cylindrical vessels (Chapter 9.2.3 '*Haniwa* Vessels'; Figure 9.9) are prominent examples of this association. In the former artefacts, the sequence of scenes depicting the conflict between nature and culture is summed up in the depiction of a building where the 'spirit' of rice (representing nature) was synthesised with the 'spirits' of the ancestors (representing culture). In the case of the latter, the characteristic curvilinear decoration would have represented that the spirit of rice was enfolded in it in order to prevent it from wandering away,[20] and the placement of the *Haniwa* vessels on the keyhole tumulus, as if enclosing the tumulus, would have symbolically represented that the enfolded spirit of rice was dedicated to the spirit of the dead buried in that spot (cf. Kondo 1983, 173); in other words, the dedication itself prevented the spirit of the dead from wandering away.

This is not intended to suggest that the onset of paddy field rice farming was the sole cause of the eventual emergence of the ancient state in Japan. However, the former certainly contributed to the latter in an important manner. The introduction of paddy field rice farming was a form of beginning as becoming. The becoming might have been situated in the continuation of the practice, but it did usher in tremendous changes which could not possibly have been foreseen when it began.

As the first step in this line of enquiry, let us determine in detail what aspects of the old life continued and what changed and then examine their implications. We begin with pottery.

3. NEW MATERIAL WORLDS: POTTERY AND OTHER PORTABLE ITEMS

As containers, pottery vessels accompany people on several important occasions for the very sustenance of their lives, such as the preparation and consumption of food in many sedentary communities. Eating is often an important occasion for reconfirming old relationships, and sometimes forging new ones, among people. Cooking is also important for ordering relationships among people in that cooking is conducted by a certain category of people in the community and hence serves to reconfirm different roles assigned to different categories of people in the community. Storing – another important function served by pottery containers – also has important implications for the way in which society is organised, in that what is stored is often the result of socially organised labour, and the organisation of the community is significantly concerned with who controls access to what is stored and how. The production of pottery, in that sense, also has important implications in that 'appropriate' pots are required for each different setting and occasion, and those who make these pots have to know how to differentiate the appearance of these pots accordingly. Moreover, pottery production itself is an important social setting because pottery making is often a gender- and rank-specific work and, hence, like cooking, serves to reconfirm different roles and positions assigned to different categories of people in the community.[21] These general observations suggest that we can investigate the process through which the elements of the Yayoi discourse came into being and spread by studying what the pottery embodied.

3.1. The Adoption of the Globular Jar (Tsubo, 壺) Shape-Type

The emergence of the globular jar shape-type (*Tsubo*, 壺) most significantly marked the beginning of the Yayoi pottery assemblage (Figure 5.4). This type of jar was originally a component of the Middle Mumun (無文)-style pottery assemblage in the southern Korean peninsula (Goto 1980). Such jars were often well burnished and painted with red, and very rarely black, pigments all over the outside of the jar, except for the bottom, and on the inside of the rim (ibid.). The specimens of the type found in northern Kyushu can be divided into two fairly distinct size categories: the large and the small-medium. The large specimens, approximately 50 centimetres in height, were occasionally used as burial jars, while the small specimens, approximately 15 centimetres in

---

20 An idea that the curvilinear pattern for enfolding the spirits of the ancestors and rice amalgamated, see Terasawa (2000, 242–243).

21 For a classic example of works concerning pottery as a medium of the reproduction of social relations and their markers, see Miller (1985).

height, were often deposited as grave goods (see Figures 5.4.2 and 5.4.A). A majority of them, however, have been excavated from non-mortuary, everyday-life contexts, including storage pits and pit dwellings, and we can infer that their basic function was storage. The fact that their inner surface is smoothened but rarely burnished might suggest that they mainly contained non-liquid substances such as cereal grains; earthenware is commonly burnished to reduce micro-holes on the wall in order to prevent the leakage of liquids. The connection between the dead (represented by the use of pottery containers as burial jars), the storage of grains (almost certainly including rice), and more importantly, the colour red (and black) suggests the metaphorical-transformative connection between the concepts of the death and regeneration of life of grains as well as of human beings, as argued earlier. We have already seen that this connection was represented by the spatial organisation of Etsuji village (Figure 5.1). It is interesting to recall that the globular jar SK17 (see Figure 5.1), deposited in such a way as if to mark the boundary between the two burial grounds – possibly of two moieties – in the village, was also painted red (see the previous section). If an infant was buried in it, the transitory nature of the location might have signified the transitory nature and/or liminality of the infant's social being and might have metaphorically represented prayers for not only the regeneration of the dead buried in those burial grounds but also a good harvest of rice.

In that case, what can we infer about the way in which the globular jar shape-type, a foreign material item, was incorporated into the indigenous assemblage? There is a suggestive phenomenon accompanying its incorporation. During the introduction stage of the globular jar shape-type to the indigenous assemblage, we find some examples of the shallow bowl shape-type – a significant member of the Final Jomon pottery assemblage – that was painted with red pigments in an identical manner to the globular jars: the shallow bowls were painted all over on the outside, except for the bottom, and on the inside of the rim (see Figures 5.4.2 and 5.4.5) (Tanaka 1986, 123).

Interestingly, both the globular jar and shallow bowl shape-types are examples of *finer wares* as regards their respective assemblages: they both are made of well-processed paste and have well-

burnished surfaces. This might suggest that the shallow bowl shape-type was chosen as a *substitute* for the globular jar shape-type, a main component of the Mumun pottery assemblage, because it occupied an identical position to the globular jar, i.e. it belonged to the finer-ware category (ibid.). It can be inferred further that these jar types occupy similar positions in the hierarchical structure/the structure of meaning content of the respective pottery assemblages or the hierarchical system of meanings signified by them (Figure 5.4) (cf. Miller 1985). Hence, the discourse regarding the production and use of pottery, as mentioned previously, assigns different pots with different appearances and requiring the investment of different amounts of time, energy and resources in their making for their use on different social occasions wherein different sets of people gather, different codes of practice area followed and different systems of meaning are activated (ibid.).

It is necessary to further elaborate on this argument. It is believed that the globular jars were primarily used for the storage of rice grains. The smaller specimens were, as mentioned earlier, often deposited in the form of grave goods, while the larger specimens were occasionally used as burial jars. The function of the shallow bowl shape-type is unknown, but from their shape, we can infer that they were used to process and/or serve foodstuffs. These specimens were often also used as lids of burial jars (Figure 5.4.B). The metaphorical connection between food and the dead is evident in the case of both the globular jar and the shallow bowl shape-types. This suggests that the positions occupied by the globular jars and bowls in the systems of meaning materialised by the Middle Mumun and Final Jomon assemblages were mutually compatible (cf. Tanaka 1986, 123).

This compatibility, I would argue, allowed the use of the shallow bowl shape-type as a *symbolic substitute* for the globular jar shape-type. If this were indeed the case, it would suggest that it was the concern with not only its function but also the meaning(s) attached to it that determined the ways in which the globular jar shape-type was used. This compatibility might also suggest that elements of the Mumun pottery assemblage were adopted in a way which would *not* lead to *destructive changes* to the preexisting discourse of pottery production and use. In order to examine the validity of this

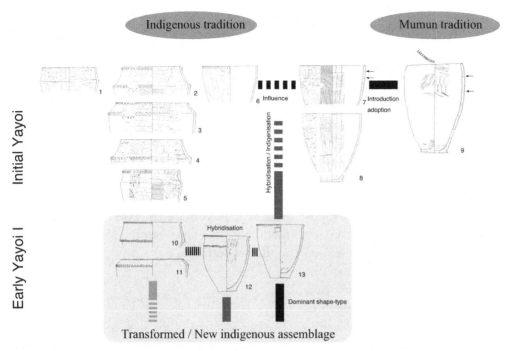

Figure 5.5. The variations of the cooking jar shape-type of the period: straight-necked, carinated, cordoned and uncordoned. Note distinct characteristics of the straight-necked type of the probable Korean origin: particularly note that the wall was built by attaching the upper ring from the outside (marked by arrows on 7 and 9). 1–8 Magarita (Fukuoka), 10–13 Iamagawa (Fukuoka) (after Fukuoka PBE 1985a, 15–77); 9 Hyam-ri (Korea; after National Museum of Korea 1990).

inference, let us now look at the changes in the cooking jar variety.

3.2. *Transformation of the Cooking Jar Variety*

Interestingly, a transformation similar to that which had occurred with the adoption of globular jars also took place with respect to the variety of cooking jars. At the time of the introduction of rice agriculture, the cooking jar variety consisted of the straight-necked shape-type and the carinated shape-type, both with incised cordons (Figure 5.5.1–6). There also were coarse, uncordoned and unincised varieties of cooking jars in use. The straight-necked shape-type typically had a cordon on its rim, but very rarely on the upper body. The carinated shape-type had a cordon on both its rim and the carination. There were a small number of specimens which had incisions on the line of carination, which was uncordoned. There also were a small number of specimens which had only incisions, but not a cordon, on the rim. There also existed another straight-necked type of cooking jar, probably originating from the Mumun assemblage, which was only distributed across northern Kyushu (Figure 5.5.7).

This is a rare type: its surface was consistently well smoothened with a wooden implement of some sort and its rim was uncordoned but incised (Figure 5.5.7).

Those pots were made of clay rings. Initially, an overwhelming majority of these cooking jar specimens were made of clay rings adhering to one another in such a way that the upper ring adhered to the lower one from the inside. What is interesting, however, is that some of the examples of the cooking jar shape-types originating from the Mumun assemblage, such as the straight-necked jars with incisions on the uncordoned rim, were made the other way round – that is, their walls were built by securing the upper ring from the outside (Figure 5.5.7, note the arrows indicating the boundaries between the rings; see Yane 1984). This new, and most likely foreign, pottery-making technique[22] was gradually adopted in the manufacture of other types of cooking pots (and other shape-types constituting the assemblage) as the Mumun-derived varieties continued to become

---

22 The cooking jar shape-types of contemporaneous Korean Mumun pottery were made in the same manner (Figure 5.5.9; Yane 1984).

increasingly popular and predominant in the cooking jar variety. At the end of this process, the straight-necked shape-type originating from the Mumun assemblage became the main component of cooking jar varieties used across the western part of the coastal northern Kyushu region, that is, in the Karastu, Itoshima and Fukuoka plains, where the paddy field rice farming communities were first established (Figure 5.5.13; Misaka n.d.).

The cooking jar varieties were regarded as the *coarse-ware* component of the assemblage. The cooking jars were used to heat and cook foodstuffs, including rice. A study of the cooking traces left behind in these jars, which involved the experimental heating of controlled substances, has revealed that grains, no doubt including rice, were cooked in these jars through the process of boiling (Kobayashi 2011). In contrast to the shallow bowl (Figure 5.4) and pedestalled bowl shape-types, which would have been used to serve food and hence would have been seen by those who gathered to eat, the cooking jar variety would have been *seen* only by those who did the cooking. However, the act of cooking can be metaphorically associated with a range of things relating to *transformations*, such as those from life to death, from death to regeneration and so on, because cooking transforms the raw into the cooked (cf. Lévi-Strauss 1970).

As long as a vessel is shaped in such a way that it can hold grains and water, and as long as its walls can withstand heat, any vessel can be used for cooking. In that sense, the late Final Jomon period's carinated cooking jar variety could continue to be used for cooking grains. In that regard, the transformation of the cooking jar variety was different from the adoption of the globular jar shape-type. There was no exact equivalent to the globular jar shape-type in the Final Jomon assemblage. However, a variety of cooking jars were already in existence at the time of arrival of the straight-necked cooking jar shape-type as part of the Middle Mumun assemblage (Figure 5.5). What happened subsequently was a case of *hybridisation*: the jar's form remained unchanged, but its rim became incised in the manner which was similar to the indigenous cordoned/carinated shape-types (Figures 5.5.6, 5.5.8, and 5.5.13). It is difficult to determine why this particular shape-type became dominant. It might have

become so popular simply because it was difficult to make carinated shape-types using the newly introduced pottery-making technique of securing coils of clay from the outside. Another possibility is that a particular system of meanings/functions represented by the different varieties of cooking jars declined as the rice-agriculture-based way of life was established. I am inclined to the latter thesis.[23] In any case, subsequent developments in pottery not only made the cooking jar shape-types originating from the Mumun assemblage the main component of the cooking jar variety but also rendered them quite different from the Mumun equivalent in their appearance.

3.3. New Pottery, New Discourse, New Reality

The introduction of the new foodstuff, i.e., rice, must have drastically changed the way in which food, in general, was prepared, served and consumed. It has been often argued that the preparation and consumption of food constitute a distinct and important discourse in which a range of sociocultural matters are differentiated, categorised and sorted out (e.g. Lévi-Strauss 1970). The storage of foodstuffs would have been part of a similar discourse, and changes in these important discourses were reflected by corresponding changes in the pottery assemblage which materially represented the structures and components of those discourses. It should be noted that these changes did not take the form of an outright replacement of the old, the Jomon assemblage, with the new, the Mumun assemblage; instead, they involved transforming both the old and the new in such a manner as to suit the new requirements, without destroying what had previously existed. In short, the new traits and techniques that had arrived from the Korean peninsula were adopted in a selective manner by drawing upon and respecting the preexisting structures, that is, the *rules* and *resources* (cf. Giddens 1984), of the earlier discourse

23 Before the introduction of the globular jar shape-type, the carinated and cordoned cooking jar shape-type was used as a burial container (see Figure 5.4.B). In this case, not only its size but also its symbolic function of transforming the raw to the cooked, being linked to regenerative transformation from death to life, would have been the reason for it to be chosen as such. It suggests that the shape-type as a coarse-ware was also imbued with symbolic meanings.

concerning pottery production and use. This mode of transformation is evident at the Etsuji village site (see the previous section).

The outcome was the creation of a new, distinct assemblage consisting of a mixture of characteristics derived from both the Jomon and the Mumun assemblages. The new assemblage would have not only mediated the new mode of food storage, preparation and consumption but also helped people identify themselves in an entirely different manner from before without putting them through destructive discontinuation.

As we have already seen, the globular jar shape-type had assumed an important role in the discourse of burying the dead. The primary function of the globular jar shape-type, as mentioned above, was to store cereal grains including rice grains, and these grains were intended either to be eaten or to be sown as seeds. If they were eaten, it could be said that the grains died in order to sustain the life of the eater. If they were sown, the grains were regenerated and reproduced themselves. Either way, as a container, the globular jar shape-type was involved in the process of transformation of grains from death to life. When larger variants of the globular jar came to be used as coffins during the Incipient Yayoi period, they contained individual dead bodies, mostly those of infants (see Figures 5.13.1–4). Hence, the death of grains and their regeneration were metaphorically associated with the death of people (infants) and their regeneration, thanks to the use of globular jars to store grains as well as contain dead bodies (of infants). To add, the liminal nature of the infant as a category would have made it easier to connect it to grains. Further, some of the globular jars, regardless of their size, were painted red or, occasionally, black (see Figure 5.13). In many ethnographic examples, the former represents life and the latter, death (e.g. Needham 1979).

The globular jar shape-type might have also had some connection with social differentiation. Small specimens of these jars were found to be buried with the dead (Figure 5.4.A). Not all the dead, however, had such jars deposited in their graves. A small number of infants, but not all of them, were buried in some of the larger globular jars, most of which were painted red. It is difficult to specify the reason for this differentiation. In most of the cases, the pots were the only artefacts to be deposited with the dead, and we have too few skeletal remains for examining any possibility of correlation between the sexes of the deceased and the presence/absence of pots. However, it can be safely argued that the globular jars potentially marked a social differentiation of some sort. In addition, with regard to the connection of the shape-type with the conception of death and the regeneration of life, the burial of the globular jars with the chosen dead tacitly, and even unconsciously, evoked the notion that *the regeneration of the life of the individual and the community was a matter concerning specific individuals.* After all, deciding who should control the distribution and use of rice grains would have become one of the most important concerns for the newly established agrarian communities. In that sense, the spatial representation of the previously mentioned metaphorical-transformative connection at Etsuji village might have also implied something similar (see the previous section): those who were in charge of the central cult-house-like building's construction might have been perceived as the caretakers of the regeneration of life – the life of rice as well as that of the community.

In any case, the creation of a new pottery assemblage became a material expression of not only a new set of realities of social life, including emergent social stratification, but also a new set of ways to cope with the changing times.

3.4. The Broader Picture

In the preceding sections, I have elaborated on how some pottery shape-types and their production technology originating from the Korean peninsula were introduced, or rather selectively adopted, in northern Kyushu. By the beginning of the Yayoi I, the new assemblage, comprising what were to become the basic components of Yayoi pottery – that is, globular jars, pedestalled bowls, shallow bowls and cooking jars with outward-curving rims – had been fully established. In addition, during the later part of the first half of the Yayoi I (the Itazuke [板付] I)-style phase in the northern Kyushu region), the assemblage began to spread eastward.[24]

24 Nobuyuki Shimojo (2002) argues that the spread was the consequence of the accumulation of cultural diffusion between neighbouring communities. However,

Situated in the wider geographical sphere of the Incipient Yayoi period, the northern Kyushu region was part of the large, internally fairly homogeneous horizon covering the whole of western Japan, which was characterised by the widespread use of incised cordoned-and-carinated cooking jars and carinated shallow bowls (hereafter referred to as the cordoned-and-carinated-cooking-jar horizon [CCH]) (e.g. Izumi 1989). Interactions between communities within the horizon would have been fairly dense, including those between supra-local groupings such as kin-based *sodalities* and dual organisations cutting across residential communities. *Sodalities* are supra-residential/communal organisations organised on the basis of kin-relations, age, gender, religious affiliation and so on. They cross-cut villages and mediate various types of inter-village/communal interactions (see Keesing 1975). *Clans* are a type of sodalities, reproducing themselves basically as exogamous (i.e. marriage between the members is prohibited) groups and functioning as units of descent, ownership of certain properties and their inheritance (ibid.).[25] *Dual organisations* cross-cut sodalities and divide them into two larger corporate groupings that are supposed to reciprocate social obligations, often related to rite-of-passage ceremonies (cf. Tuzin 2001). As illustrated previously, the existence of such kin-based sodalities and dual organisations can be inferred from the spatial structure of the Jomon settlement (e.g. the Nishida; see Figure 5.2 and related descriptions). The possible presence of a dual organisation, such as a moiety, in the Etsuji burial grounds (see preceding discussion) and the co-presence of sodality segments in the form of distinct clusters of storage pits at Itazuke (see Mori and Okazaki 1961) seem to support the model. Such inter-village/communal interactions would have contributed to the spread of information and material items through the reciprocal exchange of marriage partners and goods and the fulfilment of mutual obligations. This horizon (i.e. the CCH) extended as far as the Nobi (濃尾) Plain of Aichi prefecture to the east, and it was this horizon that witnessed the initial eastward spread of Yayoi pottery and, indeed, the Yayoi way of life.

The eastward expansion of the assemblage was initially marked by the emergence of residential communities using the Itazuke I-style or the subsequent Itazuke IIa-style assemblage, including the shape-types of globular jars and cooking jars with outward-curving rims, along the Seto Inland Sea (瀬戸内海) corridor as far east as the shore of Osaka Bay and along the Japan Sea coast as far east as Shimane prefecture.[26]

In the Kinki region, the CCH-derived cooking jars were replaced by jars with outward-curving rims, originating from the Itazuke (板付) I/IIa traditions of northern Kyushu (see Figure 5.5.13), through a process that should be examined in detail. According to Shin'ichiro Fujio, some communities chose to adopt the latter straightaway, whereas others either continued to produce and use the former or chose to copy the shape of the latter while making them by using the local traditional pottery-making techniques (Fujio 2003). This suggests that the process was one of *acculturation*. The sites showing such different patterns of Itazuke I/IIa-type cooking jar usage did not, however, show distinct distributions of such usage; the patterns were mixed together. This suggests that the process was brought about through (a) small-scale migrations, (b) intermarriage, (c) reciprocal exchanges and (d) other types of interactions

the co-presence of the villages where the Itazuke I assemblage was adopted and that where modified carinated cooking jars continued to be used in some of the floodplains along the Seto Inland Sea corridor (e.g. Kusano 2010) suggests that it was not a sole mechanism causing the spread. It is more likely that the mixture of step-model diffusion and migration across a distance resulted in the rapid spread of the fairly homogeneous pottery assemblage (Tanaka 2002). See pp. 70–74.

25 Clans are often comprised of *lineages* (e.g. Keesing 1975). Lineages are commonly defined as exogamous descent groups, like clans, and genealogical connections between the members are clearly recognised, whereas the membership of a clan is defined by the members' connection to a mythical ancestor (ibid.). In actuality there exist enormous variability in both clans and lineages in terms of membership reckoning, the mode of descent, ownership, and inheritance, and the general usefulness of the concepts itself is often disputed. However, for the sake of description and modelling, those terms will be used in the present volume.

26 The southward expansion appears to have taken place more rapidly, and some stone leaping knives have been excavated in association with potsherds dating from the Incipient Yayoi in Kagoshima and Miyazaki prefectures (see Higashi 2011, 150). Besides, iregularly-shaped paddies, dating from the Incipient Yayoi, were excavated at Sakamoto A site, Miyazaki prefecture (ibid., 154).

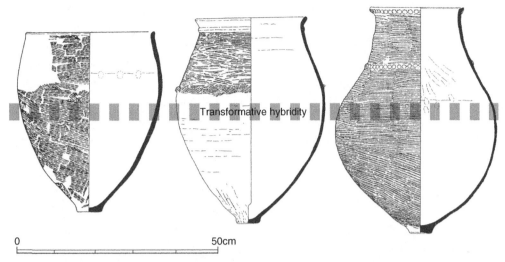

Figure 5.6. Examples of hybrid globular jars on the eastern periphery of the "cordoned-and-carinated-cooking-jar horizon" (CCH). Note transformative hybridity between cooking jar (far left) and globular jars (excavated from the Asoda-Ohashi 麻生田大橋 site [Aichi prefecture]; after Maeda and Suzuki 2002, figs. 10, 5 and 26). The hybrid shape-types of the Mikawa province shown here became the prototype of a range of globular jar shape-types with slender, S-shaped profiles, which spread across the eastern half of Honshu Island as far north as the southern Tohoku district from the Yayoi II onwards (see Figure 6.1.C and D).

between various residential communities through preexisting networks of basically kin-based connections such as sodalities and moieties (see previous discussion), both newly forged and preexisting, that criss-crossed the residential communities. People, information, knowledge and material items were frequently exchanged and were accepted and/or rejected in different manners between communities. It is interesting to note that at some sites, the CCH-derived cooking jar shape-type and/or the CCH-derived shallow bowl shape-type had been modified to form a sort of hybrid globular jar shape-type (see the similar example in the Tokai region in the following and Figure 5.6; Fujio 2003). This phenomenon can be variously interpreted. However, these modifications undoubtedly indicate that the local community modified its discourse to one which needed the globular jar shape-type as an item for its reproduction, thus suggesting that the modifications were not the result of population replacement but rather that of acculturation motivated by various strategic concerns. Different patterns of shifting from the Jomon to the Yayoi discourse, as revealed in the production and use of pottery, would have reflected *different strategic decisions* taken by the communities in maintaining their inter-communal ties. In any case, such interactions not only entailed the spread of the Yayoi way of life but also transformed the identities of the

local inhabitants, that is, the ways in which they expected themselves to behave and their behavioural expectations from others in certain social settings.

The eastward expansion of the Itazuke I-derived pottery horizon extended as far east as the Nobi Plain. However, its eastern half, that is, the ancient province of Owari, developed a unique hybrid assemblage. The characteristic S-profile of the Itazuke I-derived globular jar shape-type was incorporated into the local CCH tradition, resulting in a hybrid version of the globular jar shape-type (e.g. Kano and Ishiguro 2002) (Figure 5.6). This unique shape-type emerged by modifying the shape of the cordoned-and-carinated cooking jar shape-type by narrowing its rim diameter and lengthening the part above the carination (Figure 5.6). The modification can be understood as an attempt to copy the Itazuke I–derived globular jar shape-type while maintaining the CCH-derived local pottery-making tradition. As mentioned earlier, it is observed that similar phenomena occurred, albeit in smaller scales, across the area from the Seto Inland Sea corridor through the Kinki region to the Tokai region. However, this hybridisation phenomenon was most widespread in the Owari and Mikawa (present-day Aichi prefecture) provinces (see Figure 3.1.23). It appears that the above-mentioned networks of kin-based ties were at work, and an increasing number of sites gradually adopted the Itazuke-derived assemblage. However, the hybrid version of the globular jar shape-type also became firmly established as a significant component of the local assemblage and continued to be used into the Middle Yayoi period.

The surface of this unique hybrid globular jar shape-type was finished by scraping it with the edge of seashells or bunched sticks (ibid.) (Figure 5.6). This process left characteristic deep, parallel incisions on the surface. The custom was derived from the surface-finishing technique applied to the cordoned-and-carinated and other types of cooking jars from the latter half of the Final Jomon period in the region (ibid.). The region, as mentioned earlier, was located on the eastern fringe of the CCH horizon, extending from the Kyushu region in the west to the Ise bay area and the Nobi Plain in the east (see Figure 3.1.B). The hybrid-style assemblage established in the Owari and Mikawa provinces was, in turn, adopted by communities to the east, and the hybrid globular jar shape-type developed in Owari and Mikawa became the prototype for a range of globular jar shape-types with slender, S-shaped profiles, which spread across the eastern half of Honshu Island as far north as the southern Tohoku region from the Yayoi II onwards (see Figure 5.6, far right, and Figure 6.1.C).

This rather complicated account of the Itazuke assemblage's eastern edge of expansion has led to the interesting hypothesis that the hybrid globular jar shape-type was created to enhance the group identity of communities under pressure from the arrival of a new way of life as represented by the use of the Itazuke-derived assemblage (Komura 1983). It is difficult to discern whether there was any hostility between those communities that had manifestly adopted the Itazuke-derived assemblage and those that had not; however, such hostility is unlikely. In fact, the latter did not necessarily reject any element of the Itazuke-derived assemblage but gradually introduced an increasing number of elements from that assemblage into their own pottery traditions as the Yayoi I progressed. It is important to note, in this context, that the early versions of the hybrid globular jar shape-type occasionally bear some cooking traces in the form of soot adhering to their surface (e.g. Sato 1994). From this we can infer that such jars were used for both

storage and cooking, while the subsequent versions with slender, S-shaped profiles appear to have been used exclusively for storage. Regarding the use of the Iatzuke-derived globular jar shape-type as a storage vessel, we can say that the copying of the Itazuke-style-derived globular jar was not necessarily motivated by functional requirements; if functional requirements motivated the adoption, the globular jars would have been used solely and exclusively as storage (grain-storing) vessels, but they were used as cooking jars as well. It would suggest that the initial motivation for those who created the hybrid shape-type was an attraction to a pottery shape-type which they had never seen before, accompanied by an interest in the new way of life and new cultural values which were represented by the new shape-type. The absence of a straightforward adoption of the Itazuke-style-derived globular jar suggests that either (a) the contacts and/or ties between the communities which adopted it and those which did not adopt it were not characterised by the exchange of marriage partners or (b) the latter *rejected* the outright adoption of the Itazuke-style-derived shape-type. If the former case were true, the non-adopting communities could have still 'copied' the Itazuke-style-derived globular jar, however crudely. In that sense, the latter case is more likely, and the resultant hybridisation might have been a consequence of inter-communal rivalry; the latter communities, as far as their lithic assemblage is concerned, adopted rice paddy field farming but chose not to adopt the Itazuke-style globular jar as an *embodiment* of the newly arrived Yayoi package to signify their communal identity in their contacts and/or ties with their more Yayoi-influenced counterparts. This thesis would be feasible, considering the fact that some globular jars of the Initial Yayoi assemblage in northern Kyushu were painted red in order to symbolise the transformative connection between rice grains and human beings and between the death and the regeneration of life, i.e., the Yayoi structuring principle (see previous discussion).

From the Mikawa province to regions as far east as the edge of the southern Tohoku region, the process of adopting the Yayoi package, in terms of pottery, proceeded in the form of a gradual and selective adoption of the above-mentioned hybrid globular jar shape-type and its derivatives (cf. Takase 2004). When the process began, the Tohoku region was covered by the Obora (大洞) horizon and the Kanto and Koshin'etsu regions by the Fusen-mon (浮線紋) (relief-motifed) horizon (Hayashi 1986). As the hybrid globular jar shape-type began to be adopted and some elements of the Itazuke-derived assemblage came to be sporadically transported and/or adopted, the widespread horizons began to be segmented into local style zones, although their boundaries were not at all clear, being cross-cut by the distribution of a range of attributes (Takase 2004, 135–143).

In this regard, some peculiar changes took place in the northern Tohoku region. The region saw the incorporation of the Itazuke-assemblage-derived globular jar and cooking jar shape-types into the local Obora A′ assemblage, albeit not in a systematic and extensive manner (ibid., 111–134). This is particularly interesting in that the same did not happen in the Kanto-Koshin'etsu and southern Tohoku regions, located between the northern Tohoku region and the Mikawa province (ibid., 111–114). Kensaku Hayashi's characterisation of the mode of social networking during the Final Jomon period in the northern Tohoku region seeks to explain this phenomenon (Hayashi 1986). He argues that social networks were developed to enable purposeful transportations of source materials for ritual items such as shell armlets over a very long distance (ibid.). These would have reflected the ties formed by communities of the northern Tohoku region for the reproduction of their internal as well as external relations. Such ties would have inevitably needed reciprocity to sustain them, in addition to a certain degree of investment of time and energy. Such investments, it can be further inferred, would have had to be firmly embedded in the annual scheduling of activities; moreover, due to the risks and uncertainties involved in the transportation, such ties would have needed to be supported by pseudo-kinship-based alliances. If this were the case, in the event that some communities in the networks introduced a new subsistence technology that required them to change the annual scheduling of activities and the range of resources they could produce or procure, the others would have had to adjust to these changes in one way or another, for instance, by either accepting the new subsistence technology or changing their mode of social strategy.

From the second half of the Obora pottery style period onwards, the Obora-style finer wares were transported across the CCH, albeit on a small scale (though this distribution was limited to the eastern quarter of the CCH by the end of the Obora-style period; Shitara and Kobayashi 2007, 90–95). The fact that they were mostly finer wares suggests that their presence reflected the existence of networks such as those mentioned above. The introduction of Itazuke-style-derived shape-types and their establishment in the local pottery assemblage in northern Tohoku would have happened through those networks and through the mechanism inferred previously, that is, through reciprocal interactions coming from pseudo-kinship-based alliances.[27] According to Katsunori Takase, the Itazuke-style-derived globular jar and cooking jar shape-types were introduced through different routes (Takase 2004, 111–134). His contention is that while the former was introduced to the Tohoku region through the Pacific coastal route, the latter arrived through the Japan Sea coastal route. Although his thesis has not been fully accepted in the academia, if it were true, it would support the preceding inference: the pottery shape-types were introduced through different networks connecting different sets of communities as different non-residential pseudo-kinship-based groupings.

The question still remains: how was it that the Itazuke-assemblage-derived globular jar and cooking jar shape-types were incorporated into the local Obora A′ assemblage when the same did not occur in the Kanto-Koshin'etsu and southern Tohoku regions, located between the northern Tohoku region and the Mikawa province? According to Hayashi, the fishing communities living in the western regions of Kanto-Koshin'etsu region do not use harpoons, whereas those living in the eastern regions use them (Hayashi 1986). The absence and presence of harpoons as fishing tools would have resulted in different modes of fishing. The role played by the fishing communities would have had a significant impact on the interactions between distant communities,

27 Or, it might be the case that a kula-type long-distance exchange tie maintained by expeditionary/adventurous voyages existed, and high-quality, prestigious items were the subject of ritualised exchange (Malinowski 1984).

including both reciprocal exchanges and small-scale migrations. This role would have defined the boundary or the end-point of the sodality-based and fishing-community-aided eastward advancement of the knowledge and customs accompanying the Itazuke-style-derived pottery assemblage. In the meantime, communities on the Obora-style pottery horizon of the northern Tohoku region appear to have created and maintained pseudo-kinship-based contacts with their counterparts across northern Kyushu and western Japan. Why these communities did so, and why the communities residing in the regions in between did not, still remains a mystery. However, we can certainly infer that when the Obora-style finer wares began to arrive in northern Kyushu, at about the same time that the region shifted to the rice-agriculture-based way of life, the communities residing in northern Tohoku were attracted to some aspects of this movement (Shitara and Kobayashi 2007, 90–92). This might have been because the aggrandisers (e.g. Hayden 1995) of northern Tohoku considered it a sign of prestige to create and maintain access to the distant place where new and exotic activities were taking place.[28]

3.5. *Pots as Markers of Discourse and Identity*

When there is a change in any discourse, or the way in which a certain group of individuals think, feel and perform a certain set of activities by using a certain set of resources, both material and immaterial, the following changes are bound to happen: (a) the emergence or introduction of new resources, (b) changes in the way they are mobilised and (c) changes in the Constitution of the group. These changes are not necessarily equal in magnitude or based on the same rhythms. The extent to which the previously prevalent discourse is drawn on during this processes of change varies as well. In the case examined above – that is, the changes in pottery assemblage accompanying the onset of the Yayoi way of life – the changes took place in a highly selective manner. The word *selective*, in this context, means that the changes introduced were related almost only to those material and immaterial resources that had not already existed in the Jomon style of making, using and doing things with pottery. The selective nature of this

change in pottery styles is sufficiently attested by the frequent occurrences of hybridisation.

In that case, would it be possible to understand the onset of the Yayoi way of life, represented by the changes which occurred in the pottery assemblage of that time, as a process of gradual acculturation? Can we say that apart from some components of the preexisting culture, nothing much changed significantly? I would disagree with this perspective. One of the most prominent new additions to the assemblage, the globular jar shape-type, opened up a new range of possibilities for categorising and connecting people and resources, life and death, and the living and the dead. If one of the main functions of the globular jar shape-type, as inferred earlier, were to contain rice grains, its introduction would have opened up new possibilities of controlling access to this vital new resource; the presence of the container would have allowed communities to assign a connection between particular individuals/groups and the grain stored in such containers. Death and the regeneration of life, which was metaphorically connected to the life cycle of rice grains stored in the globular jars, in that sense, would have opened up a way for symbolically controlling some aspects of food production as well as reproduction in the community. We will see the unfolding of the potential of this metaphorical connection and the transformation of discourses mediated by the connection throughout the rest of the volume.

To sum up, the selective adoption of some components of the Mumun pottery assemblage of peninsular origin materially mediated a new categorisation of social occasions and people without drastically modifying the preexisting assemblage. In some cases, such as in northern Tohoku, these new assemblages were also mobilised as sources of prestige.

3.6. *Stone and Wooden Tools*

The lithic assemblages of that time underwent a similar process of transformation as pottery; the communities of the northern Kyushu region, which first adopted the Yayoi package in the archipelago, introduced new components, necessary for rice cultivation, that their erstwhile lithic assemblage had lacked and modified their existing assemblage to make it better suited to the uses demanded by this kind of agriculture

28 See Footnote 24 to this chapter.

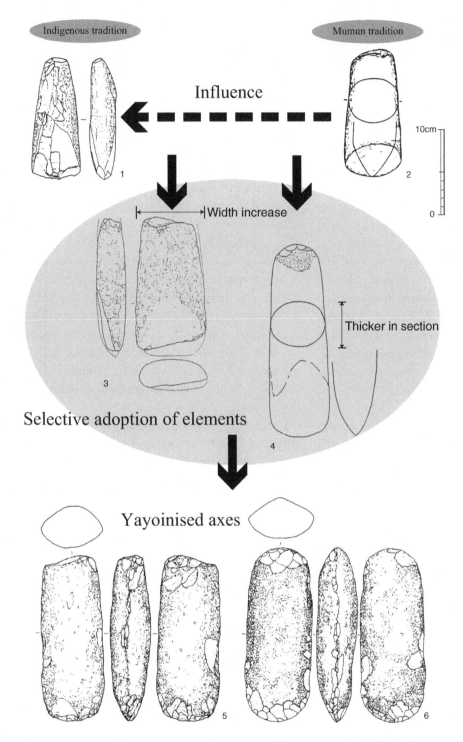

Indigenous tradition

Mumun tradition

Influence

Width increase

10cm

0

Thicker in section

Selective adoption of elements

Yayoinised axes

Figure 5.7. Tree-felling axes of the beginning of the Yayoi period. The indigenous axe was not replaced by the Mumun axe but modified by selectively incorporating the latter's elements: some specimens became larger in size, some thicker-butted. 1 Hirota (Fukuoka), 2 Songguk'ni (Korea), 3 Nabatake (Saga), 4 Itazuke (Fukuoka; after Shimojo 1986); 5 and 6 Imayama (Fukuoka; after Fukuoka MBE 2005b).

(cf. Shimojo 1986). In the case of previously existing components that could be used without modification, these were kept unchanged (ibid.).

For instance, reaping knives for harvesting the rice ears were introduced in a fairly straightforward manner from the Korean peninsula, whereas the Jomon tree-felling axes were not directly replaced by their Korean equivalents. Instead, the former were modified to become more thicker-butted by incorporating into them the latter's morphological traits (Figure 5.7; Shimojo 1985). In the case of the reaping knives, however, the implements underwent many complex transformations after the initial stage of adoption. When first adopted, there were four main sub-types: triangular-shaped reaping knives, half-moon-shaped knives with curved cutting edges, half-moon-shaped knives with straight cutting edges and almond-shaped knives (Shimojo 1986). Over the course of the Incipient and Early Yayoi periods, the triangular- and almond-shaped types disappeared, while half-moon-shaped knives with curved cutting edges became widespread in northern Kyushu, the western Seto Inland Sea and the San'in regions; in contrast, half-moon-shaped knives with straight cutting edges were more popular in the Kinki region and in the Ise province (the present-day Mie prefecture) of Tokai region (see Figure 3.1). In the eastern Seto Inland Sea region, square, chipped reaping knives continued to be used from the Final Jomon period onwards.[29] At the time of its arrival, however, the package must have included all, or at least some, of the four types of reaping knives of Korean origin. However, they were not adopted at once because the preexisting types were still preferred.

As we move further eastward from the eastern half of the Tokai region, the ratio of chipped reaping knives to the polished equivalents rises, and we find that reaping knives were rarely used in the regions east of the northern Kanto region. As mentioned earlier, long-distance contacts between communities in the northern Tohoku and the Tokai, Chubu, Kanto and Koshin'etsu regions brought Itazuke-style-derived pottery to the northern Tohoku region. In addition, excavations reveal the presence of paddies at Sunazawa (砂沢) site in Aomori prefecture (Hirosaki MBE 1991). Hence, it is intriguing that no reaping knife has yet been excavated from the Sunazawa site or, indeed, from the other sites in the northern Tohoku region where Itazuke-style-derived pots have been found. This suggests two possibilities: first, the type of knife that had originated in the peninsula, as a utilitarian tool, could easily be replaced by some preexisting functional equivalents, and second, the globular jar shape-type of peninsular origin could not be replaced by any functional equivalent(s) in the preexisting pottery

29 Some scholars infer that they were used to reap dry-cultivated rice and other crops before the Yayoi package was introduced. However, recent outcomes of the SEM analysis on seed marks on potsherds suggest caution. See Footnotes 4 and 5 to the current chapter.

assemblage because of its symbolic-metaphorical implications, already investigated at length earlier.

In any case, we can clearly observe, as was the case elsewhere to the west, that the adoption of the Yayoi package took place in a highly selective manner, and it has to be emphasised that those components which had functional equivalents in the local assemblage were not directly adopted by the local communities, whereas those which had functional equivalents but were embedded in the rice-cultivation-based system of meaning were adopted.

The preceding observations suggest that the assemblage of wooden farming tools, introduced as a component of the Yayoi package, did not undergo the process of immediate *indigenisation* (cf. Kurosaki 1985) because there was no functional equivalent in the indigenous assemblage of wooden implements, apart from some shovel-like and some other digging tools that continued to be used from the Jomon period onwards, well into the Initial and Early Yayoi periods (ibid., 82). Hence, the assemblage of wooden agricultural implements remained fairly homogeneous across the horizon within which the Yayoi package was adopted. The Yayoi wooden-agricultural-tool assemblage had spread across most of the CCH (see the section on pottery) by the end of the Initial Yayoi period and had reached the Ise Bay area and the Nobi Plain by the end of the Yayoi I (ibid.).

The assemblage consisted of task-specific tools used for different types of work necessary for the construction and maintenance of paddies and for different stages in the process of preparing the paddies for rice cultivation; the homogeneity of composition and morphological characteristics of the tools used across the horizon (ibid.) is remarkable. The assemblage nicely shows that the tools which had not existed in the Jomon repository of material items were embraced enthusiastically with the introduction of the Yayoi package.

3.7. There Is No Such Thing as 'Either Continuity or Change'

As we have seen, the process of transformation in the portable material assemblages during the Incipient Yayoi and Yayoi I periods only shows that when faced with change, life goes on by creating a new reality and adjusting to it. A new socio-technological complex was adopted during these periods; this inevitably entailed a straight-forward adoption of some components which had not previously existed, or had any functional equivalents, in the preexisting pool of habitual deeds and their material media. However, if there were any functional equivalents or similar components already in use, the alien components were not directly absorbed; instead, their preexisting equivalents were modified to fulfil the same functions. This way, as far as the material media of social practices are concerned, continuity was maintained by minimising the degree of disruptive change.

However, this does not imply that the overall changes in society and culture were minimum and negligible. On the contrary, the changes resulting from the introduction of the new socio-technological package were no doubt immense: they drastically changed the *spatio-temporal organisation* of social lives (Mizoguchi 2002, 149–152), which led to the emergence of a novel mode for the symbolic representation of social reproduction based upon the *metaphorical transformation between death and the regeneration of life and the life cycle of rice grains*. Those changes would also have led to social stratification, which was to become increasingly visible towards the end of the period considered in this chapter.

It is as if the material media of social practices served to *absorb the shocks* brought about by the introduction of the Yayoi package. Obviously, this is a gross simplification of the scenario, used only for the sake of explanation. However, it would be appropriate to say that a sense of continuity was preferred in the realm of material culture, whereas drastic changes were not only inevitable but also actively selected in the sphere of social practices and their spatio-temporal organisation. One explanation for this would be that communities might have preferred to retain the preexisting, unchanged material media for the reproduction of communications precisely because the practices they mediated had changed so dramatically.

In that case, how could this change occur without the involvement of large-scale migrations, and how could the material items remain relatively unchanged? The answer to these questions lies in the settlement structure of the Jomon period and the layers of communal ties that can be reconstructed from it.

4. NEW BUILT-ENVIRONMENTS: SETTLEMENTS AND PADDIES

4.1. *Before the Beginning: The Scenario up to the Early Final Jomon Period (c. 900/600 BC)*

As we have already seen, an enduring characteristic of the Jomon settlements – those in eastern Japan, in particular – from the Early to the Final Jomon period, was their segmentary structure. It has been pointed out that the smaller settlements also often occupied an identical spatial structure, although the number of their constituent segments was much smaller. The contents of the assemblages suggest that some of the smaller settlements were occupied only during a particular season or seasons of the year (Mizoguchi 2002, 88–92; Taniguchi 2005). On this basis, we can infer that the segments comprising individual settlements were occupied and used by some sort of corporate groups, some of which moved out of their bases (i.e. from the larger regional-centre-type settlements)[30] for a particular period (or periods) of the year, possibly either to procure a specific range of foodstuffs and resources or to reduce the subsistence pressure during the resource-poor periods.[31]

The fact that individual settlements, large and small, were often divided into a number of such groups suggests that they were a part of larger corporate groupings cutting across a number of settlements. For instance, the x-a segment of settlement A was part of a larger corporate grouping X, and the inhabitants of x-a maintained certain ties, based upon reciprocity and mutual obligations, with those of segment x-b of settlement B, those of segment x-c of settlement C and so on. Anthropologists call such larger corporate groupings 'sodalities' (see p. 70 in this chapter; Service 1962). Each individual segment of a settlement usually consists of a cluster of storage facilities, burials and pit dwellings (Figure 5.2). The fact that the inhabitants of such a segment shared a distinct burial

30 The word *region* in this case roughly indicates the area within which a majority of intra- and inter-communal activities took place. This should of course be distinguished from the 'regional' divisions of present-day Japan, mentioned in Chapter 3.

31 As an ethnographic example for this type of settlement patterning, see the case of the north-west coastal Native Americans (e.g. Johnson and Earle 2000, 204–217).

ground might suggest that they formed a 'lineage'-like grouping, having common ancestors, and that the larger groupings, or the sodality to which the group belonged, was a 'clan'-like grouping.

Interestingly, at some settlements, such segments were clustered to form two larger spatial divisions (Taniguchi 2002, 22–41). At the Nishida site, there are two rows of burials at the centre of the central open space, and the line dividing the rows also divides the settlement into two larger groupings (Figure 5.2). This suggests that the sodalities constituting a larger social unit, such as a tribal grouping, were at times divided into moiety-like dual entities.[32] If we refer to anthropological studies, such 'dual organisations' often work as a system that serves to divide and connect the halves as units fulfilling mutual obligations at certain, often ritualistic, occasions such as funerals, marriages and other rites of passage (Tuzin 2001, 79–96). Through such dual organisations help one another in preparing and organising such ceremonies, in which various social ties are created and social categories are reaffirmed, the clan-like groups which are classified into two moiety-like halves are able to form larger social networks based upon the sharing of obligations, protocols and beliefs (ibid.). As we have already seen, this type of grouping might have continued well into the Initial Yayoi period (see Section 2 in this chapter).

If the preceding series of inferences capture the social reality at that time, then those two levels of larger social groupings cutting across individual settlements – first, the clan-like groupings and, second, the dual-organisation type of group division – would have made possible the reproduction of social ties and cooperation through intermittent gatherings (including those related to rites of passage) among the members of the larger social units. In regions in the north-eastern part of the archipelago, the average distance between the larger, regional-centre-type settlements was approximately 20 kilometres, and half that distance, that is, a 10-kilometre radius, would give us an idea of the scale of such non-localised social units (Tanaka 1999).

Unlike the eastern regions, the western regions of the archipelago did not develop such extensive systems of the above-described intra- and inter-settlement divisions and groupings. How-

ever, some well-excavated examples of settlements and cemeteries in western Japan, such as the Tarozako site in Kumamoto prefecture, show traces of a segmentary spatial structure that is identical to their eastern Japanese counterparts (ibid.). These suggest that, despite the lower population density, there were similar social-organisational devices and principles in operation in western Japan as well (Mizoguchi 2010a, 24).

The widespread similarities in the ways in which various levels of social relations were maintained across almost the whole of Japan during the Jomon period are well worth further analysis. In the study of the Jomon pottery, the archipelago is commonly divided into a number of style zones. However, if we carefully analyse the way in which these style zones overlap with one another and share many attributes with their neighbouring style zones, we realise that the archipelago was covered by a much smaller number of style zones than believed, and at times, we can say that almost the entire archipelago was covered by an enormously large style zone (see e.g. Tanaka 1999). Sharing flexible modes of maintaining and enlarging social ties, as enabled by various types of sodalities, would have been one reason behind the formation of such large-scale style zones, and the sharing of material media of communication, such as a pottery style, would have supported and reinforced such flexible modes of maintaining and enlarging social ties.

In eastern Japan, the scale and number of settlements peaked in the Middle Jomon period, after which they generally declined (Imamura 1996, 93–95; 1999, 100–119). The Late Jomon period saw the disappearance of regional-centre-type settlements with segmentary structures (Taniguchi 2005). In their place, the landscape was increasingly covered with a scattering of small settlements with larger distances between them. The period also saw the widespread development of the custom of tooth extraction (Mizoguchi 2007, 192–194; Funahashi 2010). It can be inferred that maintaining the previously mentioned kind of multilayered social ties became so difficult due to the fairly dramatic population decline that this new ritualistic device was developed in order to make the rites-of-passage-like gatherings more effective for the maintenance of these ties (Mizoguchi 2007). The tooth-extraction custom, which is interpreted as having been conducted to mark social categories

---

32 See Footnotes 18 and 19 to the current chapter.

and affiliations, not only became a memorable experience but also left its trace in the recipient's body (ibid., 192–194). That means that the social affiliation marked by the rite was literary 'embodied' to remind the recipients of their social categories and belonging. This would have helped the maintenance of larger social ties and networks at a time when it had become difficult to maintain them due to lesser inter-communal contact (ibid.).

In western Japan, the scale and number of settlements remained fairly stable throughout the Jomon period. In the Late and early Final Jomon periods, western Japan saw an increase in the number of settlements, along with an increase in the complexity of their organisation, at both the intra- and the inter-site levels (Hayashi 1986); however, they declined after the early Final Jomon period and remained so until the beginning of the Yayoi period (ibid.). It should be noted that the scale and number of settlements were declining in both eastern and western Japan at the onset of the Yayoi period. However, it appears that the above-mentioned larger social ties and networks were maintained during this time. As we will see later, some Yayoi I settlements in the east show a dual spatial division (e.g. Jizoden; Figure 5.8 in this volume; Takase 2004, 168–197), and some Incipient Yayoi settlements in the west suggest the presence of both dual divisions and distinct groups within them.

The preexistence of such large social networks, i.e., the clan and moiety type of sodalities, as we noted earlier in the section on pottery, would have contributed to the spread of the rice-agriculture-based way of life and/or thinking; if a particular segment of a sodality adopted a new mode of doing and producing things, this in turn would have affected the way in which it fulfilled obligations not only with regard to the other segments of the sodality but also in terms of reciprocal exchanges with its partners in other sodalities. In this way, changes would have spread like ripples without the involvement of substantial migrations.

4.2. The Incipient Yayoi to the Yayoi I (c. 900/600 BC–400/200 BC)

OVERVIEW

The onset of the Yayoi period brought about fairly drastic changes in people's lives. At this time, a new type of house, consisting of round and rectangular sub-types, was introduced to the archipelago from the Korean peninsula. This period also ushered in the practice of enclosing settlements within V-sectioned ditches, a practice that likewise originated in the Korean peninsula. Another important change was that burial grounds came to be separated from the dwelling area. Formerly in the Jomon settlements, burial grounds were often situated at the centre of the settlement, due to which the residents were constantly aware of the presence of the dead, and possibly that of the ancestors (see Nishida as an example, mentioned earlier; see also Figure 5.2). With the onset of the Yayoi period, this level of intimacy between the living and the dead (and probably the ancestors) disappeared. The Jomon type of internal segmentation of the village (as illustrated previously) is not clearly visible in the Incipient Yayoi and Yayoi I villages. However, there are a few interesting cases in this regard. At the Jizoden site in Akita prefecture, the living area is found to have been divided into two moiety-like units, each of which contained three to four round pit dwellings (probably one or two each at a time: see the following discussion; Figure 5.8; Takase 2004, 180–181). At the Etsuji site in Fukuoka prefecture, a cluster of circularly laid out pit dwellings, not segmented into sub-clusters, was associated with two distinct clusters of burials located outside of the circle (illustrated earlier; see Figures 5.1 and 5.15.A). These suggest the continuation of clan- and/or moiety-type sodalities, whose material expression was characteristic to Jomon settlements. As argued earlier, their presence might have played an important role in the spread of the Yayoi way of life.

An interesting point is that we have not yet discovered 'colony'-like settlements whose material culture was entirely constituted by the Korean peninsula-derived items. For instance, at the Etsuji settlement site (see the following), pit houses belong to the Songguk'ni (松菊里) type (see Figure 5.9.C), but the pottery assemblage is dominated by indigenous shape-types (Shintaku 1994). As we have already seen, a similar kind of coexistence between introduced and indigenous elements is evident in many of the material items and assemblages of the time. These further confirm that components of the package were adopted by the local inhabitants rather than imposed on them to replace their existing counterparts.

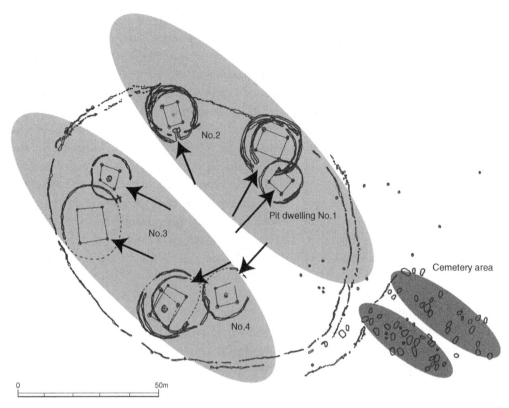

Figure 5.8. The Jizoden site, Akita prefecture. Note the dual spatial division marked by the spatial arrangement of the burials and pit dwellings. Arrows indicate the entrances of the pit dwellings (after Takase 2004 [original from Sugawara 1987], with modifications).

V-sectioned ditch-enclosed settlements initially appeared in the Incipient Yayoi; by the first half of Yayoi I, they had become widespread throughout northern Kyushu. A little later, such settlements began to appear at some spots in the Seto Inland Sea corridor and the Kinki region; by the second half of the Yayoi I, however, they had spread as far east as the Tokai region on the Pacific coast and the northern Kinki region on the Japan Sea coast (e.g. Hayashi 1986). The pattern of the diffusion along the Seto Inland Sea corridor, i.e., the diffusion of such settlement-types to other spots, coincides with the diffusion of the Itazuke I/IIa-style pottery (see Chapter 3.4). The assemblages excavated from these sites include storage and cooking jars constructed, finished and shaped in an identical manner to their northern Kyushu counterparts; however, these jars are made of local clay. Small-scale migrations, at times across long distances, would have been responsible for this kind of diffusion; the migrants would have arrived with their own ideas regarding how their villages, pottery and other material items should look like. The subsequent eastward spread of the Yayoi package, which occurred during the second half and the

final phase of the Yayoi I, would have resulted from a combination of small-scale migrations and the adoption of the migrants' customs by local communities. The new villages and assemblages began to show local characteristics; again, the presence of inter-communal networks based upon dual organisations and sodalities might have played an important role in this diffusion.

The available picture still remains obscure in the case of the regions further east. It has been pointed out that settlement concentrations moved to areas that were more suitable for paddy field rice farming in the Tohoku region (cf. Takase 2004, 168–213). It has also been argued that the increase in settlement scale which occurred along the settlement relocation reflects the reorganisation of the labour force into a form more suitable for paddy field rice farming (ibid.). As mentioned earlier, the region witnessed the introduction of selective elements of the rice-cultivation assemblage. For instance, the enclosure of Jizoden village within densely planted stakes is thought to be a result of the local inhabitants' adoption of the idea of enclosing villages – a component of the Yayoi package (Figure 5.8). However, the discovery

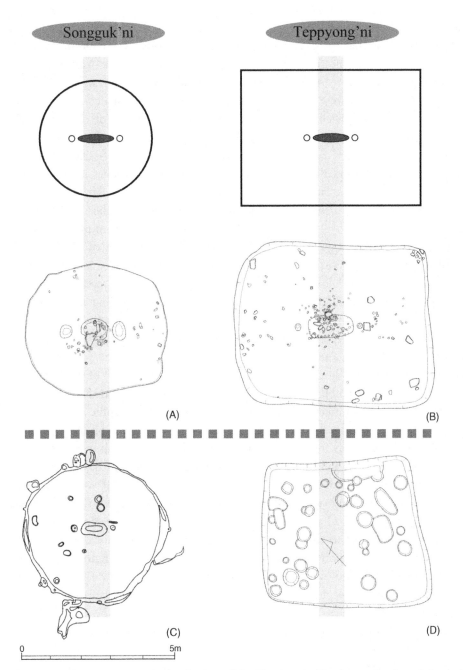

Figure 5.9. House types at the beginning of the Yayoi period in the peninsula and the archipelago. Note both the Songguk'ni (松菊里) and the Teppyong'ni (大坪里) types were introduced into the northern Kyushu region with minimal modifications. However, the material culture assemblage accompanying them were significantly modified and indigenised (see descriptions). **A** and **B**: Jinju Teppyong'ni Yubang Loc. 3 (after Gyeongsang University 2001); **C**: Etsuji (Fukuoka; after Shintaku 1994); **D**: Magarita (Fukuoka; after Fukuoka PBE 1983a).

of similarly enclosed villages from the same and even preceding periods in the north forces us to reconsider the cultural genealogy of the custom (Terasawa 2000, 61–63).

HOUSES

A new type of house, divided into two subtypes – the Songguk'ni (松菊里) and the Teppyong'ni (大坪里) types – was introduced

from the Korean peninsula (Figure 5.9; Hashino et al. 2006). The former subtype consists of round houses with a characteristic oblong pit and two posts in or close to the pit's longitudinal ends (Nakama 1987). The exact function of this pit is unknown. The excavated examples rarely show traces of their use as a hearth or a fireplace. Some of them, albeit few in number, yielded debris from the making of stone tools, leading to the idea that the pit and posts formed a facility for stone tool making. An alternative hypothesis is that the pit functioned as a mortar and a pounder hung from the beam between the posts (Nakama 1987, 614–618).[33] The examples show that the posts were set in a variety of ways. The latter type of dwelling is rectangular, with a fairly similar pit-and-posts setting at the centre. The former type tends to be distributed more densely across the western half of the southern Korean peninsula, whereas the latter type is more densely distributed across the eastern half (Hashino et al. 2006).

When these dwellings made their first appearance in the coastal floodplains of northern Kyushu, however, their distributions overlapped almost completely, even though they rarely coexisted in individual settlements (Ozawa 2006). The rectangular subtype is rarer than the round subtype. At the Magarita (曲り田) site (Fukuoka PBE 1983a, 1984), which contains only rectangular houses (Figure 5.9.D), the pottery and other assemblages are not dominated by components of Mumun culture but show the same pattern as described in our earlier investigation of pottery (see pots from the site in Figure 5.5). This shows that the village was not a colony of migrants. At Etsuji, almost all the excavated dwellings are of the round subtype (Figure 5.9.C), and the arrangement of pits and posts inside these houses is identical to that of the Korean equivalents. However, the pottery assemblage is dominated by the cordoned- and carinated-type cooking jars and includes few globular jars (Shintaku 1994). This suggests that the new house types, like some of the Mumun pottery elements mentioned above, were *adopted* by the local inhabitants. By the end of the Yayoi I, these house types, and particularly the round sub-type, had spread across western Japan (Local Organising Committee of the 55th Meeting of the Buried Cultural Properties Study Group 2006).

The phenomenon of its distribution, however, is somewhat puzzling: the adoption of a house type that eventually *replaced* the Jomon house types cannot be explained as an adoption by indigenous communities of components *they had not possessed before*. In order to comprehend this, we should refer to ethnographical findings regarding the symbolic function of the house (Bourdieu 1990, 271–283;

Carsten and Hugh-Jones 1995). It has been well understood that the house is a medium by which resident communities make sense of and cope with the complexities and contingencies of the world by materially mapping the structure of society, nature and culture; the world of the living, the dead and the ancestors; and the cosmos (ibid.). In other words, the house, in small-scale societies, is a significant device that embodies its inhabitants' cultural and social lives.

In Jomon houses, the symbolic significance of the fireplace, for instance, was emphasised in the form of frequent incorporation of phallic stones in the stone hearth setting (Mizoguchi 2002, 108–111; Taniguchi 2010, 40). This combination can be inferred to have signified the metaphorical connection between the transformative power of fire and the transformative-regenerative power of the sexual organs (Mizoguchi 2002, 108–111). This suggests that the symbolic centre of the house was the fireplace as the principle location for the regeneration of life; many ethnographic examples also suggest that the house itself metaphorically represented the human body, to which were connected various systems of meaning representing the contents of the natural and cultural worlds (Carsten and Hugh-Jones 1995). In contrast, the house types of the Initial and Early Yayoi periods, or indeed the Yayoi house types, as a whole, often neither show traces of a substantial hearth nor any significant permanent features marking various systems of meaning representing gender-related reproductive and/or regeneration forces and the contents of the natural and cultural worlds as a whole. Of course, systems of meaning can be represented through components other than hearths, such as the use of perishable items or in other intangible manners. However, it is important to note here that the Jomon dwellings traditionally included elements that represented the regeneration of life, whereas the Yayoi dwellings did not do so in a tangible, durable manner.

This might have been because the Jomon and Yayoi houses embodied different systems of meaning or because the symbolic systems of meaning that were associated with the Jomon houses might have been expressed in the Yayoi period in other ways and at places other than the dwellings.

As mentioned at the beginning of this chapter, there was no absolutely dominant spatio-temporal

---

33 The hypothesis is difficult to verify, admittedly.

locale in annual labour organisation and scheduling during the Jomon period, and people moved across diverse time-space locales. Hence, people had to categorise, make sense of and utilise different natural beings between various time–space locales. As numerous ethnographic examples suggest, and Claude Lévi-Strauss has beautifully captured in his volume *The Savage Mind* (1966), such *encultured* natural beings are used to mark and give meanings to everything that is differentiated in the conceptual and perceptible world of people, ranging from the naming of descent groups to the explanation of the origin of particular cultural habits. The Jomon dwelling space, that is, the village and the house, would have been a hugely rich bundle of all the tangible and intangible representations of such encultured natural beings signifying different human categories, including the reasons and meanings of acts and protocols as well as taboos. This is suggested by our findings of clay figurines representing not only human figures (often of pregnant females) but also various plants and animals, stone implements representing sexual organs and the pictorial representations of fantastic creatures on pottery that were excavated from the Jomon dwelling space (e.g. Mizoguchi 2002, 105–111). In contrast, the introduction of rice paddy field agriculture generated a significantly *singular* focus in the scheduling and organisation of labour, that is, activities related to paddy fields and paddy field rice cultivation, which occupied a large portion of the time-space horizon occupied by the people. Naturally, this would have reduced the range of natural beings which the people encountered, needed to make sense of and use.

In addition, the hunting-gathering activities of the Jomon did not leave behind archaeologically substantial traces of the storage of their yields (except storage pits for various types of nuts), whereas paddy field rice farming, that is, rice crops, left behind numerous traces in the form of storage facilities, storage pits and raised-floor granaries that were situated *separately* from the dwelling area. In the Jomon period, the outcomes of encounters with natural beings would have been *close* and *immediate* to those who used and consumed such yields, whereas in the Yayoi period, rice needed to be processed and stored before its consumption and exchange. In other words, the

relationship between the people in the Jomon period and the encultured natural beings they encountered, made sense of, consumed and used in order to differentiate and map their world was characterised by *immediacy*, whereas the corresponding relationship in the Yayoi period was characterised by *distantiation* because of the intrinsic nature of rice crop, that is, the need to process (and store) rice grains before consumption.

I would like to infer that it was the aforementioned sense of immediacy and diversity that made the inside of the Jomon dwelling space rich in symbolic, and often gender-related, connotations, particularly those associated with the regeneration of life. In contrast, the distantiation in the relationship between people and the outcomes of their labour, as well as the significant reduction of diversity in labour organisation, made the Yayoi dwelling space relatively simple. In other words, the new house types became popular so rapidly *because of the change in the system of meanings embodied by the dwelling space.*

The relationship between people and rice would have been denoted, made sense of and used to map the world in designated time-space locales that were separate from the arena of everyday life. The inference is also in tune with the separation of burial grounds from the inside and/or immediate vicinity of dwelling grounds, which took place in the beginning of the Yayoi period (compare Figure 5.1 with 5.2). The Jomon people appear to have perceived themselves as being in constant contact with the dead, the ancestors and many other encultured natural beings, as mentioned earlier in the chapter. In addition, living people's contact with the dead and other invisible entities appears to have been regarded as an *immediate* sort of contact, constituting *a component of everyday life* in the Jomon period. The fact that the beginning of the Yayoi period did not entail the disappearance of those invisible entities that were acknowledged during the Jomon period, albeit there might have been a shift in their meaning contents, is all too apparent if we see their depictions in the form of pictorial representations on portable material items (such as pottery and famous *Dotaku* bronze bells; see Figure 6.26) – a practice that become increasingly visible towards the end of the Yayoi I. (I examine these artefacts in detail in the next chapter.) However, these items differ from their Jomon equivalents in that they appear to have been perceived as executing their agency only in certain designated settings that were separated from those of everyday life.

I would like to argue that this fundamental change in perception led to the disappearance of tangible symbolic features and items from the Yayoi dwelling space. I would also argue that this disappearance opened up the way for certain individuals to increasingly monopolise the mediation of contacts with the invisible, encultured beings as well as the dead and the ancestors; the occasions during which their agency was executed through the mediation of certain individuals were differentiated, and this would have made the knowledge necessary for the mediation increasingly exclusive. I return to this issue later on, but for the moment, it is enough to recognise that what happened to the dwelling place corresponded with the general trend of the gradual separation or exclusion of what can be called the 'ritual' undertakings from the everyday undertakings.

VILLAGES: NORTHERN KYUSHU

The oldest example of the ditch-enclosed settlement is to be found at the Naka (那珂) site, situated on a low bed on the bottom of the Fukuoka floodplain, dating back to the Incipient Yayoi period. Reconstruction reveals that the village was about 150 metres across and enclosed within double V-sectioned ditches, round in shape (Fukuoka MBE 1994). Because there has been a severe disturbance of the living surface, no trace of houses can be determined (ibid.).

The Itazuke settlement began in the early Yayoi I as an egg-planned V-sectioned ditch-enclosed village (Figure 5.10.B). Some of the prominent ditch-encircled settlements of the Incipient and first half of the Yayoi I, notably the Naka site and the Itazuke settlement, do not show any trace of dwellings. However, the traces of storage pits, together with the discovery of some V-sectioned ditch enclosures made specifically for the storage pits – such as those found in Mitsuoka-Nagao (光岡長尾; cf. Munakata MBE 2004, 2, 4, fig. 2; Yamasaki 2008, 26–27) – dating from a slightly later date, suggests that the ditches were primarily built for the purpose of protecting the storage facilities (e.g. Kataoka 2003, 171–174). However, considering the fact that a substantial portion of

top layers have been removed from both the Naka and the Itazuke sites and that the ditch-enclosed settlements of the later part of the first half of the Yayoi I, such as the Daikai (大開), Hyogo prefecture (Kobe MBE 1993) (Figure 5.10.C), show the presence of pit dwellings as well as storage pits within the enclosed area, we can say that the primary function of the ditch would have been to protect the residents as well as the storage pits and other facilities.

Interestingly, most of the ditches show no trace of re-digging or regular clean-ups. More importantly, in the northern Kyushu region – apart from some areas of dense occupation such as the Ogori hills (Kataoka 2003) – the digging of settlement-enclosing ditches appears to have virtually ceased during the later part of the second half of the phase. The custom did not reappear until the Yayoi IV period in northern Kyushu, when the evidence suggests that tensions mounted due to a reorganisation of inter-communal relations (see Chapter 7). These observations indicate the following: the primary function of the ditch was to protect the settlement; moreover, the lack – or the relatively low intensity – of inter-communal tension made it unnecessary to maintain or re-dig the ditches, except for the protection of food storage facilities when required. This image of a relatively 'peaceful' situation supports the previously mentioned thesis that the Yayoi package would have spread fairly quickly through sodality-based inter-communal networks without involving large-scale migrations or movements of people, which in turn might have given rise to social tension. The adoption of the Yayoi package would initially have jeopardised the fulfilment of reciprocal obligations necessitated by the reproduction of sodalities, and this would have made the position of the Yayoinised community increasingly difficult. The enclosed settlements may have been occupied by such communities encountering hostility against their lifestyle. However, once the partner communities began to accept Yayoinised items and customs as reciprocated goods and deeds, these communities would also have adopted the package. In this way, the initial necessity of defending Yayoinised communities by building ditch-enclosed settlements would have rapidly ceased.

Coming back to the Itazuke settlement, a part of the enclosed area is further segregated by another

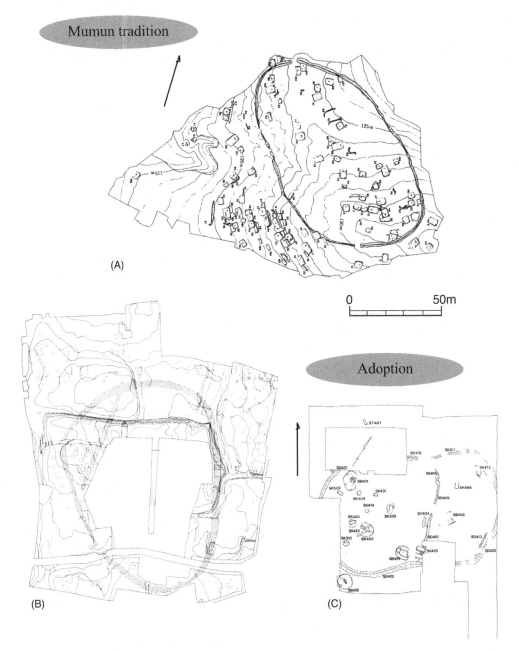

Figure 5.10. Ditch-enclosed villages of the Incipient and Early Yayoi. **A**: Geomdan-ri (Korea; after Busan National University Museum 1995), **B**: Itazuke (Fukuoka; after Fukuoka MBE 2010), **C**: Daikai (Hyogo; after Kobe MBE 1993).

straight-running ditch (Figure 5.10.B). Within the enclosed area are storage pits from which pots and carbonised rice grains have been excavated (Mori and Okazaki 1961). It is important to note that the pits form two clusters within the excavated area, which suggests that the storage pits situated in the segregated area were divided into several clusters.

The evidence from the Etsuji and Itazuke settlements would support what I proposed earlier: the inhabitants of individual settlements were members of supra-local groupings/sodalities such as

clans, and the spatial-unit clustering of houses, burials (both of which are seen at Etsuji) and storage pits (seen at Itazuke) indicates their segments. As seen in the previous section, supra-local groupings, i.e., sodalities, such as clans and dual organisations played an important role in the reproduction of social ties during the Jomon period. The absence of any mass migration in the introduction and spread of the Yayoi package means that this mode of social organisation was not implanted from the Korean peninsula (though the concept may have been included in the Yayoi package). It is more likely that the preexisting technology for the maintenance of social ties was drawn on in the process of adopting the new lifestyle. In addition, by the final phase of the Yayoi I, which is covered in the next chapter, some villages began to consist of two or more residential groupings. The phenomenon was not confined to Kyushu but spread across the horizon within which the Yayoi package spread. The residential groupings in villages would have been segments of sodalities, and they would have become visible as distinct residential groupings because of population increase.

VILLAGES: WESTERN JAPAN

With almost no exception, all the earliest Yayoi settlements in individual regions – meaning those settlements which were ditch-enclosed and/or whose inhabitants used the entire or a significant portion of the Yayoi package – were newly founded settlements (see Yamasaki 1980, 182–184). This is, in a way, quite natural: the settlements had to be situated near locations suitable for paddy field agriculture, but they were not necessarily convenient for the hunter-gatherer way of life. From a different perspective, we can say that those communities which chose to adopt the Yayoi package had to relocate themselves to more suitable places. In western Japan, ditch-enclosed settlements began to appear outside northern Kyushu during the last part of the first half of the Yayoi I. The residents of these settlements used the Yayoi pottery assemblage, which had already been adopted in northern Kyushu through the complex process outlined above; they also used most of the other traits of the Yayoi package. Almost simultaneously, moreover, there emerged some unenclosed settlements wherein residents used the same material culture assemblage as those in the enclosed settlements. Those unenclosed settlements distributed among many settlements where the residents continued to use the Final Jomon assemblage with a few traits from the Yayoi package (Kusano 2010).

At Hyakkengawa-Sawada (百間川沢田; Okayama PBE 1985, 1993), located on a natural river bank in the middle of a number of watercourses of the Asahikawa River and on the bottom of the coastal floodplain of the present-day Okayama municipality, Okayama prefecture, archaeologists have excavated at least five round pit houses, pit

or wooden-coffin burials, a circular ditch enclosure and a number of storage pits – including some probably intended for ritual purposes and some, for disposing of unwanted items[34] – inside a roughly oval-shaped area, measuring approximately 100 by 80–90 metres, enclosed within a V-sectioned ditch (ibid.; Matsugi 2001, 119). The houses are not necessarily laid out in a circular plan. The circular enclosure may well have been an animal pen (see Yamasaki 2008, 19), though some scholars have put forward the possibility that it was a burial compound.

Houses and burials, if those pits were indeed burials, appear to have been mixed together within the enclosed area, as in the Jomon settlement; this also appears to have been the case in other unenclosed settlements of the region, such as the Minamimizote (南溝手) settlement (Matsugi 2001, 120). One reason for this might be the location of the village itself – the village was situated on a slightly raised terrain at the bottom of a volatile floodplain. This may have constrained land use and may not have allowed the setting up of a separate burial ground. However, this reason seems unlikely: had they been deemed necessary or desirable, grounds would have been found elsewhere. The resultant pattern might indicate the cohabitation of the living and the dead in the dwelling space – a connection continuing from the Jomon period. This is interesting because even at Etsuji – where the Jomon-originated conception of the metaphorical-transformative connection between the death and regeneration of rice crops and human beings was embodied by the spatial structure of the village layout, the burial grounds were separated from the residential area. At the Hyakkengawa-Sawada settlement, this level of intimacy between the living and the dead, which is another crucial trait of the Jomon settlement structure, appears to have continued.

The pottery assemblage in the Tsushima (津島) site of the same region (it is unclear whether or not the site was ditch-enclosed) suggests that some of the inhabitants must have learnt pottery making

---

34 It has been pointed out and well investigated that rubbish disposal activities themselves were often incorporated into the process of reproducing symbolic systems, constituting a vital part of social reproduction, based upon such dichotomies as the polluted and the clean. See Hodder (1987).

somewhere in northern Kyushu or in the western Seto Inland Sea area (see Fujita 1982). This suggests that the process of adoption of the Yayoi package in the region involved both small-scale migrations and the selective adoption of Yayoi traits. The fact that some of the settlements of the period were not ditch-enclosed suggests the possibility that the adoption increased inter-communal tensions to different degrees between settlements. Those settlements which were ditch-enclosed might have felt stronger inter-communal tension than the others, perhaps in the form of an increased threat of raids and attacks.

To the east of this area, there is another well-excavated settlement called Daikai (大開) (Figure 5.10.C; Kobe MBE 1993). The settlement began as a small, V-sectioned ditch-enclosed village, measuring 40 metres across. At some point of time, the enclosing ditch was re-dug and the enclosed area expanded to 40 metres by 70 metres across. Only three houses existed during the first stage of occupation. Two more houses existed in the enlarged area, and one outside the enclosed area (ibid.).

The relatively small scale of the site suggests that its inhabitants constituted a small, lineage-like community (Figure 5.10.C). There is no evidence to indicate that they were further subdivided internally, and this would suggest that it was difficult or even impossible or prohibited to find marriage partners within the village. In any case, it would certainly have been impossible for the community to reproduce itself, and the necessary exchange of marriage partners would have been a part of wider reciprocal exchanges with a certain set of other localised communities. It is important to note that more than 200 arrowheads, including many Jomon-type specimens, and more than a dozen phallic stone rods have been excavated from the village (ibid.). These suggest that the inhabitants still relied heavily on hunting for their subsistence and performed a ritual, probably of regeneration, involving the use of an implement that originated during the Jomon period.

The fact that the implements used in the ritual of regeneration shifted from a combination of implements representing the sexual organs of both sexes[35] to those only representing the male sexual

organ suggests that there was a change in the gender-based focus of the ritual; however, the change was brought about through the use of a Jomon-derived implement. The identity of the inhabitants, in that sense, was a hybrid one, and their position in the network of ritual-kin-based intra- and inter-communal ties would have been an ambivalent one.

In addition, the adoption of the Yayoi package would have increased inter-communal tension, and this appears to have been felt more strongly by the inhabitants of certain villages than by others. In some inter-communal networks of reciprocal exchange, the adoption of the Yayoi package by a village or a small number of villages would have increased inter-communal tension to such an extent that some villagers found it necessary to defend themselves by building a ditch or two around their villages, whereas in other sodality-based networks, the adoption of the package by a village or a small number of villages was followed by the smooth acceptance of the package by other villages. These differences would have created a complex picture of the emulation, rejection and partial adoption of the individual components of the Yayoi package, typically exemplified by the pottery (see Section 3 of this chapter), in the area around the Seto Inland Sea and beyond.

In general, the inhabitants of V-sectioned ditch-enclosed settlements across western Japan had a greater tendency to adopt traits of the Yayoi package than those of the unenclosed villages, though the former did not have exclusive access to the package. The process of 'Yayoinisation' also occurred in the case of the latter in varying paces and by various degrees. The distribution of the enclosed villages did not go beyond the Nobi Plain (present-day Gifu and Aichi prefectures). In the regions beyond the Nobi Plain, as we saw in the case of pottery, traits of the Yayoi package were selectively adopted in ways that did not disrupt the reproduction of preexisting intra- and inter-communal ties. Moreover, some of the chosen traits may even have been transformed to emphasise the local identities as distinct from those of the

---

35 In addition to phallic stones, we have lithic implements depicting the vagina, and there also is the type which

depicts both male and female sexual organs in a combined form (e.g. *Seki-kan* [石冠], *Do-kan* [土冠]) used during the Final Jomon period across eastern Japan (see e.g. Nakashima 1995).

Yayoinised communities, as seen in the pottery (see Section 3.4 in this chapter).

THE EARLY YAYOI VILLAGE OF THE NORTH: JIZODEN

As mentioned previously, the scale and number of settlements were already declining when, in the second half of the Yayoi I, some attributes of the Yayoi package made their first appearance in eastern Japan. The resultant change appears to have been minimal in terms of the features characterising these settlements. However, when it comes to the internal structure and distribution of settlements, we can identify some important changes. Let us examine the nature of the changes which occurred in the village of Jizoden (地蔵田), one of the best-excavated sites among the early Yayoi settlements (Figure 5.8).

The duration of continuous occupation of the village can be divided into two phases (Sugawara 1987; Takase 2004, 178–179). During the earlier phase, three pit houses were enclosed by a palisade measuring approximately 60 by 46 metres across (Figure 5.8). This palisade has been found to have several gaps. Both ends of the northwest-southeast axis, which is the long axis of the enclosed area, are double-palisaded, and several gaps in these palisades appear to have been the main entrances to the settlement within. In addition, each of the three houses seems to have had an entrance nearby. Outside of the south-eastern entrance there is a burial ground, separated by another palisade running from the northeast to the southwest.

The burials are in the form of pit burials and jar burials, and the formation of two burial alignments can be recognised near the settlement entrance. They are in alignment with the long axis of the enclosed area, that is, the northwest-southeast axis, with a burial-free strip in between. This dual spatial organisation reminds us of that at the centre of the Nishida site dating back to the second half of the Middle Jomon (see Figure 5.2), where we inferred that the spatial segmentation of houses and burials at that site must have represented a dual organisation and clan-like supra-communal groupings.

The dual spatial organisation of the burial ground continues inside the enclosed area, because, as mentioned above, the burial alignments and the enclosed area are located on the same axis.

In that case, we can say that two of the houses were located in the south-western half, while one house (no. 1) was located in the north-eastern half of the site (Figure 5.8).

The layout of the palisade(s) appears to have been changed a few times, because two of the four pit houses of the later phase overlap with the line of the initial palisade. Three out of the four houses were built adjacent to the houses of the earlier phase. One house (no. 2) was built on a previously empty plot in the north-eastern half of the site, which means that there were two houses each in both the south-western and the north-eastern halves of the site. This might further support the thesis that the settlement and its burial ground spatially represented a dual organisation, because two groupings constituting such an organisation can be expected to be roughly equal in their scale. The use of the burial ground, it is believed, continued throughout the phase.

Katsunori Takase (2004) has pointed out that the houses in each of the halves have mutually different post structures: the houses in the north-eastern half are square, with posts at right angles, while those in the other half are rhombic in shape. He has further revealed that similar examples as the latter can be found distributed across the inland and Pacific Ocean coastal regions of eastern Japan, while examples of the former are distributed locally (Takase 2004, 180–181). He goes on to suggest that the settlement was formed by local residents as well as migrants from fairly remote places.

The difference in the configuration of posts is a fairly minute one, and connecting them to different groups from different regions might constitute a case of reading too much into scanty evidence. However, the existence of a dual organisation, represented spatially by the distribution of houses and burial spots, appears convincing. Takase shows that settlements that were equivalent in scale and structure to Jizoden emerged in the region during the second half of the Yayoi I, when elements of the Yayoi package were also introduced in the region, and infers that the beginning of rice farming led to a convergence ('integration', in his terminology) of communities that were, at times, quite distant. As supportive evidence, he shows that the Jizoden village site and its contemporary equivalents were much larger in population size than the settlements just before the introduction of the Yayoi elements to the region (ibid., 168–197). At this point, again, we should be cautious and not rely too heavily on the different post configurations for inferring the origins of those who occupied the two halves of Jizoden village. However, we can safely infer from the above observations that the onset of rice farming, albeit it was significantly transformed through its process of diffusion from western Japan, resulted in collaborative labour on a larger scale. Moreover, we can also infer that labour units suited to the new requirements, in terms of scale as well as organisation, could be formed through the movement of people along supra-communal ties, such as those found in dual organisations.

It is important to remember that Jomon communities were maintained and reproduced through multilayered supra-local groupings such as clan-type sodalities and dual organisations. The existence of such communities was embodied, represented and maintained by the spatial segmentation of the settlement into clusters of houses, burials and other features. In that sense, the Jizoden village site and the implications drawn from the analysis of its equivalents and surrounding conditions indicate that the discourse of dwelling in eastern Japan reacted to the changes resulting from the arrival of the Yayoi package by fully drawing upon the existing structure, that is, the preexisting multilayered communal ties, for its constitutive rules and resources; the same was true across western Japan.

THE YAYOINISATION OF THE DWELLING WORLD
The Jomon communities were connected by various types of ties based upon the fulfilment of reciprocal obligations, internally as well as externally. The introduction of the Yayoi package brought about significant changes in lifestyle in an ever-increasing number of communities situated in such multilayered networks. These changes evoked various reactions from the communities that were yet to be Yayoinised; at times, these reactions might have increased inter-communal tension. After all, communities with different annual schedules and which produced and/or procured different types of goods and foodstuffs from one another would have faced mounting difficulties in reciprocating obligations in terms of coordinating the timing of their meetings and the amount and contents of gifts to be exchanged towards the maintenance

of their ties. The coexistence of a range of villages – from the completely Yayoinised to the virtually non-Yayoinised, in terms of their spatial structure as well as material culture – reflected those difficulties. However, the difficulties were eventually tackled in one way or another, and most of the communities from Kyushu to Tohoku had adopted the Yayoi package by the end of the Early Yayoi period, albeit to various degrees and in various manners. The examination of the spatial structure of those villages has revealed that various preexisting kin and pseudo-kin networks played an important role in the process.

4.3. Paddies

EXAMPLES AND IMPLICATIONS
It was believed that the introduction of rice paddy field agriculture in the Japanese archipelago coincided with a cooling of the earth's atmosphere and a lowering of the sea level, which resulted in the development of coastal plains and marshes along coastlines and rivers (see Chapter 4.2 of the current volume; see e.g. Iseki 1983). Accordingly, until the actual discovery of Initial Yayoi paddies, it had been assumed that the earliest paddies were constructed on those marshy terrains with minimum labour and technological input in order to address the food shortage caused by the cooling. Hence, the paddies were expected to have been equipped with simple drainage, rather than irrigation, facilities. As we have seen in Chapter 4.2, regarding the traces of stabilisation of sand-dune growth, the Initial Yayoi period may well have been a period of warming, although the preceding cooler spell would have certainly given rise to the development of coastal plains and marshes. The warming – if indeed it had occurred – would have led to an increase in flooding, which would have made it increasingly difficult to utilise the coastal back marshes and the bottom of floodplains for rice farming.

The discovery of the Itazuke paddies in 1978 changed the picture quite dramatically (Yamasaki 2008). The paddies, dating back to the Initial Yayoi period, were found to have been situated on a riverine terrace, and a long irrigation canal, drawing its water supply from far upstream, was situated along the upper fringe of the terrace, irrigating the paddies situated on the downslope (Figure 5.11).

Another smaller canal ran along the main one, and this converged with the latter near a cut on the ridge irrigating a paddy. A sluice was set up at the cut to fine-tune the irrigation, while another sluice was constructed in the canal downstream to control the water level. The excavators infer that the smaller canal was used for the drainage of a paddy or paddies upstream, while the drained water was reused to irrigate paddies downstream. The paddies themselves were rectangular in shape, fitting into the contours of the terrace. In any case, the technology of water supply control was highly sophisticated. In the Yayoi I period, the paddies appear to have expanded in scale, and the irrigation canal system, it is inferred, came to be comprised of main and branch canals.

However, the paddy field structure at Itazuke was not necessarily the norm. The Nabatake (菜畑) paddies, in the Saga prefecture of northern Kyushu, were constructed at the bottom of a small valley in the beginning of the Yayoi I period (Karatsu MBE 1982).[36] It is likely that there were natural springs near the foothills sandwiching the valley, making the valley somewhat waterlogged. Although the shape and scale of the paddies cannot be confirmed, there is evidence of a canal cut at the centre of the paddy cluster – that is, at the bottom of the valley. This suggests that the canal was intended not for irrigation but for drainage. In this case, the water supply management would have involved ways and means of storing and draining ground water.

The presence of these two types of paddies with different devices for controlling water supply in the Initial Yayoi and Yayoi I periods suggests that the Yayoi package included a sufficiently sophisticated technological know-how to enable the setting up of paddies in different topographic, and probably climatic, environments. By the end of the Yayoi I period, we can even find traces of the construction of paddy terraces of some kind (e.g. Ogaki [大柿] site, Tokushima prefecture; Tokushima Prefectural Buried Cultural Properties Research Centre 1997). Clusters of extremely small paddies were constructed to fit into uneven terrains. On the whole, the technological know-how appears to have been sophisticated from the beginning, and

36 The presence of paddies during the Initial Yayoi period, which the excavators acknowledge, has been disputed by some scholars (cf. Yamasaki 1987).

it became even more sophisticated in a cumulative manner as it spread as part of the Yayoi package and reached the southern Tohoku region by the end of the Yayoi I period.

It has traditionally been emphasised that the construction, use and maintenance of paddies required a new type of labour, which in turn required an unprecedented scale of collaboration and organisational sophistication. No doubt this was the case in northern Kyushu and western Japan. In these regions, there were no large-scale Jomon structures such as settlements containing cemeteries as well as ritual centres, which were, at times, equipped with earthen works, stone structures, and wooden structures for the de-poisoning of nuts or for regular ritual gatherings (see Mizoguchi 2002, chap. 4, for examples). The construction of Jomon structures on those monumental scales would have required a considerable degree of labour mobilisation and organisational sophistication, including the felling and processing of a large number of trees for constructing wooden structures and procuring, bringing and erecting a large number of stones for constructing stone settings such as those mentioned earlier.

The following factors distinguish the Yayoi paddy fields from the Jomon structures: (1) while the Jomon structures could have been constructed in a cumulative manner, the construction of paddies, for them to be functional, would have required a *planned, single process*; (2) people have to collaborate and work together for the single purpose of growing rice over a prolonged period every year. The considerable presence of paddies in the lifeworld of the people would have shaped people's thoughts, feelings and actions to an unprecedented level of intensity; for example, the division of paddies and their scale determined the organisation of work-parties; the construction, use and maintenance of paddies required a collaboration of different scales and intensities; and most importantly, the material presence of paddies and their related features continuously reminded those who worked in them of past collaborations and the necessity of further collaborations (of various scales) in the future.

PADDIES AS YAYOI 'MONUMENTS'
The preceding observations indicate that the Yayoi package included a great deal of know-how and

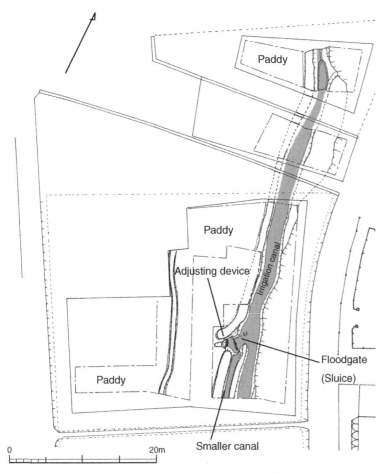

Figure 5.11. Initial Yayoi paddy fields of the Itazuke, Fukuoka prefecture. The irrigation canal is situated on the upper fringe of a riverine terrace, and a sophisticated water-level-controlling device (the combination of a floodgate and an adjusting device) is put in place (after Fukuoka MBE 1979, fig. 65, with modifications).

information that was sufficient to adapt the production of rice to various local conditions in the archipelago. The package consisted of not only material items but also important know-how for dealing with various types of local topography, appropriately and efficiently positioning the necessary features and organising labour to accomplish the required tasks. This suggests that the arrival of those who had plenty of experience in practicing sophisticated rice paddy field agriculture essentially contributed to the changes that marked the beginning of the new era. However, their mere arrival was insignificant as compared to the changes brought about by the application of their knowledge and experience in the land. As explained above, the outcome of the application of the Yayoi package, that is, the emergence of a new feature in the people's lifeworld at that time, as well as the onset of rice cultivation prepared conditions for stable social differentiation and hierarchisation.

Paddies as a newly emerging constructed environment were 'monumental' in that they not only required but also represented the mobilisation of the labour force of an entirely new character on a previously unseen scale. They would have not only reminded those who subsisted on them of the past experience and future necessity of large-scale communal collaboration but also constantly required such collaboration in the form of necessary repairs and maintenance work (cf. Mizoguchi 2002, 126–129). These occasions would have served to generate and reconfirm the mode of time management and labour organisation required for them. It is likely that these occasions also involved ritualistic activities. For instance, an entire, large, red-painted globular jar was discovered placed at the foot of one of the floodgates of the previously mentioned Itazuke paddies (Yamasaki 2008, 65–66). It can be inferred that the jar was placed when the gate was constructed, mended, opened or closed. Many ethnographies show that communal activities of this nature often involved large-scale feasting (e.g. Iwata 1970) and that the occasions themselves functioned as rituals of prayer for the regeneration of life, that is, *the yield of a good harvest*. Such rituals would have evoked particularly vivid images in the memories of those who daily encountered the agricultural way of life (ibid.).

This might partially but significantly explain the decline of the daily Jomon rituals, characterised by constant associations of the dead and the ancestors with the material embodiments of various invisible entities in houses and in settlements. The complexity of tasks involving time management and the organisation of work parties for the procurement of necessary resources varied significantly and was spread across the time-space horizon of the lifeworld in the Jomon period. Accordingly, the ritualistic activities which mediated the management of this complexity were varied and spread across the horizon of everyday life. In contrast, the complexity of tasks in the Yayoi period became increasingly centred in the paddies and the activities conducted in them. Accordingly, the ritualistic activities would also have become increasingly confined to a limited and well-defined range of time-space contexts, gradually receding from the wider horizon of the lifeworld.

The implication of this transformation brought about by the emergence of the 'Yayoi monuments' was immense in that it must have contributed, albeit partially, to the generation of authority in the form of the emergence of an organiser of the collaborative labour and its related rituals.

5. NEW RELATIONS WITH THE DEAD: CEMETERIES

5.1. *From Dolmens to Jar Burials: Northern Kyushu*

OVERVIEW

As we have already seen, the onset of the Yayoi period in northern Kyushu was marked by a separation of the dead and the ancestors from the living in terms of their spatial relationship. However, this did not include the removal of awareness of the dead and the ancestors from everyday concerns. These continued to be as mutually entangled as they had been in the Jomon period,

which is attested by the fact that the changes that occurred in the spatio-temporal organisation of Yayoi cemeteries corresponded with changes in the settlement and in other types of archaeological evidence.[37] This suggests that people constructed their own identities and determined how to behave with one another based on their ceremonial ways of treating the dead and remembering the ancestors.

By the first half of the Yayoi I, new methods for burying the dead appeared in northern Kyushu and spread southward to central Kyushu and eastward as far as the eastern part of the Seto Inland Sea region.

The structures called 'dolmens' – comprising a fairly large capstone generally supported by small stones placed on the ground over a cobble-walled chamber, or a pit, containing either a cist or a composite wooden coffin (Figure 5.12) – originated in the Korean peninsula (e.g. Hashino 2003), where they commonly formed large cemeteries with linear alignments. These structures were first adopted by the coastal communities of the northern and north-western Kyushu regions (ibid.). Shimpei Hashino has revealed that dolmens were first adopted around the Itoshima peninsula of Fukuoka prefecture and were diffused eastward, with the number of peninsula-originated attributes decreasing along the way as if following a smooth geographical cline (Hashino 2003). For instance, in the eastward diffusion from the present-day Fukuoka Plain, they lost the capstone and ended up as flat graves (probably covered by small earth caps) with a cist or a cist-like stone arrangement set around a (often composite) wooden coffin or pit burial (Figures 5.12.5 and 5.12.6) (ibid.). In this way, the original structure of dolmens did not continue, and even in the centre of their original distribution, that is, in the north-western coastal plains of Kyushu Island, they had disappeared by the end of the first half of the Yayoi I period. They were replaced by various burial customs containing some remnants of the dolmen burial attributes (such as cists and composite wooden coffins), combined with other artefacts originating from the indigenous Jomon mortuary custom (such as jar burials) showing considerable regional differences.

37 See Chapter 6.6 and Chapter 7.3.2 in the current volume.

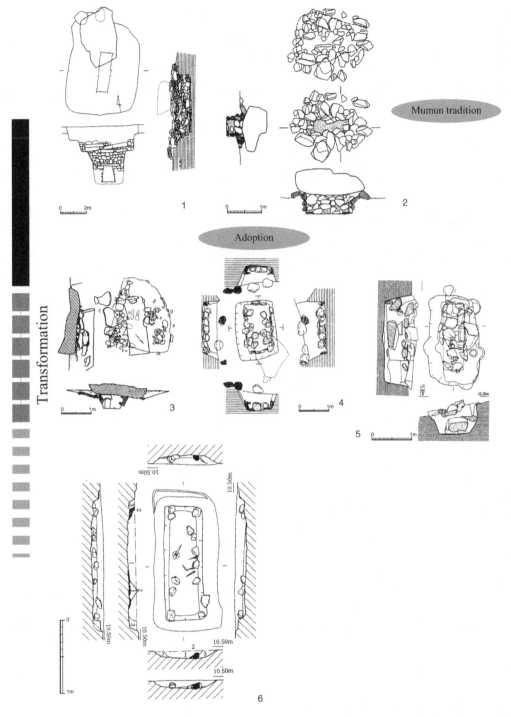

Figure 5.12. "Dolmens" and related burial facilities in Japan and Korea. Note that the essential attributes of the peninsula type were lost one by one as it was adopted initially in the western part of northern Kyushu and diffused eastward. 1 Changwon-Deokcheon'ni No. 1 (Korea), 2 Suncheon-Hanusan'ni No. 7 (Korea), 3 Ishigasaki (Fukuoka), 4 Otomo 6th excavation No. 21 (Saga), 5 Tenjin'nomori 3rd excavation No. 4 (Fukuoka), 6 Etsuji Loc. 5 SK20 (Fukuoka), (after Hashino 2003, originals from respective excavation reports).

In the western half of the northern Kyushu region, for instance, burial jars began as large globular jars containing infant remains in the Initial Yayoi, but from the first half of the Yayoi I, they became larger and their shape was modified to contain adult bodies by enlarging the diameter of the mouth and neck parts (Figure 5.13). Hence, by the end of the Yayoi I, they had become a distinct shape-type in the pottery assemblage, specifically designed for containing and burying adults (Figure 5.13).

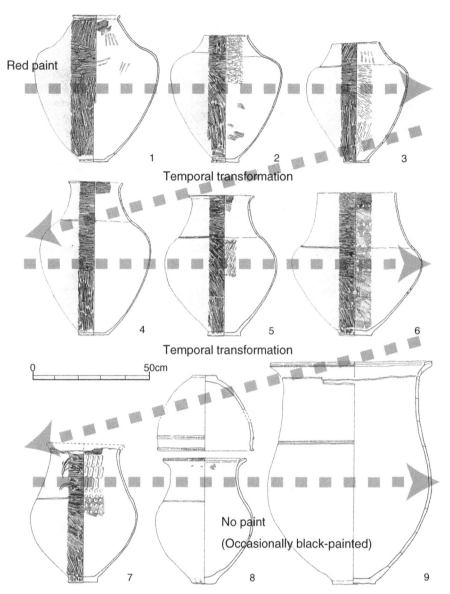

Red paint

Temporal transformation

1   2   3

Temporal transformation

4   5   6

0   50cm

No paint
(Occasionally black-painted)

7   8   9

Figure 5.13. The emergence of adult burial jars. Note gradual temporal-morphological transformation. 1 Miy-anomae (Fukuoka) 39, 2 Shinmachi (Fukuoka) II-01 trench No. 1, 3 Shinmachi (Fukuoka) 25, 4 Shinmachi (Fukuoka) 20, 5 Shinmachi (Fukuoka) 18, 6 Shimachi (Fukuoka) II-05 trench No. 2, 7 Shinmachi (Fukuoka) II-05 No. 1, 8 Kenzuka (Fukuoka) 7, 9 Magarita (Fukuoka) 10 (after Hashiguchi 1999 [originals from respective excavation reports], with additions). With kind permission from the Yusankaku Publishing Co.

This picture is consistent with corresponding changes in the other components of the Yayoi package, as we have already seen.

The custom of arranging graves in linear alignments also appears to have originated in the peninsula. After its introduction in the archipelago, however, it is interesting to note the considerable variations in the custom's implementation between cemeteries. One reason for this variance, as will be seen in the following, can be attributed to certain social and strategic factors influencing the spatio-temporal layout of graves in individual cemeteries. In any case, the active selection of arrangements appears to have been made by the indigenous communities.

Stone daggers and willow-leaf-shaped polished stone arrowheads, deposited with a very small number of individuals during the Incipient Yayoi and early Yayoi I periods, also originated in the peninsula (Figure 5.14; e.g. Shimojo 1986). This custom, again, was first introduced to northern Kyushu, from which it spread eastwards as far as

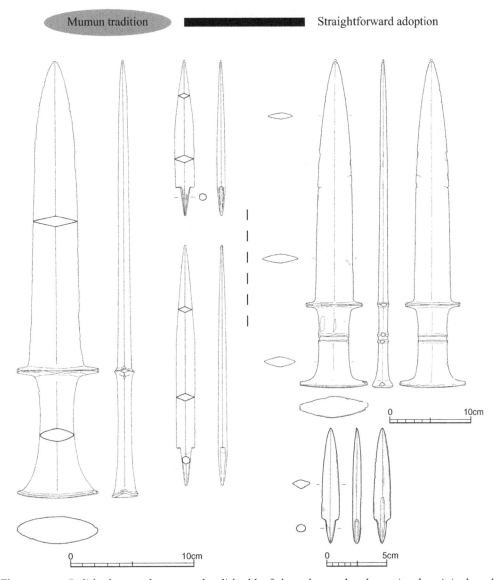

Figure 5.14. Polished stone daggers and polished leaf-shaped arrowheads: peninsula originals and adopted specimens in the archipelago. Left: from the Songguk'ni site (from Yanagida 2003, fig. 59); right: from the Zasshonokuma site (from Fukuoka MBE 2005a).

the eastern part of the Seto Inland Sea region; like the other customs, this one did not last till the end of the Yayoi I.

The aforementioned lithic weapons have attracted much interest as possible indicators of status differences. At the Mikumo-Kagaishi site, an individual was deposited along with polished stone arrowheads underneath a dolmen with a very large capstone (Fukuoka PBE 1980, 48–53), and some scholars use this as an evidence of social stratification (Yanagida 1986a, 141). However, it is unlikely that such grave goods indicate the existence of ascribed status differences; many cemeteries show

a very weak concentration, or the utter absence, of their distribution.

In fact, we should take notice of the unification of the mortuary assemblage contents in this period as compared to the Jomon equivalent: whenever graves from the Incipient Yayoi or early Yayoi I periods are found to contain portable material items, they are in the form of either globular jars, willow-leaf-shaped stone arrowheads, polished stone daggers or their various combinations. In the Jomon period, burial assemblages were more varied, probably representing a range of idealised, task-based social persona, such as those of good hunters, priests and so on.[38] However, the aforementioned early Yayoi mortuary assemblages almost exclusively represented the dead as warrior-like figures, closely associated with the storage of something that was contained in globular jars. In the section on pottery, we inferred that the globular jars used in mortuary contexts were often connected to the notion of the cycle of death and the regeneration of life, which was metaphorically connected to the life cycle of rice grains. We have already noted the model through which this set of metaphorical-transformative connections between the factors – that is, rice, death and the regeneration of life – was incorporated into the spatial structure of the settlement (see Section 2 in this chapter). If we could apply this inference to the connection between weapons and globular jars in the grave good assemblage, we would be able to infer that the themes of death and the regeneration of life, which would have been of vital concern for any community at that time, were perceived as achievable with the help of coercive power, represented by weapons.

Such a connection, if true, would be extremely interesting in that we have pictorial representations, albeit a small number, depicting figures with weapons in their hands, dating from the Middle Yayoi period (e.g. Takashima 1980). They are interpreted as depicting scenes from rituals, and it is likely that the rituals would have implied the encouragement and regeneration of life in the form of a good harvest of rice (see p. 166 in this volume). This suggests that the custom of depositing certain grave goods which were introduced at the beginning of the Yayoi period represented the metaphorical-transformative connection between the death and regeneration of life of rice grains, the dead and the *coercive power* represented by weapons; moreover, this connection probably became an important component of the Yayoi ritual discourse. An important observation in this regard is the appearance of bronze weapons as grave goods some time towards the end of the Yayoi I; these were almost exclusively deposited with males. This means that the coercive power of weaponry was attributed to the male individuals. The custom of depositing polished stone daggers and arrowheads as grave goods was not widespread

(Nakamura 2006). However, the ideological component continued to be embodied by the deposition of weapon-shaped implements as grave goods into the Middle Yayoi and beyond. For instance, in northern Kyushu, the globular jars themselves, as mentioned previously, were modified to form burial containers for adults. The elite who were buried in such jars were occasionally accompanied by bronze and iron weapons (see Chapter 6 in this volume). This association between the death and regeneration of rice crops and human beings continued in this manner, mediated by *symbols of male coercive power*, and became an important element of the structuring principle of Yayoi society. This point will be frequently raised throughout the following chapters.

SPATIO-TEMPORAL ORGANISATION OF THE 'CEMETERY-SCAPE'

The commencement of linear alignments for burials signals a significant change in the spatio-temporal organisation of graves in individual cemeteries (Figures 5.3 and 5.15). As previously mentioned, this burial custom originated in the peninsula. However, the mode of its introduction, as was the case with respect to pottery and other items, was not very straightforward and varied between cemeteries.

The Shinmachi (新町) cemetery, Fukuoka prefecture, is a case in point (Figure 5.3) (Shima TBE 1987). The typo-chronology of the globular-jar-shaped burial jars suggests that the cemetery was formed from the northern part to the south. In the northern half of the cemetery, the graves – including wooden coffins, burial jars and the dolmens covering them – are randomly arranged in terms of their direction and spatial relations (Figure 5.3). However, in the southern half, they appear to be arranged in some sort of alignment: they are all arranged in a unified direction along the northwest-southeast axis.

The somewhat chaotic arrangement of graves in the northern half of the Shinmachi site brings to mind the cemetery B at Etsuji (Figures 5.1 and 5.15.A), where graves are also arranged in a seemingly random manner. In other words, the axis of the graves, most of which would have been composite wooden coffins, varies. It can be pointed out that some graves are deliberately situated very close to others, whereas some intersect. This

---

38 See papers in Kosugi et al. (2007b).

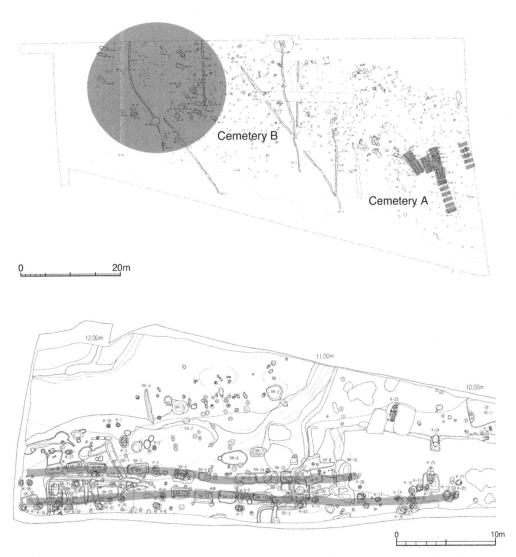

Figure 5.15. The Etsuji (Fukuoka) (**A**) and Shimotsukiguma (Fukuoka) (**B**) cemeteries. Note different spatial formations between Cemeteries A and B at the Estuji. Linear groupings are marked by shade (after Kasuya TBE 2002 [Etsuji] and Fukuoka MBE 1996a [Shimotsukiguma-Tenjin'nomori]).

suggests that the representation of some sort of connection between specific members of a community, kin-based ones or otherwise, was prioritised over the representation of internal homogeneity, and hence the unity of the entire community.

In the case of Shinmachi, the mode of spatiotemporal arrangement of graves changed over the course of time; the initial mode of representing the relationship between specific members of the community gave way to that of representing the unity of the community by unifying the axes of burials and aligning the graves along these axes. At the Shimo-Tsukiguma Tenjin'nomori (下月隈天神森) site, however, the linear alignment appears to have been planned from the beginning (Figure 5.15.B) (Fukuoka MBE 1996a). The formation began with rectangular pit graves, probably

containing composite wooden coffins, arranged in two parallel linear alignments. The oldest burials, containing small globular jars deposited as grave goods, have been dated back to the final phase of the Incipient Yayoi period or the beginning of Yayoi I (ibid.). They were gradually replaced by globular jar burials, which tended to be deposited next to older composite wooden coffin burials. Some of these are even found to overlap with wooden coffin burials, suggesting intentional positioning.

There were cemeteries with burial agglomerations rather than linear alignments in the period. However, by the end of the Yayoi I, the majority of cemeteries in the northern Kyushu region came to be constructed in linear alignments. This custom also spread across the San'in region and parts of the Setouchi region, but not to other regions. Some cemeteries of this type had two parallel linear alignments of burials, with a path-like linear space in between. In the next chapter, I examine this unique type of burial ground in more detail (Chapter 6.6.1).

COPING WITH THE NEW REALITY

As we have seen, in the northern Kyushu region, the cemeteries of the concerned period can be generally divided into three categories according to their spatio-temporal arrangement of burials:

(A) Random burials throughout the duration of the cemetery (e.g. Etsuji cemetery B; Figure 5.15.A)

(B) Unified arrangement according to a specific alignment throughout the duration of the cemetery (e.g. Shimo-Tsukiguma Tenjin'nomori; Figure 5.15.B)

(C) Shifting from the random mode to the unified mode during the course of the period (e.g. Shinmachi; Figure 5.3)

Considering the fact that a number of cemeteries in the southern coastal region of the peninsula consisted of aligned burials (basically in the form of dolmens and cists), the presence of these categories may be explained as reflecting the different degrees to which the community accepted the peninsular mode of spatio-temporal arrangement of burials. However, if we examine the correlation between those categories and compare them with other factors at individual settlements, a somewhat more complicated picture emerges. At Etsuji cemetery B, where the cemetery is an example of the type A cemetery, the houses were built like the Songguk'ni type of dwelling, which, as we saw earlier in this chapter (Section 4.2 in this chapter), originated in the southern part of the peninsula. At the Shinmachi site, where the cemetery is an example of the type C cemetery, the pottery assemblage indicated that the material culture of the community had adopted peninsula-originated items and attributes at least to the same extent as many other villages in the northern Kyushu region. This suggests that the spatio-temporal arrangement of burials in a particular community was determined by something else in addition to or apart from the degree to which

the given community had accepted the peninsula-originated influence.

I would like to argue that this specific spatio-temporal arrangement of burials, that is, arranging them along a linear alignment (type B), was adopted as a reaction to the changing social reality. As we have seen, the Yayoi package brought with it a new mode of collaborative labour: unlike the situation in the Jomon period, when the main locale of labour seasonally shifted as per the given environment and the work which was done at each of these seasonal locales required different types of expertise and collaboration, paddy field agriculture required a systematic type of knowledge, a specific type of expertise and organised labour involving the entire community, which were all invested in a specific locale in the landscape almost round the year (e.g. Nara Prefectural Kashihara Archaeological Research Institute 1987). In addition, essential tasks such as the construction of new paddies or the mending of paddy-related facilities might have required the collaboration of several communities at a time. In short, the intensity, planning requirements, duration and scale of collaborative labour increased.

The formation of linear alignments requires a long-term coordination of mortuary activities; smaller groupings constituting a cemetery-forming community have to coordinate and decide where to situate their graves in order to not block or disturb the burial alignments of one another (Mizoguchi 1995a, 1997b). The mortuary discourse, in general, is an arena in which social relations within and beyond the group responsible for burying an individual are reasserted and/or created. This discourse also involves the confirmation of long-term commitment to such collaborative relations between the concerned groups. Burial alignments would have materialised such commitment in the form of the spatio-temporal arrangement of burials and would have strongly obligated the members of a cemetery-forming community to *collaborate with each other* in other arenas of social life. In other words, the mortuary discourse can be regarded as a kind of reaction to the changes which occurred in other discourses.

Naturally, ways of reacting to these changes would have differed from community to community, and I would like to argue that this diversity is reflected by differences in the spatio-temporal organisation of cemeteries in this phase.

5.2. Rectangular Ditch-Enclosed Burial Compounds: Western Japan

The situation in the Inland Sea region is unclear in this regard. The custom of situating pit and composite wooden coffin burials in linear rows had spread across the San'in region (Yamada 2000). In the Kinki region, however, a unique burial custom emerged in the second half of the Yayoi I – the custom of burying the dead in rectangular ditch-enclosed compounds.

Rectangular ditch-enclosed burial compounds (*Hokei-shuko-bo*, 方形周溝墓), wherein adults were mostly buried in composite wooden coffins and children and infants, in either composite wooden coffins or in pots, were typically covered by low mounds. Their definite originals have not been found in the peninsula, although recent discoveries reveal that some dolmens located in linear cemeteries are situated in rectangular compounds often marked by stone settings lining the sides (e.g. D. Nakamura 2007). For now, it would be safe to infer that the custom was inspired by information included in the Yayoi package. We do not have enough evidence to recognise clear patterns in the formation process of the cemeteries of the time. Furthermore, in most of the examples, the graves have been lost due to severe disturbance and cutting. However, the following traces can be observed at the Higashi-Muko (東武庫) site, located in Amagasaki municipality of Hyogo prefecture, which dates back to the early second half of the Yayoi I (Hyogo PBE 1995): (a) the compounds are of different sizes; (b) they form clusters, resulting from the sequential adding of new compounds to preexisting ones; and (c) although there are compounds with single graves and those with more than two graves, the difference in the number of graves does not correlate with the differences in compound size (Figure 5.16). This gives rise to some extremely interesting and important questions: What type of grouping was represented by each compound and each cluster? What was the significance of the different compound sizes? While we do not have sufficient evidence to investigate these questions as yet (I return to them in the next chapter), we can

infer the following regarding the burial sites mentioned above. First, their close proximity to one another suggests that the important structuring principle of communal togetherness was embodied by the cemetery-scape. Second, relationships between the groups represented by the cluster were rather unstable, as indicated by the changing size of compounds comprising individual clusters. These changes in compound size must have resulted from a range of factors, such as the amount of help expected by a community in constructing a compound and the magnitude of the network and channels of social obligations possessed by the living people who would eventually be buried in those compounds. In other words, the social relations represented by the cemetery-scape were egalitarian ones, and they embodied not only an awareness regarding the importance of communal togetherness but also the sense of competition, reflected by different mound sizes, between the groups which constructed individual compounds.

5.3. Ancestral Bones: Eastern Japan

The available evidence is scarce, but it is possible that pit burials and occasional jar burials were the norm from the Final Jomon period onwards. The practice of depositing processed skeletal remains in globular jars (*Sai-so* [reburial] *bo* [grave], 再葬墓) (or processed bone burials, called PBB hereafter) was widespread in the Chubu, Kanto and southern Tohoku regions. This practice began in the Final Jomon period and continued until at least the Yayoi III period, possibly extending to the Kofun period (Harunari 1993, 79–82).

The Jizoden site contains a dual organisation of burials, as mentioned previously (Figure 5.8). Although not all the graves at this site are clustered into the two burial groups, the latter's prominence in the cemetery-scape is undeniable. Within those two groups and the outlying graves, we can identify some micro-clusters or micro-alignments of two or three graves. The presence of two levels of clustering brings to mind the spatial structure of the Late and Final Jomon cemeteries; there also we have larger segments, probably representing segments of supra-communal groupings such as clans, and ephemeral micro-clusters of a couple of graves (see Figure 5.2). These have been interpreted to reflect the importance of multilayered communal ties and the lack of differentiation of smaller group-ings such as households in the face of supra-local units in the settlement. With regard to the Jizoden site, the preceding interpretation strongly repres-ents the importance of dual organisations.

In the case of PBB, a fairly identical type of pic-ture emerges. According to Hiromi Shitara, some of the oldest examples of the Yayoi I PBB can be found at the Negoya (根古屋) site (Umemiya and Otake 1986); at this site, globular jars containing PBB were deposited in pits forming distinct spatial clusters, suggesting that they were made and used by different communities (Shitara 2008, 210–219). He suggests that the dead that were buried in such clusters originated from different residential groupings and usually lived separately (ibid.). As we have seen, most of the settlements of eastern Japan consisted of single residential groups with a fairly scattered distribution.[39] Kazunori Takase (2004, 144–213) has revealed that in the northern Tohoku region, the size of individual settlements increased and their distribution became less scattered in the Yayoi I, probably due to the adoption of paddy field rice farming. Traits of the Yayoi package began to appear across eastern Japan towards the end of the Yayoi I, and this may have increased the necessity of inter-communal collaboration from previously mentioned reasons. The practices concerning the PBB prolonged the process of transformation of the living body, through the transformative entity, into the ancestor, through which the attachment and relations between the living and the dead would have been confirmed, symbolically displayed and inscribed in the minds of those who were involved in the prolonged process. Such a ritual process would have served to increase the sense of communal togetherness among those who were involved in the process of reciprocating obligations with one another as well as with the dead in a number of episodes of encountering with (the remains of) the dead spread across the process.

In that sense, in comparison with the mortu-ary practices in the west – in which both the sense of communality and inter-group competi-tion were represented and played out – those in

the east emphasised the importance of commun-ality by possibly reducing the individuality of the dead.

5.4. *Communality and Differences*

In western Japan, as the preceding observations suggest, the mortuary discourse of the period expressed two contradictory themes: one, the importance of *communal unity* and *collaboration* and, two, the *differences* between individuals and between groupings smaller than the community which formed and used a particular cemetery.

The planned formation of burial alignments, which requires a certain degree of long-term col-laboration between groupings sharing a cemetery, can be recognised throughout the phase; it is visible in the dolmen/cist/wooden coffin burial cemeter-ies of the Incipient Yayoi period and those in the Yayoi I period, when new features of jars as coffins and a ditch-enclosed mortuary compound were added to them. The actual type of burial alignment, however, varied between cemeteries: in some cemeteries, burials continued to be agglom-erated in small clusters; in others, agglomerations were replaced by uniform alignments; in some other cemeteries, grave agglomerations and align-ments continued side by side. This suggests that the significance of the *themes* differed between com-munities. This would have resulted from the dif-ferent conditions in which communities initially adopted the new lifestyle and subsequently came to sustain themselves.

We have too little evidence from eastern Japan to infer the themes of the mortuary discourse and its changes. In the case of Jizoden, maintain-ing continuity with the Jomon period appears to have been a significant concern; in the representa-tion of social relations, local and supra-local com-munal ties were emphasised more than the differ-ences between individuals and between small-scale groupings. Highlighting the importance of com-munal togetherness by reducing the individuality of the dead, which seems to be the objective of the PBB-related practice, can also be regarded as a significant characteristic of the mortuary discourse of eastern Japan during this period.

During that phase, significantly, the expression of differences was not connected to any kind of hierarchy: the presence and absence of mortuary

39 According to Hideshi Ishikawa (2011b), this situation continued well into the middle phase of the Middle Yayoi period across wide areas of the Kanto region and north-eastern Japan.

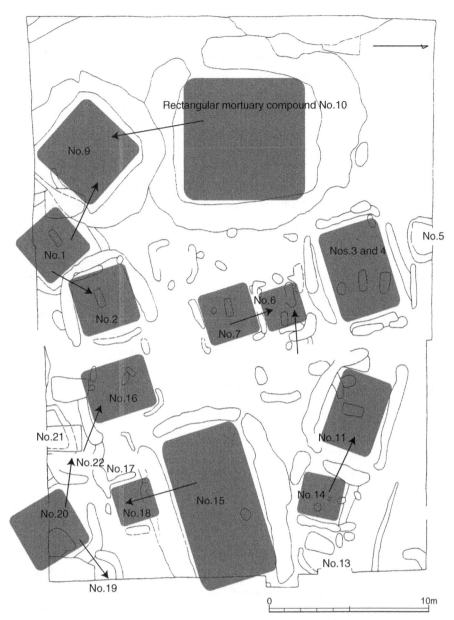

Figure 5.16. The Higashi-Muko cemetery (Hyogo prefecture) composed of rectangular ditch-enclosed burial compounds. Arrows indicate inferred formation sequences (after Hyogo PBE 1995).

goods rarely correlated to other traits of burials such as the scale and refinement of their features; burials containing mortuary goods were not concentrated in certain clusters but tended to be scattered across the cemetery. This suggests that if the expression was that of status differences, they were *achieved*, rather than *ascribed*, ones. These differences might have also been associated with gender and age differences, but the poor preservation of the skeletons, due to the soil's high acidity, makes it difficult to arrive at conclusive facts.

Paddy field agriculture necessitated an unprecedented level of social collaboration in terms of its scale and intensity. Such collaboration would have suppressed the desire and tendency of individual small social units to act selfishly and accumulate wealth. At the same time, the level of collaboration would also have required the leadership to mediate the intra-communal conflict of interests. The introduction of stone weapons to the grave good assemblage suggests that the emergent leadership came to possess an element of potential coercion by the use of physical force. However, such leaders were neither confined to certain groups nor buried separately from the others. In summary, the mortuary discourse reacted to changes in other discourses by balancing the expressions of differences, collaboration and leadership.

6. CONCLUSION

The onset of the rice-agriculture-based way of life resulted in an amalgamation of change and continuity. I have attempted to capture its essence by using the word *becoming* to describe the process of change.

The amount of surplus initially generated by the agricultural activities has been disputed (see e.g. disputes between Makoto Sahara and Kaoru Terasawa in Nara Prefectural Kashihara Archaeological Research Institute 1987). Accordingly, the thesis that competition and disputes over the distribution of surplus led to the emergence of a mediator, igniting the process towards the hierarchisation of social relations and accelerating the development of social complexity, has often been questioned. So far, this study has examined the changes that occurred in the structure of various fields of communication and social reproduction; we have learnt that the introduction of systematic rice farming brought about important changes in the spatio-temporal organisation of social life, that is, the way in which individuals organised their short-, medium- and long-term way of life and planned their lives in relation to those of others in terms of where they met, how they shared a certain set of expectations and how they collaborated.

Systematic rice farming made it inevitable that certain roles would be fixed for certain individuals. Paddy fields, irrigation systems and even the ditch-enclosed settlements, at times, worked as the media of such fixation: their construction and maintenance would have certainly required a hierarchical structure and division of tasks, and the outcome endured, i.e., it remained there to be experienced in the future. This kind of fixation would have contradicted the communal egalitarian ethos, drawn upon by the Jomon communities in their reproduction, in various ways generally associated with the organisation of things and social relations in a symmetrical manner (that is well reflected by the symmetrical-circular spatial structure of Jomon settlements; see Figure 5.2). This is because the fixation of roles within a given society ignites hierarchisation in that society. Hence, this kind of contradiction needs to be rationalised. Since rice paddy field agriculture required the investment of a considerable amount of energy and time, the possible contingencies that would need

to be dealt with began to be increasingly confined to a limited number of fields of communication, much fewer than those in the Jomon period, such as the construction and maintenance of paddies, the annual execution of rice farming activities and the maintenance of contacts and exchanges with other communities, which only accelerated the fixation of roles.

These changes resulted in the emergence of the prominent archetype of the 'warrior class' of social beings (represented by the grave good assemblage comprised of polished stone daggers/willow-leaf-shaped arrowheads), the members of which were responsible for aggressively enhancing and protecting communal interests. Such a narrowing down of the range of social archetypes from the Jomon period has clear and significant implications. Jomon mortuary practices represented a number of different archetypes, including those of good hunters, good mothers and other variously categorised beings. Coincident with the change in the range and component of complexities resulting from the introduction of systematic rice paddy field agriculture, the warrior became virtually the exclusive archetype of human categories to be marked in burial.

The ritual and mortuary fields of communication typically undertook the task of rationalising any of the arising contradictions and problems in society. Under the Yayoi package, however, people's continuous mingling with the dead ceased; the dead were fixed in their positions at the time of burial, and these positions became fixed referential points based on which the living began to identify themselves. As mentioned above, fixed positions were sometimes signified by material symbols of the individual's coercive abilities, that is, the power to harm and kill. The disappearance of *Dogu* figurines from Kyushu and western Japan and the continued presence of stone rods in the Kinki region are suggestive of this change. It is believed that the former were used in prayers for the smooth procurement of foodstuffs by metaphorically linking human fertility with that of nature. This linkage was mediated by the child-bearing faculty of the female. The latter would also have been used in similar ritual activities, but the linkage of human reproduction with that of natural resources was mediated by the role of the male (represented by phallus-shaped stone rods) in human reproduction.

The fact that only the use of stone rods continued suggests that only the male-related element of fertility rituals was selected for continuation from the repository of Jomon ritual items. This can be connected with the preceding picture as follows. Most of the sexable skeletons excavated with weapons or weapon-shaped ritual implements from the Early and Middle Yayoi periods are male (Mizoguchi 2001, 143; Yoshiyuki Tanaka, pers. comm.). From this, we can infer that the conspicuous emergence of weapons such as polished stone daggers and the polished stone 'willow-leaf-shaped' arrowheads would have reflected the increasing importance of male or male-related activities.

Ethnographic examples suggest that activities such as digging heavy soil or combat, in which masculine power played an important role, were generally exclusively performed by males (e.g. Murdock 1967). The construction and maintenance of paddies and irrigation canals, along with occasional eruptions of small-scale combats, would have increased the importance of male-related activities and correspondingly the significance of *maleness* in the symbolic representational fields of social reproduction. In addition, since these activities increasingly began to occupy significant portions and positions in the spatio-temporal organisation of social activities, those who primarily undertook them, i.e., the males in society, would have gained increasingly stable and higher positions in their communities.

In that sense, the scenario in eastern Japan appears to have been quite different: the use of clay figurines continued, while prolonged mingling with the dead continued with renewed formality in the form of PBB burials. Gender representation also appears to have continued unchanged in this region, at least for a while.

We are probably witnessing the emergence of different trajectories resulting from the introduction of the Yayoi package: one involved the emergence of a hierarchical categorisation of people and the development of a set of devices to deal with the contradictions generated by this categorisation, whereas the other involved the reproduction of the horizontal categorisation of people and the development of a set of devices to support it. Communities that followed the latter trajectory retained the basic structuring principle of Jomon society by accepting elements of the Yayoi

package in a selective manner. Communities that followed the former trajectory, however, witnessed the emergence of new social relations, identities and the way in which their members organised their lives in spatio-temporal terms. This also led to the emergence of a totally new landscape and constructed environment in which people lived, worked, died and were buried.

The structuring principle which emerged and supported this typical Yayoi trajectory can be represented in the form of a system consisting of dichotomous pairs, their transformative relations and their mediating factors, which can be described as follows:

> <*the death of rice grains : the regeneration of rice grains*> − <*the death of human beings : the regeneration of human beings*>

The relationship was *mediated by male coercive power* represented by associations between globular jars containing rice grains, the polished lithic weapons and the male dead.

The fact that males were perceived as mediators and controllers of these transformative relations suggest that the following dichotomies were added to the preceding dichotomy:

> <*the death of rice grains : the regeneration of rice grains*> − <*the death of human beings : the regeneration of human beings*> − <*female (?) : male*> − <*nature : culture*>

This system of meaning and its transformative relations were represented in various forms, including mortuary practices, agricultural rituals, the construction and use of large-scale buildings and so on, throughout the Yayoi period. These were the occasions on which various problems generated by the growth of rice farming-based communities were given certain forms such as narratives and myths, which in turn were used to comprehend and conceptually tackled these problems. By mediating the comprehension and tackling of social problems, the system predisposed people to think, feel and act in certain ways. In this way, the system was established as a dominant structuring principle which was to determine the trajectory through which the society became stratified and increasingly complex. Let us call this the *Yayoi structuring principle*. In the following chapters, I return to this principle and examine many of its aspects in further detail.

CHAPTER 6

AN ARCHAEOLOGY OF GROWTH: FROM THE FINAL YAYOI I (400/200 BC) TO THE END OF THE YAYOI IV (AD 1/50)

1. INTRODUCTION

The phase between the Final Yayoi I and Yayoi IV periods can be described as the period of maturation of rice-agriculture-based communities. The phase saw the expansion and intensification of the changes that had occurred in the previous phase. Most of the features that are regarded as representing the character of the Yayoi period, or its 'Yayoi-ness', so to say, were consolidated in terms of their nature and characteristics during this phase (Morioka 2011). Through this process, communities, both residential and nonresidential (such as clans and sodalities), became larger and began to show differences in their size and structure. In order to ensure their sustenance, the enlarged communal units either invented/adopted new devices or reinforced preexisting mechanisms. Those phenomena can be broadly described as 'growth'. Growth, like any other social process, is the continuous generation of new problems that need to be comprehended and addressed, socially as well as individually. We should not be content with merely focusing on measuring the rate of growth and connecting it with factors such as 'hierarchy' and 'complexity'; it is important to investigate the factors that brought about the growth and the conditions that resulted from such growth. Some of the problems that needed to be addressed can only be properly described as 'contradictions'. For instance, the growth and centralisation of larger settlements[1]

took place through the working of communal networks through which people, goods and information were gathered in them. However, growth of this nature inevitably led to hierarchisation, which could destroy intra- and inter-communal cooperation that was based on the sense of communal togetherness. Such problems appear to have been comprehended and addressed by communities at that time by drawing on the 'Yayoi structuring principle' (as conceptualised and defined at the end of the previous chapter) and by mobilising various material media of the principle. In other words, the society during the phase can be described as the 'society against (overt) hierarchisation' (following the title of Pierre Clastre's [1999] seminal work *Society against the State*). This chapter seeks to investigate the material traces of various reactions to such problems and contradictions that arose during this period.

2. BROAD REGIONAL TRAJECTORIES: A VERY BRIEF OUTLINE

As the process of growth progressed, three broad regional units, called 'horizons'[2] hereafter, emerged on the scene: the Kyushu, the western and the eastern horizons (Figures 3.1.A and 6.1. A–D). In archaeological terms, they are most easily identifiable as large pottery style zones. However, they were also characterised by their distinct ways of organising settlements, burying the dead and praying for the well-being of their communities. These horizons developed different sets of

---

1 The scale of typical large, regional centre-type settlements from the northern Kyushu and Kinki regions is around 10–20 hectares (1 hectare = 10,000 square metres). Small, satellite-type settlements are commonly around 1–2 hectares. A small number of extremely large settlements in northern Kyushu reach more than 100 hectares. For detail, see Footnote 36 to this chapter.

2 A 'horizon' to be loosely defined here as a distributional complex of a material culture item or a set of material culture items reflecting the recursive enactment of a certain custom/customs.

material items and built environments to mediate the reproduction of communities and their internal and external relationships. In fact, differences between those horizons – and differences between the eastern horizon and the other two, in particular – are such that one might be hesitant to lump them together under the single name of 'Yayoi'. We should be careful not to treat them as 'closed systems', however; there were dense interactions between the horizons. For instance, the raw material from which the famous *Dotaku* (銅鐸) bronze bells of the western horizon (see Figures 6.26 and 7.5) were made is thought to have been imported initially from the Korean peninsula and then from China from the Yayoi IV onwards, regardless of the shape of the material, that is, the metal was imported either in the form of ingots or as bronze implements to be melted for the production of bells (Mabuchi and Hirao 1982).[3] Such an exchange would certainly have involved the mediation of northern Kyushu communities in one way or another. Nevertheless, it is undeniable that the people's lifestyles in different horizons, as reconstructed from available archaeological evidence, show considerable differences as well as similarities between them.

Those horizons were sandwiched between the Mumun (無文, plain) pottery culture of the Korean peninsula and the 'Epi-Jomon' (or *Zoku-Jomon* [続縄文] in Japanese) culture of Hokkaido Island. The former is characterised by a relatively plain pottery assemblage; the culture shows influences of the expanding periphery of the Chinese empire's overland expansion and the development of rice-agriculture-based communities as well as bronze and ironwork. The latter derives a range of traits from the Jomon cultural tradition. Based on this heuristic perception, let us briefly examine some of the basic characteristics of the horizons before investigating the individual fields of social life in detail.

The Kyushu horizon (particularly its northern sector) (Figures 3.1.A and 6.1.A) is closest to the Korean peninsula geographically and to its

Mumun pottery culture in its traits; it is characterised by relatively plain pottery assemblages, that is, the Sugu (須玖) style assemblage and its regional variants (Figure 6.1.A), the development of various bronze weapons (including dagger-, halberd-[dagger-axe] and spearhead-shaped weapons)[4] and the prominent presence of imports from the contemporary Chinese empire of the Early Han (from the Yayoi IV onward) as well as from polities in the Korean peninsula (basically from the final Yayoi I onward). Most of the Chinese imports, including bronze mirrors and *Heki* (璧) green glass discs (see Figure 6.4.E), came through contacts with the Early Han commandery of Lelang (楽浪), situated on the north-western corner of the peninsula in 108 BC (see Chapter 4.3 of this volume; and Takakura 1995, 103–109). The distribution of Early Han imports was mostly confined to northern Kyushu during the Middle Yayoi period, and these imported artefacts were almost exclusively deposited as grave goods. We can detect an emerging hierarchical order among the burials across northern Kyushu in terms of the presence/absence of Chinese imports and other items and their quantitative and qualitative differences (see Figure 6.4), and some scholars claim that these indicate the development of a large-scale, complex, chiefdom-type organisation (e.g. Shimojo 1991; Nakazono 1991). However, it is difficult to find traces of the establishment of a hierarchy in which status was *ascribed* on the basis of descent grouping. For instance, we have not found the tangible trace of elite precinct-type structures in the large central place-type settlements of the area (Mizoguchi 2010a, 27). This suggests that the hierarchisation did not take the form of showing its representation in the sphere of everyday-life. I will return to this problem later on.

The horizon also witnessed the beginning of iron forging and the increasing use of iron implements for woodworking and occasionally as prestige/ritual goods (Murakami 1998, 53–103). For instance, iron halberds were deposited as grave goods across northern Kyushu and its peripheries (for the distribution, see Figures 6.4 and 6.19, and for an example of the halberd, see Figure 6.4.G) (ibid., 78–83). These are likely to have been

---

3 Mabuchi and Hirao (1982) infer that the *Dotaku* bells of the Yayoi V were made from ingots, consisting of lead mined somewhere in northern China, mixed with tin and copper at a fixed ratio. I come back to the issue concerning the raw material for the production of the bronze implements of the Yayoi period, including the *Dohoko* spearheads and *Dotaku* bells in the next chapter.

4 These were rarely used as combat weapons (for some rare examples of the trace of the actual combats, see Hashiguchi 2005, 1–8) and more commonly used as grave goods and ritual implements.

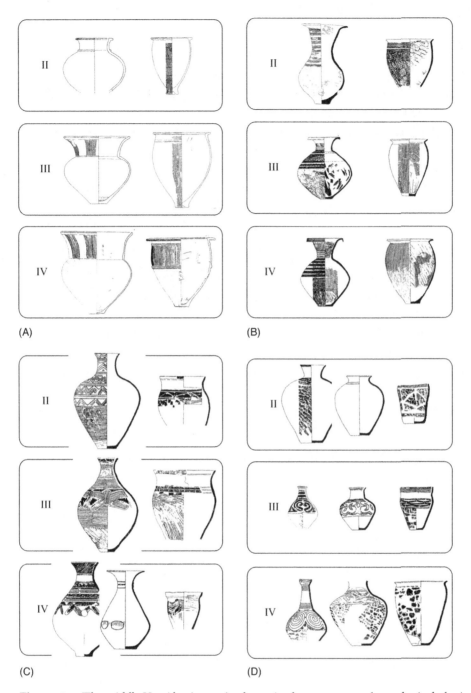

Figure 6.1. The middle Yayoi horizons: A schematized pottery typo-chronological phasing of the Kyushu (**A**), the Western (**B**), and the Eastern (**C** and **D**) "horizons". Arranged after Takesue (2003, 108–109) (for A), Wakabayashi (2003, 249–251) (for B), Ishikawa (2003, 367–368) (for C and D).

produced in the Fukuoka Plain and were probably presented to the partner-elites of surrounding areas as prestige gifts. By the end of the Middle Yayoi period, stone tools for woodworking practically disappeared in many areas across northern Kyushu.[5]

The development of settlement hierarchy was also a significant feature of this time. In northern

Kyushu, the largest settlements in individual floodplains increasingly developed a 'central-place'-like character, even though they basically remained agrarian settlements.[6] For instance, the Mikumo

5 Iron smelting did not begin before the Kofun period, however: see Murakami (1998, chap. 3).

6 The trace of bronzemaking, for instance, concentrates on those settlements. As mentioned below, they also appear to have functioned as ritual centres in that the cemeteries with rich graves attached to them are often associated with extraordinarily large buildings, probably for ancestral rituals (Shitara 2009; Mizoguchi 2010a, 27–28).

(三雲) site, which has yielded two jar burials (the Mikumo-Minamishoji [三雲南小路] site) deposited with more than fifty Early Han bronze mirrors in total and other grave goods including *Heki* green glass discs, comma-shaped glass beads, cylindrical glass beads, and bronze weapons (see Figure 6.4.A in the map and 6.4.A–F for artefacts) (Fukuoka PBE 1985b), is situated roughly in the centre of the Itoshima Plain; this location made it possible for it to function as a *node* in the flow of goods, people and probably even information.[7] However, other nodes appear to have developed because they were located on the boundaries between settlement systems; the Sugu (須玖) site (see Figures 6.4.B and 6.7), which also shows evidence of a jar burial deposited with more than twenty Early Han bronze mirrors and other grave goods similar to the Mikumo, is located on the southern bottom of the Fukuoka Plain, at a spot that is ideal for connecting the settlement systems of the Fukuoka Plain with those of the Chikushi Plain to the south and those of the Kaho Basin to the east (for the location, see Figure 6.4.B in the map; Mizoguchi 2008, 87–88). Henceforth, we shall simply describe them as 'regional centres'.[8] The centrality of those settlements as nodes for the flow of goods, people and information would have been reinforced by their function as the seat of various gatherings, including mortuary practices and other rituals. In many cases, cemeteries with extremely large jar burials (甕, jar; 棺, coffin; 墓, burial), often with separate elite mortuary compounds marked by a ditch and/or rectangular mounds,[9] were found at a corner of the regional centres (see Figure 6.6.B). A large rectangular building was often built nearby, and many such buildings were repeatedly rebuilt on the same spot (Figure 6.2).

7 Walter Christaller's (1933) original model proposes three ideal types, each of which derives from a unique principle: the marketing, the transport and the administrative. Roughly speaking, many of the Yayoi central-place-type settlements and the surrounding settlements show the pattern akin to the third principle (i.e. two-tier settlement hierarchy with no intermediary satellite settlements connecting the largest and the second-largests surrounding the former), but this impression needs to be verified.

8 The word *region* in this case roughly indicates the area within which a majority of intra- and inter-communal activities took place. This should of course be distinguished from the 'regional' divisions of present-day Japan, mentioned in Chapter 3.2.3.

9 Called *Kukaku-bo* (区画墓).

The gatherings which took place in these locales would have confirmed and renewed various types of intra- and inter-communal ties. The unique spatio-temporal configuration developed in many Yayoi II and III cemeteries of the northern Kyushu region, wherein the linear configuration comprised two rows of pit burials, composite wooden coffin burials and jar burials, may have reflected the presence of a dual organisation (Figures 6.13.B and 6.14; Mizoguchi 2008, 79–82), which might have contributed to the significant growth and sustenance of the regional centres (see Tuzin 2001); various prestations for the fulfilment of mutual obligations based upon the organisation would have taken place in larger numbers at extraordinarily large cemeteries attached exclusively to most of the regional centres of the northern Kyushu region (Mizoguchi 2006b, 2008).

The western horizon, situated between the Kyushu and the eastern horizons (Figure 6.1.B), developed intermediary characteristics. Its pottery was decorated with various comb-marked patterns (*Kushigaki-mon*, 櫛描紋) in the Yayoi II and III and with horizontal grooves (凹線紋) in the Yayoi IV (Figure 6.1.B). The horizon is also characterised by a unique custom of burying the dead in rectangular ditch-enclosed compounds. They are called *Hokei* (方形, rectangular) – *shuko* (周溝, ditch-enclosed) – *bo* (墓, burial compounds). The horizon also developed a unique bronze assemblage, including the use of *Dotaku* (銅鐸) bronze bells (for specimens dating from the Middle Yayoi, see Figure 7.5.I–III) and weapon-shaped implements (daggers and halberds). Towards the end of the Middle Yayoi period, the horizon also saw the gradual spread of iron tools. The circulation of these tools, which were mostly woodworking tools, appears to have been unstable as compared to that in the Kyushu horizon, and the shortage of such tools was compensated by the continuing use of stone tools (Murakami 1998, 74–78).

A settlement hierarchy, comparable with that in northern Kyushu, also developed during the period. Many of the regional centres, like their equivalents in northern Kyushu, had cemeteries built on a huge scale, and some of their large, rectangular buildings, just like their northern Kyushu counterparts, were repeatedly rebuilt at the same spot (Figure 6.2) (e.g. Ikegami-sone [池上曽根] site; Izumi MBE 2004). This suggests several similarities in the ways in which intra- and

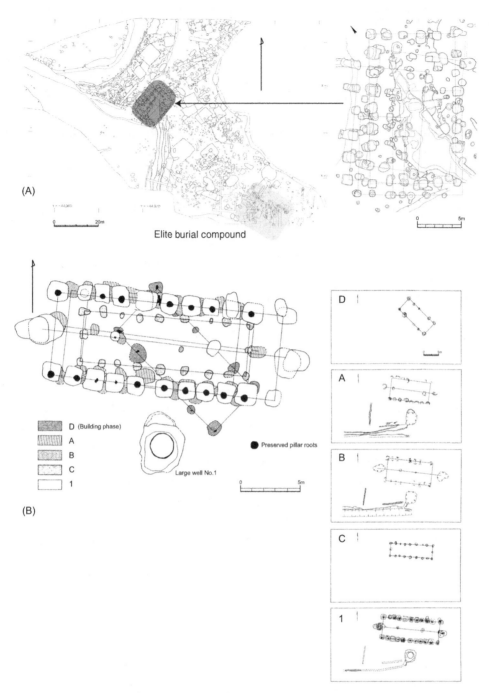

Figure 6.2. Examples of the extraordinarily large building of the Middle Yayoi period in northern Kyushu and western Japan: the Ubihon'mura (柚比本村; Saga prefecture; from Saga PBE [2003], with modifications) and the Ikegami-Sone (池上曽根; Osaka prefecture; from Izumi MBE [2004], with modifications). **A:** Ubihon'mura, **B:** Ikegami-Sone. D∼1 in B indicates the phases marked by re-buildings of the structure.

inter-communal ties were reproduced in the Kyushu and western horizons.[10,11]

It should be noted that some *Dotaku* bronze bells have pictorial representations of insects,

10 It has to be noted, however, that most of the extraordinarily large buildings of northern Kyushu were built in the vicinity of extraordinarily large cemeteries, their equivalents in the western horizon tended to be located at the centre of regional centres. I come back to the point repeatedly throughout this chapter.

11 Hiromi Shitara (2010, 11–12) implies that a more than three-tier settlement hierarchisation, reflected by quantitative and qualitative differences between chiefly burials in terms of their grave goods and features, developed in northern Kyushu whereas its development was curtailed in the Kinki region because of its reciprocity-based exchange networks. I consider the validity of this thesis in Sections 4 and 6 in this chapter.

animals, birds and human beings (see Figure 6.26). Some of these bells also have depictions of ships and raised-floor buildings, the latter most probably being granaries. In rare examples, these pictures are arranged in clearly defined panels, which lead some scholars to infer that they represent a mythical narrative (e.g. Kobayashi 1967, 212–218; Sahara 1982). Most of these creatures and other entities also appear on pots, burial jars and various wooden implements, mostly as single figures, across the Kyushu and western horizons (Harunari 1991). This indicates that the two horizons shared a basic structure of mythical narratives which were used to comprehend and cope with the problems and difficulties generated by the paddy-field-rice-agriculture-based way of life. In that sense, if we could manage to interpret the cluster of depictions on the *Dotakus*, we would be able to understand how the people in the western as well as northern Kyushu horizons perceived, comprehended and ascribed meanings to the world in which they lived.[12]

The eastern horizon, geographically farthest from the Korean peninsula, is characterised by the extensive use of cord-marked patterns on pottery (Figures 6.1.C–D), the lack (albeit not total) of bronze and iron implements and the lack of settlement hierarchy. Most of the settlements were small and homogeneous, though their clusters, some of them fairly large, began to emerge in the Yayoi III (e.g. Ishikawa 2011a, 2011b).[13] The emergence of such settlements, comprised of a number of residential units (and at times a centrally located extraordinarily large building, e.g. the Nakazato site, Kanagawa prefecture; Odawara MBE 2000), marked the establishment of a fully rice paddy field agriculture-based way of life in the Kanto region (Ishikawa 2011a). With the exception of the northern Tohoku region, the horizon also saw the extensive spread of the practice of reburial (the PBB mentioned in Chapter 5.5.3), in which

processed or excarnated bones were often contained in long-necked, S-profiled globular vessels and deposited in groups. The practice of reburial prolonged the process of encounter between the living and the dead, and this would have enhanced the sense of communal togetherness among the living, mediated by the transformation of the dead into the ancestors. The underdevelopment of settlement hierarchy and possible difficulties in maintaining inter-communal ties might have resulted in the development of this practice (Ishikawa 2000). This issue is further discussed in a later section.

Towards the end of the Yayoi III and the beginning of the Yayoi IV, an assemblage characterised by a prolific use of linear and wavy comb-marked decorations, called the Miyanodai (宮ノ台) assemblage, spread along the Pacific coast as far east as the Tone River basin of the Kanto Plain (e.g. Shinpojiumu Minami-Kanto no Yayoi-doki jikko-iinkai 2005; Ishikawa 2011b, 409–415).[14] The formation of this large-scale style zone corresponded with the spread of various traits from the western horizon, including the custom of burying the dead in rectangular ditch-enclosed compounds. The Tokai and Hokuriku regions also saw the expansion of influences from the western horizon, characterised by the expansion of the horizon of the horizontal groove-decorated pottery assemblage (e.g. Ishiguro 2011; Hori 2011). These influences marked the expansion of a broad sphere of dense social contacts from the west, and this sphere expanding into the Hokuriku was later to become the frontier of the horizon on the Japan sea coast within which the custom of building keyhole tumuli as the final resting place of the elite became prevalent (cf. Chapters 7 and 8 in this volume).

These horizons, as mentioned earlier, developed distinct broad pottery style zones. Their internal structures, that is, the way in which attribute variants and shape-types were distributed and the way in which these distributions overlapped with one

---

12 It can be inferred at this point that the narratives were related in some fundamental ways to the 'Yayoi structuring principle' analysed in Chapter 5. We will come back to the point in Section 7 later in this chapter.

13 The Yayoi III saw the sudden decrease of excavated settlement across the Tohoku region (Saino 2011, 458–459). It is suggested to have resulted from the relocation of settlements to low-lying areas due to the establishment of large-scale rice paddy fields on the bottom of alluvial plains (ibid., 470–471).

14 Roughly five style zones, including the incoming Miyanodai assemblage, spreading across the coastal areas, coexisted in the Kanto Plain in the Yayoi IV (Ishikawa 2011b, 412–415). This shows that the coming of the wave of a fully developed rice paddy-field agricultural complex stimulated both inter-regional interactions and the crystallisation of regional groupings around the Kanto Plain and beyond (ibid.).

another, however, were different: a series of mutually overlapping sub-style-zones constituted the style zones in Kyushu and western Japan, whereas the entire eastern Japan style zone, with the exception of the northern Tohoku region, was covered by the horizon of long-necked, S-profiled globular jar shape-types, cross-cutting the mutually overlapping sub-style-zones (Figures 6.1.C–D). By referring to the dual spatial division of the settlement of Jizoden (see Figure 5.8; Takase 2004), I have argued in the previous chapter that moiety-like sodalities were spreading across wide areas in the northern Tohoku region in the Yayoi I. Shitara (2008, 207–219) suggests that some of the reburial cemeteries were divided into multi-layered segments: it also suggests the functioning of *moieties* and other types of sodality-type groupings. The working of such sodalities as networks of mutual obligation-based contacts might explain the widespread formation of a horizon wherein finer wares had high ancestral ritual implications. This suggests that a unique device for the maintenance of intercommunal ties, different from that in the northern Kyushu and western Japan horizons, was at work in the eastern horizon.

In the following sections, the three aforementioned horizons will be treated separately when necessary, although the Kyushu and western horizons, which shared a wide range of traits and structural components, will often be treated as one broad horizon, hereafter described as the *broad western horizon*. In contrast, because the eastern horizon has many distinct traits from the former ones, it will generally be treated separately.

With respect to the pottery style zones, their structural differences, as mentioned above, might have been related to some fundamental differences in the ways in which the communities were organised and connected with one another, which in turn might have influenced the ways in which people categorised and identified themselves by producing and using particular material items. Let us analyse this possibility in the following section.

3. COMMUNICATION, IDENTITY AND THE MATERIAL WORLD: POTTERY

A pottery assemblage often comprises two distinct categories: one consisting of well-finished and often well-decorated shape-types made of finely processed clay, and the other consisting of relatively crudely finished and often undecorated shape-types made of plain or coarse clay, often mixed with a lot of inclusions. The former category typically consists of various globular jar shape-types, predominantly used for the purpose of storing liquid or solid substances, as well as other pottery shape-types used for serving foods such as pedestalled bowls, whereas the latter commonly consists of cooking vessels. This division is consistently seen in the Yayoi pottery and finds its clearest expression in the Middle Yayoi period (Figure 6.1).

As mentioned in Chapter 5.3, every aspect of the production and use of pottery has significant social implications, and the differentiation of an assemblage into finer and coarser categories suggests that they were given different meanings and designed to mediate different types of communication in distinct manners.[15] The finer and coarser categories would also have been referenced to indicate and reproduce the users' identities in different manners. For instance, those who were involved in cooking would have had a special sense of attachment to cooking vessels for self-identification, their expressions might have indicated various meanings related to domesticity. In contrast, ritual vessels would have ignited and mediated the communication and self-identification of either a much larger fraction of the community involved in the ritual or those who were in charge of the ritual or both. In that sense, careful examinations of the pottery assemblage and its multilayered character as the media of social communications as well as self-identification might enable us to investigate the way in which a given community was categorised, internally structured and connected with other communities. In other words, it is possible to conduct a new version of 'ceramic sociology'.

Let us now explore this possibility.

15 Daniel Miller elegantly illustrates that different shape-types with minor morphological differences were linked to a system of structural dichotomies between purity : pollution :: cold : hot, etc. and mobilised for the reproduction of a certain mode of social relations (Miller 1985).

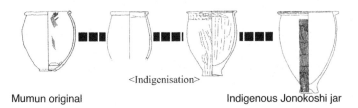

<Indigenisation>

Mumun original   Indigenous Jonokoshi jar

Figure 6.3. Transformation(/indigenization) of the Mumun pottery into the indigenous Yayoi Jonokoshi (城ノ越) style through the process of hybridization (from Takesue 2003, fig. 112–1, with additions).

3.1. Three Broad Style Zones: Northern Kyushu, Western Japan and Eastern Japan

NORTHERN KYUSHU

In Northern Kyushu, pottery was mostly undecorated. The surfaces of vessels, particularly vessels that belonged to the finer category, were intensively burnished. The custom of painting finer wares with red pigment began in the Yayoi III and had become widespread by the Yayoi IV.

The technique of burnishing pottery surfaces first developed in the Saga Plain, situated to the south of the Seburi mountain range (Tomoko Ishida, pers. comm.), where there were some prominent 'colony'-type settlements occupied by migrants from the Korean peninsula (Kataoka 1999, 103–113). Their pottery assemblage, however, quickly *hybridised* with the local Yayoi II pottery assemblage to form the Jonokoshi (城ノ越) style pottery, which suggests that the wave of migrations did not continue for long – certainly not over generations (Figure 6.3) (ibid., 114–129). The hybridisation continued with the Mumun pottery assemblage progressively incorporating elements of the local Jonokoshi assemblage, and from this, we can infer that the migrants embraced indigenous cultural traits and came to identify themselves with the indigenous culture. However, the technique of burnishing pottery surfaces appears to have been an exception; the technique was copied by local potters and quickly spread across the Chikushi Plain and the plains of the Genkai-nada coast (Ishida n.d.). It is particularly interesting that the Saga Plain is the centre of distribution of the earliest traces of bronzework (Kataoka 1999, 149–150). The emergence of the colony-type settlements and the subsequent spread of the technique of burnishing would have been concurrent with the early production of bronze implements in the Saga Plain and its subsequent spread across northern Kyushu (Ishida n.d.). Both the knowledge of bronzework and the technique of making bronze would have been perceived as traits of a 'high culture' and might have been actively and competitively copied.

The custom of painting finer wares with red pigment began in the north-eastern corner of the Chikushi Plain during the Yayoi III (Ishida 2010), where some select finer wares, mainly globular jars and pedestalled bowls, were heavily burnished and painted red (ibid.). These customs were subsequently adopted by communities in the plains of the Genkai-nada Sea to the north, and by the Yayoi IV, the Itoshima region had become the centre of the customs, followed by the Fukuoka Plain (ibid.). An interesting fact is that those two coastal plains witnessed the development of two extremely large regional centres, the Mikumo and the Sugu settlements, where certain elite individuals were buried with extremely rich grave goods including a large number of bronze mirrors imported from the Han outpost of Lelang (I come back to them later). The residents of these settlements appear to have strategically distributed bronze mirrors and other prestige items to their counterparts across northern Kyushu by presenting them in different qualities and quantities (cf. Mizoguchi 2010a, 28–30; about a hierarchy in those distributed items, see Shimojo 1991; Nakazono 1991), and interestingly enough, areas along the routes followed by this strategic gift-giving saw an increasing similarity between their pottery assemblages and those of the coastal regions (Ishida 2010). The differences in quality and quantity of artefacts presented to the elite of different communities were clearly designed to indicate the different degrees of strategic significance attributed by the elites of the Sugu and Mikumo settlements to them. For instance, three graves furnished with early Han Chinese bronze mirrors, Futsukaichi-Mine (二日市峯; Figure 6.4.7), Kuma-Nishioda (隈・西小田; Figure 6.4.9) and Higashioda-Mine

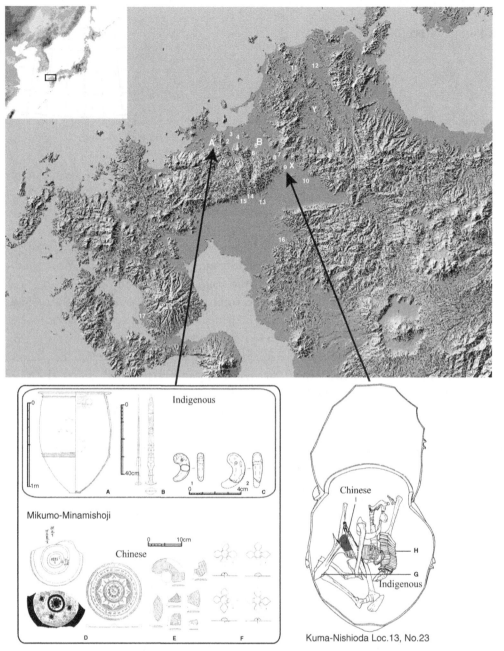

Figure 6.4. The distribution of jar burials with grave goods including Chinese bronze mirrors and other Chinese imports and/or iron weapons. Map: A and B indicate burials with a large number (more than seven) Early Han bronze mirrors and other Chinese and indigenous artefacts. X and Y indicate burials with more than two Early Han bronze mirrors and/or a small number of Chinese and indigenous artefacts. 1–16 indicate burials with either one Early Han bronze mirrors and indigenous artefacts or indigenous artefacts including iron weapons (see description on pp. 154–159). A: Mikumo-Minamishoji, B: Sugu-Okamoto, X Higashioda-Mine, Y Tateiwa-Hotta, 1: Kashiwazaki and Nakabaru, 2: Yoshitake-Hiwatashi, 3: Arita, 4: Maruodai, 5: Monden-Tsujibatake, 6: Antokudai, 7: Futsukaichi-Mine, 8: Dojoyama, 9: Kuma-Nishioda, 10: Kuriayama, 11: Fuchibaru-Umenoki, 12: Noboritate, 13: Rokunohata, 14: Futatsukayama, 15: Yoshinogari, 16: Chanokinomoto, 17: Tominoharu. Note that 16 and 17 are dated to the early Late Yayoi, but probably brought to those sites during the late Middle Yayoi. Below: A: Mikumo-Minamishoji jar burial no. 2 (lower jar), B: Bronze dagger from burial no. 1, C: Jade comma-shaped beads, D: Bronze mirrors from burial no.1, E: *Heki* green glass discs from burial no.1, F: Star-shaped gilded bronze coffin ornaments from burial no.1, G: Iron halberd from Kuma-Nishioda loc. 13, burial no. 23, H: Shell armlets, I Bronze mirror. A–F: from Fukuoka PBE (1985b), G–I: Chikushino MBE (1993).

(東小田峯; Figure 6.4.X), are clustered on the gap connecting the Genkai-nada coastal region with the riverine plains of the Chikugo River to the south (Figure 6.4). People in communities occupying the latter region and beyond had to pass through the gap, and the formation and maintenance of ties with the communities in the gap would have been a serious concern for them, which is probably why the Genkai-nada coastal communities and their elite sought to secure connections with communities in the south and allowed the entry of various goods from these regions, including half-finished shell armlets (e.g. Kinoshita 1996, 533–539). It is particularly important to analyse the difference between the Kuma-Nishioda and the Higashioda-Mine graves as regards their grave goods in order to understand the nature of the gift-giving. Despite their proximity (the graves are less than 2 kilometres apart), the latter contained two bronze mirrors (one large and one small), a decorated glass disc made from an originally larger glass disc (*Heki*, 璧) and some iron implements including an iron halberd (Yasu-cho-shi hensan-iinkai 1991, 165–176), whereas the former contained a small mirror, shell armlets, an iron dagger and an iron halberd (Chikushino City Committee for the Compilation of the History of the City 1999, 490–491). The contents of the latter are identical to those of many other graves also containing a rich assemblage, while those of the former are fairly similar in quality (not in quantity) to the assemblages with which the elite of the Mikumo and Sugu settlements were buried. Hence, we can infer that ties with the elite of Higashioda-Mine were more valued than those with the elite of Kuma-Nishioda (cf. Mizoguchi 2000, 241–242).

The red-painted finer wares were often involved in mortuary practices or practices related to the commemoration of the dead and the ancestors. For instance, at the Yubihon'mura (柚比本村) site (Saga PBE 2003), excavations in a large, shallow, oval pit measuring approximately 4 metres across have yielded more than fifty globular jars with the characteristic flared rim of the Yayoi III and IV periods, most of them unbroken, together with a small number of other shape-types (ibid., 6). Most of them are painted red from the middle of the belly up, although many of them are not very well burnished. It is inferred that all these jars

were deposited at the same time; they were located in situ, but it was not possible to determine any particular unit or agglomeration associated with their burial (ibid.). About 40 metres to the southwest of this spot, excavations reveal the presence of an extremely large rectangular building facing the cemetery; the cemetery contained a number of jar and other types of burials, some furnished with bronze daggers, dating from the Yayoi II, III and IV periods, along with two Yayoi V jar burials (ibid., 4–14). The building, repeatedly rebuilt at the same location, at least five times, during the Yayoi IV and early Yayoi V periods (Figure 6.2.A), would have had some association with the cemetery, and it is highly probable that some ritual functions, including mortuary- and ancestor-related rituals, were conducted here. It has to be noted that, according to Yoshinori Ozawa, the structure of the building appears to have been genealogically related to the central building in Etsuji (Ozawa 2006), which was discussed in the previous chapter; the building would have embodied elements of the *Yayoi structuring principle*,[16] constituted by the metaphorical-transformative relationships between the death and regeneration of rice grains, human beings and the community. It is likely that the globular jars were used during feasts or for making offerings on such occasions and were subsequently discarded in a corner of the ritual locale. In relation to the red-painted globular jars, it is interesting that from the end of the Yayoi I onwards, burial jars were occasionally painted black on the outside and red on the inside (cf. Inoue 2008, 185–190). This creates an interesting contrast with the globular jar: the colours were reversed in their case. One reason for this could be that in the case of burial jars, the power of regeneration was firmly *enclosed* and reserved for the dead, whereas in the case of globular jars, it was displayed to be shared by those who attended the ritual occasion. In any case, both the black-painted burial jars and the red-painted globular jars would have been firmly situated in the system of meaning embodying the *Yayoi structuring principle*.

It is important to note, in relation to the above observations, that specimens of the Yayoi IV finer ware category are often discovered far away from

---

16 For the detail of the definition and implications of the concept, see the concluding section of Chapter 5.

the area of their original distribution, that is, the coastal northern Kyushu region. Although some of them appear to have been imported, locally copied specimens are also common (Ishida 2010). The sites yielding them, such as the Tominoharu (富の原; Omura-shi bunkazai hogo-kyokai 1987) and Keikaen (景華園; Oda and Ueda 2004) sites in the Shimabara Peninsula, are located on transport routes for important materials and goods for the communities of the coastal northern Kyushu area and their elite. The Keikaen site is located on the route through which *Gohora* (*Tricornis latissimus*), a conch that only lived to the south of the Okinawa Islands (Nagai 1977) and whose shell was the main material of shell armlets of the Yayoi IV, would have been transported.

These materials and goods were important for the reproduction of communities and their emergent internal hierarchy in the northern Kyushu area in that the shell armlets constitute an important component of the grave good assemblage strategically presented by the elites of the Genkai-nada coastal communities to their inland peers. The finer wares that were imported or locally copied would have embodied certain meanings and values attached to contacts with the Genkai-nada coastal communities. At the Tominoharu site, for example, three iron halberds, most probably made in the northern Kyushu region, were deposited to furnish jar burials, themselves alien to the local tradition. In addition, northern Kyushu-type vessels were excavated from some nearby pits, probably associated with mortuary ritual functions (Omura-shi bunkazai hogo-kyokai 1987). Mortuary communication intensely mediates the self-identification of the living and the creation and (re)organisation of social relations. These facts suggest that the northern Kyushu material items in the grave good assemblage were *emulated* as some sort of elite material items, and competitive access to them would have partly generated and partly accelerated the hierarchisation of local communities.

The Kyushu style zone can be divided into a number of sub-zones which share an identical structure: their finer-ware categories, as mentioned earlier, include copies of the northern Kyushu finer-ware shape-types and their localised versions as well as some distinct local shape-types, whereas the coarser-ware categories pre-dominantly consist of distinctive local cooking jars, often genealogically connected to the final Jomon assemblage of the respective regions. A similar pattern can be seen in the western Japan style zone, although this region does not have a single 'centre of dominant influence' such as northern Kyushu.

This situation indicates the following possibility. The Genkai-nada coastal communities of the northern Kyushu region, which enjoyed an advantageous position in interacting, initially, with the communities on the southern coastline of the Korean peninsula and then with the Chinese Han commandery of Lelang in the north-western corner of the peninsula from some point of time around the turn of the Yayoi III, were regarded as a source of authority and prestige by the communities around them. Exotic material items produced with advanced technologies, imported from the Asian mainland, could only be obtained through the mediation of these communities. The emergent elite of these communities, competing over access to the available technologies and prestigious items, took advantage of their position and obtained different types of exotic materials, such as shells from the south, in order to enhance their authority over other competing community chiefs. The latter action would have involved strategic gift-giving, and it would have taken place at occasions such as funerals of the elite. This would explain the frequent presence of vessels imported from northern Kyushu or the local copies of the northern Kyushu equivalents in mortuary ritual contexts, where the living who buried these elite displayed their contacts with the elite of the northern Kyushu coastal region in order to establish or maintain their status. In contrast, local customs were retained in the case of more *mundane* contexts such as cooking.

This contrast between vessels used for public/sacred occasions and those used for mundane/domestic occasions can be observed in both the western and eastern Japanese style zones as well, albeit to different degrees, which indicates interesting implications for the gender relations during the phase. If we can infer that the following sets of dichotomies were in operation – that is, outside : inside :: sacred/public : mundane/domestic :: finer, non-local vessels : coarser, local vessels – we might be able to link them to the emerging dominance of males over females in various fields of social reproduction during this phase. As Hiromi Shitara illustrates, both the differential pictorial/material representations of the genders and the differential presence of males and females in elite burials point to the increasing dominance of males over females (Shitara 2007); as we will see later, the majority of those who were buried at the elite burial compounds were male (Mizoguchi 1995b, 2001). If cooking was an activity predominantly undertaken by females, as the majority of ethnographic examples suggest, and keeping in mind that many more males were buried in elite cemeteries where finer, non-local vessels were found in abundance, the differentiation of the pottery assemblage itself may well have not only reflected but also contributed to the reproduction of the emerging dominance of males over females.[17]

THE WESTERN HORIZON

The pottery assemblage of the western horizon is characterised by the use of various comb-marked decorations (*Kushi-gaki-mon*, 櫛描紋) during the Yayoi II and III and that of horizontal groove patterns (*O-sen-mon*, 凹線紋) during the Yayoi IV.

It has been revealed that variables of different attributes constituting individual shape-types show different distribution patterns (Fukasawa 1986, Mizoguchi 1987).[18] For instance, in the Yayoi IV, horizontal grooves became popular and were applied to a wide range of shape-types. The globular jars of the period can be divided into local sub-shape-types, cross-cut by the distribution of horizontal grooves (ibid.). The globular jars and other shape-types were rarely decorated in patterns other than horizontal grooves in the central Inland Sea area in the Yayoi IV, and these artefacts are found to be progressively decorated by comb-marked patterns as well as horizontal grooves as we move towards the east (Figure 6.5) (Mizoguchi 1987). The relationship between shape-types and different comb-marked patterns is complicated; they cross-cut one another in terms of their distributions. The distributions of local sub-shape-types show similar patterns: they often overlap one another to a significant degree. On the whole, it is virtually impossible to define individual style zones as clearly definable spatial units (Mizoguchi 1987, 146–153).

I would like to argue that this mixture of styles reflects the complex of interaction networks criss-crossing and cross-cutting communities, the attachment of different meanings to different shape-types and their attribute variables and the different ways in which they were mobilised to signify individual and/or communal identities. The 'exchange' of potters through inter-communal marriages would have certainly contributed to the formation of this extremely complex pattern, but that would not be a sufficient explanation for the emergence of this complex picture (Mizoguchi 1987). Further, kin-based sodalities cross-cutting villages would have played a significant role in the formation of the pattern.[19] It is possible to determine, however, the existence of some 'centres' where the distributions of a number of attribute variables overlap, such as the central Inland Sea area, the central Japan Sea coast area, the northern and southern parts of the Osaka Plain, the Nara Basin and so on (Fukasawa 1986; Mizoguchi 1987). These areas have substantial floodplains and had developed dense inter-settlement networks. The communities within each of these areas would have become increasingly interdependent in terms of the exchange of people, information and goods. Those factors would have led to the formation of local identities; however, as far as what we have seen is concerned, these identities would have been fairly loosely defined. They were also situated in a larger network of dense interactions which forms the vast style zone that is the western Japan horizon (Figure 6.1.B).

As mentioned earlier, the Kyushu region in the Yayoi IV saw the spread of certain finer ware shape-types from the coastal northern Kyushu area along

17 See Chapter 5.3 and Chapter 5, Footnote 23.
18 Although this is also true in the northern Kyushu horizon, the phenomenon is more prominent in the western Japan horizon and appears to be even more prominent in the eastern Japan horizon. The differences may reflect that in the mode of social interaction. I come back to the point in the following.

19 Yoshiki Fukasawa (2011) showed that pots used in mortuary practices that were conducted at rectangular burial compounds (see Section 6.2 of this chapter) were at times brought in from remote communities, at times more than 80 kilometres away from the compounds. He suggested that the phenomenon reflected that people had a type of social relations obliging them to attend each other's funerals that covered vast areas (ibid., 609–611). Such relations would have been mediated and supported by sodality-type connections.

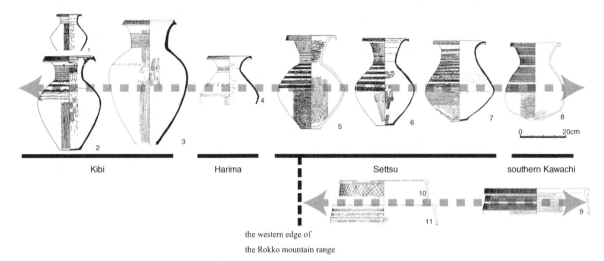

Kibi   Harima   Settsu   southern Kawachi

the western edge of
the Rokko mountain range

Figure 6.5. Above: The spatial variation of globular jars across the central Seto Inland Sea and the Kinki regions in the form of gradual changes of traits drawing a geographical cline. 1: Joto; 2: Joto; 3: Omachi; 4: Ozaki; 5: Tano; 6: Sakane; 7: Higashinara; 8: Shiroyama (1–3: from Masaoka [1992] and Takabatake [1992], originals from the respective excavation reports; 4–7: from Morioka [1985], originals from the respective excavation reports; 8–11: from Osaka PBE [1993]). Below: An example of the boundaries recognised by the spatial variation of certain pottery shape-types in the Seto Inland Sea and Kinki regions. Note that the distribution of the decorated bowl shape-type abruptly ceases around the western fringe of Rokko [六甲山] mountain range. 9: Kamei, 10 and 11: Tano (9: from Osaka PBE [1993]; 10 and 11: from Amagasaki MBE [1982]).

the routes through which goods that were important for the reproduction of the local communities and their internal as well as external relations were transported. I have argued that this reflected the emergence of an inter-regional hierarchy reproduced by the exclusive access enjoyed by the elite of the northern Kyushu coastal communities to the Han Chinese imports; these imported goods came to be used as 'prestige goods' (cf. Friedman and Rowlands 1977, 224–232), and the strategic copying, or emulation of the finer ware shape-types of the centre of distribution of those Chinese imports by local communities, which originated in the centre of distribution of these goods, would have become important for the reproduction of the local communities. The similar kind of phenomena did not occur in the western Japan horizon, where the complex scenario of the erstwhile Yayoi II and III continued. However, it is important to note that in the Yayoi IV clearer boundaries began to emerge between the areas which were recognised as some sort of 'centres'. For instance, the central Seto Inland Sea area and the area around Osaka Bay (including the northern and southern parts of the Osaka Plain) became distinctive because of the clear presence or absence of certain globular jar shape-types and a heavily decorated shallow bowl shape-type; the latter was commonly

used in the mortuary rituals of the Osaka Bay area but was non-existent in the central Inland Sea area (Figure 6.5) (Mizoguchi 1987, 148–149, 154). I would like to argue that this reflected the emergence of *regional identities* that were expressed on mortuary occasions and were mediated by different material items; instead of using the heavily decorated shallow bowl shape-type, the communities of the central Inland Sea area began to use heavily decorated pedestals in their mortuary rituals. This suggests that regional entities with distinct identities began to emerge in the western Japan horizon in the Yayoi IV, although intra- and inter-communal hierarchies were yet to develop at this time.[20]

THE EASTERN HORIZON

The horizon of eastern Japan, extending eastward from the eastern half of the Nobi Plain on the Pacific coast and in the same direction from the Hokuriku region on the Japan Sea coast, formed another large pottery style horizon. The horizon is defined by the common prevalence of the distinct globular jar shape-type, characterised by a fluent S-shaped profile and the tripartite division of the surface into distinct zones filled with

20 The subsequent development is covered in Chapter 7.

various, often highly symbolic, decorations or surface treatments (Figures 6.1.C–D, and 6.23.A–B) (for a comprehensive overview, see Ishiguro 2003, 307–316; Ishikawa 2003). Its north-eastern boundary extends to the southern edge of the northern Tohoku region in the present-day Miyagi prefecture (Figure 6.1.D).[21] The surface of the pottery in the particular shape-type mentioned above was marked either by scratched incisions made by the edge of shells, wooden implements or a bundle of glass stems or by cord-mark patterns. Cord-mark patterns were made by rolling twisted threads on the pottery surface. After applying either of those treatments, the surface was often burnished to create curvilinear/rectilinear cord-mark/scratched mark-free zones (e.g. the globular jars of the Yayoi III and IV in Figures 6.1.C–D). Various curvilinear and/or rectilinear patterns were bounded by incised lines. The use of scratched incisions appears to have ceased during the Yayoi III, and from then on, pottery surfaces were generally finished by smoothing and burnishing.

The prototype of this particular shape-type could be found in the eastern half of the Nobi Plain during the second half of the Yayoi I (Ishiguro 2003, 307–316). As mentioned earlier, the prototype, highly influenced by the Itazuke-style assemblage, was characteristically finished by scratching the surface using the edge of shells (see Figure 5.6 in this volume), and the technique continued to be used in its successors. In contrast, the distribution of cord-mark patterns was centred in the Tohoku region. The use of these three decorative patterns/surface treatment techniques, each of which has a distinct cultural-genealogical background, varies according to individual pots and shows the influence of regional trends, to some extent, in determining the frequently used patterns and their combination; for instance, the ratio of the use of cord-mark patterns increases as one moves eastward (see and compare Figures 6.1.C–D). However, these differences in pattern do not form any clearly definable style zones. In contrast, other shape-types show much wider diversities and smaller distributions. These, too, however, do not form explicit style zones and gradually shift their ratio of coexistence across the horizon.

It is always risky to read too much into the distribution pattern of material culture items. Because the relationship between material culture patterns and human thoughts and actions is not only considered highly complicated but its interpretation is also highly theory-laden, one tenable position would be to analyse it based on the context. In that regard, it is significant that the globular jar shape-type, the defining item of the horizon, was often used as a container of excarnated bones (Shitara 2008). Although it is examined in detail later, we know that the practice had already existed in eastern Japan during the Final Jomon period; however, the custom of containing bones in globular jars began in the late Yayoi I (ibid., 116). The practice of excarnation would have prolonged the engagement between the dead and the living and provided more opportunities for the living to confirm their relationships with the dead through the practice of removing small bones and using them as accessories and so on (e.g. perforated finger bone pendants from the Yatsuhagi cave site; see Shitara 2008, 22, fig. 4). This would have also provided the living with more opportunities to confirm their relationships with one another. It is also interesting to note that some cemeteries appear to reflect the presence of a clan-based segmentation (Shitara 2008, 210–219). Such a sodality-based organisation, as far as ethnographically observed examples are concerned, joins together a large number of communities and obligates their members to reciprocate each other's contributions in rites-of-passage-type occasions. Hideshi Ishikawa also suggests that a number of communities came together to process and bury the dead in individual cemeteries (Ishikawa 2000). These observations hint that the communal cooperation of many communities spread across large areas was an important theme of at least the mortuary discourse of the period. If that were true, the sharing of material items such as pottery would have been important in that it would have mediated and enabled communications between communities which did not constantly meet but had to occasionally cooperate. In that regard, the symbolic nature of some of the decorative patterns on the vessels may be significant (see the globular jars of the Yayoi III and IV in Figures 6.1.C–D). In contrast to the plain vessels of northern Kyushu and the mechanical repetition of comb-mark patterns in the decoration of western

21 The globular jar shape-type of the Tenjinbara style assemblage, for instance (see Saino 2011, 452, fig. 12.282).

Japan, many of the decorative motifs on the globular jars of the eastern Japan horizon appear to have signified something specific, and if we take the risk of circular argumentation, their use as containers of processed skeletal remains would suggest that the remains symbolised the 'spirits' of something. The excarnation of their bones might have transformed the dead individuals into the ancestors, who joined a world occupied by *various spirits* that played an important role in the Constitution of the shared world view of the communities.

There was a significant change in this large pottery horizon during the Yayoi IV period, when the so-called Miyanodai horizon began to gain popularity across the Tokai, Chubu and southern Kanto regions. The latter horizon is characterised by its distinctive globular jar shape-type (see the globular jar, right among the two, of the Yayoi IV in Figure 6.1.C). The specimens are long and flare-necked, and they are widest, i.e., with the largest diameter, on the lower half of the belly. They are often decorated with straight and/or wavy comb-marked patterns after finishing with scratches made by wooden plates (called 'Hakeme' [刷毛目], misleadingly meaning 'brush [*hake*] marks [*me*]'), but they are increasingly found to be decorated with cord-marked patterns as one moves to the east, where there also developed unique localised decorative motifs (e.g. Ishikawa 2003, 361–362). The origin of the Miyanodai horizon can be traced back to the Yayoi IV assemblages in the Owari and Mikawa provinces, and its expansion was associated with the corresponding expansion of the custom of burying the dead in rectangular-ditch-enclosed burial compounds, as also with other attributes of the western Japan horizon. The expansion also coincided with migrations on a substantial scale, including the movement of a large number of residential communities into formerly unoccupied terrains (cf. Ando 2003).[22] I shall discuss these phenomena later on in the chapter.

22 Prior to this phenomenon, it is pointed out that small groups originated in the eastern Seto Inland Sea area (i.e. ancient provinces of Harima and Settsu) migrated into the south-eastern fringe of the Tokai region and the southern Kanto region during the Yayoi III, that resulted in the establishment of fully rice-paddy-field-agriculture-based lifeways in those areas (e.g. Ishikawa 2011a). The Miyanodai phenomenon would have resulted from the subsequent population increase.

The Yayoi IV also saw the expansion of the parallel-groove-decorated assemblage to the western Hokuriku region, which effectively incorporated the region into the western Japan horizon (Hori 2011). This assemblage, as was the case in the expansion of the Miyanodai horizon, was associated with the introduction of the custom of burying the dead in rectangular-ditch-enclosed burial compounds in the region. These movements brought the eastern Japan horizon closer to the west, except for its north-eastern provinces, although the horizon continued to retain its unique characteristics.

3.2. Communication, Identity, Materiality

The three pottery horizons share a significant structural characteristic: finer wares in the assemblage tend to have larger distributions than coarser wares. The former vessels tended to be commonly used in occasions wherein people got together for feasting, funerals and other ritualistic occasions, for instance (e.g. the Yubihon'mura; see earlier discussion). In contrast, the coarser vessels tended to consist of cooking vessels and other such containers that were rarely used on public occasions. In other words, the finer wares were typically seen at and used to mediate communications during 'communal' occasions. These were also 'public' occasions in which those who were present knew how to act and communicate with one another and expected others to know the same. In that sense, these occasions served to help people find their own identity in their own eyes and in the eyes of others. The term *identity*, in this context, implies not only the conception of categories of people but also the obligations that correspond to those categories. The finer wares used on those occasions served to mediate the identification of those who were present, in a way, by embodying their communally shared morality and ethics. In addition, the materiality of those vessels preserved and activated these identities across the spatio-temporal horizon occupied by the communities that used them.

From among the three pottery style horizons, the eastern horizon, as mentioned earlier, is distinct from the other two in that the horizon is defined by the widespread use of a single shape-type across the vast area covered by the horizon, that is, the characteristic globular jar (Figures 6.1.C–D). As already mentioned, during the Yayoi II and III periods, the specimens were often used as burial containers of (processed) ancestral remains. The northern Kyushu and the western horizons are both composed of a chain of small style zones overlapping one another. Although some shape-types were more widespread than were others and were distributed across a number of sub-style-zones in these horizons, there was no shape-type like that of the globular jar in the eastern horizon, which spread across almost the whole of the horizon. This obviously does not imply that a common morality and code of ethics were shared and observed across the horizon. However, this suggests that that eastern horizon may have witnessed a mode of inter-communal communication and reproduction of identities of various types and scales that was different from those experienced by the other horizons; this mode, which occurred on a wider scale and was characterised by more flexible communal collaborations based on the fulfilment of reciprocal obligations, may have been embodied and mediated by the character of the eastern horizon.

This difference appears to be correlated with the differences in the way people organised their settlements, buried and commemorated their dead, prayed for their well-being and produced and circulated goods. Let us begin by examining the settlements.

4. ORGANISING, DIVIDING AND CONNECTING THEMSELVES: SETTLEMENTS

4.1. *General Trajectories*

THE NORTHERN KYUSHU AND THE WESTERN HORIZONS
In the horizons of northern Kyushu and western Japan, after a period of a seemingly rapid and significant increase, the number of settlements remained fairly steady during the Middle Yayoi period, though the rate of fluctuation was found to vary between regions. The significant and rapid increase in the number of settlements which occurred during the final phase of the Yayoi I and the Yayoi II appears to have largely resulted from the 'budding off' of new settlements from

pre-existing ones (e.g. Kondo 1983, 104–108; Ozawa 2006).

Of course, we have to be cautious about connecting the phenomenon of mushrooming settlements to an actual drastic increase in population size; it is possible that the population increase was neither very sudden nor very significant but only slowly reached the carrying capacity (the size of the population that can be sustained by the agricultural potential of a locality exploited using a certain technology), which may have resulted in the budding-off phenomenon within a relatively short period of time. Another distinct possibility is that the general cooling of the climate during the final phase of the Yayoi I and the Yayoi II (see Chapter 4.2) may have reduced the carrying capacity of localities, resulting in hamlet-scale groupings budding off to previously unused terrain, without much population increase. It is also possible that the preexisting necessity of 'living together', caused by factors such as the chronic threat of raids (e.g. Johnson and Earle 2000, 142–179, 179–193) and/or the necessity of collaboration in farming practices, was reduced. A tentative calculation of the sum total of the increase in number of settlement areas in a selected region during the time showed a significant increase in the size of the occupied areas (e.g. Tanaka 1991, 496). The fact that no drastic change occurred in the way the settlements were internally organised, e.g. how densely the houses were situated and so on, suggests that the population, in effect, increased quite significantly and rapidly. In addition, many of the budded-off hamlets, as will be seen in the following, banded together and formed individual villages. This suggests that the necessity of people's living together in groups was not necessarily reduced. All these points suggest that population increase, despite the cooling climate, is a likely cause of the budding-off phenomenon.

One characteristic shared by a majority of the Middle Yayoi settlements (hereafter called 'villages') of the northern Kyushu and the western horizons is that each of them commonly consists of several residential units – a pattern that became particularly visible during the Yayoi II and III, probably as a result of the above-mentioned process, i.e., the budding-off of child hamlets from the parent villages to form new villages in newly occupied areas (Figure 6.6). The scale of such a residential unit varies. In the preceding case, around five pit dwellings with storage facilities and a communal area commonly comprise one such residential unit (e.g. Kondo 1959). However, at times, such a residential unit can be much larger. Some examples of such residential units from the Kinki region, though not excavated in their entirety, are larger than an average-sized village in terms of the size of the area they occupy, and it is inferred that they comprised tens of houses at any given time (Wakabayashi 2001). Hereinafter, let us call such a residential unit simply a 'hamlet'. Yayoi villages commonly comprised a number of hamlets.

Storage facilities appear to have been communally owned and controlled by a single hamlet in most of the cases; storage pits, or raised-floor buildings that were inferred to have been granaries, were often clustered in a corner of a hamlet, and no specific connection can be determined between them and the individual houses comprising the hamlet. The fact that many such hamlets have their own burial grounds and shared storage facilities suggest that they were *corporate groupings* of some sort; each of them would have been the minimum unit of ownership, conducting their own mortuary and ancestor rituals (Figure 6.6).

I would like to posit that those hamlets comprising individual Middle Yayoi villages were parts, or 'segments', of larger, kin-based corporate groups cross-cutting a number of villages. In the previous chapter, we tentatively called them 'sodalities' (Service 1962, 13–15, 115–121) and inferred that they were part of larger descent groups, such as 'clans'. Such groups would have functioned as units in which various social obligations were fulfilled, and hence they would have mediated the inter-village networks through which goods, people and information flowed along the principles of reciprocity. The presence of a number of segments of such *sodalities* in individual villages would have been advantageous to the village in many ways. Such kin-based sodalities are commonly *exogamous*, prohibiting marriage between their members (ibid.; Keesing 1975, 39–42). The presence of many segments of such *sodalities* in individual villages would have allowed marriages between the residents of a village as long as they

lived in different hamlets and hence belonged to different sodalities (ibid., 41, 43, fig. 17). This would also have made the maintenance of inter-village relations easier, because the sodalities would have connected the villages which they cross-cut by various mutual obligations, commonly concerning the rites of passage of the members and conflicts with other sodalities (Tuzin 2001). Various goods, pieces of information and people would also have moved through such sodality-based networks. This would have enabled the reproduction of identities in terms of three different natures and scales: the village-membership-based identity, the sodality-membership-based identity and the local identity shared within the area covered by the sodalities.

By the Yayoi III, larger settlements with the characteristics of regional centres, such as the distribution centres of goods and materials, centres of production, centres for intensive ritual activities and so on, emerged in major flood plains of the northern Kyushu and western horizons (Akiyama 2007, 699–803). These regional centres often have an extremely large cemetery which cannot be associated with any one of the hamlets located in the centre (Figures 6.6.B and 6.9; Mizoguchi 2006b). Such a large cemetery might have been co-owned by the hamlets constituting the regional centre. Alternatively, it might have functioned as the 'necropolis' of the entire regional community; the residents of the other villages constituting the regional community may have brought their dead to be buried in the large central cemetery. This is an important piece of information concerning the way in which individual regional communities were structured and their members connected and identified themselves with respect to one another.

After the Yayoi I period, the settlements of the northern Kyushu horizon are rarely found to have been enclosed by a ditch. Towards the end of the Middle Yayoi, i.e., the Yayoi IV, there were some settlements, mostly regional centres (such as the Yoshinogari [吉野ヶ里] settlement in Saga prefecture), that became enclosed by a (often V-sectioned) ditch or ditches. Some of these ditches are more than 5 metres deep, and their defensive potential is all too apparent. In the Hie-Naka (比恵—那珂) settlement, an extremely large settlement occupying the centre of Fukuoka Plain

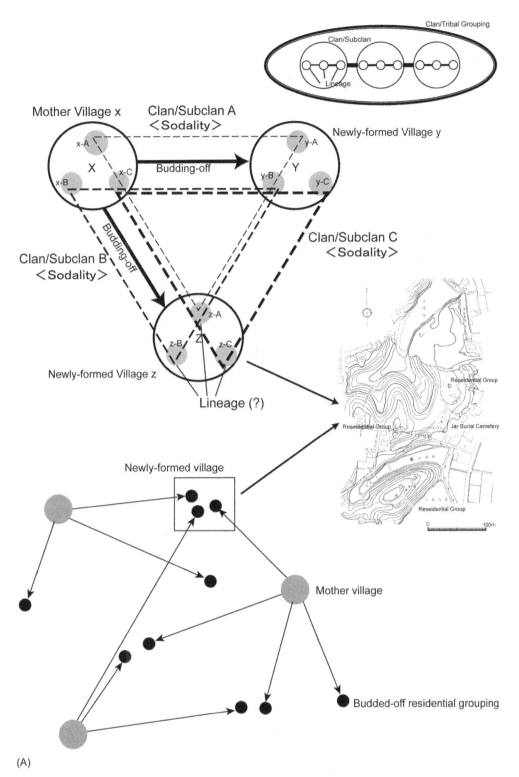

Figure 6.6. A: A schematised model for the formation of villages as comprised of residential groupings (hamlets) that have budded off from preexisting settlements, with the plan of the Takaradai (宝台) settlement (Yayoi III and IV), Fukuoka prefecture (after Fukuoka MBE 1970). **B**: A schematised model for the development of large central-place-type settlements and allied facilities attached to them, with the plan of the northern burial mound (Yayoi III) of the Yoshinogari (吉野ヶ里) settlement (after Saga PBE 1997).

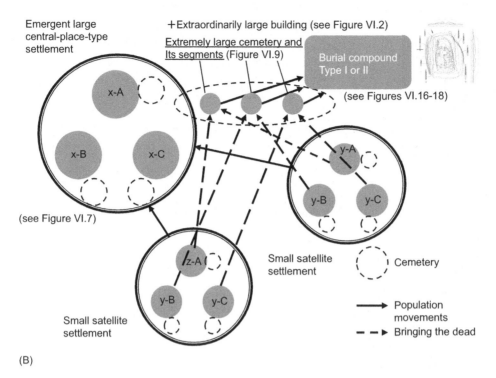

Figure 6.6 (*continued*)

in northern Kyushu, it is argued that deep V-sectioned ditches were cut to not only enclose but also systematically divide the residential groupings constituting this huge residential community, which occupied approximately 100 hectares of land (Kusumi 2008). The available evidence is patchy because the picture is comprised of an accumulation of small-scale urban rescue digs. However, it appears certain that the community was comprised of distinct large-scale residential units, possibly individually enclosed, and that each of them probably comprised a number of sodality segments/descent groupings (see the preceding discussion and Figure 6.6). This has led some to categorise the site, and the Sugu site also located in the Fukuoka plain (Figure 6.7), as *urban* settlements (ibid.). In the western horizon, from the Yayoi II onwards, many of the regional centres were either partially or completely enclosed by ditches (e.g. Morioka 2011, 282–291). Some of these ditches show traces of water-logging, from which some scholars infer that they functioned as drainage ditches. Indeed, it is entirely possible that some of these ditches might have been used for drainage, but others would have performed defensive functions, keeping in mind that the ditches were, at times, dug on a higher ground or even on a slope (e.g. in the Kamo

[加茂] site in Hyogo prefecture; ibid., 285, fig. 6, 286).

The significant increase in the number and scale of settlements during the phase leads to the inference that a degree of social complexity and hierarchy were achieved by the Yayoi IV. It has been argued that as many as four hierarchical layers of leadership – that is, the village leadership, village group leadership, floodplain-scale group leadership and regional-scale (consisting of more than two neighbouring floodplains) group leadership – developed during the Middle Yayoi period (Terasawa 1990). In fact, it is often emphasised that this hierarchy of leadership emerged out of chronic conflicts (in the case of northern Kyushu; Terasawa 2000, 145–163) and the need to mediate the increasing flow of goods, people and information. Kazuo Hirose argues that the regional centres were formed by the will of such leaders, forming their own rank-based corporate grouping (Hirose 2003, 43–56). However, it should be noted that those large, central-place-type settlements lack any clear trace of internal hierarchisation (Mizoguchi 2010a, 27; pp. 34–35, footnote 6). In other words, there are no clear indications of either the differentiation of the descent-group-based elite or the ascription of their status. So far, archaeologists have neither discovered any clear example of an elite-precinct-type of compound (with the exception of a possible rectangular ditch-enclosed compound discovered in the Mikumo settlement of northern Kyushu, the inside of which has not yet been explored; Sumi 2006, 20–21) nor found traces of a separate sector with larger houses and greater storage facilities continuing over a certain period of time.[23] Instead, they have discovered extremely large rectangular buildings at the centre of the sites in the Kinki region and at locations close to the high-ranked cemeteries in northern Kyushu (Figure 6.2). Many northern Kyushu examples, from their structure, can be inferred to have been genealogically derived from the Etsuji central building (Ozawa 2006), as discussed in the previous chapter. This connection suggests that during the Middle Yayoi period, these were the buildings where the metaphorical-transformative connection between the death and regeneration of rice grains and human beings was confirmed and encouraged through ritual practices. The Kinki examples are often associated with traces of rituals regarding various production and subsistence activities. The Ikegami-Sone site, for instance, has yielded octopus-fishing jars deposited in a pit and a well situated in front of an extremely large rectangular building with a raised floor (Figure 6.2.B; Akiyama 2007, 473–474). In front of the building, there was a large well furnished with a huge, hollowed tree trunk about 2 metres in inner diameter (ibid., 449–450). This indicates that the extremely large rectangular buildings of the Middle Yayoi period in western Japan were not elite residential buildings but buildings used for communal rituals, probably to ensure the successful reproduction of the communities and their subsistence activities.

23 Takeo Kusumi (2006) argues that the Ichinomachi (一の町) site of Itoshima municipality, northern Kyushu, comprised of large-scale buildings, some raised-floored, some walled, possibly surrounded by stakes to form a rectangular compound, is an early example of such elite precincts. However, the duration of the possible compounds, known from excavated relative-datable pots, spans from the Early Middle Yayoi to the Late Yayoi (Kawai 2009; Mizoguchi 2010a, 34–35 [note 6]). It is an exceptionally long duration, and suggests that the compound may have been a public-communal facility like the extraordinary large buildings, whose functions investigated earlier (Mizoguchi 2010a, pp. 34–35, footnote 6).

Some ethnographic works have also revealed that in order to sustain a residential community of over a certain scale, for example, more than a couple of hundred individuals, it is necessary to develop certain specific mechanisms, such as internal hierarchisation, or devices, such as dual organisations, in order to sustain and enhance communal cohesion (Tuzin 2001). The presence of extremely large rectangular buildings in many of the large regional centres of western Japan and their inferred function suggest that the latter was the aim: the communal cohesion of those large-scale residential communities was probably maintained through the performance of communal rituals involving rice, other foodstuffs, the dead and the ancestors conducted in and around those buildings. Besides, some of those buildings show the trace of rebuiliding for a number of times within a relatively short period of time. For instance, at the Ubihon'mura, as illustrated above, an extraordinarily large rectangular building was repeatedly rebuilt at almost exactly the same spot, adjacent to an elite cemetery, for at least five times (Figure 6.2.A: see preceding discussion and Saga PBE 2003). As will be seen later, dual organisations might also have been involved in the maintenance of communal cohesion.

In summary, the archaeological evidence from the northern Kyushu and western horizons shows that the villages (1) commonly comprised a number of hamlets and (2) can be broadly classified into two strata in terms of their scale, that is, larger and smaller villages, and their function, that is, regional centres and satellite settlements (Figures 6.6 and 6.7). The evidence also suggests that (3) the former often contained an extremely large cemetery (Figure 6.9), which might have functioned as a shared necropolis for the regional community of which the concerned village functioned as the centre, and that (4) despite some signs of hierarchisation, including the emergence of differences in the treatment of the dead, there is no discernible, definite sign of social hierarchy, for example, the emergence of elite precincts, in the villages.

The end of the Middle Yayoi and the beginning of the Yayoi V saw a widespread change: many of the smaller settlements disappeared, which threatened the continuation (and in some cases, the enlargement) of the regional centres as well as particular hamlets associated with them in northern Kyushu; this was accompanied by the emergence of settlements of a considerable scale located on hilltops across the regions around Osaka Bay in western Japan (e.g. Kosobe-Shibatani [古曽部-芝谷] site of Takatsuki municipality, Osaka prefecture; Terasawa 2000, 200, 210–211). In many areas, the latter phenomenon appears to have coincided with the abandonment of many preexisting settlements located at the bottom of floodplains. The cause of this change is commonly attributed to the rising social tension caused by (a) the steadily increasing population pressure worsened by climatic deterioration and/or (b) heightened competition over access to vital resources for the sustenance of developing agrarian communities. With regard to (a), we have already inferred that climatic change was a contributory factor. The period might have experienced a colder spell with larger precipitation after a period of relatively high temperature (Chapter 4.2). Traces of large-scale flooding have been confirmed in the layer formation of sandy deposits covering living surfaces in some of the regional centres around the Osaka Bay and Nara Basin areas.[24] This flooding might have become serious enough for the inhabitants to decide to relocate their villages. However, many of the large-scale hilltop settlements located in the vicinity of the Osaka Bay area were short-lived, and most of the smaller abandoned settlements were reoccupied after a short while in northern Kyushu (Ozawa 2000). Because of this relocation, we cannot simply attribute the cause of the change solely to the climate. With regard to (b), the western horizon and the regions around the Osaka Bay area, in particular, saw the increasing use of iron tools, competition over access to them and attempts to dominate or monopolise their circulation (Negita 1998). As we shall see in the following, however, the centre for the circulation of iron source materials and iron tools firmly remained in northern and central Kyushu, without moving eastward to the eastern Seto Inland Sea region. Because the iron-circulation thesis is also difficult to sustain, we will attempt to determine

the most feasible model for the phenomenon in Chapter 7.

THE EASTERN JAPAN HORIZON

In the eastern Japan horizon, the picture is quite different. During the Yayoi II, the settlement scale remained fairly small, with each village commonly consisting of a single residential unit (Takase 2004, 168–197).

The Yayoi III saw the gradual incorporation of Hokuriku region into the western Japan horizon. The village-scape of the region became akin to that of the western horizon (cf. Yasu 2009), also coinciding with the expansion of the comb-marked pottery horizon into the region (Kawai 2003). On the Pacific coast, the recently discovered site of Nakazato (中里) in Odawara City of Kanagawa prefecture, dating from the mid-Yayoi III, shows an identical village-scape to the contemporaneous settlements in the western Japan horizon (cf. Odawara MBE 2000; Takesue 2002, 43–45; Ishikawa 2011a, 106–108); an extraordinarily large rectangular building (rebuilt on the same spot at least a couple of times) was at the centre of the site surrounded by at least five clusters of pit dwellings with storage buildings, and scholars claim that this site shows traces of direct interaction, possibly involving small-scale migrations, with the Kansai region (specifically with the northern part of the Osaka Plain and the eastern Seto Inland sea area, based on the pottery analysis; ibid.).[25]

During the Yayoi IV, some settlements in the Nagano Basin of Chubu region contained a number of residential units and their associated burial grounds, like the settlements in the west (e.g. Baba 2008). One of them, the Matsubara (松原) site, suddenly became a large settlement at some point of time during the Yayoi IV, and Shin'ichiro Baba argues that this sudden growth was caused by the immigration of a number of formerly separate communities into the region (ibid.). In this site, similar to the northern Kyushu and western Japan counterparts, archaeologists have not found any

24 The famous northern sandy deposit band of the Karako-Kagi (唐古-鍵) site of Nara prefecture (Suenaga [1943] 1976) was a layer caused by a severe flooding, taking place sometime in the Late Middle Yayoi (i.e. the Yayoi IV), and destroying large extents of this largest central-placed-type settlement of the Nara Basin.

25 Ishikawa (2011a, 108) points out that the pots brought in from the eastern Seto Inland Sea area include a significant number of globular jars suitable for the storage of liquid substance or grains, and argues that they do not necessarily reflect migrations but rather suggest interactions between the areas through direct movements of people, probably by sea.

clear indication of established ascribed hierarchy (ibid., 157–158).

The Yayoi IV also saw the expansion of the Miyanodai pottery assemblage horizon, which had originated in the eastern periphery of the western Japan horizon, to the east as far as the river Tone. This movement coincided with the reorganisation of settlements (e.g. Ando 2003). The hills along the Tsurumi River on the western coast of Tokyo Bay saw the sudden emergence of a large number of ditch-enclosed, single-residential-unit settlements in the Yayoi IV (ibid.). The scale and contents of these settlements were fairly identical, apart from the presence of some particularly large settlements, and one of these – the Orimotonishihara (折本西原) settlement – had an extremely large ditch-enclosed rectangular mortuary compound situated at its centre (Yokohama-shi maizo-bunkazai chosa iinkai 1980), as if to represent the ties and social integration among those settlements (Ando 2008, 66–67). That they disappeared again after a fairly short time, probably moved to elsewhere, suggests that the group formed a large corporate grouping of a 'tribal' kind. Such movements can be recognised in the Kanto region from the Yayoi IV through the Early Kofun period in different areas in different timings. In the eastern half of the eastern horizon, that is, in the Tohoku region, however, the picture was not much different from that in the previous phase: the settlements appear to have basically continued to be composed of a single small residential unit.[26]

The development of a large pottery horizon and of the custom of burying processed bones in stylistically quite similar pottery vessels (illustrated in the previous section) may have been organically related to the general picture of the east. The sharing of certain material items would have helped in reproducing shared identities, which in turn would have helped in reproducing communications which were not very regular or frequent. Prolonging the engagement of the living with the dead through the practice of reburial (e.g. Shitara 2008, chap. 1) would also have increased the num-ber of occasions on which people from separate residential communities gathered together, which would also have helped the maintenance of social networks. Moreover, such gatherings would have been organised on the basis of large-scale sodalit-ies such as moieties, which would have connected sparsely distributed single-residential-unit villages together. Instead of developing into villages and regional centres made up of multiple residential groups, communities of the east, and those in the north-eastern half of this horizon, in particu-lar, developed specific types of practices and their media which could be used to reproduce social networks despite the fact that these communit-ies were not able to meet frequently and interact densely. In that regard, the fact that the disappear-ance of the practice of processed bone burials took place around the time when the eastern horizon began to see the expansion of the type of settle-ments, each of which was comprised of a num-ber of residential units, is suggestive. The residen-tial units comprising such a settlement, as argued, would have been segments of sodalities spreading across a number of settlements, and their func-tion would have made the reproduction of social ties through the fulfilment of various social oblig-ations more efficient and effective than before. That may have made redundant the prolongation of contacts with the dead that was a tacit func-tional characteristic of the processed bone burial custom.

4.2. Why and How Did the Regional Centres Emerge, and How Were They Sustained?

I have already considered the question of why indi-vidual villages in the northern Kyushu and West-ern horizons consisted of a number of hamlets; as a tentative answer, we have posited that the hamlets constituting a village were segments of clan-type corporate groupings, or sodalities, cross-cutting a number of villages. We have also inferred some functional advantages of the presence of a number of such segments in individual villages: it allows intra-village marriages to take place, because clans are commonly exogamous and marriage partners in such villages can be found from segments of clans other than one's own (Keesing 1975). Such a social structure allows for the reproduction of at least three different levels of identities, that is,

---

26 However, the Yayoi III saw the establishment of large-scale rice paddy fields on the bottom of alluvial plains (Saino 2011, 470–471). Saino infers that sud-den decrease of excavated settlement across the Tohoku region during this period (ibid., 458–459) have resulted from the relocation of settlements to low-lying areas.

the clan-based identity, the village-based identity and the regional-group-based identity (a regional group being comprised of the sodalities whose segments are present in the villages constituting the regional group) (Figure 6.6); moreover, it allows an efficient inter-settlement flow of things, people and information. In addition, it allows the formation of a large-scale corporation for rice paddy field farming. However, as mentioned earlier, the cohabitation of more than a certain number of individuals would have proved to be difficult, if not impossible, without the implementation of certain mechanisms to maintain the cohesion of the grouping (Tuzin 2001, esp. 66–77). This number would have varied according to the infrastructural-technological and cultural-historical conditions. However, it is commonly accepted that a couple of hundred villagers is a common upper limit, above which it would have been difficult to maintain group cohesion based on face-to-face contact (ibid.). In many small-scale societies, however, this number appears to have been much smaller (ibid.).

Individual hamlets constituting a village often consisted of around three to five pit dwellings and some storage facilities, and we can infer from the size of the floor space that such a dwelling was occupied by around five or six individuals. That means that around thirty individuals occupied a hamlet. The Sugu site, another extremely large regional centre in the Fukuoka floodplain of northern Kyushu, is said to have been comprised of approximately around forty such hamlets in the Middle Yayoi period (Inoue 2009). If each of them were occupied by 30 individuals, it turns out that between 1,200 and 1,500 individuals lived in this settlement, covering a 2-kilometre-by-1-kilometre piece of land situated on low-lying hilltops and the surrounding floodplains (Figure 6.7). This is certainly an extreme example. However, the regional centres of western Japan in the Middle Yayoi period often contained more than three or four hamlets, which are often much larger than the five-pit-dwelling unit (Wakabayashi 2001). This suggests that many of them exceeded the magic number of a couple of hundred in terms of number of inhabitants.

The preceding figures indicate that the regional centres of western Japan in the Middle Yayoi period were unusual, to say the least. This is even more significant because, as mentioned earlier, there is no clear trace of internal centralisation and hierarchisation in them. In order to understand the nature and character of these large settlements, we have to investigate (a) why so many people decided to live together and (b) how their cohabitation and communal coherence were sustained.

Let us now return to the Sugu site. Most of the forty to fifty hamlets in the settlement were built in the Yayoi III (Inoue 2009, 122–128). Before that, only five or six settlements had existed in the area, and they were spread out in a scattered manner (ibid., 121–122). This indicates that the sudden emergence of so many hamlets during the Yayoi III cannot be explained as the result of population growth in the preexisting settlements in the area; the phenomenon can only be understood as a result of migration. Moreover, the fact that the migrants chose to live in separate hamlets with distinct burial grounds attached to each of them strongly suggests that they came from *different sodalities*. The area, which covers a low-lying hill sticking out of the mountain range separating the Fukuoka Plain from the floodplains of the Chikugo River to the south, has many small valleys. It would have been possible to construct paddies at the bottom of these valleys without the input of much labour; since spring water would have taken care of their irrigation, it would not have been necessary to dig substantial irrigation ditches. However, the same conditions were to be obtained at many other foothills of the mountain range. In addition, even if large-scale collaboration would have helped in the construction and maintenance of paddy fields, large-scale cohabitation would have generated many risks, such as famine – caused by either flooding or drought – which could easily have negated the advantages of large-scale cohabitation.

It seems much more feasible that the high 'centrality' of the location as a natural node of inter-communal networks attracted migration when the network began to function in a substantial manner. Following the Yayoi II period, which witnessed the sudden increase in the number of settlements, as mentioned earlier, due to population increase and the budding off of small hamlets from preexisting residential communities in many floodplains across western Japan, the Yayoi III saw an increase in the flow of goods and products made of rare

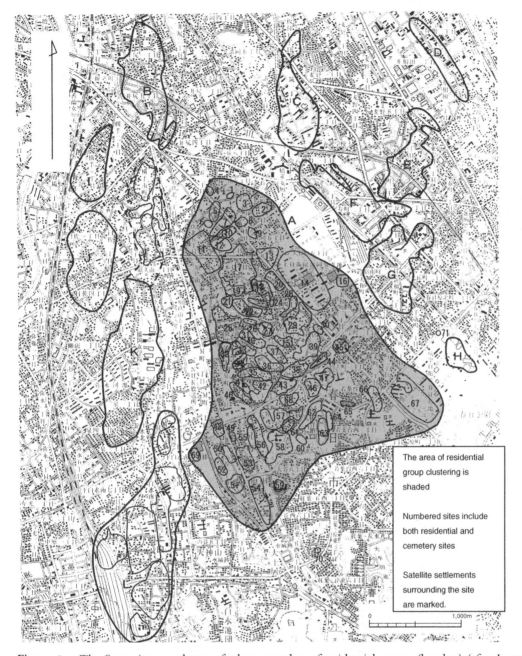

Figure 6.7. The Sugu site as a cluster of a large number of residential groups (hamlets) (after Inoue 2009). This is one of the largest of all the Yayoi period settlement sites in the archipelago. Many of the residential groups constituting this extraordinarily large settlement site are associated with storage facilities and cemeteries, and inferred to have been communal groupings probably having characteristics of lineage groupings. See Figure 6.6.

sources, such as lithic tree-felling tools made of volcanic (basalt) stones, whose distribution was limited (e.g. Shimojo 1985; also see Section 5.1 in this chapter). The period also saw an increase in the production and circulation/distribution of bronze implements, including weapons deposited mainly as grave goods in northern Kyushu and *Dotaku* bronze bells and other bronze implements deposited as ritual tools across the Seto Inland Sea and Kinki areas. Many of the regional centres exis-

ted in locations which could be easily accessed from a number of areas separated and bounded by rivers and/or mountain ranges. The Sugu site, for instance, was located on the southern end of Fukuoka Plain, connecting the communities of the plain with the networks of settlements beyond the surrounding mountain range extending to the east, south-east and south-west (Figures 6.4.B and 6.7). The other mega-settlement of the Fukuoka Plain, the Hie-Naka settlement, was situated between Sugu and the coast, connecting the former with the coastal settlement communities.

It has been pointed out that regional centres were distributed along regular intervals, often at a distance of about 5 kilometres from other settlements (Figure 6.8; Sakai 1984). In large floodplains such as the Kawachi Plain and the Nara Basin of the Kinki region, which had a dense distribution of a number of central-place-type villages,[27] the situation appears to have been much more complicated because the individual residential groups (i.e. hamlets) constituting individual central-place-type villages were as populous as the average-sized settlements found elsewhere (Wakabayashi 2001), and their sizes significantly changed through time. However, the areas surrounding these central settlements, as if forming linear networks with the settlements, were distributed along fairly regular intervals (Sakai 1984). This suggests that a sort of 'cumulative effect' initiated by minute differences between settlements culminated in the differentiation of the regional centres from the smaller 'satellite' settlements (Mizoguchi 2008, 87–88).[28]

In the case of the network of settlements practising jar burial(s) furnished with grave goods including Early Han Chinese bronze mirror(s), the *centrality* of the individual settlements in the network, calculated using a network-theory-based formula, shows some interesting outcomes pertaining to the situation (for details concerning the following discussion, see pp. 154–159 in this chapter; for details regarding this method and its underlying theoretical premises, see Chapter 8.3). This centrality is calculated purely based on the *topological* position of individual settlements as nodes in the network by taking into account how many other nodes were connected to a particular node, how many other nodes had to pass through a given node during the shortest journey to those

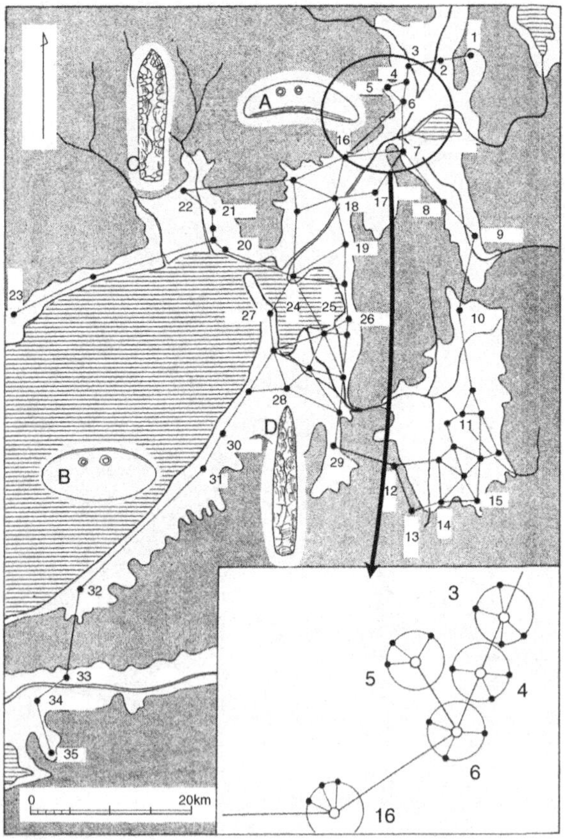

Figure 6.8. The distribution and the network of regional centre-type settlements in the southern Kinki region (after Tsude [1989] with additions and alterations; created by Tsude by referring to Ryuichi Sakai's [1984] model). Site names: 1: Nakatomi, 2: Fukakusa, 3: Nakakuze, 4: Morimoto, 5: Imasato, 6: Kotari, 7: Yawata, 8: Okamidani, 9: Wakudenomiya, 10: Saki, 11: Karako, 12: Takenouchi, 13: Kamotsuba, 14: Niizawa, 15: Daifuku, 16: Ama, 17: Tanokuchiyama, 18: Shibou, 19: Uzumasa, 20: Tanou, 21: Miyanomae, 22: Kamo, 23: Kusunokiarata, 24: Morishoji, 25: Uryudo, 26: Kitoragawa, 27: Morinomiya, 28: Uriwari, 29: Kishi, 30: Yotsuike, 31: Ikegami, 32: Otokosato, 33: Kitatai, 34: Otakuroda, 35: Okamura. Characteristic local products: A: black slate-made reaping knives, B: crystalline schist-made reaping knives, C: Nijosan mountain Sanukitoid-made stone spearheads, D: Kanayama mountain Sanukitoid-made stone daggers. Note that the inter-settlement relations indicated in the inset is too simplistic (see Figure 6.6). With kind permission from the Iwanami Shoten Publishing Co.

27 See Footnote 6 to this chapter.

28 Yoshiyuki Tanaka's (1995) osteoarchaeological investigations have revealed that the dominant kin-organisation of the period is bilineal, that suggests that a newly married pair could choose either wife's or husband's original village to live. That would have resulted in widening differences in scale between settlements, and contributed to the emergence of regional centres and their acquirement of central-place functions.

other nodes and so on (Borgatti, Everett, and Freeman 2002). However, the calculations do *not* take into account any other attribute of the given node such as its potential carrying capacity and so on. The Sugu settlement appears to have been the most central node according to many of the measurements. Its extremely high score in the betweenness

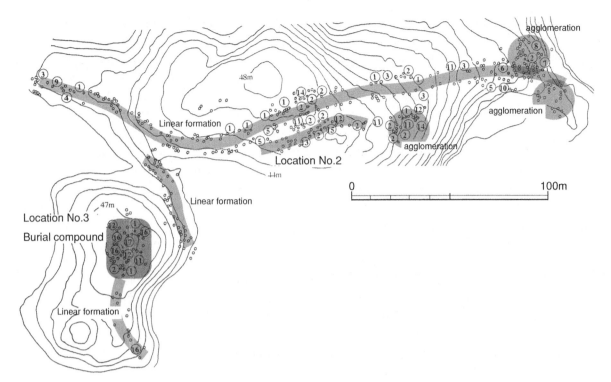

Figure 6.9. The Kuma–Nishioda loc. 2 and 3 cemeteries, Fukuoka prefecture. Numbers in the circles: mt-DNA types. Note rows of burials developed along probable paths (marked by shades) connecting hamlets comprising the Kuma-Nishioda settlement. Location no. 3 is a burial compound situated on a hilltop. There is no substantial feature, such as an earthen mound, to mark it. Agglomerations of burials basically formed in the Yayoi IV, after the Yayoi III when the burial rows developed (after Shinoda and Kunisada 1994).

centrality measurement (see Table 6.6) indicates that the site was the most significant *mediator* of interactions in the network. The Mikumo settlement, the other paramount centre of the network in terms of the number of Early Han Chinese bronze mirrors found buried with its elite, however, comes consistently below Sugu in the centrality calculation, and in some measurements even below some other settlements where only one Early Han bronze mirror was buried with their elite (see Table 6.1–5). These observations suggest that basically their high *network centrality* led to the rapid expansion of the regional centres, though some other factors, such as differential accessibility to outside (and hence precious/prestigeous) resources such as Han-imported goods, would have also contributed to it. I come back to the issue later in the chapter.

In that case, how was *cohesion* sustained among the ever-increasing population occupying the individual regional centres? As mentioned earlier, archaeologists have not yet discovered any clear evidence of separate elite residential areas/ compounds in the regional centres of western

Japan, with very few possible exceptions.[29] This suggests that cohesion among inhabitants was sustained by means *other than* the hierarchisation of social relations and the emergence of a decision-making system – one of the most common solutions used to cope with problems generated by the increasing population. If we consider the means used by inhabitants to cope with the potential problems of cohesion and order that would have been generated by the large-scale cohabitation, we have recourse to two unique traits of the regional centres: extremely large burial grounds (Figure 6.9) and extremely large rectangular buildings (Figure 6.2).

The former are commonly not associated with any particular hamlet that is part of a regional

29 It has recently been reported that a straight-running ditch, which might be marking a side of a square compound dating from the Yayoi IV, was discovered in the Mikumo site of Fukuoka prefecture (Sumi 2006, 21, 23). Hiroyuki Sumi infers that the compound, if it were indeed the case, was a elite residential sector. In order to investigate the validity of the claim, however, we have to wait for further excavations to take place.

centre, and at times, the number of dead persons buried there exceeds one thousand (e.g. the Kuma-Nishioda [限·西小田] locations 2 and 3 [Chikushino MBE 1993; Shinoda and Kunisada 1994] and the Shiwaya-Yon'notsubo [志波屋四ノ坪] cemetery at the Yoshinogari site [Saga PBE 1994, 63–65, 72]). The hamlets constituting individual regional centres have their own burial grounds, mostly situated right next to them, suggesting that those who were buried in the extremely large burial grounds were not necessarily residents of the regional centres but could have originated from elsewhere (Figure 6.6.B; Mizoguchi 2006b). These large cemeteries were often associated with square burial compounds wherein certain select individuals, at times buried with grave goods such as bronze weapons and, in the Yayoi IV, Early Han Chinese bronze mirrors, and/or shell armlets, iron weapons and so on, were laid to rest (see Figure 6.4). Some of these individuals are buried under very low burial mounds, though the mounds of some of the larger examples, such as the Yoshinogari north tumulus (see Figure 6.17), are quite substantial (Saga PBE 1997, 29–44); in the case of the Yoshinogari tumulus, the mound is estimated to have at least been 4.5 m high (Figure 6.17; ibid., 29).[30]

Kuma-Nishioda location 3 is an example of such square tumuli, located close to the extremely large linear cemetery at Kuma-Nishioda (限一西小田) location 2. Mitochondrial DNA (mt-DNA) was successfully extracted from eleven skeletal remains contained in burial jars and deposited in those burial grounds. While thirteen different sequence-types were found in location 2, six sequence-types – including two sequence types which were absent from location 2 – were found in the tumuli-like hilltop burial grounds of location 3 (Figure 6.9; Shinoda and Kunisada 1994). This can be interpreted to indicate that these individuals originated from distant communal groupings and were either married into the community which buried its dead at that particular burial ground or brought from distant communal groupings to be buried here. In any case, we know that people who did not originally reside in the village were buried in this burial ground. This supports the idea, albeit indirectly, that the extremely large burial grounds

were places where even the dead of people who did not reside in the large villages were brought for burial (Figure 6.6.B; Mizoguchi 2006b). It is most natural to assume that the large cemeteries were places where a number of clan-type sodalities spread across a number of villages brought their chosen dead for burial. If we keep in mind that burials are occasions wherein various social obligations are fulfilled and many social relations are forged and/or reconfirmed,[31] we realise that the large cemeteries served as locales wherein relationships within and between the sodalities constituting individual regional groupings were structured and reproduced. If this were indeed the case, we can also infer that the dead who were buried in the square burial compounds commonly attached to the large cemeteries would most likely have been leaders of the sodalities comprising the regional community, and their burials would have been occasions for the further reproduction of the internal order of such groupings as well as that of the regional community.

With regard to the burials, it is extremely interesting that most cemeteries in northern Kyushu, not only the extremely large ones but also the cemeteries attached to individual hamlets during the Yayoi II and III, were structured in a unique linear formation consisting of two (or occasionally more) rows of burials (see Section 6.1 in this chapter). At location 3 of Kuma-Nishioda site, for instance, the mt-DNA sequences of the deceased show that each row of burials might have represented some kind of descent grouping; the northern row has seven type-1 mt-DNA sequences out of sixteen, whereas the southern row has seven type-2 mt-DNA sequences out of twenty-two (Figure 6.9; Mizoguchi 2008). The cemetery appears to have been co-owned and co-used by the hamlets comprising the Kuma-Nishioda village or by the sodalities spread across the regional community in which the Kuma-Nishioda was the centre, suggesting that those hamlets were divided into two descent groupings, either internally within each hamlet or between the hamlets (ibid.). In any case, the two groupings can be inferred to have been *moieties* of a *dual organisation*. Dual organisations cut across a number of communal groupings, dividing

---

30 I examine them in detail in Section 6.1 in this chapter.

31 Of course, we should not forget that these obligations and relations can also be challenged and, at times, transformed through mortuary practices.

them into two sections, i.e., moieties, and creating mutual obligations between their members, who are expected to reciprocate both labour and gifts obtained on various occasions of communal importance, such as those related to the rites of passage (e.g. birth, initiation into new age grades, marriage and death). A dual division is often multilayered: hamlets, villages and regional communities can all be divided into moieties. Moreover, this multi-layered nature of the dual division makes each individual occasion for the fulfilment of reciprocal obligations an occasion in which the order and cohesion of communal groupings is symmetrically confirmed and reinforced on all levels (Tuzin 2001).[32]

This is a very efficient mechanism for maintaining group cohesion without developing hierarchy (ibid.). In other words, this mechanism enables order-generating self-regulation. If the widespread use of the linear form of spatial structure of cemeteries during the Yayoi II and III in northern Kyushu is considered an indication of the operation of dual organisations, this would have perfectly suited the rising functional requirements of the time: the generation and maintenance of social cohesion and communal integration in and between individual villages forming individual regional communities. Meanwhile, the regional centres increased in size and scale; hamlet-scale groups budded off from preexisting settlements, and it was necessary to maintain the sodalities that had formed between them (Mizoguchi 1995a); in other words, new villages were formed of hamlet-scale groupings budding off (see Figure 6.6.A). In such circumstances, the presence of a dual organisation in the three layers of communal integration, that is, (a) the intra-village level, (b) the inter-village level and (c) the sodality level, would have been extremely advantageous.

Let us continue our analysis of the people's customs pertaining to burying the dead. In the Yayoi IV period, there emerged some kind of 'burial sequences', formed by situating new burials right next to preexisting ones in a repetitive fashion (see Figure 6.16, and Section 6.1 in this chapter). This type of square burial compound should be separately treated from those prevalent in the Yayoi III,

where the central burial spot was surrounded by a number of burials that did not intersect with one another (Figure 6.17); let us refer to the elite burial compounds of the Yayoi III as the elite burial compound Type I and that of the Yayoi IV, the Type II (Figures 6.13.C, Type I, and E, Type II; 6.16, Type II; and 6.18, Type I; Mizoguchi 2001, and see Section 6.1 of this chapter). The sequences were found to be particularly developed in the burial compounds attached to the large cemeteries of the regional centres (in the case of the Kuriyama location C, see Figure 6.16; see Figure 6.4.10 in the map). The sequences can be interpreted as having represented genealogies, or the lines of inheritance, of an identity, social role or status. The phenomenon can be hypothetically interpreted in the following ways:

(1) Elite segments came to be differentiated from individual clan-type sodalities, and their leadership was exclusively inherited through genealogical lines.
(2) The function of clan-type sodalities needed to be enhanced as the amount of goods, people and information being exchanged through them increased, and their leadership – which was still achieved rather than ascribed – came to represent the stable reproduction of the sodalities.

Elite-precinct-type compounds clearly emerged in the larger settlements/regional centres only in the second half of the Late Yayoi period (i.e. the Yayoi V), suggesting that the latter possibility (2) was more likely; in that case, leadership would have been an achieved position, not an ascribed/inherited one, which suggests that the sodalities were not yet internally segmented and hierarchised. It is interesting to note that the emergence of the burial sequences coincided with the construction of the large buildings in the northern Kyushu horizon. These were often located adjacent to the burial compounds in the large central-place-type settlements, from which we can infer that the buildings were most probably related to an increasing consciousness regarding the significance of the ancestors. If this were true, the phenomenon nicely fits into the hypothesis: the large buildings were communal locales where the ancestor-leaders of the communities were commemorated.

32 Also see Footnotes 18 and 19 and related parts of Chapter 5.

Recent excavations have revealed the presence of many large rectangular buildings at the regional centres in the Kyushu and western Japan horizons. In the former horizon, they are often located close to the square burial compounds, where, as suggested above, the leaders of the clan-type sodalities would have been buried. At the Yubihon'mura site near Tosu City in Saga prefecture, for instance, an extremely large rectangular building is situated next to a cemetery which contains a number of jar burials and other types of burials furnished with bronze daggers dating from the Yayoi II, III and IV, along with two jar burials dating from the Yayoi V (see Figure 6.2.A; Saga PBE 2003, 4–14). The building, which was rebuilt at least five times at the same location during the Yayoi IV and early Yayoi V, would have been associated with the cemetery, and it is highly probably that some ritual functions, including mortuary- and ancestor-related rituals, were held in that building. The repeated rebuilding itself might have been a ritual act in which the participants might have prayed for renewing the power of the ancestral spirits (cf. Tuzin 2001, 104–107).[33]

In the latter horizon, these buildings are often located at the centre of large central-place-type villages. The Bunkyo (文京) site at Matsuyama City in Ehime prefecture includes three extremely large buildings (they would not have existed contemporaneously) which are not associated with any of the residential units constituting the village but located at the nodal point between them (Tasaki 2006, 33–34). The Ikegami-Sone (池上曽根) site at Izumi City in Osaka prefecture features another large building, again rebuilt a number of times (five times to be exact), which was closely associated with pits containing various production and food-procurement tools including octopus-fishing pots

and so on (Figure 6.2.B; Izumi MBE 2004). It has been suggested that these pits are related to some ritualistic practices. Nevertheless, it cannot be confirmed whether these items themselves served any ritual purpose or they were deposited after the performance of some other rituals in which they had been used. However, it can be inferred that the building and its surroundings formed a communal area rather than a segregated residential area for the elite. This is suggestive of the real purpose of the large buildings in northern Kyushu. Many of them were associated with the ancestor-leaders, and if they were like their western horizon equivalents, they would have been communal buildings in and around which the rituals, probably involving some kind of ancestor worship, were conducted. Interestingly, these buildings can be genealogically connected with the Etsuji central building, which we inferred was related to rituals concerning the dead and the ancestors (see Ozawa 2006, 17–18). This is suggestive of the character of the large buildings in the regional centres of the Western horizon: they might also have been used for rituals concerning the dead and the ancestors as well as those pertaining to the regeneration of rice grains.[34] In that regard, it is suggestive that some of the extraordinary large buildings of northern Kyushu are also located close to the areas where bronzeworking is inferred to have been conducted (e.g. Naka [那珂] site of Fukuoka prefecture; see Kusumi 2008, 244). Bronzeworking involved the transformation of the ores to metal. The process can be metaphorically linked to the transformation of rice from seed to foodstuff. Behind the extraordinary large buildings would have laid the *Yayoi structuring principle* that was based on the cyclic transformation from something lifeless to something filled with life (see Chapter 5.6). The repeated rebuilding on the same spot, as observed in the Yubihon'mura, Ikegami and Etsuji sites suggests that the rebuilding itself could have been perceived as a ritual for regenerating the power of the ancestors as well as the rice grains.

Traces of rituals conducted at the regional centres are not confined to the large buildings. We often come across a large number of wooden

---

33 Shitara (2009) argues that the extremely large buildings of northern Kyushu, commonly situated adjacent to rich cemeteries (see Figure 6.2.A), emerged under the influence of the Han Chinese custom of building ancestral mausolea-type buildings (陵 or 寝). However, as mentioned in Chapter 5.2 (p. 58), a genealogical roots of those buildings can be traced back to the beginning of the Yayoi period, when the central large building of the Etsuji site was built on an fairly identical plan to the large buildings of Lgeum-dong in the Korean peninsula, that were build adjacent to the cemetery area of the site (cf. Hashino et al. 2006, fig. 9). That suggests that those Middle Yayoi buildings do not necessarily have to be connected to the Han Chinese influence.

34 See arguments on the metaphorical connection between the death and regeneration of human being and that of rice grain in Chapter 5.2.

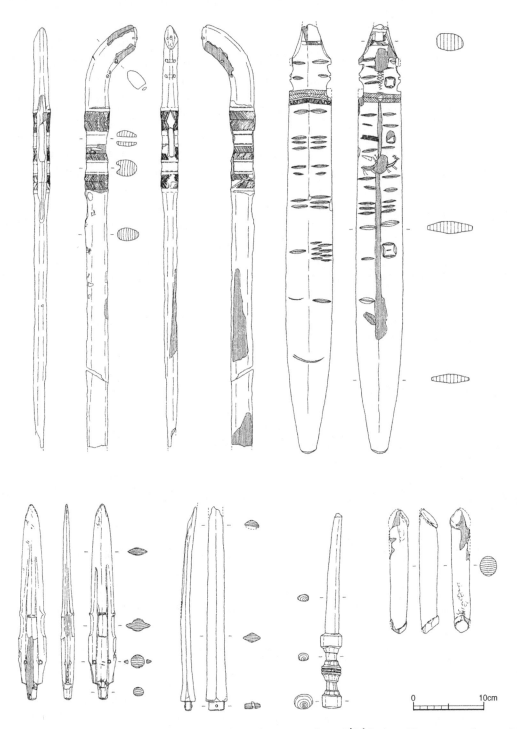

Figure 6.10. Wooden ritual implements from the Minamikata (南方) site, Okayama prefecture (after Okayama MBE 2005).

implements of unknown, non-utilitarian functions lying discarded in a sector of a village-enclosing ditch. These implements are often in the shape of weapons, such as bronze weapons, or are fashioned in the form of birds or human figures (e.g. Okayama MBE 2005). They also sometimes include staff-like items with elaborate carvings (Figure 6.10) or richly curved and lacquer-painted shields (ibid.). They were most likely used in ritual gatherings in which, at times, certain members of the participating communities carried wooden weapon-shaped implements and decorated shields; sometimes, certain items depicting animal and/or human shapes, probably representing spirits – ancestral as well as those of natural creatures – were displayed and used in these rituals (Figure 6.10). A vast number of unbroken vessels discarded in a village-enclosing ditch may have been used in ritual feasting (e.g. Hie [比恵] site fifty-third excavation SD (ditch) 10; Fukuoka MBE 1996b). In any case, it seems certain that such occasions occurred much more often in the regional centres and involved the mobilisation of not only the images of ancestors but also those representing the spirits of natural creatures, probably associated with the reproduction of life and the order of the world. The presence of ancestral images (Shitara 2007) suggests a reference to the *Yayoi structuring principle*: if this were the case, ritual acts involving the use of weapon-shaped implements may have encouraged/coerced the spirit of rice grains to regenerate bountifully.[35] *Dotaku* bronze bells and various bronze (weapon-shaped) implements may have been used on such occasions before being deposited elsewhere (see Section 7 in this chapter). Needless to say, these must have been the occasions on which different categories of people in the assembly were assigned different tasks and obligations; through this, the social categorisation and order would have been partially but significantly displayed, confirmed and internalised through the mediation of the Yayoi structuring principle and the enactment of protocols based on it.

Let us now return to the regional centres of the northern Kyushu and western horizons. These centres were the nodes for the flow of goods, people and information. They were also the centres of various ritual activities and, as we will see later, doubled up as production and distribution centres. Needless to say, they were large – this seems to have been an important point.[36] Because they were situated either at the centre of emerging individual regional settlement systems or on the boundaries between them, they naturally began to function as regional centres, attracting more people, goods and information. This means that more births, more initiations and more deaths took place in these centres. For each of these occasions, people assembled, fulfilled their mutual obligations by offering certain types of labour, material items and information, and confirmed their relations as members of specific groups. The regular occurrence of such occasions would have prompted the invention of various means and protocols for their smooth and repeated enactment (Mizoguchi 2008). In other words, the regional centres served as locales for the mediation, regulation and reproduction of certain modes of social relations, where disputes were mediated and problems were solved more often in more formalised ways.[37]

Despite all this, it is important to note that social relations do not appear to have been fully hierarchised during the Middle Yayoi period. Even though the mortuary evidence suggests the gradual emergence of an elite class, this group had not yet marked its presence in the spatial structure of the village. In other words, the regional centres did not contain a segregated elite precinct, although there were some focal points of specific *discourses*, such as those pertaining to the large rectangular buildings, which differentiated between those who were allowed to enter and those who were not; in the case of the northern Kyushu examples, these discourses connected the *chosen* living with the *chosen* dead and the ancestors (Mizoguchi 2010a, 27–28). In other words, the chosen few were not so differentiated from the others, as yet, as to materialise those differences by living an upper-class life in segregation.

All in all, it appears that the large regional centres of the northern Kyushu and the western horizons were locales wherein the complexity

35 For a collection of concise ethnographies of rice agriculture-related ritual practices, various material items used in them, and their symbolic contents/implications, see (Iwata 1970).

36 The scale of some regional centres in northern Kyushu and Kiniki during the Middle Yayoi are as follows: Hie-Naka: more than 100 hectares (1 hectare = 10,000 square metres), Sugu: more than 100 hectares, Yoshinogari (吉野ヶ里; Saga prefecture): about 20 hectares, Karako (唐古; Nara prefecture): about 30 hectares (14.8 hectares excluding circumference ditches), Ikegami-Sone: about 25 hectares (7.2 hectares excluding circumference ditches). For information concerning the Karako and Ikegami-Sone, see Morii (2001).

37 The present author pointed out that the mega-centres of northern Kyushu such as the Hie-Naka and Sugu had more than two type I/II burial compounds (see Section 6.1 in this chapter), and argued that, because those burial compounds would have functioned as locales where various social relations were negotiated and reproduced by referring to the elite dead and ancestors, differences in scale between regional centres were correlated with the scales of the regional communities the internal and external communications of theirs the regional centres mediated and reproduced (Mizoguchi 2008).

of contemporaneous society was crystallised in an intensive manner. Accordingly, the people of that time developed the necessary devices and implemented them in order to regulate and reduce the complexity of their living conditions. As described earlier, many of the settlements were situated at critical locations in the networks of flow of people, goods and information. People were attracted to those locations because of the range and amount of goods accumulated there and the variety of human contacts and chances available there, and they would have moved, if they could, to those locations through the network of clan-type sodalities to which they belonged. The sudden emergence of the Sugu settlement in the Fukuoka Plain[38] (Figure 6.7) and the rapid expansion of many large settlements across northern Kyushu and western Japan, as mentioned, can be explained based on the attractiveness of their locations in the developing networks of flow of people, goods and information.

This implies that in those settlements, negotiations over the exchange of people and goods, and decisions regarding whom to select in order to mediate these exchanges and take charge when necessary, would have been much more numerous and much more complex than before. Moreover, the outcomes of these negotiations would have affected not only the prosperity of the residential groups of the concerned settlements but also that of the clan-type sodalities spread across a number of settlements (Figure 6.6).

The elite burial compounds and extremely large cemeteries attached to the large regional centres, in that sense, would have served as materialised devices for reducing the complexities and problems arising in the society of the period (see Figures 6.6.B and 6.9).[39] In addition, they would have worked as materialised devices which could be used to manage the *contradictions* generated between the inevitable hierarchisation within and between the clan-type sodalities and the necessity to maintain communal egalitarianism. The latter need would have been acutely felt, in particular, because the functional efficiency of sodalities as a dominant network medium for the flow of

increasing amounts of goods, people and information was dependent upon the communal and egalitarian nature of society. In this context, we will fully investigate the mortuary evidence in a subsequent section.

Before analysing that evidence, however, let us look at the ways in which goods were produced and circulated in and among villages in order to further examine the concrete nature and character of the complexity and contradictions mentioned earlier.

5. PRODUCTION AND CIRCULATION

5.1. Stoneworking

It has long been regarded as an evidence of the 'maturity' of the social complexity of the northern Kyushu society that the bulk of supply of stone axes across the region between the Yayoi II and III relied on a single source of stone – the volcanic outcrop or hill called Imayama (今山) – then almost an island connected to the mainland by a sandbar (Figure 6.11). The utilisation of stone (basalt) from Imayama definitely began during the Jomon period (Fukuoka MBE 2005b, 184–187), but a large-scale production of axes on and near the hill did not begin until the second half of the Yayoi I (Shimojo 1975). Stone axe production reached its peak in the final Yayoi I and the Yayoi II and thereafter decreased, and virtually ceased quite suddenly in the Yayoi IV (Mori 2010a, 2010b).

One significant characteristic of the production is that, during the Yayoi II and III, pecked and almost-finished products were brought into settlements across northern Kyushu, where they were finished by fine polishing and then used (Shimojo 1975).[40] The distribution of stone axes coincides fairly well with the horizon of the jar burial custom (Figure 6.11; Shimojo 1989). It also coincides fairly well with the distribution of bronze weapons, which were commonly deposited as grave goods during the Yayoi II and III (ibid.).

38 The Sugu settlement in the Yayoi II comprised only six hamlets. However, by the Yayoi III, the number jumped to forty-two (Mizoguchi 2010a, 34).

39 See Footnote 37 to this chapter.

40 During the Yayoi I, the horizon was not yet formed, and it is suggested that some communities scattered across the floodplains around the hill, such as the Hie and the Arita (有田), visited it and brought back stone to make axes (Mori 2010a, 2010b); stone axe production debris as well as used axes have been excavated from the settlements of these communities (Fukuoka MBE 2005b, 181–182).

These facts appear to point to a centralised distribution network based upon an inter-regional hierarchy, which is possibly reflected by the concentric distribution of jar burials containing plenty of graves goods with different grades of richness that emerged in the Yayoi IV.[41] The seeming concentric distribution of rich grave goods (Figure 6.4) has also led to the widely-shared image that the production and supply of Imayama axes, although it almost ceased in the Yayoi III, contributed to the rise of the Mikumo settlement, which reached the highest position in the inter-regional hierarchy in the Yayoi IV (Takesue 1985, 403).

It is often inferred that the production of Imayama axes and their circulation were controlled by the elite residing in Mikumo settlement – one of the largest settlements of the entire northern Kyushu region, located approximately 6 kilometres to the south-west of the hill (ibid.). Situated in the south-western corner of the Mikumo site is the rich Mikumo-Minamisyoji cemetery (see Figures 6.4.A, 6.13.G and 6.20), dating from the Yayoi IV (see Section 6.1, p. 158 in this chapter), that is, after the Imayama axe production had ceased. Some scholars infer that the prominence of the Mikumo settlement was achieved, albeit partially, by controlling the production as well as distribution of the stone axes (ibid.).

In reality, however, the picture is much more complicated. The ratio of the use of Imayama axes is consistently more than 70 per cent within the distribution with some site clusters, quite remote from the Imayama, showing notably high concentration (Figure 6.11; Mori 2010a). However, along the north-western coastline of the region, where

41 As shown in Section 3.1 (pp. 111–113), the apparent hierarchy was formed by strategic gift-giving by the elite, who were probably residing in the Mikumo and Sugu settlements on the Genkai-nada coastal plains; the gifts included early Han Chinese mirrors and other precious goods. This hierarchy, however, did not necessarily indicate actual domination and subordination in the community. At the Yoshinogari site in Saga prefecture, we find a mirror that was deliberately broken and packed in the clay sealing the joint between two burial jars constituting a coffin. At the Mikumo, Sugu and other burial sites where Early Han Chinese mirrors were found to be deposited as grave goods, the mirrors were placed on one or both sides of the body in the coffin. This suggests that there was no consistent rule enforced for the treatment of goods presented by the elite of the Mikumo and Sugu settlement, which was supposed to indicate the status difference of the elite.

the settlements were distributed along fairly equal intervals without any significant regional centres, a typical fall-off pattern can be seen (ibid.). Besides, the fall-off corresponds with an increase in the rate of curation and reuse (ibid.); this indicates a typical distribution pattern suggesting the operation of a chain of gift exchanges between neighbouring settlements. Meanwhile, the sites showing unusually high concentration – the site clusters around the Mikuni (三国) hill and Haji (土師) (marked as Futsukaichi and Kaho, respectively in Figure 6.11; Mori 2010a) – share the common characteristic that they all suddenly appeared in the form of a large number of residential units on bed-like low-lying hills between the second half of the Yayoi I and Yayoi II. Their formation, probably resulting from the colonisation of a number of groups that budded off pre-existing settlements (see Figure 6.6.A), would have required large-scale forest clearance. The two clusters are located at a distance of approximately 32 kilometres and 39 kilometres from the hill, respectively. The high concentration of axes in these settlements, which is anomalous to the natural fall-off pattern, might be explained by the higher demand: the intense and extensive forest clearance undertaken by the communities compelled them to secure the supply of a much higher number of axes. However, it is difficult to determine how they managed to secure this supply; the three main possibilities are as follows: (a) The communities lying between the hill and the Mikuni and Haji communities were involved in a chain of gift-exchange activities with those communities, and the latter actively accumulated the products by tactfully involving themselves in such activities. (b) Some communities settled between the hill and the Mikuni and Haji settlements, such as the Hie and Naka, suddenly expanded in the Yayoi II, acted as intermediaries in the transport of these goods, since they were situated in a location that made it convenient for them to visit both the hill and the two communities in question. (c) Another possibility is that the two communities regularly dispatched procurement parties to visit the communities involved in the production of stone axes. Hypothesis (a) might be unlikely in that the supply would have been erratic and unstable; hypothesis (b) is possible, as the rapidly achieved prominence of the Hie and Naka would be partially explained if the communities were involved in acquiring the

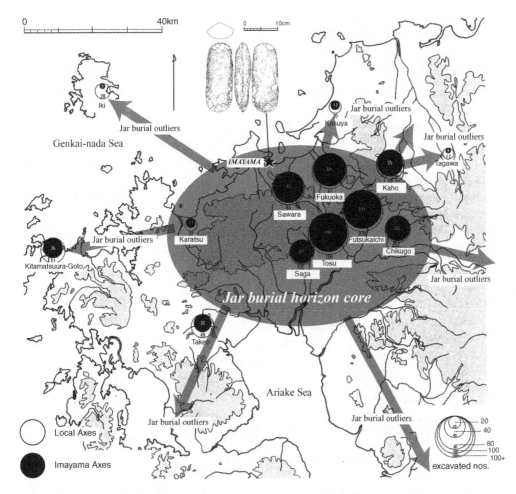

Figure 6.11. Imayama hill (marked by a star), the distribution of the jar burial custom (shaded) and that of the Imayama axe. Note that the ratio of the Imayama axes to locally made axes remains constant within the jar burial core horizon whereas that drops suddenly outside it. It should be noted that the perimeter of the distribution of the Imayama axe coincides with the outliers of the jar burials, marked by arrows coming out of the core horizon. Those observations suggest that the circulation of the axe was achieved through sodality-type ties symbolised by the sharing of the jar-burial custom (arranged after Mori 2010a). With kind permission from the Yusankaku Publishing Co.

half-finished products from their producers and exchanging them with the Mikuni and Haji communities for something else, along with a certain profit margin – similar to the Siassi trade sphere of Papua New Guinea as explained by Marshall Sahlins ([1974] 2004, chap. 6), for instance. A problem with the thesis is that the Hie and Naka themselves have not yielded a large number of Imayama axes. Hypothesis (c) may also be possible: ethnographic records indicate that some communities did, in fact, dispatch parties for exchange activities. In that case, the parties must have crossed the territories of a number of communities on their way to the hill; it is also possible that the parties relied on sodality-based ties and alliances for the acquisition of the stone axes. It is important to note that the two communities' use of Imayama axes was not significantly supplemented by the use of axes made of locally available stones, which suggests that the communities had secured a *constant* supply of these axes in one way or another. In fact, it is also possible that both the mechanisms, that is, hypotheses (b) and (c), were involved in the procurement of the axes.[42]

42 Yoshinori Mori's (2010b, 12–13, figs. 13 and 14) work revealed that hypothesis C was the case for some communities of the Sawara and Fukuoka plains during the Yayoi I: the size of the axes excavated from those areas are different statistically significantly. Some sites of those regions also yielded production debris such as basalt chips of the Imayama origin (Fukuoka MBE 2005b, 181–182).

In the Yayoi II, at the peak of axe production, it appears that the axes were made in several locations on the slope and foothills of Imayama (Shimjo 1975), often in an intensive manner.[43] Both quarried stone and stone pieces of appropriate sizes lying around were used for making these axes. Although the difference in source materials led to variations in the quality and size of the products, it has been pointed out that the overall variability decreased with the commencement of the Yayoi II (Mori 2010b). This strongly suggests that a number of groups/units were involved in the production, though they interacted one another very well. The picture would bring to mind a structure commonly shared by the settlements of the Middle Yayoi, that is, settlements with a number of residential units and cemeteries attached to them (Figure 6.6). We have inferred that these units were segments of different clan-type non-residential corporate groupings, that is, sodalities (see Section 4 in this chapter). If the same were to be applied in this case, it would suggest that the different production sites were used by different production groups belonging to different corporate groupings from a village or that from some villages.[44]

If this were the case, sodality-based networks, as suggested earlier, might indeed have played a significant role in the production and circulation of the axes. This might also explain the mechanism behind the anomalous concentrations: the communities may have used their sodality-type networks to procure the axes from far away by taking help from the fellow communities of their respective sodalities. In that case, this 'help' could have involved either acting as the intermediary or

protecting the procurement party dispatched by the remote communities. In any case, it is highly unlikely that there was any unified, 'axe-factory' type of production or that any single group, such as that residing in the Mikumo settlement, controlled the distribution of those axes (contra e.g. Takesue 2002); it is much more likely, considering the available evidence, that kin-based connections, including sodality-type ones, played an important role in the production, circulation and acquirement of the axes. The dense distribution of the axe confined within the core distributional horizon would support the model; the kin-based connections, regardless genuine or fictive, would have been symbolised by the sharing of the jar burial custom (see Figure 6.11, and its caption in particular). Interestingly, the axes were made at sites quite close to the hill, such as the Imajuku-Aoki (今宿青木) site (Fukuoka MBE 1987b, 1993), where axes were produced out of much smaller stones than used at 'workshops' on the slope or at the foot of the hill apparently brought from the hill. The products, naturally were much smaller than that produced at those workshops. This suggests purposeful exportation of the products from those workshops on the slope and those at the foot of the hill and might further reinforce the hypothesis of the involvement of kin-based, including fictive ones, connections spread wide across the northern Kyushu region.

If the preceding were indeed the case, the abrupt ending of the production at some point of time in the Yayoi IV would need to be interpreted along the same lines. Evidence suggests that the production and circulation of stone axes stopped quite suddenly. The situation was partially compensated for by the small-scale production of axes made of locally gathered stone, but this substitution did not occur at all the settlements that had formerly used the Imayama products. Without doubt, the total quantity of tree-felling axes in circulation considerably decreased at this time. As mentioned previously, the phenomenon coincided with an increasing use of iron and the emergence of rich graves with abundant Early Han Chinese imports and their hierarchical distribution.

Northern Kyushu saw the emergence of socketed and flat iron tree-felling axes in the Yayoi III, which became widespread by the Yayoi IV

43 The eighth rescue excavation, carried out along the eastern foothills of Imayama near the shoreline, yielded a couple of pits with large concentrations of stone chips and flakes in them. The excavator argues that these were the result of an intensive production activity conducted within a short period of time, probably resulting in the production of about three hundred almost-finished axes (Fukuoka MBE 2005b, 183).

44 Excavations have revealed traces of a settlement on the sandbar connecting the hill to the mainland; these include some burials (one such – probable – burial yielded a bronze dagger and a jade comma-shaped bead) and other features (Fukuoka MBE 1981, 5–9). Archaeologists have yet to confirm the scale and structure of this particular settlement.

(Murakami 1998, 68–69). The specimens dating from the Yayoi IV are robust enough for heavy use (ibid.), though it is difficult to determine whether they were available in sufficient quantities to replace their stone counterparts. The Yayoi IV, as we have seen, did not definitely witnessed the establishment of a stable, kin-based social hierarchy. However, with the continuing development of large, regional-centre-type settlements, it is evident that intra- and inter-communal relations would have moved towards increasing hierarchisation. It is quite feasible that the increasing use of iron tools and the social tendency towards hierarchisation was coupled with the probable, but admittedly unconfirmed, decrease in regular and extensive tree felling in the villages. In the Yayoi III period, a tendency was widely shared across northern Kyushu that a specific settlement or settlements in individual local settlement systems tended to be equipped with an entire range of tool kits for woodworking, whereas others seem to have only part(s) of the possible range (Yoshihisa Watanabe pers. comm.). This suggests that a kind of settlement-scale 'specialisation' tendency concerning woodworking had already appeared before the end of the Imayama axe circulation. Such a tendency, if accelerated, would have reduced the total number of axes required to be in regular circulation.

Ironworking would have been performed by groups of artisans who were most likely to have been under the care and control of the emergent elite. Iron weapons, which were new additions to the grave good assemblage in the Yayoi IV, were confined to the second-tier burials (in terms of richness), below the Mikumo-Minamishoji and Sugu-Okamoto burials (Figure 6.4; also see Section 6.1 in this chapter); these would have been presented by the chiefly figures of the time, residing in the Mikumo and Sugu, to their peers (Mizoguchi 2010a). As the use of iron tools for woodworking became gradually widespread, the degree of involvement of the emergent elite in their circulation was also enhanced. This may well have contradicted the kin-/sodality-based circulation system of the Imayama stone axes. I do not suggest that the intervention of the emergent elite disrupted the circulation of Imayama axes in a substantial manner. I would like to emphasise,

however, that the combination of those factors, pointing towards an increasing degree of specialisation and control over production activities, would have hastened the demise of the Imayama axe production.

The use of a particular source of raw material and the involvement of kin-/sodality-based exchange networks characterised the Imayama axe production and circulation in northern Kyushu. The situation appears to have been fairly similar elsewhere in western Japan, although there were cases in which only finished products (e.g. stone reaping knives from the Tateiwa [立岩] site, Fukuoka prefecture[45]; cf. Shimojo 1975, 1989) or only raw materials were circulated (e.g. Sanukitoid stone procured in the Kanayama [金山] mountain, Kagawa prefecture; Takehiro 2010). In these cases, too, we can presume the involvement of kin-/sodality-based exchange networks. For instance, Naoto Teramae shows that dominant stone leaping knives were made of stones procured from different sources between different residential units in the large central-place-type settlement of Karako-Kagi (唐古鍵) in the southern Kinki region during the Yayoi III and IV and suggests that those residential groups acquired the raw materials for the knives through different social networks (Teramae 2006, 113–118).

Sanukitoid or *Sanukaites* (a type of granitoid) sourced from the Nijo-san (二上山) mountain was widely used as raw material for stone tools, most notably stone reaping knives. Throughout the Middle Yayoi period, the procurement of raw materials was undertaken by communities settled near the source (Sakai 1974), and it is argued that raw materials were brought into the central settlements of individual regional settlement systems, where they were made into roughouts and then taken to the other settlements, given finishing touches and then used (ibid.). Scholars have yet to fully examine the extent to which raw materials were brought into the regional centres exclusively to be made into rough-outs, but they are certain

---

45 In this one of the regional centres of the riverine basin of the Onga, all the hamlets constituting the village yielded some traces of the production of the stone knife, though one particular hamlet, the Shimonokata (下方), was the most prominent production centre (Kojima 1977, 27).

that a highly stable and reliable network of inter-communal exchanges was in place and operational at that time (e.g. Negita 1998), and kin-/sodality-based groupings cutting across a number of settlements would have played some role in reproducing the network as one of mutual expectations and obligations.

The Chubu region of eastern Japan has yielded traces of intensive axe production at the Enokida (榎田) site in Nagano prefecture (Nagano Prefectural Buried Cultural Properties Research Centre 1999). The axes were made of basalt, procured from a source approximately 500 metres away from the site and were distributed up to areas as far away as 200 kilometres (Machida 2010, 81). In this case, half-finished products were circulated, and the final polishing was undertaken in the sites of the consumption (Machida 2010), the pattern identical to the Imayama axes of northern Kyushu (see the previous discussion). One of the most prominent nodes of the distribution of the Enokida axes is the Matsubara (松原) site of Nagano prefecture. It is notable that the drastic growth in the size and internal structural complexity of the village has been shown to have resulted from the agglomeration of a number of residential groups (Baba 2008). As argued previously, this would have resulted from the cumulative advantages generated by the given settlement's location as a node of various types of interactions (see Section 4.2 in this chapter). If this were indeed the case, we can then deduce that the increased production of goods would have constituted one of these advantages, and the circulation of the products would have been mediated by the kin-/sodality-based networks meeting at the site.

Based on the preceding discussion, we can conclude the following: (1) the involvement of kin-/sodality-based networks remained significant in the production and circulation of stone tools during the Middle Yayoi period; (2) in many cases, half-finished products were circulated and subsequently finished at the settlements where they were intended to be used; (3) both gift-exchange-type and strategic-acquirement-type mechanisms were involved in the formation of the distribution patterns; (4) intra- and inter-communal relations became increasingly centralised and gradually even hierarchised due to such production and

circulation towards the end of the Middle Yayoi period.

5.2. Metalworking

BRONZE

The basic technology of bronzeworking and its raw materials were introduced to the archipelago from the Korean peninsula; bronzeworking appears to have begun in northern Kyushu by the Yayoi II, and it spread across western Japan in the Yayoi III (Iwanaga 1980). An intriguing outlier among sites showing evidence of bronzework is the Katada (堅田) site in Wakayama prefecture, where excavations have revealed a mould of a wood-shaving tool (*Yarigan'na*) and a hearth, reportedly dating back to the final Yayoi I and the second half of the Yayoi I, respectively (Gobo MBE 2002). The terminus post quem of the mould of the oldest type of bronze dagger from the Yoshinogari site is said to date back roughly to the final Yayoi I; however, considering the available evidence, it would seem more reasonable to date it to the Yayoi II (cf. Kataoka 1999, 189).

The colony-type settlements (e.g. the Habu [土生] site in Saga prefecture; Kataoka 1999, 110–111) or the residential areas in individual settlements (e.g. the Yokoguma-Nabekura [横隈鍋倉] site in Fukuoka prefecture; Kataoka 1999, 108) of migrants from the Korean peninsula – identified by the traces of their material culture, most prominently represented by the Late Mumun (dating mainly from its first half; Kataoka 1999, 103–113) pottery assemblage – emerged in parts of northern Kyushu in the Yayoi II.[46] Another interesting point is that the area of their concentration appears to have coincided with the distribution of the earliest traces of bronzework, in the form of stone-made casts (ibid., 176–201). It is possible that the smiths may have arrived in northern Kyushu through communal ties maintained by the migrant communities with their parent

46 Interestingly, the inhabitants do not appear to have kept in close contact with the communities of their origin in the peninsula, based on the apparent lack of continuous influx of migrants. Consequently, their material culture became hybridised with and was absorbed by the local material culture fairly quickly, within a couple of pottery typo-chronological phases (Figure 6.3; also see Kataoka 1999, 114–129).

communities in the Korean peninsula. The available evidence suggests that initially the smiths were quite mobile and attached themselves to residential communities that were not necessarily extraordinary in their scale or contents (ibid., 193–194). This suggests that their decision of where to reside was not made on the basis of simple factors such as economic advantage but more likely based on information brought through the networks created by the migrants who had settled down in certain parts of northern Kyushu. As time went by, and as the Mumun settlers increasingly absorbed local customs and lost their distinct material culture traits during the Yayoi III, the smiths set up their residences in some corner of the emerging large, regional-centre-type settlements (ibid., 191–195). This phenomenon can be observed both in the northern Kyushu and southern Kinki regions (e.g. the Yoshinogari in the former [ibid., 193] and the Karako-Kagi in the latter; Mametani 2008, 219–220). The products they made – mainly daggers, spearheads and halberds in the former and bronze bells and halberds in the latter – were fairly evenly spread in their respective horizons and were deposited mainly as grave goods in the former area and in manners suggesting their ritual use in the latter area, i.e., deposited somewhere away from the sphere of daily life such as on a hill slope facing a valley (e.g. Shimane PBE 1996, 379–429). The production and distribution of bronze artefacts remained fairly dispersed in the Yayoi III, suggesting that their circulation was not tightly controlled by the emergent elite but instead took the form of prestige *gift* exchange in that era. For instance, in northern Kyushu, at the recently excavated cemetery site of Hashimoto (橋本), eighteen bronze weapons were excavated from jar burials dated to the Yayoi II and III (Shin Nagaya pers.comm.) The cemetery was not attached to a regional centre-type large settlement, but situated on a nodal position connecting the three neighbouring floodplains, namely, the Itoshima, Sawara, and Chikushi. It can be inferred that the community was approached and presented prestige gifts by the communities in those floodplains in order for them to secure safe passage for interactional activities.

In the Yayoi IV, as some regional-centre-type settlements located at the interaction network nodes became extremely large in both northern Kyushu and the southern Kinki region (see the previous section) the production began to be concentrated at those settlements, while it continued in other settlements in increasingly smaller scales (Tajiri 2001). The Sugu and its nearby settlements became the centre of production in northern Kyushu (Kasuga MBE 1994, 137–149), while sites such as Higashinara (東奈良), and possibly Karako-Kagi (唐古鍵), became centres of production in the southern Kinki region (Harunari 1992).

By this time (i.e. the Yayoi IV), in northern Kyushu, the dominant metal items deposited as grave goods were iron weapons, and bronze weapons – the spearheads, in particular – came to be deposited in contexts strongly suggesting the involvement of ritual activities (cf. Takesue 1990a): they were commonly deposited on a slope facing a valley, sometimes in the vicinity of regional centres, other times far away from any settlement (Shimane PBE 1996, 379–497). In some cases of the latter, connections with watercourses, such as near the point where a river flew out of the mountain range, are pointed out. In the Kinki region and its neighbouring regions, scholars have pointed out the wide distribution of bronze bells made from a similar mould and produced in major central-place-type settlements of the southern Kinki region (Harunari 1992). This might suggest the involvement of strategic gift-giving rather than a chain of gift exchange. The concentration of production locations and the increase in possibly strategic gift-giving do not necessarily indicate that the elite were in control of distribution, however; the presence of an outlying production site, the Nagoyama (名古山) site in Hyogo prefecture (Harunari 1992, 19), located far away from the production centres suggests that the smiths might have still enjoyed some freedom of movement between communities. However, it has also been pointed out that the raw material for the production of bronze bells, from the Yayoi IV onward, was almost entirely procured in mainland China, surmised to be somewhere in the present-day Hebei (河北) province (Mabuchi and Hirao 1982). The homogeneity of the chemical contents of this raw material led to the inference that the material was imported in the form of ingots (ibid.). Before that (i.e. during the Yayoi II and III), lead isotope analysis conducted by Hisao Mabuchi and Yoshimitsu Hirao suggest that most of the bronze implements were made from materials brought from the Korean peninsula (ibid.), though locally-procured materials may have occasionally been used. It is suggested that bronze implements imported from the peninsula were melted and reused (ibid.). From the Yayoi IV, imports from China may also have been reused, albeit not so in large amounts (e.g. Morioka 2010). In any case, raw material acquirement by the production centres would have required a degree of inter-communal coordination, and possibly led to the formation of a loose network of raw material exchange; the dominant raw materials shifted from that imported from the Korean peninsula to that originated in China across western Japan, and it is more likely that they were imported through a single channel than that there existed a number of coexisting channels across western Japan.[47] If it were the case, a significant portion of the material would have been acquired from/through the mediation by northern Kyushu communities and needed to be brought across a long distance. It is difficult to determine whether those bronze bell–producing communities in the Kinki region sent any procurement parties for collecting this material.[48] In sum, we can say that bronze implements and their production significantly contributed to the increasing centralisation and sophistication of intra- and inter-communal collaboration of various scales in the Yayoi IV.

IRON

The time of introduction of iron implements has been the subject of much dispute in recent times. It seems certain that during the Yayoi I, cast-iron implements, mostly socketed axes, were imported, most likely from one of the Chinese warring

states, Yen (燕), via the peninsula (Murakami 1998, 56–60); the broken fragments of various sizes and shapes of these implements were reworked by polishing them, like stone tools, for use as small woodworking tools across northern Kyushu (ibid., 58–60).

By the Yayoi II or III, forged iron production began in northern Kyushu (ibid.). The production did not leave any significant traces, such as hearths, during the Yayoi II and III; one possible reason is that the production would not have been very substantial in its scale, and the smiths might have been quite mobile, like their bronzeworking counterparts (see the preceding discussion).

In the Yayoi IV, hearths for forging iron came to be built from northern Kyushu to as far east as the Yano (矢野) site in the Tokushima prefecture of the eastern Inland Sea region (ibid., 84). Interestingly, the structure of the hearths of this period, according to Yasuyuki Murakami (1998, 85–87), was extremely sophisticated, with a pit filled alternately with charcoal and earth for drainage and covered by a carbon bed and charcoal for forging; the structure was later progressively simplified (ibid.). A substantial iron forging workshop with clear traces of production in the form of a specially made hearth, the Nioute (仁王手), has been found at one of the residential units in the Sugu site (Figures 6.4.B and 6.7), one of the largest central-place-type settlements in the coastal northern Kyushu region (Figure 6.12) (Kasuga MBE 2004). The settlement increasingly became the centre of bronzeworking in the region during the Yayoi IV, and some of the iron products, namely, iron spearheads and halberds, would have been given as gifts, possibly as funerary gifts, to the emergent elite, mainly of the inland communities, by the elite residing at the Sugu. The fact that iron weapons replaced bronze daggers, spearheads and halberds as metal grave goods suggests that iron was accorded higher value due to its novelty. This means that iron was used to manufacture prestigious items, on the one hand, while it was simultaneously used to manufacture working tools, mainly for woodwork, on the other. The elite of the region would have exerted some degree of control over the production of the former. However, as Murakami suggests, they would not necessarily have sought to control the latter (Murakami 1998, 90). This may be the reason why traces of iron

47 If a number of channels coexisted, both Korean and Chinese raw materials would have continued to be imported.

48 There is a possibility that procurement expeditions might have been organised, based on a simple chiefdom-like organisation and the communal unity. The kula exchange, although its nature and character are non-utilitarian and different, shows that a simple chiefdom-type community can organise long-distance, large-scale exchange parties (Malinowski [1922] 1984).

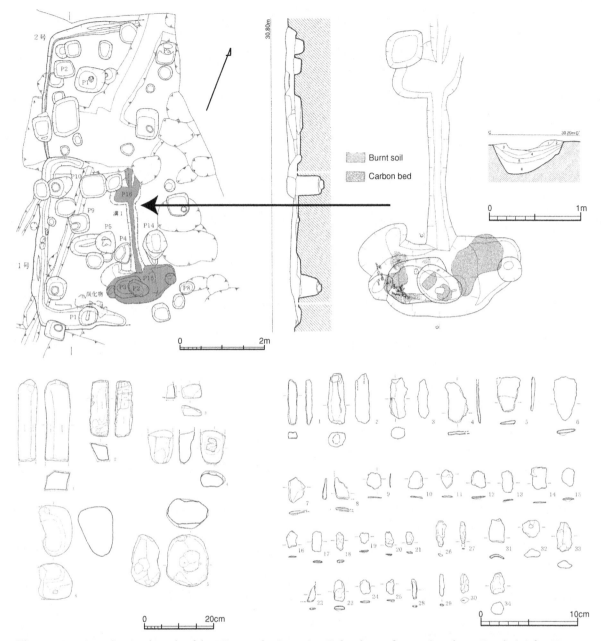

Figure 6.12. Iron forging hearth of the Nioute, the Sugu site, Fukuoka prefecture (northern Kyushu) (after Kasuga MBE 2004). Below left: whetstones and hammer stones. Below right: iron fragments generated from ironworking.

production are neither as tangible nor as concentrated at the Sugu site as those of bronzework: the elite might have controlled only the production of *prestigious* iron items, while allowing communities to continue manufacturing daily working tools in a dispersed manner.

In the Yayoi V, unlike bronzework – which came to be further concentrated in Sugu, where a large number of workshops were operational – ironwork remained dispersed, although there seems to have emerged a clear differentiation between the settlements producing iron tools and those that did not (Watanabe 2007); Takashi

Watanabe revealed that the whetstones for iron implements excavated from the Naka site, a regional centre of the Fukuoka plain, included that for both rough-finishing and final sharpening during the Middle Yayoi whereas in the Late Yayoi they only included the latter. It suggests that the production of iron implements took place in the site during the Middle Yayoi but ceased in the Late Yayoi, and the site came to solely rely on the supply from elsewhere. In the next chapter, I deal with this matter in more detail, but at this point, we can see that the picture supports the preceding inference.

As mentioned earlier, iron-forging technology had reached as far east as the Yano site of Tokushima prefecture by the end of the Yayoi IV; however, it did not reach the Kinki region (Murakami 1998, 73–78). This is interesting in that the horizon of northern-Kyushu-made bronze spearheads spread as far east as the Kagawa and Tokushima prefectures without reaching Kinki. It might be dangerous to read too much into this concurrence, but it might also be possible that the movement of ironsmiths was determined by preexisting sodality-type networks, the largest extension of which, reflected by the use of the particular ritual tool, had not quite reached the Kinki region.

5.3. Inseparability of Production and the Reproduction of Social Relations

The production and circulation of goods appear to have been based upon kin-/sodality-based inter-communal ties throughout the Middle Yayoi. These ties gradually became multilayered: goods produced with novel technologies became the subject of strategic gift-giving, and the artisans involved in their production were increasingly brought under the direct control of the emergent elite. However, in the case of goods needed for daily labour and/or produced with more common/traditional technologies, the principle of reciprocal exchange between peers appears to have continued.

However, the emergence of large, regional-centre-type settlements generated and enlarged differences between regional centres and their satellites; what had once been egalitarian, non-centralised inter-communal relations reproduced through the latter type of circulation now became increasingly centralised and hierarchised. This might have led to the heightening of contradictions in society. On the one hand, the relationship between the supplier and the supplied would have inevitably become that between the dominant and the subordinate, while on the other, the network through which goods were distributed was founded on kin-/sodality-based principles of egalitarianism/reciprocity. It would have become necessary to deal with this contradiction in one way or another, and mortuary practices appear to have been one of the arenas where it was addressed.

6. DEALING WITH THE DEAD AND COPING WITH THE WORLD: MORTUARY PRACTICES AND CEMETERIES

6.1. Northern Kyushu: The World of Jar Coffin Cemeteries

As we have already seen, the practice of burying the dead in large burial jars began in the northern Kyushu region during the Early Yayoi period. The practice continued to develop in the Middle Yayoi period, as the jars, standardised in shape and their size differences, were increasingly employed to indicate different positions accorded to the dead (Shimojo 1991; Nakazono 1991; for the size differentiation of jars in individual sites, see Mizoguchi 2005). Some of them – importantly, often the larger ones in individual burial grounds – were painted black, and occasionally red, on the outside, with an occasional coat of red on the inside.[49] Keeping in mind the metaphorical-transformative connection between the death and regeneration of rice crops and human beings as represented by the globular burial jars in the Initial and Early Yayoi periods (see Chapter 5.2–3, esp. p. 66), we can say that the connection continued and, concerning the correlation between the larger burial jars and their being painted black and red, became increasingly connected with the higher-ranked dead. Jar burial cemeteries of various scales and characters were also formed during this time, and they can be classified into several distinct categories based on different spatio-temporal patterns which resulted from the cumulative addition of jar burials to individual cemeteries (Mizoguchi 2000, 2001). The last point is of particular importance for our study, because the emergence, continuation and disappearance of those cemetery categories would sensitively reflect the transformation of the way in which the dead were socially treated and relationships among the living confirmed (or challenged) through mortuary practices.

---

49 Red ochre was often sprinkled over the bodies deposited in the jars. In rare cases, red mercury was painted on the inside of the jars, often containing rich grave good assemblages including early Han bronze mirrors (e.g. the Sugu-Okamoto and the Mikumo-Minamishoji [Fukuoka PBE 1985b]) (see Figure 6.4).

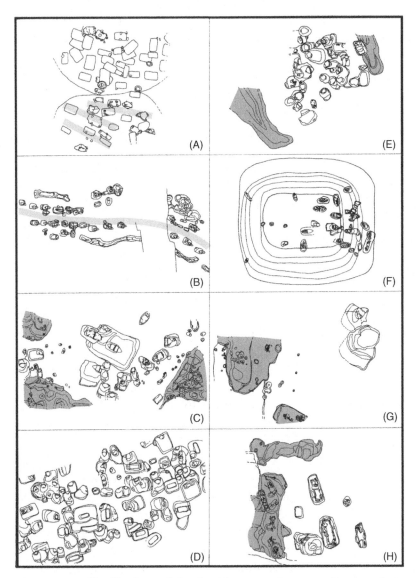

Figure 6.13. Classification of jar burial cemeteries according to the spatio-temporal formation process. Pits/ditches marked by darker shade, and linear path/arrangement marked by lighter shade. **A**: Linear cemetery A (Initial Yayoi~Yayoi III; Shinmachi cemetery), **B**: Linear cemetery B (Yayoi II~III; Nagaoka), **C**: Burial compound type I (Kuriyama loc. D), **D**: Agglomerated sequential burial cemetery (late Yayoi III~early Yayoi V; Kitsunezuka), **E**: Burial compound type IIa (Yayoi IV) (Kuriyama loc. C), **F**: Burial compound type IIb (Yayoi IV) (Yoshitake-Hiwatashi), **G**: Richly-furnished burial compound for specific individuals (Mikumo-Minamishoji), **H**: Burial compound type III (Mikumo-Teraguchi) (from Mizoguchi [2001] with additions, original plan drawings from the excavation reports traced and modified by Mizoguchi).

TYPES OF JAR BURIAL CEMETERIES

Similar to the Incipient Yayoi and the Yayoi I periods, the cemetery-scape of this phase went through several transformations. We can identify distinct modes, or principles, of cemetery organisation in terms of the spatio-temporal layout of the burials and the ways in which the mourners participated in and experienced them. To a certain extent, it is possible to reconstruct the mourner's experiences by reconstructing the formation process of individual cemeteries and their cemetery-scapes. Burial jars, from which the relative dates can be accurately determined (Hashiguchi 1979), enable us to reconstruct the formation process accurately. Based on these reconstructions, four distinct modes, or principles, of cemetery-scape organisation can be recognised as follows: the linear formation, the micro-sequence formation and two distinct modes of "burial compound" (*Kukaku-bo*, 区画墓) formation (Figure 6.13).

LINEAR FORMATION (IN THE YAYOI II AND III)
This manner of spatio-temporally organising the cemetery-scape, as mentioned earlier, originated in the Initial Yayoi period, developed further in the Yayoi I and continued into the Yayoi II and III (Figure 6.13.A–B).

The most typical example of this mode of cemetery-scape formation can be found at the Nagaoka (永岡) site (Figure 6.14; Fukuoka PBE 1976, 1977; Chikushino MBE 1981, 1990). The cemetery is situated on a hill slope running up to the ridge. The linear space does not coincide with the contours or line of the ridge. This suggests that the linear spatial structure was not forcibly based on the topography (Mizoguchi 1995a; the following analyses are based on its work). The formation began with the placement of several wooden coffin burials at a spot which was later to become the northern end of the linear space during the Yayoi II period. Interestingly, a pit marks the entrance to the linear space, dug at the beginning of the cemetery's formation, and a globular jar dating back to the Yayoi II was placed at the bottom of the pit. The cemetery gradually grew southwards from its lower, northern end, but the burials were not placed in a strictly cumulative, sequential manner (Figure 6.14.B). The coffins, mainly wooden coffins during the Yayoi II and jar coffins during the Yayoi III, were situated linearly, as if following a preexisting path running up the hill, on top of which there appears to have been a large-scale settlement; this settlement, however was subsequently destroyed and has not yet been fully examined by archaeologists (Takesue 1999, 443–445). The two rows of burials were further lined by pits, some of which had globular jars and a small number of cooking jars placed at their bottom (Figure 6.14.A). Although it is difficult to decipher the customary practices that were conducted around these pits, we can safely infer that the practices referred to the *collective* dead, not to specific individuals; there are much fewer pits than burials, and the former are not directly related to any specific burial spatially. During the final stage of the formation process, when the burials were situated around the higher, southern end of the linear space, two shallow linear ditches were dug to line the two burial rows. Again, archaeologists were able to unearth some globular jars from these ditches. A large number of jar coffins containing

the bodies of infants are present. The number (109 out of 153) exceeds that of the adult jar coffins (44 out of 153) (Chikushino MBE 1990, 157). The infants' jar coffins were often situated as if exactly marking the outline of square grave pits containing adult jar coffins, thus suggesting that the grave pits were covered by small earth caps, roughly square in shape (Figure 6.15). Most of the infant coffins were inserted into the structure of the adult grave pits from the inside of the path-like linear space in between the lines of the adult graves, suggesting that the inside of the linear space was the main 'mortuary activity area' (Figures 6.14 and 6.15). In fact, it is obvious that the inner side of the linear space was actually a path, through which funeral processions probably proceeded. If this were the case, the customary practices conducted around the pits and ditches lining the linear space and the rows of burials from the outside might have been independent of the other burial practices conducted inside of the rows in terms of their timing, and it is quite possible that they constituted *ancestral*, not *mortuary*, rituals.

There are examples of burial sites with more than two rows of burials. However, the presence of a path-like linear space between rows of burials is a common trait shared by the cemeteries of the time. This suggests that the linearity of the linear cemeteries derives from the (pre)existence of a path. In terms of their formation processes, there are examples such as the Nagaoka, the Monden (門田), the Kuriyama (栗山) and other cemeteries where the formation process progressed in a cumulative but fairly random manner (Mizoguchi 1997b). As a result, those linear cemeteries do not contain any clear clustering of burials, though some of them show some traces of clustered burials. The scale of such clusters varies. Some of them consist of only four or five burials, and may have represented households. However, the majority of burial clusters are larger than that, and it is possible that they represent lineage-scale groupings. At the Shiwaya-Yon'notsubo (志波屋四ノ坪) cemetery at the Yoshinogari site, around a couple of thousand burials appear to have been divided into not more than ten to twenty clusters (Saga PBE 1994, 62–76). In this case, the clusters would most probably have represented clan-scale, rather than lineage-scale, groupings.

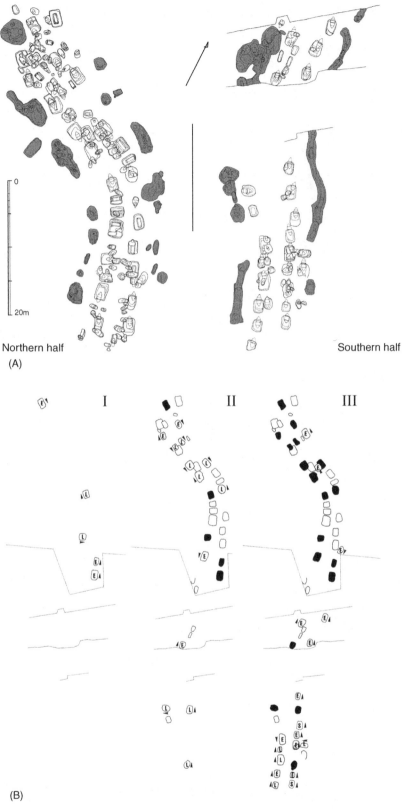

(A)

Northern half   Southern half

(B)

Figure 6.14. Nagaoka cemetery, Fukuoka prefecture: general plan (A) and formation process (B). A-left: Northern half, A-right: Southern half. Note that most of the infant burials are inserted from the inside of the path-like linear space flanked by the lines of adult graves, suggesting that the linear space was indeed the activity area (also see Figure 6.15). B-I: Yayoi II, B-II: first half of the Yayoi III, B-III: second half of the Yayoi III. E: Earlier burials, L: Later burials. Arrows indicating the direction to which the burial jars are inserted to the burial pits, effectively indicating the vista of the mourners (see Figure 6.16). After Mizoguchi (1995a), original plan drawings from Chikushino MBE (1990), traced and modified by Mizoguchi.

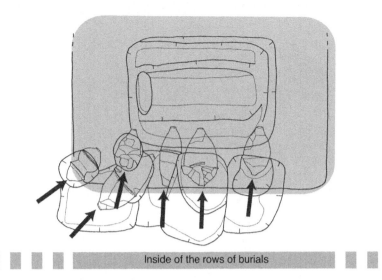

Inside of the rows of burials

Figure 6.15. Infant burial jars inserted to the adult grave, the Nagaoka cemetery. Arrows indicate the directions to which the jars were inserted to their burial pits. The presence of a square earthen heap covering the grave (shaded) can be inferred from the configuration of the former (after Mizoguchi [1995a], with additions).

From this, we can infer that irrespective of their scale, communal groupings buried their dead in an orderly manner, that is, buried them along paths, which resulted in the formation of linear cemeteries. I would like to argue that this linear formation along a common path holds a vital clue to the understanding of why this unique cemetery-scape formation was particularly preferred during the Yayoi II and III. The (pre)existence of a path necessitates the formation of a procession, along which people have to move. As John Barrett (1993,

9–39) points out, processions necessitate coordination while simultaneously deciding who will lead and who will follow. This suggests that the linear cemeteries served as locales where the *coordination* and *internal hierarchy* of various communal groupings were generated and reproduced (Mizoguchi 1995a).

If this were the case, such a cemetery-scape can be regarded as having been 'functionally' fit for dealing with some of the difficulties that faced the communities of the Yayoi II and III periods. As mentioned earlier, the Yayoi II in northern Kyushu saw small residential groups budding off from the settlements that had emerged in either the Incipient Yayoi or the Yayoi I (Figure 6.6.A). This would have required the implementation of special devices to maintain communal, collaborative ties between the parent and child settlements. It would also have led to the formation of new villages consisting of residential units that had budded off from different parent villages, which in turn would have necessitated the creation of new communal togetherness between the formerly separate communal segments (see Figure 6.6). The formation of inter-village networks would have also been vital for the supply of goods and raw materials, including the Imayama axes (see the preceding discussion). The period also witnessed an increased frequency of inter-communal violence. From among the fifty-three skeletal remains excavated from the third excavation of Nagaoka, three had traces of injuries, two in the form of tips of bronze daggers stuck in bones and one in the form of a severe cut in the forehead, some of which appear to have been fatal (Nakahashi 1990). For instance, the adult male skeleton excavated from the jar burial no. 100 had the tip of a bronze dagger stuck in his sacroiliac joint (ibid., 199). According to the reconstruction by Takahiro Nakahashi, his death resulted from a fatal stabbing from behind (ibid.). It is possible that this particular adult male had been involved in a pitched battle and was trying to escape from the enemy. In fact, the areas where the number of settlements increased steeply over a relatively short period because of the accumulation of budded-off settlements, such as the Kuma-Nishioda site in Fukuoka prefecture (Takesue 1985, 448), appear to have yielded a greater number of skeletal remains with traces of combat injuries (Takesue 1999, 448). This suggests that the increasing violence was the result of increasing competition over various resources, ranging from lands suitable for constructing paddies to marriage partners, and the situation was, at times, further exacerbated by overpopulation. This would have increased the importance of a stable communal leadership working to maintain the internal cohesion and corporation of individual residential communities and the clan-type kin-based sodalities, on the one hand, while leading combatants in the inter-village/communal battles, probably small scale, on the other. The leaders generated and represented by the organisation of processions would have been naturally equipped with the kind of faculties needed to deal with these contradictions, that is, the ability to be the *communal mediator* as well as a *strong leader*.

MICRO-SEQUENCE FORMATION (IN THE YAYOI III AND IV)

The linear formation of cemetery-scapes was phased out towards the end of the Yayoi III (Figure 6.13.A and B). Instead, burials began to be situated in the form of densely packed clusters that were arranged in a seemingly chaotic manner (Figure 6.13.D). A careful reconstruction of the formation process of the clusters, however, reveals that the clusters consist of 'micro-sequential clusters' of burials (Mizoguchi 1995b; the following analyses are based on this work).

At location C in the Kuriyama cemetery of Fukuoka prefecture, we find seven such clusters formed over the period of three jar burial typo-chronological stages spanning the end of the Yayoi III to the end of the Yayoi IV (Figures 6.13.E and 6.16) (ibid.). A new jar burial was located right next to a preexisting one. The jar coffin was inserted into the horizontal pit adjacent to the primary rectangular pit, and its direction, without doubt, pointed to the preexisting grave (Figure 6.16). As we have seen in the case of linear cemeteries, the graves appear to have been covered by small earthen heaps, which would have enabled the insertion of jars in exactly the direction of the preexisting graves. Repeated acts of this kind resulted in the formation of sequences of graves, which can be described as 'materialised genealogies' (Mizoguchi 2005); those who attended and/or were involved in such acts would have been reminded of and/or impressed with the ties between the person they were burying and those who had been buried in the preexisting graves (Figure 6.16).

The structure of grave pits allows us to reconstruct the manner in which mourners stood around the pit during a funeral. The presence of steps leading down to the bottom of the pit suggests that the mourners would have stood around the edge of the pit, looking in the direction of the jar's insertion (Figure 6.16). In such a case, the mourners' eyes would have been directed to the earthen heaps covering the preexisting graves. Hence, we can infer that they would have seen the heaps not as merely heaps of earth but as the *materialised memories* of the lives of those who were buried underneath the heaps. In that sense, the micro-sequential clusters of burials were, indeed, like materialised genealogies inscribed in the ground (Mizoguchi 2005).

As regards the cause of emergence of such a mortuary custom, it is important to note that the average 'length', that is, the number of burials comprising individual micro-sequential clusters, is different between ordinary cemeteries and the 'compound' cemeteries. The latter, which were commonly rectangular in shape with shallow ditches surrounding them, would have been the elite burial compounds (see the following discussion); they were not only clearly marked and differentiated as locales but also often contained burials with grave goods, larger grave pits and larger coffins (Mizoguchi 2005). The micro-sequential clusters in the mortuary compounds tend to be 'longer' than those in the ordinary cemeteries; the former commonly consist of three or four burials, and in the case of location C in the Kuriyama site, seven burials, whereas most of the latter consist of two or three (compare Figures 6.13.D and 6.16). This suggests the emergence of differences between the 'elite' and the 'commoners' in the way of reckoning their genealogical-generational depth and continuity (ibid.).

BURIAL COMPOUND FORMATION

Burial compounds emerged in the Yayoi II, became widespread in the Yayoi III and continued throughout the rest of the Yayoi period (Figure 6.13.C, E–H), although the oldest burial compound dates back to the Yayoi I (Yasu-cho-shi-hensan-iinkai 1991, 159–162; Mizoguchi 2001). They are generally square in shape, commonly enclosed by a shallow ditch, with one or two bridges connecting the inner regions of the compound with the rest of the cemetery; most of the compounds are covered by low, flat-topped mounds, although some of them have had no mound covering them.

The way of situating burials inside the compounds transformed during the period from the Yayoi II and III (Figure 6.13.C) to the Yayoi IV (Figure 6.13.E). During the Yayoi II and III, the spatial arrangement of burials commonly began from the central grave (Figure 6.17). At the northern burial compound of the Yashinogari site, the compound and its covering mound had already been built when the central grave was dug (Figure 6.17; Saga PBE 1997, 29–44, Mizoguchi 1998). At location D of the Kuriyama site (Figure 6.13.C), however, the digging of a grave, later to be the central grave, appears to have marked the beginning of the construction of a square burial compound (Mizoguchi 1998, 66). This was commonly followed by other burials situated in circles around the central grave. With almost no exception, the burial jars were inserted into the grave pits as if pointing towards the central grave. At the northern burial compound of the Yoshinogari site in Saga prefecture, the central grave contained a bronze dagger and seventy-nine glass cylindrical beads, probably parts of a headband, and seven out of thirteen satellite burials contained bronze daggers (Figure 6.17; Saga PBE 1997, 29–44). The presence of several burials during each burial jar typo-chronological phase suggests that many elite members or a group of chiefly figures were generally buried there every generation, not just one elite member or chief (Mizoguchi 1998). With regard to the sexable skeletal remains excavated from the burial compounds, almost all of them were found to be adult males.

Although the Yoshitake-Takagi (吉武高木) cemetery has some unique features, it is basically similar to the Yoshinogari cemetery. Here, dug-out wooden coffin burials as well as jar coffin burials are situated as if paired together or forming a number of rows within a roughly square area (Figure 6.18; Fukuoka MBE 1996c; Mizoguchi 2008, 83). Many graves within the square area contain rich grave good assemblages, variously comprised of bronze weapons, bronze armlets, bronze mirrors, comma-shaped beads, cylindrical beads and so on. At the wooden coffin burial no. 3, which contains the richest assemblage, the deceased was buried with two bronze daggers, one bronze spearhead, one bronze halberd, one bronze mirror with complex geometric motifs (*Tachu-saimon-kyo*, 多紐細紋鏡), one comma-shaped jade bead, ninety-five cylindrical jasper beads and a globular jar (Figure 6.18; Fukuoka MBE 1996c, 76–84). The person,

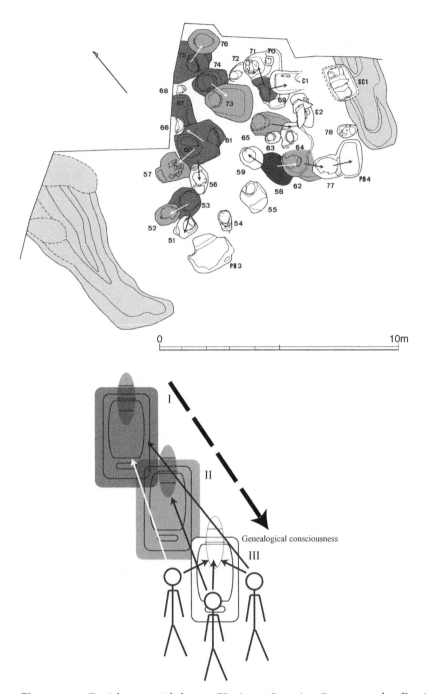

Figure 6.16. Burial sequential clusters (Kuriyama Location C, an example of burial compound type II). Differently coloured shades indicate different phases determined by burial-jar morphology-based relative chronology, with darker shades indicating older burials and arrows indicating the progression of the formation of 'burial sequences' (after Mizoguchi 1995b, 2005, with alterations). Below: the vista the mourners would have had (indicated by arrows), memory and the generation of genealogical consciousness through sequentially depositing the dead (schematised drawing).

whose body and skeleton have long since disintegrated and disappeared because of the highly acidic soil, wore a necklace made of the above-mentioned beads and was buried with a bronze dagger and a halberd to his or her left and another dagger, a spearhead and a mirror to his or her right (Figure 6.18). Considering their positions, the bronze weapons could not have had hilts or been attached to their shafts when deposited. The necklace and the mirror might suggest that the person was a priest-like character; the surface of the mirror is slightly incurved and would have created a spectacular visual effect when reflecting the sun. The weapons might also have been deposited not

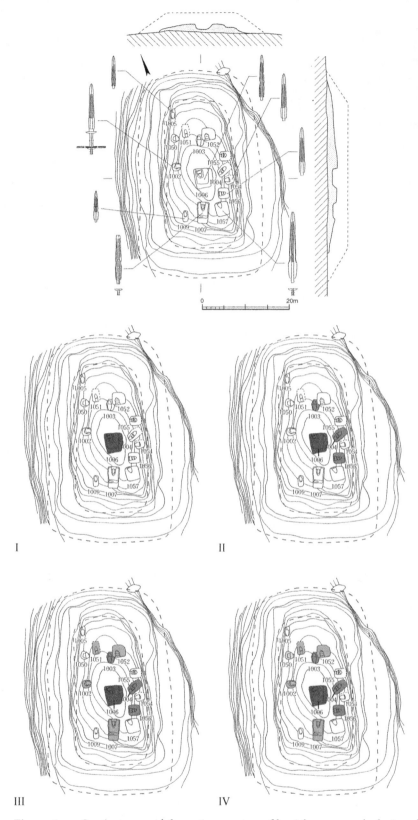

Figure 6.17. Spatio-temporal formation process of burial compounds during the Yayoi II and III: Burial compound type I, the northern burial mound of the Yoshinogari (after Saga PBE [1997], with additions and alterations). Top: General plan with the indication of bronze dagger-yielding jar burials; I~IV: Formation phases. New burials in each phase are colored differently than that of the previous phases.

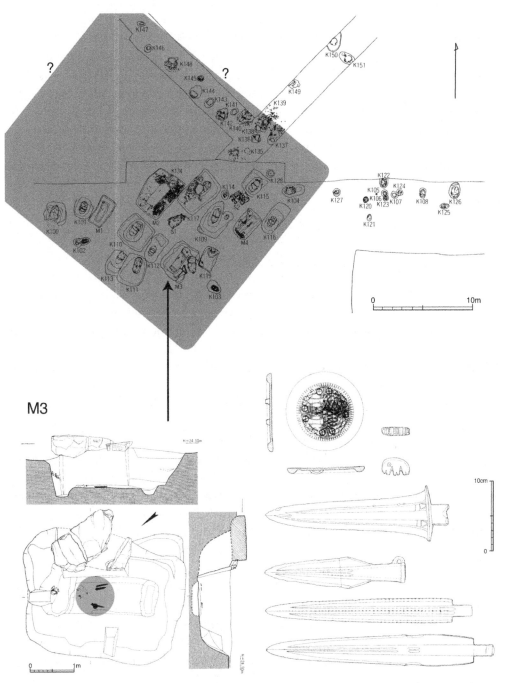

Figure 6.18. The probable square burial compound of the Yoshitake–Takagi (Fukuoka prefecture) and the grave goods composite wooden-coffin burial no. 3 and two bronze daggers, one bronze spearhead, one bronze halberd and a bronze mirror with two handles and complex geometric motifs deposited in it; after Fukuoka MBE 1996c). The possible compound area, inferred by the spatial configuration of the jar burials and the direction to which the jars are inserted to their pits, is shaded.

to indicate the person's status as a warrior-leader but to signify polythemic meanings, including the position of leadership in combat and in ritual occasions. Together with the fact that some of the other deceased found here were also buried with a combination of weapons and necklaces as their grave goods, their dualistic nature, that is, priest-like figures and *potential* leaders in combat, appears significant. In this case, again, we find the burials of a few chiefly figures per generation, not that of a single chief. The available pieces of information point to the image of collective leaders chosen as firsts among equals. This inference might further be reinforced by the fact that there were only a few jar burials of infants/children within the square area, whereas a number of them were situated to the east of that area (Figure 6.18): they seem to have been treated not as the future chiefs who died young but as those who were bemoaned and commemorated communally. This would indicate that higher statuses of some sort, as represented by those buried in the demarcated area, did not fully become *ascribed* ones but continued to be *achieved* ones.

Towards the end of the Yayoi III, however, micro-sequential clusters began to be formed in the burial compounds, as mentioned above. At location C in Kuriyama (Figure 6.16), a detailed reconstruction of the formation process has revealed the presence of at least seven burial micro-clusters, consisting of burials situated adjacent to one another to form visual sequences of graves, probably capped by small soil heaps (Figure 6.16; also see Figure 6.15 for the presence of small soil heaps) (Mizoguchi 1995b). The intentional formation of such clusters, as mentioned above, not only brings to mind but also represents the continuation of the genealogical lines of the deceased. An important point to be noted here is that the length of the clusters, that is, the number of burials constituting the clusters formed within the compounds, tends to be longer than that of the clusters outside the compounds (Mizoguchi 2001). Similarly, the burials inside the compounds tended to have grave goods more often than those outside the compounds (Mizoguchi 1995b, 2001). These grave goods came to include iron weapons such as spearheads, daggers and halberds; accessories including armlets made of the shell *Tricornis latissimus* (*Gohora* in Japanese; see Figure 6.4.H), and, in rare cases, early Han Chinese imports such as bronze mirrors and green glass discs (Figure 6.4. D–F). The majority of the sexable skeletal remains excavated from these graves are those of males, similar to the corresponding burial compounds in the Yayoi II and III; however, these had by now begun to include a small number of females and infants.[50] The compounds, almost without exception, were situated in or near extremely large

cemeteries attached to the large regional-centre-type settlements of individual settlement systems, similar to their Yayoi II and III equivalents.

These changes can be understood as a reaction to the emergent hierarchisation between the sodality segments residing in the regional centres and in smaller settlements that were increasingly becoming dependent on the former. As I have already argued, the central-place-type characteristics of the regional centres became more prominent during the Yayoi III and IV, and the increasing circulation of raw materials and goods such as iron tools would have consolidated the function of the sodality-type inter-village ties through which they were circulated (Figure 6.6.B; see Section 5 in this chapter). This would have necessitated a stable leadership for the individual sodalities. The formation of burial micro-sequences in the burial compounds indicates that the concept of genealogical continuity was emphasised as a way to address the situation (Figure 6.16). In this way, the stability of leadership of individual sodalities and continuing collaboration between the sodalities would have been ensured by the use of a common elite burial ground in the form of burial compounds situated in the regional centres (Figure 6.6.B) (Mizoguchi 2008). As mentioned earlier, the extremely large cemeteries attached to the regional centres may have functioned as *regionally shared necropolises* (Figures 6.6.B and 6.9). In that case, they would have functioned as locales where the *solidarity* of the sodalities comprising individual, tribal-group-like regional groupings was confirmed and reproduced; hence, they functioned as a sort of *monument* for embodying and representing the sense of regional communal togetherness. The burial of sodality leaders in those burial compounds would also have enhanced the sense of solidarity and communal togetherness.

THE EMERGENCE OF INTER-REGIONAL HIERARCHY

Only a small number of the deceased buried in the burial compounds (and very rarely in ordinary burial grounds) were deposited with grave goods. In the Yayoi II and III periods, the grave goods comprised bronze weapons and accessories such as necklaces made of comma-shaped and cylindrical beads, armlets made of shells exclusively sourced from the seas around the Okinawan

---

50 At location C of the Kuriyama site, the burial sequence no. 2 (Mizoguchi 1995b), the longest burial sequence in this compound cemetery comprising seven burials, includes a female with fourteen shell armlets made of *Conidae* (*Imogai* in Japanese).

islands and so on (see Figures 6.17 and 6.18). In the Yayoi IV, early Han Chinese mirrors and other Chinese products – most probably imported from the Han commandery of Lelang (see Chapter 3.2.4) – became part of the grave good assemblage, apart from iron daggers, spearheads, halberds, and, in rarer cases, glass comma-shaped beads and cylindrical beads (Figure 6.4.D–F).[51]

It has been pointed out that there existed an inter-regional hierarchy indicated by the different contents of grave good assemblages (e.g. Shimojo 1991; Nakazono 1991). At the top of this hierarchy are two extremely rich burial compounds, the Mikumo-Minamishoji and the Sugu-Okamoto burial compounds, located in the extremely large regional centres of Mikumo and Sugu (Figure 6.4.A–B). Two jar burials in the former, only burials situated in it, as mentioned (see Figures 6.13.G and 6.20), were found to contain around fifty-two early Han Chinese bronze mirrors in total, a number of bronze weapons, eight gilded bronze ornaments, at least eight *Heki* (壁) green glass discs, about fifteen glass comma-shaped beads, numerous glass cylindrical beads, and so on (Figures 6.4.A–F and 6.20).

Situated below these burials in terms of hierarchy of grave-good richness, we can classify the other grave good assemblages into the following categories: (A) those comprising more than two mirrors, including large one(s) (> about 16 cm; Figure 6.4.X and Y); (B) those comprising one large bronze mirror (> about 16 cm; Figure 6.4.Y, 5, 13 and 14); (C) those comprising one small bronze mirror (> about 10 cm or smaller; Figure 6.4.2, 3, 7, 9, 10 and 15) and (D) those without any bronze mirrors. Category A can be further subdivided into two: (A-1) bronze mirrors plus bronze and iron weapons (Figure 6.4.Y) and (A-2) bronze mirrors plus iron weapons/tools (Figure 6.4.X). Category C can also be subdivided as follows: (C-1) a small bronze mirror with bronze weapons (Figure 6.4.7); (C-2) a small bronze mirror, iron

weapons/tools and shell armlets (Figure 6.4.9); (C-3) a small bronze mirror with iron weapons/tools (Figure 6.4.2 and 10) and (C-4) a small bronze mirror only (Figure 6.4.3 and 15). Category D can be subdivided into three subcategories as follows: (D-1) iron weapons/tools and shell armlets (Figure 6.4.6), (D-2) only iron weapons/tools (Figure 6.4.8, 11, 12, 16 and 17) and (D-3) only shell armlets (numerous). Bead accessories were, at times, added to all of the above-mentioned subcategories.

An analysis of the distribution of these categories reveals the following: (1) the distribution of category B and the others is widespread, whereas that of the richest is confined to the coastal areas; (2) the distribution of A, B and C is confined to the areas surrounding the Sefuri mountain range, whereas that of D overlaps the above, with some outliers. What is particularly interesting is that examples of A and B appear to be situated at strategically important locations in the network of burials with the grave goods. The Tateiwa-Hotta (立岩掘田) site (Figure 6.4.Y) is located near the confluence of two rivers, the Honami and the Kama, and at the meeting of routes connecting the communities of the Fukuoka and Chikushi plains, including those living in the Sugu, Futsukaichi-Mine (二日市峯) and Higashioda-Mine (東小田峯) settlements to the east, that is, the western Seto Inland Sea area and beyond. The Higashioda-Mine settlement (Figure 6.4.X), where two early Han Chinese bronze mirrors, one large and the other small, a small disc-shaped implement made of a *Heki* (壁) green glass disc made in China, an iron halberd, an iron dagger, and an iron implement of an uncertain function were deposited in jar burial no. 10 as grave goods, is located on the meeting of routes connecting the communities of the Fukuoka and Saga plains, including the Sugu (Figure 6.4.B) in the former and the Futatsukayama (二塚山; Figure 6.4.14) in the latter, to those of the floodplain of the Onga River, including the Tateiwa (Figure 6.4.Y), and to those of the eastern Chikushi Plain, including the Kuriyama (栗山; Figure 6.4.10). The Futatsukayama settlement (Figure 6.4.14) is located on the crossroads connecting the communities of the Fukuoka and Itoshima plains, including the Sugu (Figure 6.4.B) in the former and the Mikumo (Figure 6.4.A) in the latter, to

51 The source glass of which the comma-shaped beads were made was imported, most likely from China (Fujita 1994, 44–49). The cylindrical beads are also inferred to have been made of the material of Chinese origin, but the place of their production remains uncertain (ibid., 71–86). The iron implements might include some specimens made in the Korean peninsula.

TABLE 6.1. *Degree centrality scores of the jar burial cemeteries with grave goods. For the theoretical assumptions of and method for the calculation of the score, see Chapter 8, pp. 229–230, of this volume*

Rank	Node	Degree
1	Futatsukayama	5
1	Mikumo	5
1	Yoshinogari	5
4	Futsukaichi-Dojoyama	4
4	Higashioda Mine-Fukita	4
4	Rokunohata	4
4	Sugu	4
4	Tateiwa	4
4	Yoshitake	4
10	Arita	3
10	KumaNishioda	3
10	Maruodai	3
13	Antokudai	2
13	Fuchibaru	2
13	Kashiwazaki-Nakabaru	2
13	Kuriyama	2
13	Monden	2
13	Noboritate	2
19	Noda	1
19	Tominoharu	1

TABLE 6.2. *Bonacich centrality scores of the jar burial cemeteries with grave goods*

Rank	Node	Power
1	Yoshitake	182.7117
2	Arita	174.271
3	Higashioda Mine-Fukita	162.5672
4	Mikumo	145.4643
5	Tateiwa	141.8231
6	Maruodai	140.3661
7	Futsukaichi-Dojoyama	139.752
8	Kuriyama	112.1951
9	KumaNishioda	91.36418
10	Futatsukayama	65.32209
11	Kashiwazaki-Nakabaru	44.69597
12	Sugu	43.74958
13	Noboritate	29.13192
14	Yoshinogari	23.92769
15	Rokunohata	0.409286
16	Fuchibaru	−3.55927
17	Tominoharu	−8.03617
18	Noda	−19.7954
19	Antokudai	−21.8688
20	Monden	−29.0597

those of the Saga plain, including the Yoshinogari (Figure 6.4.15) and the Rokunohata (六ノ幡; Figure 6.4.13). An examination of the *centrality* of those sites by applying several methods of Network analysis[52] shows that their score is higher than those of the neighbouring communities (Figure 6.19, Tables 6.1–6). Therefore, it can be deduced that these well-connected communities would have become regional centres by attracting more people, goods and information to pass through them through the working of sodalities and other inter-communal ties (also see Figure 6.6.B). In the case of the elite of the Mikumo and Sugu settlements, which enjoyed consistently high centrality scores among the coastal communities and across the entire network of communities respectively (Tables 6.1–6), forging and maintaining ties with them by strategically distributing prestige gifts and possibly exchanging marriage partners would have secured them access to

various resources such as shells for making armlets from the south and stone reaping knives made in Tateiwa. In the case of the Sugu, its extremely high betweenness centrality score (Table 6.6) indicates

TABLE 6.3. *Closeness centrality scores of the jar burial cemeteries with grave goods*

Rank	Node	Closeness
1	Rokunohata	44
2	Futatsukayama	45
3	Futsukaichi-Dojoyama	46
3	KumaNishioda	46
5	Sugu	47
6	Maruodai	49
6	Yoshinogari	49
6	Yoshitake	49
9	Higashioda Mine-Fukita	52
9	Mikumo	52
11	Antokudai	53
11	Monden	53
13	Arita	54
14	Tateiwa	58
15	Fuchibaru	61
15	Kashiwazaki-Nakabaru	61
17	Noda	62
18	Kuriyama	67
18	Noboritate	67
18	Tominoharu	67

52 Network analysis calculates how each of the units ('nodes') comprising a network is well connected to the others ('centrality score') by using topological mathematical formula (Borgatti et al. 2002). For a short methodological introduction, see Chapter 8.3.2, pp. 229–230.

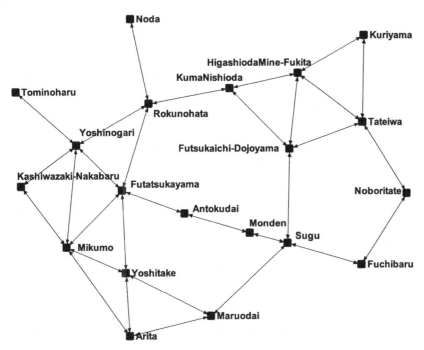

Figure 6.19. Network of rich jar burials of the Yayoi IV. 'Edges' are basically drawn between the neighbouring 'nodes', but other archaeological-contextual information is also taken into account (after Mizoguchi 2010a). The graph is generated by NetDraw (in UCINET Ver. 6.239; Borgatti et al. 2002), and the locations of the edges do not reflect their exact locations on the site distribution map, provided in Figure 6.4.

the settlement to be the most important 'mediator' in the network of exchange and interaction. In the case of the Mikumo, however, the centrality scores are consistently lower than some of the inland sites such as the Yoshinogari, the Futatsukayama and Higashioda-Mine (Tables 6.1–6), all located a sort of 'gateway' locations connecting the coastal and inland floodplains, and it suggests that

TABLE 6.4. *Reach centrality scores of the jar burial cemeteries with grave goods*

Rank	Node	Reach
1	Futatsukayama	11.44999981
2	Rokunohata	11
3	Yoshinogari	10.98333359
4	Sugu	10.78333187
5	Futsukaichi-Dojoyama	10.74999905
6	Mikumo	10.68333244
7	Yoshitake	10.44999886
8	KumaNishioda	10.24999905
9	Higashioda Mine-Fukita	9.999999046
10	Maruodai	9.916666031
11	Tateiwa	9.599999428
12	Arita	9.449999809
13	Antokudai	9.11666584
14	Monden	9
15	Kashiwazaki-Nakabaru	8.599999428
16	Fuchibaru	8.516667366
17	Noboritate	8.133333206
18	Kuriyama	7.950000286
19	Noda	7.733333588
20	Tominoharu	7.600000381

TABLE 6.5. *Eigenvector centrality scores of the jar burial cemeteries with grave goods*

Rank	Node	Eigenvector
1	Mikumo	0.44731
2	Futatsukayama	0.428956
3	Yoshinogari	0.395506
4	Yoshitake	0.357763
5	Rokunohata	0.273709
6	Arita	0.26734
7	Kashiwazaki-Nakabaru	0.225118
8	Maruodai	0.19582
9	Antokudai	0.131676
10	KumaNishioda	0.127168
11	Sugu	0.108026
12	Futsukaichi-Dojoyama	0.107838
13	Tominoharu	0.10564
14	Higashioda Mine-Fukita	0.094556
15	Tateiwa	0.073985
16	Noda	0.073108
17	Monden	0.064025
18	Kuriyama	0.045018
19	Fuchibaru	0.036754
20	Noboritate	0.029579

TABLE 6.6. *Betweenness (flow betweenness) centrality scores of the jar burial cemeteries with grave goods*

Rank	Node	FlowBet
1	Sugu	120.0667
2	Tateiwa	62.66667
3	Rokunohata	62.56667
4	Yoshinogari	60.46667
5	Futatsukayama	55.83333
6	Antokudai	39.73333
6	Monden	39.73333
8	Mikumo	39
9	Fuchibaru	38.83333
9	Noboritate	38.83333
11	Higashioda Mine-Fukita	29
12	KumaNishioda	26.16667
13	Maruodai	25.23333
14	Futsukaichi-Dojoyama	17.83333
15	Yoshitake	13.06667
16	Arita	8.566667
17	Kashiwazaki-Nakabaru	1.9
18	Kuriyama	1.5
19	Noda	0
19	Tominoharu	0

the prominence of the Mikumo community and its elite was achieved by its control over access to the Han commandery of Lelang where it obtained the prestige goods (Mizoguchi 2010a, 28–29).

The practice of differentiating themselves, probably initiated by the elite of the Mikumo and Sugu settlements, from those of the other communities who were buried with simpler grave good assemblages shows the former's strategic intention and manipulation of their position by seeking exclusive access to the source(s) of exotic goods, such as the Lelang commandery. These elite were not buried in micro-sequential clusters but individually interred in the centre of the mound; in the case of the Mikumo-Minamishoji burial compound, they were buried in two adjacent graves (Figures 6.13.G and 6.20).[53] The other graves with grave goods, particularly those with early Han Chinese bronze mirrors, were situated either in micro-sequential burial clusters in the burial compounds (e.g. Tateiwa-Hotta; The committee for the investigation of the Tateiwa site 1977) or in ordinary burial grounds (e.g. the Kashiwazaki-

[53] In the case of the Sugu-Okamoto site, the situation is unclear because the site was discovered and destroyed by farmers in the year 1899 (cf. Nakayama 1922, 1927).

Tajima [柏崎田島]; Horikawa 1982). These findings suggest that those who were involved in the burial of the Mikumo and Sugu elite attempted to differentiate and emphasise their dead chiefs' unique positions by burying them individually rather than situating them in sequential burial clusters.

However, whether their status was an *ascribed* rather than an *achieved* one remains uncertain; as yet, we have not uncovered any clear trace of status differentiation among the living elite in the form of separate living quarters, or elite precincts, furnished with facilities and goods suggesting the residents' stable high status. In addition, excavations have not yet revealed any burial compounds for the successors of the deceased who were buried in those extremely rich burials. This suggests that their status would have certainly been recognised and marked as higher than that of any other elite within the horizon of inter-communal ties but would not have been regarded as one meant to be inherited by their offspring or other fellow descent-group members. Alternatively, their status might have been genuinely achieved by their securing exclusive access to various source(s) of exotic items in addition to their ability to deal with various social problems, and due to some momentary discontinuation in the supply of goods (I return to this issue in the next chapter), their status could not be maintained and/or inherited.

In any case, the practice of representing the position of the elite by their manner of burial was a transitional one. This is well attested by the contradictory coexistence of two characters in one individual person: the accessories deposited with the deceased, such as shell armlets and comma-shaped beads, suggest their shamanistic character, whereas the mirrors and other Chinese imports emphasise their connection with regions far away and their position of dealing with a completely different type of uncertainty from that generated by the paddy field rice farming-based way of life (artefacts bracketed as 'Chinese' in Figure 6.4.D–F and I). The region became exposed to this new 'Other', by which I mean a new identity whose operation defied the conventional sets of expectations, including occasional disruption of the smooth running of everyday life, which the people previously had drawn upon.

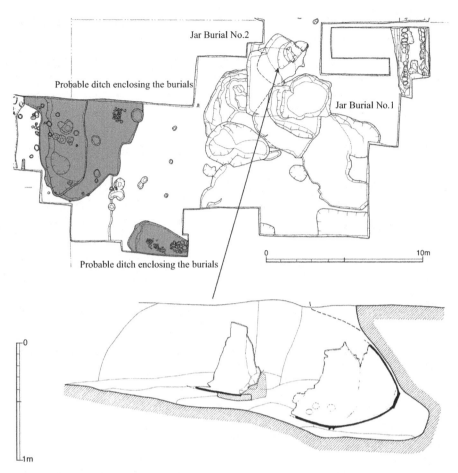

Figure 6.20. The Mikumo-Minamishoji, Fukuoka prefecture (after Fukuoka PBE 1985b). Jar burial no. 1 was disturbed thoroughly in the Edo period. The section drawing is that of jar burial no. 2, excavated by the Fukuoka PBE. The shaded depressions are parts of the ditch probably enclosing a rectangular earthen mound (possibly 30 metres by 20 metres) covering the burials. For some artefacts recorded to be from no. 1 and excavated from no. 2, see Figure 6.4.

The operation of the new other, that of Lelang, was in the realm of human being, hence negotiable and controllable to a degree, differing fundamentally from the operation of nature, that was non-negotiable and uncontrollable. Meanwhile, because it is the operation of human being, hence already definable, access to the former by means of negotiation can be monopolised.

6.2. Houses of the Dead? – The World of Rectangular Ditch-Enclosed Mortuary Compounds (Hokei-Shuko-Bo, 方形周溝墓)

As we have seen, rectangular ditch-enclosed burial compounds emerged in the Yayoi I, and they most significantly characterise the mortuary evidence of the regions around the Osaka Bay area of western Japan during the Middle Yayoi period (Figure

6.21). The cemetery-scape they typically form is characterised by the agglomeration of micro-clusters of compounds. This leads to the picture that cemeteries were 'villages of the dead'; a cemetery was the burial ground for the inhabitants of a village, and its micro-clusters represented the households in the village. This model assumes that successive generations of members of a household were buried in the individual mounds forming a micro-cluster (Harunari 1985; Terasawa 1990, 22–23).

Based on this assumption, it is widely assumed that we can attempt to reconstruct the social organisation of the time. For instance, when a pair or pairs of interments, most often buried in wooden composite coffins, are found in individual mounds, they are almost automatically inferred to be husbands and wives, and it is further inferred

that individual households had already begun functioning not only as the basic unit of social reproduction but also as that of the inheritance of
wealth and rights/obligations (Harunari 1985).
This also implies that the emergence of rectangular ditch-enclosed burial mounds reflected the
commencement of internal segmentation of corporate groupings such as clans or lineages into
smaller units, which were to become the building blocks of an emergent social hierarchy (ibid.).
According to the Marxist-inspired perspective (see
Chapter 2.2.2), hierarchical order is thought to
have emerged due to the development of inequality between small-scale kin groups, resulting from
the collapse of larger, internally egalitarian corporate groups. The mortuary archaeology of the Yayoi
period, drawing on this model, assumes that the
spatial patterns that can be analytically extracted
from Yayoi cemeteries directly reflect the residential pattern and kin organisation of the living
community.

However, an in-depth investigation into the
formation process of individual cemeteries, the
spatio-temporal configuration of the burials and
the age and sex of those buried in individual burial
mounds refutes these theory-driven inferences.

COMPLEXITY OF THE FORMATION PROCESS
Let us first examine the formation process of individual cemeteries consisting of rectangular ditch-
enclosed burial compounds. An examination of
the formation process of some exemplary cemeteries revealed the following (Figure 6.21): (1) the
burial mounds form *sequential clusters*, (2) each
cluster consists of mounds of *various sizes*, and
(3) *sequences are often divided* during the course of
their development. The temporal order of the construction of mounds can most often be confirmed
by the intersecting and/or overlapping of ditches
(Figure 6.21).

If we regard mortuary practices as a unique and
autonomous part of social practices, these observations would suggest the following. The fact that
the mounds formed sequential clusters by probably intentionally intersecting and/or overlapping
with ditches suggests that each sequential cluster
represents the conscious and continuous separation
of a field of social practices from the others; each
sequential cluster was formed as a consequence of
the cumulative enclosing of spaces wherein mortu-

ary practices were conducted and the dead buried,
also in a cumulative manner.

An important recent investigation also shows
that a gathering involving the use and disposal of
a large number of pottery vessels and occasionally
wooden statuettes (possibly representing ancestral
figures; cf. Terasawa 2000, 121–123) occurred at
the time of mound construction and enlargement
(e.g. Oba 2001). Many of the vessels show traces
of being heated, which indicate that the activity involved collective feasting (Oba 2007, 73–77).
This suggests that the boundaries of the field of
mortuary-related social practices were marked not
only spatially by physical markers, such as ditches
and low earthen mounds, but also temporary by
events such as ritualistic gatherings and collective
feasts.

The mounds, as enclosed spaces constituting
individual sequential clusters, are of various sizes
(Figure 6.21). In addition, the sequential clusters
are often found to be divided into two during
the course of their formation (Figure 6.21). These
observations suggest that the theme(s), strategy of
practice, and the character and scale of the unit
conducting them changed from time to time during the formation process of individual sequences.
With regard to the varying mound size, there
are intriguing examples of changes in the size of
mounds in neighbouring sequential clusters, as if
those who built them were competing against one
another (Figure 6.21; compare ups and downs in
the mound size of the sequential cluster composed
of A2, A3, A4, and A5 and that composed of
B1, B2, B3, B4 and B5). Such cases suggest that
the varying mound size in individual sequential
clusters was related to some sort of inter-group
competition. Those who were in charge of the
construction of relatively large mound in individual cemeteries would have enjoyed relative
dominance indicated by the number of people
they could mobilise for the construction of the
mounds and conducting funerals. However, such
position would have been difficult to sustain for
more than a couple of generations. Accordingly,
the next time when a new mound had to be
constructed, its scale did not necessarily match up
with the previous one.

In this section, we have already noted two
important observations: (1) the formation of individual sequential clusters of burial mounds was

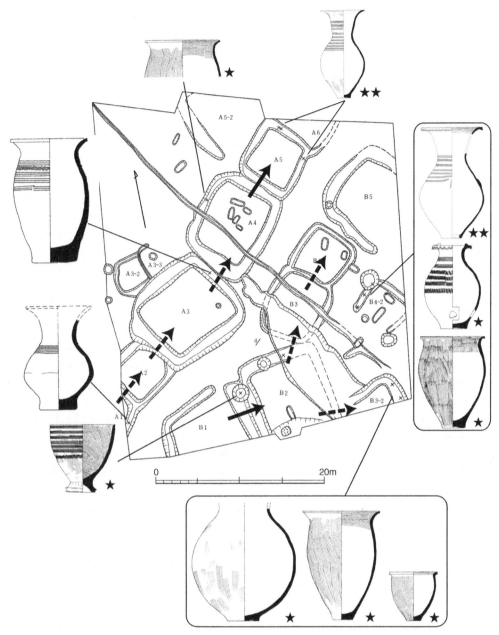

Figure 6.21. An examples of the clusters of rectangular ditch-enclosed burial compounds: the Ama (安満) site of Osaka prefecture (after Takatsuki MBE 1977). Pots from the bottom of ditches, probably used in ritual occasions, dated to the Yayoi II (marked with one star). Two-starred pots dating from the Yayoi III. Arrows indicate confirmed superimposition; dotted arrows indicate probable order of construction. Note sequences B3–B4 and B3–2 came out of sequence B1–B2.

the consequence of an intentional undertaking to maintain a symbolically as well as physically bounded field of mortuary and related social practices, and (2) the theme(s) and strategy of mortuary and related practices performed during the construction and use of burial mounds and the character and scale of the unit performing them changed, often several times, during the formation process of the sequential clusters.

How and why did these aspects change, and how can we make sense of the changes? In order to answer these questions, we need to investigate the nature and character of the practices performed and what they represented, and for that, we need to examine the remains of those who were interred in the individual mounds.

First, in order to examine the commencement of individual fields of mortuary and related practices, we need to examine the age and sex of the *first interment* in the individual burial mounds. It appears that there were no strict or fixed rules in this regard; while male individuals were most often chosen to be the first interment in a mound, there were cases in which female individuals or infants were chosen as first interments as well (e.g. Kosaka ponpu-jo [小坂ポンプ場, Kosaka pumping site]) No. 10 rectangular ditch-enclosed mortuary compound (Uryudo-iseki chosa-kai 1982; Harunari 1985, 16) for the former, and Kitoragawa (鬼虎川) No. 26 rectangular ditch-enclosed mortuary compound for the latter.

Interestingly, the first interments were found to be deposited at various locations on the flat tops of the individual mounds: they were frequently deposited on the fringes as well as in the centre of the flat tops. This observation coincides with the fact that many mounds containing multiple burials show no traces of a central grave. The examples in which burials were placed on the fringes of the mound, with the central area remaining empty, suggest that the number of interments and their locations in the mound were already planned at the time of construction of the mound; someone who was still alive during the mound's construction might have planned for his/her own burial to be located in the mound, or indeed at the centre of the mound, but for some reason, this plan was never accomplished. In fact, such plans for using a particular mound as a locale for successive burials appear to have been changed quite often; it is impossible to determine any straightforward correlation between the number of interments and the size of the mound. Had the pre-devised plans been retained until the termination of the use of the mounds, larger mounds would have contained more interments than smaller ones. However, it was not the case. At times, only one or two interments were found to be buried at the fringes of a large mound, after which the mound was no longer used. In other cases, a considerable number of burials were literary packed into a relatively small mound (A4 in Figure 6.21; see e.g. Uryudo-iseki chosa-kai 1982).

These observations suggest the following: (1) it appears that at the time of construction of a mound, there was some planning as to who were to be buried in the mound; (2) however, these

plans appear to have changed quite often, and (3) this tendency to change the original plan is well illustrated by the fact that there is no significant correlation between the size of the mound and the number of interments in it.

COMPETITION IN THE BURIAL OF THE DEAD
Based on the preceding observations, I would propose the following:

(1) The sequential clusters of rectangular ditch-enclosed burial mounds did not 'reflect' the life-course of well-defined units such as 'households'; instead, they were used as arenas for the performance of mortuary practices with changing *themes and agenda*.

(2) Each mound was constructed with a certain plan in mind, in terms of who were to be buried in the mound and at what location.

(3) Such planning does not appear to have 'reflected' the actual power, wealth and/or the position(s) of those who were involved in the construction. It is more likely that the plans were strategically devised in response to inter-group competition over positions in larger corporate groupings. The size of the mound would have been influenced by a combination of factors including not only the number of individuals who willingly participated in or could be mobilised for the construction of the mound but also the strategic decision of *outdoing* rivals by constructing larger mounds than those constructed by the rival groups (note the case of location no. 9 of the Ama site, as mentioned earlier; see Figure 6.21).

(4) The trajectory of formation of each sequential cluster of rectangular ditch-enclosed burial mounds represents the material traces of the trajectory of changing strategies and positions chosen and occupied by each group, at a time when the scale and content of groups tended to change constantly.

6.3. Prolonged Liminality: Depositing Processed Skeletal Remains in Pots in Eastern Japan

The custom of depositing processed skeletal remains, often in densely decorated globular jars,

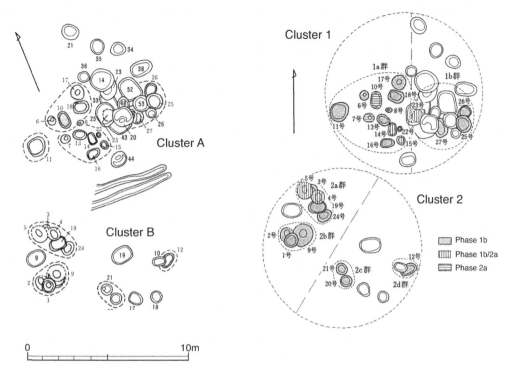

Figure 6.22. Oki cemetery (Gunma prefecture) and the spatial segmentation reconstructed by Harunari (left; after Harunari [1993], with additions) and Shitara (right; after Shitara [2008], with additions).

was widespread in eastern Japan, particularly from Chubu and Kanto to south-western Tohoku, during the Yayoi II and III periods (Figures 6.22–23).

Considering the character of the discourse embodied by this practice, it is important to note the presence of segmentary divisions at some cemeteries. For instance, the Oki (沖 II) site in Gunma prefecture is clearly divided into two groups, separated by two shallow ditches running side-by-side between the groups (Figure 6.22.A; Harunari 1993, 50–52). Shitara argues that those groups are further divided into two distinct sectors (Figure 6.22.B; Shitara 2008, 212–213, 215, fig. 101). Although the accurate recognition/reconstruction of distinct burial clusters is in many cases difficult,[54] it can be accepted that most of the cemeteries comprised of processed skeletal remains burials consist of a number of segments (e.g. Harunari 1993; Ishikawa 2000; Shitara

2008, 210–219). If the segments identified at those cemeteries were indeed sodality-like units, it suggests the presence and reproduction of sodalities cross-cutting a number of localised residential communities, bringing them together into wider units functioning as the units of mutual help and fulfilling reciprocal obligations (cf. Shitara 2008, 218).

As explained earlier, one of the most significant characteristics of the practice is the prolongation of social engagement with the dead. We cannot conclude that the final deposition of the remains marked the transformation of the dead into the ancestors. However, practices such as the extraction of small bones and teeth from the remains and their use as accessories (e.g. the Yatsuhagi [八束脛] cave site in Gun'ma prefecture; ibid., 22) indicate that the practice guaranteed the maintenance and perpetuation of intimate connections between the living and the dead. Together with the previously mentioned observations, it can be inferred that the practice generated and reproduced a discourse that helped maintain the sense of communal togetherness, with a strong egalitarian overtone.

The practice of processing the body and burying its skeletal remains began in the western half of

54 The reconstruction by Harunari (1993, 75, fig. 13) and by Shitara (2008, 215, fig. 102) of the Izuruhara (出流原) cemetery (Figure 6.23), for instance, disagree with one another quite significantly, whereas the former reconstructs the cemetery to comprise four clusters, the latter, eight.

eastern Japan during the Final Jomon period. The body was either burnt or deposited and then re-excavated (Yamada 1995). In some examples of the latter process, long bones were first arranged in the shape of a rectangle, within which the rest of the bones were arranged. It is interesting to note, however, that the bones were rarely kept in jars.

It might be a case of reading too much into the limited evidence, but one is tempted to speculate that the metaphorical connection between globular-jar-shaped storage vessels, the rice grains contained in them, and the death and regeneration of life embodied by the grains, that is, the *Yayoi structuring principle*, was accepted in the east as well. However, the image of the dead does not appear to have been solely connected with the death and regeneration of rice grains. The jars were often decorated with motifs apparently signifying either some actual/imaginable creatures and/or some concrete images (see Figures 6.1.C and 6.23.B). With respect to ethnographic examples, the latter might have included features of natural landscapes. The decoration of the jars varies between individual contexts; the fact that the decorations draw from different mythological narratives and landscapes for every deceased individual indicates that the deceased were somehow related, in a transformative manner, to various actual/imaginable living creatures. This is a completely different horizon from that embodied and signified by the jar coffins of northern Kyushu, deriving genealogically from the red-painted globular jars of the Initial Yayoi period. In the latter, the dead were related in a transformative manner to rice grains, which could be possessed and mobilised. In contrast, in the former, the dead were situated in a mythical world wherein they were mutually related, interchangeable and hence equal to various creatures living in it. This 'worldview' expressed through the prolonged treatment of the dead drew upon the reciprocity-based 'cold' tribal world (see works by Lévi-Strauss) in which social contingencies were not dealt with through hierarchical decision making but absorbed on the basis of reciprocal mutual help between equal participants. This picture also nicely fits into the presence of a dual organisation and other reciprocity-based social divisions inferred to have been in operation, based on the spatial structure of the burial grounds (see earlier discussion).

Some composite wooden coffins in the rectangular burial compounds of Kinki region were found to have red pigments sprinkled inside them. As mentioned, the Yayoi IV in the region, marked by the widespread of the Miyanodai assemblage, witnessed the introduction of the custom of the rectangular burial compound to the region. This suggests that the metaphorical-transformative connection between the death and regeneration of rice crops as well as human beings was emphasised in the mortuary practices followed in the region. If it were also true that the people's world view was intrinsically connected with hierarchical social relations, as embodied and expressed in the mortuary practice of the rectangular burial compounds, it would clearly suggest that the introduction of rectangular burial compounds in the eastern horizon marked the end of the practice of secondary burials.

7. PRAYING

7.1. Ritual Horizons and Bronze Implements

OUTLINE

During the Yayoi II and III, northern Kyushu and western Japan saw the development of ritual horizons characterised by the use of bronze implements which differed from one horizon to another. The former horizon covered the area from northern Kyushu to the present-day Shimane prefecture on the Japan Sea coast and the Hyogo and Kagawa prefectures on the Seto Inland Sea coast to the east, while the latter extended from the Kinki region to the Shimane and Hiroshima prefectures to the west. The former is characterised by the manufacture and use of daggers, spearheads and halberds. The centre of distribution was northern Kyushu, where these items were mainly found deposited as grave goods. Bronze halberds with some characteristics that distinguished them from their northern Kyushu counterparts were also manufactured and used in the southern Kinki region, and daggers, particularly those with holes for hafting, were probably made somewhere in the regions around the Seto Inland Sea (Iwanaga 1980). The distribution of *Dotaku* bells centres

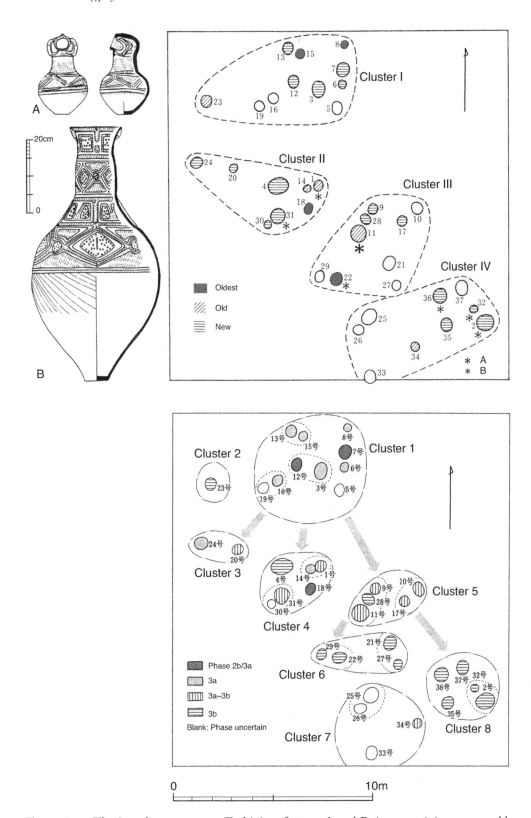

Figure 6.23. The Izuruhara cemetery, Tochigi prefecture. **A** and **B**: jars containing processed bones (from Harunari 1993). Above: the spatial segmentation reconstructed by Harunari (1993), with additions. Below: by Shitara (2008) with additions.

consistently in the Kinki region,[55] and it expanded to the west in the Yayoi III.

The bronze weapons which had originated in the Korean peninsula appear to have lost their function as tools for killing and came to be transformed into ritual implements very quickly (Iwanaga 1994, 48–49).[56] By the Yayoi III, the daggers, spearheads and halberds were being entirely locally produced (Iwanaga 1994), and they gradually lost their functionality as they became increasingly larger, at the cost of the sharp cutting edge and the function of hafting. The paucity of evidence makes it difficult to fix the precise point in time when the indigenous production and use of the *Dotaku* bronze bells began, though circumstantial evidence suggests that their manufacture had begun sometime in the Yayoi II/III periods. By the Yayoi IV, fairly large specimens were being manufactured in some regional centres across the southern Kinki region (see Figure 7.3; Harunari 1992); their original function as bells was compromised as they were increasingly decorated not only with complex geometric decorations but also occasionally with pictorial representations (see the following discussion). Interestingly, pictorial representations almost disappeared during the Yayoi V, while geometric motifs increased in complexity. In my opinion, this was related to the fact that the knowledge of ritual practices involving the *Dotaku* bells and the meanings signified by them had, by then, became esoteric and *abstract*, and it was probably related to that the ritual involving the use of the *Dotaku* bronze bells increasingly became under control of the elite of an ever decreasing number (cf. Iwanaga 1997, 149–150). I return to this issue in the next chapter. The pictorial representations, in their turn, most probably signified 'mythological' beliefs and/or narratives. Let us examine them in the following section.

THE TRANSFORMATION OF RITUALS

Northern Kyushu In northern Kyushu, daggers, spearheads and halberd were mainly deposited as grave goods during the Yayoi II and III. Depositional practices outside of the mortuary context began, rather interestingly, on the peripheral regions of northern Kyushu (e.g. the Hama [浜] site of Oita prefecture, the Imakoga [今古閑] of Kumamoto prefecture, and so on (Iwanaga 1994, 51) in the Yayoi III, from which they spread elsewhere. As mentioned earlier, the centre of production for these weapons was northern Kyushu. This might point to a situation in which the scarcity of their supply made the implements suitable for occasional rituals for communal well-being in the peripheral areas, whereas they were used for indicating the status of certain individuals as representatives of communal well-being in the centre of their production. It is highly probable that wooden weapon-shaped implements were used in ritual practices (Figure 6.10; also see preceding discussion) in which many other types of wooden implements, including figurines probably representing ancestral images, were also used (e.g. Shitara 2008, 252). Such rituals, often conducted in the regional-centre-type settlements (see Section 4 of this chapter), would have mobilised the image of the ancestors and the spirit of the rice crop, which, as argued previously, were interchangeable and transformable; these spirits would have been further 'encouraged' by the performance of ritual acts using mock weapons. In that sense, in areas where bronze weapons (as scarce items) were deposited outside mortuary contexts, their deposition would have been accompanied by prayers for a good harvest of rice crops and the well-being of the community, whereas in areas where they were deposited as grave goods, the well-being of the community would have been perceived to be represented by the body of the elite.

Interestingly, when the depositional practice of this probably ritual character began in northern Kyushu, the new types of items, enhanced in terms of size for a greater visual presence, tended to be deposited in ritual contexts, whereas those which were deposited as grave goods maintained their more functional, weapon-like appearance (they may well have been inherited over some generations; Iwanaga 1994, 45–47). Furthermore, in the Yayoi IV, the latter were almost exclusively deposited with the dead, who were also given a large number of bronze mirrors which were probably imported from the Early Han commandery of Lelang (see Figure 6.4). These mirrors,

---

55 The earliest specimens distributed on peripheral areas of Kinki, such as Fukui, Hyogo, and Shimane prefectures, however. See Sahara (2002, 197).

56 Some of the specimens from the peninsula show the sign of losing their functionality (Shozo Iwanaga, pers. comm.)

along with several other exotic items, as mentioned already, were generally buried in much larger jar coffins than usual in burial compounds covered by earthen mounds (e.g. at the Mikumo-Minamishoji site [Fukuka PBE 1985b] and at location D of the Sugu-Okamoto site; e.g. Takakura 1995, 145–148). In comparison, (a not so large number of) the elite from other communities in northern Kyushu were buried with iron weapons such as iron daggers and halberds, some of which might have been imported from the Korean peninsula, though many of them would have been produced in the regional-centre-type settlements in coastal northern Kyushu among which the Sugu was probably the production centre (see Figure 6.4.G; Murakami 1998). This suggests that the elite from some of the coastal northern Kyushu communities, who would have intentionally mediated the import and distribution of those iron implements and controlled their production, continued to retain the old-styled (bronze) implements, whereby they probably sought to display their status as 'authentic' representatives of the well-being of the communities in the network.

In relation to this inference, it is important to mention that some extremely large buildings, some of them with raised floors, were built near the elite burial grounds. At the Yubi-Hon'mura site in Saga prefecture, as mentioned, a large, rectangular raised-floor building was built in the Yayoi IV in the vicinity of the elite burial ground, which possibly formed an elite burial compound (Figure 6.2.A; Saga PBE 2003). The oldest burial in this compound, a large composite coffin made of slate stones and wooden plates containing a dug-out log coffin (which has rotted away), with a bronze dagger equipped with a stone-made pommel and metal hilt guards, probably dates back to the Yayoi II or early Yayoi III (Saga PBE 2003, 10–11). Six jar burials with bronze daggers and other items followed this burial (ibid., 11–12). They date back to the late Yayoi III. The burial ground continued to be used until the early Yayoi V, although from the late Yayoi III period onwards, the number of burials in each phase started decreasing. This means that the large building, located in the vicinity of a huge square pit in which more than fifty red-painted flared-rimmed globular jars were found deposited (ibid., 6), was actually built *after* the peak phase of the formation and use of the

burial ground, which obviously was the late Yayoi III. From this, we can deduce that the building had something to do with the *remembrance* of and/or *reference to* the dead who were buried long before its construction.

We now have identified three phenomena which might have been three different representations of a single factor – the generation of a sort of *genealogical consciousness*:

(1) As we have seen in the section on mortuary practices, the period witnessed the emergence of burial sequences (see Section 6.1 of this chapter). In addition, differences in the length of individual sequences in terms of how many burials constituted them, as shown, appear to have been correlated with status differences between the deceased (Mizoguchi 2005); the burials of emergent elites tend to contain more graves than those of the commoners, and this phenomenon can be understood to reflect the materialisation of a developing sense of genealogical continuation of the elite segments of communities (ibid.).

(2) The continual use of old-style bronze implements as grave goods among the limited elite can also be understood as a strategy of materially representing the continuation and authenticity of the status and authority assumed by the elite segments of communities; the old-style implements would have emphasised the elites' connection with 'traditional' material items.

(3) The construction of extraordinarily large, raised-floored buildings in the vicinity of the elite burial grounds which had already begun to operate long before the construction of the buildings, as argued above, can also be understood as a reflection of the increasing importance of referring to the ancestors, who were perceived as having made significant contributions to lay the foundation for (the prosperity of) the communities.

It would have been possible to associate the preceding practices with the increasing differentiation of particular groups who gradually formed an elite rank in the process of acting as representatives of the communal well-being.

The Dotaku *Bronze Bell Horizon* The custom of using *Dotaku* bronze bells in ritual practices during the Middle Yayoi period spread in regions around the Kinki region as far as the Shimane, Hiroshima and Kagawa prefectures and the eastern half of Kochi prefecture to the west as well as to the Fukui and Aichi prefectures (Figure 6.24). The fact that the bells were often heavily worn – as a result of ringing them using a bronze bar (called *zetsu*, 舌, meaning 'tongue' in Japanese), which can be observed on a raised band inside the bells – suggests that most of them were rung on a number of occasions before being deposited. In cases where more than two *Dotakus* were deposited together, the bells belonged to the successive temporal phases (Iwanaga 1987): this suggests that the bells were deposited from time to time, and not all at once. It is difficult to determine if the depositional practice itself was as important as, or more important than, the ritual performance involving the bells. It is also difficult to determine if they were deposited and then dug up repeatedly (cf. Sahara 2002, 67– 68). We cannot dismiss the possibility of the latter; there is a confirmed example in which a bronze spearhead of the Yayoi V period was deposited in a corner of a large rectangular pit house and then dug up for a number of times (at the Shigetome [重留] site in Kitakyushu City of northern Kyushu; Kitakyushu-shi-kyoiku-bunka-jigyo-dan 1999). The spearhead, however, is a different type of bronze ritual implement, and it dates from a different period (the mid-Yayoi V). The bells were never deposited inside houses; there are mostly found on or near the slopes of hills/mountains. Some of them appear to have been deposited at locations that are hidden from the view of nearby settlements. However, the Shigetome example at least confirms the practice of underground storage of bronze ritual implements.

It is interesting to note that, especially in comparison with the use of bronze ritual implements in northern Kyushu during the Yayoi IV, most bells in use during the Yayoi IV appear to have been deposited towards the end of the period and were never dug up again. This is revealed by the fact that the III type of bells, which emerged in the later part of the Yayoi IV, and IV-1 type of bells (see Figure 7.5), which emerged in the earlier part of the Yayoi V, were rarely deposited together,

whereas other sequential types were often deposited together before and after this 'lapse' (Fukunaga 1998, 220–222). This discontinuation also coincides with a reorganisation of the groupings of artisans; it is argued that the artisan groups – which were attached to a number of communities dispersed fairly widely across the southern Kinki region and possibly a part of Tokai region – converged to form two artisan 'schools' at this time, one of which was based somewhere in the southern Kinki region (most likely in the present-day Osaka or Nara prefectures), while the other was based somewhere in Tokai region (Sahara 1960, 99–102). This also coincides with the near-disappearance of pictorial representations from the surface of the bells (see preceding discussion). As I argue in the next chapter, this change in artistic style probably reflects the increasing abstraction of the meaning content of ritual practices and the esotericisation of ritual knowledge. These phenomena would have been related to changes in the relationship between the elite and the rituals they were responsible for performing. The lapse would have marked the beginning of the establishment of stable elite segments in the concerned communities. The same seems to have occurred in northern Kyushu slightly earlier, but here this phenomenon was manifested in the form of references to the past and the claiming of (genealogical) continuity from the past, as we have seen above. Just like the ritual practices involving the use and deposition of bronze weapons in northern Kyushu and elsewhere, the use and deposition of the *Dotaku* bells would have referred to the connection between the ancestors and the spirit of rice grains (see the following discussion). This would have made it easy to connect the ritual knowledge with the genealogical continuity of the emergent elite groups.

SHARED STRUCTURE AND TRAJECTORY
This co-transformation occurring within a small gap of time might suggest that the two 'ritual horizons' archaeologically represented by the use of different types of bronze ritual implements were not entirely mutually exclusive and antagonistic. For instance, it has been confirmed that some specimens, at least, of a particular type of *Dotaku* bell – the Fukuda (福田) type, named after the

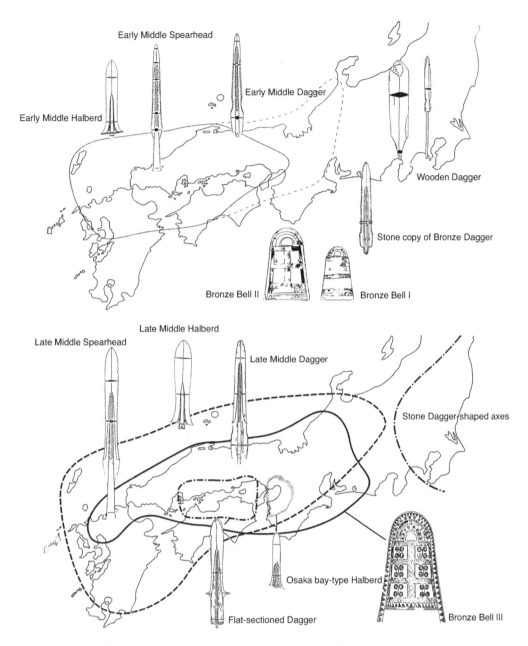

Figure 6.24. The horizons of the bronze ritual implements of the Middle Yayoi. Above: the Yayoi II–III. Below: the Yayoi IV (from Terasawa [2010, figs. 92 and 93], with modifications). With kind permission from the Yusankaku Publishing Co.

eponymous site in the present-day Hiroshima pre-fecture – was produced and used in northern Kyushu (cf. Saga PBE 2002).

We can explain this phenomenon as follows. It has become increasingly clear that the bronze ritual implements of the Middle Yayoi period were copied predominantly in wood and less often in clay. The range of wooden ritual imple-ments, however, includes unique implements which were never made of bronze or iron (Figure 6.10). Considering the frequency of presence and distribution pattern of these implements, the dif-ferences between the bronze and the other, that is, wooden and clay, implements, in terms of their use and life cycle, would have been related to a certain hierarchy in the system of rituals and the selection of implements mobilised for them (e.g. Takesue 1990a). The distribution of bronze ritual implements is sparse, and the dis-tance between their depositions often extends over multiple settlement clusters (Kobayashi 1967, 230–235). In northern Kyushu, for instance, bronze weapons appear to have been deposited in the vicinity of regional-centre-type settlements: more than twenty-three bronze halberds were accidentally discovered at location seven of the Kuma-Nishioda site, a large regional-centre-type settlement comprising at least fourteen residential units and an elite burial containing an early Han Chinese bronze mirror, an iron halberd, an iron sword, and forty-one shell armlets as grave goods (see Figure 6.4; Chikushino City Committee for the Compilation of the History of the City 1999, 383–394). In contrast, the other implements are rarely found deposited in such a formal manner; they were possessed and used by most of the settlement communities. These observations suggest a significant difference in the scale of gatherings which involved the use and/or deposition of certain ritual goods: a considerably larger number of people from many more settlements would have gathered to participate in ritual practices involving the use (and deposition) of bronze ritual implements.

From this, we cannot directly conclude that those who were in charge of the ritual practices involving bronze implements occupied a higher status between communities; such practices may well have been jointly organised by those who typically used non-bronze implements for such activities in their own individual villages. If this were the case, it might indicate that the bronze implements were co-owned by the communities that jointly organised the ritual practices and the elites who conducted them. However, with regard to the fact that in northern Kyushu, the elite of some specific communities began to differentiate themselves from those of other communities by exclusively collecting/retaining old-style bronze implements and being buried with them (i.e. the Mikumo-Minamishoji and Sugu: see above), added to the emerging genealogical consciousness in the form of references to the memory of the ancestors – both of which occurred during the Yayoi IV – it would be natural to suggest that hierarchisation within and between the communities, and indeed the clear emergence of an elite class, may well have been underway. Nevertheless, it should be noted that the hierarchisation had not yet led to the centralised production of bronze ritual implements; these implements were still being manufactured in a number of regional-centre-type settlements in the northern Kyushu

and southern Kinki regions (Harunari 1992; Tajiri 2001), and until the Yayoi V, their production had not been centralised and restricted to a small number of extremely large settlements, such as the Sugu settlement on Fukuoka Plain in northern Kyushu. This suggests that the Middle Yayoi period, particularly Yayoi IV onwards, was a transitional period in the sphere of ritual practices across northern Kyushu and western Japan, during which the communities changed from the communal-egalitarian mode to the moderately hierarchised mode.

It should also be added that the communal sharing of a basic set of ritual items and symbols, except for the bronze ritual implements, would have formed a base to sustain a broad sense of sameness across northern Kyushu and western Japan. As mentioned above, weapon-shaped wooden ritual implements and *Dotaku*-bell-shaped clay implements were widespread across northern Kyushu and western Japan, suggesting that the contents of ritual practices conducted in individual villages and communities were fairly identical across those regions. In addition, the widespread tendency to depict shamanistic figures taking an identical gesture and holding identical implements such as a shield and a halberd (Figure 6.25) suggests that the physical appearance of shamanistic figures was common in those regions (e.g. Shitara 2007). This indicates that the self-identity of the people, as it was marked and reproduced in the rituals, would have been multi-layered.

The case of northern Kyushu is of particular importance in this regard. In this region, as Nobuyuki Shimojo (1975, 1989) points out, the horizon of the practice of burying the dead in unique burial jars roughly coincided with the circulation of stone axes made of basalt procured from the volcanic outcrop of Imayama (Figure 6.11; see preceding discussion). The axes were circulated in the form of roughouts, produced in a fairly standardised manner, and were polished at the settlements of their use (ibid.). The phenomenon suggests a typical situation, according to Marshall Sahlins ([1974] 2004), wherein economic and utilitarian activities, including the exchange of utilitarian goods, cannot be separated from the ritual activities, in a broad sense, through which intra- and inter-communal relations are reproduced. My inference is that the half-finished products were either transported through ties between kin-based

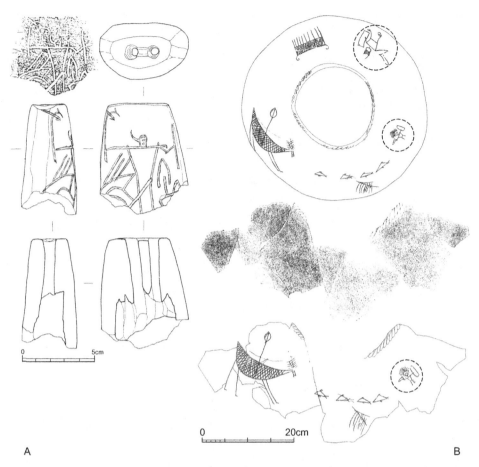

A   B

Figure 6.25. Shamanistic figures taking an identical gesture and holding identical implements from Kyushu and Kinki. A: A human figure with a head decoration and a weapon (possibly halberd) and a shield on a *Dotaku* bronze bell-shaped clay implement (from Kawayoriyoshihara [川寄吉原], Saga prefecture) (from Saga PBE 1981; also see Takashima 1980). B: Human figures depicted without facial features, but apparently with a handle-attached halberd and a shield held in their hands, inscribed on pots from Shimizukaze (清水風; from Fujita 2006, with minor alterations).

sodalities or brought to fairly remote communities by caravans with the help of kin-based sodalities (see previous discussion). The sodalities extended across wide areas, and in order to bind the regional communities together, it would have been necessary to maintain a sense of communal togetherness by sharing ritual practices that involved the assembly and participation of members of the various different communities scattered across the wide areas. In that sense, we can infer that the ritual practices involving bronze implements *functioned* to reproduce both intra- and inter-communal ties by creating and reproducing a shared identity, whereas the village/individual-community-level ritual practices involving non-bronze items basically served to reproduce individual-community-level identities. It should be added, however, that their functioning drew upon the *Yayoi structuring*

principle, that is, the life, death and regeneration of people and community being perceived as one and same with that of rice (as conceptualised and defined at the end of Chapter 5). When the bronze and other ritual items were used, they would have mediated the enactment of something which can be called the Yayoi 'myth', to which now we turn.

7.2. Understanding the Basic Structure of the Yayoi 'Myth'

The preceding indicates that ritual practices of different levels functioned to create and reproduce the different scales and implications of communal identities. In any case, for any ritual to work and be perceived as such, it needs to have a narrative framework which enables the participants to forge a relationship between what they do as part of the ritual and what they can expect as its effect(s). Such narratives commonly share a *mythical* nature that serves to explain not only the origins of the basic elements and the commonly accruing events of social life but also the reasons why they work and why they occur as such (e.g. works by Lévi-Strauss). In that sense, our attempt to understand the ritual practices of the Middle Yayoi period has to involve the reconstruction of the mythical narratives of the time.

The analyses in the current and previous chapters suggest that some of the themes of the formalised practices which can be described as *ritual* in the Middle Yayoi were certainly associated with the dead and the ancestors, on the one hand, and with success in (probably predominantly) paddy field agricultural practices, on the other. Pictorial depictions of insects, birds, animals, buildings and human beings conducting various tasks can be found on some *Dotaku* bells, though these are few in number.[57] These findings serve as a window into the ancient past, through which we can glimpse some of the images and conceptual units comprising the structure of mythical narratives and what they might represent.

Quite naturally, such narratives have been interpreted from a wide range of perspectives. Two of the animal species that are predominantly depicted – deer and wild boar, for instance – have been studied in terms of their ratios of occurrence in the excavated assemblage of hunted animal bones, their behaviour patterns and their depiction in ancient literary sources. An interesting and significant point is that deer are depicted more frequently than are wild boar; however, studies have revealed that wild boar were hunted and consumed in significantly greater quantities than were deer. Both these creatures inhabited the foothills of mountains, quite close to human activity areas, and their uneven presence in the bone assemblage might reflect differences in either the manner or purpose of their being hunted; it might even represent the different manners in which they were encountered by people or were involved in human activities. The latter point has several implications, including the possibility that boar might have been

kept in settlements for consumption; according to Hiromasa Kaneko, around 80 per cent of boar remains in the assemblage from the Ikegami site in Osaka prefecture belonged to animals which were around two years old and which might have been killed en masse in early summer (Kaneko 1997, 146–147), which leads him to infer that these boar might have been kept within the settlement for meat consumption (ibid., 147). Kaneko also points out an interesting example from the Karako-Kagi site in Nara prefecture in which young and adult female boar were selectively killed, consumed and their mandibles hung from the branch of a tree, probably for some ritualistic purpose (ibid., 145–146). He infers that their selection would have been associated with some ritual of agricultural regeneration and fertility (ibid.), although it is obvious that many more such examples need to be collected and examined in order to verify this thesis. In any case, it is unlikely that boar were significantly less prominent than deer in the daily lives of people. This suggests that the uneven representation of those animal species on the *Dotaku* bells was intentional and might reflect different meanings attached to and/or signified by those animal species.

There is a suggestive mythological narrative in the *Harimanokuni-fudoki* (播磨国風土記) document (a record of the culture, geography and legends of the province of Harima [coinciding largely with the south-western part of present-day Hyogo prefecture] compiled by the decree of the empress Genmei [元明] sometime during the early eighth century AD) which describes how rice plants grew overnight from a paddy field after blood from the guts of a deer was sprinkled over the field (e.g. National Museum of Japanese History 1997, 165). Other mythological narratives in other *Fudokis* describe connections between deer and the growth and harvest of rice (ibid.). There is a gap of at least 700 years between the production of *Dotaku* bells at the end of the Middle Yayoi period, that is, the Yayoi IV, and the compilation of the *Fudokis*, and even if it were possible to assume a direct historical connection between the two time periods, there is too little evidence to make any specific inference about what was implied by the depiction of deer on the *Dotaku* bells. However, the accounts at least support the view that deer and boar were associated with, represented and

___

57 According to Hideji Harunari, as of February 1997, approximately 470 such bells have been found, of which 62 have pictorial depictions (National Museum of Japanese History 1997, 68).

signified different things, meanings and concepts in the ritualistic domain. In other words, the deer and boar were depicted as *transformations* of something else. If this is true, then we can assume that the other depictions on the bells are transformations of something else, too.

This implies that the meaning(s) signified by the bells were generated through a process of transformation between systems of signifiers. In other words, the figures depicted on the bells formed a distinct system of meaning by not only differing from one another as pictorial representations but also being representative of something else; that is, they themselves constituted a distinct system of meaning. In short, in order to understand the meaning behind the depictions, we have to reconstruct the system in which the depictions are situated. For this purpose, we have an excellent material – a set of four *Dotaku* bells with their surfaces divided into clearly defined panels showing different (combinations of) pictorial representations (Sahara 1982; National Museum of Japanese History 1997, 216–223). Two of them were excavated from the Sakuragaoka (桜ケ丘; Kamika, 神岡) site of Kobe city, one was allegedly sourced from Kagawa prefecture and one was formerly owned by the Edo-period painter Buncho Tani (谷文晁; National Museum of Japanese History 1997, 216–223). Circumstantial evidences date them to the Yayoi IV.

The Sakuragaoka (Kamika) nos. 4 and 5 bells have four panels on each side of their body (Figure 6.26.S4 and S5; ibid.). The Buncho Tani bell also has four panels on each side (Figure 6.26.BT; ibid.), while the Kagawa bell has six panels on each side (Figure 6.26.K; ibid.). Yukio Kobayashi was the first to point out that a certain narrative was represented by the arrangement of different depictions on the different panels of individual bells (ibid.). Kobayashi (1967) argued that the depictions on the panels form a sequential narrative progressing from the upper to the lower panels, with insects and amphibians tending to appear in the upper panels and birds, deer, boar, human beings and buildings (probably granaries) tending to appear in the lower panels. He concluded that the narratives depicted the natural cycle of the strong eating the weak and the termination of that cruel cycle due to the onset of rice paddy field agriculture. Makoto Sahara (1982) conducted further research

on this idea by systematically examining the correlations between the representations on the panels in individual bells and between different bells, concluding that the bells shared a set of codes based on which the depictions were placed in different panels. Sahara first noticed that a panel depicting a spider and a mantis was always situated on the upper right corner of one side of the bells. Then he noticed that a man with an I-shaped implement in his hand (see S-4-Y-c, S-5-Y-a, BT-Y-c, K-Y-c in Figure 6.26; for principle for naming the panels, see the following description) was always depicted in a panel on the left column of the side opposite to the spider-mantis panel (S-4-X-b, S-5-X-b, K-X-b in Figure 6.26; ibid.). This panel, depicting the man with an I-shaped implement, was always associated with another panel to its right, depicting a hunter and a deer (S4-Y-d, BT-Y-d, K-Y-d in Figure 6.26; ibid.). Moreover, in the Kagawa bell, which has six panels on each side (whereas the others have only four panels on each side), the two panels on the bottom row of the side containing the man-with-I-shaped-implement panel depict a scene wherein two human figures are husking rice grains next to a raised-floor building with a ladder, probably a granary (K-Y-e and f in Figure 6.26; ibid.). By putting together these new findings, Sahara concluded that since Kobayashi's thesis was consistent with the findings, it was feasible (ibid.); the sequence of the strong killing (and eating) the weak was terminated by the onset of rice farming, symbolised by the scene showing the husking of rice and its storage.

I agree with Kobayashi and Sahara on the following points: the arrangement of the panels is sequential and follows a narrative-like flow; in addition, all four bells represent basically the same flow. In my view, the panels that are situated in a same position, i.e., on the same row and column on the same side (the latter, as Sahara [1982] pointed out, can be determined by the presence or absence of the man-with-an-I-shaped-implement panel), can be inferred to have depicted the same scene and signified the same meaning(s).

Let me explain my argument further. For the sake of clarity in the following argument, I shall label each of the panels on all four bells (Figure 6.26). As for the Sakuragaoka (Kamika) no. 5 bell, the panel on the upper row, left column of the side containing the man-with-an-I-shaped-implement

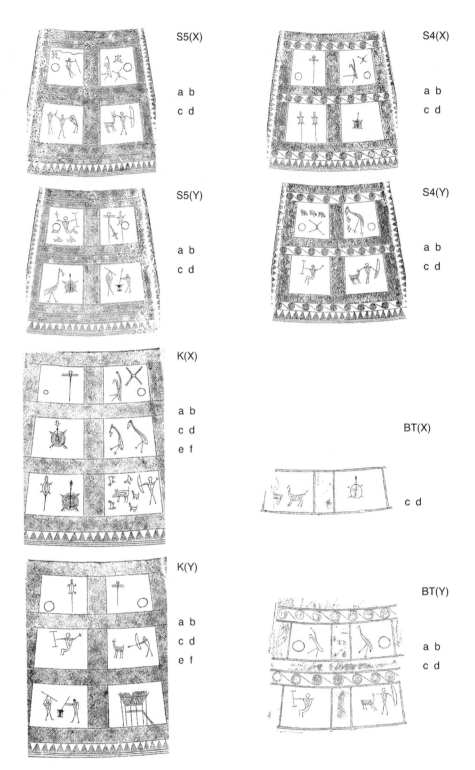

Figure 6.26. *Dotaku* bronze bells with sequential pictorial depictions. S4 and S5: Sakuragaoka nos. 4 and 5 bells, K: the bell allegedly excavated elsewhere in Kagawa prefecture, BT: the bell formerly owned by the Edo period painter antiquarian Buncho Tani (after National Museum of Japanese History 1997).

panel is labelled S-5-Y-a. The panel on the upper row, right column of the same side is labelled S-5-Y-b (see Figure 6.26.S5(Y)). The panel on the lower row, left column of this side is labelled S-5-Y-c, while that on the lower row, right column is labelled S-5-Y-d (Figure 6.26.S5(Y)).

The respective panels on the other side are labelled correspondingly as follows: S-5-X-a∼d (Figure 6.26.S5(X)). Based on the same scheme, the panels of the Sakuragaoka (Kamika) no. 4 bell are accordingly labelled as S-4-X-a∼d (Figure 6.26.S4(X)) and S-4-Y-a∼d (Figure 6.26.S4(Y)).

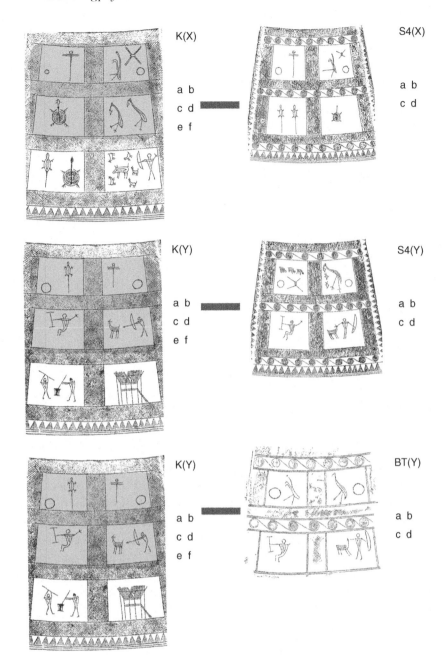

Figure 6.27. Analysis of the pictorial depictions (1). Relevant 'panels' for the purpose of comparison are shaded.

The Buncho Tani bell does not have upper panels on side X; therefore, the rest of the panels are labelled as follows: BT-X-c~d (Figure 6.26.BT(X)), and BT-Y-a~d (Figure 6.26.BT(Y)). The panels of the Kagawa bell are labelled as K-X-a~f (Figure 6.26.K(X)) and K-Y-a~f (Figure 6.26.K(Y)).

A comparison between the panels of the different bells reveals the following (Figures 6.27 and 28): the upper two rows on both sides of the Kagawa (K) bell are basically similar to the corresponding panels of the Sakuragaoka (Kamika) no. 4 (S-4) and Buncho Tani (BT) bells (Figure 6.27). Furthermore, the lower two rows on the Y

side of the Kagawa bell are basically similar to the corresponding panels of the Sakuragaoka (Kamika) no. 5 (S-5) bell (Figure 6.28). This means that if there are different depictions in the panels that are supposed to contain the same depictions, then those depictions are likely to signify the *same things*; that is, they are *interchangeable*. Drawing upon this assumption, let us first compare the K and S-4 bells.

The panels on the lower row of side Y in S-4 and those on the middle row of side Y in K contain the same depictions: a man with an I-shaped implement on the left panel and a deer and a hunter on the right panel (Figure 6.27). However, the panels

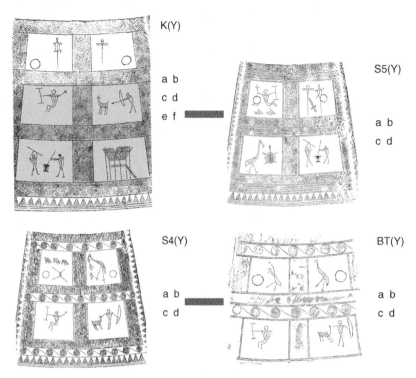

Figure 6.28. Analysis of the pictorial depictions (2). Relevant 'panels' for the purpose of comparison are shaded.

situated above them contain different depictions; S-4-Y-a depicts a spider and three other animals, whereas K–Y-a depicts a newt; moreover, S-4-Y-b depicts a bird eating a fish as well as two other fishes, whereas K–Y-b depicts a dragonfly. If these figures are interchangeable, then the newt is interchangeable with the spider (and the animals of an unidentifiable species), while the dragonfly is interchangeable with the bird of an unidentifiable species (and the fish). This can be summarised as follows: newt means spider/spider means newt; dragonfly means bird/bird means dragonfly. The interchangeability of these figures appears to stem from their 'intermediary' nature: newts live both in water and on land, while spiders live in the air, but close to the earth; dragonflies and birds both fly in the air and rest on earth.

The differences on side X are simpler (Figure 6.27). S-4-X-c depicts two newts, while K-X-c depicts a soft-shelled turtle eating a fish; S-4-X-d depicts a soft-shelled turtle, while K-X-d depicts two birds, each eating a fish. The position of the soft-shelled turtle is reversed between the bells, while the two newts would be interchangeable with the two birds. In this case, too, the intermediary nature of the figures is apparent: as mentioned earlier, newts live in water and on land, while birds

fly in the air and rest on earth; soft-shelled turtles, like newts, live in water and on land.

Let us now examine the BT bell. Sahara has already pointed out that the depictions on the four panels of side Y are almost identical to their counterparts in S-4-Y, *except* for the fact that BT-Y-a depicts a mantis where S-4-Y-a depicts a spider and three animals of an unidentifiable species (Figure 6.28). K-Y-a, as mentioned earlier, depicts a newt (Figure 6.27). This suggests that the figures of the mantis, spider and newt are interchangeable. Based on these findings, most of the creatures depicted have 'intermediary' characters in that the three creatures discussed above were regarded as interchangeable because of their ability to survive on stems of grass, between the earth and the sky (mantis), in the air but close to earth (spider) and in water as well as on land (newt). If we turn to side X, BT-X-c depicts two deer, while S-4-X-c depicts two newts (Figure 6.29). K-X-c depicts a soft-shelled turtle, while K-X-d depicts two birds eating fish. These orders are reversed in the case of S-4-X-c and d. Therefore, we can infer the following interchangeable relations: deer means newt means bird. We have already discussed the intermediary characters of newts and birds. What about deer? Sika deer (*Cervus nippon*, Japanese deer) live

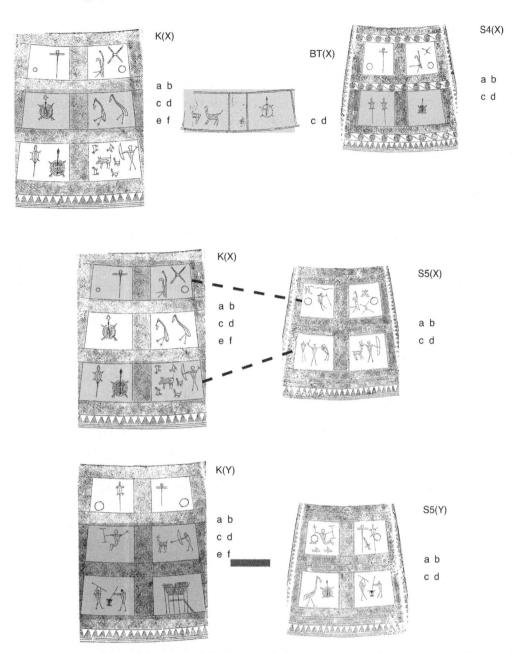

Figure 6.29. Analysis of the pictorial depictions (3). Relevant 'panels' for the purpose of comparison are shaded and connected by arrows.

in the forests on the foothills of mountains, sometimes wandering into the vicinity of human settlements. In that sense, they also have an intermediary character, living in the forest and in territories inhabited by people.

Based on the preceding findings, it can be deduced that virtually every creature depicted has an intermediary character, as is evident in the S-4 and BT bells and the panels on the upper two rows of the K bell (Figure 6.26). Accordingly, we can surmise that both the man-with-an-I-shaped-implement panels and those depicting a deer and

a hunter also represented intermediary characters. The meaning behind the man-with-an-I-shaped-implement motif (S-4-Y-c, S-5-Y-a, BT-Y-c, K-Y-c in Figure 6.26) has been variously interpreted as follows: some claim that the I-shaped implement was used for weaving, while others believe it was a tool for measuring the flatness of the surface of rice paddies or a reel for fishing. S-5-Y-a depicts a man-with-an-I-shaped-implement as well as three fishes – one of which appears to have dropped from the man's hand (Figure 6.26). This points to the likelihood of the fishing thesis, a probability that would be further enhanced by the intermediary-character thesis: if S-5-Y-a indeed depicts a fishing scene, then it is possible that the man was 'transporting' fish from water to land; that is, the panels show the movement of the fish from water to land. If this interpretation were to be accepted, then we can say that the intermediary character of the fish was created by the *act* of a man.

This makes an interesting parallel to the scene depicted in the panel next to the man-with-an-I-shaped-implement panel in the S-4, BT and K bells (Figure 6.26). The scene concerns a hunter and a deer, and in K-Y-d, the hunter is about to shoot the deer with an arrow; in S-4-Y-d and BT-Y-d, the hunter appears to be taming the deer by holding on to its antlers (Figure 6.26). If the hunter's action, like the fisherman's, is intended to transform the character of the deer, it would change the deer from a *wild* creature to a *tamed* one. Here, the emphasis of depiction has possibly shifted from the intermediary character of the creature to the creature's transformation from a wild to a tamed character through the *intervention* of the hunter as an active agent. It is important to note this active role assigned to human beings, which is potentially of significant importance for understanding the undercurrent behind the somewhat mythological 'theme' of the pictorial representations on the four bells. It should also be noted at this point that the transformation from the *wild* to the *tamed* can also be interpreted as a transformation from *nature* to *culture*, which is one of the basic motifs of myths, according to scholars such as Lévi-Strauss (e.g. 1966, 1970).

Let us now compare the S-5 and K bells. The former, with its sides divided into four panels each, like the S-4 and BT bells, is different from them in that its panels depict more than two human figures in the same scene. The four panels on side Y of S-5 are comparable with the lower four panels of side Y of K (Figure 6.29): both S-5-Y-a and K-Y-c depict a man-with-an-I-shaped-implement, and S-5-Y-d and K-Y-e depict a scene of two women husking rice.

The four panels on side X of S-5, however, cannot be directly compared with the lower four panels of K-X. The fact that both K-X-b and S-5-X-b depict a mantis and a spider (the latter panel also includes a frog) and that both K-X-f and S-5-X-d depict a human being and animal(s)

(the former panel depicts a hunter, a boar and five dogs, whereas the latter depicts a hunter and a deer) suggest that K-X-a, b, e, f and S-5-X-a, b, c, d can be compared as equivalent panels (Figure 6.29). Based on this, the depiction of a man with a stick of some sort and a frog (some suggest that this is a snake) in S-5-X-a would be interchangeable with the depiction of a dragonfly in K-X-a, and the scene in S-5-X-c, wherein a man is about to hit a woman with a stick while another woman is trying to stop him, would be interchangeable with the depiction of a newt and a soft-shelled turtle in K-X-e. The latter interchangeability, if it were to stand, is highly suggestive for studying the representation of gender differences across the four bells. Let me elaborate.

It is an accepted fact that round-headed human figures are typically depicted as being involved in male-oriented labours such as hunting, while triangular-headed ones are generally involved in female-oriented labours such as husking grains (Sahara 2002, 290–292). Based on this, the depiction of a newt and a soft-shelled turtle in K-X-e, which is interchangeable with that of human figures in S-5-X-c, would represent an activity between a male and a female, because S-5-X-c contains a representation of both the sexes – that is, a man about to hit a woman with a stick and another woman trying to stop him (Figure 6.29). There is no direct evidence to indicate which represents the male and which represents the female principle in the figures of the newt and the soft-shelled turtle in K-X-e. However, a vagina-like representation on the back of the newt and possibly a penis-like representation on the head of the soft-shelled turtle (see K-X-e in Figure 6.29) might allow us to infer that the newt represents the female while the turtle represents the male. In that case, the juxtaposition of a bird with a soft-shelled turtle in S-5-Y-c might be understood as representing the turtle as male and the bird as female. If we develop this theory further, we can interpret all the panels depicting more than two different types of creatures as representing activities between the two sexes. For instance, hunters are always depicted in juxtaposition with either deer or boar, and if the preceding theory were to be applied to these depictions, the deer and boar would emerge as consistently representing the female. Even the scene of two female figures husking grain might symbolise an activity between the two sexes: the two female figures in S-5-Y-d and K-Y-e are pounding husked rice grains using pounding sticks. The latter can be metaphorically interchanged with penises, representing maleness, and the act of husking grain by pounding it can also be metaphorically compared to the act of sexual intercourse.

The findings, observations, inferences and speculations that we have arrived at, so far, can be summarised as follows:

(1) Virtually every creature depicted in the panels of the four bells has an intermediary character.

(2) The creatures, due to these intermediary characters, represent interfaces between two different realms, such as water and land, earth and air/sky, forests and paddies, rice grains with and without husks, men and women and so on.

(3) Human figures appear to be depicted as agents who activate the creatures' transformation from one realm/state to another.

(4) The transformational faculty attributed to human figures involves the faculty of physical reproduction.

(5) Human figures tend to be located in the lowest row of the panels.

(6) This location of human figures suggests that the arrangement of panels might represent the various stages of transformation of creatures, who reach the final stage through human intervention.

(7) One possibility is that the transformations represented in these panels might symbolise the transformation from nature to culture: <nature : culture :: water : land :: earth : air/sky :: grains with husk : grains without husk :: women : men>.

What would the above pairs suggest for investigating the '*mytho-logical* reality' of social life in the Middle Yayoi period? In my opinion, the most important aspect of these figures is the fact that they represent the process of *transformation* from nature to culture through the mediation of creatures/scenes having *intermediary characters*; this theme is consistently repeated throughout the panels of all the four bells. It is equally important to note that the active intervention of human beings

in the transformation process has been attributed a unique, possibly privileged position in the entire system of meanings signified by the four *Dotaku* bells. As mentioned earlier, the transformation from nature to culture is an important common theme in myths across the world (see works by Lévi-Strauss [e.g. 1966, 1970]), and the mythologies and world view of a people are widely regarded as constituents of a sort of *tribal peoples' social theory*, by which I mean that people in small-scale societies made sense of the beginning of things and their workings by referring to/living through their myths, which somehow helped them cope with the difficulties they often encountered. It would surely be a case of reading too much into scanty evidence if I argued that this proves that the Middle Yayoi society was a tribal society. However, it can certainly be inferred that the users of the four *Dotaku* bells made sense of the world's reality and coped with life's difficulties in ways that were not very different from those of many other tribal groups in the (not-so-distant) past and present.

The presence of human figures and the important role ascribed to them, that is, as active agents causing transformations, is notable. In the pictorial representations of the Jomon period, human figures are rarely juxtaposed with other creatures. Some of the figures are interpreted as representing the scene of childbirth; if this is true, then they can be said to represent a kind of transformation. However, the human beings in those representations *do not intervene* in the activities of other creatures and/or the workings of realms apart from the human realm. In relation to this point, it should be noted that the involvement of agents in the transformation of rice grains appears to be treated as a particularly important theme if we consider the position of the panel depicting the scene in the system of panels in the four *Dotaku* bells (S-5-Y-d, K-Y-e in Figure 6.26). The scene depicting the two women husking rice grains by pounding them with pounding sticks, as suggested, is possibly a metaphorical representation of sexual intercourse and its result, that is, reproduction. In that case, it would be natural to infer that the transformation from nature to culture in that period represented – and was represented – by the production and consumption of rice, and the latter significantly mediated the reproduction of basic social relations such as gender relations. This leads to the inference that rice paddy field agriculture generated many problems that needed to be addressed, and the communities which practiced rice farming made sense of the world and coped with its realities by using a sort of a mythological framework as represented by the pictorial representations on the *Dotaku* bells and other such devices.

Another, probably most important point is that the sequence represented on those panels is an 'evolutionary' one: the dichotomous relationships, that is, those between female and male, nature and culture and so on, signified on individual panels are transformable between the panels, but the relationship between neighbouring panels consistently seems to be an evolutionary one in that the creatures depicted in the next panel are always those which typically kill (and eat) the creatures depicted in the previous panel (see Lévi-Strauss 1966, chap. 8). In that sense, this is a way of introducing *asymmetrical* relationships into an otherwise *symmetrical* world in which the general relationship between the creatures, including human beings, was transformable, and hence interchangeable and symmetrical. Borrowing Lévi-Straussian terminology, we can say that the world view depicted in those panels can be described as a transitional one that can be situated between *cold* and *hot* societies, in the latter of which occurrences in the world were reacted to in a way which changed the world. In cold societies, in contrast, occurrences in the world were reacted to in a way which maintained the preexisting order by drawing on a preexisting, internally symmetrical system of meaning in which various occurrences and various creatures were transformable and interchangeable. In hot societies, occurrences in the world were treated as events that needed a higher order to deal with/mediate them. In the case of the *Dotaku* panel depictions, the interventional faculty of male human beings and rice paddy field agriculture represented such an order. If that order were connected with an actual group of individuals, it would have implied that the order of the world was mediated by them. The creatures living in and around rice paddies, including human beings, were still regarded as intimately related and interchangeable, but the (male) human beings were situated in a higher realm. Societies that used such a world view to make sense of the difficulties generated

by the rice-agriculture-based way of life also tended to select certain categories of people to mediate these difficulties. In that manner, asymmetrical relationships became implanted in the world view of these societies.

8. CONCLUSION: GROWTH AND CONTRADICTIONS

The changes occurring in the lifeworld of people during the period were most vividly marked by the development of new settlement systems characterised by the emergence of larger settlements, increasingly acquiring central-place-like attributes. The increase in sedimentation at the bottom of floodplains, caused by warmer temperatures and a rise in the sea level, coincided with and significantly contributed to an increase in population; the ongoing sedimentation at the bottom of floodplains across the archipelago would have resulted in frequent flooding, which would, at times, have taxed the carrying capacity of individual settlements. Most of the time, the problem appears to have been solved by the segments budding off these settlements, probably kin based, to new lands. Across western Japan, the movement resulted in an increase in the number of such settlements along the foothills of the mountain ranges surrounding individual floodplains.

The formation of these new settlements coincided with the emergence of the basic structure of the Yayoi settlements in western Japan: each settlement commonly consisted of a number of distinct residential units. As mentioned previous, they would have constituted segments of clan-type sodalities (Figure 6.6.A). These residential units, in themselves, would have been either lineage- or sub-clan-based residential corporate groupings, and they appear to have been internally egalitarian; each of them commonly consisted of a number of pit dwellings, ranging from four or five dwellings to tens of them in number, and they often shared a storage area with storage pits and/or raised-floor granaries. During the Middle Yayoi period, there were few significant differences between the residential units forming a settlement in terms of their scale and facilities; as we have already seen, the types of tools used and the activities performed by communities were basically homogeneous. This suggests that both individual clan-type sodalities cross-cutting settlements and individual settlements were basically internally egalitarian, corporate groupings of different scales, characters and functions.

As mentioned earlier, the clan-type sodalities appear to have functioned as networks for movement of source materials, finished goods, information and people. The natural result of this was that the larger settlements, with more residential units than the smaller ones, increasingly acquired central-place-like attributes throughout the Middle Yayoi period (Figure 6.6.B). I have pointed out that many of the large central-place-type settlements of western Japan occupied locations with topological advantages, such as the natural meeting point of many interaction routes or locations close to the boundaries between different social networks. These location-based advantages made those locales increasingly attractive to those who wished to migrate to new regions, for instance, after marriage. An osteo-archaeological analysis indicates that the dominant system of descent at that time was bilateral (Tanaka 2000), which suggests that the dominant post-marital residential rule at the time would have been *bilocal*. This implies that a newly married couple could choose whether to reside in the husband's or wife's family's village. If either of these happened to be the central-place-type settlement of the region, the couple would have obviously chosen to move there. Such a system would have established and continued mutually enhancing parallel processes, that is, an increase in population and an increase in the amount of source materials, finished goods and information flowing into those larger settlements (Figure 6.6.B).

It was also pointed out that these settlements generally tended to have square, and often mounded, burial compounds, extremely large cemeteries and large buildings associated with them, sometimes with raised floors (see Figures 6.2, 6.9, and 6.16–18). These would have been locales for regulating, defining and reducing the increasing complexity of the life-world in the form of an increasing range and frequency of social negotiations and decision making (see Figure 6.6.B); practices confirming a person's death and situating that person in the world of the dead/ancestors would also have become communal occasions in which various social relations and categories could be negotiated and confirmed by the living indicating their relation with the dead. Because the deceased buried in

those large square burial compounds (Figures 6.16, 6.17 and 6.18) also tended to be buried with several grave goods (Figure 6.4), we can safely infer that they were part of the emergent elite. Before the Yayoi IV, there was no trace of genealogy marking in mortuary practices and cemetery formations; based on this, it was argued that the status of the elite was an achieved one during the Yayoi II and III periods. The elite would have been chosen based on their ability to mediate negotiations and take successful decisions, and they would have been buried as social heroes and heroines symbolising the togetherness and well-being of the clan-type sodalities in the regional corporate units whose centres constituted those larger settlements.

Initially, changes in the spatial organisation of clan-type sodalities necessitated an emphasis on communality in the ritual and mortuary fields of social reproduction. Their internal cohesion, which would have fluctuated because of the relocation of preexisting settlements and new ones budding, needed to be reorganised and restored. In such a situation, dual or bilateral organisations and moieties would have worked as an effective means to achieve this internal cohesion. However, once the process of reorganisation was more or less completed, sodalities appear to have begun functioning as the units and media for the flow of goods and information as well as units of production and ownership. As the quantity of production and flow of goods and information increased, the internal structure of sodalities had to become increasingly sophisticated and complex, which appears to have led to the generation of genealogical consciousness in the Yayoi IV in northern Kyushu, as reflected by the formation of micro-sequential burial clusters (Figure 6.16).

The internal hierarchisation of the clan-type sodalities would have also been accelerated as larger settlements increasingly acquired central-place-like characteristics and functions and their residents became increasingly powerful. By the end of the Yayoi IV, dominant lineage-scale segments may well have emerged in individual sodalities, and the deceased buried in extremely rich burials and type II burial compounds in the northern Kyushu region might have been members of such elite segments.

However, it appears that the elite status was regarded as representative of communal interests.

As we have seen, most of the examples of burial compounds, types I as well as II, were located in large settlements, as if symbolising the unity of the community centred on the settlement. The mt-DNA analysis of the Kuma-Nishioda locations 2 and 3 suggests that non-residents of the settlements were also buried in type I burial compounds of the site, that is, in location no. 3 (Figure 6.9). The formation process of these cemeteries clearly indicates that there were a number of burials during each phase and that the type II burial compounds comprised a number of burial sequences. This shows that both intra- and inter-sodality communalities were represented and reproduced in those cemeteries.

At the same time, the social roles played by the elite appear to have needed some enhancement and formalisation. The increased circulation of lithics, now including source materials and half-finished products as well as finished lithics, and the increase in other types of inter-settlement divisions in production, including the production of wooden and bronze implements, would have increased the significance of mediation and control of production by the elite. In northern Kyushu, the Yayoi IV period saw the beginning of the purposeful, probably ritual, deposition of bronze implements, predominantly spearheads. Meanwhile, the grave goods of the elite came to include Early Han Chinese bronze mirrors and iron weapons, some of which would have been imported from the newly founded Early Han outpost of Lelang and from communities living in the Korean peninsula (Figure 6.4). These phenomena might reflect the differentiation of a formalised ritual sphere in which an emergent hierarchical order was mediated. The deposition of bronze weapons from northern Kyushu and *Dotaku* bronze bells from western Japan (Figure 6.24) would have served to portray those who were in charge of this sphere as representatives of the interests of the communities involved in it. The myths which can be reconstructed from the pictorial representations on the *Dotaku* bells also suggest that the world view represented by those bells accommodated both *symmetrical* and *asymmetrical* relationships between the living beings in that world: the relationship was basically egalitarian in that the positions were basically interchangeable, but there existed one

category, that is, the human male, which was designated as the mediator of all the relationships. Thus, there emerged a *contradiction* between the increasing fixation of certain social roles to certain individuals and the existing ethos of communality, which continued to grow, along with the increasing necessity of dealing with such contradictions within society.

In the east, however, a different picture emerged. In the early part of the Middle Yayoi period, settlements were commonly comprised of a single residential unit, sparsely distributed, and unlike the regions in the west, these regions did not develop differences between larger and smaller settlements. A unique mortuary practice developed here, that is, the custom of secondary burial (再葬墓), which prolonged the phase of transition from the state of the living to that of the dead and effectively allowed the living to negotiate and confirm their relations with one another at deeper and denser levels (Figures 6.22 and 6.23). This would have helped the reproduction of inter-communal ties, which must have been relatively hard because of the difficulties involved in organising frequent communal gatherings in such sparsely inhabited settlement systems. The decorative motifs on the globular vessels containing the processed remains of the dead, as interpreted, also suggest that social relations, as symbolically depicted, were egalitarian; because the beings signified by them were depicted as interchangeable, their relationships were symmetrical. In other words, the eastern horizon did not recognise a specific category, like the human male in the west, which was designated to mediate the relationships between living beings in this world.

This egalitarian world and its world view, however, changed towards the end of the Middle Yayoi period, when the expansion of the Miyanodai style zone penetrated deep into this region, bringing with it a complex of customs, features and items that had originated in the west, including the custom of burying the dead in rectangular ditch-enclosed burial compounds (方形周溝墓). Following this, the east was incorporated into the hot world in which occurrences in the world were no longer absorbed by a symmetrical order but instead contributed to the renewal and development of further complexity and hierarchy.

CHAPTER 7

AN ARCHAEOLOGY OF HIERARCHISATION: FROM THE FINAL YAYOI IV TO THE YAYOI V PERIODS (AD 1/50–200)

1. INTRODUCTION

As we saw in Footnote 17 to Chapter 3, the boundary between the Yayoi IV and V periods involves a problem of synchronisation across the regions of the archipelago which are covered by the current volume. The Yayoi V period in northern Kyushu, defined by its pottery, began at a time when western Japan was still in the second half of the Yayoi IV, and the Yayoi V in western Japan began during the second half of the early Yayoi V in northern Kyushu. As we will see later in this chapter, the sudden disappearance of a number of settlements in northern Kyushu during the early Yayoi V (the Takamizuma [高三潴] pottery style phase), in fact, coincided with similar occurrences in western Japan in the final phase of the Yayoi IV. In both the northern Kyushu and Kinki regions, it is suggested that the residents of those disappeared settlements moved to preexisting regional centre-type settlements in the former and to newly established large hilltop settlements in the latter. We shall come back to the issue in detail, but, here, let us think a little bit further about the cause(s) of this intriguing phenomenon for the general understanding of the historical background of the period, in which the trajectory of China came to play an increasingly important role.

In terms of absolute chronology, this transitional phase appears to coincide with the turmoil caused at the end of the Early Han period in China by the establishment of the Xin dynasty by Wang Mang (王莽), which only lasted from AD 9 to AD 23. Wang Mang adopted a policy of non-appeasement towards the polities and groups on the periphery of its domain and stopped the practice of awarding status items to their chiefs (Nishijima 1983, 1985,

23–28). He also lowered the status of many of the chiefs on the periphery of its domain from king (王) to lord (侯) and tried to reissue the official seals representing their status accordingly (Nishijima 1985, 26–27). These moves caused a lot of trouble across the peripheral areas, where the elite were dependent in various ways upon the authorisation by the empire of their status embodied by the seals and other exotic Han goods for achieving and maintaining their positions (ibid.).[1] The effects included the short-lived independence of the commandery of Lelang (楽浪郡) from the Han rule, which lasted between circa AD 25–30. The supply of Lelang-imported items to the archipelago – which included bronze mirrors, most significantly – would have dried up for a while. After a lapse lasting for a single pottery style phase, that is, the first half of the early Yayoi V (the first half of the Takamizuma phase), Han Chinese bronze mirrors appeared again, deposited in a small number of jar burials in northern Kyushu which are dated to the second half of the Takamizuma-pottery-style phase. Those mirrors, including the so-called TLV-patterned (方格規矩) mirrors and *naiko-kamon* (内行花紋; inward arc chain-patterned) mirrors (e.g. Okamura 1993), were produced in China during the first half of the first century AD. This suggests that a possible TPQ

---

1 As mentioned in Chapter 4.2 and in the following, the turmoil across the north-eastern borders of the Han empire might have been caused/exacerbated by a possible cold spell around this period (possibly reflected by a small plateau and a couple of spikes in the calibration curve before and after AD 1 in Figure 4.1.B). The climatic deterioration, if it indeed happened, would have caused some changes in the way communities of the archipelago were organised.

(terminus post quem; the earliest possible date) of the later half of the Takamizuma phase (which coincides with the final Yayoi IV of Western Japan and beyond) is AD 30.[2]

Climatic evidence, as mentioned in Chapter 4.2, indicates that there might have been a cold spell around this period (c. 1–50 AD) as well. Either or both of the previously mentioned events might have led to the disappearance of a large number of settlements across northern Kyushu and western Japan. Considering the authority and prestige that the access to the Lelang commandery brought to certain coastal northern Kyushu communities (represented by the bronze mirrors and other items; see Chapter 6), it may be more likely, at least in northern Kyushu, that this phenomenon was caused by the demise of the Lelang commandery than by climate change; the network analysis conducted in the previous chapter revealed that the centrality of one of the two centres of distribution of Chinese imports, that is, the Mikumo settlement, did not necessarily imply that the settlement was the best connected by the networks of residential communities who deposited the early Han Chinese mirrors as grave goods, and this can be understood as an evidence of the importance of access to the Chinese authority in the formation of network hierarchies (see Chapter 6.6.1, 'The Emergence of Inter-Regional Hierarchy'). The disappearance of vital media for the reproduction of inter-communal relations, albeit momentarily, might have heightened inter-communal tension, and might have resulted in the above-mentioned settlement convergence. The production from sometime in the Yayoi V onward of *Dotaku* bronze bells and other bronze items produced in western Japan is also suggested to have relied on the supply of source material from China: a series of lead isotope analyses undertaken by

Hisao Mabuchi and Yoshimitsu Hirao have shown that the examined bells typo-chronologically categorised as the latest in the sequence (proposed by Makoto Sahara in 1960 and has since become widely accepted from accumulated circumstantial evidences) and dated to the Yayoi V include the lead most likely acquired somewhere in northern China, mixed with tin and copper on a standardised ratio (e.g. Mabuchi and Hirao 1982). How the raw material was imported and in what form are the subject of ongoing debate, but it can safely be assumed that the mediation of the Lelang commandery was essential for the acquirement of northern Chinese raw materials in any case (regardless, the further mediation of the northern Kyushu communities monopolising access to the commandery was necessary or not). If the supply of the raw material for the *Dotaku* production also dried up, the maintenance of inter-communal relations within its horizon would have been threatened.[3] The settlement disappearance and convergence within the distribution of the *Dotaku* bronze bell, in that regard, can also be explained by the independence of the Lelang commandery. However, the scale of the phenomenon also suggests that the possible cooling (or some other environmental factors) might have also been a contributing factor/factors.[4]

After this event, interestingly, the preexisting order – in terms of the networks between settlements – appears to have been restored in northern

---

2 The custom of depositing a large number of Chinese-imported mirrors as grave goods, began in the Yayoi VI, with the mentioned lapse, continued in northern Kyushu. The Iwara-Yarimizo (井原鑓溝) jar burial, accidentally excavated in the Edo period (the Tenmei (天明) era, 1781–1788; Aoyagi 1976), yielded at least twenty-one TLV-patterned mirrors, three Tomoe (巴)-shaped bronze implements, and some iron weapons. The overt display of status difference and wealth of some sort, however, did not take place in western Japan except northern Kyushu before the final phase of the Yayoi V and the Yayoi-Kofun transitional period. See below.

3 The possible mass deposition of bronze bells that is inferred to have taken place around this time (mentioned in p. 168 of Chapter 6; Fukunaga 1998, 220–222) might have been related to this temporal stoppage of the supply of the source for the production of the bells.

4 It is interesting that regions such as the southern Shikoku and central Inland Sea coastal regions did not see a decline in the number of settlements: on the contrary, the number and the scale increased in the regions during the very phase (e.g. Dehara 1999). In the latter region, there also appeared a number of hill-top settlements showing traces of normal subsistence and production activities, for instance, in the form of a small hilltop shell midden and evidences of stone reaping knife production (e.g. Kondo 1983, 87–88; Matsugi 2001). This suggests that inter-communal tension might also have risen and that some communities might have chosen to relocate themselves to hilltop locations. These observations suggest that the cause of this widespread phenomenon and the reaction to it were complex and different from one region to the next, to say the least.

Kyushu, even though many of the preexisting large regional-centre-type settlements disappeared or significantly reduced in size in the Kinki region and its surrounding regions (e.g. the Ikegami-Sone [池上曽根] settlement in Izumi province; Izumi MBA 2004). As if to replace them, some large-scale hilltop settlements emerged during the period of settlement decline; these consisted of a number of separate residential groups, like their equivalents situated on the floodplains (e.g. the Kosobe-Shibatani [古曽部・芝谷] settlement in the northern part of present-day Osaka prefecture; Takatsuki Municipal Buried Cultural Properties Research Centre 1996). However, they did not flourish for very long. Except some large regional centres in the Nara Basin such as the Karako-Kagi (唐古・鍵) settlement, most of the regional centres in areas around the Osaka Bay became much smaller or eventually disappeared.

I examine the cause of these changes later on in this chapter, but it should be mentioned here that the 'restoration' of the settlement system in northern Kyushu coincided with the establishment of the Later Han dynastic rule and the reopening of contacts with it, through the Lelang commandery (which, as mentioned, became independent during the short-lived Xin dynasty of Wang Mang but put back under Han's control in AD 30), by certain northern Kyushu coastal communities. The Houhanshu (後漢書) chronicle, the official document chronicling events during the Late Han dynasty, records that the king of Na (奴), the main polity of the present-day Fukuoka Plain, sent a delegation to the emperor (emperor Guangwu [光武]) in AD 57. The date probably corresponds to some time in the second half of the early Yayoi V period, roughly coinciding with the beginning of the restoration of the settlement system in northern Kyushu and the establishment of the new settlement order in Kinki region. The record in the same chronicle that the king of Wa (倭) and others sent a delegation to the emperor An (安帝) in AD 107 suggests that increasingly wider areas in western Japan became centralised and integrated from the second half of the early Yayoi V to the late Yayoi V periods; Wa is the generic name used by the Chinese imperial chronicles to describe the polities of the archipelago before the late seventh century AD, when the newly established ancient state began to refer to itself as Riben

(日本), and the use of the word *Wa*, in this context, suggests that the Later Han dynasty recognised the king of Wa as the representative of a number of polities constituting the larger, integrated political entity.

An important point is that the late Yayoi V saw the emergence of a clear indication of hierarchisation in the form of elite-precinct-type compounds in settlements across northern Kyushu and western Japan (Takesue 1990b; Mizoguchi 2000, 2001). At times, the precincts have exclusive storage facilities inside them, which are often enclosed by a ditch and clearly separated from the other residential units, all of which together constitute individual settlements. Simultaneously, the number of the people given formal burials dropped sharply at this time, and those who were buried in archaeologically traceable ways were found to be buried in clearly defined burial compounds that were commonly square in shape (Mizoguchi 2000, 2001). The deceased in individual compounds include not only adults but also infants and children, significantly, who were buried in the same manner as adults, suggesting that their membership was not *achieved* but *ascribed* as a birthright. This also suggests that the elite status was now occupied and inherited by certain communal segments, probably lineage- or sub-lineage-scale groupings, which controlled the storage of things, probably both foodstuffs and goods; for instance, at the Sendoyama (千塔山) site in Saga prefecture, northern Kyushu, a number of iron tools were excavated from the ditch enclosing a residential compound which was the only compound in the settlement to have raised-floor granaries (Kiyama Town Site Excavation Team 1978).

The stratification appears to have been accelerated by, and accelerated, the development of production and circulation of products. At the same time, the organisation of labour and the mode of ritual activities suggest that it became crucial to not only maintain the sense of communal togetherness and collaboration, most likely based on an egalitarian ethos, but also enhance it. These trends contradicted one another and thus would have required some resolution. As we will see later, the degree of collaboration required in the construction and maintenance of a large unit of rice paddy fields on the floodplains of the large alluvial plains in Kyushu, western Japan and the western half of eastern Japan, extending up to the Kanto region, is significant in this regard. The development and formalisation of various ritual practices, including the deposition of an increasingly large number of bronze implements in the northern Kyushu and Kinki regions and the construction of increasingly large tumuli in the San'in, northern Kinki and central Inland Sea regions, can be interpreted as a way of addressing the rising contradictions.

In short, this chapter deals with the causes and outcomes of the emerging hierarchisation and how the societies of the time dealt with the phenomenon. Let us begin by examining hierarchisation as a consequence of developing production and circulation, and their involvement in social reproduction, which would also reveal the ambivalent nature of society's reaction to hierarchisation.

2. PRODUCTION, CIRCULATION AND SOCIAL REPRODUCTION

2.1. *Rice Paddy Field Agriculture and Communality*

By this time, substantial portions of the major floodplains in western Japan were covered by paddies watered by sophisticated irrigation systems. The latter often consisted of large irrigation canals and/or triangular-sectioned dams of substantial scales constructed by compositing logs across small rivers. At the Naka-Kun'ryu (那珂君休) site in the Fukuoka Plain,[5] for instance, a roughly triangular-sectioned structure constructed by substantial wooden piles (many of which were reused construction materials for houses and other features) dammed up a river of substantial scale (Figure 7.1; Fukuoka MBE 1987a). To what extent this kind of large-scale water-controlling features, requiring large labour force and sophisticated engineering for their construction, were widespread, and whether they were locally invented or were introduced from the outside, from Korean peninsula, for instance, remains unclear. However, it can at least be said that the technology of rice paddy field agriculture developed to

such an extent that its organisational management came to require a new level of sophistication.[6]

At the Hyakkengawa (百間川) site in Okayama prefecture, more than a kilometre-long stretch in the excavation was found to be almost entirely covered by paddies divided by bunds (Okayama PBE 1980; Kondo 1983, 42–44, 97). The stretch cut across naturally formed raised riverbanks and buried former watercourses, and different means were used to ensure that all the paddies would be evenly irrigated, mainly by constructing smaller paddies on uneven terrains and larger ones on flat terrains (ibid.). Such differentiation in the size of paddies, based on the topography of the terrains, had already begun in the Yayoi I, and came to be applied in such a large scale and organisationally sophisticated manner (Figure 7.2).[7] While the paddies situated on buried former watercourses appear to have been in a semi-waterlogged condition, those located on raised riverbanks had to be irrigated by canals (Okayama PBE 1980; Kondo 1983, 42–44). In order to irrigate these separate units of paddies, situated on several natural riverbanks, it would have been necessary for a number of communities to coordinate and collaborate with each other, to some extent, to design the course of the canals and dig them.

At the same site, excavations revealed several sophisticated water-distributing features, highly suggestive of the level of organisation involved in the use and maintenance of paddies (Okayama

---

5 The site was originally excavated as the Naka-Kyuhira (那珂休平) site, but turned out to be a part of the Naka-Kun'ryu. Therefore, it is reported as the former (Fukuoka MBE 1987a).

6 It has been pointed out that large scale irrigation canals cutting low-lying hills and reservoir-like features constructed by damming a stream on the bottom of a small and shallow valley began to be constructed in parts of northern Kyushu in the late Middle Yayoi period (e.g. Yoshidome 2005). It might suggest that the degree of the organisational sophistication in putting together labour force from a number of communities, that the following will suggest to have been achieved across western Japan in the Yayoi V, had already been reached in northern Kyushu during the Yayoi IV.

7 At the Ogaki (大柿) site in Tokushima prefecture, which dates back to the final Yayoi I, for instance, small paddies were situated on a gentle slope to form a kind of 'stepped paddies', whereby flat paddy beds could be obtained with minimum labour investment (Tokushima Prefectural Buried Cultural Properties Research Centre 1997). This suggests that the rice-agriculture-based techno-complex introduced at the beginning of the Yayoi period had already developed a sufficient range of techniques and know-how to cope with different topographical conditions.

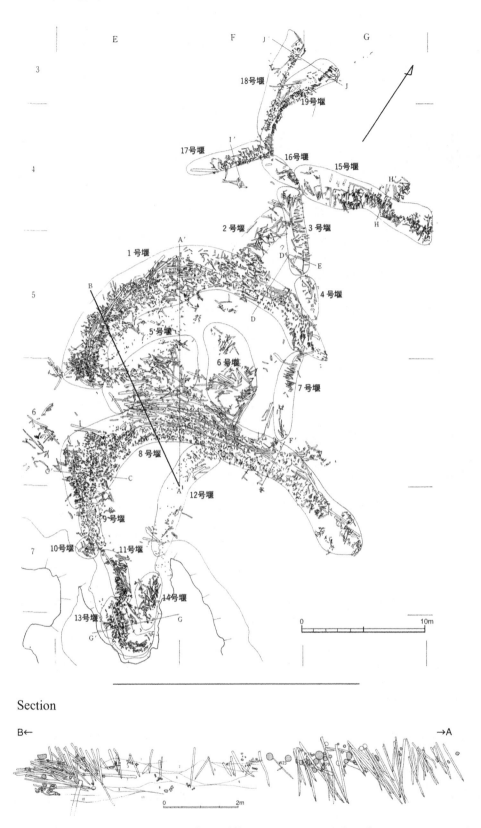

Figure 7.1. A triangular-sectioned dam of the Late Yayoi period: Naka-Kunryu site, Fukuoka prefecture (after Fukuoka MBE 1987a). Above: the dam complex. Below: section drawing of the axis A–B marked in the above.

Figure 7.2. Paddy fields excavated at Hyakkengawa site, Okayama prefecture (after Okayama PBE 1980). Above: excavated paddies dating from the Middle Yayoi and that from the Late Yayoi. Note the increase in the number of paddies and the sophistication of adjusting the shape of paddies to micro-topography. Below: the Late Yayoi paddies in the present-day landscape.

PBE 1980). At Hyakkengawa-Haraojima (百間川 原尾島) site, a water-distributing canal was split into two, as if to form the letter *Y* (Figure 7.3). A complex structure was implemented at the point of the split as well as upstream in the canal. The canal was first divided into two parallel-flowing sub-canals before the splitting point. At the splitting point, the eastern sub-canal continued as before, while the western one was split into three sub-canals. If the western sub-canal is not dammed at the Y-shaped splitting point, water flows into the paddies adjacent to the canals. Otherwise, those four canals bring water some distance away. Kazuo Hirose infers that each of these sub-canals was

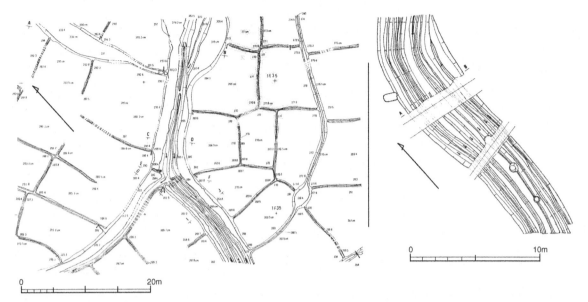

Figure 7.3. Complex canal system excavated at the Hyakkengawa-Haraojima site, Okayama prefecture (after Okayama PBE 1980). Left: Note the complexity of the way a canal is divided into a number of parallel-running canals. Right: an example of parallel-running canals.

designed to water a separate set of paddies at their end (Hirose 1997b, 46). This is suited for watering different terrains such as what were mentioned above. Also, this, I would like to argue, is a device highly suited for maintaining *communal egalitarianism*; by distributing water in this way, paddies located around the downstream areas would not have suffered from water shortage because an equal amount of water was allocated to each separate canal for watering a separate set of paddies, regardless of whether it was located around the upstream or downstream areas. At the Ikeshima-Fukumanji (池島・福万寺) site in Osaka prefecture, it has been pointed out that a cluster of three or four spatial units each comprised of a number of small paddies functioned as an independent unit of water supply during the Yayoi V (Inoue 2005). The complex structure that the Ikeshima-Fukumanji paddies took would have also been for achieving communal egalitarianism amongst those communities which constructed, used and mended the paddies.

The implementation of such schemes would have required considerably greater labour force and technological sophistication/investment than that required to build a single canal system for simply distributing water to paddies along the way. It is quite possible that such a scheme was invented as a consequence of the development of wooden earth-digging and earth-moving tools. These tools began to be equipped with iron blade edges in the northern and central Kyushu regions

in the Yayoi V period; however, their prevalence declined as one went east (Murakami 1998, 60–73), where U-shaped and 'eggplant-shaped' digging tools, which were invented around the Yayoi IV period, might have contributed more significantly to rice paddy field agriculture in that area (see e.g. Terasawa 2000, 79–84). The invention of such a paddy irrigation scheme, however, was not necessarily utilised to further the interest and economic autonomy of individual communal segments, that is, sub-lineages, lineages or sub-clans, which would have been allocated individual *sets* of paddies in the case of Hyakkengawa. Instead, such inventions and technological improvements would have been utilised to maintain the integrity of communal groupings, probably based on an egalitarian ethos.

These occurrences in the central Seto Inland Sea region are particularly interesting in that the region, together with the San'in and northern Kinki regions, developed the custom of burying the elite and their family members in clearly defined, often mounded, burial compounds which were commonly situated on hilltops (e.g. Kondo 1983, 148–167, 177–187). As we will see subsequently in this chapter and in the next chapter, the period saw the development of four major 'ritual horizons' in western Japan (Figure 7.4): the first was characterised by the use and deposition of *Dohoko* (銅矛) bronze spearheads and extended from northern Kyushu to the south-western portion of Shikoku Island; the second was characterised by the use and deposition of *Dotaku* bronze bells and covered the Kinki region and the western portion of Tokai region; the third was characterised by square burial mounds with characteristic tail-mounds sticking out of the four corners, and this horizon covered the San'in region; the fourth horizon spread over the central Seto Inland Sea region, where there developed a unique elite mortuary custom involving the construction of substantial tumuli and mortuary rituals involving lavishly decorated pottery pedestals (e.g. Matsugi 1998).[8] The first two horizons can be said to display elements of 'communal' ritual practices; their enhanced visual appearance suggests that those ritual implements would have been displayed in communal occasions which took place before their deposition. However, the last two clearly reflect the emergence of elite segments; the deceased commonly consisted of several adults and a couple of infants/children (Mizoguchi 2000, 243–257). It is particularly worth noting that the infants/children were buried in the same manner as the adults; in most cases, the deceased were buried in cists, though those used for children/infants were smaller than the ones which contained adult bodies. This suggests that their status was ascribed rather than achieved. However, the characteristics of the mortuary ritual suggest its communal nature; for instance, the presence of a large number of vessels, including a substantial number of pedestalled bowls and globular jars, most typically seen in examples in the San'in region (Shigematsu 2006; Furuya 2007), suggest large feasts conducted on top of or around the mounds.[9] This suggests that burials in these communities would have also been occasions for praying for the well-being of the entire community represented by the

deceased person, rather than merely an occasion to lavishly display the person's distinct status (see Section 3.2 in this chapter). By this time, a small number of communal segments would have begun to be treated as 'higher-ranked' by birthright, but they would have been perceived as *representing* the interests of the communities of which they were a part. This picture appears to coincide fairly well with the situation in Hyakkengawa. The ongoing technological development made it possible to build and maintain paddy fields on significantly larger scale than before. However, this also necessitated a higher degree of coordination and cooperation between individual communal segments which were allocated individual sets of paddies. Performing daily agricultural labour in certain paddies would have enhanced the sense of attachment between each communal segment and the paddies it was responsible for, and this would have given rise to a sense of natural right of possession over the produce yielded by the paddies. The contradiction between (X) the heightened necessity of intra-communal coordination and (Y) the rising sense of possession felt by individual communal segments of the paddies for the produce they yielded would have become increasingly acute. This contradiction, in itself, must have been initially generated much earlier. However, the invention and implementation of sophisticated devices for distributing water in an egalitarian manner, such as the irrigation system at the Hyakkengawa site, suggest that the contradiction was about to reach a critical point. The emergence of elite segments, buried in the tumuli of the central Seto Inland Sea, San'in and northern Kinki regions, would have been a reaction to this contradiction: the segments would have served as a stable pool of 'mediators' who embodied the interests of the entire community and managed the intra- and inter-communal tensions generated within the community by increasing the 'force of production' and encouraging the autonomy of individual communal segments cultivating individual units of paddies, such as the examples at the Hyakkengawa site.

If we shift our attention to the wider picture, even those settlements that were not so large, and definitely not as big as the regional-centre-type settlements, such as the settlement at the Toro (登呂) site in Shizuoka prefecture, eastern Japan, began cultivating very large paddy fields at the

8 Those four horizons were amongst roughly eight ritual horizons emerged across western Japan and the western portion of eastern Japan (see Chapter 8.3.1, esp. Figure 8.6).

9 In contrast to the San'in examples, in the central Seto Inland sea region, certain types of the vessels had their bottoms bored after firing (Shigematsu 2006, 20). It suggests that those vessels were not actually used as food-serving vessels but used to *symbolically gesture* dedicating offerings. We will come back to some implications of the difference observed in the way the ritual on the tumuli was conducted between the San'in and the central Seto Inland Sea regions later (Section 3.2 in the current chapter).

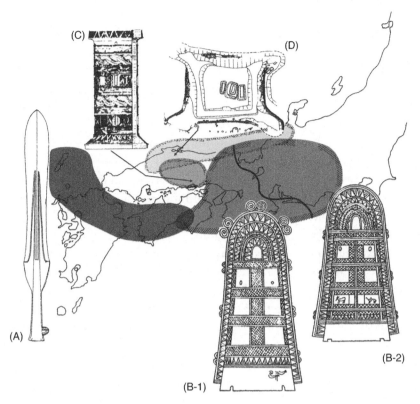

Figure 7.4. Four ritual horizons emerged in the Late Yayoi period (after Matsugi 1998, with modifications and additions). **A**: bronze spearheads type W (see Figure 7.5), **B**: *Dotaku* bronze bells type IV (see Figure 7.5), **C**: heavily decorated pedestal used in mortuary rituals from the area around the ancient Kibi province, **D**: an example of the rectangular tumulus with four tails sticking out of the corners from the area around the ancient Izumo province. With kind permission from the Kadokawa Shoten Publishing Co.

bottom of floodplains by flattening the minute bumps on the surface of the floodplains (e.g. Okamura 2008). At Toro, situated on the western fringe of eastern Japan, approximately 70,000 square metres of land was divided into more than fifty paddies, the largest of which measured approximately 2,000 square metres; a 2-metre-wide canal equipped with floodgates and other facilities to control the water level ran through the centre of this paddy field system (ibid.). Some scholars point out the significance of the fact that the paddies extended so far outside the excavated areas, suggesting that they were constructed and maintained by the collaboration of the Toro and several other settlements, such as the Shioiri (汐入), which were situated in the vicinity (ibid.). If this were the case, it would further confirm the thesis that rice paddy field agriculture increased the importance of large-scale communal collaboration during the Yayoi V period.

It should be noted that eastern Japan, except for its northernmost regions (i.e. the northern Tohoku region), also saw the steady spread and development of rice paddy field agriculture. Interestingly, the traces of rice paddy field agriculture seem to have disappeared from the prominent paddy field site excavations in the northern Tohoku region such as the Sunazawa (砂沢; see Saino 2005) and Tareyanagi (垂柳; ibid.) settlements during the Yayoi V. The region saw the introduction of rice paddy field agriculture, along with some of the relevant techno-complex from western Japan, during the Yayoi I (see Chapter 5.3.4), and large paddies equipped with water-distributing devices that were as sophisticated as their equivalents in western Japan were constructed and used during the Early and Middle Yayoi periods. Hirohiko Saino has pointed out that the paddies of those sites are characteristically small despite their being situated on fairly flat terrains; according to him, this was intentionally done in order to keep the water level as high as possible when the paddies were filled, which prevented the water temperature from dropping below the temperature which ensured the healthy growth of rice (ibid.). Despite such efforts to adapt the farming technology to an environment that was harsh for rice paddy field agriculture, the communities of the region appear to have eventually abandoned it. This coincided with an increase in contact between the communities of that region and those inhabiting Hokkaido Island, where the Epi-Jomon (続縄文) culture was continuing and the inhabitants of which led a hunting-gathering-based way of life. From now on, the communities in the region began to steadily increase their affinities with their northern counterparts, and in the Kofun period, a fairly clear sociocultural and technological boundary, which appears to have also coincided with the emergence of two distinct 'identities', emerged between them and their southern counterparts, who embraced a large portion of the range of customs characterising the *Kofun way of life* (Fujisawa 2004a).

In short, the study of paddies in the Yayoi V period (mainly in Kyushu and western Japan) reveals that (1) the scale of rice paddy field agriculture increased significantly, (2) the complexity generated by this would have required more sophisticated coordination of labour organisation and water distribution on a larger scale than before and (3) this did not necessarily imply increasing autonomy for individual communal segments but rather appears to have led to the development of new devices for maintaining the egalitarian-ethos-based communal integration, such as certain mortuary rituals involving large-scale feasting and ritual practices involving the deposition of bronze implements (see the following).

Hunting and gathering activities continued during this period, though the communities' degree of reliance on them for subsistence appears to have declined significantly. In the Chubu and Kanto regions, circumstantial evidence suggests that some communities or sub-groups residing in mountainous regions did devote a certain amount of time to hunting activities (Kaneko 1997). The data from the Yugura (湯倉) cave in Nagano prefecture suggest that young deer were specially hunted for their fine, soft hide (ibid., 149). It has also been pointed out that deer antlers were transported elsewhere, possibly to villages located on terrains suitable for rice agriculture, for processing and use (ibid.). In addition, it appears that deer hunting had

been considered of greater importance than was wild-boar hunting in eastern Japan ever since the Jomon period, and it remained significant until the Yayoi V (ibid., 150). This is particularly interesting because in western Japan, deer hunting began to decline with the onset of the Yayoi period and became secondary to wild-boar hunting (Kaneko 1997). As mentioned in Chapter 6.7.2, it might have something to do with the change in the symbolic positions of those animals. The depiction of deer is far more frequent and prominent in the pictorial representations on the *Dotaku* bronze bells (Morita 2008, 49, table 2), whereas the jaw bones of predominantly female and young wild boars were hung on sticks, probably for ritual purposes (ibid.). It is interesting to note that this norm could not be observed in eastern Japan, where the composition of hunting animals had not changed much from the Jomon period; this gives us an idea about the differences between western and eastern Japan during the periods analysed in the current volume.

The development of selective hunting and the intensive use of animal parts for specific production activities might reflect the progressing differentiation of hunting communities from farming communities.

2.2. Metalworking, Distribution and the Nature of the Ritual Sphere

BRONZE

The scale and organisation of bronzeworking developed across northern Kyushu and western Japan.

In those regions, the size of the main ritual implements – *Dohoko* bronze spearheads in northern Kyushu and *Dotaku* bronze bells in Kinki region – increased at an accelerated pace (Figure 7.5; Tanaka 1970), indicating the increasing importance attributed to the ritual spheres involving those implements as their media. We have already inferred earlier that the sense of communality would have been enhanced through such rituals and that the modification of the implements was a kind of reaction to the developing hierarchisation and necessity to maintain communal collaboration. The fact that their deposition, mainly conducted far away from the settlements during the Middle Yayoi, became increasingly conducted

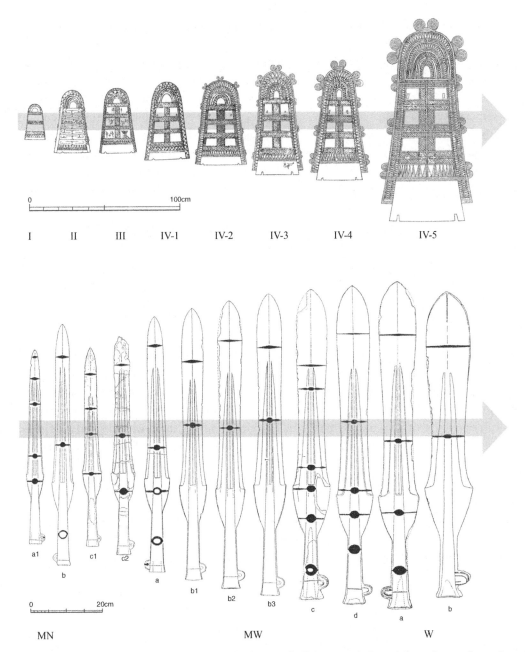

Figure 7.5. Temporal change of the *Dotaku* bronze bell (arranged from Sahara [2002, fig. 13]) and the *Dohoko* bronze spearhead (from Iwanaga [1986, fig. 3], with additions and modifications).

nearby the settlements, often on their boundaries (Adachi 2011, 174), would probably support the inference; more people would have been easily gathered to the latter locations. Their production, which was carried out in a number of settlements on a relatively small scale during the Middle Yayoi period, appears to have increasingly become concentrated in a limited number of large regional-centre-type settlements.

In northern Kyushu, during the Middle Yayoi period, the production of bronze spearheads and other bronze ritual implements was carried out in the central-place-type settlements of the northern Chikushi Plain and the Fukuoka Plain, with a number of outlying settlements also participating in the production (Kataoka 1999, 149–150). In the early Middle Yayoi period, the centre of production was the Saga area in the northern Chikushi Plain, where, as mentioned earlier (p. 111 in Chapter 6), there had been an influx of migrants from the Korean peninsula (ibid.), who settled in that plain and were gradually absorbed by the indigenous communities during the Yayoi II and III. In the Yayoi IV, however, the centre of bronzeworking began to shift to the north, and in the Yayoi V, the Sugu (須玖) site cluster and other sites in its vicinity became the dominant centre of bronzeworking (Hirata 2003), although these implements were produced on a much smaller scale across northern Kyushu (Tajiri 2001).

A typical workshop at the Sugu site, such as the Sugu-Sakamoto (須玖坂本), consists of a rectangular structure with a roof, which is possibly without walls and is enclosed by a shallow ditch, probably to drain rainwater and keep the inside dry (e.g. Kasuga MBE 2010, 2011). The absence of any substantial hearth in the excavations probably suggests that the scale of work undertaken at each time in each workshop and the technological sophistication involved were not very significant, though the amount of bronzeworking-related debris, including fragments of stone moulds, clay cores, pouring vessels, and so on, excavated from them is significant (ibid.). An interesting finding about the Sugu site is that a number of such workshops were found to be simultaneously operating in the northern sector of the site (Hirata 2003). Limited rescue excavations make it difficult to reconstruct the entire picture, but it is likely that each of these workshops was attached to separate residential units, some of which may have been ditch-enclosed and square in shape (Kasuga MBE 2010, 2011). There is no significant difference between the excavated workshops in terms of the types of bronzeworking-related equipment and the items produced using them, including spearheads, arrowheads, mirrors and so on. The image of the production does not suggest a centralised production system based on the division of labour/different tasks allocated to different workshops. It would be more feasible to infer that some members of the residential units, probably representing lineage-scale groupings, in this large village undertook bronzeworking as a part-time skilled work. In addition, it is difficult to determine the extent to which the distribution/circulation of the products was under the control of the elite residing elsewhere in the settlement.[10] These implements, particularly bronze spearheads, were distributed across a large horizon extending eastwards

through the coastal north-eastern Kyushu region to the south-western portion of Shikoku Island (Figure 7.4; Shimojo 1982). Some scholars argue that the horizon indicates the spatial extension of the 'political influence' of northern Kyushu (ibid.). However, the ways in which these implements were used appear to have varied from region to region; for instance, the bronze spearheads were deposited in different manners in different areas within the horizon (Takesue 1982). This suggests that the distribution of the products did not necessarily correspond with the distribution of the mode of their use. Jun'ichi Takesue has pointed out that within the horizon, the ways in which the spearheads were deposited varied. In northern Kyushu, spearheads were often deposited with the blade edge set vertically and the head and socket set alternatingly (ibid.). In Tsushima Island, spearheads deposited in various manners, including spearheads deposited in the manner crossed against one another, coexisted with those deposited in the typical mainland northern Kyushu manner (ibid.). In Tsushima, some of them were deposited as grave goods as well. In the eastern fringe of the horizon, that is, in the western half of Tosa province (which largely coincides with present-day Kochi prefecture), they were often deposited singly (ibid.). The bronze spearheads were circulated as ritual goods, and their distribution would have certainly indicated the horizon within which they were perceived as such. However, this does not necessarily prove that the communities constituting the horizon shared a unified belief system and a uniform mode of ritual.

This means that their distribution does not indicate the presence of a ritual horizon of some sort, let alone that of a tight social integration under the control of a dominant community and its elite in that horizon. However, considering, for instance, the *Dotaku* bronze bells' dense distribution on their south-western, south and south-eastern periphery, that is, the southern Shikoku region, where a clear boundary can be drawn between the horizon of spearheads and that of *Dotaku* bells, present-day Wakayama prefecture, and the area around the lake Hamana, respectively (Figure 7.4; see e.g. Harunari 1982), it might be said that strategic gift-giving to the peripheral polities was involved in the formation of this distribution pattern. I will come back to this issue later.

---

10 No elite precinct-type residential compound has been excavated yet in this extremely large site, covering about 200 hectares of low hills and surrounding floodplains (see Figure 6.7).

The *Dotaku* bronze bells developed to such an extent in terms of size that they were rarely used as bells; this is indicated by the fact that the band on the lower inside of the bell, which was heavily worn due to repeated ringing in the bells dating back to the Middle Yayoi period, rarely shows any trace of wear in the case of the Yayoi V bells. It is widely believed that by this time, the bells were used solely for display on ritual occasions (Tanaka 1970). It is interesting to note that pictorial representations on these bells, interpreted in the previous chapter as having signified elements of mythological narratives of transformation between the elements implicated in the system of rice-paddy-field agricultural practices, and seen throughout the Middle Yayoi period, had almost disappeared by the Yayoi V (e.g. National Museum of Japanese History 1997). This can possibly be interpreted as reflecting that the message signified by the use of the bells gradually became *esoteric*: the meaning(s) indicated/generated through the use of the bells would have become not explained by pictorial representations but exclusively known by chosen few. According to Makoto Sahara (1960), the stylistic analysis of these bells reveals the emergence of two distinct schools: the first, as far as the distribution of its specimens is concerned, emerged in the central Kinki region, whereas the second emerged in the Tokai region (Figures 7.4.B-1 and B-2). The differences between these schools are quite minute; for example, in specimens of the latter school, protruding bands dividing the surface into panels cross with one another, whereas in specimens from the former school, they do not and so on. Based on this, we can infer the following: (1) *Dotaku* bells were widely used as ritual implements across those regions; (2) the stylistic differences in the bells do not appear to have been used to indicate the existence of distinct ritual-based identities between the regions; and (3) their production was centralised to the extent that the attributes indicating their respective schools were rigidly maintained and rarely mixed in individual specimens. This might be further supported by the fact that the prototypes of the bells representing those schools were derived from a particular group of bells with protruding bands dividing the panels on their surface, produced by means of highly sophisticated artisanship in the Yayoi IV somewhere in the central Kinki region (ibid.; Harunari 1992). The *Dotaku* bells of

the Yayoi IV varied stylistically, and the fact that the specific group mentioned above almost solely became the prototype of the bells in the Yayoi V suggests that the groups of bronzesmiths involved in the *Dotaku* production, formerly scattered across the central Kinki region, were reorganised and its production was centralised (ibid.).

By the second half of the Yayoi V, the Tokai school disappeared, and as if to replace the ritual involving the *Dotaku* bells, the custom of burying the dead in a keyhole tumulus with a square rear mound spread within the erstwhile horizon of the Tokai school bells and extended beyond, to the east. At the same time, scholars have pointed out that the distribution of *Dotaku* bells was increasingly concentrated in the fringe areas of their distribution: the Oiwayama (大岩山) deposition, which consists of twenty-four bells, and the findings that a large number of these bells were distributed in the Ki'i province (present-day Wakayama and a part of Mie prefectures) and the Awa province (present-day Tokushima prefecture), only reinforce this impression.[11]

A currently influential thesis posits that the depositions of the bells in the regions on the fringes of the horizon were intended to ritualistically mark the boundary of the emergent body of political integration or alliance against its potentially hostile neighbouring communities, that is, the central Seto Inland Sea, San'in, and Tokai regions beyond the line of the river Tenryu, which had started displaying their distinct local identities in the form of customs involving the burial of their elite in uniquely shaped tumuli in the former two and in the form of developing a distinct pottery style (e.g. Harunari 1982; Terasawa 2000, 221–224). Some of the proponents of this thesis suggest that the *Dotaku* bells of the Middle Yayoi were deposited in a fairly short while some time towards the end of the Yayoi IV (Fukunaga 1998) and emphasise that such a deposition was not a normal practice but one representing a ritual reaction to a contingency with significant implications on the well-being of the concerned communities (Terasawa 2000, 221–224). Kaoru Terasawa, for instance, argues that the

---

11 It has to be noted, however, that Shin'ya Fukunaga (2001, 44) argues that the distribution as currently seen might be distorted due to the practice of destroying and recasting the *Dotaku* bells, which might have been followed in the central areas of the latest *Dotaku* horizon.

depositions which occurred at the end of the Yayoi IV were a reaction by communities living along the Seto Inland Sea corridor and in the Kinki region to the rising influence of northern Kyushu polities which monopolised the import of Chinese bronze mirrors and other prestige goods and items from the continent by exclusively controlling access to the early Han commandery of Lelang (ibid.). By emphasising the political nature of the *Dotaku* deposition, Terasawa and others argue that the eventual concentration of their distribution on the fringes of the horizon was the consequence of ritually marking the boundaries of the newly emerging, internally unified polity by its increasingly centralised authority which controlled the production and distribution of the *Dotakus* (Wada 1986).

However, another important finding has revealed that individual depositions only include neighbouring temporal types (Iwanaga 1987, 464–465). This strongly suggests that the depositions of *Dotaku* bells in the Middle Yayoi period were not a one-off event but took place regularly and continuously (ibid.). This would further suggest that the depositional practice constituted only *a part of* the ritual system and process involving the *Dotaku* bells. This means that the *Dotaku* depositional practice in the Yayoi V also need not necessarily be understood as a one-off political reaction against pressures from the neighbouring polities. In contrast, the observations point to an alternative interpretation: the *Dotaku* bells which ended up in the peripheral communities were presented to those communities in order to retain them in networks of denser interaction and exchange than those forged with the neighbouring communities beyond, to the west and to the east. As we have seen earlier, and will discuss again in the current chapter, the Yayoi V period saw the emergence of intra- and inter-communal hierarchisation based on the segmentation of lineage-scale groupings as the basic unit of social hierarchy. This would have led to the formation of a conical structure within and between the communities. It has long been suggested that such communities commonly have a tendency to continually expand their horizons through further segmentations, budding off newly segmented communal units and/or the marrying out of redundant elite individuals who cannot occupy higher positions in their own communities

(Friedman and Rowlands 1977, 224–228). We can certainly infer that such movements occurred during the Yayoi V. The *Dotaku* bells deposited by communities across the periphery of their horizon might have been presented to those on the 'frontiers' of such expanding horizons comprising actual or fictive kin-networks as gifts for forming and/or maintaining such ties. In any case, the use of the bells varied and was hardly uniform across the regions; some were deposited at a remote place from the sphere of daily life (e.g. at the Oiwayama site in Shiga prefecture; cf. Sahara 2002, 7–9), while others were deposited singly within a settlement area, with some structures built above them (e.g. at the Yano [矢野] site in Tokushima prefecture; Tokushima Prefectural Buried Cultural Properties Research Centre 1993). This suggests that the bells were used not to confirm ties with their distributor(s) but in ways that seemed to fit the necessity of the individual communities which used and deposited them. The *Dotaku* shows an identical picture to the *Dohoko* bronze spearhead in terms of use, as we saw earlier.

The formation of horizons characterised by the deposition of *Dohoko* bronze spearheads and *Dotaku* bronze bells indicated the rising importance of a communal ritual sphere on various scales. The horizons, however, were not internally integrated nor can be characterised as 'ritual horizons'; instead, they might have reflected developing *networks* based on actual and/or fictive kin ties and gift giving, and they would have still heavily drawn on the communal, egalitarian ethos.

IRON: THE SPHERE OF DAILY TOOLS
The use of iron tools in the archipelago, as briefly mentioned in the previous chapter, began with the use of imported cast iron tools such as socketed axes; even their broken pieces were reused. It has been revealed that a large number of flat iron axes and other variously shaped tools with a cutting edge, widely used across Kyushu and western Japan during the early Middle Yayoi period and reaching as far east as Kanto region by the end of the Middle Yayoi period, were, in fact, reworked broken pieces of cast-iron socketed axes and other tools (cf. Murakami 1998, chap. 2). An interesting and important feature of these reworked tools is the fact that they were reshaped and polished using the techniques and tools used to shape and

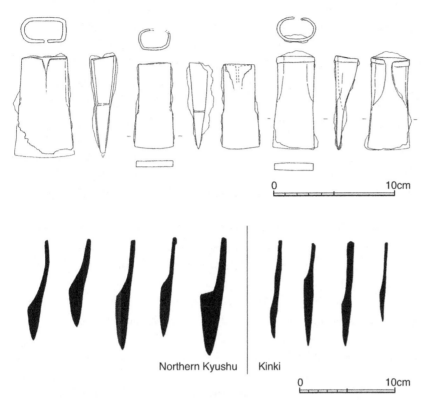

Northern Kyushu | Kinki

Figure 7.6. Regional variations of flanged forged iron axes (arranged from Murakami [1998], with additions). With kind permission from Aoki Shoten Publishing Co.

polish stone tools; this indicates that the functional supremacy of iron tools was recognised by this time, even if cast-iron tools were easily broken, the desire for acquiring them was such that even very small broken pieces were reshaped and reused (ibid.).

The forging of iron appears to have begun in the late Yayoi III, and by the Yayoi IV, the production of forged iron tools was widespread across Kyushu and western Japan (Murakami 1998, chap. 2). The production technology was most advanced in northern Kyushu. For instance, flanged forged iron axes needed to have a thickened body and blade-base in order to be effective in cutting down thick tree trunks. Such axes were produced in northern Kyushu, whereas from the western Seto Inland Sea region eastward, the body and blade-base became increasingly thinner, and the axes became functionally less effective than their northern Kyushu equivalents (Figure 7.6; ibid., 68). This technological deterioration from the west to the east is also generally visible in the variety, quality and quantity of iron implements in use and circulation. According to Yasuyuki Murakami (1998, 84–87), there were three distinct types of hearth used for ironworking at that time. Murakami's type I hearth consists of a substantial pit filled with alternate layers of earth and charcoal and a superstructure. The inside walls of the pit were commonly dried and hardened by fire, and the layers of earth and charcoal were designed to keep the superstructure of the hearth dry (ibid., 84). The superstructure, which rarely tends to survive the passage of time, would have consisted of a layer of crushed charcoal under a pile of charred logs (ibid.). The type II hearth consists of a shallow pit and a superstructure, whereas type III consists only of a superstructure (ibid., 86). Both types I and II emerged in northern Kyushu in the Yayoi IV, and while the former continued until the end of the Yayoi period (ibid.), the latter became widespread across Kyushu and the western Seto Inland Sea region in the Yayoi V. The type III hearth appears to have emerged in Kansai region under the technological influence of the west, and it diffused eastward as far as Tokai region (ibid.). The functional efficiency of these hearths, in terms of the maximum temperature obtainable from them, decreases from type I to type III. Interestingly, this maximum temperature, inferred from the degree of hardening of the hearth-floor caused by fire, gradually dropped through time (ibid, 86–87), suggesting a kind of *technological devolution*.

This last finding is highly indicative of the nature and character of ironworking in the Middle and Late Yayoi periods. Murakami also adds that the roots of the type I hearth can be traced back to the technological tradition of sophisticated ironworking by artisans closely associated with the elite of the Korean peninsula, whereas those of the type II hearth derive from the less sophisticated ironworking practice commonly practiced in ordinary villages across the peninsula (Murakami 1998, 89–91). The technological complex represented by the use of the type I hearth appears to have been closely attached to the emergent elite of northern Kyushu in the Yayoi IV, and the technology was probably used to produce iron halberds, which appear to have been presented as prestige gifts to the elite of communities across northern Kyushu (see pp. 142–144 in Chapter 5). However, the type I hearths were not widely adopted, and most of the uncentralised ironworking prevalent at the time involved the use of type II hearths (Murakami 1998, 84–87). This vividly demonstrates that agriculture and other production activities intensified to such an extent that ironworking and the procurement of iron tools could not have been centralised under the control of the elite. This is in stark contrast with bronzeworking, which became increasingly centralised location-wise in the northern Kyushu and Kinki regions and was increasingly mobilised for strategic use by the elite who sought to consolidate their position as organisers of intra- and inter-communal collaboration and mediators of intra- and inter-communal conflicts (see the previous section).

Even so, in northern Kyushu, there appear to be some indications that ironworking and the circulation of iron products were in the process of being centralised during the Yayoi V. Takashi Watanabe's work shows that at the Hie-Naka (比恵-那珂) site, there was a decrease in the ratio of whetstones with rougher surfaces for the initial sharpening of iron implements immediately following the process of forging, accompanied by an increase in the ratio of whetstones with fine-grained surfaces for resharpening those implements during the Yayoi V (Watanabe 2007). This probably indicates that the type of ironworking

that was practised at the site during the Middle Yayoi period had ceased by the Yayoi V and that the community now relied on the supply of finished iron implements from elsewhere (possibly from the Sugu site cluster located a couple of kilometres to the south). A similar situation may not have occurred in other regions, however. Ironworking in middle and southern Kyushu and the western Seto Inland Sea region developed to such an extent that those regions began to develop distinct local iron assemblages (Murakami 1998, 65–84). From the central Seto Inland Sea region eastward, however, there was relatively little technological development and intensification of iron production throughout the Yayoi V period.

The last finding is well attested by the continuing use of stone tools. Scholars have long emphasised that the quantity of stone tools excavated from individual sites dropped fairly dramatically from the final Yayoi IV onwards across western Japan. However, the composition of tools used in the tool-kits for woodworking and agricultural production remained the same (Murakami 1998, 63–65). In northern Kyushu, in contrast, stone tools almost entirely disappeared in the Yayoi V, and those that remained were not part of a toolkit but used as ad hoc substitutes for iron tools (ibid.). This suggests that the supply and circulation of iron source materials and products were unstable and that communities across western Japan could not abandon the certain composition of toolkits comprising stone tools, with the exception of those in northern Kyushu (ibid.). At the same time, however, it is evident that the growing attraction of iron tools led to a steady decline in stone tool production and circulation. Yoshio Negita, for instance, argues that the increasing use of iron tools, whose production almost totally relied upon the supply of raw material from outside the system of inter-communal exchange, led to its collapse; he contends that this resulted in the disappearance of many settlements and the emergence of large hilltop settlements in the Kinki region in the early Yayoi V period, because the reproduction of the inter-communal exchange network of the Early and Middle Yayoi periods significantly relied upon the circulation of raw materials for stone tool production procured from a (limited) number of local sources, whereas the raw materials for iron tools would have been procured from a single source (Negita 1998, 87–98). The underdevelopment of the technological-functional sophistication of iron tools and their use, in terms of the quantity of tools used, however, makes this interesting hypothesis difficult to accept in its entirety, though it is likely that the gradual increase of iron tools and source materials in circulation would have contributed to the transformation of the exchange networks in terms of structure and scale.

The distribution of the type III hearth extended as far as Kanto region to the east, although the technological-functional sophistication of the iron and ironworking tools excavated from the region is found to be even less impressive than that in Kinki region. The use of the type III hearth across the communities in this region and the corresponding similarities in the types of iron tools produced suggest that ironworking technology and iron tools were diffused to the region from the Kinki region (Murakami 1998, 102–103). This would have occurred through the existing inter-communal networks, which appear to have formed a broad cultural horizon characterised by the sporadic presence of *Dotaku* bronze bells either transported from the west or locally produced as much smaller and cruder copies (*Sho* (small)-*Dotaku* [小銅鐸]; see e.g. Matsui 2004), showing the loose sharing of customs originating from the Kinki-Tokai regions.[12]

The preceding picture continued more or less unchanged until the early Kofun period when the Nara Basin, the Osaka Plain and surrounding areas of the Kinki region, or the 'Kinki-core region' (KCR), gradually became the centre of ironworking in the archipelago in terms of technological

sophistication and quantity of production. I discuss further the cause and consequences of this change in Chapters 8 and 9.

2.3. Expanding Production, Hierarchisation and Communality

The quality and quantity of production, in general, continued to develop with the passage of time. With respect to the centralisation of production, however, is it essential to exercise a degree of caution in our analysis. The stylistic standardisation of the *Dotaku* bronze bells progressed to such an extent that two stylistic 'schools' emerged – one in the Kinki region and the other in the Tokai region. They were later unified, and the distribution pattern, showing concentrations in peripheral regions of the horizon centred around the present-day Nara and Osaka prefectures, is interpreted by some scholars that the specimens were made at production centres controlled by the dominant elite and strategically presented to the elite of the peripheral communities in order to mark the boundary of the newly formed political alliance, which was centred around the elite of the Nara Basin and the southern Osaka Plain, and to symbolically defend its borders against rival polities in regions such as northern Kyushu, the central Seto Inland Sea and San'in (Harunari 1982; Terawasa 2000, 221–224). However, as argued earlier, the distribution can also be explained as the consequence of competitive gift-giving practised to expand the network of kin-based sodalities, either virtual/pseudo or genuine. If the latter were the case, we would not have to assume that an integrated political unit was established across this domain, controlled by some dominant elite members.

The situation of rice paddy field agriculture is interesting in that the advanced technology of water distribution was not necessarily solely used for increasing productive efficiency but for maintaining communal egalitarianism in terms of the equal distribution of water to every part of individual paddy field units.

Sea salt production, which began in the central Seto Inland Sea region and later spread to the western coastal regions of Kinki region during the Yayoi V period, also appears to have been carried out not by specialised groups but by segments of those who resided in ordinary rice farming

12 It has to be noted that the small *Dotaku*, in contrast to the ordinary *Dotaku*, was rung in the ritualistic occasions in which it was used after the latter lost its function as a bell and became a symbolic material item designed to be seen as a visually spectacular item. This suggests that whereas the latter became an item to be displayed with its meaning(s) not known but a chosen few (see above) the former retained its original function as a bell and mediated a particular ritualistic experience of the many. It might suggest that communities of eastern Japan, where a large number of *Sho-Dotaku* bronze bells were in use during the Yayoi V and VI/Shonai phase, relied on communal experience rather than monopolised esoteric knowledge (that characterised the *Dotaku* ritual of western Japan in the Yayoi V) in their ritual.

settlements (Shiraishi 1997); sea salt was produced either inside or within the vicinity of ordinary coastal settlements (ibid.; Okayama PBE 1974, sec. III). This suggests that its production was undertaken as a part of the system of communal labour and was not really centralised; it also suggests that sea salt was circulated through kin-based sodality-type inter-communal ties.

The amount of flow of these products no doubt increased through the Yayoi V period, and this in turn would have increased the necessity of centralising the mediation and coordination of this flow. It would also have resulted in the sudden emergence of extremely large settlements on the nodal locations of such quickly developing networks through which products, information and people were being transported towards the end of the Yayoi V ('port-of-trade-type settlements'; see Chapter 8.2). It is important to note, however, that this was not preceded by the centralisation of their production and circulation. Instead, it appears that such centralisation was stimulated and accelerated by the increase in the scale of horizons within which the products were circulated. This is an important finding for our research on the mechanism of formation of a large, and seemingly hierarchised, inter-regional alliance that was forged in the Yayoi–Kofun transitional period, which is investigated in Chapter 8.

3. DWELLINGS AND BURIALS

3.1. Dwellings

GENERAL TRENDS AND CHANGES

The early Yayoi V saw the widespread, though temporary, disappearance of pre-existing settlements across northern Kyushu and western Japan. In the former region, the larger, central-place-type settlements, however, not only continued flourishing but also expanded in scale (Ozawa 2000). According to Yoshinori Ozawa, this expansion took the form of an increase in the number of houses constituting each one of the preexisting residential units of individual settlements but not an increase in the number of distinct residential units themselves (ibid.). This coincided with the disappearance of smaller, 'satellite' settlements, which suggests that the widespread disappearance of settlements in northern Kyushu was the result of

population concentration: it might have been the case that the population did not drastically decline but that the residents of the satellite settlements abandoned them and moved to the centres. The fact that the number of distinct residential units constituting individual settlements did not increase and that the number of houses constituting the preexisting residential units of individual settlements increased instead suggests that the movement took place through the preexisting sodality-based ties; clan members living in larger and smaller settlements by forming lineage-like segments came to live together in the former (ibid.; see also Figure 7.12).

This time coincides with the trend of enclosing many of the larger, central-place-type settlements within V-sectioned ditches (the Yoshinogari [吉野ヶ里] and the Sugu, for example). At the Ominami (大南) site of the Sugu site cluster, we also find ditches that internally divide the residential area (Ozawa 2000). Intra- as well as inter-settlement community divisions were enhanced by the digging of these ditches. The defensive character of the V-sectioned ditch cannot be denied, and it certainly appears to indicate an increase in inter-communal tension.

Across the southern Kinki region, many of the large central-place-type settlements shrank in scale or virtually disappeared; instead, there emerged large hilltop settlements consisting of a number of residential units, similar to the erstwhile settlements on the floodplains before their disappearance (e.g. Wakabayashi 2006). These new settlements also served as a kind of central place; precious material items such as iron tools and bronze implements that were typically exchanged at that time tended to concentrate in them. This suggests that some residents of the large settlements on the floodplains moved to the hilltop locations (e.g. Terasawa 2000, 200). In addition, many of these new settlements were enclosed within V-sectioned ditches. Again, the increase in inter-communal tension can be safely assumed to be the reason behind this phenomenon.

As always, it is difficult to pin down the single, undisputable cause behind the increase in inter-communal tension which occurred almost simultaneously across substantial areas of northern Kyushu and western Japan. The period might have overlapped with the cold spell which occurred around the early part of the first century AD, as far as a plateau and a spike in the calibration curve dated to the period (between c. 1 and 50 AD) is concerned (Figure 4.1.B; see Chapter 4.2). This period, as mentioned earlier, would have seen a temporary halt in the supply of Chinese prestigious items (caused by the establishment of the short-lived dynasty of Xin and the independence of the Lelang commandery [between c. 25–30 AD]; see earlier discussion) which conspicuously characterised the strategic gift-giving performed by the emergent elite of the coastal plains of northern Kyushu; this would explain the turmoil in northern Kyushu, even though it could not have been the sole reason for the widespread nature of the phenomenon, which covered not only northern Kyushu but also western Japan. The period also saw the onset of the flow of metal items made in northern Kyushu reaching the eastern Inland Sea region and beyond: bronze spearheads and small bronze mirrors created by copying the Chinese originals began to appear in these areas, and at times in the large hilltop settlements themselves (e.g. Omoteyama [表山] site of Hyogo prefecture; cf. Negita 1998, 89).

It is quite likely that a combination of all the three previously mentioned reasons caused the increasing tension. The effect of the cold spell upon intra- and inter-communal relations in the form of, for instance, bad harvests and the resultant increase in tension might have been enhanced by the shortage of material means of mediating, that is, the early Han Chinese prestigious goods. In terms of absolute chronology, this transitional phase coincides with the turmoil caused by Wang Mang's establishment of the Xin dynasty at the end of the Early Han period in China; this dynasty only lasted from AD 8 to 23. Wang Mang adopted a policy of non-appeasement of polities and groups on the periphery of its domain (Nishijima 1985). This caused a lot of trouble across the peripheral regions, where the elite were dependent, in various ways, on the constant supply of exotic Han goods, which they used in order to achieve and maintain their positions. One of the consequences of this action was the short-lived independence of the commandery of Lelang, lasting between circa AD 25–30. The supply of items imported from Lelang to the archipelago, most significantly including bronze mirrors, appears to have dwindled for a

while. Hidenori Okamura classified the Han mirrors into seven typo-chronological categories (e.g. Okamura 1999). According to Okamura's scheme, the Yayoi IV of northern Kyushu, coinciding with Okamura's stage III of his typo-chronological scheme, saw a surge of Han mirror imports (Figure 7.7). However, the number of imported Han mirrors momentarily but significantly dropped in the beginning of the Yayoi V. Climatic evidence, as mentioned in Chapter 4, indicates the possibility of a cold spell during this period. The disappearance of a large number of settlements across northern Kyushu and western Japan might have resulted from either of those events, or even both. Considering the authority and prestige brought to certain coastal northern Kyushu communities by their access to the Lelang commandery, embodied by the bronze mirrors and other items, it is more possible, at least in northern Kyushu, that this phenomenon resulted from the demise of the Lelang commandery than from climate change. As we have already seen, the network of inter-communal interactions formed throughout the Middle Yayoi period began to be hierarchised towards the end of this period in the form of increasing differentiation between central-place-type and satellite settlements; the relations between the coastal communities of northern Kyushu and their inland exchange partners were based on the practice of strategic gift-giving by the elite of the coastal communities to their inland partners (see pp. 154–159 in Chapter 6). These acts would have generated a sense of mutual obligation and honour for each other's trust, and the suspension, albeit momentarily, of their material media would have upset the system significantly and caused a widespread panic; at times, it would have resulted in the breakdown of inter-communal ties, which in some cases would have ended up in violence. Had the occurrence of such situations become common, the very existence of individual residential communities would have become difficult. The widespread disappearance of satellite settlements and the relocation of their residents to central-place-type settlements, most likely through clan-type sodality-based networks, together with the digging of enclosing ditches around many of the central-place-type settlements, can be understood as a reaction to this critical situation.

The development of the practice of depositing bronze spearheads in remote places that were
removed from the domain of daily life might have
been accelerated to compensate for this situation
(see previous discussion). Meanwhile, due to the
frequent fluctuation of the flow of goods, the inter-
communal network formed and reproduced during the availability of the early Han Chinese prestigious goods began to open itself up to contacts
from the east: it is difficult to determine what
kind of goods were received in exchange for the
metal items made in northern Kyushu, but the
beginning of their flow eastward ignited the reorganisation of inter- as well as intra-communal relations, first in the Inland Sea region, and then across
western Japan. Broken pieces of Han Chinese mirrors began to distribute along the Seto Inland Sea
corridor as far east as the central Kinki region
(Figure 7.7), and local copies of a particular mirror
type dating from the final Early Han period and
would have been imported sometime in the early
Yayoi V (inferred above to be sometime after AD
30) emerged in the eastern Inland sea and Kinki
regions (Morioka 1989).

In the southern half of eastern Japan, the number of settlements also decreased momentarily in
the beginning of the Yayoi V across this horizon
(Ishikawa 2011b, 415–417). This would be an evidence supporting that the cooling was at least a contributing factor to this widespread phenomenon.
Kazuaki Matsui (2001, 203–208) observed that the
Middle Yayoi V and the Late/Final Yayoi V were
two phases which saw the emergence of ditch-
enclosed settlements and a fairly large number
of hilltop settlements across the Pacific coastal
regions of the horizon. He interprets those episodes as reflecting heightened inter-communal tension, and relates them to the trajectory of the Kinki
region and the regions to the west. I examine the
latter episode in the next chapter. The former may
have been related to a movement represented by
the expansion of the *Dotaku* horizon to the east
and the formation of a concentrated distribution
around the lake Hamana and the western bank of
the lower flow of the river Tenryu: if we understood the concentrated distribution as a result of
strategic gift-giving from some communities of the
Kinki and/or Tokai regions to incorporate those
communities which were presented the bells into
their domain of influence, communities to the

east which would have had contacts with those
communities would have had to be reacted to the
move. The previously mentioned introduction of
iron-forging hearths to the region, which took
place around this period, would have been a part
of the general expansion of communication and
exchange networks from the west, and it would
have shaken and led to a restructuration of preexisting inter-communal ties.

In the northern half of eastern Japan, that is, in
Tohoku region, settlements remained small-scaled
and comprised a single residential unit (Takase
2004). As mentioned earlier, the communities of
the northern Tohoku region appear to have abandoned rice paddy field agriculture and returned to
the hunting-gathering-based way of life.

THE EMERGENCE OF ELITE PRECINCTS
The emergence of elite-precinct-type compounds
within settlements marks the beginning of the
explicit expression of social hierarchy in *mundane*
fields of social reproduction. These precincts were
typically enclosed by a ditch, and they often contained larger pit dwellings than those situated outside, along with occasional walled structures and
storage buildings.

The settlements of Kyushu and western Japan,
as mentioned earlier, continued to be formed
of several residential units, and the compounds
often consisted of one of those units, which
was enclosed. At sites like the Sendoyama site in
Saga prefecture, raised-floor storage buildings were
exclusively situated inside the ditch-enclosed compound (Figures 7.8 and 7.12; Kiyama Town Site
Excavation Team 1978). At the same site, iron agricultural and woodworking implements were also
exclusively found in the vicinity of the compound,
predominantly from the bottom of the enclosing
ditch (ibid.). Another interesting fact is that only
this compound has a substantial number of burials
in the form of stone cists in its vicinity; the other
two residential units, both unenclosed, have only a
couple of burials or no burial at all in their vicinity
(ibid.; Mizoguchi 2000).

These findings suggest several things. First, it
appears that the elite of a lineage-scale grouping
(who lived in a ditch-enclosed compound such as
that of the Sendoyama) began to display their dominance over the other communal segments constituting individual settlements by living in a clearly

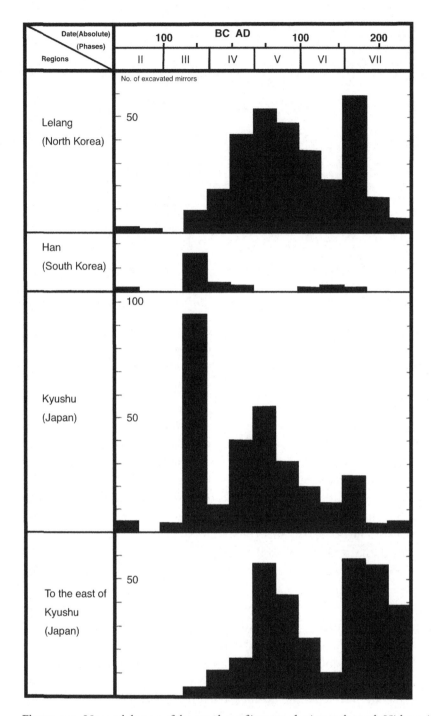

Figure 7.7. Ups and downs of the number of imported mirrors through Hidenori Okamura's seven-phase chronological periods and their distribution period by period (from Okamura [1999], with modifications and additions). With kind permission from Yoshikawakobunkan Publishing Co.

marked compound. This shows their status was now stabilised to the extent that they could not be suddenly replaced by one of the other communal segments forming the settlement. Second, they now controlled the storage of products, and possibly the distribution of goods acquired through exchange; the concentration of iron tools in the vicinity of the elite compound of the Sendoyama site supports the latter inference. Third, the fact that the compound was enclosed by a ditch suggests that the elite were perceived as protectors of the fruits of the residents' communal labour in the individual settlements. This leads to the inference that they were perceived as the representatives of common interests shared by the members of the settlement.

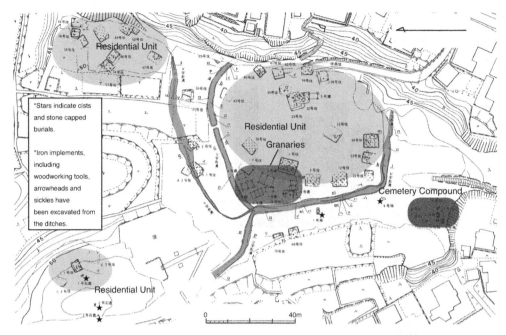

Figure 7.8. Sendoyama site (Saga prefecture) and its residential segments (from Kiyama Town Site Excavation Team [1978], with additions). Note residential blocks, a cluster of granaries and a cemetery compound marked. Individual burials distributing outside the compound are starred.

In relation to the last point, the coexistence of two inner compounds in the Yoshinogari settlement is highly suggestive (Figure 7.9). As we have seen, the Yoshinogari settlement was formed in the Initial Yayoi/Yayoi I period and developed into a central-place-type settlement during the Middle Yayoi period. In the final phase of the Yayoi IV, a V-sectioned ditch was dug around the settlement, and two ditch-enclosed compounds were created within the settlement some time during the late Yayoi V period (Saga PBE 1994). The southern compound was oval in shape, enclosed by a box-sectioned ditch and possibly an earthen wall (Figure 7.9.B–C). Parts of the ditch-line protruded outwards, and six-pillared rectangular structures were situated there. These are inferred to have been watchtower-like structures, though the validity of the reconstruction disputed. Inside this oval compound were rectangular pit dwellings and some raised floor buildings, probably granaries, with an empty space at the centre (ibid.).

The northern compound was roughly triangular in shape, albeit with rounded corners (Figure 7.9.A; Saga PBE 1997, 44–68). The ditch-enclosed space had two entrances with a structural device to hide the inner layout from the direct gaze of outsiders. The inside of this compound was dominated by an exceptionally

large raised-floor building. It is difficult to infer the exact function of the complex: it might have been an elite residential complex or a structure of a ritual nature. However, circumstantial evidence possibly points to the latter. As mentioned earlier, there were also some exceptionally large rectangular buildings, some with raised floors, built in northern Kyushu during the Yayoi IV period (see Figure 6.2.A; see Chapter 6.4). Most of them appear to be burial related, based on their relations with the other features at the given site; these buildings in both the Yubihon'mura (柚比本村) site and the Yoshitake-Takagi (吉武高木) site are situated right next to the type I burial-compound cemeteries yielding rich grave goods. Behind the former building, excavations have revealed a huge pit containing a substantial number of red-painted globular jars, probably showing traces of numerous ritual practices relating to the dead and the ancestors (see Figure 6.2.A). This might suggest that the large raised-floor structure in the northern compound of the Yoshinogari site was also related to rituals pertaining to the dead and the ancestors. In addition, there was a bronze halberd (dagger-axe) deposited on the bottom of an older enclosing ditch that was apparently filled when the enclosing ditch was dug (Figure 7.9.A). This is an extremely rare example of the

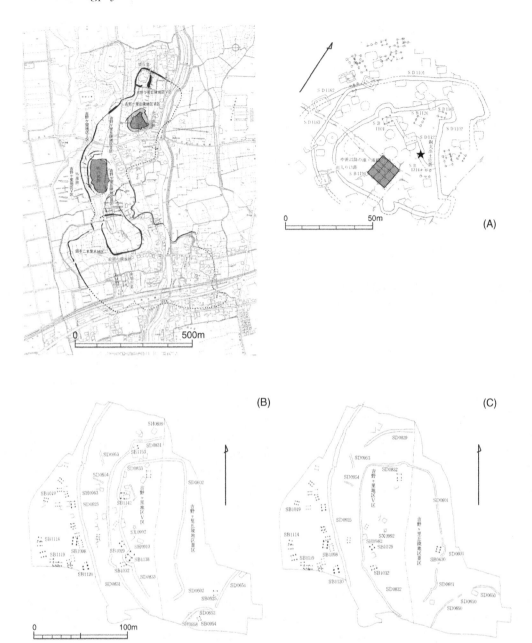

Figure 7.9. Yoshinogari settlement (Saga prefecture) in the Yayoi V. Above left: the general plan (northern and southern compounds are shaded), **A**: northern compound (the extremely large building is shaded, and the location of the deposition of a bronze halberd is starred), **B**: southern compound in the early and middle Yayoi V, **C**: southern compound in the late Yayoi V and Yayoi VI (after Saga PBE [1994], with additions).

deposition of bronze ritual implements in this manner, which would certainly reinforce the idea that the function of the compound was such that it needed to be symbolically marked and bounded/protected by a ritual deposition.

If we accept the inference that the southern compound was the elite residential compound and the northern compound was the ritual compound, we can deduce the following: the elite who occupied the residential compound (i.e. the southern compound; Figure 7.9.B and C) also conducted

rituals relating to the dead and the ancestors, among other communal concerns, in the ritual compound (the northern compound; Figure 7.9.A); in addition, the members of the elite group were perceived to represent the interests of the kin-based, clan-type sodalities constituting the emergent regional polity centred around the Yoshinogari settlement. However, it is difficult to determine the relationship between the elite segment of regional central-place-type settlements such as the Yoshinogari settlement and that of second-tier settlements such as the Sendoyama settlement (see Figure 7.12). Within a particular regional polity, the elite group may have belonged to a single clan-type sodality which became dominant over the other clan-type sodalities in the regional polity. Alternatively, the elite may have belonged to different clan-type sodalities that competed with each other within a regional polity. If we refer to the mortuary evidence, as we will see in the following, the latter appears to have been more likely.

Outside of northern Kyushu, in fact, it is difficult to confirm the presence of elite precincts (for general information, see Hirose and Iba 2006). This is certainly partly due to the fact that the settlement evidence from the Yayoi V is rather scarce in many parts of western Japan. However, evidence from San'in region, for instance, leads us to conclude that the differentiation of the elite – clearly indicated by the development of a unique variant of burial compounds, called 'Type III' in this volume (see the next section) – did not have an equally clear expression in the settlements. At the Mukibanda (妻木晩田) site, for instance, the residential units constituting this large-scale regional-centre-type settlement are homogeneous in their contents and internal structure: each of them consisted of a set of less than ten pit dwellings, some walled storage facilities and other large-scale walled structures slightly separated from the former structures (Hamada 2009). Those large-scale walled structures show few traces of residence, and we can infer that they were used for some kind of communal function, that is, 'cult houses' of some sort, for instance. Each residential unit appears to have had its own burial ground, but there is one large burial ground where there is a concentration of larger rectangular tumuli with tails sticking out of their four corners. All the units contain traces of iron production and some other production activities, and the overall picture is an aggregation of functionally homogeneous residential groupings (e.g. Hamada 2006). The integration and internal cohesion of each residential unit would have been reproduced by communal, and probably ritualistic, acts performed in the large-scale walled structure(s), and the entire settlement's integration would have been represented by the burial of a few chosen individuals – by this time forming elite segments, possibly from the individual residential units – at the largest burial ground, Donohara

(洞ノ原) cemetery, which was not attached to any particular residential unit.

The situation around the Seto Inland Sea corridor remains somewhat unclear, although it is quite likely that the picture was rather similar to that in San'in region, characterised by the emergence of some extremely large settlements comprising a number of residential units of a basically homogeneous structure and function. Type III burial compounds of increasingly large scales tended to be situated on hilltops, and the integration of intra- and inter-localised communities would have been reproduced through large-scale, increasingly sophisticated and abstract mortuary rituals that were conducted in an intensive manner (Kondo 1983, 148–167, 177–187).

The situation in the Kinki region, again, is not so clear, though some regional-centre-type settlements indicate the presence of separate, roughly rectangular compounds bounded by a ditch and containing large walled structures and traces of special activities, including rituals and/or bronze-/ironworking. A particularly interesting example can be found at the Ise (伊勢) site in Shiga prefecture, on the south-eastern shore of Lake Biwa, where large walled structures were built to form a circle. Hiroshi Kondo (2006, 26) points out that the areas between the structures, which appear to have been specifically marked by a large ritual pit nearby, offer the vista of a distinct cone-shaped figure, Mt. Mikami. Scholars have not yet sufficiently explored the area inside the circle to determine how the space was used, but we can safely infer that some kind of ritual function was performed here. Considering the scale of the settlement, it is possible that the structure functioned as a centre of regional ritualistic gathering.[13]

Farther east, there were fewer differentiated ditch-enclosed compounds. An interesting observation is that in these areas, there was one or a couple of extremely large-scale rectangular pit houses, some reaching 198 square metres in floor size (Y32 dwelling of Moritohara [森戸原] site; Kuze 2001, 35), in each individual ditch-enclosed settlement or attached to each of the clusters of pit dwellings constituting such a settlement (e.g. ibid.,

13 We are reminded by the Ise of the northern compound of the Yoshinogari, which is situated in a regional-centre-type settlement and inferred to have fulfilled ritualistic functions (see preceding discussion).

31–45). They often have more than two fireplaces, and are often rebuilt on the same spot and on the same structure (ibid., 38). Besides, some examples show the trace of being deliberately burnt down (ibid., 37). Those point to the possibility that these houses were used for ritual functions rather than as elite dwellings. The rebuilding on the same spot reminds us of what we saw in some extremely large buildings of the northern Kyushu and western Japan horizons in the Yayoi IV (e.g. that of the Yubihon'mura and Ikegami-Sone), where we inferred that the custom was designed to revitalise connections with the ancestors whereby to revitalise the integration of the community (see Figure 6.2 and Chapter 6.4).

All in all, apart from northern Kyushu, regions in Japan had not developed a way of explicitly differentiating the elite from the commoners in everyday settings during the Yayoi V. The mortuary evidence, as we have briefly seen earlier and again discuss in the following, suggests that the differentiation of this ascribed elite status took place across western Japan and probably in the western portion of eastern Japan. The emergent ranking was not subject to overt display in everyday settings in those regions. I would like to argue that in those regions, the emergent elite needed to be perceived as well as displayed as 'firsts among equals' who embodied the well-being of the entire community. In contrast, in northern Kyushu, the elite were perceived as the chosen few who had an ascribed right to exercise more control over the mobilisation of resources than did others. That perception would have certainly been accompanied by the notion that their doing so was for the well-being of the entire community; the development of communal rituals involving the deposition of a number of bronze weapons would have worked as an arena in which the elite portrayed themselves as the representatives of communal interests. Although it may not have been necessary to extend this portrayal to everyday settings, showing that the elite were *dominant*, even in everyday settings, now was perceived as *necessary* for the well-being of the community.

It is extremely difficult to determine the reason for such inter-regional differences. They might have derived from northern Kyushu's proximity to the Asian mainland, which, as we have seen in the previous chapters, led to greater development

in the northern Kyushu society in terms of force of production and made the society more complex. Alternatively, the proximity to the Asian mainland might have compelled the northern Kyushu communities to choose a different way in which to deal with a widely shared problem, or 'contradiction': how to cope with the increasing necessity of regulating intra- and inter-communal collaborations (requiring a degree of control) and mediating the intra- and inter-communal tension (requiring the enhancement of the sense of equality and unity). The important and interesting point to note in this regard is that, when a much wider horizon of networks emerged in the Yayoi-Kofun transitional period (which is dealt with in the next chapter), the northern Kyushu elite did not become dominant over the elite of other regions. This suggests that factors different from the development of the force of production and greater social complexity contributed to the development of wider social integration and inter-regional hierarchisation towards the beginning of the Kofun period.

3.2. Burials

This period – and its second half, in particular – saw the emergence of burial compounds in which around five adults and a couple of infants/children were commonly buried in areas across the whole of western Japan and in parts of the western part of eastern Japan. In order to compare and contrast them with the burial compounds of northern Kyushu in the Middle Yayoi period, called burial compounds type I and type II in this volume (see pp. 150–154 in Chapter 6), I would like to refer to them as burial compound type III (Mizoguchi 2000, 2001).

These compounds were commonly topped by rectangular mounds, and they were often situated on hilltops, particularly along the Japan Sea coastal regions and across the Seto Inland Sea corridor. In the central Japan Sea coastal region, the rectangular tumuli often had four small tail-like rectangular formations sticking out of the four corners (Figure 7.10) (四隅突出型墳丘墓; e.g. Shimane Prefectural Ancient Culture Research Centre 2007). There were some equivalents with regional characteristics in the Hokuriku region (e.g. Obayama no. 4 tumulus; Furukawa 2010).

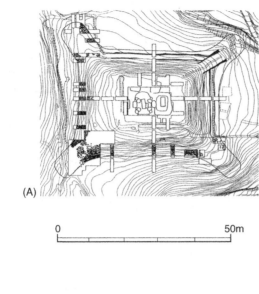

(A)

0   50m

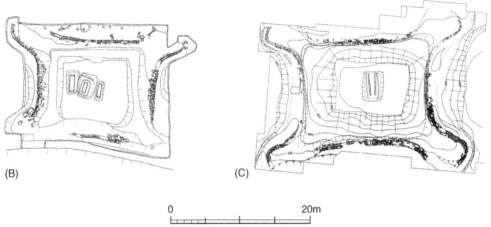

(B)   (C)

0   20m

Figure 7.10. Some examples of the rectangular tumulus with four rectangular features sticking out of the four corners (*Yosumi-tosshutsu-fun*, 四隅突出墳). **A**: Nishitani No. 3 (after Furukawa et al. [2010], original from Izumo MBE [2000]), **B**: Chusenji No. 9 (after Furukawa et al. [2010], original from Tanaka [1988]), **C**: Miyayama No. 4 (after Furukawa et al. [2010], original from Matsumoto [2003]).

While some of them were situated singly, they also sometimes formed clusters (Figure 7.11). In the latter case, the number of compounds constituting individual clusters varied, and they often took the form of small tumuli. They also were often arranged in a linear formation, regardless they were situated on a ridge (e.g. the Sasaka [左坂] of Kyoto prefecture; Omiya TBE 2001; Figure 7.11.A) or a flat ground (the Mukaida [向田] of Fukuoka prefecture; Honami TBE 1992; Figure 7.11.C). The number of deceased buried in one compound – around five adults and a couple of infants/children – suggests that each compound was the burial ground for a household or lineage segment (Mizoguchi 2001, 153–155). The fact that the infants/children were buried in the same manner as the adults, as mentioned earlier, suggests

that their status was an *ascribed* status, rather than an achieved one, based on the fact that they were members of a chosen household/lineage segment. In the case of a cluster which comprised a number of such compounds, they may have been the burial grounds of the higher-ranking families of a number of distinct lineages or clans comprising a tribal group-type local communal grouping (Figure 7.12). It is difficult to determine whether they all resided in the village, which often was a regional-centre-type settlement, to which the cemetery was attached, or some of them represented the chiefly families of the smaller, satellite villages. If the latter were the case, it would have been that the chiefry families of the villages, that were subordinate to the regional-centre-type village of a tribe-like regional corporate grouping, brought their dead to

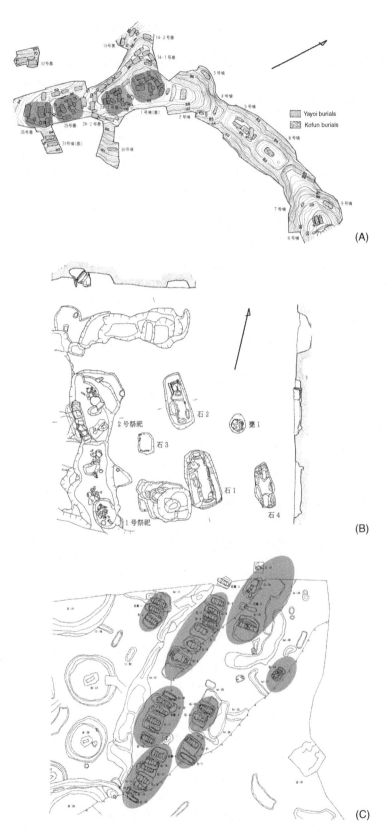

Figure 7.11. Cemeteries of the Yayoi V. **A**: Sasaka (from Omiya TBE [2001], with additions), **B**: Mikumo-Teraguchi (from Fukuoka PBE 1983b), **C**: Mukaida (from Honami TBE [1992], with additions).

the latter and buried them there (Figure 7.12). In that case, it can be further inferred that the sense of togetherness of the tribal grouping was enhanced by the sharing by the higher-ranking segments of its clan-type segments of their burial grounds. In the case of a singly situated compound (e.g. the Akasaka-Imai [赤坂今井] of Kyoto prefecture; Kyoto Prefectural Research Centre of Buried Cultural Properties 2001), the deceased may have been members of a segment situated at the helm of a number of lineages/clans, together constituting a localised, tribal-group-type communal grouping. In any case, it appears that the structure and scale of the hierarchy of localised communal groupings varied, reflected by differences in the way cemeteries were organised (Figures 7.10–12).

The coexistence of cemeteries containing different numbers of type III burial compounds with different qualities and quantities of grave good assemblages within individual regions suggests the *emergent* nature as well as *immaturity* of intra-regional social integration and hierarchies; there cannot be recognised a stable pyramidal hierarchy composed of conically situated villages and cemeteries. Rather, it is inferred that competition by the higher-ranked segments of sodalities over dominance in their tribal grouping was rife; in most of the clusters of type III burial compounds, no particular compound achieved overall dominance over the other compounds in terms of the quantity and quality of grave goods deposited, and the number of deceased buried varies between them as well (Figure 7.11). It also suggests that, in such a circumstance, it is unlikely that inter-regional hierarchies, covering a number of regional communities, developed quickly. Instead, the available evidence suggests that *competitions* of various scales, ranging from the intra-settlement level to the inter-regional community level, emerged during this time. It is virtually impossible to reconstruct conically structured intra- and inter-communal hierarchies in which the largest compound with the richest grave good assemblage is situated on the top, and the other, less-well-equipped compounds are situated below in a descending order (contra e.g. Terasawa 1990). Even if there existed either a singly located large tumulus or a larger tumulus with richer burials than the others together comprising a cemetery,

they rarely showed stability in inheriting higher-ranked positions.

Despite the instability and fluidity that can be observed in the intra- and inter-regional structures formed by the burial compounds, or probably because of them, the contents of the burials and the characteristics of the compounds increased in affinity across western Japan and the western portion of eastern Japan. As mentioned earlier, the deceased commonly consisted of around five adults and a couple of infants/children. In many cases, there are traces of mortuary practices, including feasting – in the form of a substantial number of whole and/or fragmented pots found on the flat tops or around the mounds. In some cases, we find certain selected vessels with holes that were deliberately drilled in their bottom or lower half, before as well as after firing (e.g. Shigematsu 2006). In the latter case, it might indicate that the vessel was marked and differentiated from the others as a vessel used for dispatching the dead and was not supposed to be used again. In the former case, the meaning of the vessel might have been 'abstracted': it did not contain actual offerings for the dead but nevertheless signified the conception and act of dedication to the dead. In any case, there was an increasing formalisation of mortuary practices, as reflected by the increasing scale of mortuary rituals and the growing sophistication of some of the vessels involved in them as the media of mortuary communication. This trend can be connected with an increasing number of burial compounds situated on hilltop locations, some of which, interestingly, were associated with standing stones/stone settings (e.g. Tatetsuki [楯築] tumulus; Kondo 2002; and Iyobeyama [伊予部山] cemetery; Soja City Cultural Promotion Agency 1996). It is possible that these were markers of contacts with, or the presence of, the *transcendental* realm, including the ancestors or the force(s) behind the success and failure of the general reproduction of community (Mizoguchi 2000, 257–261). In that case, such transcendental beings were now seen as embodied by the deceased; in other words, the elite who were buried in the burial compounds were seen as mediators of the relationship between the community and the transcendental. If this were the case, it would explain the changes in the pottery obtained from the top of and around the mounds; first, the

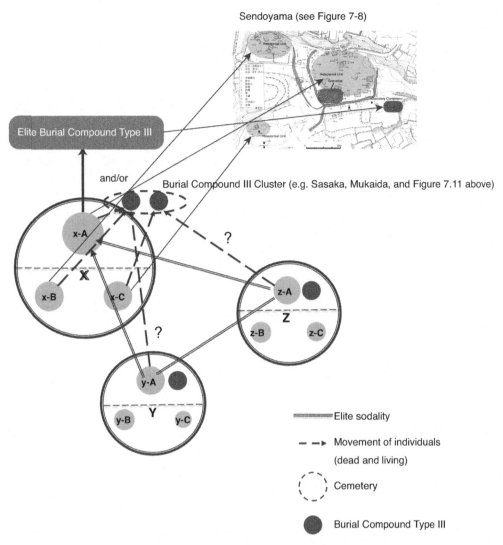

Figure 7.12. Possible relationships between burial compound type III clusters, settlements, and kin/communal-groupings. X, Y, Z: Settlements, A, B, C: Sodalities (constituting residential groups/lineage groupings in individual settlements), Dominant residential groups/lineages of different settlements would have formed an elite sodality/an endogamous elite group, and their dead may well have been brought to the central place-type settlement of a regional community where they were buried in a elite burial compound type III. As an example the structure of the larger settlement is compared to that of the Sendoyama (see Figure 7.8 and related descriptions). An example of the regional centre-type settlement, the Yoshinogari, ranked higher than the Sendoyama in a regiona settlement hierarchy, should also be referred to (see Figure 7.9 and related descriptions).

deceased would have been perceived as the representatives of communal interests, and feasts were organised on their mortuary occasions to display and confirm the sense of togetherness between the dead and the living. Then, gradually, the deceased themselves – probably perceived as the ancestors – came to be recognised as members of the transcendental realm, and the notion of *eating with them* was replaced by a display of *dedication* to them in the form of specialised and sophisticated vessels, some of them containing deliberately drilled holes.

This trend can also be understood as a part of the wider process of change mentioned above. The development of rice farming did not lead to an outright social stratification but first enhanced the sense of communality. The increase in the scale of networks associated with the flow of goods, information and people stimulated the centralisation of bronze production, which in turn led to the formation of distinct ritual horizons (Figure 7.4). The rituals involving the deposition of *Dohoko* bronze spearheads and *Dotaku* bronze bells would have enhanced the sense of communality and served to portray those who were in charge of conducting the rituals as the representatives of communal interests. The elite, who were being increasingly differentiated as higher-ranking segments of communal groupings, (a) acted as the mediators of the escalating intra- and inter-communal negotiations and (b) had to portray themselves not as rulers but as representatives of the communal will and interest. Factor (a) would have necessitated the adoption of a mechanism for creating and enhancing the sense of communal togetherness between ever-widening communities, and the formation of fictive kin networks, which would have been expanded by the sharing of increasingly similar mortuary practices, must have perfectly suited the 'functional' requirement. The commemoration of the deceased buried in the type III burial compounds, who were portrayed first as the representatives of communal interests and well-being and then as members of the transcendental realm[14] that influenced the well-being of the community, would have fit the functional requirements of factor (b).

The growing incidence of factor (a) would also have accelerated the expansion of inter-communal networks while simultaneously intensifying the intra- and inter-communal competition over the position of the mediator.

4. CONCLUSION

The Yayoi V period can be characterised as a time of increasing contradiction and intensifying intra- and inter-communal competition. The scale of production and exchange and the intra- and inter-communal collaboration between communities increased during this period. Meanwhile, the society's response to the trend could not have taken the form of outright and overt stratification of the decision-making systems.

By this time, individual sodalities had become segmented into hierarchically ordered units, and

14 At the Iyobeyama (see preceding discussion; Soja City Cultural Promotion Agency 1996), a group of large rocks, rearranged of their original positions to form a structure, occupied a corner of the cemetery. Such stone arrangements are commonly called *Iwakura* (磐座), and inferred to have functioned as the material media in which transcendental beings were believed to have occasionally descended to take residence.

in northern Kyushu, this order was evident in the form of elite-precinct-type compounds in individual settlements (Figures 7.8 and 7.9). The elite groups, which were lineage-scale groups based on the reconstructed number of people occupying such a precinct, that is, around thirty to forty, appear to have not only mediated the flow of information and goods, including iron tools and bronze ritual implements by this time, but also begun to exclusively control agricultural products.

However, it was still necessary to maintain the preexisting communal collaboration and ethos; individual villages continued to be comprised of a number of residential units, and each of these units – which were again probably lineage-scale groupings – could not have functioned as independent units of production and consumption. Accordingly, in some spheres of social reproduction, the egalitarian communal ethos was given an enhanced representation, for example, the seemingly unnecessarily sophisticated water distribution systems of the Hyakkengawa paddies (Figures 7.2 and 7.3), the prevalence of large walled structures and raised floor buildings (Figure 7.9.A) for some ritualistic functions across western Japan and the extremely large pit houses of probably the same nature in the western portion of eastern Japan.

In the course of time, there would have been greater contradiction between the hierarchisation of social relations and the necessity of maintaining communal collaboration and the egalitarian ethos, which would have needed to be addressed accordingly. There emerged two contrasting modes of response to such a situation: one involved enhancing the formalisation of communal rituals, while the other sought to enhance the character of the elite as exclusive mediators of communal interests with supernatural entities. We have already seen an example of the operation of the former mode in the form of the mass deposition of bronze implements and that of the latter mode in the form of the type III burial compounds and their equivalents which emerged in many places across western Japan and in the western portion of eastern Japan (Figure 7.4). An interesting point in this regard is that the process of enhancement of the modes of response occurred across the same horizon which saw the spread of the earliest keyhole tumuli and allied facilities and material items during the Yayoi-Kofun transitional period (discussed in the next chapter). This suggests that the emergence of the keyhole tumulus – which occupies such an impressive and prominent place in the available archaeological evidence used to characterise and define the period of its use as an elite burial mound – was the culmination of various modes of reaction to the increasing contradiction mentioned above. This also suggests that the representation and reproduction of communality through rituals associated with the burial of dead leaders fit the purpose more effectively than those involving the deposition (and effective consumption) of bronze ritual items. The complexity and contradictions of the world, and the contingencies generated by them, would have reached such a critical point as to render communal decision-making-based reactions somewhat ineffective; in such a situation, individual decision-making-oriented frameworks came to be increasingly preferred. Such a trend would probably have necessitated the display of prestige goods, which marked the individuals' access to the source and which led to the trend of collecting increasingly exotic goods in order to indicate one's prestigious status.

CHAPTER 8

AN ARCHAEOLOGY OF NETWORKS: THE YAYOI–KOFUN TRANSITION (THE SHONAI [庄内] POTTERY STYLE AND THE EARLIEST FURU [布留] POTTERY STYLE PHASE, AD 200–250/275)

1. INTRODUCTION

The Yayoi-Kofun transitional period continues to generate a huge amount of interest and fascination in academic circles, predominantly because the emergence of the keyhole tumulus (the next chapter discusses these tumuli in further detail) is tacitly (and even explicitly, at times) equated with the origin of the genealogical line of the imperial family (Fujisawa 1966; see Chapters 1 and 2 of this volume). This is supposedly supported by the following observations:

(1) Some of the early keyhole tumuli are gigantic; the Hashihaka (箸墓) tumulus, inferred by some scholars to be the tomb of Queen Himiko (卑弥呼),[1] is approximately 280 metres long, which is at least four times the length of the largest examples of mounded tombs from the Late Yayoi V period: the Tatetsuki (楯築) tumulus in Okayama prefecture, which is the largest Yayoi tumulus consisting of a round central mound conjoined by two oblong mounds, dates from the second half of the Yayoi V and is approximately 72 metres in length.

(2) The tumuli were initially distributed along the Seto Inland Sea corridor and then became widespread across western Japan and the western half of eastern Japan. The emergence of the horizon and its expansion can

apparently be related to the entries depicting the establishment and expansion of the rule of the imperial ancestors in the *Kojiki* and *Nihonshoki* chronicles.[2]

(3) There appear to have been size differences based on rank among the early keyhole tumuli. The largest examples can be found in the Nara Basin and the second tier examples are distributed along the Seto Inland Sea corridor and northern Kyushu, while the third tier and so on are found in various other places. This suggests that there already existed a centralised hierarchical order of some sort, which was under the control of the elite of the Nara Basin, where, according to the *Kojiki* and *Nihonshoki* chronicles, the courts of the early emperors were situated.

(4) The grave goods of the early keyhole tumuli, consisting of Chinese and Korean imports as well as indigenous products (e.g. Matsugi 2007, 167–173), appear to have been assembled by the elite of the Nara Basin and the surrounding areas and distributed to the elite of other regions. In this case, again, there appear to have been ranked differences in the quantity and quality of goods presented to the different elite, which only confirms the previous observation.

All in all, it appears that an inter-regional, conically structured hierarchy emerged within a fairly short

---

1 In my opinion, the potential of archaeology as the study of the materiality associated with human actions can sometimes be better utilised by not relating a set of archaeological evidence with the historical records pertaining to it, and I believe the tumulus represents such a case. The reason would be made apparent by the argument presented throughout this chapter.

2 Yukio Kobayashi, who laid the paradigmatic foundation of the study of the period back in the 1950s and 1960s, tacitly but clearly referred to the chronicles in order to show that the patterns he found in the relevant archaeological evidence coincided well with the entries in the chronicles; see e.g. Kobayashi (1961).

period between the end of the Yayoi period and the beginning of the Kofun period. The shared picture is neat and coherent, but we need to carefully examine whether it accurately reflects a situation that can be confirmed by archaeological evidence. We have seen that inter-communal relations in the Middle and Late Yayoi period were based upon kin-based sodalities cross-cutting settlements and criss-crossing within and between regional units. The hierarchisation of social relations progressed within and between such sodalities as well as villages. A segment of a particular sodality might have been dominant in one village but not necessarily in the other villages constituting the regional unit, and competitions over access to and control over the flow of goods, people and information would have assumed a complex form. At one level, the competition appears to have accelerated the diffusion and sharing of certain ritual customs across wide areas; by the late Yayoi V period, as mentioned in the previous chapter, four such 'ritual horizons' emerged in Kyushu and western Japan (see Figure 7.4 in the previous chapter; Matsugi 1998, 178–186). The sharing of certain ritual items and customs would have secured the flow of goods, people and information *in spite of* the intensifying competition. At the same time, the emerging elite, whose status was gradually shifting from an achieved to an ascribed one through the escalating competition (see the previous chapter), would have attempted to take advantage of this situation and consolidate their positions by gaining control over the rituals. These factors would have contributed to the accelerated pace of development of distinct regional ritual customs and allied paraphernalia (i.e. bronze spearheads in northern Kyushu, bronze bells in Kinki and Tokai, and more sophisticated, large-scale mortuary practices in the areas in between) of the Yayoi V (ibid.).

If we turn our attention to the intra-regional phenomena, it is impossible to get a clear picture of the situation. To start with, regional characteristics abound in the seemingly homogeneous package consisting of the keyhole-shaped mound, burial facilities and grave goods (hereafter abbreviated as the Initial Kofun Package, IKP), often said to be 'distributed' by the elite of the Nara Basin and its surrounding regions across the horizon (e.g. Organisation Committee of the General Meeting of the Japanese Archaeological Association 2002,

277–362). The intra-regional distribution pattern of the early keyhole tumuli (which date from the first half of the Early Kofun period; see Footnote 1 in Chapter 9) does not point to a smoothly developing regional integration and hierarchisation. They were often constructed too close to one another for them to be identified as the resting places of chiefs 'governing' a region larger than the supposed individual regional units of integration of the Yayoi period, which was marked by the presence of regional-centre-type settlements; on the contrary, in many cases, it is more likely that the chiefs competed for dominance over such a region (roughly the scale of an ancient province, for instance). In addition, the largest tumuli of such a region did not necessarily form a single genealogical sequence; they tend to have been constructed in different locations at different phases. This suggests that the chieftainship of the region was not only the subject of competition but also actually changed hands between competing groups. For instance, in the ancient province of Bizen (roughly coinciding with the southeastern portion of present-day Okayama prefecture), the Urama-Chausuyama (浦間茶臼山) tumulus (keyhole-shaped with the round rear mound, approximately 138 metres long) and the Bizen-Kurumazuka (備前車塚) tumulus (keyhole-shaped with the square rear mound, approximately 48 m long) were built almost simultaneously. Although small, the latter contained thirteen bronze mirrors, including eleven *Sankakuen-shinju-kyo* mirrors (三角縁神獣鏡, triangular-rimed mirrors decorated with motifs of deities and beasts), a constitutive element of the IKP, probably given by the elite of the southern Kinki area. These tumuli are located at a distance of about 7.5 kilometres from one another. Only a couple of regional integration units could have existed between these locations during the Yayoi period; most likely, they were constructed by two neighbouring, and probably competing, communities.

It should also be noted that the image of a neat conical hierarchisation relies heavily upon the assumption that a unilinear descent system had been established by the time the IKP was widely adopted (e.g. Kobayashi 1961, 135–159); based on this image, what was actually hierarchised was the relationship between the elite lineages of individual regional polities, and as a chieftain ascended the ladder of hierarchy, the image indicates that the scale of the area under his or her control exponentially increased. The *Kojiki* and *Nihonshoki* chronicles indicate that a male-line-based unilinear descent was firmly established at the very beginning of the imperial genealogy, and this notion tacitly supports the image (ibid.). However, it is contradicted by the Chinese chronicle *Weizhi*, which records the events that occurred around the beginning of the Kofun period; this record mentions that two unnamed male chiefs who failed to be good leaders were later replaced by the queens Himiko and Iyo (Ichiyo, 壱与), which suggests that the descent system was *bilinear/bilateral*. Yoshiyuki Tanaka's osteo-archaeological reconstruction of the kinship system of the time also supports this inference; the existence of biological kin relations that were closer than those of brothers and sisters has been confirmed in most of the skeletal remains from multiple burials dating from between the Yayoi V and the Early Kofun periods, based on Tanaka's (1995) examination; many examples indicate the presence of both sexes. The chronic competitions over chieftainship, as mentioned earlier, could also have resulted from the instability caused by the bilinear descent system.

How can we accommodate those two seemingly contradictory phenomena, that is, the conical hierarchisation of the horizon and the ongoing inter-communal competition, in our understanding of the Yayoi-Kofun transition? I believe that the issue can be clarified by examining the phenomena in detail, in terms of the formation and transformation of inter-communal and inter-regional *networks*. Let us begin by examining the newly emerged 'nodes' of the inter-communal and inter-regional communication networks, that is, the port-of-trade-type settlements, where people would have encountered a new lifeworld reality and contradictions it generated.

2. THE EMERGENCE OF PORT-OF-TRADE-TYPE SETTLEMENTS

The period saw the emergence of new large settlements across western Japan and the western fringes of eastern Japan; in these settlements, there was an abundance of material items which either were brought in from remote regions or were made by copying the originals from remote regions.

In many such sites, we find conspicuous existence of pots of non-local origin (often including both transported and locally produced ones). The assemblage (commonly called the Shonai [庄内] assemblage, after the eponymous site), which originated from certain locations in the Kinki region, that in San'in region, that in the ancient Kibi province of Sanyo region, that in the ancient province of Omi (coinciding with present-day Shiga prefecture) and the Nobi Plain, was particularly conspicuous at such sites.[3]

A majority of the non-local pots found at those sites are cooking jars. This suggests that groups who had their own distinct way of cooking with those pots travelled a certain distance to relocate to those sites, at least for a while. A set of cooking jars and vessels used for other purposes and belonging to different regional traditions were often used in a particular dwelling (e.g. Nishijinmachi [西新町] Location D, Nos. 4 and 7 pit dwelling; Figure 8.1; Fukuoka MBE 1982). Interestingly, many 'hybrid' vessels, showing signs of a combination of production techniques and/or visual attributes of both local and remote origins began to appear in these new sites (Figure 8.1.B). This suggests that both local and migrant populations lived together in these sites and that they formed a community in which the formerly distinct customs were mutually influenced, and at times modified, to form

---

3 The Hakata Bay area of northern Kyushu already witnessed the presence of pots, stylistically originated from the Kinki region and the ancient Kibi province, but apparently produced locally in the second half of the Yayoi V (e.g. Fukuoka MBE 1996b, 61–64). This shows that small-scale migrations to certain spots in the Hakata bay area, the gateway region to the Korean peninsula and mainland Asia already begun before the Yayoi VI (i.e. the Shonai phase). However, there were some significant differences. Those non-local pots became quickly absorbed by the local-style assemblage in the second half of the Yayoi V, whereas in the Shonai phase and thereafter they continued as stylistically distinct assemblages and gradually replaced the northern Kyushu style assemblage (see the following and Mizoguchi 1988). Non-local pots in the second half of the Yayoi V concentrated in preexisting regional-centre-type settlements, whereas that in the Shonai phase and thereafter concentrated in newly-emerged coastal settlements ('port-of-trade-type' settlements; see the following discussion). They suggest that the migrations of the Yayoi VI would have been ignited by the rapid and significant increase of the flow of goods, people and information between the communities of western Japan as a sort of 'equal partners'.

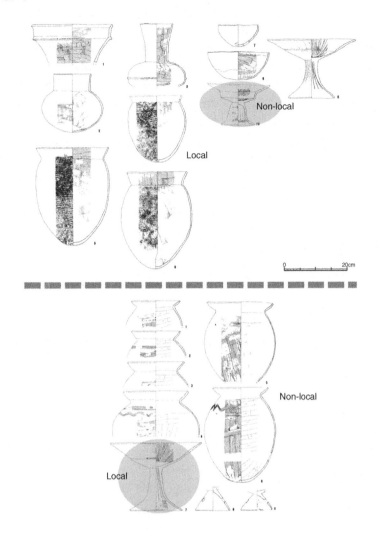

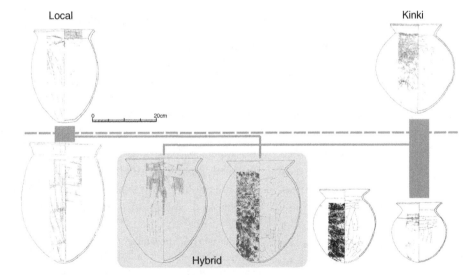

Figure 8.1. Potteries of non-local stylistic characteristics and origins excavated from a port-of-trade-type settlement, the Nishijinmachi, Fukuoka prefecture (after Fukuoka MBE 1982) **A (top):** assemblage from No. 4 pit dwelling in Loc. D, **A (bottom):** assemblage from No. 7 pit dwelling in Loc. D. Note differences between local and non-local shape-types coexisting in individual dwellings. **B:** Hybridisation in cooking jars.

a unique hybrid custom pertaining to everyday activities. In certain sites in the northern Kyushu region, and most notably the Nishijinmachi site in the Hakata Bay area of Fukuoka prefecture, excavations have revealed not only pots and material items from across western Japan but also some unique features for dwellings originating from the southern coastal region of the Korean peninsula and beyond. In order to understand the nature of those sites and the roles they played, let us examine the Nishijinmachi site in detail.

The Nishijinmachi site is situated on a sand dune near Hakata Bay (Fukuoka MBE 1982, 17–22). The discovery of a well at the site indicates that the inhabitants had a fairly secure water supply (Fukuoka PBE 2003, 26–33). However, there is no land suitable for paddy field rice farming in the vicinity; the lagoon behind the dune would have been swampy at the time of the dune's occupation, and even if it had been possible to construct small paddies on its fringes, their productivity would have been low. This strongly suggests that the inhabitants would have relied upon the supply of food from elsewhere, albeit partially.

The settlement was established sometime in the second half of the late Yayoi V period, when the south-western quarter of the site was occupied, and the centre of the residential area shifted to the north-west as the scale of settlement expanded (Fukuoka PBE 2009, 127–133). Quite unlike the regular 'norm' of the Yayoi settlements, the Nishijinmachi settlement did not comprise clearly distinguished residential units. However, during the Yayoi-Kofun transitional phase, that is, the Shonai phase and the earliest Furu (commonly called the Furu 0 [zero] type) phase, it might have been very loosely divided into neighbourhoods inhabited by those who mainly used local cooking and serving vessels and those who used cooking and serving vessels originating from elsewhere, in terms of their style and/or techniques employed for making them, such as the Kinki-core region (KCR), the San'in region and so on (Mizoguchi 1988, 109).[4] Interestingly, there was no

clear boundary with respect to pottery use; there were many houses where both local and non-local pots of various appearances, qualities and functions were used in various ratios (ibid.). In addition, somewhat later (during the earliest Furu, i.e. the Furu 0, phase and the early Furu phase), there emerged a small number of hybrid vessels, including cooking jars whose rim shape, along with the manufacturing and finishing techniques employed to make them, corresponded with that of the earliest and early Furu-style cooking vessels originating from the Kinki region; however, their form (especially their almond-shaped body) was that of the local cooking jar (Figure 8.1.B; Mizoguchi 1988, 103–104). This suggests that the inhabitants identified themselves in a relaxed, inclusive manner, even though they would probably have loosely maintained their original identities (hence the two loosely and vaguely separated 'neighbourhoods').

Houses facilitated with a Korean-style cooking stove suddenly emerged in the earliest Furu phase, and their distribution does not show any significant concentration (Fukuoka PBE 2009, 99).[5] A little later, there emerged a number of vessels produced in the southern Korean peninsula, although their distribution, interestingly enough, does not exclusively coincide with that of the cooking-oven-facilitated houses. Excavations have also revealed traces and debris of glass-bead manufacture (including a mould for making comma-shaped beads), which was carried out using technology from the Korean peninsula (Fukuoka PBE 2009, 103–106).

These traces suggest that inhabitants from mainly the southern Korean peninsula not only brought goods of their daily use into the settlement but also lived and worked here. Interestingly, they also appear to have retained their own identity in a relaxed, flexible manner; they fitted their houses with the cooking stoves that they were accustomed to back in the peninsula, but they did not rigidly

---

4 Takeo Kusumi (1999, 113–116) has revealed that a considerable number of the Shonai style and Furu 0 (zero)–style pots would have been produced in the Hie-Naka (比恵-那珂) site cluster, located at the centre of the adjacent Fukuoka plain. This suggests that a certain number of migrants from the KCR settled in the major

settlements of the Hakata Bay area and that the local population adopted the migrants' material culture to a significant extent. Kusumi has also suggested that some of the San'in style pots excavated from the Nishijinmachi settlement were produced locally, probably within the settlement (pers. comm.).

5 Jun'ichi Takesue (pers. comm.), however, points out that there is a loose concentration of Korean-style cooking stove-facilitated pit dwellings with not-so-clear boundaries.

stick to their peninsular way of life and gradually adopted local customs in the form of using local cooking and serving vessels.

The other artefacts excavated at this site, apart from those mentioned above, include a bronze mirror (a broken piece), bronze Chinese coins, numerous glass beads, comma-shaped stone beads (both finished and unfinished) and various iron implements, including swords, arrowheads, knives, sickles, woodworking tools and so on. What is interesting is that they include not only items that were produced and used in the settlement but also the probable remains of items that were transported in and out of the settlement; iron swords (Fukuoka PBE 2000, 250–252), for instance, are rarely excavated from settlements and are more likely to be found in burial contexts, and it is quite possible that these were brought into the settlement with the intention of exchanging them for other items. The presence of various fishing tools, including stone and pottery net-sinkers and octopus-fishing pots, is also prominent, and the large stone net-sinkers, a significant component of the fishing-tool assemblage of the settlement, would have been used for large-scale offshore fishing (cf. Shimojo 1984; Fukuoka PBE 2009, 107–116). This suggests that the inhabitants of the settlement were involved in offshore fishing activities, which also indicates that they were involved in the transportation of goods, and probably of people and information, by using the navigation technology which they nurtured through their subsistence activity. They would have crossed the Tsushima Strait and maintained constant contacts with communities in the southern coastal regions of the Korean peninsula. This special ability and the contacts they had made with the peninsular people would have put them in a unique position: they would have become the mediators between the inland agrarian communities of the archipelago and the peninsula, and their villages (I have used the plural form, because there were several other villages like the Nishijinmachi settlement along the Hakata Bay coast, such as the Imajuku [今宿], the Hakata [博多] and the Tatara-komeda [多々良込田] villages) thereby acquired a unique position in the functioning of the regional social system and beyond (Kusumi 2007).

In many senses, those settlements were situated on the *interface* of many spheres, including the cultural, traditional, communicative, exchange and subsistence spheres, among others.[6] A number of cultural and traditional spheres interfaced with one another, which generated hybridised ways of life mediated by hybridised material items and their configuration; for instance, many of these inhabitants lived in houses equipped with kitchen ovens of Korean origin but used pots deriving from a mixture of traditions from various parts of the archipelago (including the Kinki and San'in regions, among others). Many inhabitants would have been involved in both fishing and exchange activities, although their involvement in the latter would not have helped them ascend the ladder of social hierarchy. In fact, very loose, group-identity-based divisions can be identified from the distribution of pots deriving from different traditions, the distribution of kitchen ovens[7] and so on; this suggests that different communities were not arranged in a unified hierarchical order but mingled with one another as equals. Many of these settlements, and particularly those located on sand bars (e.g. the Nishijinmachi settlement), would have required an external supply of rice and other foodstuffs, simply because these sites did not have sufficient land in their vicinity for the cultivation of rice or other crops.

In short, these coastal villages constituted port-of-trade-type settlements (Polanyi 1966). The experience of living in them would have created self-identities and perceptions of the lifeworld among their inhabitants that had not previously existed. Some of those who came from remote places might have been 'assigned' the task of obtaining exotic goods and advanced technologies, predominantly imported from the Korean peninsula, by the elite of their respective communities of origin. Although their customs and interests varied, they needed to live together, and they managed to do so. The inhabitants of such ports-of-trade would have negotiated their respective identities and interests with respect to those of others. Their hybrid lifestyles and material items of

6 This distinguishes the phenomenon from the small-scale migrations that took place in the second half of the Yayoi V (see Footnote 3 to this chapter). The latter concentrated in pre-existing regional centre-type settlements where the identities of the newcomers became quickly absorbed by the indigenous culture.

7 See Footnote 5 to this chapter.

various characters were the consequences of such negotiations, and they would also have mediated such negotiations. This suggests that the ports-of-trade formed a unique communicative setting where individuals needed an entirely new framework, or a referent, with which to decide how to get on with the others, and indeed with a new reality; they came from communities far away which had different customs and interests, and since they came all the way in order to interact with, or against, the people in the archipelago, it was essential to interact in such a way as to not cause excessive frictions. This would have led to the realisation of the necessity of developing a shared system of values and code of conducts. I would argue that the elite (mortuary) communicative horizon, which was materially embodied by the keyhole tumuli and allied mortuary assemblage (the Initial Kofun Package; the IKP hereafter), was generated out of this novel reality.

Such ports-of-trade occupied the nodal positions of the coastal regions of Kyushu and western Japan and were distributed particularly densely along the Seto Inland Sea corridor. The major examples of such settlements include, from west to east, the Miyamaegawa [宮前川] settlement of the Matsuyama Plain, the Tsudera [津寺] settlement cluster of the Okayama Plain, and the Kosakaai [小坂合] settlement of the Kawachi Plain (Figure 8.2; e.g. Tsugiyama 2007). The pottery assemblages of those sites comprise as diverse a range of pots deriving from different traditions as those of the ports-of-trade along Hakata Bay, though traces of migrants/visitors from the peninsula become fainter and the quality and quantity of goods/source materials imported from the continent declined as one went east.

Kusumi points out that in the early Furu phase, the distribution of pots imported from the southern Korean peninsula was concentrated in the Nishijinmachi settlement even as it almost disappeared from the other major settlements in the Hakata bay area, such as the Hie-Naka (比恵-那珂) settlement (Kusumi 2007). This might have resulted from the imposition of a degree of control on the organisation and behaviour of the communities in the interface settlements. In order to regulate the quantity and quality of the flow of goods, people and information passing through those settlements, it might have

been advantageous, and even necessary to limit those who were directly involved in the flow to a small number of designated settlements. It would have become increasingly stressful for the residents of the central-place-type settlements to cope with the influx of people from various parts of western Japan, some sent by the elite of the communities to which they belonged, and to regulate the negotiations between these people while fulfilling a wide range of requirements; the stress and problems generated by this situation would have been reduced by developing interfaces and negotiations with remote communities in the designated settlements.[8]

The period witnessed the rise of the ancient provinces of Kawachi and Yamato (the KCR) as the node of flow of an increasing range of goods and technology from overseas as well as from regions across western Japan and the western half of eastern Japan. The region also became the centre of IKP distribution. In other words, the elite of the KCR gradually acquired the position of the supreme mediators of the flow of goods, people and information across the newly emerging horizon covering significant portions of the archipelago. This indicates the increasing influence of those who originated from the KCR in the negotiations that took place at the port-of-trade-type settlements – an influence that was faithfully reflected by the adoption of the region's pottery styles by communities across northern Kyushu and the Seto Inland Sea area. How and why did this happen?

3. NETWORKS, DIFFERENTIAL TOPOLOGICAL POTENTIALS AND THE EMERGENCE OF THE KEYHOLE TOMB HORIZON

3.1. The Causes of Hierarchisation

The distribution of the earliest keyhole tumuli roughly coincides with that of the port-of-trade-type settlements in Kyushu and western Japan. The construction of the earliest examples of these tumuli – the largest of which, that is, Hashihaka (Hashinakayama,箸中山; Figure 8.3), is approximately 280 metres long – undoubtedly required

8 See Footnotes 3 and 6 to this chapter.

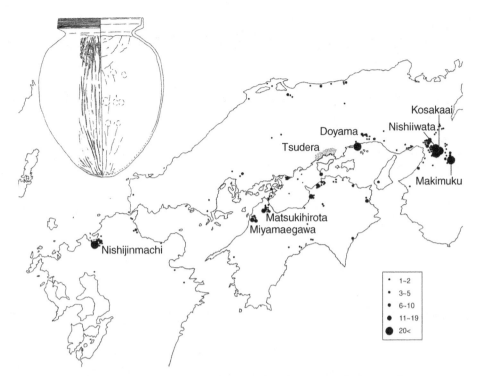

Figure 8.2. The distribution of typical port-of-trade-type settlements of western Japan indicated by the distributional nodes of the so-called Kibi (吉備)-style cooking jar (from Tsugiyama [2007], with additions and modifications). 'Ports-of-trade'-type settlements are named.

a vast labour force. The deceased were buried in these tumuli along with a homogeneous set of grave goods, including bronze mirrors, bronze and iron tools and weapons; slightly later, these goods came to include the characteristic jasper/green tuff products (e.g. Kondo 1983, 175–196). This set of tumuli, representing the earliest forms of the keyhole-shaped mounds with allied features such as a stone-built mortuary chamber pit, compose the IKP.

There were certain variations in the earliest keyhole tumuli, including the Makimuku [纒向]-type tumuli (Figure 8.4.8–10; see Hojo 2000, 99–109), and some scholars treat them as prototypes of the keyhole tumuli and do not recognise their construction as marking the beginning of the Kofun period. Instead, they regard the construction of the Hashihaka tumulus as the defining epoch of the period's onset (Figure 8.4.A; e.g. Kondo 1983). However, the earliest keyhole tumuli, and particularly the Makimuku-type tumuli, were as widespread as the Hashihaka derivatives (Terasawa 2000, 258–260; Barnes 2007, 118–124). The earliest examples of the Makimuku-type tumuli date back to the later part of the Shonai-style pottery phase, preceding the earliest Furu-style pottery phase, as Hashihaka itself was built during the earliest Furu-style pottery phase (Nara Prefectural Kashihara Archaeological Research Institute 2002). In the following text, the earliest keyhole-shaped burial mounds, including the Makimuku-style mounds, are treated as examples of the keyhole tumulus, which marked the beginning of the phenomenon which is covered under the *sign* 'the Kofun period'.[9]

9 The beginning of the formalisation of the IKP was marked by the emergence of the Makimuku-type tumuli, though their spread to spots across western Japan and the western portion of eastern Japan did not result in the instant elimination of unique regional mortuary and other ritual practices. In fact, distinct regional traits continued into the Earlier Kofun period (see Chapter 9). The construction of the Hashihaka tumulus marked the beginning of the trend in which the largest keyhole tumulus in the IKP horizon in each generation was constructed somewhere in the Kinki-core region. In that sense, the period between sometime in the Yayoi VI/the Shonai style pottery phase, which witnessed the emergence of the Makimuku-type tumuli, and the earliest Furu pottery phase, which witnessed the construction of the Hashihaka tumulus, was, indeed, a transitional period.

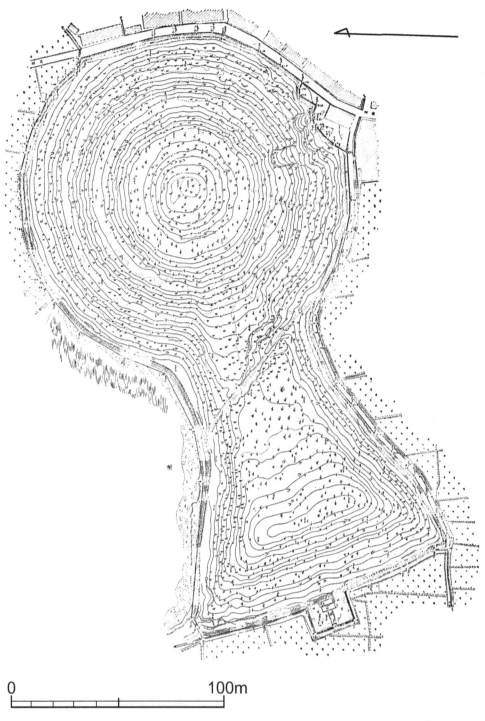

0   100m

Figure 8.3. Hashihaka (Hashinakayama) tumulus (from Suenaga [1975], original produced by the Imperial Household Agency). With kind permission from the Imperial Household Agency and Gakuseisha Publishing Co.

Therefore, the IKP, in the present volume, includes both the Makimuku-type tumuli and their allied features and artefacts, including bronze mirrors with deity-beast motifs (*Gamontai-shinjyu-kyo*, 画紋帯神獣鏡) dating from the late second to the early third century AD (Okamura 1999, 134–144; Fukunaga et al. 2003, 147–158), as well as the Hashihaka derivatives and their allied features and artefacts, including triangular-rimed bronze mirrors with deity-beast motifs dating from circa the early third century to the early/mid-fourth century AD (Fukunaga et al. 2003, 86–127). The

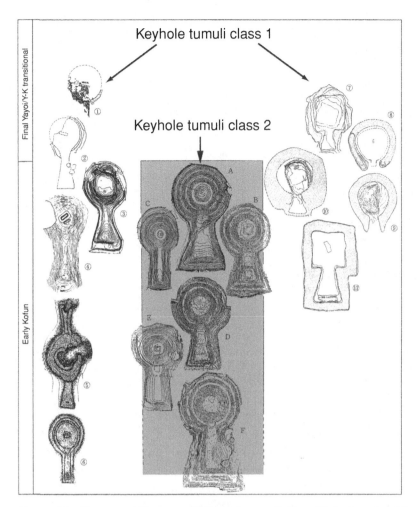

Figure 8.4. Type 1 and Type 2 early keyhole tumuli (from Hojo [2000], with additions). 1 Hagiwara (Tokushima prefecture), 2 Tsuruojinja No. 4 (Kagawa), 3 Yoro-Hisagozuka (Hyogo), 4 Takamatsu-Chausuyama (Kagawa), 5 Nekozuka (Kagawa), 6 Ishifunezuka (Kagawa), 7 Hoshoji (Shiga), 8 Godo No. 5 (Chiba), 9 Godo No. 4 (Chiba), 10 Makimuku-Ishizuka (Nara), 11 Toba (Shiga), A Hashihaka (Hashinakayama), B Nishitonozuka, C Sakurai-Chausuyama, D Andonyama, E Mesuriyama, F Shibutani-Mukaiyama (A–F: Nara). With kind permission from Aoki Shoten Publishing Co.

transition from the former to the latter implies a range of important issues (e.g. Fukunaga et al. 2003), which I discuss subsequently.

The largest examples of these tumuli, as mentioned above, were built in the present-day Nara Basin (Figures 8.4 and 8.5), which was to later become the seat of successive capitals of the ancient Japanese state, established in the late seventh century AD. It appears that many of the mortuary items constituting the IKP were distributed to other regions from the polity/polities occupying the present-day Nara Basin and Osaka Plain of the KCR (e.g. Kondo 1983, 175–196). These facts suggest that the onset of the Kofun period marked the emergence of a centralised and hierarchical alliance of polities (Gina Barnes characterises this alliance as 'stratified peer polit-

ies'; see Barnes 2007, 173–177), reflected by the IKP horizon, the core of which extended along the Inland Sea corridor (Figure 8.5; Kondo 1983, 175–210). This centralised alliance was later to become the foundation of the ancient Japanese state, fully equipped with its own bureaucracy, systems of taxation and conscription, and administrative institutions.

Scholars have long debated the factors leading to the formation of the KCR-centred hierarchical alliance. To begin with, during the preceding Late Yayoi (Yayoi V) period, as illustrated in the previous chapter, intra-regional integration and hierarchisation had progressed fairly evenly between the regions, including the KCR, and these regions were later to be stratified under the control of the KCR (e.g. Matsugi 1998; Mizoguchi 2000).

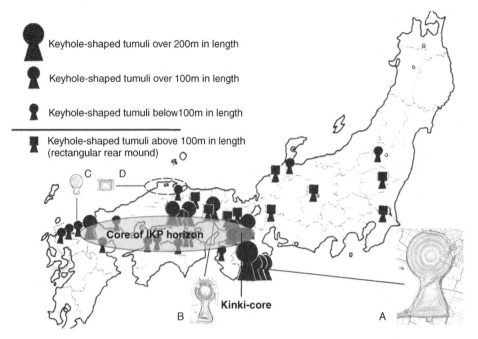

Figure 8.5. Size differences and distribution of the early keyhole tumuli and the IKP horizon (after Hirose [2003], with additions). Distribution and size differences of the earliest keyhole-shaped tumuli (from Hirose 2003 with modification). **A:** Hashihaka (Yamato (G) in Figure 8.6); **B:** Yoro-hisagozuka (Harima: between Kibi (D)) and Kinki-core (G)); **C:** Haraguchi (Tsukushi (B)) and **D:** Onari (Izumo (C)). The core of the IKP horizon and the location of the Kinki-core are indicated. With kind permission from Kadokawa Shoten Publishing Co.

Although there is no evidence of any militaristic conquest made by those in the KCR (cf. Matsugi 2007, 128; Terasawa 2000, 233–236), some scholars argue that competition over access to resources from overseas, such as Chinese mirrors and Korean raw materials for iron production, gave rise to tensions between the KCR and the northern Kyushu regions (e.g. Fukunaga 1998, 240–241). Further, there is no evidence to indicate that the KCR had monopolised the exploitation of, or access to, critical resources – either symbolic (e.g. bronze mirrors)[10] or functional (e.g. raw materials for iron production) – during the Yayoi V (cf. Murakami 2000). In fact, the northern Kyushu region (the ancient province of Tsukushi; see the following discussion) was much better positioned for access to Chinese and Korean prestige items (Figure 8.6.A) as well as the sources of raw materials for iron production, believed to be found in the southern Korean peninsula (Murakami 1998).

The northern Kyushu region was clearly the centre of distribution of Chinese bronze mirrors and iron artefacts throughout the Yayoi period (e.g. Terasawa 2000, 204–220).[11] Moreover, there were only small and scattered floodplains suitable for paddy field farming in the horizon covered by the IKP (Figure 8.6.B), and the Wittfogelian thesis, according to which centralised hierarchies emerge necessarily through the centralised control of irrigation systems (Wittfogel 1957), is invalid in this case. The only viable theses put forward so far, with regard to the preceding observations, are as follows: first, the KCR enjoyed a high carrying capacity because its large and stable floodplains were suitable for paddy field farming, which helped extend its politico-cultural influence across adjacent regions and beyond (e.g. Kondo 1983, 128–136); second, the Nara Basin in this region occupied the nodal position between western and eastern Japan, which naturally led to the formation of a Nara-centred hierarchical alliance (e.g. Kondo 1983, 128–136; Matsugi 1998, 185).

Greater productivity and carrying capacity would have given the region an added advantage; these conditions would have enabled the communities of the KCR-based units to outdo

10 The KCR polity/polities might have exclusively distributed the *Gamontai-shinjyu-kyo*-type mirrors across the KCR itself and the eastern Seto Inland Sea region in the second half of the Yayoi VI (e.g. Fukunaga et al. 2003, 226–246), but other types of bronze mirrors continued to be imported to northern Kyushu at least during the first half of the Yayoi VI (e.g. Okamura 1999, Fukunaga et al. 2003, 148–158).

11 See Footnote 10 to this chapter.

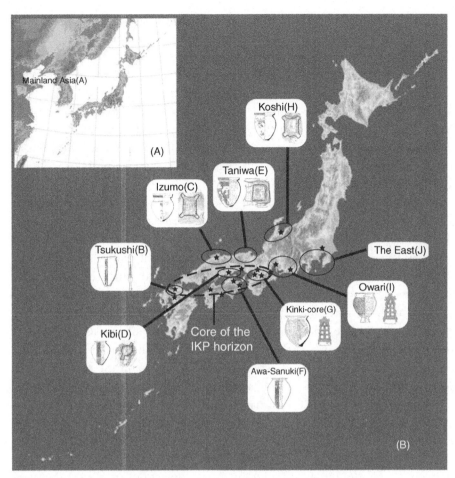

Figure 8.6. The location of Japanese archipelago in East Asia (A) and ancient provinces as "nodes" relevant to the investigation (B). Boxes show the characteristic mortuary mound forms/ritual items and pots of the respective regions. Stars indicate major floodplains in and around the core of the IKP horizon (see relevant descriptions; from Mizoguchi 2009).

the others in competitive gift-offering/exchange (Friedman and Rowlands 1977, 206–224). However, such an advantage would have been enjoyed only in the relationships with regions which were in direct and constant contact with the KCR. Moreover, many regions which were later to be incorporated into the IKP horizon developed their unique ritual devices during the late Yayoi V period and, in fact, broke away from the KCR-centred bronze-bell-ritual horizon (e.g. Matsugi 1998, 178–182; Terasawa 2000, 238–240). These observations effectively invalidate the first thesis, thus making the second thesis the only viable hypothesis.

The second thesis has a significant feature: it does not try to find the advantages enjoyed by the KCR due to its attributes; rather, it emphasises the region's *locational advantage*. In other words, the advantage of the region was generated, rather than acquired or attained, from the relations it could naturally forge with other regions because of its location. This is in accordance with the premises of the social network analysis mentioned above and is worth investigating further.

Based on the preceding observations, the following sections examine if there was any *topological* advantage enjoyed by the KCR over the other regions constituting the hierarchical alliance formed in the IKP horizon; this involves the application of some basic network analysis methods. The study will also investigate whether the hierarchical positions of other regions in the IKP horizon coincide with their topological positioning using calculations based on social network analysis methods.

The regional units of the Late Yayoi (Yayoi V) period, which later formed the KCR-centred hierarchical alliance, can be recognised by the high concentration of sites with their own distinct pottery styles (e.g. Terasawa 2000, 275–298; Morioka and Nishimura 2006) and can therefore be treated as distinct nodes (Figure 8.6.B). Interactions (represented by 'edges') between them can be identified based on the stylistic similarity and/or movement of pots (carried by those who moved between nodes) and the sharing of (attributes pertaining to) mortuary traditions between the nodes. The networks that had existed *before* (i.e. the second half of the Late Yayoi V period, c. the late first to second centuries AD) and *during* the widespread IKP (i.e. the Initial Kofun period, between at some point in the Yayoi VI and the earliest Furu pottery style phase, c. the late second/early third to late third centuries AD) can be defined by these nodes and edges, and the 'centrality' (indicating the influence, dominance, dependency and power) of the KCR and the other nodes can be calculated based on various measurements. The outcomes of the calculation are compared with the patterns indicated by relevant archaeological evidence, and this is used to examine the validity of the network-theory-driven hypothesis, that is, the emergence of the KCR-centred hierarchical alliance due to the topological structure of the network and the centrality enjoyed by the KCR in that network.

Network analysis is used to examine the structure of relations between the nodes constituting a network (e.g. Scott 2000; Carrington et al. 2005; Hanneman and Riddle 2005). The nodes and edges connecting each other form a network which can be visualised as a graph. In such graphs, different numbers of edges (commonly represented by straight lines) emerge from the nodes (commonly represented by dots), connecting them to other nodes. In a given network, the *topological* character of a node is constituted by a range of factors such as the number of nodes that are connected, or 'adjacent', to it, the number of nodes that can be accessed from the given node by moving along a certain number of nodes and edges, and the number of nodes that need to be connected to that particular node in order to be further connected to certain other nodes. These topological factors constitute the centrality of a given node, which determines how *influential*, *dominant* or *dependent* the node is with respect to the other nodes in the network. In other words, the centrality of a node indicates the given node's power over the others in the network, and this centrality is measured by using various methods to quantify the node's topological position in the network (Borgatti et al. 2002).

In this analysis, Net Draw 2.074 (Borgatti et al. 2002) has been used to draw graphs to indicate the archaeologically relevant regional entities of the Late Yayoi V period (c. the late first to the second centuries AD) and the Initial Kofun period (the Shonai to the earliest Furu pottery style phase, c. the late second/early third centuries AD to the late third century AD) as nodes and the archaeologically recognisable interactions between them as edges.

During the late Yayoi V period, both western Japan and the western part of eastern Japan, later to be covered by the IKP horizon, were divided into a number of regional units characterised by distinct pottery styles and rituals (Figure 8.6.B). During this period, there emerged a certain degree of social integration and hierarchisation, as reflected by the differentiation of burials into two or three strata, in terms of the quality and quantity of grave goods deposited and the scale of burial features and mounds, and by the sharing of similar mortuary/ritual customs across individual regions (e.g. Matsugi 1998). Although it appears that there was continuous competition between local chiefs over the hegemony of each of these regions (see Chapter 7), there was also a steady development in the process of centralisation of decision-making bodies in the form of the emergence of the paramount regional chief (Mizoguchi 2000; Terasawa 2000, 231–240).[12] In that sense, the regional units can appropriately be treated as distinct nodes.

The northern Kyushu region, or 'Tsukushi' – if we use its ancient provincial name recorded in the Ritsu-ryo regal-administrative code issued in AD 701 – was characterised by the use of bronze spearheads, often in ritualistic contexts (Figures 7.4 and 7.5) (see Chapter 7.2; also see e.g. Terasawa 2000, 222–224). Tsukushi almost monopolised the archipelago's interactions with mainland Asia (Figure 8.6.A), although there does appear to be some traces of sporadic direct contact between other nodes and mainland Asia. This chapter treats China and the polities of the Korean

---

12 This was, as illustrated in Chapter 7, based on the internal segmentation and hierarchisation of individual clans and the stabilisation of the membership of higher-ranked lineages in them. This phenomenon correlates with the expansion in scale of regional horizons within which goods, information and people were exchanged and moved around. For the detail, see Chapter 7.3.

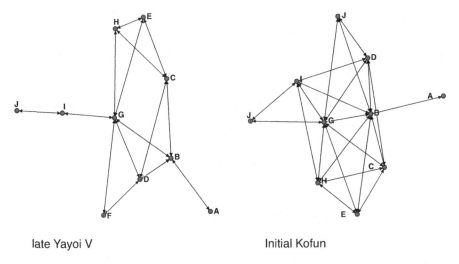

late Yayoi V   Initial Kofun

Figure 8.7. The nodes and the edges: for the actual locations of the nodes, see Figure 8.6.

peninsula as one node and draws an edge between this node and Tsukushi (Figure 8.7).

The northern central shore of the Inland Sea, where the province of Kibi was located, and the coastline of the Sea of Japan, surrounding the ancient province of Izumo in the present-day San'in region, developed the mortuary practice of burying the dead in large earthen mounds (Terasawa 2000, 236–238). In the former region (i.e. the province of Kibi), the mounds were commonly rectangular in shape; however, the famous Tatetsuki tumulus – a large central mound with two rectangular tails – was built towards the end of the Yayoi V period. Some scholars argue that the tumulus was the direct prototype of the keyhole tumulus with a round rear mound (ibid., 238–246). In the latter region (i.e. the San'in region), the corners of the rectangular mounds often characteristically protruded like four tails. The bases of the four-tailed mounds were commonly covered with cobbles (see Chapter 7.3.2).

Interestingly, four-tailed tumuli were also built in the present-day Hokuriku region, or the ancient Koshi province, though the cobble cover, common in Izumo, was not found in Koshi (e.g. Furukawa 2010). However, the regions in between, that is, the present-day northern Kinki region or the ancient Taniwa province, did not see the construction of four-tailed mounds; instead, rectangular tumuli were built in these regions, and some of them contained exceptionally rich grave goods, including iron weapons and glass artefacts (Kyoto Prefectural Research Centre of Buried Cultural Properties 2001; Terasawa 2000, 239).

Sandwiched between the Kibi and Kinki regions, the ancient Sanuki and Awa provinces, situated on the southern shore of the Inland Sea, developed a distinct pottery style and the custom of constructing stone-built pit mortuary chambers. These regions developed a characteristic type of stone-built pit burial chamber, the prototype of the IKP component (Sugawara 2006), and some of the earliest keyhole tumuli with a distinct local mound form can be found here (Hojo 1999b; Okubo 2006). This volume treats these regions as one node, even though their pottery and other material cultural traits show a few differences. These regions exerted a powerful influence over the ancient province of Harima, located across the Inland Sea. However, during the Yayoi V period, the region was covered by the horizon of cultural traits originating from Kinki, and during the Initial Kofun period, it became a junction of interactions between the Kibi, Sanuki, Awa, Kinki and possibly the Tsukushi regions (Morioka 2006); hence, it is not treated as an independent node in this volume.

The present-day Kinki and Tokai regions were characterised by the use of *Dotaku* bronze bells, which were so developed in terms of their size and visual impressiveness by that time that they no longer functioned as bells (see Figures 7.4 and 7.5). These regions can be subdivided into a number of smaller sociocultural zones, of which the present-day Kawachi and Yamato plains formed the sociocultural core (cf. Shiraishi 1999, 72–78). The integration of those plains into a unified polity is well attested by the fact that the larger tumuli of the Initial Kofun period are concentrated in the south-eastern corner of the Yamato Plain, not in the Kawachi Plain; the chieftains of those plains would have been integrated into a unified hierarchical structure, due to which they built their tumuli at a specific location (ibid.).[13] This integration process would have already begun during the Yayoi V; hence, this study treats those areas as a single node, called the 'Kinki-core'. This region saw the development of keyhole tumuli with a round rear mound during the Shonai pottery style phase,[14] which is considered to mark the beginning of the Initial Kofun period in this volume (Figures 8.4 and 8.5). At roughly the same time, the ancient province of Owari developed the style of building keyhole tumuli with a square rear mound, thus differentiating itself from the Kinki region (e.g. Terasawa 2000, 281–283). The area to the east of Owari, later to constitute the periphery of the IKP horizon (Figures 8.5 and 8.6.B), loosely shared a distinct pottery style with Owari (Terasawa 2000, 279–286). This large area, consisting of the ancient provinces of Mikawa, Totsuomi and Suruga, is heuristically treated as a single node and called 'the east'.

The present-day Hokuriku region, or the ancient province of Koshi, as mentioned earlier, constitutes the Sea of Japan's coastal periphery of the IKP horizon. This region is also treated as a node (Takahashi 2005).

These regions began to develop distinct pottery styles in the Yayoi V period (Morioka and Nishimura 2006). In the Initial Kofun period, they had already consolidated their distinct characteristics (e.g. Morioka and Nishimura 2006), although most of them (except Izumo and Owari: see below) eventually became incorporated into the IKP horizon (Figure 8.6). This period also saw an explosive increase in inter-regional interactions, which can be archaeologically traced through the movement of pots, some of which were carried across great distances (Kusumi 1999, 2007; Morioka and Nishimura 2006). Excavations also reveal pots made in the styles of remote regions but from local clay (ibid.). This phenomenon suggests the movement of people/potters.[15] Mutual influence between 'foreign' and local pottery styles is also evident in many regions in the

13 The so-called Oyamato (オオヤマト) tumuli cluster (see pp. 281–286 in the present volume).
14 The so-called Makimuku type. See Figure 8.4.8~10.
15 See Section 2 of the present chapter.

form of stylistic hybridisation (Mizoguchi 1988). In this way, we can identify edges by tracing the movement and inter-regional stylistic hybridisation of pottery, among other types of archaeological information.

This study represents the edges identified in the Late Yayoi V and the Initial Kofun periods as matrices in which the presence and absence of edges between the nodes are represented as 1 and 0, respectively, and then uses these matrices to calculate the various types of centrality pertaining to individual nodes.

Some network analysis methods designed for measuring various types of centrality (degree centrality, Bonacich power centrality, closeness centrality, eigenvector centrality and betweenness centrality measures; see Hanneman and Riddle 2005) have been applied to the graphs representing the networks of the late Yayoi V period and the Initial Kofun period. The UCINET network analysis software was used to draw the graphs and calculate the centralities (Borgatti et al. 2002).

This study compares the outcomes of these analyses with the patterns shown by the available archaeological evidence, through which it seeks to examine the validity of the previously mentioned hypothetical premise while considering the reasons behind the KCR's transformation into the centre of the emergent hierarchical alliance.

3.2. Measuring the Topological Potentials of the Regions

THE LATE YAYOI V (C. THE LATE FIRST TO SECOND CENTURIES AD)

The interactions between the nodes in this period were basically confined to adjacent nodes (Figure 8.7), although the flow of Chinese and Korean imports from one node to the next, starting from Tsukushi, appears to have steadily increased during the period (e.g. Terasawa 2000, 204–207). It is interesting to find that Kinki-core appears to have had direct contacts with Tsukushi, as is indicated by the excavation of some Kinki-core-style pots from the Hie-Naka site, one of the central-place-type settlements of Tsukushi (Fukuoka MBE 1996b, 61–64). Takehiko Kusumi highlights the fact that the Hie-Naka site also reveals some attribute-level influences, albeit a small number, of the Kinki-core style on the locally made indigenous pots (ibid., and see Footnote 3 of the present

TABLE 8.1. *Matrix indicating the presence and absence of edges between the nodes in the late Yayoi V*

	Mainland (A)	Tsukushi (B)	Izumo (C)	Kibi (D)	Taniwa (E)	Awa-Sanuki (F)	Kinki-core (G)	Koshi (H)	Owari (I)	East (J)
A	0	1	0	0	0	0	0	0	0	0
B	1	0	1	1	0	0	1	0	0	0
C	0	1	0	1	1	0	0	1	0	0
D	0	1	1	0	0	1	1	0	0	0
E	0	0	1	0	0	0	1	1	0	0
F	0	0	0	1	0	0	1	0	0	0
G	0	1	0	1	1	1	0	1	1	0
H	0	0	1	0	1	0	1	0	0	0
I	0	0	0	0	0	0	1	0	0	1
J	0	0	0	0	0	0	0	0	1	0

chapter). These factors suggest the migration of people from Kinki-core to Tsukushi. Therefore, we can draw an edge between the Kinki-core and Tsukushi nodes (G and B, respectively, in Figure 8.7). In all other cases, edges are only drawn between adjacent nodes in this period; as mentioned above, the Yayoi V saw the development of distinct regional pottery styles (Figure 8.6.B), and though we can observe mutual influences and occasional transportations of pots between neighbouring regions, stylistic/technological influences and transportation of pots across farther regions were very rare (Morioka and Nishimura 2006).

The matrix representing the situation is provided in Table 8.1.

MEASURING CENTRALITY

The *degree centrality measure* shows that Kinki-core had the largest number of edges emerging from it; Tsukushi, Izumo and Kibi followed, with four edges each (Table 8.2).

The *Bonacich power centrality measure* (Table 8.3), which takes into account how well connected are the nodes directly connected to the given node in measuring the centrality of that node, shows that Izumo was the best-connected node in the network, followed by Kibi and the Kinki-core.

The *closeness centrality measure* (Table 8.4), which shows a given node's closeness to all the other nodes in the network in terms of the number of edges that have to be crossed in order to reach all the other nodes from that node, generates a picture that is almost perfectly consistent with the findings of the degree centrality measure: the Kinki-core ranks first, followed by Tsukushi, Kibi, Izumo, Taniwa and Koshi.

The *reach centrality measure* (Table 8.5), which indicates the smallest number of edges that one needs to pass through in order to reach all the other nodes in the network from one given node, shows that the Kinki-core, again, is best connected, followed by Tsukushi, Kibi, Izumo, Koshi and Taniwa.

TABLE 8.2. *Degree centrality scores of the edges*

Rank	Node	Degree
1	Kinki-core	6.000
2	Izumo	4.000
2	Kibi	4.000
2	Tsukushi	4.000
5	Koshi	3.000
5	Taniwa	3.000
7	Owari	2.000
7	Sanuki-Awa	2.000
9	East	1.000
9	Mainland Asia	1.000

TABLE 8.3. *Bonacich centrality scores of the edges*

Rank	Node	Power
1	Izumo	55.122
2	Kibi	51.777
3	Kinki-core	51.359
4	Taniwa	46.481
5	Koshi	46.481
6	Tsukushi	45.505
7	Sanuki-Awa	31.568
8	Mainland Asia	12.753
9	Owari	0.906
10	East	−9.547

TABLE 8.4. *Closeness centrality scores of the edges*

Rank	Node	Closeness
1	Kinki-core	12.000
2	Tsukushi	15.000
2	Kibi	15.000
4	Izumo	17.000
4	Taniwa	17.000
4	Koshi	17.000
7	Sanuki-Awa	18.000
7	Owari	18.000
9	Mainland Asia	23.000
10	East	26.000

TABLE 8.6. *Eigenvector centrality scores of the edges*

Rank	Node	Eigenvector
1	Kinki-core	0.492
2	Kibi	0.405
3	Izumo	0.387
4	Tsukushi	0.375
5	Taniwa	0.326022238
6	Koshi	0.326022148
7	Sanuki-Awa	0.243
8	Owari	0.144
9	Mainland Asia	0.101
10	East	0.039

Next, let us consider the *eigenvector centrality measure* (Table 8.6). This method uses factor analysis to calculate the eigenvectors of individual nodes. The algorithm is complicated, but the method can be used to capture the overall patterns concerning a given network, thus summarizing what the other measures of centrality individually represent. Higher scores on this measure indicate that nodes are 'more central' to the main pattern (reflected by the factor 1 eigenvectors) of distances among all of the nodes in the network. Again, the Kinki-core ranks first, followed by Kibi, Izumo, Tsukushi, Taniwa and Koshi.

Finally, let us consider the *betweenness centrality measure* (Table 8.7). Higher scores indicate that more nodes depend on a given node to make connections with other nodes in the network. In other words, a higher score indicates that a given node *mediates* interactions between more nodes than do other nodes in the network. The Kinki-core's centrality is quite significant on this measure,

followed by the usual group of Tsukushi, Izumo, Kibi and so on. Interestingly, Owari ranked second on this measure, since all the other nodes had to pass through Owari to proceed to the east.

SUMMARY AND DISCUSSION

The nodes that consistently rank higher on the centrality measurements, that is, the Kinki-core, Tsukushi and Kibi regions, were later to form the core of the IKP horizon (e.g. Tsude 1998, 37–41). From among them, the Kinki-core's location in the network made it the central-most node in terms of its *connectedness* to all the other nodes in the network and its *mediation* of interactions between other nodes. This suggests that once the interactions between the nodes in a network exceeded a certain volume and reached a *critical point*, the Kinki-core's supreme centrality in the network inevitably exerted its influence on, and hence its power over, the other large nodes in the network. This would particularly have served to

TABLE 8.5. *Reach centrality scores of the edges*

Rank	Node	Reach
1	Kinki-core	8.500
2	Kibi	7.333
2	Tsukushi	7.333
4	Izumo	7.083
5	Koshi	6.667
5	Taniwa	6.667
7	Owari	6.167
7	Sanuki-Awa	6.167
9	Mainland Asia	5.083
10	East	4.667

TABLE 8.7. *Betweenness centrality scores of the edges*

Rank	Node	Betweenness
1	Kinki-core	40.000
2	Tsukushi	17.500
3	Owari	16.000
4	Kibi	8.167
5	Izumo	6.500
6	Koshi	3.667
6	Taniwa	3.667
8	Sanuki-Awa	1.000
9	East	0.000
9	Mainland Asia	0.000

sustain and enhance the quality as well as quantity of interactions taking place between the nodes, because the centrality of the Kinki-core significantly derived from its position as the most prominent *mediator* of interactions between the other nodes, as was indicated by the betweenness centrality measure.

It is also notable that the Bonacich power measure indicated that the Izumo node was best connected to other, better-connected nodes (Table 8.3). This fact is interesting in that Izumo not only developed the unique four-tailed mortuary mound during the Yayoi V period (Figures 7.10 and 8.6.B) but also remained out of the IKP horizon while maintaining its distinct pottery and mortuary mound styles during the earlier Kofun period (Figure 8.5.D) (c. the fourth century AD to the late fifth century AD; e.g. Ikefuchi 1997). The elite in Izumo were buried in large square or rectangular mounds rather than in keyhole-shaped mounds. Moreover, not only were the distinctive Izumo-style pots carried widely across the network, but their influence also played a significant role in the emergence of Furu-style pottery (Tsugiyama 2007, 26). Furu pottery originated in Kinki-core and became widespread as a component of the IKP.

All in all, the outcomes of the centrality analyses are in accordance with the available archaeological evidence.

THE INITIAL KOFUN PERIOD (C. THE EARLY THIRD TO THE LATE THIRD CENTURIES AD)
During this period, there was a drastic increase in the movement of pots between the nodes. A considerable number of cooking jars made in the Kibi region, for instance, were brought into the central-place-/port-of-trade-type settlements along the coastline of the Inland Sea. According to some scholars, this suggests that seafaring groups of Kibi were involved in mediating the interactions that took place along the Inland Sea corridor (Tsugiyama 2007). The Shonai-style and the earliest Furu-style pottery assemblages also became widespread at this time. They originated in the Kinki region, and the specimens spread extensively in the network (e.g. Morioka and Nishimura 2006). These specimens are different from the Kibi pots in that they came to be produced locally in many nodes and influenced local pottery

styles, resulting in widespread stylistic hybridisation (see Section 2 of this chapter; e.g. Mizoguchi 1988; Kusumi 1999; Morioka and Nishimura 2006). This phenomenon appears to have been particularly significant in Tsukushi (Figure 8.1),[16] suggesting the existence of a particularly intense interaction between Tsukushi and the Kinki-core which involved the migration of people from the Kinki-core to Tsukushi.

The nodes of Izumo, Kibi, Sanuki-Awa, Taniwa, Koshi and Owari also started directly interacting with Tsukushi, which involved further movement of people, albeit on a smaller scale than that from the Kinki-core. This movement, again, is indicated by the distinctive nature of the pots brought into the central-place-type settlements of Tsukushi, such as the Hie-Naka and Nishijin-machi settlements (cf. Kusumi 1999, 2007).[17] A slightly different network matrix diagram can be drawn from these observations (Figure 8.7; Table 8.8).

This period also saw the widespread appearance of the keyhole tumuli that originated in the Kinki-core and Owari regions (Figures 8.4 and 8.5) (Terasawa 2000, 258–264). The tumuli that originated in the KCR had a round rear mound[18] (*Zenpo* [front rectangular]–*koen* [round rear]–*fun* [tumulus], 前方後円墳), while those that originated in the Owari region had a rectangular rear mound (*Zenpo* [front rectangular]–*koho* [rectangular rear]–*fun* [tumulus], 前方後方墳). Such tumuli were distributed widely across the IKP horizon, with significantly overlapping individual horizons, though tumuli with rectangular rear mounds were found to be much more densely distributed in the area to the east of Owari (Figure 8.5). The increasing distribution of the tumuli did not bring the local mortuary traditions to an immediate end (Hojo 2000,

16 Almost exact copies of the Shonai- and Furu-style cooking jars were also produced in the Hie-Naka settlement of the Hakata Bay area of the region. See Footnote 4 to this chapter.

17 Pots were also brought into northern Kyushu from the ancient province of Chikatsu-afumi (present-day Shiga prefecture), but the region did not develop its own distinct ritual (mortuary or otherwise) practice and hence is not treated as a distinct node in this chapter.

18 A larger part of the mound is customerily described as the rear mound whereas a smaller part the front. See Chapter 9.

TABLE 8.8. *Matrix indicating the presence and absence of the edges between the nodes in the Initial Kofun period*

	Mainland (A)	Tsukushi (B)	Izumo (C)	Kibi (D)	Taniwa (E)	Awa-Sanuki (F)	Kinki-core (G)	Koshi (H)	Owari (I)	East (J)
A	o	I	o	o	o	o	o	o	o	o
B	I	o	I	I	I	I	I	I	I	o
C	o	I	o	I	I	o	I	I	o	o
D	o	I	I	o	o	I	I	o	I	o
E	o	I	I	o	o	o	I	I	o	o
F	o	I	o	I	o	o	I	o	o	o
G	o	I	I	I	I	I	o	I	I	I
H	o	I	I	o	I	o	I	o	I	o
I	o	I	o	I	o	o	I	I	o	I
J	o	o	o	o	o	o	I	o	I	o

104–109).[19] However, by the end of the transitional period, keyhole tumuli with a round rear mound were an established form, best exemplified by the Hashihaka tumulus in the present-day Nara Basin (Figure 8.3); this became the dominant form of burial mound in most of the nodes in the network, with the exception of Izumo (Figure 8.5; see the previous discussion). More importantly, almost all the features of the IKP were formalised in the KCR, along with the emulation and/or incorporation of the local customs of the nodes into the package, many of the latter being prominent in the previous period (in Tsukushi, Kibi and Izumo; Terasawa 2000, 264–267). The pit mortuary stone chamber of Sanuki-Awa was also emulated; however, the node did not enjoy a particularly significant centrality in the Yayoi V period.

Drawing on the premise of the network analysis conducted earlier, this phenomenon can be explained as the consolidation of the Kinki-core as the paramount *mediator* of the interactions occurring in the network; its mediation of interactions between the nodes (particularly the prominent ones) of the network were symbolically materialised and expressed by the IKP.

MEASURING CENTRALITY

The degree centrality measure (Table 8.9) showed that the Kinki-core and Tsukushi had the highest number of edges connected to them, followed

19 The Makimuku-type itself includes variations in mound shape (cf. Hojo 2000, 99–103), suggesting that various modes and items for the mortuary ritual of the elite were being invented and 'tested out' during the transitional period.

by Izumo, Kibi, Koshi and Owari. The rise in Tsukushi's prominence was due to the onset of direct interactions between Tsukushi and the distant nodes. Koshi's prominence rose due to the commencement of direct interactions with Tsukushi and Owari.

The Bonacich power centrality measure (Table 8.10) showed a slightly different picture from that in the previous period: the Kinki-core was best connected in the network, followed by Izumo, Tsukushi and Koshi. Again, Koshi's rise was notable in this regard. Interestingly, Kibi, which was highly prominent in this measure in the previous period, fell to the sixth position with regard to its connectedness in the network.

The closeness centrality measure (Table 8.11) also generated a slightly different picture from that in the previous period: the Kinki-core and Tsukushi were followed by Izumo, Kibi, Owari and Koshi. Izumo overtook Kibi, while Owari rose in terms of centrality ranking.

TABLE 8.9. *Degree centrality scores of the edges*

Rank	Node	Degree
I	Kinki-core	8.000
I	Tsukushi	8.000
3	Izumo	5.000
3	Kibi	5.000
5	Koshi	5.000
5	Owari	5.000
7	Taniwa	4.000
8	Sanuki-Awa	3.000
9	East	2.000
10	Mainland Asia	1.000

TABLE 8.10. *Bonacich centrality scores of the edges*

Rank	Node	Power
I	Kinki-core	3.783
2	Izumo	3.746
3	Tsukushi	3.652
4	Koshi	3.619
5	Taniwa	3.401
6	Kibi	3.037
7	Owari	2.656
8	Sanuki-Awa	2.236
9	East	1.220
10	Mainland Asia	0.826

TABLE 8.12. *Reach centrality scores of the edges*

Rank	Node	Reach
I	Kinki-core	9.500
I	Tsukushi	9.500
2	Izumo	8.000
4	Kibi	8.000
5	Owari	8.000
5	Koshi	8.000
7	Taniwa	7.500
8	Sanuki-Awa	7.000
9	East	6.333
10	Mainland Asia	5.833

The reach centrality measure (Table 8.12) generated exactly the same picture as that of the closeness centrality measure.

Next, let us look at *the eigenvector centrality measure* (Table 8.13). With regard to this measure, the Kinki-core occupied the first rank, followed by Tsukushi and Izumo. Interestingly, Koshi overtook Kibi once again.

Finally, let us look at the results pertaining to the *betweenness centrality measure* (Table 8.14). Higher scores indicate that more nodes depend on the given node to connect with the other nodes in the network. In other words, a higher score indicates that a node mediates interactions between more nodes than do others in the network. Tsukushi's centrality is quite significant with regard to this measure, followed by the Kinki-core's. However, Izumo and Kibi considerably fell in prominence as compared to their ranks in the previous period, while, rather interestingly, Owari ranked third.

SUMMARY AND DISCUSSION

The consistent prominence of the KCR in the graph coincides well with the centrality of the region in the widespread IKP throughout the network; the KCR's emergent dominance is indicated by the quantitative differences in the contents of the package between the Kinki-core and the other nodes (Figure 8.5).

The outcomes also reveal remarkable coincidences in terms of the increase in the prominence of Izumo, Owari and Koshi. As mentioned earlier, Izumo not only retained its distinct mortuary practices (Figures 8.5 and 8.6.B) but also extended its influence, reflected by the widespread use of its pottery style. Owari became the centre of a widespread distribution of keyhole tumuli with a rectangular rear mound (Figure 8.5; Terasawa 2000, 258–264).

Koshi was to become the supplier of characteristic armlets made of jasper/green tuff and allied items, which constituted the basic contents of the early Kofun mortuary assemblage (i.e. the

TABLE 8.11. *Closeness centrality scores of the edges*

Rank	Node	Closeness
I	Kinki-core	10.000
I	Tsukushi	10.000
3	Izumo	13.000
3	Kibi	13.000
3	Owari	13.000
3	Koshi	13.000
7	Taniwa	14.000
8	Sanuki-Awa	15.000
9	East	17.000
10	Mainland Asia	18.000

TABLE 8.13. *Eigenvector centrality scores of the edges*

Rank	Node	Eigenvector
I	Kinki-core	0.450
2	Tsukushi	0.440
3	Izumo	0.343
4	Koshi	0.341
5	Kibi	0.329
6	Owari	0.315
7	Taniwa	0.292
8	Sanuki-Awa	0.226
9	East	0.142
10	Mainland Asia	0.082

TABLE 8.14. *Betweenness centrality scores of the edges*

Rank	Node	Betweenness
1	Tsukushi	10.833
2	Kinki-core	7.833
3	Owari	2.250
4	Kibi	0.917
5	Izumo	0.583
5	Koshi	0.583
7	Mainland Asia	0.000
7	Sanuki-Awa	0.000
7	Taniwa	0.000
10	East	0.000

developed form of the IKP), distributed from Kinki-core to the heads of regional polities in the subsequent Early Kofun period (Hojo 1996, 320).

The relative decline in Kibi's prominence may also explain why the region became firmly incorporated into the IKP horizon and lost the cultural distinctness it had displayed in the previous period; in the late Yayoi V period, this region saw the development of the *Haniwa* cylindrical jar prototype (see Figure 9.9) and the construction of the Tatetsuki tumulus (Figure 8.6.B), which, according to Kaoru Terasawa, was the prototype of the keyhole tumuli (Terasawa 2000, 260).

Tsukushi's centrality rose due to its establishment of direct contacts with many other nodes of the network (Kusumi 1999, 2007). However, judging from the archaeological evidence, its sociocultural autonomy appears to have significantly reduced during this period: its communities adopted the IKP as their elite mortuary culture, and its pottery assemblage became hybridised with the Kinki-originated Shonai and the earliest Furu assemblages (Figure 8.1; see Section 2 and Footnotes 3 and 4 in this chapter), which eventually almost entirely replaced the original assemblage (Mizoguchi 1988). This appears to contradict the outcomes of the centrality analyses. However, this may not necessarily be the case; the direction of contacts indicates that Tsukushi was predominantly the receiving side of the interactions (Kusumi 2007). This might even have led to the internal fragmentation of the region (Mizoguchi 1988), which would have undoubtedly reduced its integration and centrality.

On the whole, the outcomes of the centrality analyses certainly support the archaeological

evidence: the ups and downs in the centrality of the nodes coincide with the prominence/positions of the regions in the centralised hierarchy of the Initial Kofun period. The nodes that stayed out of the IKP, that is, Izumo and Owari, increased in prominence with regard to their centrality measurements, whereas the nodes that became firmly incorporated into the IKP, such as Kibi and Taniwa, decreased in prominence correspondingly.

Therefore, we can conclude that the emergent inter-regional hierarchy can be explained, to a considerable extent, as caused by the different locations of the respective nodes situated in the network and the different topological characteristics possessed by those nodes. In other words, other factors such as a particular node's increasing dominance over the exploitation of raw materials and its access to and distribution of symbolic and/or subsistence resources/items (and even their *consequences*) were not very significant reasons for the emergence of inter-regional hierarchy in the Initial Kofun period (Mizoguchi 2000). This implies that the KCR-centred hierarchisation, which took place in a short time during the Initial Kofun period, was the realisation of the *potential* of the region, which it already possessed by virtue of its topological structure within the network.

3.3. Networks, Topological Differences and the Contingent Generation of the Kinki-Core Centrality

The period was a watershed in the history of the archipelago. The communal ritual sphere, which involved the use and deposition of bronze spearheads in the northern Kyushu and southwestern Shikoku regions and bronze bells in the Kinki and Tokai regions and formerly constituted an independent field of social reproduction, was replaced by the sphere of elite mortuary practices. This coincided with the widespread construction of keyhole tumuli. The custom of constructing keyhole-shaped mounds and burying the elite in them was adopted by many elite groups across western and eastern Japan as far east as the southern Kanto region.[20]

20 There are, for instance, three successively-constructed Makimuku-type tumuli, Godo (神門) Nos. 3–5 tumuli, in the ancient Kazusa province, present-day Chiba prefecture (cf. Tanaka 1984).

The phenomena further coincided with the increasing distribution of bronze mirrors and allied items imported from China, along with products imported from the Korean peninsula and locally produced goods, to regions as far east as the Chubu region; at the same time, there was an increasing distribution of iron implements across western Japan and wide areas of eastern Japan (Murakami 1998). Imports from the southern regions of the Korean peninsula began to reach regions as far east as the southern Kanto region. In addition to all this, as we have already seen, port-of-trade-type settlements emerged across the horizon, which were to be shortly marked by the widespread construction of keyhole tumuli.

As observed earlier, the quantity of flow of goods and information appears to have constantly increased throughout the Yayoi period. Its mediation and control, together with the management of various production activities, led to the increasing hierarchisation of social relations and the increasing segmentation of sodality-type corporate groupings. The widespread distribution of keyhole tumuli and the increasingly formalised allied mortuary practices resulted in the formation of a widespread elite mortuary interaction sphere. The fact that its horizon roughly coincided with the widening distribution of various goods and items that had formerly been limited to either northern Kyushu or western Japan suggests that the formation of the sphere was related to not only the increase in the flow of goods and information but also changes in the nature of the flow.

It has been mentioned that the topological locations of the regional polities, rather than their character and content, significantly influenced hierarchisation in the individual polities as well as the formation of a centralised hierarchy in the Initial Kofun period. Both the positions of the regional polities in the hierarchy and the ups and downs they experienced from the late Yayoi V to the Initial Kofun periods have shown a remarkable coincidence with the results of the centrality measures in terms of the topological positions of the nodes in the graphs representing the networks of the Yayoi V and Initial Kofun periods.

This fact does not, however, refute the importance of the strategies employed by the emergent elite in each of the polities. For instance, as mentioned earlier, distinct elements of mortuary traditions that had developed in the polities, which were later to become prominent members of the hierarchised alliance, were deliberately combined to form the IKP (Hojo 1999a, 2000, 87–90; Terasawa 2000, 264–267). It is an indisputable fact that the ingenious strategy of the elite groups which led to the formation of the centralised hierarchical alliance also resulted in the creation of this sophisticated mortuary communication medium. It has also been suggested that during the earliest phase of the Initial Kofun period (i.e. the Shonai pottery style phase following the Yayoi V), the Kinki-core had established contact with the northern Yellow Sea coast, where the Chinese Wei empire's commandery of Daifeng was later to be reestablished (see Chapter 4.3; Fukunaga et al. 2003, 147–158). Based on this, some scholars argue that the establishment of this contact, reflected by the presence of bronze mirrors of a certain type (those with deity-beast motifs, called *Gamontai-shinjyu-kyo*, which date back to between the late second and the early third centuries AD; Okamura 1999, 134–144; Fukunaga et al. 2003, 147–158), placed the chief(s) of the Kinki-core in the advantageous position of being granted the paramount chieftaincy of the domain represented by IKP distribution by the Wei emperor (Okamura 1999, 134–144; Fukunaga et al. 2003, 147–158). The strategic presentation of exclusive diplomatic ties with such an exotic source of authority as the Wei Empire might have been sufficient for the chief of the Kinki-core to ascend to the top of the emergent hierarchy. However, it is also necessary to realise that the effectiveness of a chosen strategy would have been strongly influenced by the resources that could be mobilised by the agents for the implementation of that strategy and by the way in which the strategy was received by other agents sharing the arena of competitive interactions. Keeping in mind the fact that the regional polities in the process of hierarchisation were equally integrated and hierarchised internally, the latter factor; i.e., the way in which a given strategy was received by other agents sharing the arena of competitive interactions, would have been particularly important. The topological position of the node in which the agents acted would have strongly influenced these factors.

If we relate this issue to the conceptualisation of power, it is important to remember that power implies two facets: the first is 'power over', whereas the second is 'power to' (cf. Miller and Tilley 1984, 5–8). The former constrains those who are subjected to the exercise of power in making choices and doing things. The latter, in contrast, expands or transforms the range of people's thoughts and actions. This is the power to make the improbable probable (Miller and Tilley 1984). By doing something regarded by many as natural, a powerful agent can make a thing that was formerly improbable not only probable but also perceived as something that is necessary. Further, this kind of power is often generated rather than imposed.

Drawing on the implications of 'power to', we can relate this notion to the emergence of the *enabler* and the *enabled* in an emergent network. The KCR was situated in such a location in the network that it could become the paramount mediator of the interactions that took place between the nodes in the network; this implied that the KCR was the paramount enabler as well. Once recognized as the paramount mediator, through actual gift-givings, various negotiations and exchanges that took place in the port-of-trade-type settlements, for instance, the network could not function without the mediation of the KCR, and its intervention in the interactions between the polities would have increasingly been regarded as necessary and even natural. Under these circumstances, the KCR's exclusive access to the Wei dynasty and its prestigious items, such as certain types of bronze mirrors, and the strategic distribution of these items would have further strengthened its status as the paramount mediator authorised by the external 'superpower' (i.e. the Wei dynasty). The formation of the IKP and its distribution from the KCR to the elite of the other polities, the latter being the lesser enablers of interactions within the network, also reflects this fact.

This process began in the late Yayoi V period, circa from the late first to the late second centuries AD, and continued until the end of the fifth century AD, by which time the scale difference between the largest keyhole tumuli of the KCR and that of the other polities had become decisively widened and a primitive bureaucratic organization had emerged (Shiraishi 1999, 141–168; see Chapter 9 of the present volume). The process was, as illustrated, set in motion by an increase in the flow of goods and information from mainland Asia. It has to be emphasised that it was not a polity's wilful attainment of dominance over others that *solely* led to centralised hierarchisation; it was the network system in which the polities were situated and its topological structure that hierarchised *itself* by differentiating the mediator/centre from the mediated/dependent. From this point of view, the rise of a centralised hierarchy, in Japan at least, can be partially but significantly explained as a *self-organised phenomenon*.

4. CONCLUSION: THE BEGINNING OF A NEW WORLD

To conclude this chapter, let us discuss why the gigantic keyhole tumuli were built and what were their intended functions.

I would argue that the tumuli were designed to serve as symbolic focal points for the creation and reproduction of the order of the world. The unique mound shape was created by combining and modifying several regional mounded burial traditions. The same was true in the case of burial facilities (Hojo 2000, 87–90).

The grave good assemblage was again created by putting together and modifying the regionally developed assemblages. Significantly, some of the exotic items were transformed by using different materials to make them; for instance, various armlets, originally made of exotic shells that could only be procured from regions around the Okinawa islands (see Chapter 6), came to be made of jasper or green tuff procured from the Hokuriku region. Shells were imported from the periphery or even outside the sphere of normal contact during the Yayoi, and items made of rare stones were brought in from the north-eastern edge of the distribution of the earliest keyhole tumulus. These might have metaphorically represented the deceased persons' control over contacts with the *edge of the world* within which the communities (and their elite) could potentially communicate with one another and beyond.

The contents of the assemblage were of a particular symbolic-metaphorical significance: the iron tool assemblage often consisted of (a) weapons, (b) woodworking implements, (c) agricultural implements and, albeit rarely, (d) fishing implements – an interesting component (see Figure 9.5 and relevant descriptions). These appear to represent the dominant spheres of social life in terms of all the important types of labour, that is: (a) communal defence; (b) making various wooden implements, including those used for agricultural work; (c) agricultural activities; and (d) fishing activities, respectively. The iron tools, in that sense, metaphorically represent significant interfaces with different types of complexities and contingencies generated by both the natural and cultural environments experienced by the people. In addition, the tools classified under (b), (c) and (d) might also have represented the three components of the entire lifeworld, with (b) representing the mountain, (c) representing the floodplain and (d) representing the sea.

The assemblage also often included mirrors called Sankaku (triangular)–en (rimmed)–shinju (deity-beast-motifed)–kyo (mirror). At present, scholars are involved in a fierce debate on whether the typo-chronologically earlier categories of the specimens were made somewhere in the domain of the Chinese Wei dynasty or in the centre of their distribution, that is, the present-day southern Kinki region (Fukunaga, et al. 2003; Terasawa 2000, 305–316). Regardless of where they were made, however, we can safely say that they represented an alien system of meanings and contacts with an authority and power residing outside the domain within which the communities (and their elite) could potentially communicate.

On the whole, many of the attributes of the earliest keyhole tumulus metaphorically represented the *world* – whose integration, working and history were symbolised by the tumulus. The attributes also represented the three main components of the lifeworld, that is, the mountain, the floodplain and the sea, and the distinct activities conducted in them. Moreover, the keyhole tumulus was utterly new in terms of its gigantic scale, beyond comparison with its regional predecessors, as well as its shape; hence, it was alien to even those who constructed it and buried their elite dead for the first time. In short, the earliest keyhole tumulus represented the beginning, the history of the integration and the working of the world across which the tumulus and the mortuary custom embodied by it were adopted.

As we have seen, the time leading to the emergence of the earliest keyhole tumulus witnessed the formation of an extremely wide interaction network covering the areas which were later to form the horizon wherein the earliest keyhole tumuli were constructed and reacted to by subsequent generations. This was ignited by (a) the differentiation of elite lineage-scale segments in clan-type sodalities across the areas; (b) the increasing density and frequency of inter-communal contacts and the growing reliance on them by the communities, and particularly their elite, for their reproduction; (c) the intensification of inter-communal competition over dominance in such contacts and over the exchange of goods, information and people; and (d) the rise of the Chinese empires as the ultimate source of authority for legitimising the dominance. These emergent factors would have necessitated the sharing of a unified structure enabling the reproduction of an elite communication sphere, within which the increasingly differentiated and stabilised elite groups competed against one another over dominance, on the one hand, and collaborated with each other for the constant, uninterrupted flow of goods, information and people for the reproduction of their communities, on the other.

Such a structure, ensuring the continuation of the elite communications, would have needed to symbolically and metaphorically embody the traditional values formerly followed while integrating them with a totally new value so as to represent the *order of the world* which transcended the differences between those old value systems. In that regard, the newness and alien nature of the earliest tumulus, as mentioned above, seems particularly significant. In a number of mythical narratives describing the origin of chieftainship/kingship, the first chief/king is supposed to have come from *outside the domain* (e.g. Sahlins 1985, chap. 2). This kingly individual, in the narratives, destroyed the old order and established a new one, as if re-creating the world.

The fact that the reproduction of the elite interaction sphere relied predominantly upon the unification of mortuary practices provides another important clue to our understanding of the social processes which occurred in the Yayoi-Kofun transitional period. The flow of goods, people and information, as argued above, sharply increased in the late Yayoi V period. The phenomenon coincided with the beginning of people's movement across long distances, for instance, between the Kinki and the northern Kyushu region (represented by the presence of Kinki-originated Yayoi V vessels at the Hie-Naka site, along with local-styled vessels partly made using techniques originating in the Kinki region; Fukuoka MBE 1996b; also see Footnote 3 to this chapter). As mentioned earlier, the late Yayoi V saw the consolidation of the differentiation between large, central-place-type settlements and smaller, satellite-type ones (see Figures 7.8, 7.9 and 7.12), and the former increasingly became the nodes of long-distance interactions. This suggests that in the central-place-type settlements of regional communities, negotiations over the exchange of goods (and possibly people) increasingly involved people from distant places who did not share the same set of customs and expectations as the local population. The emergence of such a situation would have made communications pertaining to the exchange of goods increasingly difficult and stressful. One of the most effective solutions for tackling this problem would have been to forge fictive-kinship ties among those who were involved in the negotiations, regardless of their genuine backgrounds and community affiliations. Marshall Sahlins ([1974] 2004) beautifully illustrates the correlation between increasing kin-distance and the shift of the mode of exchange from sharing through gift-giving/equal-value exchange to strategic exchange, and suggests that the stress and risk of the breakdown of relationships tended to increase as the kin-distance increased and the mode and norm of exchange became increasingly strategic and profit-oriented. Those involved in negotiations that occurred at the central-place-type settlements would have been mutually perceived as belonging to different tribal groupings, and Sahlins observes that exchange acts between tribal groupings tend to be strategic, profit-oriented exchanges that often result in the total breakdown of the relationship (ibid.). In order to avoid this possibility, it would have been preferable to forge fictive-kinship ties, as suggested above. In this regard, ritual practices involving the deposition of bronze items, that is, bronze bells in and around the Kinki region and bronze spearheads across the northern Kyushu and southern Shikoku regions, used to pray for the well-being of the living community, would *not* have been very effective in forging fictive-kinship ties (see Figure 7.4).

Clearly, the burial of the dead would have served as a significant occasion wherein various kin-based social ties were confirmed, restructured and newly forged. In that sense, the sudden emergence of variously shaped tumuli across western Japan in the late Yayoi V (Figures 7.4 and 8.6.B), the subsequent, and quite sudden, abandonment of the rituals involving bronze bells and bronze spearheads in the Shonai pottery style period and the beginning of the formalisation of keyhole tumuli during the same period can all be understood as correlated phenomena that were part of a unified reaction to the rising difficulties generated by the increasing long-distance interactions and the ever-widening sphere of the exchange of goods, people and information.[21]

In that sense, I am tempted to speculate that the construction of the Hashihaka (Hashinakayama) tumulus, the largest among the earliest keyhole tumuli (it is about 280 metres long; Figure 8.3), was a massive ceremonial event marking, and re-enacting as well, the birth of the world consisting of criss-crossing (fictive) kinship ties. I would further like to speculate that the elite groups and members of their communities involved in the formation of the new order and its network might have willingly volunteered to construct the tumuli: designing the mound shape and deciding how to furnish the mound and the mortuary facility/facilities, what grave goods to bury and how to conduct the ceremonies would have all acquired ritualistic-magical meanings associated with prayers for ensuring the well-being of the (fictive) kinship-tie-based communities involved

21 The port-of-trade-type settlements, as discussed above, would have been established by the elite of respective regions in order to ease the problems generated by the increasing presence of people from remote regions in their central-place-type settlements. These artificially created locales were expressly formed to facilitate negotiations between people from different backgrounds and with different communal affiliations, and a range of etiquettes would have been observed in these places. In that sense, it is natural that their reason for existence ceased once the flow of goods was stabilised by the establishment of centralised exchange networks under the increasing control of the elite of the KCR; following this, the ports-of-trade were abandoned – their maintenance would have been costly for the regional communities and their elite because those settlements, due to their coastal locations, needed to be supplied foodstuffs and almost all the other subsistence goods.

in the interaction network and of the network itself. Without doubt, those who presided over the ceremony would have assumed the position of the supreme mediator and kin-based-community-leader of the network. This would have signalled the beginning, not the conclusion, of the consolidation process of inter-communal/regional community hierarchisation.

We might be led to infer that a sophisticated hierarchical organisation consisting of multilayered systems for mobilising people/labour force would have constituted a necessary precondition for the construction of such a vast, monumental structure (e.g. Kondo 1983). We might also naturally assume that a system of coercion, albeit not very sophisticated, was in place at the time. However, if we turn our attention to some classical ethnographies of communally organised large-scale projects, such as a Kula voyage by a Trobriand Island chief (Malinowski [1922] 1984), we find several historical instances wherein a vast number of people, at times over a thousand, have gathered without any coercion in order to accomplish a certain task(s). In the Trobriand case, people come together to fulfil their kin obligation to the chief of a relatively simple stratified organisation. Each of a number of stages comprising such projects is often associated with a specific ritual conducted by either the chief or a shamanistic figure. The members often firmly believe that the honour and prosperity of their community is dependent on the success of the project (ibid.).

Obviously, a similar picture would have been seen in many other 'public' projects apart from the construction of keyhole tumuli, but I would like to particularly highlight the fact that it is possible to assemble a large-scale labour force with a relatively simple organisation for fulfilling a communal obligation and ensuring communal prosperity.

In the case of one of the earliest, but not the oldest, keyhole tumuli with the IKP, the Tobi (外山; Sakurai, 桜井) Chausuyama (茶臼山) tumulus (approximately 208 metres long), scholars have pointed out the possibility that people from the Tokai region to the east were involved in its construction; the Sotoyama (外山) location of the Shikishima (城島) site, situated 250 metres to the north of the tumulus, yielded wooden implements and pots, including large cooking vessels,

which appear to have been either brought from the Tokai region or made in the style of the region. It has also been suggested that the double-rimmed and narrow-necked vessels placed to mark the rectangular earthen platform with a long stone cist containing a coffin at its centre[22] might show connections with the Tokai region; they were frequently used in the region at the time that the use of *Haniwa* cylindrical vessels (see Chapter 9) became prevalent in most of the Kinki-core (Takahashi 2008, 119). The tumulus was possibly the largest tumulus across the IKP horizon amongst the tumuli constructed roughly at the same archaeological temporal horizon and was located at the entrance of a valley connecting the Nara Basin to the Tokai region. These factors suggest that the construction of the tumulus was a massive ceremonial occasion involving a large number of people from the Tokai region. Regarding the presence of the possibly Tokai-originating traits, they might have been moblised for the fulfilment of inter-communal obligations, possibly based on kin-ties forged between the respective elite of the Nara Basin and the Tokai region. They are unlikely to have been forcibly mobilised by the order of the elite of the former; the latter continued to bury their elite dead in keyhole tumuli with a square rear mound and maintained their traditional cultural traits, making it highly unlikely that the communities of the region were under tight control/rule of the elite of the Nara Basin/KCR.

In any case, the centrality of the Kinki-core was reinforced by the elite communication sphere, materially marked by the IKP and the keyhole tumulus, the construction of which was a spectacular ceremonial event representing the beginning, history and working of the lifeworld, crisscrossed by actual and fictive kin ties. The status of the elite of the communities situated in the vast, newly emerging network of interactions and the well-being of those communities would have been regarded as contingent on the successful performance of the ceremony, and a massive amount of labour and essential symbolic and material

---

22 The latest excavation of the platform has revealed that it was surrounded by about 150 logs, standing possibly as high as more than 2 metres (Higashikage 2011, 90–91).

resources were mobilised for it. By this time, the material reproduction of the communities had become increasingly dependent on the ceremonial mediation by the centre, which in turn would have increasingly enhanced and secured the position and status of the elite presiding over the ceremonial sphere. The next chapter mainly discusses the ways in which this emergence of the *supreme/paramount-mediator figure* affected the trajectories of the fields of social reproduction.

CHAPTER 9

AN ARCHAEOLOGY OF MONUMENTS: THE EARLY KOFUN (AD 275–400) AND MIDDLE KOFUN PERIODS (AD 400–500)

1. OVERVIEW

As we have seen in the previous chapter, the Yayoi–Kofun transitional period witnessed the generation of the elite interaction network/sphere, the reproduction of which was materially mediated and embodied by the Initial Kofun Package (IKP). The IKP comprised a range of material items, including portable and monumental items, as well as the technologies to mobilise them, many of which can be found in their prototypes from the Yayoi period, as mentioned in the previous chapter. These items and technologies were assembled together in the Kinki-core region (KCR; also see the previous chapter); however, their widespread distribution does not appear to have been *imposed* on others by the particular group(s) of the KCR. Instead, they were *adopted* and *shared* by the emergent elite of individual regions who tried to achieve dominance over the other elite in their respective regions by joining the elite communication sphere. In the previous chapter, I had suggested that the progression of the differentiation of sub-clans or lineages within individual clan-type sodalities and their hierarchisation accelerated this *competitive emulation* of a new material-technological package symbolising the elite communication sphere, mediated by the sharing of uniform modes of worshiping certain *ancestral, transcendental* spirits and of enacting the history of the beginning, integration and working of the world (e.g. Kondo 1983; also see Chapter 8.4). In addition, the presence of kin-based sodalities, regardless genuine or fictive, formed through the exchange of marriage partners and criss-crossing individual settlements and sometimes forming very long-distance networks of flow of people, goods and information served as the

infrastructure for the formation and reproduction of this large elite interaction sphere. The previous chapter also maintained that the very formation of these large-scale networks, on which the regional communities increasingly relied for their reproduction, necessitated the formation of the IKP horizon (cf. Mizoguchi 2000; Hirose 2003; also Chapter 8.3–4).

The process which had begun in the Yayoi–Kofun transitional period continued into the Early (from the late third century to the late or end of the fourth century AD) and Middle Kofun (from the end of the fourth or early fifth century to the end of the fifth century AD) periods.[1] The KCR appears to have increasingly consolidated its domination over contacts with the outside world, that is, the polities of the Korean peninsula, during the

---

[1] The Early and Middle Kofun periods are commonly divided into phases. Seigo Wada, for instance, divides each of them into four phases, while numbering them from I to VIII (Wada 1987). Phases I–IV constitute the Early Kofun period, while Phases V–VIII represent the Middle Kofun period. In this volume, for the sake of simplicity, I have referred to the earlier two phases of each period (i.e. Phases I and II, Phases V and VI) as the 'first half' and the later two phases (i.e. Phases III and IV, Phases VII and VIII) as the 'second half' of that respective period. Therefore, a phenomenon that occurred during Wada's Phase II will be described as having occurred during the first half of the Early Kofun period, and during Phase VII, as having occurred during the second half of the Middle Kofun period. The absolute dates can be determined by referring to the datable artefacts imported from the Korean peninsula and mainland China, but these only indicate the terminus post quem (TPQ) of the artefacts. This, and other related issues that inevitably introduce a degree of speculative argumentation, imply that the absolute dates mentioned are quite likely to contain a fair margin of errors (cf. Hishida 2007, 22–36).

Early Kofun period, and during the Middle Kofun period, the *Book of Song* (宋書) and other works have recorded that five successive paramount chiefs of the KCR (*Wa-no-go-oh*, 倭五王) had dispatched their emissaries to the Jin (晋) and the Liu Song (劉宋) dynasties of China (e.g. Yoshida 1998; see also Chapter 4.3). The contact with the latter appears to have been monopolised by the KCR, though some local polities forged and maintained ties with the communities of the peninsula throughout the periods.[2]

The KCR also constantly added new items to the mortuary package (Hirose 2003). This practice can be characterised as the constant renewal of the contents of the package, which effectively maintained the process of competitive emulation among those who were given the items, those who copied them and those who relied on them. The package was distributed across the horizon, which extended from the Osumi province of south-eastern Kyushu to the southern and northern edges of the southern Tohoku region and covered the present-day Sendai Plain (Fujisawa 2004a) while extending farther north during the Middle Kofun period.[3] The largest keyhole tumulus of the KCR was generally also the largest in the entire archipelago, and the tumuli size continued to increase fairly consistently, with some notable ups and downs (which I discuss later). To sum up, the previously mentioned process can be described as the increasing dominance of the KCR over the other regions within the expanding horizon of the keyhole tumuli. The previous chapter mentioned that the construction of individual tumuli metaphorically marked the beginning of a new world. In that case, the preceding suggests that the continuous renewal – and indeed the well-being – of the world depended upon the way in which the elite of the KCR buried their dead chiefs. By emulating the KCR elite,

the elite of the other regions ensured the well-being of their own worlds and reconfirmed their own identities.

However, this appears to be too simplistic a picture, which seems to overemphasise the degree of centralisation and stratification in the relationship between the KCR elite and those of the other regions, while it underestimates the significance of their strategic interdependence. To begin with, the relationship between the elite of the dominant groups of the KCR may not have been stabilised despite the achievement of a certain degree of intra- and inter-communal stratification; during a phase in the first half of the Early Kofun period (c. the end of the third century), the largest and the second-largest tumuli were almost of the same size (i.e. the Nishitono-zuka [西殿塚], approximately 219 metres long, and the Sakurai [桜井; Tobi 外山] Chausuyama [茶臼山], approximately 208 metres long), but shaped quite differently. Something similar again occurred during another a phase in the beginning of the Middle Kofun period (the late fourth century to the beginning of the fifth century) with regard to two other tumuli (i.e. the Suyama [巣山], approximately 220 metres long, and the Tsudo-Shiroyama [津堂城山], approximately 208 metres long), both within the KCR. This suggests that the succession of paramount chieftainship was either disputed or destabilised at the time, suggesting that more than two chiefs claimed the paramount chieftainship. There was also a phase in the first half of the Middle Kofun period (the end of the fourth or beginning of the early fifth century to the early fifth century) when the two largest tumuli were constructed contemporaneously, one in the KCR (the Kami'ishizu Misanzai [上石津ミサンザイ] tumulus) and the other in the Kibi province (the Tsukuriyama [造山] tumulus), both measuring approximately 360 metres in length. In this case, we can assume the same possibilities as we did earlier. These suggest a persistent instability in inter-elite relationships within the KCR as well as between the KCR and certain other regions as regards the succession to the paramount chieftainship, provided that it was indeed represented by the largest mound size. As mentioned in Chapter 8.4, the construction of these gigantic tumuli itself was an important ceremonial occasion that would have involved the participation of a number of

2 For instance, as we will see later in the present chapter, polities of northern and central Kyushu forged and maintained ties with that of the south western part of the peninsula (later to become the ancient state of Paekche [百済]), that led to the introduction of the custom of burying the dead in gallery chambers to the former regions in the second half of the Early Kofun period.

3 The Tsunozuka (角塚) tumulus, situated in the Kitakami river basin of present-day Iwate prefecture is the northern most keyhole tumuli, dating from the first half of the Late Kofun period.

communities, some residing quite far from the place of construction. The presence of more than one such tumulus constructed contemporaneously, in that sense, would imply the splitting of the regional communities' allegiance to the 'candidates' that contested the paramount chieftainship.

Individual keyhole tumuli continued to consist of a matrix of traits with different genealogies: some of them derived from KCR-originated traditions, but they also contained many locally unique traits (Hojo 2000, 87–90; Terasawa 2000, 264–267). This reinforces the impression that the relationships between the regions and the communities constituting them were not rigidly centralised and hierarchised but still remained fairly fluid, though influences of the KCR would have been felt increasingly strongly in the other regions. The relationship might be better described as a kind of interdependence which was sustained to reproduce the order of individual regions and communities, including the ones comprising the KCR itself, on their own terms.

The introduction of sophisticated construction, manufacturing and agricultural technologies from the Korean peninsula, which was accelerated in the second half of the Early Kofun period and reached its peak in the Middle Kofun period, resulted in the emergence of certain communities – often including large numbers of migrants from the peninsula – who carried out ironworking, *Sue* stoneware production, horse rearing, salt production and so on (e.g. Hishida 2007). It has been argued that in the KCR, Kibi and Tsukushi provinces, the manufacturing communities were strategically situated so as to fall under the increasingly tight control of the elite of those regions, and some scholars even argue that those polities had by then acquired the characteristics of the primitive/inchoate state (e.g. Hishida 2007, 39–63, esp. 62). This also shows that some of the regional polities at this stage were autonomous. In any case, the new manufacturing technologies would have transformed the lives of both the elite and the commoners by generating new desires, identities and opportunities for competition, all of which needed to be dealt with at the social level. On the whole, the well-being of individual communities/polities would have been perceived as depending significantly upon successfully burying the dead in a highly formalised, monumental manner, leaving behind monumental

tumuli as the material trace of the practice as well as the embodiment of the materialisation of their beliefs. The practice was perceived and designed to maintain harmonious intra- and inter-polity relations, but it also provided societies the resources and opportunities to compete with and challenge the dominant societies.

Let us begin our exploration of these periods of monumental tumuli construction by examining the Kofun tumuli themselves, because the transformation of social life during these periods and the problems and contradictions generated by this transformation appear to have been well embodied by the contents of the contemporaneous tumuli and their transformations. In addition, it is evident that their construction and related (ritualistic) practices would have been a reaction to the problems and contradictions generated by the changing times.

2. IMPLICATIONS OF THE KEYHOLE TUMULUS

The keyhole tumulus is not only the most prominent archaeological material available for the study of the periods but also embodies the uniquely ritualised discourse of the time that represented the way in which various concerns of the people of the time – both the elite and the commoners – were negotiated and settled in highly symbolic manners. The absence of any other equivalent to the regional-centre-type settlements of the Yayoi or any administrative-centre-type site apart from the elite residential sites,[4] which were often situated near the keyhole tumuli (e.g. Mitsudera [三ツ寺] site, Gunma prefecture; Gunma PBE 1988, 1991), suggests that the construction of the tumuli itself played a significant role in reproducing social cohesion and maintaining social networks (see e.g. Hojo 2000, 128–131). The macro- and micro-distribution patterns of the tumuli reflect the genealogical dynamics of chieftains and their changing political relations and hierarchies.

---

4 The KCR, the Kibi and the northern Kyushu regions, however, saw the formation of complexes of elite residential compounds, special production settlements (e.g. for Iron and stone-ware productions), and keyhole tumuli clusters in the Middle Kofun period (see pp. 291–294 in the present chapter, and Hishida 2007, 54–63).

Besides, as argued in the previous chapter, the tumuli symbolically embodied the 'world' in which those who were buried and those who buried their leaders resided. It suggests that the changing contents of the tumuli – the grave good assemblage, burial facilities, mound size and shape, and various other items and features placed on and around the mound – represent the changing meanings attached to the tumuli and their construction. The following section explains some basic facts concerning those traits and factors and attempts to capture their implications.

2.1. Mound 'Shape-Types'

There are some other mound shape-types apart from the keyhole type among the tumuli constructed during the Kofun period; these are described as follows (Figure 9.1).

In addition to the keyhole type (the K type), the Kofun period also saw the construction of some round (R) and square (S) types of tumuli. As we have already seen, the K-type tumuli consist of two sub-categories – those with a round larger part (K-1) and those with a square larger part (K-2). The larger part of a tumulus is customarily called the *rear* mound, while the smaller part is called the *front* mound; hence, in Japanese, the K-1 type is called the *Zen* (前, front) *po* (方, square) – *ko* (後, rear) – *en* (円, round) – *fun* (墳, tumulus; 前方後円墳), and the K-2 type *Zen* (前, front) – *po* (方, square) – *ko* (後, rear) – *ho* (方, square) – *fun* (墳, tumulus; 前方後方墳).

There also exist a few unique and important variants that are derived from or related to the K-1 category: K-1 tumuli with a very small frontal square part (widely called the *Hotategai-gata* [帆立貝形, scallop-shaped type, SC]) and those with two square mounds conjoined to the round central mound, in which one mound is sometimes smaller than the other (called the square-round-square type, SRS, 双方中円墳).

In addition, there are a small number of tumuli with a round mound placed on top of a square base (SR; 上円下方墳) and a much smaller number of octagonal tumuli (O; 八角墳).

The K, R, S and SRS types of tumuli were constructed from the beginning of the Kofun period to almost its end, though the R type appears to have (re-)emerged slightly later than the K (e.g.

Shiraishi 1985, 33–39).[5] The SC type might have emerged during the Early Kofun period, but the majority of SC type tumuli were built between the beginning of the Middle Kofun period and the first half of the Late Kofun period (Shiraishi 1985, 39–40). The previous chapter has already touched upon the different but significantly overlapping distributions of the K-1 and K-2 types during the Early Kofun period. The distribution of the SRS type was mostly confined to the Sanuki province (present-day Kagawa prefecture), but there is a large example of this type in the Nara Basin (the Kushiyama [櫛山] tumulus, approximately 152 metres long, dating from the second half of the Early Kofun period; Figure 9.1.E). It is possible that these differences between types of tumuli were mobilised to signify some sort of (*ancestral*) group affiliation or group-related identities of the deceased, though they also appear to have been used at times to indicate the status differences between the deceased (see the following discussion). The SR and O types of tumuli emerged towards the very end of the Kofun period, by when the construction of the K type had ceased, except for in the Kanto region (see Chapter 10.4 of this volume). Their emergence is widely understood to mark the end of the social order and its maintenance mechanisms symbolically embodied by the K-1 tumuli (Kondo 1983, 363–381). An increasing number of scholars differentiate this phase from the Late Kofun period, referring to the former as the Final/Terminal (終末期) Kofun period (Table 3.1; see Chapter 11 of this volume).

The mound shape of the K type changed over time. Researchers have investigated this changing mound shape from various viewpoints, including the planning stages (Ueda 1969), the units of measurement used for the planning (ibid.), the function(s) fulfilled by the rear and front mounds

5 The tradition of small round tumuli distributed across the eastern Seto Inland Sea region from the late Middle to the end of the Yayoi, but it appears to have ceased in the beginning of the Kofun. When they re-emerged at the end of the first half of the Early Kofun, they were equipped with facilities similar to that of the K type, occasionally with less sophistication. They may have been reinvented to represent status/categorical differences of the buried from that of the K type. The emergence of the SC type has also been explained similarly (Ugaki 2004).

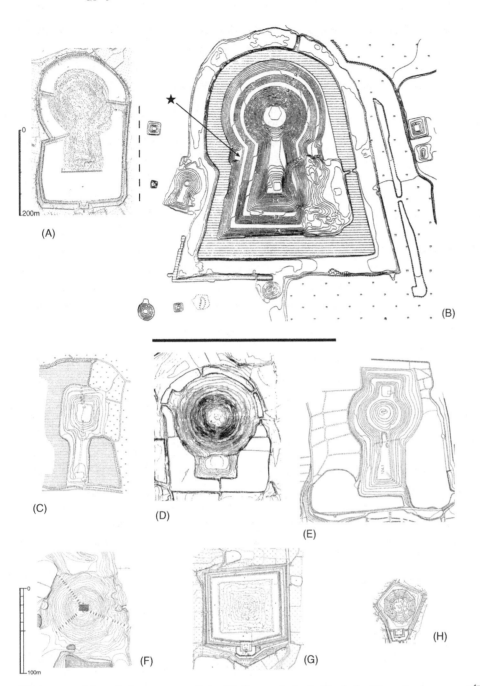

Figure 9.1. Mound shape-types of the Kofun period. **A**: Keyhole (K-1; Andonyama [行燈山], after Suenaga [1975], dating from Phase II; see Footnote 1), **B**: Keyhole (K-1; Konda-Gobyoyama [誉田御廟山], after Suenaga [1975], dating from Phase VI), **C**: Keyhole (K-2; Shimoikeyama [下池山], after Suenaga [1975]), **D**: Scallop (SC; Otomeyama [乙女山], after Kondo [1992, 533]; original in Nara Prefectural Kashihara Archaeological Research Institute [1988]), **E**: Square-round-square (SRS; Kushiyama [櫛山], after Suenaga [1975]), **F**: Round (R; Tomio Maruyama [富雄丸山], after Kyoto National Museum [1982]), **G**: Square (S; Kasuga-Mukaiyama [春日向山], after Suenaga [1975]), **H**: Octagonal (O; Noguchi Onohaka [野口王墓], after Shiraishi [2000]; original from Suenaga [1975]). One of the *Tsukuridashi* platforms of the Konda-Gobyoyama (B), characteristic attribute of the keyhole tumuli of the Middle Kofun period, is marked with a star.

(e.g. Kobayashi and Kondo 1959, 11–15), how they were used in the mortuary rituals (Kondo 1983, 194–196) and so on. The general trend can be described as follows: (1) the height of the rear mound was greater than that of the front mound in the beginning, but by the end of the Middle Kofun period, the latter became greater than the former; (2) the width of the frontal end of the front mound became wider as its height increased, and by the Late Kofun period, it far exceeded the diameter of the rear mound (e.g. Kobayashi and Kondo 1959, 11–15). It is difficult to ascertain the determinant cause of this trend. Yukio Kobayashi and Yoshiro Kondo, for instance, have related the enlargement of the front mound to the actual reduction in the size of the rear mound due to the introduction of the gallery mortuary chamber; it was a common practice to situate the main room of the gallery mortuary chamber, which contained the coffin(s), at the centre of the rear mound and to situate the base of the chamber on the bedrock. Therefore, since the normal length of such chambers rarely exceeded 16 metres, the diameter of the rear mound could only measure around 30 metres, or 60 metres at most (ibid., 13–15). However, the diameter of the rear mound of some of the largest tumuli built during the Late Kofun period – such as the Imashirozuka (今城塚) tumulus – exceeds 60 metres (the mound length: about 190 metres; the diameter of the round rear mound: about 100 metres; Kondo 1992, 280–281), thus falsifying the above-mentioned thesis. The thesis also disregards the fact that the trend of enlargement of the front mound had already begun in the Early Kofun period.

Two factors can help us to infer the cause of this trend: first, the progression of the trend corresponded with an increase in the general height of the whole mound, as also in the steepness of the mound; second, the front mound would, in fact, have been the *front side* of the mound, while the main burial facility, without exception, was situated in the rear mound. Synthesising these two factors, we can observe the following: the progression of the trend enhanced the visual impact of the mound while effectively concealing the place of burial of the deceased. The front mounds, which became increasingly higher and steeper, effectively hid the rear mounds from view, thus concealing the burial place of the dead chief when seen from the front side or from the foot of the front mound. This trend can be connected with the establishment of facilities such as moat(s) and banks surrounding and bounding the mound and the changes in the way the body of the dead chief was buried (the latter will be described in detail below). The resting place of the chief, as argued in the previous chapter, was probably designed as the miniature

materialisation of the world, while the body of the dead chief was used to embody the order of the world and hence became the focal point of praying for the well-being of the community and the world. The second half of the Early Kofun period saw the beginning of the practice of surrounding the mound with a moat and/or other facilities in the KCR, while the Middle Kofun period saw the establishment and formalisation of the custom and its (uneven) spread outside the KCR (e.g. Wada 1987). This can be understood as the increasing sophistication of the idea of representing the tumulus as a miniature of the world, featuring metaphorical representations of the sea (i.e. the moat) and the land (or mountain, i.e. the mound). The general increase in the height and steepness of the mound can be understood in relation to this trend. The specific development of the height of the front mound can be understood in relation to the transformation of the way in which the dead chief was portrayed in the mortuary rituals, from (X) the *embodiment* of the order of the world and the focal point of prayers for the well-being of the community and the world to (Y) the *commander* in charge of organising labour activities among the commoners for the well-being of the community and the world. Mode X required the resting place of the chief to be widely visible, from the frontal part of the mound, in particular, whereas mode Y would have made it preferable for the resting place of the chief to be generally known but still invisible, in reality, whereby to enhance its sense of *untouchability* and *inaccessibility*. Considering that the mound was intended to be seen from its frontal side, that is, the frontal side of the front mound, the rear mound became *invisible* at some point in the Middle Kofun period. This period, as we will see in the following, also witnessed the development of the custom of depositing a large quantity of tools and weapons either in compartments in the burial cist or in facilities specifically built for their deposition (see the following Shiraishi 1985, 79–81). These grave goods would have represented the chief's ability to amass such a quantity of tools and weapons for defending the community and ensuring its well-being. In other words, the chief gradually became perceived and portrayed as a *ruler* figure. I would like to argue that the gradual transformation of chiefs into *rulers* progressed in tandem with the enlargement of the front mounds.

If we consider the mound shape-types, it is widely agreed that the K, R and S types form a loose hierarchy in which K-1 (i.e. with the round rear mound) occupies the top position, followed by the K-2 (with the square rear mound) and SC (scallop-shaped) types, respectively. The R and S types form the bottom layer of the hierarchy (Figure 9.1). The SRS type was at the highest-ranked type in the Sanuki province at the onset of the Early Kofun period (Okubo 2004), but it was an exception. As I have mentioned in the previous chapter, in many regions from the Tokai and Hokuriku regions eastward, K-2 occupied the top position at least during the Early Kofun period, although there were communities in those regions where K-1 type of tumuli were the most preferred for burials of the elite (Fujisawa 2004b).

From the Middle Kofun period onwards, many regions showed the presence of the SC, R or S types in the highest position in their respective regional hierarchies. According to some scholars, the phenomenon resulted due to interventions from the KCR seeking to control the elite of those regions (e.g. Onoyama 1970). The fact that this happened fairly contemporaneously across a number of regions (see e.g. Ishino 1995) suggests that there was a common reason for the same. However, it is important to carefully examine whether the change was the result of coercion or of voluntary decisions. We shall return to this issue in a subsequent part of this chapter. In this regard, it is interesting to note that the end of the Early Kofun period witnessed the onset – while the beginning of the Middle Kofun period saw the development – of the construction of tumuli clusters consisting of variously shaped tumuli of several sizes, particularly in the KCR (see Figure 9.14.B–E; e.g. Hirose 1987, 1988). Such clusters can be understood to have represented the entire structure of the hierarchy marked by different mound shapes and sizes, and it would be possible to suggest that the emergence of the previously mentioned differences, including the invention of the SC type, attempted to refine the representation of the hierarchy (e.g. Ugaki 2004, 242–243).

Towards the end of the sixth and seventh centuries, the popularity of the K type rapidly decreased from among the tumuli of the top elite who were granted the construction of a burial mound (Kondo 1983, 374–381).

It should be noted that the S type, as mentioned earlier (Chapters 6 and 7), was the typical mound shape of the Yayoi mortuary compounds, whereas the R type also emerged and gained popularity in the Harima province (coinciding largely with the south-western part of present-day Hyogo prefecture) during the Late Yayoi period. Interestingly, the S type continued to be preferred in the Izumo province during the Early Kofun period as the mound shape for elite burials (Otani 1995; Ikefuchi 1997). The province also saw the development of the characteristic rectangular tumuli with four tails sticking out of their corners during the Yayoi V and the Yayoi-Kofun transitional period (Figures 7.10 and 8.6.B; see Chapters 7 and 8 of this volume), and throughout the rest of the period, the elite were buried in the K-2 type of tumuli (Otani 1995); it should be noted that the elite of the region did not choose to adopt the keyhole mound with a round rear mound as the preferred shape-type.[6]

It is also important to add that very small square burial compounds, along with a smaller number of round ones, with very low mounds continued to be constructed throughout the Earlier Kofun period (e.g. Wada 2007). They can be genealogically connected with the rectangular ditch-enclosed mortuary compounds (*Hokei-shuko-bo*, 方形周溝墓) of the Yayoi period (ibid.). Their relative rarity in comparison with their Yayoi predecessors suggests that they were not simply the burial facilities of the commoners. Moreover, the fact that they were rarely equipped with *Haniwas* (埴輪; see the following) and other characteristic features of the K types further suggests that some of them were constructed by commoners, probably relatively higher ranked in their communities, and that their construction was neither sanctioned by the higher elite (those who were buried in the original K types) nor designed to symbolically represent the deceased person's ties with these elite. The construction of such tumuli ceased in the

---

6 This supports the idea that the nature of the centralisation and the hierarchisation of inter-polity relations was that which can be described as 'alliance' of some sort, at least before the second half of the Middle Kofun period, as suggested in the previous chapter and maintained in the rest of the present volume.

Late Kofun period, and as if to replace them, there emerged an enormous number of clusters of R types (the packed tumuli clusters [*Gunshu-fun*, 群集墳]; see Chapter 10.2), suggesting that some of the commoners acquired the ability and probably the *sanction* from the elite to construct small round tumuli as their resting places. Some scholars refer to the latter as the later packed tumuli clusters (*Shin-shiki gunshu-fun*, 新式群集墳) and the former, as the earlier packed tumuli clusters (*Ko-shikigunshu-fun*, 古式群集墳). I return to the issue of who sanctioned the construction of the later clustered tumuli in Chapter 10.2.

The situation described so far can be very roughly summarised as follows:

(1) The R and S types emerged as the chosen mound shape-types of the Yayoi mortuary compounds, which were very small in comparison with the Kofun tumuli.

(2) The emergence of the K type marked the beginning of the Kofun period.

(3) The K-1 type gradually came to be regarded as ranked higher than the K-2 type in most of the regions to the west of the KCR during the Early Kofun period, while the S type continued to mark the resting places of the elite of communities that did not adopt the K-1 type (the elite of most of the communities of the Izumo province were buried in the S type; see earlier discussion and Chapter 8.3).[7]

(4) The hierarchical order of tumuli types, with K-1 at the top, followed by K-2, SC, R and/or S, in that order, was established in the Middle Kofun period, as revealed by the fact that some of the examples of K are

surrounded by much smaller R, S, SC and, very occasionally, K types of tumuli.[8]

(5) The Late Kofun period saw a decline in the construction of K, along with a drastic increase in the construction of very small specimens of R (often clustered in tens of tumuli, and sometimes even in hundreds; see Chapter 10.2 of this volume), particularly from the latter half of the period onwards (i.e. from the mid-sixth century onwards).

(6) The construction of substantial mounds for burying the dead ceased in the final part of the Late Kofun period, or the 'terminal' Kofun period, except for the construction of very few SR and O types of tumuli for the highest-ranking elite of the region.

(7) The construction of the K and other types of tumuli, however, continued in parts of the Kanto region until the beginning of the eighth century.

This complex picture suggests that the different mound shape-types represented not only some kind of (ancestral) group affiliation but also a hierarchised system of meanings, values and categories; further, it indicates that the system underwent several changes during the Kofun period. From among these mound shape-types, the keyhole type of mound (i.e. the K type) occupied the topmost position in the hierarchy until the late sixth century, when its construction was discontinued throughout the archipelago, except for in the Kanto region (see relevant chapters in Ishino 1995). In addition, the possibility that the keyhole tumulus with a very small frontal mound (i.e. the SC type) was invented in order to further refine the mound-shape-based hierarchy (Ugaki 2004) suggests the significance of the position of the keyhole tumulus as the *ideal type* among the entire range of mound shape-types (Kondo 1983, 175–177). However, merely the presence of a keyhole-tumuli-centred system of hierarchy (with mainly the K-1 type occupying the topmost position)

---

7 It has to be noted, however, that in some cases K-2 type tumuli were furnished better than K-1 type tumuli coexisting in individual regions (e.g. the Bizen-Kurumazuka [備前車塚], K-2 type, with thirteen bronze mirrors, including eleven *Sankakuen-shinju-kyo* mirrors (三角縁神獣鏡), and Urama-Chausuyama [浦間茶臼山], K-1 type, robbed, with fragments of a late Han bronze mirror and other grave goods, tumuli mentioned in the previous chapter on p. 215). Those cases suggest that the logics behind the choice between the K-1 and K-2 types was more complicated than mere concern with the indication of the status differences of the deceased.

8 Some of these 'satellite' tumuli contained burials, while a small number of them, mainly in the KCR, were specifically built for depositing extremely large quantities of weapons (cf. Kondo 1983, 226–228).

does not indicate whether the system was forcefully imposed by a centralised authority or it was voluntarily adopted or emulated. The latter implies the possibility that the formation of the hierarchy was a consequence of the local people's voluntary expressions of *deference* to the elite of the KCR as the *supreme mediators* (see Chapter 8.3–4), which may indeed have been the case. As we will see subsequently in this chapter (see 'Ideal Types and Variations', pp. 271–272), there are numerous variants in terms of their similarities to and differences from the mound shape constructed, the facilities provided and the grave goods deposited in the largest keyhole tumulus of each phase of the Kofun period – all of which, without exception, existed in the KCR. This suggests that the construction of the keyhole and other types of tumuli was undertaken through a *combination* of possible instructions by the KCR elite and voluntary copying of the KCR mortuary customs by the regional elite, with the inclusion of regional modifications. If this were the case, the question regarding the size of the vast labour force that needed to be mobilised for the construction of the keyhole tumuli, and their gigantic examples, in particular, would be answered as follows: the mobilisation of the labour force included the *voluntary*, and probably *willing*, participation of the members of those communities that had (fictive) kin relations and/or ties of some other kind with the KCR.[9] The same interpretation can be applied to the emergence of the vast number of clustered tumuli in the Late Kofun period (see Chapter 10.2). In addition, the continuation (well into the seventh century) of the construction of keyhole tumuli in the Kanto region, long after it had ceased elsewhere (i.e. during the sixth century), suggests the region's unique position in the matrix of control imposed by the KCR and the strategies used by the local chiefs of the region to compete as well as forge alliances with each other. I return to this issue in Chapter 10.3.

Keeping all these points and possibilities in mind, let us now discuss the burial facilities and grave goods associated with the tumuli.

9 For an additional supportive argument, see the interpretation in the previous chapter concerning the labour mobilisation for the construction of the Tobi-Chausuyama tumulus (see p. 239).

2.2. Burial Facilities and Grave Goods

THE EARLY KOFUN PERIOD

The standard burial facility in the first half of the Early Kofun comprised a cist made of slate stones constructed in an oblong plan (Figure 9.2). Several types of cists can be differentiated based on their ways of wall-construction and formation of the capping (Okabayashi 2002); these types can be traced back to their prototypes dating from the Late Yayoi and the Initial Kofun periods (ibid.). The bottom of a cist was typically covered by a thick layer of clay in which a dugout log coffin (*wari* [割, split] *take* [竹, bamboo] – *gata* [形, shaped] *mokkan* [木棺, wooden coffin]) was laid.

The process of construction of a typical cist can be reconstructed as follows (Figure 9.2; Shiraishi 1985, 75–76): A large rectangular pit was dug on top of the mound, and the bottom centre of the pit was covered by a bed of clay; the space around the bed was filled with cobbles. Following this, a dugout log coffin (a composite wooden coffin in rare cases) was laid on the bed and the body was laid in the coffin, along with the deposition of some grave goods in the coffin; thereafter, the coffin was closed, and further grave goods were deposited around it. Meanwhile, walls made of slate (in some cases, of large cobbles; e.g. the Tsubai Otsukayama [椿井大塚山] tumulus; Kobayashi and Kondo 1959, 27) were gradually built around the coffin; slate and cobblestones were commonly laid in alternate layers behind the walls in order to support the walls. When the walls and the layers of slate and cobblestones behind them reached a sufficient height to completely cover the coffin, they were again covered by a layer of clay (at times, some grave goods were packed in the clay, while red pigments were sprinkled on the clay a number of times to form layers in it), after which the cist was capped by large flat stones; another layer of clay was laid on this to seal the capping stones, and the rest of the pit was filled with soil. The side of the pit facing the frontal mound was often cut open to make a sloping path to the top of the frontal mound in order to allow clay, stones and other mortuary paraphernalia to be brought in (for a well-excavated example, see Higashikage 2011, 75–76). Certain people involved in the sequential stages of construction would have used this sloping path to enter the structure, themselves forming a part of the ritual process; iron weapons were often enclosed in the walls and/or the layers supporting the cist, and individual slate stones on the walls were sometimes entirely painted with red pigments (e.g. the Sakurai [Tobi] Chausuyama tumulus; Nara prefectural Kashihara archaeological research institute 2009; Higashikage 2011, 73–83). This procedure suggests that even piling the stones for the construction of the tumulus would itself have had ritual implications (Kobayashi and Kondo 1959, 26). I discuss this point further in the following.

Excavations have revealed regional variations in construction at each of these stages, and at times regional traditional features, such as a composite slab coffin (e.g. the Akatsuka [赤塚] tumulus, Oita prefecture [Umehara 1923]), were used as burial facilities. In addition, the elite of many other communities apart from those who adopted the keyhole-tumulus-related mortuary practices continued to bury their dead in square, low-mounded tumuli containing several composite slab coffins, including some for infants, during the early Kofun period: this was basically a continuation of the customs derived from the burial compound type III of the late Yayoi V (see Chapter 7.3.2), which well illustrates the voluntary and strategic nature of adopting the keyhole tumulus and its allied mortuary paraphernalia and practices.

At some point of time in the first half of the early Kofun period, a custom emerged according to which the coffins were packed in the clay bed (粘土槨) but not enclosed in a cist (called clay-packed coffins hereafter) (Figure 9.3.1). The practice might appear as a more economical alternative to building a cist, but this type of mortuary installation was not necessarily confined to the burial of the minor/vassal elite. At the Simanoyama (島の山) tumulus (approximately 195 metres long) of the Nara Basin, which dates back to the second half of the Early Kofun, c. the late fourth century, a clay-packed coffin was located on top of the rectangular frontal mound (Nara Prefectural Kashihara Archaeological Research Institute 1997). A hundred thirty-two variously shaped armlets, mostly made of green tuff, were deposited on it as if to literally cover the clay packing

of the dugout log coffin, and the deceased person is inferred to have been a female of a shamanistic character (Shiraishi 1999, 86–91). These differences in tumuli type appear to have been used in a flexible manner to indicate various characters of the deceased, although when a cist and a clay-packed coffin are co-present in individual tumuli, the latter type appears to have been regarded as lower ranking in the value system of the time.

Some of the cists and clay-packed coffins were equipped with a cobble-packed drainage facility (Shiraishi 1985, 83–84), suggesting that the body was intended to be preserved. As we have seen, the body was packed and concealed in a secure manner. At the Sakurai (Tobi) Chausuyama, the square platform situated on the top of the round rear mound, as mentioned earlier briefly, was not only marked by well-made, double-rimmed jars but also surrounded by more than one hundred and fifty logs, densely planted and standing possibly as high as more than two metres (Nara Prefectural Kashihara Institute of Archaeology 2009; Higashikage 2011). Based on this, we can infer that packing and enclosing the body of the chief was one of the most important concerns for those who were in charge of the construction of the tumuli – it was part of the ritual process. The fact that they intended to preserve the body suggests that the body was not regarded as an empty substance: it would have been perceived as still containing a *force* of some sort which had the potential to influence the community of the living, either for good or evil. In the case of the former, the packing and enclosing of the body would have been intended to protect the entity buried in the tumuli, so that it would do something to benefit the community. In the case of the latter, the process would have been intended to prevent the entity from harming the community in some way. Considering the fact that the *Haniwa* vessels, as we will see in the following, came to represent offerings of various facilities that the dead chief was expected to live on, the former intention, that is, protecting the entity buried in the tumuli do that it could benefit the community in some way, is more likely to have been the case. However, such forces, as many ethnographic examples indicate, also often had evil elements. In that sense, the packing and enclosing would have been intended

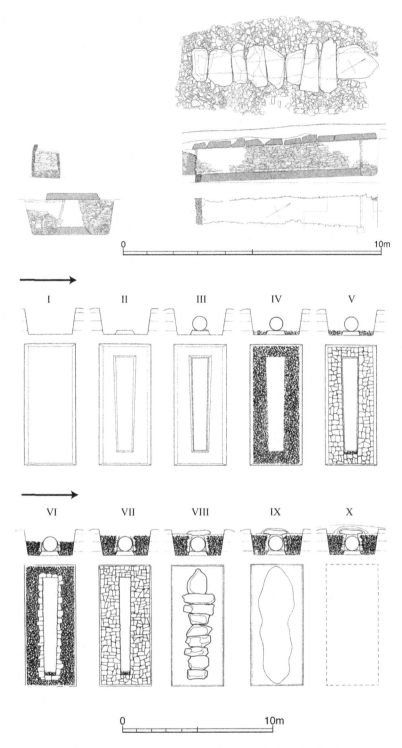

Figure 9.2. The construction process of a typical cist: the Ikeda Chausuyama [池田茶臼山], Osaka prefecture (after Katata [1964], with additions).

to prevent the evil spirit from wandering out as well.[10]

To support this view, we find that in some earlier Kofun period tumuli, the walls of the cists were painted with red pigments. This brings to mind the colour dichotomy between red and black

10 Yasumasa Hozumi (2007) points out that some shield-shaped *Haniwa* vessels enclosing the top of some tumuli under which the dead were buried are situated to face to the inside of the enclosure. He argues that it was designed to prevent the evil spirit of the dead elite from wondering out of the enclosure.

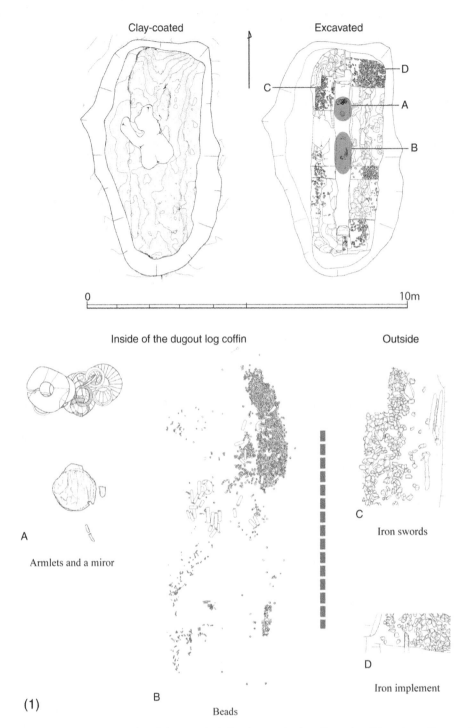

Figure 9.3. An example of the *Nendo-kaku* clay-packed coffins: the Shiramizu Hisagozuka (白水瓢塚) tumulus, Hyogo prefecture. 1: clay-packed coffin and grave goods. 2: Grave goods (after Kobe MBE 2008).

which we saw in the Yayoi period (see Chapter 5.2). The inner surfaces of some burial jars of the Middle Yayoi period in northern Kyushu were painted red, whereas their outer surfaces were painted black. In the Initial and Early Yayoi periods, the outer surfaces of globular jar coffins were painted red, and it was inferred that they represented the following series of dichotomies – death : death

regeneration of life :: black : red – and that they were connected with the death and regeneration of the life of rice grains as well as human beings (see Chapter 5.2.1). In the case of the burial jars whose inner surfaces were painted red, they were often found to contain the elite, i.e., those who were buried with grave goods, and we had interpreted that burying the elite in this manner

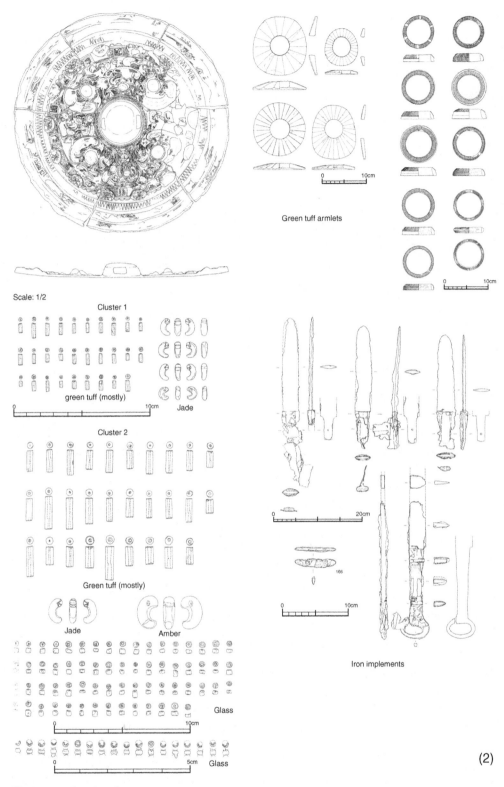

Figure 9.3 (*continued*)

represented a form of prayer for the well-being of the community (see Chapter 6.6.1). In those examples, the bodies of the dead would have been perceived as possessing some powers to represent the well-being of the community, based on their connection with the regeneration of rice grains, and because of that, the bodies would need to be preserved so that they could work for the well-being of the community. The preservation and retention of some powerful force by covering the

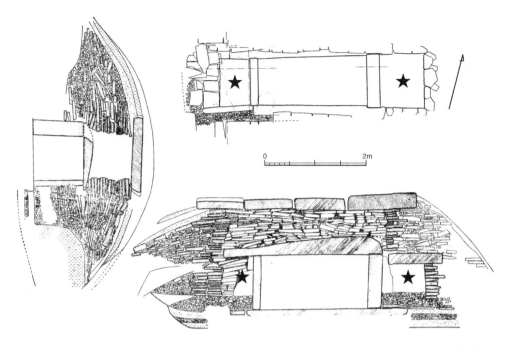

Figure 9.4. An example of the cist with compartments for grave goods: Myokenzan (妙見山) tumulus, Kyoto prefecture (after Kyoto PBE [1955], with additions). Compartments are starred.

dead body of the elite, as illustrated in the following, continued in the form of the wrapping motif of the prototypical *Haniwa* cylindrical vessels enclosing the tumuli (see Figure 9.9); wrapping the dead body would have prevented that powerful force from wandering away. In that sense, the metaphorical-transformative connection between the death and regeneration of rice grains as well as (elite) human beings (the 'Yayoi structuring principle' repeatedly mentioned in Chapters 5 and 6) continued from the beginning of the Yayoi onwards and came to be represented in the form of various facilities employed for enclosing the elite body (see Kondo 1983, 167–194). By doing this securely, the communities involved in the burial of the dead within the tumuli effectively prayed for and secured their own well-being.

THE MIDDLE KOFUN PERIOD

The long dugout log coffins were eventually replaced by various types of stone coffins which were shorter than their dugout log equivalents and could thus be packed in much shorter cists (Shiraishi 1985, 79–83). This change corresponded with the onset of building compartments in the cist for containing grave goods (Figure 9.4; ibid.). However, the preservation of the body and the protection/enclosure of the force perceived to

be residing in it (see earlier discussion) appear to have continued to be the most significant requirements in the construction of tumuli at the time.

The emergence of separate compartments for grave goods, however, marked an important change. These often contained a number of weapons as well as tools for farming, woodworking and, albeit rarely, fishing, which were laid inside and outside the log coffin during the Early Kofun period (Figure 9.5; e.g. Fukunaga and Sugii 1996). They would have represented the categories of work necessary for the sustenance and well-being of the community embodied and represented by the deceased (see earlier discussion). Since these grave goods were few in number and placed in particular patterns, their placement in and around the coffin, and even around the body, would have been carried out by a limited number of individuals, probably specifically chosen for the task. The careful placement of different goods at different spots around the body in the coffin and around the coffin itself suggests that the body of the elite was used as the focal point for the metaphorical representation of tasks needed for the maintenance and well-being of the community. Through the patterned practice of placing certain items representing the essential elements of everyday life around the body of the dead chief, the body

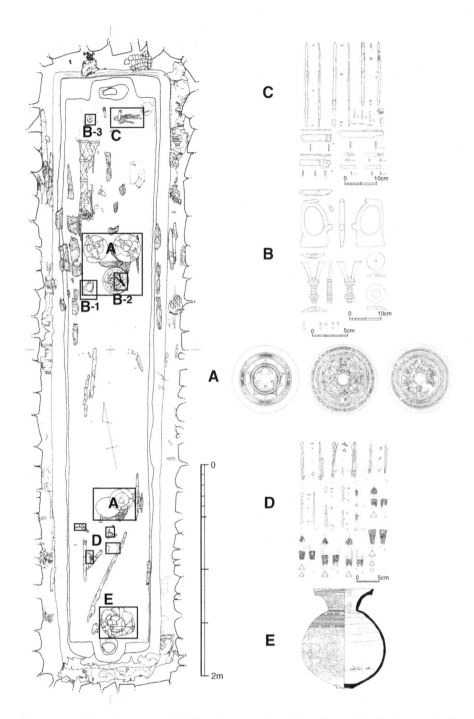

Figure 9.5. The placement of different categories of artefacts with distinct symbolic meanings: the Yukinoyama tumulus, Shiga prefecture (after Fukunaga and Sugii [1996], with additions). **A:** Bronze mirrors. **B:** Stone implements. **C:** Iron woodworking tools. **D:** Iron fishing implements. **E:** Pottery globular jar.

was made the embodiment of the functioning of the entire community. In contrast, in the Middle Kofun period, in cases where large quantities of grave goods were deposited in specifically designated compartments outside the coffin (Figure 9.4), a much larger number of individuals would have been involved in the deposition, and it is possible that the body of the elite did *not* remain the

intimate focal point for metaphorical networking and the generation of certain meanings; apart from the timing of deposition, the placement of grave goods became detached from the act of placement of the body. It would have been possible for a number of people to bring grave goods to the mound and deposit them in the compartments in the cist.

This suggests that the meaning of the practice itself underwent a transformation. In the Early Kofun period, the grave goods would have signified whatever activities the body and the force residing in it would have performed by using them; in the Middle Kofun period, however, their meaning(s) shifted to signify whatever activities could be potentially performed by those who were *controlled by* the body and the force residing in it, i.e., those who brought the grave goods and deposited them in the compartments. In the former case, the body and the force would have been perceived to be *representing* and *embodying* the communal will and interests; in the latter case, the body and the force would have been perceived to be *in charge of* integrating and achieving the communal will and interests. On the whole, we can clearly determine a shift in the image of the dead chief, as signified through the burial process, from that of the *representative* of the community's will and well-being to that of the dominant individual being in charge of the *execution* of the communal will and the defence of communal well-being (as signified by the large quantity of weapons deposited in the compartments). I return to the implications of this shift in the following sections.[11]

GALLERY MORTUARY CHAMBER

Before proceeding further, however, let us examine another important tradition and its commencement: the construction of the gallery mortuary chamber. The oldest of these, built in northern Kyushu at the turn of the Early Kofun period (c. the late fourth or early fifth centuries AD; hereafter called the 'northern-Kyushu type'), was a cist-like chamber with a rectangular pit-like entrance (Figure 9.6; e.g. the Roji [老司] tumulus in Fukuoka prefecture; Fukuoka MBE 1989). The bottom of the entranceway, dug into the constructed mound, was level with the mouth of the entrance pit. It was reopened at least twice after the construction of the chamber and the burial of the original deceased in order to accommodate

---

11 If we speculate further, we can infer that in the world represented by the tumulus, which was also inhabited by the powerful force (i.e. the spirit of the dead chief; see the subsequent section on the *Haniwa* vessels), the force would have been believed to *distribute* those weapons and tools among its followers to undertake tasks necessary for the well-being of the community.

---

additional burials (ibid.). The genealogical origin/prototype of the oldest type of gallery mortuary chamber is disputed: some scholars suggest that the type was a hybridisation of the traditional cist chambers and the Korean-peninsula-derived custom of re-opening the chambers to bury additional deceased, while others argue that its genealogical roots can be traced back to the type of gallery chambers built in the Korean polity of Paekche when its capital was located in Hansong (漢城; Yanagisawa 1982). Shortly afterwards, a different type of chamber with a proper gallery entranceway emerged in the central Kyushu region (hereafter called the 'central-Kyushu type'). The main chamber of this type was often characteristically compartmentalised using slabs; its origin can also be reportedly traced back to a prototype in Paekche (ibid.). During the second half of the Middle Kofun period, there emerged another type of gallery chamber in the KCR; its entranceway was attached to the left-hand side of the chamber wall facing the entranceway. According to some scholars, its genealogical roots can again be traced back to the chambers built in Paekche when its capital was located in Unjin (熊津; Morishita 1986). At around the same time, the Kyushu-type gallery chambers appear to have been adopted in the region. The supposition that they originated in Paekche is disputed on the grounds that there are some gaps in their absolute chronological positions, but the morphological similarities between the structures seem persuasive (Yanagisawa 1980). The introduction of this type of chamber allowed the re-opening of the chamber for additional burials; I come back to its implications in the next chapter. At this point, we will concentrate on the fact that both the northern-Kyushu and central-Kyushu types spread to regions across western Japan and the Tokai and Hokuriku regions in eastern Japan (see papers in Yokoanashiki sekishitsu kenkyu-kai 2007). Some of the examples are identical to their Kyushu equivalents in terms of the way in which their walls and inner compartments were built, and we can infer that their construction involved those who already had some experience with building or using them in Kyushu (e.g. Yanagisawa 1982). In any case, their presence indicates the existence of ties between communities of northern and central Kyushu and those across western Japan and parts of eastern

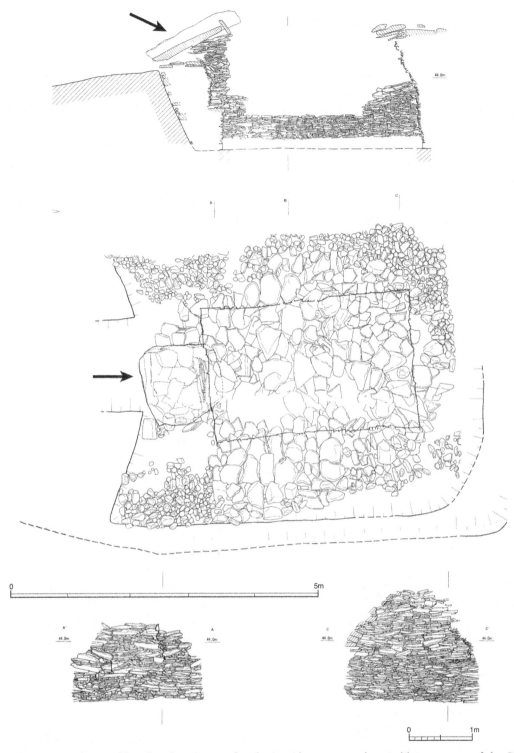

Figure 9.6. The cist-like chamber (no. 3 chamber) with a rectangular pit-like entrance of the Roji tumulus, Fukuoka prefecture (from Fukuoka MBE 1989). Arrow indicates the capping stone of the rectangular pit-like entrance.

Japan, and we can also infer, based on the fact that it was a shared mortuary custom, that they would have signified (fictive or real) kin ties forged and maintained between the communities. This is suggestive in understanding the nature of the KCR-centred hierarchisation of inter-regional relation-ships, that still included ones not mediated by the KCR elite.

The time of their spread corresponded with the intensification of interventions by the archipe-lago communities in the inter-polity conflicts of the Korean peninsula (see Chapter 4.3); it also corresponded with the formation of local complexes of activities such as constructing elite residences, farming, manufacturing and conducting rituals – all involving sophisticated technologies that had originated in the peninsula, which were applied in northern Kyushu, the province of Kibi and the KCR (Hishida 2007, 60–63). This suggests that those regional 'polities' would have centralised their internal power structure and developed a certain internal hierarchy. In this process, those polities would have sought to forge contacts and alliances with an ever-increasing number of remote communities.

This phenomenon indicates the following: although an archipelago-scale centralisation and hierarchisation had not been achieved, the archipelago's interventions in the peninsula stimulated the development of some of the regional polities in it. However, with regard to many other sociocultural elements, the KCR occupied a very powerful position among them.

GRAVE GOODS

The set of grave goods deposited with the dead also changed according to the previously mentioned shift in the image of the dead chief.

The Early Kofun Bronze Mirrors: During the first half and early second half of the Early Kofun period, the grave goods deposited around the body, both inside and outside the dugout log coffin, included bronze mirrors; armlets of various types basically made of green tuff; other items of unknown functions with presumed symbolic meanings also made of green tuff; bronze arrowheads; iron weapons including swords, spearheads, arrowheads, body armours and helmets; iron tools including farming, woodworking and fishing equipments; and so on (Figure 9.5).

The bronze mirrors included imported (X) Chinese mirrors of various styles, (Y) the *Sankakuen-shinju-kyo* (三角縁神獣鏡) type of triangular-rimed mirrors with beast-and-deity motifs, and (Z) shortly afterwards, mirrors made in the archipelago by adopting, modifying and combining the traits of the Chinese mirrors (e.g. Tsujita 2007, 231–278). The X, Y and Z categories of mirrors were treated differently: the X and Z types were often placed near the head of the body, whereas the Y types were often laid on the sides

of the body and/or used to line the sides of the coffin (Figure 9.7).

It is possible that some of the specimens of X may have been imported at some time in the Yayoi V or the Yayoi–Kofun transitional period, and hence were deposited in full recognition of their distinct meanings from that of Y.[12]

According to some scholars, the Y type of mirror includes the hundred mirrors presented by the Wei (魏) emperor to Queen Himiko (卑弥呼) of the Yamatai-koku (邪馬台国) polity, as recorded in Wei-zhi (Kobayashi 1961, 95–133). Their presence is conspicuous during the first half of the Early Kofun period, and their distributional centre was clearly the KCR (ibid.). The strategic nature of their distribution has already been emphasised (e.g. Fukunaga 1999); they appear to have been presented by the KCR elite to the chiefs of communities – sometimes even fairly obscure communities, not only the dominant ones – in individual regions, as if to check the behaviour of the recipients. Since no exact specimen of this type has ever been excavated in the mainland, there is an ongoing dispute in academic circles concerning whether the mirrors were produced within the domain of the Wei dynasty or made by artisans who had migrated to the archipelago (cf. Fukunaga et al. 2003; Terasawa 2000, 305–316). The fact that a special meaning appears to have been attached to this type of mirror, which was frequently used in strategic gift-giving activities, leads some scholars to suggest that the oldest specimens of that type were, indeed, presented by the Wei emperor, whereas the others would have been produced by migrant artisans located somewhere in the archipelago, probably in the KCR (cf. Tsujita 2007, chap. 4). The specimens were placed around the body, inside as well as outside

12 It has to be noted, however, that the distribution of the Late Han mirrors (X type) excavated from Yayoi V contexts concentrates in northern Kyushu (e.g. Tsujita 2007). Combining this important observation with other types of relevant information, Jun'ichiro Tsujita argues that most of the Late Han mirrors deposited with the *Sankakuen-shinju-kyo* type were imported from the Yayoi-Kofun transitional period onward (ibid.). If it were the case, it would suggest that the X type of mirrors deposited in Kofun tumuli were imported together with the Y type by the elite of the KCR, and were given a different meaning from that of the Y type and distributed. See the argument on the meanings given to the X, Y and Z types in the following.

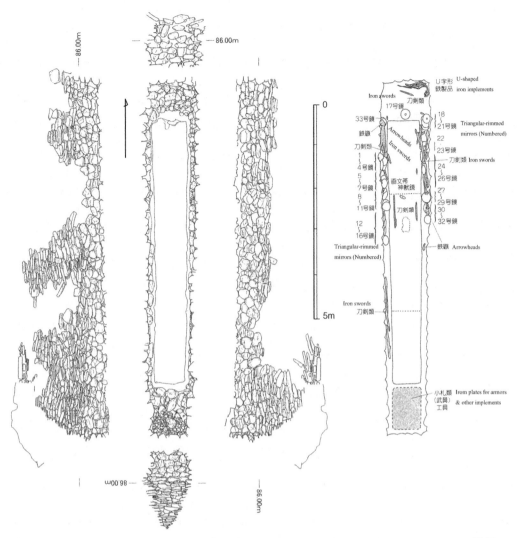

Figure 9.7. The placement of the *Sankakuen-shinju-kyo* mirrors in the cist: the Kurozuka (黒塚) tumulus, Nara prefecture (from Nara Prefectural Kashihara Archaeological Research Institute [1999], with additions).

the coffin, as if to display the number of such mirrors presented by their giver to the deceased, although they would also have been placed in that manner in order to protect/conceal/contain (see earlier discussion) the body (and the force residing in it; Figure 9.7 and see Footnote 10).

Many of the specimens of the Z type are larger than their X and Y counterparts, and their decorative traits include non-Chinese elements, that is, motifs not signifying the deities of Chinese cosmological schemes or religious beliefs but probably representing creatures from indigenous mythical narratives/beliefs. The snake-like motif on the *Banryu-kyo* type of mirror is an example of these. The hybridisation of Chinese and non-Chinese motifs would have been intended to blend the references pertaining to the source of authority overseas and the indigenous conceptual creation

of the transcendental realm (for the significance of this reference to the transcendental realm, see Chapter 8.4). They were also often treated differently from Y, and rather like the X. Hitoshi Shimogaki has shown that the size of the Z type of specimens generally reduces in direct proportion to the distance of the tumulus wherein they are deposited from the KCR (Shimogaki 2003). It can be inferred that this phenomenon was the consequence of the accumulation of strategic gift-giving carried out by the elite of the KCR to mark the differences in the importance of their ties with chiefs outside the KCR (ibid.; Tsujita 2007).

These points suggest that the X, Y and Z types of mirrors were assigned different meanings as prestige goods: X, if they were given by the KCR elite, may have been designed to show the history of the KCR's exclusive access to successive

Chinese dynasties; Y may have been designed to display the power authorised by the Wei; Z may have been designed to show the status of the KCR elite as the supreme mediators dealing with the transcendental realm.[13]

In any case, these meanings were signified in relation to the body of the dead chief: as argued, the dead chief was portrayed as the representative of the communal will and communal interests in contacts and negotiations with the KCR elite, and through them, with the domain that lay outside the horizon of normal contacts, that is, the Chinese dynasties, and with the realm of the transcendental.

Armlets: Armlets in the Early Kofun period were initially made by copying the shell armlets of the Yayoi period. The Yayoi shell armlets, which appeared towards the end of the Yayoi I, were made in various shape-types during the Middle Yayoi period, and in the Yayoi V, some of them were copied in bronze (Yanagida 1986b). The shells used for making the original armlets, as mentioned earlier, could only be procured from the seas around the Okinawan islands. This would have attributed a symbolic significance to the armlets as something from outside the horizon of normal contacts, or from the *outer/other world*. This feature of their other-worldliness was again replicated by the exotic nature of bronze towards the end of the Yayoi period (ibid.). Following this, when the armlets were incorporated into the mortuary paraphernalia of the Early Kofun period, the other-worldliness of this artefact was again represented by making the specimens out of another new material – green tuff; these armlets were mostly produced in the Koshi province in the present-day Hokuriku region (Figure 9.3.2; e.g. Hojo 1999a). Accessories made of green tuff were mainly produced in the Hokuriku and San'in regions during the Yayoi period. However, in the Early Kofun period, their production in the latter region diminished for a while, whereas the former region became the main production centre of the armlets (ibid.).

The Koshi province was, again, located on the periphery of the horizon of normal contacts: the distribution of the keyhole tumuli during the first half of the Early Kofun period extended as far east as the present-day Nigata prefecture (see relevant chapters of Ishino 1995), but no farther. The distribution of the armlet-production centres around the KCR suggests that the products were brought in from the Koshi province and then redistributed (e.g. Kawamura 2010). In that sense, like the bronze mirrors, the armlets would have signified contacts with the periphery of the horizon of normal contacts, i.e., the outer world, inevitably mediated by the elite of the KCR. The dead chief would have been perceived to mediate contacts with remote places, which had become increasingly necessary for the reproduction of the community, by maintaining contacts with the KCR elite, and this, in turn, was symbolically signified by depositing the armlets, which would also have been worn in ritualistic occasions, around the body of the dead chief.

Weapons and Tools: Weapons and tools signify both the high technology involved in their production and the tasks undertaken using them. In that sense, they would have embodied not only the maintenance of contacts with the remote places from where the technology and raw materials were imported but also prayers for the smooth operation of certain sectors of daily life.

From the Yayoi–Kofun transitional period to the beginning of the Early Kofun period, a specific type of bronze stemmed arrowheads with a mid-rib became prevalent across wide areas and is believed to have been distributed by the KCR elite. However, archaeologists have pointed out the existence of minute regional variations within the KCR itself, which suggest that the production of these specimens was not centralised (Ikefuchi 2000). The bronze and iron arrowheads from the first half of the Early Kofun period were often copied in green tuff, thus indicating that they were attributed certain symbolic meanings. Iron helmets from the first half of the Early Kofun period are observed to have had stylistic affinities with certain Chinese equivalents (Matsugi 2007, 170). The rarity of their presence as grave goods suggests that they fulfilled the same function as the X- or Y-type bronze mirrors – symbolically signifying connections with the Chinese authority.

The presence of woodworking, framing and fishing tools would have signified not only the

13 See Footnote 12 to this chapter.

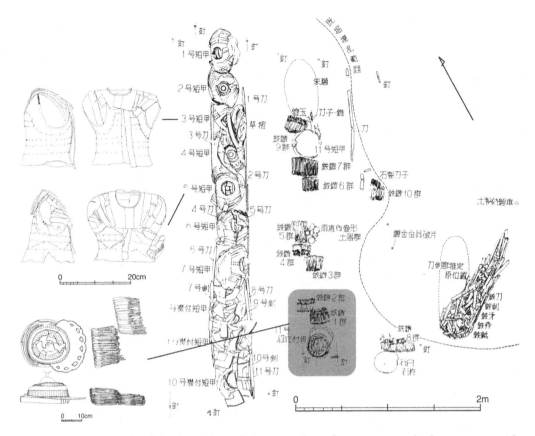

Figure 9.8. An example of the deposition of a large number of iron armors and other weapons without the body: the Nonaka Ariyama (野中アリ山), Osaka prefecture (after Osaka University Section of Japanese History [1964], with additions and modifications).

three main sectors of daily work but also possibly the three elements of the world: the plains, the mountain and the sea. By placing those items at certain spots around the body of the dead chief (see Fukunaga and Sugii 1996), prayers for the well-being of the community, including its defence, were portrayed as being embodied by the chief.

In the second half of the Early Kofun period, while swords continued to be placed around the body as grave goods, spearheads and daggers were gradually placed away from the body, at times in a separate cist which did not contain the body or in the previously mentioned compartment(s) situated in or above the cist (Figure 9.4; Shiraishi 1985). Takehiko Matsugi (2007, 173) argues that the phenomenon must have reflected the differentiation of those who used swords from those who used spears and daggers in combat. I would like to propose, however, that this clearly shows the beginning of a shift in the social identity of the chief from that of the representative of the community's destiny to that of a powerful figure executing

the will of the community by *commanding* its members.

The period also saw the emergence of body armour made of a number of rectangular iron plates (Figure 9.8). These items would have been made in the archipelago by copying the originals from the Korean peninsula (Yoshimura 1988). Their rarity suggests that they would have been worn only by the elite as status items, like the Chinese-style iron helmets. It should be noted, however, that the source of authority and prestige had shifted from China to the peninsula at that time. It is particularly interesting in that the militaristic interventions by communities of the archipelago in the inter-polity conflicts of the Korean peninsula are recorded as having begun around this time (cf. Inoue 1960), and the phenomenon can be understood in this context (Matsugi 2007, 153–208). This also implies that the source of authority and prestige shifted from the *mediation* of contacts with the authorities to the *act* of intervening in the matters of remote places.

The latter obviously required the chief to *command* his subordinates. In any case, the beginning of interventions by the archipelago communities in matters pertaining to the peninsula, from this period onwards, was to have a significant influence on the structure of the mortuary discourse henceforth, and undoubtedly on the other discourses constituting the society.

The Early Kofun Period – A Summary: The changes that occurred in the different categories of grave goods during the Early Kofun period are correlated with one another, and they clearly point to a significant change in the entire structure of the mortuary discourse of the time. That change can be summarised as a shift from the material media signifying the body of the dead chief as a *communal* body to that signifying it as a *commanding* body. In the first half of the Early Kofun period, the grave goods were mostly placed around the body of the dead chief or in places where the meaning(s) of the items were signified *in relation to* the body. Accordingly, there were relatively few such goods deposited in and around the cist, with the exception of bronze mirrors (Figures 9.3, 9.5 and 9.7). In the second half of the period, however, certain categories of grave goods, including bronze mirrors and swords, continued to be placed around the body, whereas others such as daggers and spearheads tended to be deposited in compartments built for this purpose, located away from the body (Figure 9.4). It is possible that the goods were now treated as offerings signifying the submission of those who offered them – these people were probably also those who had worked (or fought) using these items under the command of the chief. Accordingly, their quantity increased progressively during the second half of the period. In the case of the armlets, their quality declined with time, as they increasingly began to be made of talc. The trend gradually led to the situation wherein those who were buried in the larger tumuli, and hence would have had more followers than the others, were also offered more items for the fulfilment of social obligations.

The Middle Kofun Period: The trend set in motion in the second half of the Early Kofun period reached its zenith in the Middle Kofun period. A particularly significant finding is that a large quantity of weapons and certain tools such as U-shaped ploughshares were often deposited in small, mostly rectangular and round tumuli surrounding the gigantic keyhole tumuli at the Saki (佐紀), Furuichi (古市), and Mozu (百舌鳥) sites, some without any other trace of burials (Figure 9.8) and the others, in clay-packed log coffin burials (e.g. Kondo 1983, 226–228). Their presence implies that the scene of their offerings was made visible, probably perceived as a way of expressing subordination to the dead buried in the gigantic tumulus. At the same time, the scene would have also been perceived to symbolically signify the undertaking of important daily activities, including combat, under the command of the chief.

A significant change which occurred in this period was the replacement of helmets and body armour of Chinese origin with those that had originated in the Korean peninsula. The migrants who entered the KCR probably brought with them the technology for producing these items (see the following discussion), and their production was undertaken exclusively by certain artisan communities of the KCR under the command of the dominant clans (see the following discussion). At the same time, Matsugi (2007, 153–208) has shown that there was an increasing preference for the Korean equivalents of other weapons such as spearheads. Records indicate that by this time, there were constant militaristic interventions by communities of the archipelago in the inter-polity conflicts of the Korean peninsula (see Chapter 4.3; Inoue 1960), and the phenomenon can be understood as the natural progression of the strategy that was initiated in the second half of the Early Kofun period, as mentioned earlier (Matsugi 2007, 153–208). In any case, regardless of whether they were mobilised by the KCR elite or offered their voluntary participation, a number of communities in the archipelago – particularly in Kyushu and western Japan – came in contact with the communities in the peninsula (cf. Park 2007), and the set of new contingencies generated by this experience would have contributed to/accelerated the transformation of the image of the chief from the *mediator* of communal well-being to the *executor* of the communal will in order to achieve communal well-being.

2.3. *Haniwa* Vessels

Haniwa vessels were a constant feature of the Kofun tumulus.[14] Meanwhile, the vessels themselves went through a number of significant changes, which suggests that the vessels mediated the Kofun mortuary discourse as an important component of its structure; as a consequence, they changed as the discourse was transformed through time.

CHARACTER AND EMERGENCE OF THE *HANIWA* VESSELS

As mentioned earlier, in order to understand the meanings attached to and/or generated by the practices conducted at the keyhole-shaped mounds and in the associated facilities around them, which can be described thus the 'Kofun discourse', it is essential to examine the role played by the *Haniwa* cylindrical jar, which provides us with a very significant clue.

The seminal work on the origin of these jars by Yoshiro Kondo and Hideji Harunari (1967) convincingly elaborates on the process through which a specific pedestal shape-type, uniquely developed in the Central Inland Sea region during the Late Yayoi, developed into the *Haniwa* vessels – literary thousands of these vessels encircled the mounds.

The pedestal shape-type was densely decorated with a complex curvilinear motif comprised of a combination of incised lines and comma-shaped holes (Figure 9.9). The motif is interpreted to have symbolically depicted the wrapping of something. The shape-type was designed to support a globular jar shape-type with a long flared neck and a number of M-sectioned cordons. The combination of the pedestal and the globular jar began to be used as an important mortuary item during the Late Yayoi. The original function of the globular jar was probably to contain rice grains given as offerings to the ancestors.

At this point, we should recall the ways in which the globular jar shape-types of the Early and Middle Yayoi periods were used. We have already seen the metaphorical connection between the life cycle of rice grains and the death and regeneration

14 Their characteristics had become stylistically formalised by the beginning of the second half of the Early Kofun period, and the custom of placing them in a particular manner originated in the KCR and spread widely thereafter.

of human beings which emerged in the beginning of the Yayoi and which continued to be increasingly sophisticated through the subsequent periods. During the final phase of the Late Yayoi, the bottom of the vase was perforated before the firing. From this, we can interpret that the ritual involving the offering of grains became formalised to such an extent that the mere presence of the vase was sufficient to signify a prayer to the ancestors, without the actual offering of any rice grains. Another possibility is that the hole may have been made to allow the free movement of the *spirit* of the rice grains. The latter thesis might come across as a little too far-fetched. However, since the spirits of the ancestors as well as those of rice grains appear to have been traditionally considered the same (see earlier discussions on the Yayoi structuring principle) – and as spirits which needed to be wrapped up in order to prevent them from wandering away (see earlier discussion) – the latter might indeed be the case. Another likelihood is that the two possibilities mentioned above may not contradict one another: the formalisation of the ritual might well have been both the cause and the effect of the emergence of the notion of the *wandering* spirits of rice grains and the dead/ ancestors.

This *abstraction* of the contents of the rituals pertaining to the death and regeneration of rice grains and human beings (the elite) roughly coincided in timing with the formalisation of the Kofun discourse. In the discourse, the abstracted offering of rice to the dead in the form of prayers for agricultural success, and hence for communal well-being, began to function as a physical marker of the boundary between the inside and the outside of the discourse. By now, literary thousands of *Haniwa* cylindrical jars were being placed around the places where the prayers for communal well-being were conducted, which would have also metaphorically represented the commoners' mass-participation in the prayers to the elite dead and the ancestors for their communal well-being.

One possible proof of the use of *Haniwa* vessels to metaphorically represent the commoners' mass participation in the prayers to the ancestors for their communal well-being can be found in the pictorial representations on the vessels. Such representations are very rare, but interestingly enough, their depictions distinctly coincide

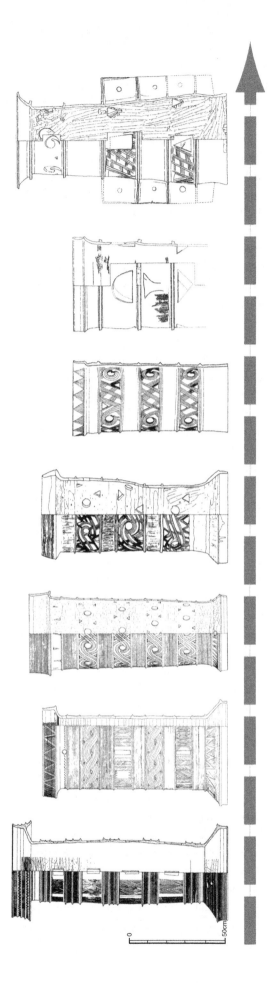

with their Yayoi equivalents – both of which depict deer, hunters, ships and so on (Takahashi 1996, 60–61). As we have already seen, the above representations are often incised on pots from the Yayoi IV and V periods and also appear on *Dotaku* bronze bells (and occasionally on other types of bronze ritual implements; see Figure 6.26). As mentioned above, the themes conveyed by the combination of those motifs would have been related to the cyclic rejuvenation of rice as well as the rice-agriculture-based world view (see Chapter 6.7.2). The fact that those items of the Yayoi period were used in *communal* rituals conducted for communal well-being suggests that the production of thousands of *Haniwa* jars and their placement around the tumuli represented as well as evoked the sense of communal participation in the prayers for communal well-being. This thesis is reinforced by the fact that deer, which are commonly inscribed on *Haniwa* vessels, were otherwise rarely depicted in the animal *Haniwa* assemblage which emerged in the Middle Kofun period (Morita 2008, 49–51). According to the statistical analysis carried out by Katsuyuki Morita, the deer depictions amount to 7.5 per cent (i.e. 13 out of 173) of the known animal *Haniwa* assemblage, whereas those of horses amount to 68.3 per cent (i.e. 118 out of 173). There are virtually no line-inscriptions of horses on the *Haniwa* vessels, suggesting that the system of meanings and values underlying the placement of animal *Haniwa* assemblages on the mounds differed from that underlying the inscription of pictorial figures on the *Haniwa* vessels. This might also suggest that the discourses behind them were different: the pictorial inscriptions would have been

Figure 9.9. Some proto-types of the *Haniwa* cylindrical vessel. From old to new: Tatezaka (立坂) type (Tatetsuki [楯築], from Tatetsuki kanko-kai 1992), Tatezaka type (Nakayama [中山]; from Ochiai TBE 1978), Muko-gimi (向木見) type (Yadani [矢谷], from Hiroshima PBE and Hiroshima Prefectural Buried Cultural Properties Research Centre 1981), Miyayama (宮山) type (Miyayama [宮山], from Takahashi et al. 1987, Tot-suki (都月) type (classified as the oldest *Haniwa* type; Totsuki, from Kondo and Harunari 1967, fig. 7), early Haniwa type from the Nishitonozuka (西殿塚) tumulus (from Hirose 2008, fig. 35.1; original from Tenri MBE 2000), early *Haniwa* type from the Higashitonozuka (東殿塚) tumulus (from Hirose 2008, fig. 35.6; original from Tenri TBE 2000).

the products of the *commoner* discourse, while the placement of various types of *Haniwa* vessels on the mound would have constituted a part of the *elite* discourse symbolised by all the contents of the tumulus. The artisans involved in the production of *Haniwa* vessels (these artisans probably worked on a part-time basis and were occupied in farming activities when not producing *Haniwas* for the elite) would have expressed their prayer for the successful execution of their agricultural activities in the form of occasionally inscribing those creatures on the vessels.

It is suggestive that the custom of enclosing the mound using *Haniwa* jars was phased out in the Later Kofun period. The period, as we will see, saw the transformation of the keyhole tumuli from locales for the offering of prayers for communal well-being to the indicators of the social status of the deceased (Kondo 1983, 363–374). This may also support the above thesis; I return to this point in Chapter 10.

Ironically, the establishment of the custom of enclosing the mound using *Haniwa* jars coincided with the exclusion of commoners from the actual performance of mortuary rituals for the dead chief; this also coincided with the disappearance of archaeological traces of mass feasting on and/or around the mounds (Furuya 2007; also see Shigematsu 2006). The conceptual inclusion of commoners into the Kofun discourse, metaphorically signified by the placement of *Haniwa* jars, was associated with their physical exclusion from the performance of the mortuary ritual itself, which became increasingly esoteric in nature.

Another important source for understanding the meaning content of the *Haniwa* jars and its transformation is the curvilinear decoration applied to many specimens of the pedestal shape-type, the prototype of the *Haniwa* jars (Figure 9.9). It is important to note that the same type of curvilinear decoration was found to have been applied to two stone artefacts from the Tatetsuki tumulus (Figure 9.10; Kondo 2002). The tumulus itself, as we have seen, offers us with some insights into the mortuary ritual discourse prevalent at the beginning of the Kofun period. However, the artefacts themselves yield equally significant information. One of them has been preserved as the deity stone of a kiosk situated on the top of the tumulus, and pieces of another have been excavated from the layer covering the main burial facility, a wooden chamber containing a composite wooden coffin, together with smashed pots including a large number of pedestalled bowls. Both these artefacts depicted a creature with a human face wrapped in a piece of cloth in a highly complex, elaborate and stylised manner (Figure 9.10). The director of the excavation, Yoshiro Kondo, infers that the creature represents the materialised form of an ancestral spirit, and depicting it as wrapped in something, he suggests, would have been of vital importance for the ritual involving the use of those artefacts (e.g. Kondo 2002, 50–51). If we accept Kondo's inference that the wrapped up creature represents an ancestral spirit, and if we assume that the respective spirits of rice grains and the ancestors converged over the course of time (Kondo 1983, 167–174; also see earlier discussions on the Yayoi structuring principle), we can infer that the artefacts were used for praying for human and crop regeneration. Moreover, we can further infer that the act of wrapping the spirit(s) was crucial for the success of the prayers. This suggests that the importance of *wrapping* the crop-ancestral spirit was transformed and/or translated into the importance of *enclosing* and *bounding* the locale wherein the mortuary rituals for the dead chief were performed. In this case, again, the original meaning content/use of the pedestal shape-type became increasingly abstracted as the nature of the ritual requiring the use of the item shifted from the communal to the exclusive, esoteric and hierarchical sphere (see Figure 9.9).

In short, the keyhole-shaped mound needed to be encircled and bounded by the placement of *Haniwa* jars in order for it to represent (1) the embodiment of communal participation in the rituals performed for ensuring communal well-being, (2) an effective locale for the ritual involving prayers for the successful regeneration of the *crop-ancestral spirit* and (3) the exclusive locale where esoteric practices could be performed and witnessed by the elite.

OTHER TYPES OF *HANIWA* VESSELS

In addition to the cylindrical *Haniwas*, there were other types of *Haniwa* vessels depicting objects ranging from architectural structures, weapons and armours to various animal and human figures (Figure 9.11).

Figure 9.10. The stone artefact inferred to have been excavated from the Tatetsuki tumulus (Okayama prefecture) of the Late Yayoi V period (from Inoue 2010; original Tatetsuki kanko-kai 1992).

Haniwa buildings included house structures and storage buildings which were span-roofed in various forms. They can be differentiated based on the presence and absence of window-like openings. The ones with these openings appear to have depicted elite residences, and the others would have depicted storage buildings attached to elite residential compounds. There are *Haniwa* buildings with raised floors and no walls, which are interpreted as depicting architectural structures built for some ritual-performance purposes (Takahashi 2008, 105–109). There also are fence-shaped *Haniwas* with a series of triangles lined up on their top; their horizontal sections are oval, and they are joined together to surround

the compounds depicting elite residences. There are unique *Haniwas* depicting a walled compound with an entrance and likewise a series of triangles lined up on their top (ibid., 109). Some examples of *Haniwas* depict a building with a well or with drainpipes situated inside it. The excavation at the Gokurakuji-Hibiki (極楽寺ヒビキ) location of the Nango-O'higashi (南郷大東) site in Gose City in the south-eastern corner of the Nara Basin, located in the heart of KCR, confirmed that water-related rituals[15] were carried out in that spot using exactly the same type of

---

15 Possibly to do with the washing of the dead body of the chief(s) (Yasumasa Hozumi, pers. comm.).

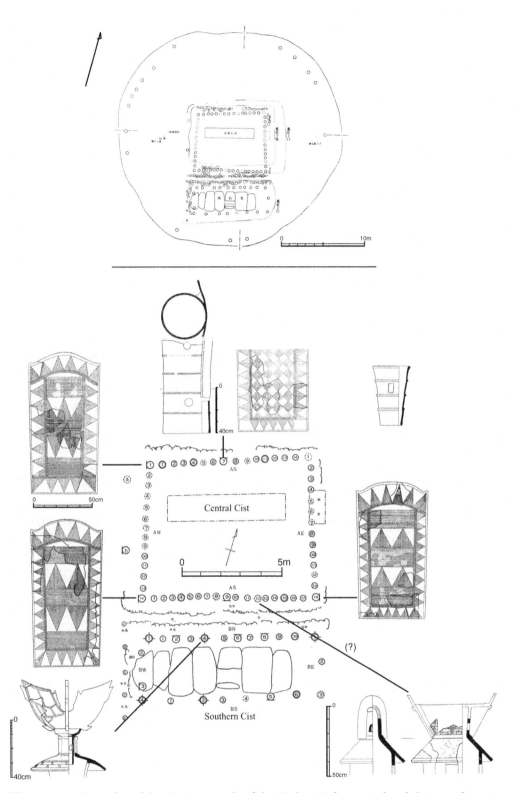

Figure 9.11. Examples of the *Haniwa* vessels of the Earlier Kofun period and their configuration on top of the round rear mound of the keyhole tumulus: the Kanakurayama (金蔵山) tumulus, Okayama prefecture (from Nishitani and Kamaki [1959], arranged by the author).

facilities (Nara Prefectural Kashihara Archaeological Research Institute 2007).

Armour-shaped *Haniwas* include types depicting shields as well as body and head armour, while weapon-shaped *Haniwas* include those depicting arrow containers and variously hilted swords. There are also *Haniwas* depicting ships.

In addition, there are some *Haniwas* with depictions which cannot be fully identified or explained. The *Kinugasa*-type (see Figure 9.11, bottom left) and *Sashiba*-type of *Haniwas* are interpreted as depicting items indicating the presence of the living elite.

Animal *Haniwas* include those depicting horses, wild boar, dogs and deer (Takahashi 1996). Horses are depicted most frequently, followed by wild boar, dogs and deer, in that order. There are also very few depictions of cattle; other *Haniwas* depict various species of birds.

Human *Haniwa* figures depict a range of social categories, including warriors in full armour, priests and priestesses, *Koto*-playing figures, falconers, servants, seated figures probably representing the elite and so on.

Haniwa buildings emerged in the middle phase of the Early Kofun period. Most of the bird-shaped *Haniwas* emerged during the early phase of the Middle Kofun, except for the hen-shaped *Haniwas*, the prototypes of which had emerged earlier on in the Initial Kofun period. Armour-shaped and weapon-shaped *Haniwas* emerged towards the end of the Early Kofun, though hilted-sword-shaped *Haniwas* did not emerge before the Late Kofun period; at around the same time, there emerged *Haniwas* depicting various items symbolising the presence of the elite. *Haniwas* depicting human figures emerged in the early phase of the Middle Kofun period and became the main components of the *Haniwa* assemblage placed on and around the mounds in the Late Kofun period, although other types of *Haniwas* also continued to be placed (Takahashi 1996).

This cumulative process suggests that the *Haniwa* assemblage formed a distinct discourse, which was also transformed through time in an evolutionary manner.

THE *HANIWA* 'DISCOURSE' AND ITS TRANSFORMATION

It is observed that the cumulative transformation of the contents of the *Haniwa* assemblage, as explained above, corresponded with cumulative changes in the way in which the *Haniwas* were placed on the mound.

The continuing placement of cylindrical *Haniwas* on the mounds (and on the banks surrounding the moat[s], when the latter exist) thus effectively defining the boundaries of the mounds, suggests that the fundamental function of the *Haniwas* was to metaphorically make offerings to the spirit that resided in the mounds. *Haniwas* were also placed on top of the rear mound, where a square platform was commonly located, under which the burial installations were situated. Cylindrical *Haniwas* were placed on the four sides of the platform (Figure 9.11). In some cases, composite-rimed vase-shape vessels with a hole in the bottom were chosen to be placed on the platform instead of the cylindrical *Haniwas* (e.g. the Tobi-Chausuyama tumulus in the Nara Basin, KCR).[16] Various *Haniwa* buildings, which emerged in the middle phase of the Early Kofun period, were placed inside the compound defined by the cylindrical *Haniwas* on the platform (Figure 9.11). The fact that the *Haniwa* buildings placed inside the compound include residential buildings, storage buildings and those used for other functions suggest that together they depict an elite residential compound. Armour-shaped *Haniwas*, which emerged in the second half of the Early Kofun, were often placed outside the cylindrical-Haniwa-enclosed compounds, suggesting that they symbolised the presence of soldiers defending the compound. This shows that although human figures were not represented as *Haniwa* figures, their presence was signified by the depiction of items used by human beings. That allows us to infer that the *Haniwas* indicating the presence of the elite, such as the *Kinugasa*-type and *Sashiba*-type *Haniwas*, indeed represented the presence of the elite. Such *Haniwas* were often placed either inside the compound or in between the cylindrical *Haniwas* enclosing the compound, and they would have been intended to symbolise the presence of the elite. This indicates that the

16 This large tumulus, which is approximately 208 metres in length, is situated about 4.5 kilometres away to the south of the Oyamato (大和/オオヤマト) cluster where the majority of the largest tumuli of the first half of the Early Kofun period were located. The tumulus is situated on an important direct route to the Tokai region. The custom of using composite-rimed vase-shape vessels with a hole in their bottom for mortuary rituals was widespread in the Tokai region, and their use might suggest the deceased's connection with the elite of the Tokai region (Takahashi 2008, 118–119). See Chapter 8, p. 239.

absence of human figures was intentional. I return to this point shortly.

The beginning of the Middle Kofun period (c. the late/final fourth century) witnessed the addition of square platforms situated either off the mound and connected to it by an earthen bridge or in the moat detached from the mound (both these types are hereafter referred to as the 'island-type platforms') or attached to the boundary between the front square and the round/square rear mound.[17] The platforms attached to the boundary between the square front and the rear mounds became a standard feature of the keyhole tumulus: these are commonly called *Tsukuridashi* (造り出し; hereafter called the *Tsukuridashi* platforms: see Figure 9.1.B). As mentioned earlier, this period also saw the emergence of the *Haniwa* assemblage depicting water-related rituals, and this assemblage was commonly placed on the gully dividing the front and rear mounds (Kohama 2008). *Haniwas* built in the shape of aquatic birds are often found placed on the island-type platforms, though *Haniwa* buildings and other *Haniwas* used to enclose the *Haniwa* compound on top of the rear mound were also often placed on this spot (ibid.). These phenomena can be viewed from two different perspectives. According to one perspective, the island-type platforms may have depicted islands; the presence of aquatic-bird *Haniwas* on some of them increases this possibility. The other perspective, however, emphasises the fact that the compound depicting the elite precinct, which was located only on top of the mounds previously, also came to be placed at the foot of the mound in some cases, that is, the *Tsukuridashi* (造り出し) platforms (see Figure 9.1.B, indicated with a star) as well as the island-type platforms were connected to the mound by an earthen bridge.

These perspectives can both be understood on the basis of their shared factors as follows. First, the platform locations ensured that the *Haniwa* assemblages placed on them became visually more accessible than the compound on top of the rear mound. Second, the platforms appear to have some connection with the prevailing

17 Keyhole tumuli with both round and square rear mounds coexisted, although their distributions were different, as I have mentioned in the previous chapter (also see Figure 8.5). I reconsider this phenomenon subsequently in the current chapter.

rituals/religious beliefs; aquatic birds, as we saw in Chapter 6, were depicted in the array of pictorial representations on the *Dotaku* bronze bells of the Yayoi period (see Figure 6.26), and the *Haniwa* assemblage depicting water-related rituals is commonly located on the gully dividing the front and the rear mounds, and hence is located near the *Tsukuridashi* platforms.

I would argue that the placement of these platforms would have added to the *Haniwa* discourse a visual element that depicted its actual working. The *Haniwa* discourse is about the role of the elite as the representatives of communal interests and the chief mediators with the transcendental realm who prayed for communal well-being; the *Haniwa* compound atop the rear mound would have represented this role played by the elite after their death. The symbolism behind the wrapping of the crop-ancestral spirits, as embodied by the prototype of cylindrical *Haniwas* (Figure 9.9), was continued through the placement of the cylindrical vessels, and the ancestral spirits – all wrapped up and tied to one place by the enclosing vessels – would have been perceived as carrying on with the duties performed by them before their death, i.e., praying for the well-being of the community. The setting up of the *Haniwa* assemblage depicting the elite residential compound would have provided a concrete visual representation of this perception.

The addition of the platforms and the placement of the previously mentioned types of *Haniwas* on them would have visualised prayers as ritual performances in the form of miniaturised ritual facilities in a miniaturised setting. The aquatic-bird-shaped *Haniwas*, as suggested by the fact that aquatic birds were included in pictorial representations on *Dotaku* bronze bells as items used for agricultural rituals during the Yayoi period, would have signified an important inclusion in the prayers for successful agricultural cycles and the well-being of the community.

If the preceding interpretation were valid, the conspicuous absence of depictions of the elite in the form of human *Haniwa* figures would need some explanation. It is highly unlikely that this absence was caused by the lack of sufficient technological sophistication necessary for the making of human *Haniwa* figures; considering the degree of sophistication required for making and firing the aquatic-bird-shaped *Haniwas*, there would have been no problem in making human *Haniwa* figures during the second half of the Early Kofun and the beginning of the Middle Kofun periods. I would argue that the absence of human *Haniwa* figures during those periods was a deliberate omission, perhaps because the invisible *spirit* of the deceased considered to reside in the compound was supposed to conduct the rituals for the well-being of the community in the facilities placed on the gully between the front and rear mounds and on the *Tsukuridashi*-type and island-type platforms.

The emergence of human *Haniwa* figures is thought to date back to the first half of the Middle Kofun period (Takahashi 2008), and they were initially placed neither on top of the rear mound nor on the platforms but on the bank surrounding the mound. These figures are understood to have depicted the people involved in various activities in the service of the deceased. There are competing theses concerning the activities purportedly being performed by the human *Haniwa* figures. According to one interpretation, these figures are associated with the enthronement of the new chief who inherited the status from the deceased buried in the tumulus on which the *Haniwas* were placed. Another thesis suggests that they depict various scenes that occurred during the reign of the deceased buried in that particular tumulus, while a third thesis posits that they depict activities conducted in and around the compound in which the deceased resided when alive. Another inference is that they represent activities carried out for the spirit of the deceased. The advocates of each of these theses attempt to justify them based on interesting semiotic readings of the assemblages, including human *Haniwa* figures as well as most of the other types of *Haniwas* (e.g. Takahashi 1996; Osaka Prefectural Chikatsu Asuka Museum 2008).

It is obviously very difficult to verify one thesis and dismiss the others, but there are some clues that might help us narrow down the possibilities. First, it is evident that the figure of the deceased is never depicted in the form of a human *Haniwa* figure. Second, the most common feature of the human *Haniwa* figure assemblage from the earliest phase of its existence is the *Haniwa* priestess (Takahashi 1996). These observations suggest that the tradition continued from an earlier era, while *the spirit of the deceased continued to remain invisible.* In that case, the human *Haniwa* figures would have depicted those who served the deceased and/or its spirit and helped it to pray for the well-being of the community which had constructed the tumulus. In other words, those who were represented by the human *Haniwa* figures mediated the relationship between the deceased and the community. In one sense, they represented the interests of the community which had constructed the tumulus. However, they were depicted in the *Haniwa* assemblage as subordinates of the deceased who were in the service of the deceased. In that sense, the emergence of human *Haniwa* figures marked the beginning of the visual representation of domination and subordination in society.

Human *Haniwa* figures remained inconspicuous during the Middle Kofun period, although the way in which *Haniwas* were to be placed appears to have been established in this period; these placements continued into the Late Kofun period, when human *Haniwas* became the main component of the *Haniwa* assemblage. They were placed on the bank of the moat surrounding the mound; therefore, they would have been relatively visible from the outside. If the top of the mound and the platforms can be described as *esoteric* spaces, the moat banks can be described as *exoteric* spaces. It is interesting to note that the emergence of the exoteric presentation of the *Haniwa* assemblage coincided with the representation of dominant and subordinate relations in the form of human *Haniwas*. In addition, those who are depicted in the *Haniwas* are shown as working for the well-being of the community which had constructed the tumulus. At the same time, however, they are doing so by serving the dead chief. In these cases, we can identify a kind of dialectic of domination at work: human *Haniwas* effectively represent the emerging perception that working for communal well-being has to take the form of serving and being subordinate to the chief and the elite.

The aforementioned transformation of the *Haniwa* assemblage in terms of its contents and its placement can be divided into the following three stages: (1) the stage in which the *Haniwa* compound was established atop the mound in order to represent the elite residential precinct; (2) the stage in which platforms were added to places where *Haniwas* depicting elite residential facilities, ritual facilities and other agricultural ritual-related features/animals were placed; and (3) the stage in which human *Haniwas* were added to the assemblage and were placed on the moat banks. These stages were accompanied by corresponding changes in the burial goods assemblage (see the preceding discussion). During stage 1 of the transformation of the Haniwa assemblage, the grave goods assemblage mainly consisted of items used for ritual performances, including bronze mirrors, sceptre-like rods with jasper decorations, various types of jasper armlets and so on. Stage 2 saw the increasing emergence of talc-made miniatures depicting various ritual tools such as mirrors, weapons, production items and so on, whereas stage 3 saw the emergence and establishment of the custom of depositing a considerable quantity of armour and weapons as part of the assemblage. Scholars argue that these changes reflect the transformation of the image of the dead chief from the priest-king type of figure through the process of its formalisation to a figure with warrior-ruler type of characteristics. Although it does seem farfetched to characterise this figure in stage 3 as 'despotic', the process can certainly be described as the process through which the chief's character was transformed from that of the *shamanistic leader* to that of the *ruler*.[18] The *Haniwa* discourse illustrated above was co-transformed along with the discourse constituted by the selection of the grave goods assemblage, and hence can be interpreted to reflect the transformation of the way in which the position of the elite was perceived by the elite themselves as well as by the commoners.

The onset of the Late Kofun period saw the emergence of human *Haniwas* which appear to depict the chiefs, mainly in the Kanto region. This suggests that the transformation process of the discourse had reached the point where the depiction of the relationship between the elite and the commoners came to finally include the figure of the dominant group. I discuss this case and its implications in more detail in the next chapter.

18 See the interpretation of the transformation of the identity/perception of the chiefly figure from the Early to the Middle Kofun period discussed earlier (pp. 258–262).

2.4. Ideal Types and Variations

So far, we have examined the attributes of the keyhole (and other types of) tumuli as if there was very little variation between them. This view is not necessarily 'wrong' – the keyhole and other types of tumuli can be lumped together as a single 'polythetic' classificatory category (Clarke 1978, 35–37). What is more important, in this context, is how we explain these variations. This issue is of crucial importance for the understanding of the nature and character of the inter-communal and inter-regional relationships of the Kofun period.

To begin with, we must confirm the fact that the largest keyhole tumulus of each phase of the Kofun period was, without exception, constructed in the KCR in the present-day Nara and Osaka prefectures (see Figure 8.5). Another consistent occurrence throughout the Kofun period was that all the changes in the mound shape, related facilities, burial installations and grave good assemblages initially originated in the KCR. In other words, the trajectory of transformation in the mortuary discourse embodied by the keyhole tumulus and its attributes was determined by those who presided over the burial of the elite of the KCR. In that sense, the variations in the individual traits of the keyhole tumuli reflect the different degrees to which the different communities outside the KCR followed the KCR's 'lead'.

The largest tumulus of each phase, all located in the KCR, can be regarded as constituting a sort of ideal type (hereafter called the 'A type'). Then there are tumuli with mound shapes that are identical to those of the A type but with different facilities and/or grave goods (hereafter called the 'B type'). In addition, there are tumuli with facilities and/or grave goods identical to the A type but with different mound shapes from the A type (hereafter called the 'C type'). Finally, there are tumuli with mound shapes as well as facilities and/or grave goods that differ from those of the A type (hereafter called the 'D type').

The replication of identical keyhole mounds must have been technologically highly challenging, and considering that it would have been accomplished by employing simple devices such as ropes and stakes, it must have required the involvement of individuals who either were involved in the construction of the largest tumuli in the KCR or had learnt the technology of their planning as well as the plan itself directly from the former. This suggests that the construction of the B-type tumuli involved a group or groups of some sort of specialists/artisans based in the KCR or those who had learnt how to build the tumuli from such specialists/artisans. I have described them as 'some sort of' specialists/artisans because it is highly likely that the planning, as well as the other stages of the mound construction, constituted a ritualistic occasion which involved esoteric knowledge and was surrounded by taboos. In that sense, the technology they possessed would have also been regarded as a package of esoteric religious know-how. The same can be said about the examples in which identical coffins, burial chambers, *Haniwas* and so on were replicated locally. In addition, the possibility that the esoteric religious know-how mentioned above was connected with the rituals pertaining to the dead and the ancestors strongly suggests that the sending of group(s) possessing and applying this package of esoteric religious know-how, from the KCR's point of view, and their acceptance by the local elite implied the forging of ties based upon (pseudo) kin relations (Kondo 1983, 188–196). However, the fact that both the B- and C-type tumuli have some elements that are *not* identical to those of the A type suggests that the mortuary discourse embodied by the keyhole tumuli traits was not forcefully imposed by the elite of the KCR but was *adopted* by the local elite. If the former had been the case, the tumuli builders would have constructed only A-type tumuli, not the B- or C-type tumuli.

Interestingly, the B-type tumuli include specimens such as the Goshoyama (御所山) tumulus of Kanda township (in Fukuoka prefecture) on the coast of the western Seto Inland Sea area; in this tumulus, the burial chamber was constructed in a local (Higo [an ancient province situated in the present-day Kumamoto prefecture] style; Yanagisawa 1980, 482, fig. 5.4). We can infer that the structure of the burial chamber and coffin(s) would have directly reflected the living people's perceptions and beliefs regarding the dead and the ancestors and the relationship between them. It shows that even if the KCR elite were directly involved in the construction of the tumulus, in the form of probably sending the group/groups

of specialists/artisans to build them, this did not necessarily indicate that the local elite were subordinated to those of the KCR. Instead, it is possible that the authority of the KCR elite may have been a religious one reinforced by the exclusive possession of esoteric know-how to which those who were in charge of constructing the B-, C- and D-type tumuli sought access.

This view can be further validated by the following example. The keyhole tumuli constituting the Dairizuka (内裏塚) cluster in the present-day Chiba prefecture in Kanto region were built from the second half of the Middle Kofun period to the very end of the Kofun period, with a short recess in their construction during the first half of the Late Kofun period (Hirose 2009). The change in the mound shape progressed according to the corresponding changes in the KCR. However, it has been pointed out that the mounds of the Dairizuka cluster were much lower than their KCR contemporaries. This further bears out the choices made by the local elite in referring to/adopting the KCR-originated esoteric know-know (ibid.).

Unlike the above picture concerning the construction of the B-, C- and D-type tumuli, the construction of the A-type tumuli indicates the almost complete acceptance of the KCR-originated esoteric know-how/burial process. However, in the case of the B-, C- and D-type tumuli, we should not jump to the conclusion that the construction of A-type tumuli indicated the subordination of the local elite or even their replacement by someone sent by the KCR. It may have been the case that the local elite's intention to entirely adopt the KCR-originated burial process was met with the KCR elite's strategic decision to send the entire, rather than a partial, range of specialists. Let us now investigate the 'elite histories' embodied by keyhole tumuli while keeping the above-mentioned points in mind.

2.5. Reading the Elite Histories from the Keyhole Tumuli

The largest keyhole tumulus in the present-day Nara and Osaka prefectures (in the KCR) of each phase is larger than its counterparts in the other regions (Figure 8.5). The general trend constituted a steady increase in the mound size of these largest tumuli (see Figure 8.4.A–F) until the early second half of the Middle Kofun period (c. the mid/late fifth century AD), when the Daisen (大仙) tumulus, designated as the mausoleum of Emperor Nintoku (仁徳), was constructed. It is also observed that after the mound size had reached its peak in the construction of the preceding tumulus, it gradually began to decrease, with an increasingly wider gap in mound sizes between the KCR tumuli and their other regional equivalents (e.g. Shiraishi 1999, 148–152; also see Figure 10.1). However, the mound sizes of the largest tumuli between the mid-third and mid-/late fifth centuries AD changed from one phase to another. Moreover, in some phases, there were more than two fairly similar-sized largest tumuli constructed in different locations in the KCR. The differences in mound size certainly reflect corresponding differences in the scale of labour force mobilised for the tumuli construction. In that sense, it would be possible to relate the size difference to some kind of hierarchical order; since larger tumuli needed the involvement of a larger labour force than did the smaller ones, those who were buried in the former or those who ordered their construction could mobilise larger numbers of people and hence were higher ranked than those who built or were buried in the smaller tumuli. However, this line of thinking alone cannot help us determine the reason for the *fluctuating* sizes of the tumuli over the course of time; if the size difference had been designed to signify different ranks in the hierarchy, and if the hierarchical order (its system of signification as well as its concrete structure) had needed to be stable (which would certainly have been desirable for the higher-ranked), it would have been rather inconvenient for the size of the largest tumulus, which was meant to function as the yardstick, to fluctuate from one phase to the next. However, the fact that these fluctuations did occur suggests the following: (1) the hierarchy indicated by the size difference between the mounds was not very rigid; (2) the mound size was determined by concerns other than merely the indication of hierarchical differences; (3) the mound size might have possibly been ultimately determined based on the number of communities who willingly offered their labour towards the tumulus construction. The last point derives from the contemporaneous existence of more than two tumuli that could be called the

largest – it suggests that a certain amount of competition was involved in their construction, which would also have involved competition over the competitor-faction's size of following.

In order to investigate the validity of these inferences, we need to examine (a) how the mound itself functioned, (b) whether there is any recognisable pattern in the fluctuation of the mound size over phases and (c) whether there is any factor, archaeological or otherwise, that shows a co-relation to or co-transformation with the fluctuation.

CHANGING SIZE OF THE LARGEST TUMULI
Facts: The following is a list of the largest and second-largest tumuli (measured in metres) of each phase between the mid-third and the mid-/late fifth centuries AD:[19]

(a) Hashihaka/Hashinakayama (箸中山) 276 (280) // Nakayama-Otsuka (中山大塚) 120

(b) Nishitonozuka (西殿塚) 219 // Tobi-Chausuyama (外山茶臼山) 207

(c) Mesuriyama (メスリ山) 250 // Andon'yama (行燈山) 242

(d) Shibutani-Mukouyama (渋谷向山) 300 // Gosashi (五社神) 275 (?: date disputed; might be re-dated to (e) or (f))

(e) Horaisan (蓬莱山) 227 // Saki-Ishizukayama (佐紀石塚山) 218 (//Saki-Misasagiyama (佐紀陵山) 207)

(f) Suyama (巣山) 220 // Tsudo-Shiroyama (津堂城山) 208 (//Saki-Misasagiyama 207)

(g) Nakatsuyama (仲津山) 290 // Ichiniwa (市庭) 250 (// Muro-Miyayama [室宮山] 240)

(h) Mozu-Misasagiyama (百舌鳥陵山; Ishizuoka-Misanzai) 360 (365) = Zozan (造山; Kamo-Tsukuriyama, Okayama prefecture) 360 // Konabe (コナベ) 207

(i) Konda-Gobyoyama (誉田御廟山) 425 // Sakuzan (作山; Misu-Tsukuriyama) 286

19 The accurate determination of the mound length is difficult in that the base of the mound is often buried or submerged in the moat, or, simply, destroyed. Accordingly, the determination remains to be 'estimation'. In that sense, the figures are commonly accepted ones and have to be treated as 'estimated figures'. Even so, the outcome of the following work, focussing on the long-term trend rather than the mound size itself, would not be severely affected by possible margin of errors involved.

(Okayama; date uncertain) (// Uwanabe 255)

(j) Daisen (大仙) 486 // Sakuzan (Misu-Tsukuriyama) 286 (Okayama; date uncertain)

(k) Haji-Nisanzai (土師ニサンザイ) 288 // Ichinoyama (市野山) 227, Ota-Chausuyama (大田茶臼山) 227 (// Hishiage [ヒシアゲ] 220) (// Ryoguzan [両宮山] 194 Okayama prefecture])

(l) Oka-Misanzai (岡ミサンザイ) 242 // Nanakoshiyama (七興山) 146 (Gun'ma prefecture)

A comparison of the respective mound sizes of the largest and second-largest tumuli of each phase reveals an intriguing pattern (Figure 9.12.A–B). The mound size of the largest tumulus continued to decline after the construction of the first large tumulus, the Hashihaka tumulus (a), until there was hardly any difference between the mound sizes of the largest and the second-largest tumuli (Figure 9.12.A). The Mesuriyama tumulus (c) is thought to date from the early fourth century AD, and the Andon'yama tumulus (c) is widely believed to have been constructed immediately afterwards. However, as far as the available information is concerned, both date back to the same quarter of the fourth century AD. The mound of the Mesuriyama tumulus is 31 metres longer than that of the Nishitonozuka, the largest tumulus of the previous phase (b), while that of the Andon'yama is just 8 metres short of the mound of the Mesuriyama. The 300-metre-long mound of the Shibutani-Mukouyama (d), widely thought to have been constructed after the Mesuriyama, appears to have been specifically made larger than that of the second-largest tumulus due to the ongoing competition; the second-largest tumuli of the phase, the Gosashi (the date disputed, possibly replaced by the Horaisan), was 25 metres longer than the Mesuriyama, the largest tumuli of the previous phase, and as if to outdo all the other competitor(s), the Shibutani-Mukouyama tumulus exceeded the 300-metre-mark for the first time. The Shibutani-Mukouyama tumulus, incidentally, was the first tumulus to surpass the size of the very first big tumulus – the Hashinakayama (Hashihaka) (a).

It should be noted that the Gosashi tumulus was constructed some 18 kilometres to the north of the tumulus cluster containing the previous largest and second-largest tumuli – the tumulus cluster of Oyamato (大和/オオヤマト; Figures 9.13 and 9.14.A and B). We shall shortly discuss the issue of the changing locations of the largest and second-largest tumuli of each phase, but now let us continue with the examination of tumuli sizes. The size of the largest tumuli of the next phase declined again: the Horaisan tumulus (e) measures 227 metres and Saki-Ishizukayama (e), 218 metres. Then, the size difference between the largest tumulus and the second-largest tumulus narrowed down further: both the Suyama and the Tsudo-Shiroyama measure around 210 metres.

The Horaisan, Saki-Misasagiyama and Saki-Ishizukayama tumuli are located in the Saki cluster in the north-eastern edge of the present-day Nara Plain (Figures 9.13 and 9.14.B), while the Suyama tumulus is located in the western part of the same plain (the Umami cluster: Figures 9.13 and 9.14.C). The Tsudo-Shiroyama tumulus is located where the present-day Kawachi Plain opens into Osaka Bay (the Furuichi cluster: Figures 9.13 and 9.14.D). Although the Ikoma and Kongo mountain ranges separate the Nara and Kawachi plains, the Yamato River flows through both of them (Figure 9.13).

After the construction of those tumuli of fairly identical sizes, the earlier half of the fifth century AD saw a mounting difference between the respective mound sizes of the largest and second-largest tumuli of each phase. For instance, the Nakatsuyama tumulus (g), located to the south-east of the Tsudo-Shioroyama tumulus (Figure 9.14.D), measures 290 m, which is about 40 m longer than the Ichiniwa tumulus (g), located in the same cluster as the Gosashi, Horaisan, Saki-Misasagiyama and Saki-Ishizukayama tumuli (Figure 9.14.B). The Mozu-Misasagiyama tumulus (h), measuring approximately 360 m, was matched in size by the Zozan (Kamo-Tsukuriyama) tumulus (h) in the present-day Okayama prefecture. Following this, the two largest tumuli ever were successively constructed: the Konda-Gobyoyama (i) at 425 m and the Daisen tumulus (j) at 486 m (Figure 9.14.C and D). The Sakuzan (Misu-Tsukuriyama) tumulus (i) (in Okayama prefecture) was the second-largest tumulus after the Konda-Gobyoyama in the same phase,[20] again located

20 Possibly dated to the parallel position to the *Daisen*.

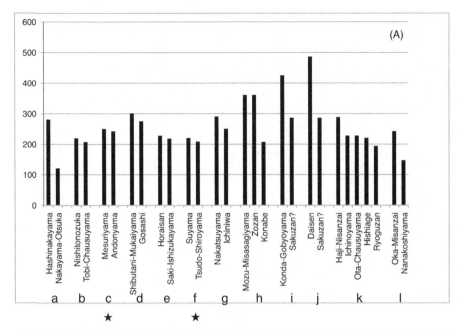

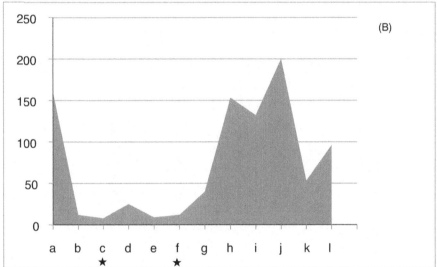

Figure 9.12. The largest and second-largest tumuli in each phase by mound length (**A**), and the difference between them plotted phase by phase (**B**). The 'phases of competition' starred (see relevant discussions).

in the present-day Okayama prefecture (286 metres), followed by the Uwanabe tumulus at 270 metres, situated in the same cluster as the Gosashi, Horaisan and other tumuli (Figure 9.14.B). The gap between mound sizes widened to more than 200 metres (Figure 9.12.B). The trend reached its zenith as the 486-metres-long mound of the Daisen (j) was constructed.

After the construction of the Daisen tumulus, the size of the largest tumulus of each phase declined drastically (Figure 9.12.A), along with that of the second largest, and the gap narrowed but remained significant (though the sudden narrowing of the gap in the phase K, with fairly similarly sized tumuli coexisting, should be noted). Towards the end of the Kofun period, two very large tumuli were built – the Kawachi-Otsukayama (河内大塚山; 335 m) and the Mise-Maruyama (見瀬丸山; 310 m) tumuli.[21] We shall return to a more detailed discussion of this intriguing episode in the history of the keyhole tumuli in a subsequent chapter (Chapter 11). At this point, let us concentrate on the continuous fluctuation of the size of the largest tumulus of each phase.

21 The date of the former is undetermined, and some infer that the tumulus was abandoned under construction.

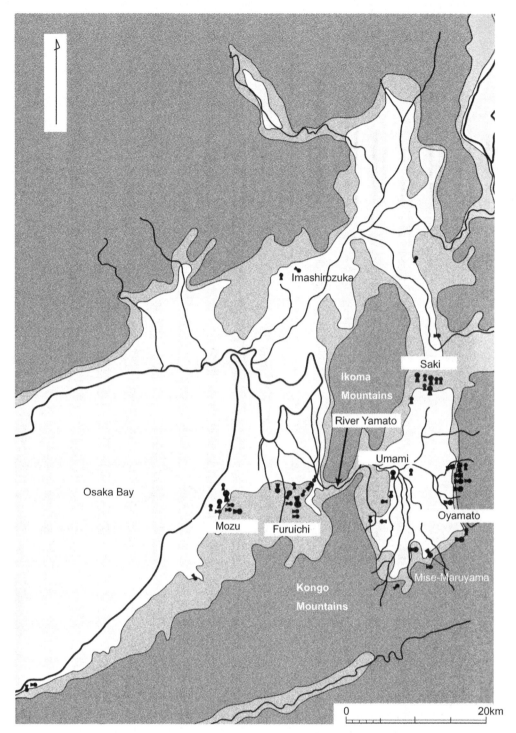

Figure 9.13. Major tumuli clusters of the KCR (Kinki-core region): distribution (from Hirose 2003). With kind permission from the Kadokawa Shoten Publishing Co.

Interpretation: The size-fluctuation patterns described above show the following characteristics:

(1) The size of the largest tumulus significantly increased when there was a narrow gap in scale between it and the second-largest tumulus of the same or previous phase (phases d and g).

(2) The rate of enlargement of the largest tumulus increased (g afterword) after the phase wherein three identical-sized tumuli, i.e., the Saki-Ishizukayama, Suyama and Tsudo-Shiroyama tumuli, were constructed (f).

(3) As if to surpass all the 'prior competition', the Zozan tumulus in the present-day

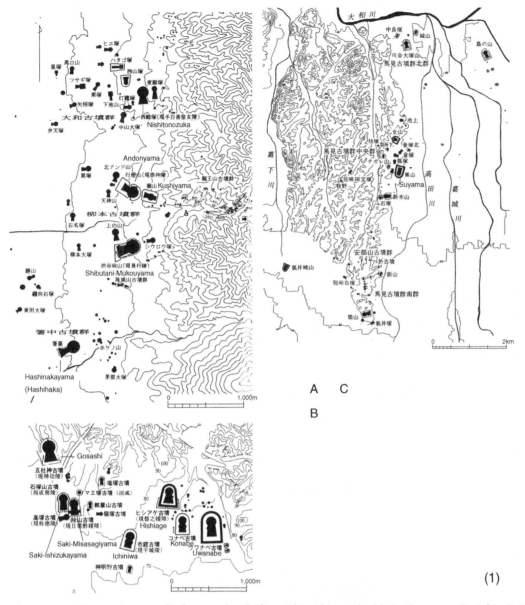

Figure 9.14. Five major tumuli clusters: detail (from Shiraishi 2000). (1) A: Oyamato, B: Saki, C: Umani. (2) D: Furuichi, E: Mozu. Note the names of the tumuli mentioned in the sentences are Romanised. With kind permission from Professor Taichiro Shiraishi and the Hanawa Shobo Publishing Co.

Okayama prefecture and the Mozu-Misasagiyama tumulus were both constructed of the same size, that is, about 360 metres (phase h).

(4) Following the construction of the above tumuli, the two largest tumuli ever built were the Konda-Gobyoyama (phase i) and the Daisen tumuli (phase j), and the gap between them and the second-largest tumulus of their respective phase further widened to exceed 150 metres (Figure 9.12.B).

Observation 1 suggests that some sort of competition over the scale of the mound contributed to a steady increase in the mound size; this competition would have occurred between individuals/groups. In this case, the 'units' involved in the competition can be hypothesised to have been the individuals or groups who were in charge of planning the construction of the mounds and mobilising the labour force to that end. These units could have been a part of separate *factions* (Brumfiel and Fox 1994), or they could also have been successive generational units forming a single lineage/clan. However, the fact that those tumuli which appear to have been built 'out of competition' (i.e. constructed in the same phase or successive phases with mound-size

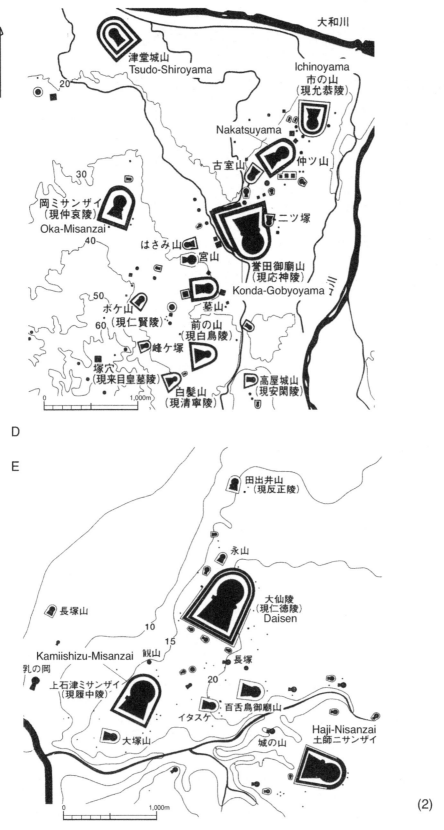

D

E

Figure 9.14 (*continued*)

(2)

differences of less than 50 metres) are located in different clusters (Figures 9.13 and 9.14) suggests that the former was the case.

This observation and its interpretation suggest some important implications for understanding (X) the reason behind the construction of the gigantic tumuli, (Y) the nature of the clusters in which those tumuli are situated and (Z) the reasons for the changing locations of the largest tumuli from one phase to the next.

Concerning X, the reason behind the construction of the gigantic tumuli, the observations suggest that it related to the symbolic representation of the position of the deceased buried. This might seem to be a truism; however, it is very important to consider the way in which, and why, the position of the deceased was represented by the size of the mound. To begin with, who decided the size of the mound? The deceased themselves might have been involved in this decision, if the planning and construction of the mound had been initiated when the individual to be buried in it was still alive. As mentioned earlier, some examples do indicate the possibility that the mound construction was partially completed at the time of death of the person(s) buried in that tumulus (Yoshidome 1992). However, we cannot assert that the construction of every one of the gigantic tumuli had begun before the death of the person(s) buried in those tumuli. In any case, it can be said that those who decided the tumuli size would have tried to ensure that their own mound was larger than that of their 'opponent'; in other words, the decision was conscious and strategic. Scholars have already pointed out that the foundations of most of those tumuli were built on preexisting hills. However, the patterns mentioned in the above observations make it difficult for us to claim that the mound size was solely determined by the size of those preexisting hills.

With regard to Y, the nature of the clusters in which those tumuli are situated, there are two theses that currently attempt to explain this aspect. The first argues that the cluster in which the largest tumulus was constructed at each phase was strategically chosen by the (already established unilinear) lineage of paramount chiefs (Kondo 1983, 295–306). The thesis also argues that throughout those periods, the residence and power-base of that lineage was continuously situated in the vicinity of the cluster where the largest tumuli of phases (a) to (e) were situated, that is, in the south-eastern corner of the Nara Basin (the Oyamato cluster; Figure 9.14.A, and see the next section).

The second thesis argues that the cluster in which the largest tumulus was constructed at each phase was close to either the residence or the power-base of the paramount chief of that phase. Taichiro Shiraishi, the main proponent of this thesis, observes that the area of Saki – located on the northern edge of the Nara Basin, where the largest tumulus of phase (e) was situated – was occupied by a clan from which the wives of successive early paramount chiefs hailed, according to the old imperial chronicles. Shiraishi argues that deepening ties between the paramount chiefs whose residences and tumuli were constructed in the south-eastern corner of the basin and the clan residing in the Saki area led to the change in location of the resting place of paramount chiefs from the former region to the latter (Shiraishi 1999, 118–127).

With regard to the further change in the location of the largest tumuli from the Saki to the Kawachi Plain along the Osaka Bay (Figure 9.13), Shiraishi argues that by that period, the local clans that had begun to play an increasingly important role in the interactions, including militaristic interventions, with the polities of the Korean peninsula, had also assumed the paramount chieftainship; it was these clans that began to construct the largest tumuli from phase (g) onwards. An important point is that phases (e) and (f) – which saw fierce competition over the size of the largest tumuli (characterised by the construction of three tumuli with fairly similar sizes, that is, the Saki-Ishizukayama, Suyama and Tsudo-Shiroyama tumuli, located in three different clusters) – also saw the construction of the Tsudo-Shiroyama tumulus, which measured 208 metres in length and was only 12 metres shorter than the Suyama, dated contemporaneous to it.[22] In addition, Shiraishi adds that the largest tumuli of phases (a) to (d) – all of which are situated in the south-eastern

---

22 The excavations conducted after Shiraishi's research have confirmed that the Suyama tumulus is actually 220 metres long, which means that it is the largest tumulus of the phase: Shiraishi assessed it to be as large as or smaller than the Tsudo-Shiroyama (Koryo TBE 2005).

corner of the Nara Basin – were actually constructed in different subgroups (Figure 9.14.A; also see the next section). He infers that those subgroups constituted burial grounds for different kin groups, which leads to the inference that the paramount chieftainship was not exclusively assumed by a single lineage. The preceding observations, according to Shiraishi, suggest that the paramount chief was chosen by a group of clans that formed a 'ruling confederacy'. In that case, the changing locations of the resting place of the paramount chiefs can be explained as the natural result of the selection of the new paramount chieftain from a new or different clan from the previous one.

The observations in the current investigation, pointing to the competitive construction of mounds that were larger than those built by the opponents, support Shiraishi's inferences. The fact that the 'phases of competition', by which is meant that similarly sized 'largest tumuli' of a phase were situated in different clusters (i.e., phases c and f; Figure 9.12), preceded or coincided with the changes in location of the resting place of the paramount chief (Figures 9.13 and 9.14) suggest that a number of clan-type groups formed a ruling confederacy and competed for the paramount chieftainship. For these clans, or their elite segments, the sheer size of the labour force that they could mobilise would have been important for displaying their power and authority to their rivals. In that sense, the actual standing of those who were buried in the tumuli built by the ruling confederacy may not necessarily have been *reflected* by the size of the mounds; instead, the size may well have been determined by the *potential* and *desire* among those who buried their dead chiefs to become the paramount chieftains. This further implies the possibility that the size of those tumuli might have been significantly determined by the number of communities that voluntarily participated in their construction in order to fulfil the social obligations that were generated through the display of various forms of generosity, including generous gift-giving. If this were the case, the construction of those tumuli would have involved gigantic celebratory occasions, which might well be the reason why the excavations do not reveal any traces of camps or villages for the 'construction workers' of those tumuli. Except for the traces of workshops producing the necessary paraphernalia for their

construction, such as *Haniwa* kilns (e.g. the Konda-Hakucho [誉田白鳥] kiln in the *Furuichi* cluster [see the next section]; Hishida 2007), researchers have been unable to find any clear traces of residential areas housing those who were involved in the construction of the gigantic tumuli, despite undertaking extensive rescue excavations around the tumuli. This might be because these residences were indeed ephemeral, in the form of temporary camps. The construction parties, coming from a community having ties and social obligations with those who were in charge of the tumuli construction, might have arrived as ritual expeditions in order to pay back their social debt and obtain new honour and privilege. For those who were in charge of the construction, the reception of such parties would have been an occasion to display their generosity by providing plentiful food and show their ritualistic authority by conducting various religious performances, ranging from planning the shape of the mound to rituals marking distinct stages of the construction, each of which would have been characterised by a distinct taboo. The parties may not have resided at the construction sites for a very long period: instead, it is quite possible that a large number of such parties came and went while the construction was in progress. This might be the very reason why there were no permanent settlements around the tumuli: the residences of the construction workers might have been ephemeral, temporary structures.

IMPLICATIONS: THE NATURE OF THE PARAMOUNT CHIEFTAINSHIP AND THE SYSTEM OF SUCCESSION

The preceding observations and inferences can be compared to the outcome of an important investigation conducted by Yoshiyuki Tanaka (1995) into the status of kinship in the Kofun period and its transformation. According to Tanaka (1995), who has reconstructed the descent system of the Kofun period, the period covered by the current investigation saw the gradual transformation of the concept and principle of kinship from a bilinear-oriented descent to a unilinear male-line descent. By examining the morphological affinity of tooth-crown measurements (proved to be a sensitive indicator/genetic marker of the existence of kinship) of individuals buried either in individual burial facilities or in individual tumuli, Tanaka has revealed that those who were buried together in individual burial facilities or in separate burial facilities of a given tumulus were most often brothers and/or sisters during the period from the third to the late fifth centuries AD, strongly suggesting the dominant system of descent being *bilineal* (ibid.).

The bilinear descent system is inherently unstable because on the occasion of succession, it allows both the father's kin and the mother's kin to offer their candidacy for succession and compete for stronger influence. Moreover, in cases where there are more than two candidates, and if they were born of different mothers, the succession decision will be very difficult and can potentially generate a feud between the kin groups.

If this general tendency was present in the period under investigation, that is, the period between the mid-third and mid-/late fifth centuries AD, when those gigantic tumuli were built, it would further strengthen the thesis that the increase and decrease in the size of the largest tumuli over the period reflected inter-group competition over the paramount chieftainship and that the trend of increasing the mound size was accelerated by this competition.

The preceding suggests that the Kofun discourse for the groups forming the ruling confederacy during the Earlier Kofun period was partially but significantly structured around competition over inter-group (or clan) dominance and its projective expression.

One possible supportive evidence can be obtained from the production and distribution, in the form of strategic gift-giving, of certain types of bronze and iron arrowheads (Matsugi 1996). Those arrowheads are small, and the shape of their hafts, in particular, indicate that they were likely to have been made not for actual use as weapons but as weapon-shaped symbolic implements (Matsugi 2007, 168). Taking into account the facts that these arrowheads are homogeneous in their traits across their horizon, that they are conspicuous in the mortuary assemblage of the early keyhole tumuli and that the centre of their distribution lies in the KCR, we can infer that they were distributed by the KCR elite as part of strategic gift-giving for forging/maintaining their relationships with the elite of the other regions (ibid.). However, with regard to the presence of minute morphological variations which can be classified into a number of subcategories (e.g. Ikefuchi 2000) and taking into account the presence of these variations among the tumuli of different subregions of the KCR, we can entertain the possibility that the different elite groups competing for the paramount chieftainship of the KCR had their own workshops for producing those arrowhead types and strategically distributed these arrowheads among the different elite groups of regions outside the KCR as a means to achieve a position of dominance within the local sphere.

THE FORMATION PROCESS OF TUMULI CLUSTERS AND THEIR CHANGES

In addition to the changes occurring in various features of the tumuli, the contents of the tumuli clusters and their corresponding changes reflected how those who buried their elite dead decided the location of the tumulus in relation to the preexisting tumuli, whereby to spatially display their own relationship with the deceased. Let us now examine the following clusters of the Nara Basin and the Kawachi Plain: (a) the Oyamato, (b) Saki, (c) Umami, (d) Furuichi and (e) Mozu clusters (Figures 9.13 and 9.14; cf. Hirose 1987, 1988):

(a) *The Oyamato* (大和/オオヤマト) *cluster* is located in the south-eastern corner of the Nara basin. It is located on the foothills of the Miwa Mountain where, according to the *Kojiki* and *Nihonshoki* chronicles, various rituals were performed by those who were related to the paramount chieftainship. This location is also near the mouth of a valley connecting the basin with the regions around the Ise Bay plains and the Tokai region. This cluster was mainly built from the beginning of the Kofun period to the second half of the Early Kofun period, though sporadic constructions of tumuli continued into the first half of the Late Kofun period.

(b) *The Saki* (佐紀) *cluster* is located at the northern edge of the Nara Basin, at the bottom of the hills dividing the basin and the riverine plain of the Kizu River; it can be conveniently accessed from the Osaka Bay via the Kizu and Yodo rivers and from the Tokai and Hokuriku regions via the Yodo River and Lake Biwa. This cluster began with the construction of the Gosashi (the exact date of construction disputed) or Horaisan tumulus in the second half of the Early Kofun period and expanded until the second half of the Middle Kofun period.

(c) *The Umami* (馬見) *cluster* is located in the south-western corner of the basin and stretches from the region near the mouth of the valley, through which the Yamato River flows out of the basin and into the Osaka Bay via the Kawachi Plain, to the south-western end of the plain. The cluster formation began in the first half of the Early Kofun period and continued until almost the end of the Kofun period, though the construction of large keyhole tumuli became sporadic from the end of the Middle Kofun period onwards.

(d) *The Furuichi* (古市) *cluster* is located near the other end of the valley through which the Yamato River flows out of the Nara Basin. The river connects the location to both the Nara Basin and the Osaka Bay. While some scholars have disputed the genealogical relationship between the cluster and the keyhole tumuli successively constructed during the Early Kofun period on Tamateyama (a hill) to the east, which overlooks the Yamato River as it flows out of the mountain range dividing the Nara Basin and the Kawachi Plain, the cluster formation itself began in the beginning of the Middle Kofun period. The construction of large keyhole tumuli lasted until the first half, and possibly extended into the second half, of the Late Kofun period.

(e) *The Mozu* (百舌鳥) *cluster* is located to the west of the Furuichi cluster. The gigantic tumuli constituting this cluster are located not far from the eastern coast of Osaka Bay and must have been clearly visible from the ships sailing into the bay. The cluster formation began in the beginning of the Middle Kofun period and abruptly ended at the end of the same period.

A brief review of the most prominent clusters of the KCR indicates the following:

(1) The beginning and duration of the cluster formation differ as if the construction activities were shifted from one to the other, with significant overlaps in between.

(2) The shift started from (a) the Oyamato cluster and moved to (b) the Saki to (d) the Furuichi to (e) the Mozu cluster, while the duration of (c) the Umami cluster significantly overlapped with those of the other four.

(3) During the Early and Middle Kofun periods, clusters (a), (b), (d) and (e) saw the constructions of successive largest tumuli among their contemporaries, whereas (c) possibly saw the construction of only one such tumulus, that is, the Suyama tumulus (approximately 220 metres), dating back to the turn of the Early Kofun period, which is likely to be contemporaneous to the Tsudo-Shiroyama tumulus (approximately 208 metres) in cluster (d) (see relevant discussions in the previous section).

(4) The above points suggest that the burial (and ritual-ceremonial) base of the paramount chiefs and their peers of some sort moved from clusters (a) to (b) to (d) to (e), whereas cluster (c) continued, during the Early and Middle Kofun periods, to be the base of the second-highest chieftain figures (who were also possibly contenders to the paramount chieftainship).

Based on these four points, we can suggest the following:

(a) The spatio-temporal configuration of clusters (a), (b), (d) and (e) would have reflected the way in which those who buried the paramount chieftains and their peers decided on the location of the tumulus in relation to the pre-existing tumuli, whereby to spatially display their own relationship with the deceased.

(b) If it is possible to identify any significant changes in the spatio-temporal configuration of the tumuli clusters, these would reflect the temporal changes that occurred in the meaning(s) that were attached to not only the paramount chieftainship and the position of the chief's peers but also the organisation of the power structure of the KCR.

Let us now investigate if we can recognise any changes of this kind by examining the spatio-temporal configuration of the tumuli clusters (a), (b), (d) and (e) in that order (Figure 9.13).

(a) *The Oyamato Cluster* (Figure 9.14.A). The cluster can be divided into four sub-groups, the durations of which significantly overlap with one another, although the southernmost sub-group, with Hashinakayama being the largest tumulus in it, is older than the rest. Each of those sub-groups contains a largest tumulus dating back to a particular phase in the Early Kofun period. This suggests that the cluster served as the burial and ritual-ceremonial ground for a number of groupings and that the paramount chieftainship rotated from one such grouping to another (Hirose 1987). Each group consists of a number of fairly large keyhole tumuli, and the northern-most sub-group includes those with a square rear mound (e.g. the Shimoikeyama (下池山), approximately 120 metres long, and the Hatagozuka (波多子塚), approximately 140 metres long, among others). The Kushiyama (櫛山) tumulus, located in the northern central sub-group, is approximately 152 metres long and dates back to the second half of the Early Kofun period; it is unique in that the round rear part of the mound is attached to a smaller square mound. The genealogy of this unique mound shape might be traced to the Nekozuka (猫塚) tumulus in Kagawa prefecture in the eastern Inland Sea region, dating back to the first half of the Early Kofun period, and even further back to the Tatesuki (楯築) tumulus of Okayama prefecture in the same region, dating back to the Late Yayoi V. The presence of the Kushiyama and the keyhole tumuli with square rear mounds suggest that the display of connections, including (possibly pseudo/fictive) kin relationships, with a community/communities in the eastern Inland Sea, the Tokai region and the east was considered important by those who were involved in the formation of the cluster.

Scholars have pointed out that when the Hashihaka was constructed, there were no contemporaneous tumuli of a significant scale across the KCR, except for the Tsubai-Otsukayama (椿井大塚山) tumulus (approximately 170 metres; Shiraishi 1999, 74–77). They have also pointed out that this situation persisted throughout the duration of the cluster formation (Hirose 1987, 1988). Based on these facts, it is possible to infer that the cluster was used as the burial site for the elite of dominant communities across the KCR (ibid.); moreover, as previously stated, Shiraishi (1999, 86) argues that they formed a ruling confederacy, choosing the paramount chieftain from among themselves (see also Hirose 1988, 72–73). The fact that the largest tumuli of different phases during the cluster formation were constructed in different sub-groups supports this inference. The presence of the Kushiyama and the keyhole tumuli with square rear mounds suggests that the dominant communities, probably clan-type groupings, would have had pseudo-kinship-tie-type relations with the elite of remote communities.

On the whole, the characteristics of the cluster indicate that a certain amount of significance was attributed to the display of *collaboration* and *togetherness* within and between the communities who buried their chiefs in that cluster; it was also considered important to maintain networks with remote communities.

(b) *The Saki Cluster* (Figure 9.14.B). This cluster appears to have been divided into two sub-groups. However, considering the erstwhile location of the Ichiniwa tumulus – the square front mound of which was destroyed during the construction of the Heijo palace (平城宮) in the eighth century – and the locations of certain other tumuli which were also destroyed by the construction, all of which were situated between the apparent clusters, it would be safe to assume that the cluster did not consist of distinct sub-clusters. The formation process generally progressed from the west to the east. There also is an outlier – the Horaisan tumulus (approximately 227 metres long, dating back to the end of the Early Kofun period) – located to the south-west of the cluster.

In contrast to the Oyamato cluster, the eight keyhole tumuli exceeding the 200-metre-mark were constructed in a successive manner, not forming distinct sub-groups containing smaller keyhole tumuli like the Oyamato. Instead, the largest tumuli were attached to much smaller round and/or square tumuli. This custom began when the earlier four of the eight tumuli – the Horaisan, the Saki-Misasagiyama (approximately 207 metres), the Saki-Ishizukayama (approximately 218 metres) and the Gosashi tumuli (approximately 275 metres)[23] – were successively constructed in the second half of the Early Kofun period, and the custom of building tumuli exceeding 200 metres in length continued into the Middle Kofun period, when the Ichiniwa (approximately 250 metres), the Konabe (approximately 207 metres), the Uwanabe (approximately 255 metres) and the Hishiage (approximately 220 metres) tumuli were built. These 200-metre-plus Middle Kofun tumuli of this cluster were constructed at around the same time as those in the (d) Furuichi and (e) Mozu clusters, where many of the 200-metre-plus tumuli were also surrounded by small round, square and at times keyhole tumuli (*Baizuka/Baicho* [陪塚: 'satellites']). Some of these tumuli had no grave goods apart from specific types of artefacts such as weapons. Therefore, those who were buried in them would have certainly occupied different positions from those who were buried in the smaller keyhole tumuli of the Oyamato cluster. Whereas the latter are likely to have been the chiefs of the clans, the former may well have represented the elite belonging to lineages subordinate to the chief lineage in the clan. In that sense, those who were buried in the small tumuli surrounding the gigantic keyhole tumuli might be described as the sub-chiefs of the paramount chiefly clan or the chiefs of clans subordinate to the paramount chiefly clan, and those small tumuli located outside the terrace encircling the moat(s) of the gigantic tumuli – wherein at times no bodies appear to have been buried – might have been designed to symbolically represent the tasks undertaken by those sub-chiefs.[24] In any case, this new custom began with the formation of the Saki cluster (e.g. Shiraishi 1999). In addition, this cluster contains neither any keyhole tumulus with a square rear mound nor one with any additional square part like the Kushiyama tumulus in the Oyamato cluster.

In short, the characteristics of the cluster show the significance of representing the lineage-like succession of chiefs buried in keyhole tumuli exceeding 200 metres in length and the possibility of a hierarchical relationship between the chief's lineage and the subordinate's lineages of the clan which constructed each of those gigantic tumuli. As far as the lineage-like successive constructions of gigantic tumuli are concerned, the paramount chief was materially portrayed by the tumuli forming a *single* genealogical line. It is important to note that the chief's connections with remote communities were not overtly represented in these tumuli any longer.

(d) *The Furuichi* and (e) *the Mozu Clusters* (Figures 9.14.D–E). The formation process of these clusters was basically similar to that of the Saki; gigantic tumuli exceeding 200 metres in length – including the Tsudo-Shiroyama (approximately 208 metres), Nakatsuyama (approximately 290 metres), Konda-Gobyoyama (approximately 425 metres), Ichinoyama (approximately 230 metres) and Oka-Misanzai (approximately 242 metres) tumuli located in the Furuichi cluster and the Kamiisizu-Misanzai (approximately 360 [365] metres), Daisen (approximately 486 metres) and Haji-Nisanzai (approximately 288 metres) tumuli located in the Mozu cluster – were successively constructed to form a genealogical sequence in the respective cluster. They were commonly surrounded by small tumuli of various shapes and sizes, some of them with burials and others without, and containing artefacts (in many cases, weapons and tools including body armour, spearheads, swords, arrowheads, sickles and socketed axes – all made of iron), often in an extremely large quantity. As in the case of the Saki cluster, those who were buried in these tumuli can be inferred to have been sub-chiefs subordinate to the deceased buried in those gigantic tumuli.

It is important, however, to note that those clusters also contained a number of fairly large keyhole tumuli, scale-wise exceeding 100 metres in length, some of which were constructed adjacent to the gigantic tumuli, while others were quite independent of them. These particular tumuli did not form sequential sub-groups. In other words, their construction was sporadic, and the character of the deceased buried in them is difficult to

---

23 The exact dating of the tumulus is now disputed, and may be relocated to a slightly later date.

24 They can be understood to have been the extension of the custom of depositing large amounts of artefacts in separate compartments of the burial facility of the main tumuli. See pp. 254–256 in this chapter.

discern. One possibility is that they are the burial tumuli of the chiefs of some dominant clans of the KCR who were subordinates of the paramount chief and his clan (e.g. Hirose 2009).

The *Umami Cluster* (c) (Figure 9.14.C). It was built at around the same time as the Furuichi and Mozu clusters, also contained some gigantic tumuli, but the keyhole tumuli in this cluster were consistently smaller than the contemporary largest (except at the end of the second half of the Early Kofun period, which saw the construction of the Suyama tumulus, approximately 220 metres); based on this, we can infer the presence of a clan which represented its position and identity in the power relations of the KCR by successively constructing gigantic keyhole tumuli in the Umami cluster as well as the existence of many other clans also involved in the power relations but which did not built their own tumuli clusters. These clans probably constructed the tumuli of their chiefs only when certain conditions were met; in this way, we might be able to explain the sporadic nature of construction of the 'fairly large' tumuli in the Furuichi and Mozu clusters.

In short, in the Furuichi and Mozu clusters, the paramount chieftainship appears to have been portrayed by the successive construction of gigantic tumuli forming a genealogical line. The internal hierarchy of the clan(s) of the paramount chieftain continued to be symbolically represented by small tumuli of various shapes and sizes built around the gigantic tumuli. The power relations among the dominant clans of the KCR might have been represented by the construction of fairly large tumuli in a sporadic fashion in these clusters. These reflect the increasing complexity of the power relations and hierarchy of the KCR and the unilinearity of succession of the paramount chieftainship, at least in its *representation*. However, in this interpretation, we encounter a problem: the Furuichi and Mozu clusters are located about 12 kilometres away from one another. It is certainly interesting to note that they each occupy an area measuring approximately 4 kilometres by 4 kilometres, and that their northern and southern limits fairly well correspond with one another in terms of latitude (Figure 9.13). Some scholars argue that these clusters were designed as one large area that would form the resting ground of the successive

paramount chieftains. However, the presence of a large gap between the clusters cannot be denied. Moreover, they include archaeologically contemporaneous gigantic tumuli. One possible reason for this might have been that the gigantic tumuli were alternately built between the two clusters in order to form a unified genealogical sequence. Even so, we still have no reason indicating why they were constructed in those separate locations. By referring to the *Kojiki* and *Nihonshoki* chronicles and pointing out that the 'recorded' locations of the successive paramount chiefs' (*O-kimi*) residences were mostly in the Nara Basin during the Middle Kofun period, that is, between the end of the fourth/beginning of the fifth and the end of the fifth centuries AD, some scholars argue that the locations of the clusters were entirely determined on a political basis in order to display the authority of the paramount chieftainship and the power structure around it (e.g. Kondo 1983, 295–306). Because of the cluster's proximity to the eastern coast of the Osaka Bay, several scholars have argued that the gigantic tumuli of the Mozu cluster were designed to impress emissaries from remote places, including the polities of the Korean peninsula (ibid.). However, this argument contradicts the fact that many such gigantic tumuli also continued to be built in the Furuichi cluster, located far away from the coast. In addition, considering the necessity of various facilities for the construction of gigantic tumuli, it would have been more efficient not to constantly relocate the designated area for the construction of the resting place of the paramount. Hence, it would be reasonable to infer that the coexistence of those clusters reflected some kind of competition between two *groupings*,[25] though it is difficult to discern the nature, character and scale of those groupings.

Summary of the Argument. The shifting locations of the resting place of the paramount chieftains

25 To add, when the Kamo-Tsukuriyama was constructed in the ancient province of Kibi, present-day Okayama prefecture, concerning its size (about 360 metres, almost identical to that of the Kamiishizu-Misanzai) and mound shape (also almost identical to the Kamiishizu-Misanzai), the person buried there and those who were in charge of its construction were also in direct competition with those who were in charge of the formation of those tumuli clusters.

from the Oyamato to the Saki (and possibly temporarily to the Umami, reflected by the construction of the Suyama in the cluster) to the Furuichi and Mozu clusters corresponded with changes in the way power relations among the dominant elite clans of the KCR and beyond were structured and represented. This trend can be summarised in phases as follows: (I) it represented communal collaboration among the elite clans (the Oyamato phase) through (II) an attempt to portray the paramount chieftainship as unilinearly inherited (the Saki phase onward); (III) it also involved inter-group competition represented by the competitive constructions of ever-larger tumuli, wherein each group attempted to outdo its competitor and thus challenge the paramount chieftainship by constructing the largest tumuli in the two clusters situated in the Kawachi Plain (the Furuichi and Mozu phase).

Phase I of the aforementioned trend was also characterised by the representation of connections with remote communities (as we saw in the form of the presence of some large K-2 and SRS type tumuli in the Oyamato cluster), while phase II was characterised by the emergence of 'satellites' overtly representing and visualising the stratification of the internal structure of the clan from which the paramount chieftain was chosen. This phase also saw the beginning of the display of independence of dominant clans in the KCR, which was reflected by the development of the Umami cluster and the large keyhole tumuli constructed in areas that were later to become part of the Furuichi and Mozu clusters. Phase III was characterised by the further development of the hierarchy and the continuation of inter-dominant-clan competition over the paramount chieftainship, now including that of the province of Kibi (reflected by the successive construction of the largest, the Kamo-Tsukuriyama, and second-largest, the Misu-Tsukuriyama, tumuli). Interestingly, this change appears to have nicely correlated with the change in the image of the chief as revealed by the investigation of the mortuary paraphernalia above – that is, the change in the image of the chief from the representative of communal well-being to the commander-executor of the communal will. These changes can also be related to the beginning and expansion of interventions within the Korean peninsula (see

Chapter 4.3). As argued earlier, these interventions would have generated a new set of contingencies which would have initiated and accelerated those changes; the chiefs were now required to deal with unprecedented and incalculable risks that would normally never have been generated by agricultural activities and interactions among communities within the archipelago, and their mere ability to mediate with the transcendental realm would have become insufficient to overcome these new contingencies.

THE BROADER PICTURE

If we consider the cluster formation in the regions outside the KCR, we can recognise some significant patterns.[26]

First, the Early Kofun (c. the late third–fourth century) witnessed the formation of keyhole tumuli clusters in many of the major flood plains in the Kyushu, Shikoku and Honshu islands, except for the southern Kyushu and northern Tohoku regions. A notable exception to this was the ancient province of Izumo, which remained independent of the IKP (see Chapter 8.3) horizon and continued constructing rectangular tumuli. During the fourth century, this region saw the construction of square tumuli as well as keyhole tumuli with a square rear mound (see Figure 8.5; Otani 1995; Ikefuchi 1997); the latter type continued to be predominantly built from the Tokai region on the Pacific coast to the Hokuriku region to the east (see Figure 8.5; Fujisawa 2004b). Many of the larger tumuli of this type were constructed in the northern Kanto region (ibid.), while a small number of them continued to be constructed in the regions west of those regions (ibid.).

Second, the construction of some of those clusters which continued to form genealogical sequences came to an abrupt close at the beginning of the fifth century (the end of the second half of the Early Kofun and the first half of the Middle Kofun), whereas others continued to grow. However, only a few of them saw the formation of genealogical sequences continuing into the sixth century.

Third, many clusters began to be formed during the fifth century, but very few of them

---

26 See Ishino (1995) for a concise summary of the overall trend.

continued into the sixth century (the Late Kofun). Notable exceptions include the ancient provinces of Fusa (largely coinciding with the present-day Chiba prefecture) and Kamitsukenu (largely coinciding with the present-day Gunma prefecture) in Kanto region, where the formation of genealogical sequences of relatively large keyhole tumuli continued throughout the fifth and sixth centuries AD.

Fourth, the formation of many keyhole tumuli clusters ceased towards the beginning of the sixth century AD (the beginning of the Late Kofun), particularly in the regions around the KCR. In many of the still-continuing clusters, the size of the tumuli drastically decreased. The Kanto region was an exception to this trend, wherein many of the older clusters continued growing, while a number of new clusters with relatively large keyhole tumuli were even newly constructed.

Finally, some clusters of keyhole tumuli that had either suddenly emerged or had continued developing from the fifth century became prominent due to the construction of relatively large keyhole tumuli during the sixth century AD.

These patterns, in terms of their timing, correspond with the locational shift of the cluster consisting of the largest tumuli in KCR from the southeastern corner of the Nara Basin to the northern bottom of the same basin (c. the mid-fourth century; shift I), then to (II) the Kawachi Plain (c. the end of the fourth and the beginning of the fifth centuries) and then to (IV) the southern bottom of the Nara Basin (the late sixth century) via (III) the northern edge of the Osaka Plain (the early sixth century). The end of the formation of many sequential clusters at the beginning of the fifth century and the simultaneous onset of the formation of a number of new sequential clusters in different regions coincided with shift II mentioned above, and the cessation of the formation of a large number of the sequential clusters at the beginning of the sixth century, particularly significant in and around the KCR, coincided with the above-mentioned shift III.

These patterns are also correlated with the changing nature of the keyhole tumulus and of the mortuary practices conducted there (see earlier discussions in this chapter). As mentioned above, shift I coincided with the new trend of using *Haniwa* vessels depicting the residential compound and ritual facilities of the elite, along with the paraphernalia

symbolising their status. This shift also coincided with the transformation of the *Sankakuen-shinjukyo* mirror-centred mortuary assemblage into that consisting of a large quantity of jasper- and talc-made paraphernalia, as well as the possible inclusion of iron armour and weapons (see earlier discussions in this chapter). The end of the formation of many sequential clusters at the beginning of the fifth century and the simultaneous onset of the formation of a number of new sequential clusters in individual regions coincided not only with the intensification of this trend but also with shift II; the *Haniwa* assemblage of the time came to include shields and armours (see Figure 9.11 and relevant discussions), and by now a vast quantity of iron armour and weapons were being deposited as grave goods, at times, in cists specifically constructed for containing them (see Figure 9.8 and relevant discussions). As we have seen, after a period wherein there was a very narrow gap between the respective sizes of the largest, second-largest and third-largest tumuli, from the beginning of the fifth century onwards, the gap became increasingly wider (except in the case of the Kamo-Tsukuriyama and Misu-Tsukuriyama tumuli, which were almost as big as the contemporaneous largest tumulus in the KCR and were successively built in the ancient province of Kibi in the mid-fifth century), while the size of the largest tumulus increased significantly (see Figure 9.12 and relevant discussions). The above-mentioned shift III and the halt in the formation of a large number of sequential clusters correlated with the decrease in the size of the largest tumulus of that period as well as other changes which occurred in the nature of mortuary practices carried out on and around the mound. I discuss this aspect in the next chapter.

How can we make sense of these co-transformations? The following clues might help us understand the changes.

In the ancient province of Sanuki, largely coinciding with the present-day Kagawa prefecture, the late third and fourth centuries witnessed the formation of a large number of sequential clusters containing mostly small keyhole tumuli. Some unique regional characteristics were evident in their shape, such as the long and slender square front mound, whose origins can be traced back to the Initial Kofun period (see Figures 8.4.1, 8.4.2, 8.4.4,

8.4.5 and 8.4.6; Hojo 1999b). Then, when the formation of a majority of the clusters came to a halt at the beginning of the fifth century AD, the region saw the construction of a large tumulus, the Tomita-Chausuyama (富田茶臼山), equipped with KCR-derived characteristics, including a moat, an earthen terrace encircling the moat and the KCR-derived *Haniwa* assemblage. It should be noted that the mound shape of this tumulus is different from those of the contemporaneous keyhole tumuli of the KCR in that it has a narrower front square mound than the latter. It is 139 metres long, and is not only the largest tumulus in the region but also the largest tumulus to be constructed in the entire Shikoku region during the whole of the Kofun period (Okubo 2004).

Following its construction, most of the clusters either ceased to be formed or continued with the successive construction of round tumuli or round tumuli with a short square mound attached to them (ibid.). Interestingly, no large keyhole tumulus was constructed in the vicinity of the Tomita-Chausuyama tumulus thereafter, or elsewhere in the region. In fact, until the latter half of the Late Kofun period, virtually no keyhole tumulus was constructed in this region.

As in the case of the Sanuki province, many regions outside the KCR in the period between the end of the fourth and the mid-fifth centuries AD witnessed the construction of the largest or one of the largest tumuli of the entire Kofun period. In many cases, those tumuli were also the largest in their individual regions. The Osumi province in the south-eastern regions of Kyushu region, on the south-western fringe of the distribution of the keyhole tumulus, was no exception to this trend. Two exceptionally large tumuli built in this province – the Tojin-Otsuka (唐仁大塚) and the Yokose (横瀬) tumuli – are dated back to the end of the fourth or the early fifth centuries and to the mid-fifth century, respectively. The former tumulus is approximately 140 metres long, whereas the latter is approximately 134 metres long.[27] While the former was surrounded by a single dry moat, the latter was possibly surrounded by double moats.

Their composition of traits in terms of their cultural-traditional affiliations is complicated. The

27 According to Tatsuya Hashimoto et al. (2008), they were originally 154 metres and 140 metres long, respectively.

Tojin-Otsuka tumulus has a disproportionately long and low square front mound (Hashimoto et al. 2008, 21–22), which is quite different from the mound shapes of the other large tumuli of that period in the KCR; in fact, it is more similar to the mound shapes of some of the fourth-century keyhole tumuli of the neighbouring Hyuga province. The mound of the tumulus has *Haniwa* vessels placed on it, and the grave goods include a set of iron body armour that is highly likely to have been made in a workshop in the KCR. The mound of the Yokose tumulus has been subjected to severe modification, and it is difficult to reconstruct its original shape (ibid., 23–25). However, this tumulus is certainly not very different from the tumuli built in the KCR during the same period. The moat, possibly partially surrounded by another one, however, is keyhole shaped, whereas many of the large KCR tumuli of the same period have a single or double water-filled moat surrounding the mound like a square box with a round side curving along the round rear mound (see Figures 1.2 and 9.1.B). The Yokose also has *Haniwa* vessels placed on the mound, possibly including human *Haniwa* figures (ibid.). Interestingly, the cylinder-shaped *Haniwa* vessels have a number of traits in common with the local pottery assemblage called the Narikawa (成川) pottery style (ibid.). Like the Tojin-Otsuka tumulus, the Yokose tumulus is said to have had a set of iron body armour included in its grave goods. If this were true, it is highly likely that the armour was manufactured in a KCR workshop.

The Kimotsuki Plain, which contains exceptionally large tumuli, saw the onset of the construction of keyhole tumuli during the Early Kofun period. There are several tumuli clusters formed during the Middle Kofun period. Interestingly, the unique mortuary tradition of burying the dead in an underground dugout chamber (*Chikashiki* [underground] – *yokoana* [dugout chamber] – *bo* [grave]; 地下式横穴墓) developed during the Middle and Late Kofun periods. These chambers sometimes form clusters and contain relatively rich grave goods including sets of iron body armour and other iron weapons. In at least one round tumulus in a tumuli cluster (the Okazaki [岡崎] cluster), the dead were buried in underground dugout chambers situated beneath the mound (Hashimoto et al. 2008). It should be noted that the Yokose tumulus is situated alone on a sand dune near the coast, whereas the Tojin-Otsuka tumulus is situated slightly inland and among a cluster comprising more than 130 tumuli, including several other keyhole tumuli.

How can we interpret these cases? The case of the Sanuki province can be summarised thus: the construction of a large keyhole tumulus with many KCR-derived attributes effectively marked the end of the formation of many sequential keyhole tumuli clusters that had continued throughout the Early Kofun period. Thereafter, in clusters that were still seeing construction, the keyhole tumuli were replaced by round or clam-shaped tumuli (SC type: see Figure 9.1.D). The case of the Osumi province can be summarised thus: the construction of two exceptionally large keyhole tumuli with a mixture of KCR-derived and local attributes acted as significant episodes in the ongoing development of a number of sequential clusters comprising keyhole and other types of tumuli, again with a mixture of local and KCR-derived traits.

Based on these observations, I would like to interpret the scenario as follows.

The Early Kofun period, following the formation of the elite interaction sphere in the Initial Kofun (Yayoi-Kofun transitional) period, saw the competitive construction of keyhole tumuli by the elite of a number of clan-type sodalities that constituted the individual regional communities. The ever-increasing importance of intercommunal interaction and exchange, including the exchange of raw materials for producing iron implements, and the functioning of the elite interaction sphere as the medium of this interaction and exchange would have accelerated this competition. The IKP, which included a unique mound shape and its own set of symbolic items (see Chapter 8 of the present volume), was sought after as the material indication of some sort of 'membership' of the sphere, and its chief provider, i.e., the dominant polities of the KCR, would have been perceived as the *paramount mediators* of the interaction and exchange (see Chapter 8.3–4).

Through the recursive provisions of the IKP, the relationship between the KCR elite and the elite of the other regions in the IKP distribution became hierarchised and eventually stabilised. By the end of the Early Kofun period, this relationship assumed such a form that the former could exert an increasingly strong influence over the functioning of the latter. For the latter, main-taining their ties with the KCR elite would have become increasingly important for maintaining their status as representatives of the communal interests, because the items provided by the former (including bronze mirrors, jasper items and, subsequently, iron armour; see e.g. Kondo 1983; Matsugi 2007) became essential constituents of the funerary events conducted by the successors of the dead chiefs as important occasions for praying for communal well-being.

The situation in the Sanuki province, in my view, represents a case in which the KCR elite exerted a powerful *influence* over the local elite who were in charge of constructing the Tomita-Chausuyama tumulus and conducting the mortuary practices regarding the deceased (hereafter called the 'Tomita-Chausuyama chief'). The cessation of the formation of a number of sequential clusters in the region and the replacement of keyhole tumuli by round tumuli in most of the remaining clusters might reflect either (a) that the local elite and their communities became subordinated to the Tomita-Chausuyama chief and this stratification was represented by the former adopting the round or the SC type tumuli in place of the erstwhile keyhole tumuli or (b) that the elite and their communities in the entire region became subordinated to the KCR elite, and the Tomita-Chausuyama chief was entrusted the responsibility of governing that region or (c) that the elite and their communities in the entire region became subordinated to the KCR and the deceased chief who was buried in the Tomita-Chausuyama tumulus was assigned that position and sent by the latter to govern that region; he was later expected to be buried according to the KCR's funerary procedure.

Hypothesis (c) is unlikely in that the construction of the Tomita-Chausuyama was not followed by successive constructions of large tumuli equipped with KCR-derived traits in the region. In contrast, after the construction of the Tomita-Chausuyama, no other large tumulus, let alone a keyhole one, was constructed in the vicinity of the Tomita-Chausuyama. If the deceased had been a person assigned by the KCR elite to govern the region, the governor's successors would have constructed the largest keyhole tumuli of the region and equipped it with KCR-derived traits, even if the location of the construction shifted from the vicinity of the Tomita-Chausuyama to elsewhere in the region. In reality, after the construction of the Tomita-Chausuyama, as mentioned above, the construction of keyhole tumuli ceased for a while – to be exact, until the second half of the Late Kofun period, c. the late sixth century AD.

Both hypotheses (a) and (b) are possible; in fact, they can be seen as two sides of the same coin. The other elite's subordination to the Tomita-Chausuyama chief might have been achieved by the chief's forging strong ties with the KCR elite. It is difficult to investigate this situation archaeologically, but we cannot rule out the possibility that some militaristic aide was provided by the KCR elite to the Tomita-Chausuyama chief. However, regarding the symbolic significance attached to the items provided by the KCR elite and the importance of their mediation in the maintenance of inter-communal interactions, through which the local communities obtained many items of vital importance for their own reproduction, only a monopolisation of ties with the KCR elite would have enabled the chief to achieve regional dominance. The problem in this regard, however, is the question of why that earned dominance and its material expression – i.e., the construction of large keyhole tumuli – disappeared.

Tetsuya Okubo (2004) argues that the elite groups of the local communities of the Sanuki province not only became subordinate to but also were directly controlled by the KCR elite. He adds that the same kind of phenomenon can be observed in the Harima province across the Seto Inland Sea (ibid.). His points may be valid. After the early fifth century AD, which witnessed the construction of exceptionally large keyhole tumuli in many regions (see Shiraishi 1999, 92–99), the size of the largest tumuli only continued to increase in the KCR (and, for a while, in Kibi) for a while (Kondo 1983, 306–314). This might suggest that the KCR elite managed to subordinate the elite of the regions where the formation of keyhole tumuli sequential clusters had ceased. In regions such as the Sanuki province, the local elite's achievement of regional supremacy based on their ties with the KCR, ironically, might have lead to their subordination to the KCR and their eventual downfall.

In the case of the Osumi province, the picture is somewhat different. As discussed earlier, the local autonomy was strong. The KCR-derived traits and items appear to have been used as resources to reinforce and legitimise the rising dominance of the elite. To begin with, the mound shape and other visually prominent traits of the two exceptionally large tumuli were derived either from the local prototypes or from heavily modified versions of the KCR prototypes, though the mound shape of the Yokose tumulus might have been derived from the KCR prototype. The deposition of portable items either obtained from or presented by the KCR, such as iron body armour, is prominent not only in those large tumuli but also in smaller tumuli and in underground dugout chamber graves. This can be understood as the result of an increasingly sophisticated prestige-item-distribution-based hierarchy in the region, and regarding the regional characteristics found in the Tojin-Otsuka and Yokose tumuli, the hierarchy was possibly instigated neither by the KCR elite nor under their control. It is more likely that the regional paramounts, who were successively buried in the Tojin-Otsuka and Yokose tumuli, were voluntarily involved in the alliance network formed around the centre represented by the KCR elite. Involvement in the network, in some cases, resulted in the shift from an initial voluntary participation for achieving regional supremacy to the subsequent unintended subordination to the KCR. However, the Osumi province retained a degree of autonomy throughout the Middle Kofun period.

On the whole, we can say that the KCR elite tried to incorporate local chiefs into their sphere of control, and the local elite, themselves competing with or wishing to consolidate their own dominance over their rivals, *voluntarily* joined the shared elite communication sphere; through this, they attempted to take advantage of their connections with the KCR elite, importing new prestigious goods and technologies into their own regions in order to achieve regional dominance. In some cases, the relations of mutual dependence resulted in the continuous enlargement of the size of the largest keyhole tumuli from phase to phase; in other cases, these relations resulted in the decline of local chiefs, who became subjugated to the KCR. The latter pattern becomes more prevalent as one approaches the KCR, even though the Kibi province showed the progression of the former trend until the middle phase of the

Middle Kofun period (see earlier discussions in this chapter). Meanwhile, it appears that some remote regions became subject to deliberate intervention by the KCR. It is difficult to fully explain the sudden emergence of large keyhole tumuli in terms of the actual mechanisms behind it. However, this would not have been possible unless the KCR had provided the technical and material complex required for the construction of these tumuli. By drawing on the position of supreme mediatorship, initially achieved due to their highest centrality in the network of communications that emerged in the beginning of the Kofun period (see Chapter 8.3–4), the KCR elite gradually transformed their position from that of the *mediator* to that of the *ruler*.

3. SETTLEMENT, RITUAL, PRODUCTION AND CIRCULATION

The traces of dwelling themselves became inconspicuous in the archaeological evidence from the Earlier Kofun period. Towards the end of the Yayoi period, as mentioned in the previous chapter, extremely large, 'port-of-trade'-type settlements suddenly emerged across the horizon which was later to become the horizon of the earliest and early keyhole tumuli and the IKP (see Chapter 8.2). During the second half of the Early Kofun period, however, most of these settlements declined and eventually disappeared. Many of the remaining villages appear to have been single-residential-unit villages, while those which were composite villages, that is, villages comprising a number of residential units, appear to have become much smaller than their Yayoi counterparts. It has to be noted that the elite-precinct-type residential compounds, which clearly emerged in the second half of the Yayoi V, in many cases as one of the residential units constituting individual villages (see Figure 7.8 and relevant discussions), were now often spatially separated from the residential units of the commoners (Tsude 1984, 150–153). Individual, large Yayoi composite villages, which we have already described as 'regional centres', functioned as a hub for the flow of goods, people and information and also mediated various levels of conflicts and tensions (see Chapter 6). The fact that these centres of mediating and regulating various levels, scales and types of social

relations disappeared and elite precincts came to be differentiated from the commoners' residential units, as if replacing the regional centres, suggests that the mode of mediation of social relations and the tensions generated through them shifted from that based on communal will and decision-making to that based on the actions and decision making of the elite. The circulation of goods and people would have been communally regulated through the network of sodalities which came together in individual regional-centre-type settlements during the Yayoi (see Chapter 6). These centres-as-elite-residential-compounds, however, were less reliant on the workings of sodalities and instead would have been regulated by redistribution mechanisms increasingly under the control of the chiefs. The construction of keyhole tumuli, which would have been a regular, recurrent event, itself would have served to regulate relations among the groups that were intensively involved in it; the construction would have involved the well-planned mobilisation of a vast labour force and the procurement of various natural and artificial material resources – such as a large number of cylindrical *Haniwas* to encircle the mound and an enormous amount of pebbles to cover the mound – which were, at times, brought from remote locations (Nishiguchi 1987). While it is possible that the construction was organised during the agricultural off-season, it would certainly have required the supply of a substantial amount of foodstuffs. The range of tasks and obligations, undertaken and fulfilled under the leadership of the chief(s), would have been perceived as a duty required for communal well-being, effectively consolidating the position of the chief(s). In short, the functions fulfilled by communal decision-making undertaken in the large, regional-centre-type composite settlements of the Yayoi were now fulfilled by decisions taken by the elite residing in their precincts and by the construction of their tumuli undertaken by themselves and their predecessors (see Hojo 2000, 128–131).

Let us now look at the situation in the Nara Basin, at the heart of the KCR. Yasushi Ban's summary of this region's situation shows some interesting trends (Ban 2008). During the late third to the fourth centuries AD, most of the site clusters belonged to settlements which had continued from the Yayoi. It is interesting to note, however, that some of them now showed traces of migrant groups moving in from the Tokai region to the east, the Hokuriku region to the north-east and the San'in region to the west. As mentioned earlier, these regions showed unique changes in the transitional period from the Yayoi to the Kofun periods (see Chapter 8.3): Tokai was the centre of distribution of the keyhole tumulus with a square rear mound, Hokuriku was the centre of production of jasper implements, particularly armlets, which formed one of the core items of the IKP (see Kawamura 2010) and San'in retained its cultural independence by not adopting the keyhole tumulus but constructing square tumuli as the resting places of their leaders (Otani 1995; Ikefuchi 1997; also see discussions in Chapter 8). The presence of pots in the Nara Basin either brought in from those regions or manufactured in the unique styles of those regions suggest that people came to the Nara Basin from those regions and lived there for more than a certain length of time.

It is difficult to infer why these people came to the basin and what they did there. Some of them might have come to participate in the construction of the gigantic tumuli. The Sotoyama location of the Shikishima (城島) site, located 250 metres to the north of the Tobi Chausuyama tumulus (see p. 239), yielded a large number of wooden digging implements and pots made in the style of the Tokai region (Chiga 2005). This site is believed to have been a settlement for those who were involved in the construction of the tumulus, and it reveals that there was a substantial inhabitation of people coming from the Tokai region.

As far as the distribution of mortuary paraphernalia is concerned, long-distance inter-communal ties, which emerged in the Yayoi-Kofun transitional period, were further strengthened. It is difficult to infer whether, and to what extent, they reflected the acceleration of the circulation of mundane goods. It is more likely that these goods were circulated within individual regional units. In that case, why did people of those regions come to the Nara Basin and settle in a number of areas there, not in one particular area? One clue to this situation is the fact that the elite of the basin increasingly monopolised contacts with China and the Korean peninsula (see earlier discussion and Chapter 4.3 in the present volume). This brought new technologies as well as prestige goods under their control first, and the elite of the regional polities would have desired to obtain these goods and technologies whereby to strengthen their own positions; as already discussed, competition over their position, as regards the formation of regional tumuli sequences, continued to be fierce. In order to secure the stable flow of mundane as well as symbolic resources that were essential for achieving and sustaining regional dominance, it would have been increasingly important for the regional elite to form and maintain ties with the elite(s) of the Nara basin and its surrounding regions, i.e., the KCR. My inference is that this would have involved the utilisation of the preexisting device used to reproduce inter-communal ties, that is, *kin-based sodalities*. The local elite who were competing for dominance would have voluntarily formed actual or fictive kin ties with the KCR elite and sent their members/subordinates to the KCR. Some of these people were involved in the KCR activities, including the construction of large keyhole tumuli. Hence, their arrival would have taken the form of the fulfilment of social obligations and would have been perceived as a voluntary participation in the tumuli construction, as was the case in most of the ethnographically recorded large-scale projects organised by the chiefs of stratified communities.

During the fifth century AD, some of those site clusters developed manufacturing sectors specialising in the production of stone accessories, iron weapons and armour, and so on (Ban 2008). Gigantic tumuli were constructed in their proximity, even though the largest clusters were now located in the Kawachi Plain (the Furuichi and Mozu tumuli clusters; see earlier discussion). This suggests that the elite of those communities were part of the confederacy of powerful clan-type communities which dominated other communities across a large portion of the archipelago and that they mutually divided and undertook the responsibility of manufacturing products necessary for sustaining their dominance; these products included iron weapons and armour as well as accessories. As far as the situation during the fourth century is concerned, the elite would have utilised their long-distance inter-communal ties in order to procure through them labour force and raw materials for their own manufacturing activities.

The actual sites of the elite residences remain elusive. However, fragmentary pictures can be gleaned from the accumulation of rescue excavations in such areas as the Katsuragi (葛城) site in the south-western corner of the Nara Basin. In that area, inferred to have been the home base of one of the dominant clans whose elite were buried in the Umami cluster of gigantic keyhole tumuli (see above), the excavated sites appear to have fulfilled different functions and are situated in a hierarchical structure (see Ban 2008, 42). Some of them are clearly residential, whereas others seem to be combined residential workshops used for various manufacturing activities such as ironworking (ibid.). The hierarchies of the former can be classified based on the size of the buildings and the spatial configurations they form. A small number of these sites appear to have been assigned ritual functions, including mortuary rituals and those related to the control of water sources.

Excavations in other regions have revealed traces of elite precincts enclosed by a stone-wall-lined moat (Figure 9.15; e.g. the Mitsudeara [三シ寺] in the province of Kamitsukenu in the present-day Gun'ma prefecture; Wakasa 2007). The inner areas of these precincts were divided into separate sectors, and one or a few of them appear to have been used exclusively for ritual purposes, often involving, again, rituals associated with water sources. This would have reflected the importance of controlling the water sources for not only farming activities but also various types of manufacturing activities involving the sophisticated use of fire. It should also be noted that water would have played an important role in purification rituals of various sorts. In that sense, the elite residence would have embodied the function of the elite as mediators of contacts with the transcendental realm to ensure the general well-being of the community. This makes an interesting contrast to the image of the chief as the commander-executor of communal will in the Kofun discourse of the Middle Kofun period, as mentioned earlier. Although archaeologists rarely find clear spatial divisions demarcating individual elite precincts, Kazuhiro Tatsumi (2006) points out that many

elite residences, comprising a combination of elite residential compounds and commoner residential sectors, are commonly divided into 'sacred' and 'profane' sectors.

One interpretation of this would be that the spatial configuration formed by the units fulfilling distinct residential, manufacturing and ritualistic functions embodied the conical, segmentary structure of the clan (composed of both genuine and fictive kin ties). It appears that the manufacturing groups, as regards their technological sophistication and genealogical origin, included migrants from the Korean peninsula, and they would have been either accommodated by the lineages of the indigenous artisans or allowed to form their own lineages.[28] Those lineages would have formed individual residential groupings and would have obtained subsistence goods and foodstuffs from other non-manufacturing lineages situated on floodplains, at times fairly remote ones. In contrast, it appears that the manufacturing groups tended to be situated close to the elite residential complex, allowing the elite absolute control over the behaviour of the manufacturing groups.

Such a large-scale *residential-farming-manufacturing-ritual complex* appears to have emerged in northern Kyushu, the province of Kibi, and in parts of the Kawachi plain and the Nara Basin in the KCR (Hishida 2007, 54–63). The regions which saw the emergence of these complexes also witnessed the development of a specific type of tumuli cluster consisting of a combination of fairly large (and in the case of the Kibi province, gigantic) keyhole tumuli and smaller tumuli, much like their contemporaneous equivalents in the KCR (see earlier discussions and Figure 9.14.C–E). This suggests that in certain regions of the archipelago, particularly across its western portion, various elements of the developing stratified social relations came to be visualised in terms of not only the size hierarchies of the keyhole and other tumuli forming individual tumuli clusters but also the spatial configuration of differentiated units in the residential-farming-manufacturing-ritual complexes located

28 The clans that originated from the Korean peninsula were later to be recorded and listed in documents compiled by the ancient state (*Shinsen shoji roku*, 新選姓氏録).

near the clusters. The internal conical structure of these residential-farming-manufacturing-ritual complexes was based on mutual reliance; the residential units which conducted special production activities needed a constant supply of staple foods and other daily resources, and vice versa. There would have been a similar relationship between the residential-farming-manufacturing-ritual complexes and the ordinary settlements. In other words, the intra- and inter-communal relations became even more 'organic' in nature (Durkheim [1893] 1997). This trend would have further consolidated the position of the elite of the powerful regional polities mentioned earlier, in general, and those of the KCR, in particular.

With regard to rituals, the Earlier Kofun period witnessed the formalisation of ritual practices, which also became unified to some extent. The most significant case in this regard can be found in the Okinoshima (沖の島) Island, situated between northern Kyushu and the south-eastern coastline of the Korean peninsula. On this island, which is better described as a gigantic rock, rituals began to be performed some time towards the end of the first half of the Early Kofun period. These involved the use and/or offering of assemblages almost identical to the grave good assemblage deposited in the contemporary large Kofun tumuli, comprising bronze mirrors; iron weapons including swords, daggers and knives; and various accessories including comma-shaped jade beads, cylindrical beads made of green tuff, glass beads, green tuff armlets, iron armlets and various talc beads (e.g. Oda 1988). It is suggested that the assemblage contents, in terms of quality, are only comparable to the grave good assemblage of the larger tumuli in the KCR, which indicates that the rituals were conducted by the KCR elite rather than by the elite of the northern Kyushu communities (ibid.). In many other rituals – commonly conducted at important spots along interaction routes such as mountain paths, on the foothills or near mountains with the characteristic conical shape, near or on watercourses or water sources such as springs and so on – the combination of mirrors, swords, daggers and various beads and accessories was fairly strictly observed, although the items were commonly copied in talc (e.g. Koide 1966). The formalisation of this practice appears to have continued throughout the Earlier Kofun period.

There is an important, noteworthy difference between the ritual assemblage and the grave good assemblage: the latter commonly consisted of iron, and later increasingly talc-made, tools used for woodworking, farming and so on, including various axes, whereas the former very rarely included them. The ritual assemblage rarely diverged from the combination of mirrors, swords and accessories (see Koide 1966). If these items were regarded as offerings as well as mobilised for some purpose in the ritual acts, the difference would have reflected the emerging differentiation between the objectives of the mortuary practices and those of the rituals for the transcendental being(s) other than the dead elite. Because the body of the dead elite, as argued earlier, would have embodied and symbolised the orderly working of the sectors of everyday life, the transcendental being(s) for whom the above-mentioned rituals were conducted would have embodied the various contingencies of the world, for example, the danger of travelling across land and the sea, the fear of agricultural failure and so on. In other words, these separate rituals might have marked the differentiation of *deities*, who could influence various types of risks and contingencies, from the ancestors, who embodied the communal will. Significantly, the Okinoshima rituals came to be performed more often with the commencement of interventions, including militaristic ones, in the Korean peninsula (Oda 1988; also see Chapter 4.3). The contingencies experienced through them would have been entirely different from those experienced by the people thus far through activities such as farming, interactions *within* the archipelago and so on; this would have led to the differentiation of contingencies which could only be managed with new perceptions and new devices. I would not argue that this was the sole reason for the differentiation of the transcendental(s) from the dead elite, but the correlation appears to be significant enough to suggest that the interventions in the peninsula contributed significantly to the emergence of deities and the formalisation of their rituals.

This trend might be related to the phenomenon of an increasingly clear spatial segmentation of elite precincts into areas for mundane activities and those for ritual activities, which began from the Middle Kofun period onwards. Kazuhiro Tatsumi

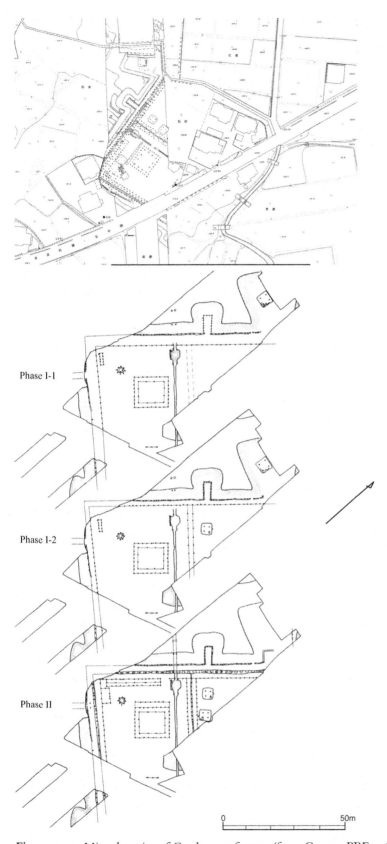

Phase I-1

Phase I-2

Phase II

0   50m

Figure 9.15. Mitsudera site of Gun'ma prefecture (from Gunma PBE 1988).

points out that some individual precincts were internally segmented to form such areas, whereas some precincts were exclusively reserved for ritualistic activities (Tatsumi 2006).

The differentiation of those deities and a formalisation of the ways in which they were deified appear to have occurred in the KCR (Koide 1966). This would have increased the local elite's reliance on the KCR elite as regards the performance of their ritual practices and would have reinforced the authority of the latter as the paramount mediators of various social relations.

4. CONCLUSION

The keyhole tumulus was invented as the material medium of the elite communication sphere that initially spread across a vast area covering Kyushu, western Japan and the western portion of eastern Japan; it was 'selected', through accumulated experiences of social negotiations, for solving contradictions between the increasing social hierarchy, the segmentation of communities and the necessity of maintaining communal collaboration and the communal ethos. The mound of the tumulus and its related paraphernalia constituted an arena for performing a set of formalised collaborative activities suitable for the previously mentioned purposes. Through these activities, the body of the dead chief was made to embody prayers for ensuring the success of important sectors of daily life and the communal well-being, and the various paraphernalia used for this purpose became increasingly sophisticated during the first half of the Early Kofun period.

The structure of the mortuary discourse started changing when communities across the horizon of the keyhole tumulus, under the leadership of the KCR elite, began to intervene in the inter-polity conflicts of the Korean peninsula. This generated a completely new set of contingencies, quite different from those generated by the usual range of farming, general production and exchange activities, which the elite had to deal

with in order to maintain the well-being of their respective communities. At the same time, various ties were forged between the communities in the archipelago and those in the peninsula – all of them were not necessarily mediated by the KCR elite. Based on these ties, many migrants came to settle down in various parts of the archipelago, bringing with them a range of high technologies for production and construction. This led to the formation of residential-farming-manufacturing-ritual complexes across Kyushu and western Japan, most notably in the KCR, the Kibi province and northern Kyushu.

The contradictions among the erstwhile communal ethos, the deepening stratification and the ever-widening range of contingencies transformed the image of the chief from the embodiment of the communal will and communal well-being to the commander-executor of the communal will and interests. This transformation, moreover, progressed concurrently with the differentiation of the transcendental(s) underlying various sources of contingency and the formalisation of their rituals. This was reflected by the rituals associated with water sources, often conducted in or near elite residential precincts.

On the whole, the number of distinct fields of communication, each of which generated its own set of contingencies and required the formation of a distinct structure, continued to increase. At the same time, the spatial extension of those fields also increased to the extent that some of them now included communities in Korea. In order for such communications to continue after a temporary break, it became necessary for societies to have hierarchised social relations, conceptualise some transcendental being(s) as the ultimate referential point for making sense of things across different communications and institutionalise certain communications. The establishment and transformation of the Kofun mortuary discourse and some other changes, as discussed so far, can be understood as social responses to those difficulties.

CHAPTER 10

AN ARCHAEOLOGY OF BUREAUCRACY: THE LATER KOFUN PERIOD (AD 500–600)

1. OVERVIEW

After a frenzy of constructing truly gigantic key-hole tumuli, the structures slowly began to be *downsized*. The size of the largest tumulus of individual sub-phases decreased significantly over the course of time.[1] At the same time, interestingly, there was an ever-widening difference in size between the largest tumuli built in the Kinki region and those in other regions (Figure 10.1; Shiraishi 1999, 148–153). The distribution of the largest tumuli in the Kinki region also changed. As we have seen (see Chapter 9, pp. 281–286), the locations of the largest tumuli shifted from one phase to the next: they were initially built in the south-eastern corner of the Nara Basin, from which they were moved to the northern end of the same basin at some time in the latter half of the fourth century; then they were moved out of the basin altogether into the Kawachi Plain at the end of the fourth century. From the beginning of the fifth century onwards, the largest tumuli were constructed in two locations on the Kawachi Plain – the Furuichi area to the east and the Mozu area to the west. The latter was directly connected to the Osaka Bay, and the largest of all the keyhole tumuli, the Daisen (大仙) tumulus – designated by the Imperial Household Agency to be the mausoleum of Emperor Nintoku (仁徳) – was built in this area. These sites, i.e., the Furuichi and the Mozu, continued to be used for the construction of the largest tumuli in the archipelago for about a century. Then, in the beginning of the sixth century, the location of the largest tumulus of the period was suddenly shifted to the northern fringe of the Osaka Plain, some 30 kilometres to the north of the Furuichi and Mozu areas.

The Imashirozuka (今城塚) tumulus, widely considered to be the tumulus of Emperor Keitai (継体), was approximately 190 metres long and encircled by double moats and platform banks (see Figures 9.13 [for the location] and 10.7). The shape of the mound and its allied features show remarkable continuation from those of its Furuichi and Mozu predecessors, except for the fact that the tumulus has no small, satellite tumulus, while most of the Mozu and Furuichi tumuli are encircled by these. The continuation of the erstwhile features suggests that those who were in charge of constructing the mound and burying the deceased intended to portray the deceased as the successors to the genealogy of the paramount chieftains who were buried in the Mozu and Furuichi clusters. Nevertheless, the fact that the tumulus was located far away from those tumuli clusters suggests some event which disrupted the continuation of the material representation of the preexisting genealogy of the paramount chieftains, which was already involved in competitions between the two groupings represented by the successive and almost alternate construction of gigantic tumuli at the Mozu and Furuichi sites (see Chapter 9.2.5).

The scale of the two tumuli built after the construction of the Imashirozuka tumulus, that is, the Kitsui-Shiroyama (狐井城山) and the Takaya-Shiroyama (高屋城山) tumuli, showed a general decline (approximately 140 meters and 122 metres, respectively). The fact that they were constructed in the Nara Basin and back in the Furuichi cluster, respectively, suggests that there was continuing instability in the succession of the

---

[1] This section briefly charts what happened, detailed descriptions of which will follow with full citations in the subsequent sections.

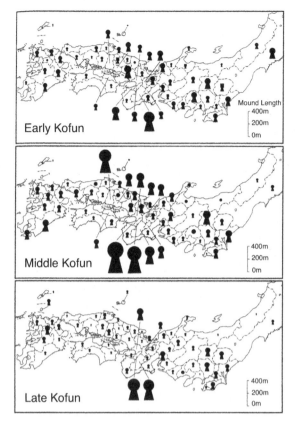

Figure 10.1. Size differences between the largest tumuli of individual regions across the archipelago: the Early, Middle, and Late Kofun periods (after Shiraishi [1999], with additions). With kind permission from the Bungeishunjusha Publishing Co.

paramount chieftainship, which would have correspondingly caused instability in the material representation of the genealogical continuation of the paramount chieftainship. Following this, the gigantic Mise-Maruyama (見瀬丸山) tumulus was built at the southern bottom of the Nara basin (about 318 metres; see Figure 9.13 for the location), and the construction of the gigantic keyhole tumuli ceased, except for in the Kanto region (e.g. Sasaki 2007). Thereafter, the tumuli of the paramount chieftains were built in a rectangular shape, and later in an octagonal shape (Shiraishi 1999, 184–196), but these are discussed in the next chapter.

The disruption in the continuous formation of the materialised genealogy of the paramount chieftainship, i.e., the successive constructions of the largest tumuli in the Furuichi and Mozu areas, reflected an event which marked the beginning of the end of a system. The reproduction of the system itself significantly relied on the successive constructions of the large keyhole

tumuli, and this was coming to an end. This decline was accompanied by the emergence and prevalence of clusters of numerous small, round tumuli, called 'packed tumuli clusters' (*Gunshu* [clustered] – *fun* [tumuli], 群集墳; PTC hereafter), across the horizon extending from Kyushu to the southern Tohoku region (Figure 10.2). This phenomenon is interpreted to have reflected that the extended family-scale, or sub-lineage-scale groupings, became differentiated as stable units of self-identification, that is, the unit of ownership and inheritance of certain rights and possessions (Tanaka 1995; Wada 2007). We shall need to examine this phenomenon in detail in order to check whether this thesis is feasible. If it does emerge feasible, it would mean that those stable units would have increasingly acquired autonomy from the corporate groups to which they belonged and begun to accumulate wealth. This would have weakened the position of the chiefs of such corporate groupings who had formerly enjoyed a guaranteed status as the representatives of communal well-being. This might also have been the very reason behind the emergence of the PTC: the extended family-scale groupings became powerful enough to emulate the chiefly habit of constructing tumuli (Kondo 1952).[2] On the other hand, the emergence of such units might have provided the communal chiefs a new opportunity to impose tighter control over the corporate groups; they could use those small, newly differentiated but stable social units as units from which they could claim services and on which they could impose a primitive form of taxation. Either way, this significant change in the way in which the ordinary members of the communities identified and organised themselves would have led to a fundamental change in the ways in which the hierarchy for the reproduction of social orders was maintained.

This change can also be understood as a transformation of the way in which people identified themselves. Those who were buried in the stone-built gallery-type mortuary chambers of the small tumuli constituting the PTC (Figures 10.2 and 10.4) were buried not only because they were members of a sub-lineage-scale grouping but also

2 Another influential thesis is that those groupings were sanctioned to build tumuli and effectively incorporated into the hierarchical structure of control (see e.g. Nishijima 1961).

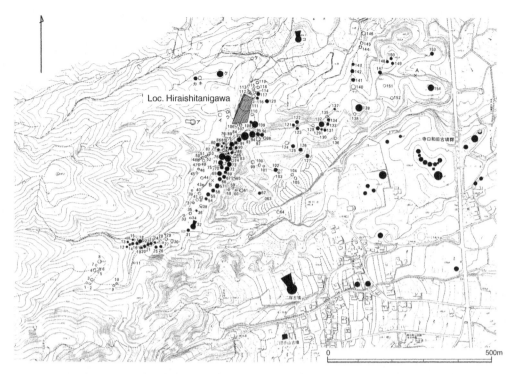

Figure 10.2. An example of the packed tumuli clusters (PTC): the Teraguchi-Oshimi (寺口忍海), Nara prefecture (Nara Prefectural Kashihara Archaeological Research Institute and Shinjo TBE 1988). The Hiraishitanigawa (平石谷川) location (see Figure 10.4 and relevant descriptions and analyses) is shaded.

because as individuals, they had done and achieved certain things in their lifetime; the *biography* of the buried individual came to be represented in the form of differences in the grave goods deposited with the individuals who were buried together in individual chambers (see Figures 10.4 and 10.5). This custom also appears to have been applicable to the elite. The grave goods deposited with them changed from those emphasising their character as representatives of the communal fate and well-being by depicting them as shamanistic (in the third and fourth centuries, the Early Kofun period) and as warrior-chief-like figures (in the fifth century, the Middle Kofun period) to those indicating their personal status in an increasingly sophisticated system of public signification of a hierarchical order (e.g. Niiro 1983).

This significant transformation in the perception and representation of self-identity coincided with several important changes. First, it coincided with the onset of the clear differentiation of roles between the dominant clans of the Kinki-core region (KCR) who were responsible for organising various activities for the maintenance of power structures. Second, interventions in the chronic conflicts between the polities of the Korean peninsula appear, on one hand, to have resulted in the previously mentioned fluctuation and centralisation of power relations among the KCR elite and between them and those in the other regions, and on the other hand, to have led to increased contacts with the peninsular polities, particularly Paekche (百済). Mobilising the commoners to participate in militaristic campaigns and involving them in production activities such as iron production appear to have been carried out by utilising fictive kin ties forged between the dominant elite groups of the KCR and the local communities, which is indicated archaeologically by the presence of not only KCR-originated material items but also stone gallery chambers which could have only been built with the involvement of KCR artisans (Figure 10.3; Yokoana-shiki-sekishitsu kenkyukai 2007). In addition, the militaristic interventions appear to have brought in an increasing number of migrants from the peninsula, and their incorporation into the KCR and other regional communities may have accelerated the above-mentioned segmentation and formation of fictive kin ties between them and the dominant kin groups of the KCR. The mounting daily presence of migrants embodying a range of things alien, including previously unknown high technologies and information from the peninsula with 'political' implications, would have affected the way in which the elite and the commoners perceived the world; their presence would have been a living reminder of the existence of contingencies other than those generated by the rice-cultivation-based agricultural cycle; these new contingencies also needed to be addressed, and this realisation would have necessitated the invention of a range of new technologies to cope with them. Buddhism, as a formalised framework that could be used to refer to a unified transcendental value system, was introduced during this phase,[3] and it can be understood as one of these new technologies. The differentiation of distinct sectors assigned to cope with newly differentiated types of contingencies was another. The latter can be described as a primitive form of bureaucratisation of the power structures. A significant characteristic of this organisation was that each sector was assigned to a dominant kin group of the KCR, and the KCR elite also sought to exert control over the regional communities by utilising their pseudo/fictive-kin-ties originally forged with those communities through the exchange of goods, information and people during the previous period (see Chapter 9).

At this point in history, we are poised just one step before the formation of the entity called 'the state'.

2. THE EMERGENCE OF A NEW MORTUARY DISCOURSE AND A TECHNOLOGY OF SELF-IDENTIFICATION: THE PACKED TUMULI CLUSTER (*GUNSHU-FUN*, 群集墳)

The Later Kofun period saw the emergence of a vast number of new tumulus groups. The actual number of tumuli constituting such a group often

3 There are two competing theses concerning the date of the official introduction/acceptance by the paramount and the vassals of Buddhism from Paekche (百済), one dating it to 538 (*Jogu-shotoku-hohoh-teisetsu*, 上宮聖徳法王帝説) and the other (*Nihonshoki*) to 552. The dispute is caused by confusion concerning the date of the enthronement of the emperor Kinmei (欽明), which is recorded in the latter to have been in 540, whereas the former put it to 531. Both of those documents agreed that the introduction/acceptance took place under the reign of Kinmei. It is widely agreed that some political confusion surrounded the enthronement of the emperor Kinmei, causing the contradictory recordings (see e.g. Inoue 1974, 111–119).

reaches the region of hundreds, sometimes even thousands. The Hiraoyama (平尾山)-senzuka (*senzuka*, 千塚, means 'a thousand tumuli') group, for instance, is said to consist of around 2,000 tumuli (Shiraishi 1966). Some of them include keyhole, square and large round tumuli, and sometimes their formation began with the construction of those types of tumuli. Most of them, however, consist of only round tumuli, mostly around 10 metres in diameter (Figures 10.2 and 10.4), covering gallery-type mortuary chambers, often made of large, roughly rectangular stones (Figure 10.3).

This phenomenon roughly coincided with the previously mentioned decline in the size of the largest keyhole tumuli, which continued to be constructed in the KCR. This corresponded with the ever-widening gap in the sizes of the largest tumuli of the KCR and those of other regions (see Figure 10.1; Shiraishi 1999, 148–153). The phenomenon also coincided with the disappearance of the extremely small, low-mounded round tumuli, whose genealogy can be traced back to the square mortuary compounds (*Hokei-shuko-bo*, 方形周溝墓) of the Yayoi period (Wada 2007; also see pp. 247–248 in this volume). These would have been constructed by the relatively higher-ranked commoners who had neither the permission nor any intention to symbolically indicate their ties with the KCR elite (ibid.). All these roughly contemporaneous phenomena can be interpreted to reflect the strengthening power and authority of the paramount chieftainship of the KCR and the tightening and widening web of control exerted by the paramount chieftain over the commoners. It is assumed, though not necessarily explicitly stated (except, for instance, in Wada 2007), that the construction of tumuli of even the smallest size needed to be *sanctioned* by the paramount chieftainship. The questions as to who constructed those small round tumuli, who were buried there and why did people suddenly begin to bury their dead in that manner have to be answered while keeping the above-mentioned assumption in mind. At the same time, this new phenomenon is likely to have represented the emergence of a new mortuary *discourse* in which a new set of socially coded expectations would have been confirmed and a new set of social identities, reproduced.

With this in mind, let us examine the characteristics of the packed tumuli clusters (PTC)

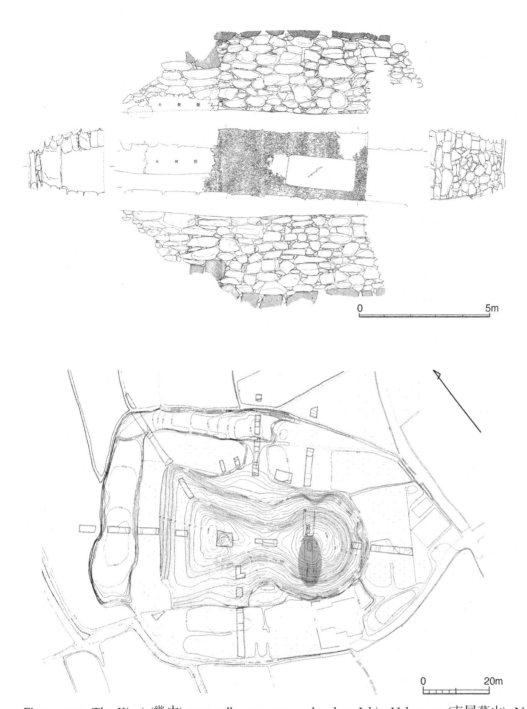

Figure 10.3. The Kinai (畿内)-type gallery mortuary chamber: Ichio-Hakayama (市尾墓山), Nara prefecture (Nara Prefectural Kashihara Archaeological Research Institute 1984). Note the mound shape typical of the Phase IX (see Chapter 9, Footnote 1, and Table 3.1).

in terms of their formation processes. Reconstructing this formation process would allow us to investigate the structure of the discourse, that is, which items (including the body, grave goods etc.) were mobilised in what manner and in what settings (including gallery mortuary chambers, spatial relationships between the preexisting and the newly constructed tumuli etc.) and how they were transformed through time. This examination, it is hoped, will reveal the characteristics of the

discourse and their relation (or lack of it) to the control exerted by the paramount chieftainship over the commoners.

2.1. The Formation Process of the Packed Tumuli Cluster

Scholars have increasingly come to realise that the formation processes of the PTC show quite significant variations (e.g. Migishima

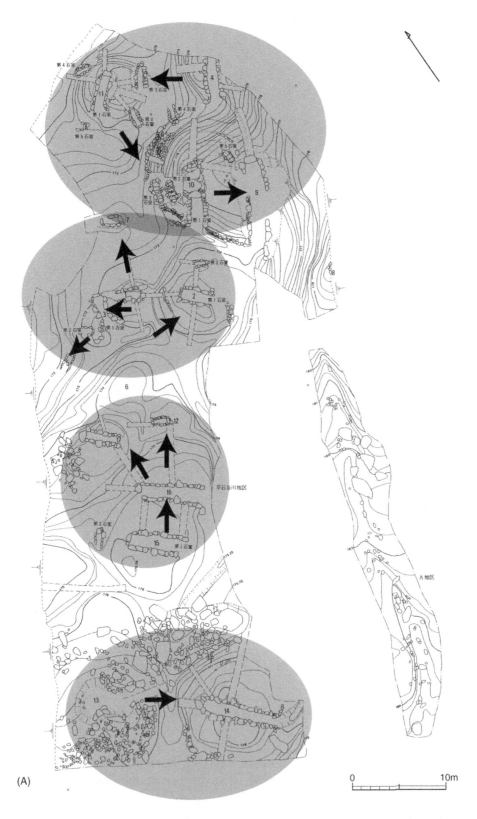

Figure 10.4. The structure and formation process of the packed tumuli clusters: Location Hiraishitanigawa (平石谷川), Teraguchi-Oshimi, Nara prefecture (Nara Prefectural Kashihara Archaeological Research Institute 1991; also see Figure 10.2). **A**: Micro groupings (S-scale groups) are marked by shades (The location itself comprises an L-scale group). Arrows indicate the order of construction. **B**: The formation process. Possible pre-constructed path is marked by shade.

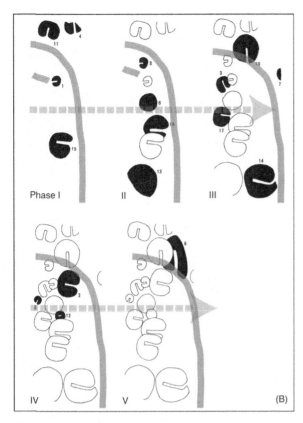

Figure 10.4 (*continued*)

leaders' resting places through the generations; the number of tumuli and micro-groupings in each such sub-group varies considerably, and they are not necessarily constructed in an orderly, successive manner, such as one by one from one end to the other. Each tumulus that is part of such a group commonly contains a gallery-type stone mortuary chamber (hereafter called 'gallery chamber'), though some rare tumuli contain a number of gallery chambers (see the following). In most cases, a number of people were buried in these tumuli, and it was not very uncommon for the bodies of the previously buried individuals and their grave goods to be shifted to one side in order to make room for new burials. In addition, the number of people buried in individual chambers varies significantly. Moreover, it was not necessarily the case that a particular tumulus in a sub-group or micro-grouping continued to accommodate individuals with rich grave goods: the quality and quantity of grave goods buried with the individuals often vary considerably within a chamber.

Yoshiyuki Tanaka's (1995) osteo-archaeological investigations have revealed that the deceased individuals from individual gallery chambers of the PTC included both those who had close blood ties with each other and those who did not. By examining the relevant information, he concludes that these individuals included husbands and wives marrying into the group as well as other kin members (ibid.). Based on these findings, it can be suggested that the unit responsible for constructing each individual micro-grouping of tumuli was a lineage or an even smaller grouping such as a household (called 'S-scale group' hereafter; Figure 10.4). This unit was situated in a larger group (called 'L-scale group' hereafter; Figure 10.4), described above as a sub-group, and members of such a group – probably a clan or a sub-clan – might have come together to construct the tumuli. In any case, the presence of the L-scale group suggests that some characteristics of corporate grouping were maintained in this society. However, the relationship between the units (S-scale groups) constituting such a corporate group (L-scale group) were not egalitarian, as indicated by the different mound sizes and differences in the mortuary assemblages in the clusters.

2009).[4] Some began with the construction of a fairly large keyhole tumulus, at times (see e.g. Kimoto 2008), whereas others included a number of keyhole tumuli in the cluster, constructed either consecutively in a certain location or in different locations in the cluster. Most of them consist of sub-group and at times they can be further divided into micro-groupings consisting of about two to four tumuli (Figures 10.2 and 10.4). These sub-groups and micro-groupings in the clusters are sometimes situated as if they were connected by pre-constructed paths (Figure 10.4.B; Mizuno 1975). However, this may not directly indicate that the spaces were pre-allocated to certain groupings for the successive constructions of their deceased

In addition, the 'stability' of the S-scale groups as units of inheritance of some sort tended to

---

4 As mentioned in the previous chapter, packed tumuli clusters with rich grave goods emerged in the second half of the earlier Kofun period, circa the mid-fifth century AD (the 'earlier packed tumuli clusters' [古式群集墳]; see Chapter 9.2, pp. 247–248). They are understood to have been the resting places of the vassal elite of individual regional communities, who were previously not buried in conspicuous tumuli (Kondo 1983, 252–261). This phenomenon reflects the progression of rank differentiation within the elite kin-groupings and needs to be separately discussed from the current topic of PTCs which we are dealing with in this chapter.

vary; as mentioned earlier, the number of tumuli representing the S-scale groups varies significantly (Figure 10.4).

These points lead to the following observations:

(1) Each of the micro-clusters of tumuli constituting the sub-group was formed to represent the genealogy of a small corporate grouping such as a lineage or a household, that is, an S-scale group.

(2) However, the genealogy often appears to have been unstable; it would be disrupted at times, and the mound scale fluctuated during the formation process of a microcluster.

(3) Genealogical consciousness must have existed and was materially represented by that time, but the grouping (the S-scale group) which was meant to be the unit of genealogical continuation, probably implying inheritance, was not yet stable enough to firmly support this consciousness.

2.2. Implications: The Emergence of a New Social Identity

The order which can be found in the spatial structure and formation process of a sub-group of individual PTCs can be neither entirely explained as an artificially imposed one nor described as a naturally generated one, i.e., generated through the 'evolution' (or evolutionally segmentation) of communities.

The smallest unit, the S-scale grouping, which we defined in the preceding analysis, was made up by those who had neither constructed nor been buried in tumuli before. Yoshiro Kondo argues that the development and eventual independence of such a grouping from a larger corporate grouping was the main cause of the emergence of the PTC of the Later Kofun period (Kondo 1952; 1983, 346–353). However, the grouping often appears insufficiently developed to function as an independent unit that was able to construct and maintain the tumuli; as we saw earlier, many micro-clusters of tumuli show interruptions or disruptions in their formation processes, and there exist many tumuli outside of these clusters – the groups which constructed them might not have been stable enough to continue constructing new tumuli which would

eventually form micro-clusters. In other words, those S-scale groups which stopped constructing new tumuli would have ceased to function as independent units of production, consumption, storage and human reproduction. At the same time, the L-scale grouping – either on the scale of a clan or a sub-clan consisting of a number of S-scale groups – was relatively stable, and constituted, together with other sub-groups, of an entire group of PTCs; within that grouping, the location and status of L-scale groups were clear and stable. These observations suggest that the L-scale groups were stable corporate groupings such as clans or sub-clans, whereas the S-scale groups, probably lineages or households, were instable as a basic unit of social reproduction, ownership and inheritance.

The mortuary assemblage sometimes includes material items, such as iron slugs, salt-making vessels and so on (Kondo 1983, 337–345), which indicate the occupation of the deceased. Their presence suggests that the identity of the deceased buried in individual tumuli was differentiated and marked not only by their kin affiliation but also by what they did for a living. There are also cases in which a tumulus that seems quite ordinary, in terms of its mound size and the size and structure of the mortuary chamber, is found to contain rather spectacular material items such as long iron swords with gilded hilts, an arrow container with gilded frames and so on (Figure 10.5). Some of them would have been imported from the peninsula, while others are likely to have been produced in the workshops under the control of the elite of the Kinki region. These would have been given by the elite of the clan-type kin organisation to which the deceased belonged. In some cases, these elite received the prestigious, at times imported, items from the elite of the Kinki region, who increasingly monopolised contacts with their equivalents in the peninsula. These facts suggest that the identity of the deceased was differentiated and marked by (a) their kin affiliation, (b) their 'profession' and (c) their relationship with the elite.

The fact that very few persons were given such prestigious items suggests that such items were awarded by the elite to those who had performed distinguished deeds. This further suggests that the relationship between them and the elite was of a personal nature, which means that the value of

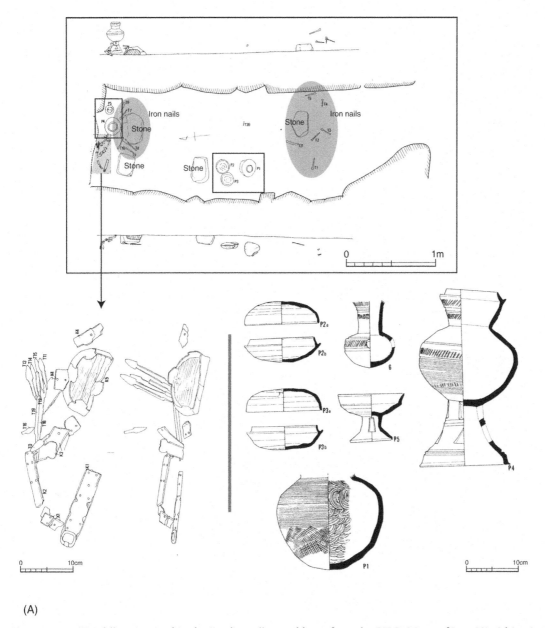

(A)

Figure 10.5. "Rich" grave good in the "ordinary" assemblages from the PTC: No. 3 of Loc. Hiraishitanigawa, the Teraguchi-Oshimi, Nara prefecture (after Nara Prefectural Kashihara Archaeological Research Institute [1991], with arrangements by the author). **A**: context (bottom left: an arrow container with gilded frames, bottom right: Sue stonewares), **B**: detail of the parts of the arrow container.

such deeds was not calculated in terms of how it benefited the communal well-being of the clan; rather, the value was measured based on how far the deed *benefitted the elite*.

All of these facts point to the following: the clan elite were no longer acting as representatives of the communal well-being. On the contrary, they ruled the community, which was by now internally segmented into lineages or households which competed for favours from the ruling elite.

The contents of the mortuary communication themselves are also suggestive of this fact. A large number of *Sue* (須恵) stoneware (and occasionally a few *Haji*, 土師, wares) are often found close to individual bodies buried in the chamber. Remains of foodstuffs, for example, fish bones, can be found in these wares, and the vessels are of various shape-types, which suggests that they contained food as well as drink – probably for the consumption of the deceased in their afterlife (Figure 10.5). The fact that the individual dead were provided food and drink for their afterlives implies that their individuality was maintained even after their death – in the memory and perception of the living. The

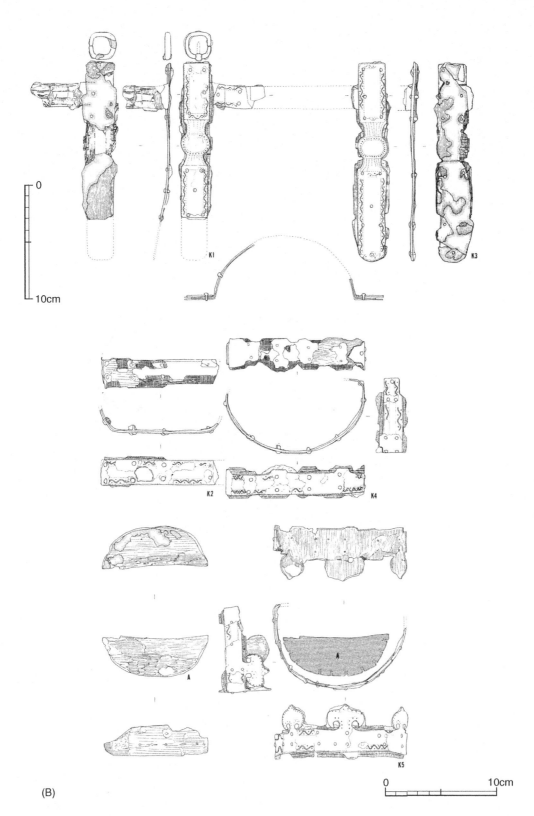

(B)

Figure 10.5 (*continued*)

large number of vessels containing these offerings to the dead is also suggestive in this regard. There does not appear to be any fixed number of vessels to be offered. On the contrary, it appears as if there was some kind of competition for offering more and more vessels filled with food and drink for the consumption of the dead. These facts suggest that the living identified themselves through their connections with the dead, whose individuality was retained even in their afterlives. This also suggests that the above notion of individuality became a source of competition between household-scale (i.e. S-scale) groupings represented by the deceased buried in individual small tumuli.

On the whole, this newly emerged mode of mortuary communication, materialised by the PTC, marked a significant departure from the previous mode, which was based on the presentation of communality. In the previous mode of mortuary communication, the dead and the living were regarded as situated in a larger community in which the dead did not retain their individuality for long. Commoner cemeteries in the Earlier (i.e. the Early and Middle) Kofun period were chaotic clusters of burial pits situated very close to one another without forming any micro-clusters (Fukunaga 1989). At the keyhole tumuli, the dead were buried through communal ritual performances designed to promote communal well-being (see Chapter 9). In that sense, the elite dead were treated as the representatives of their communities.[5] In the Later Kofun period, however, allotment-like spaces were allocated to household-scale groupings, and the dead came to retain their individuality. The sequential constructions of small tumuli in individual mortuary allotments marked the differentiation and continuation of household genealogies, and the living competed for positions in the clan-scale community by serving the elite and by attempting to outdo the others by conducting increasingly lavish funerals. The relationship between the elite and the commoner household members became also direct and personal and was no longer mediated by *communality*.

In that case, were those who built the PTC and buried their dead there directly sanctioned by the elite to build them? Did the elite allow them to build those tumuli in order to incorporate them into the artificially created fictive kin groupings headed by the KCR elite? The answer would be yes and no. The above-mentioned instability of the formation processes of many micro-clusters of tumuli (i.e. the S-scale groupings) suggests that the household-scale grouping which constructed the tumuli was a natural kin-grouping

rather than an externally defined one. It is more likely that these groupings were segments, possible *semi-independent* units of production and reproduction, of larger corporate groupings such as clans or sub-clans. The segmentation appears to have begun, albeit sporadically, during the final phase of the Earlier Kofun period. Some of the 'earlier packed tumuli clusters' (see Chapter 9, pp. 247–248), which yield rich grave good assemblages, have been interpreted to be the resting places of the emergent 'bureaucratic' class which supported the chiefs who became powerful enough to establish a despotic regional rule (Kondo 1983, 252–261; Wada 2007). However, these tumuli were not necessarily situated in the vicinity of the largest tumuli of individual regions. In the Munakata area of the present-day Fukuoka prefecture in the northern Kyushu region, for instance, Hiroyuki Okada has shown that the distribution of the earlier packed tumuli cluster was located at a distance from the area that saw the genealogical-formation-like successive constructions of large keyhole and round tumuli (Okada 2004). Such examples suggest that the segmentation was a natural process that had slowly progressed since the final phase of the Middle Kofun period (c. the late fifth century AD) to reach the point when it resulted in the widespread formation of PTCs.

Those segmented groupings, as argued, would have functioned as semi-autonomous, mutually competing units of production and reproduction, albeit still fairly unstable. This would have made their relationships easily hierarchised. Then, if the KCR elite managed to incorporate the emergent chiefly household into their system of control through a range of rewards including the presentation of prestigious items, it would have been easily possible to further incorporate the other households constituting the group. In fact, such intentional incorporation of newly internally segmented corporate groups into the web of direct control exerted by the KCR elite appears to have been underway in many regions; PTCs are, in many cases, situated away from the genealogical sequence of large keyhole tumuli in individual regions, and they often include small keyhole tumuli within them (see e.g. Kimoto 2008). Those who were buried in these small keyhole tumuli would have been the newly emerged lesser chiefs, who were sometimes strategically

---

5 Although the identity and the perception of the elite dead buried with those performances transformed through the period from that of the embodiment of communal well-being to that of the figure in charge of the conduct of the community for its well-being; see Chapter 9.

incorporated into the KCR elite's web of direct control.

Such a process would have, albeit partially, paved the way for the eventual implementation of the registration and direct control of the commoners by the KCR elite. This would have been crucial for generating an institutional structure of the social organisation which can be described as the 'state'. Before situating the implications of this change in a wider picture, however, we need to examine the correlated changes which occurred with regard to the keyhole tumulus construction.

3. TRANSFORMATION OF THE KEYHOLE TUMULUS

The keyhole tumulus was no longer the locale for the confirmation and presentation of the communal character of the deceased chief. Instead, the tumulus became the *machinery* for the representation, and hence the maintenance, of actual social order.

EVIDENCE 1: THE DECLINE OF THE *HANIWA* VESSELS

During the Earlier (i.e. Early and Middle) Kofun period, *Haniwa* vessels either embodied prayers for communal well-being or formed material settings for rituals conducted for communal well-being (see Chapter 9, pp. 263–271). Cylindrical *Haniwa* vessels, which enclosed the mounds, were occasionally inscribed with pictorial representations similar to those found on Yayoi pots and *Dotaku* bronze bells. These were used in rituals involving prayers for a good harvest of rice and communal well-being. Representational *Haniwa*s, including building-, armour- and weapon-shaped as well as human *Haniwa* figures, which appeared later during the Earlier Kofun period, depicted the life and (ritual) activities of the dead chief who represented communal well-being. At times, clay miniatures of food offerings were laid on the chief's burial mound amid representational *Haniwa*s.

The Later Kofun period saw the decline of the custom of surrounding the tumuli with cylindrical *Haniwa* vessels. This period also saw a transformation in representational *Haniwa* assemblage, which came to mainly consist of various human *Haniwa* figures, including the explicit depiction of the chief and those who served the chief (e.g. Taka-

hashi 1996, 128–142). The services depicted are mostly those of a ritualistic nature, and it is quite possible that the role played by the chief in such rituals would still have been that of the mediator of communal prayers to the supernatural beings. However, as regards the actual depictions represented by the *Haniwa* vessels, the chief was the person to be served, not the one who served.

These observations suggest a significant change in the set of meanings embodied and represented by the *Haniwa* vessels. The cylindrical *Haniwa* vessels, as interpreted earlier, were initially used as the material representations of vessels containing offerings to the dead chief and the spirit of rice grains (Kondo 1983, 171–174). They also were originally used to enclose the resting place of the dead chief in order to restrain the chief's wandering spirit (see Chapter 9, p. 263). In other words, they were used to ensure the communal well-being of those who participated in the burial of the dead chief and the construction of the burial mound. Later, the building-shaped *Haniwa* vessels represented the life of the dead chief as the representative of communal interests. Clay miniatures of food offerings, laid with the representational *Haniwa* vessels, would have symbolised offerings made by the chief as the mediator between the community and the supernatural realm (Wada 2009, 255–256). However, those communal elements faded from the meaning symbolised by the *Haniwa* vessels during the Late Kofun period. Instead, the Late Kofun *Haniwa* assemblage came to depict scenes in which the chief was *served* by others, even when the chief was depicted as conducting a ritual for *communal* well-being. In short, this change reflects the chief's transformation from the people's representative to the ruler.

EVIDENCE 2: CHANGES IN THE GRAVE GOOD ASSEMBLAGE

There were a number of significant changes in the grave good assemblage at this time. First, the custom of depositing a large, and at times vast, number of weapons and tools in the tumuli ceased. This custom, as suggested in the previous chapter, was intended to represent the dead chief as the commander-executor of the communal will and interests, and the *offering* of those items in a vast quantity would have indicated and confirmed the subordination of the commoners to the chief for the sake of the community's well-being. In the Late Kofun period, the grave goods were chosen to indicate the *status* of the dead chief and were therefore beautifully and spectacularly wrought items; various status items, including many imported from the peninsula or made by emulating Korean originals, such as gold or gilded crowns and shoes with small, clover-leaf-shaped decorations hanging from their soles (e.g. Park 2007), were either draped on the body or placed around it. This suggests that the chiefs were buried in the status they had occupied when they were alive, or at least the status that they had hoped to occupy.

Scholars are divided on the opinion of what the dead were perceived to become. The fact that the dead were buried in the gallery mortuary chamber, Seigo Wada argues, does not necessarily mean that the person was perceived to live on *inside the chamber* (Wada 2008). However, as a continuation from the Earlier Kofun period, the dead, regardless of whether they were perceived to become 'spirits' or not, appear to have been perceived to live on; a number of Sue wares, including many vessels offering food, were often placed in the chamber, at times with actual traces of food in them. Regardless of whether or not these vessels were used in the feasts marking the dead person's initiation into the community of the dead (cf. Kobayashi 1976), the food traces suggest that the dead were believed to eat, just like they did when they were alive. This further suggests that the dead chiefs would have been perceived to act as they did when they were alive to fulfil the obligations required by their status, as indicated by the status items surrounding them in the chamber.

The status items used in the Late Kofun period included a range of items whose different traits could be used to indicate minute status differences; for instance, different lengths and features on the hilts of iron swords, as shown by Izumi Niiro (1983), were typical indicators of such differences (Figure 10.6). These suggest that as regards the socially constituted identity, there was no significant transformation from the state of living to that of the dead as far as the elite of the period were concerned. During the Earlier Kofun period, the body of the dead chief was used to embody the destiny of the community. In the Late Kofun period, the body of the dead chief was used to signify that the system of hierarchical governance

continued after death. In the former, the dead became part of the abstract, transcendental realm. In the latter, the dead became individualised and humanised.

EVIDENCE 3: CHANGES IN THE CEREMONIAL PRACTICES

The prevalence of the gallery mortuary chamber changed the sequence of events involved in the construction of the tumuli. During the Earlier Kofun period, the pit containing the cist was dug on top of the mound after the mound had been constructed. In contrast, the gallery mortuary chamber was commonly built along with the base terrace of the mound; after that, the construction of the chamber and the mound progressed together. As a result, the top of the mound could no longer function as the platform for performing the sequential (ritual) acts involved in the placement of the coffin, the construction of the cist, its concealment and the setting up of the rectangular terrace for placing the *Haniwa* vessles and performing other rituals (e.g. Wada 2009 and Chapter 9 in this volume).

Of course, a range of performative acts would have characterised the mortuary rituals conducted inside and in front of the chamber. However, those performative acts which were associated with and derived from the implications of the shape of the keyhole mound and the meanings attached to its parts would have been phased out. In other words, the keyhole mound and its paraphernalia lost their meanings as the symbolic-metaphorical embodiments, i.e., the miniature representations, of the world (see Chapter 8.4). From now on, the original meanings of the mound and its paraphernalia either ceased to exist or were lost; for instance, by the mid–Late Kofun, *Haniwa* vessels were no longer placed on the mound (Kondo 1983, 370–374). From now onwards, the mound became the *monumental indicator* of the status of the deceased.

4. TRANSFORMATION OF THE KEYHOLE TUMULI CLUSTERS

The Situation in the Centre: The transformation of the character of the keyhole tumulus was accompanied by simultaneous transformations in the formation pattern of keyhole tumuli clusters.

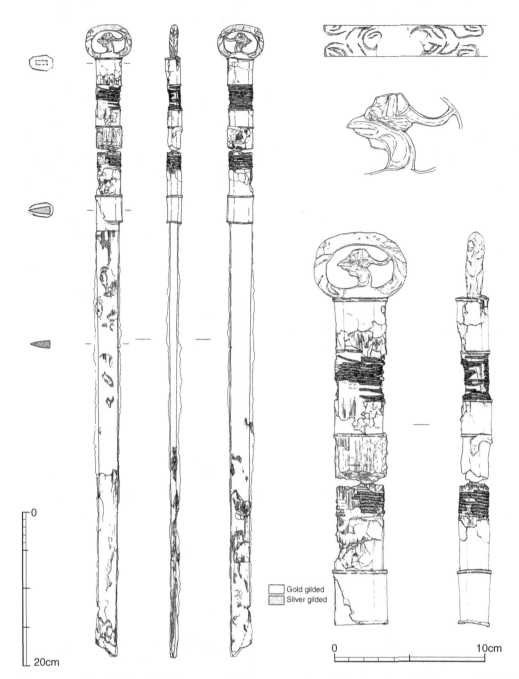

Figure 10.6. Late Kofun hilted iron swords: No. 8 tumulus of the Kuwabara-Ishigamoto (桑原石ヶ元) tumuli cluster, Fukuoka prefecture (after Fukuoka MBE 2003b).

In many regions around the KCR (Harima, Tajima, Tanba, Tango, Settsu, Kawachi, Izumi, Yamato, Yamashiro, etc. [roughly coinciding with the present-day Kinki region]), the formation of many of the keyhole tumuli clusters was terminated during the first half of the sixth century AD (cf. Ishino 1995).[6] The construction of fairly large round tumuli continued at some of these regions, and from the end of the sixth century onwards,

there were sporadic constructions of square tumuli. At the same time, a small number of clusters saw the continuous construction of keyhole tumuli. Some keyhole tumuli were even constructed in locations that were far away from any preexisting keyhole tumuli clusters. Interestingly, they often saw the formation of large PTCs nearby. In this regard, it is interesting that in many cases, the formation of PTCs began with the construction of a keyhole tumulus (e.g. Kimoto 2008). This suggests that the character of those who were buried in the 'untraditional' keyhole tumuli (meaning

6 In Sanuki and Awa, this termination had occurred earlier, during the fifth century AD. See Okubo (2004) and Chapter 9, pp. 287–291.

0   100m

Figure 10.7. The Imashirozuka tumulus, Osaka prefecture (after Shiraishi [1999], original produced by Takatsuki MBE). With kind permission from the Bungeishunjusha Publishing Co.

that they were not constructed in the preexisting [hence 'traditional'] keyhole tumuli clusters) was different from that of those who were buried in the 'traditional' keyhole tumuli.

In relation to the 'identity' of those who were buried in the untraditional keyhole tumuli, it is important to note that, as interpreted earlier, the traditional keyhole tumuli were built as monumental manifestations of communal togetherness embodied by the chiefs who represented the well-being of their respective communities during their lives and probably guaranteed it (or were perceived to do so) after their death. In that sense, the traditional keyhole tumuli cluster would have served not only as the locale where the continuation of a community represented by its successive chiefs was repeatedly confirmed and monumentally represented but also the locale which guaranteed (or was perceived to guarantee) the well-being of the community. In that case, the termination of the 'use' of such locales and the emergence of non-traditional keyhole tumuli could be interpreted as reflecting the end of the notion of communal well-being which had continued from the Yayoi period.

As we have seen, the first half of the sixth century AD saw a fairly significant reduction in the size of the largest keyhole tumuli (Figure 10.1; Shiraishi 1999, 148–153). Their locations also shifted from the previous clusters of the largest tumuli, that is, the Furuichi and Mozu clusters; for instance, the Imashirozuka tumulus, dated back to the early sixth century, as we have seen, was

constructed in northern Settsu (Figures 9.13 and 10.7). From the construction of the Imashirozuka tumulus onwards, the gap in scale between the largest tumulus and the others became wider, except for in the Kanto region, where the formation of traditional keyhole tumuli clusters continued throughout the sixth century AD (ibid.).

By putting together these pieces of information, a clear picture emerges: the conception of the chieftain as the representative and guarantor of communal well-being either declined or was in a process of transformation; this coincided in timing with the possible foundation of a new lineage of paramount chiefs (marked by the construction of the Imashirozuka tumulus in Settsu, far away from the previous resting places of the paramount chiefs, that is, the Furuichi and Mozu clusters of Kawachi; Figure 9.13) and the paramount chief's establishment of much more significant authority over the regional chieftains than before, as suggested by the significantly widened gap between the largest tumuli and the others (see Figure 10.1). The traditional chieftainship and its genealogy, manifested by the traditional keyhole tumuli (see above), were losing their traditional communal support base; large, individual clusters of small round tumuli (L-scale group; see earlier discussion) comprising PTCs represented a group of clan-like groupings in which internal competition between lineages or smaller groupings for the favour of the chief was rife (see Section 2 of the present chapter) – this would have been related to the decline of the erstwhile notion of communal well-being. Such clan-like groupings were also often the units of specialised production, such as salt or iron production (ibid.); those who were buried in the nontraditional keyhole tumuli would have been the chiefs of such groupings, and these nontraditional/new chiefs might have been *directly* entrusted by the paramount or the elite of the KCR to control the specialised production necessary for maintaining the power-base of the paramount chief and the KCR elite as well as that of the 'new' local chiefs. As mentioned above, most of the prestige items, such as gilded equestrian gear or swords with gilded hilts excavated from clusters of small round tumuli, were produced in the KCR workshops. These local chiefs might be described as *primitive local bureaucrats*, though they would have still been perceived as the chiefs of kin-based communities.

The Situation in the Surrounding Regions: It is interesting to note that the general trend is that as we go further away from the KCR into the surrounding regions, we find that keyhole tumuli clusters continued to be constructed into the sixth century (see Ishino 1995). This trend is most significant in the Kanto region, where not only did the preexisting keyhole tumuli clusters continue to grow but also new ones, consisting of a number of large-scale keyhole tumuli, emerged (ibid.). The size of the keyhole tumuli did not necessarily decrease but even increased in many areas in the Kanto region (ibid.).

Some of these regions saw the sudden emergence of new keyhole tumuli clusters, for instance, the cluster on the north-eastern edge of the Hizen province (coinciding with the present-day Saga and Nagasaki prefectures) of northern Kyushu and the Sakitama cluster (in Saitama prefecture) of Musashi (coinciding with the present-day Tokyo, Saitama and a part of Kanagawa prefectures) (Ishino 1995, 24–27, 150–153; 2005, 115–137). These newly formed clusters of this period often show traces of direct contacts with the KCR. The former cluster is characterised by the presence of *Haniwa* vessels showing strong affinities to their KCR equivalents (e.g. the Okadera [岡寺] tumulus; Tosu MBE 1984). It is difficult to determine if there was any direct involvement of artisans either who were based in the KCR or had learned their craft somewhere in that region; however, it is clear that there was some kind of direct human connection between the KCR and the group that constructed the tumuli. The Sakitama cluster is famous for the deposition of a sword which bears an inscription recording the service offered by the successive chiefs of the clan to the paramount chieftains of the KCR (Saitama PBE 1980). However, unlike the nontraditional keyhole tumuli built in the KCR and its surrounding regions, the new clusters continued to be built in the traditional form; that is, they consisted of one or more sequences of large keyhole tumuli (Shiraishi 1999; Hirose 2009). This was the consequence of either the intra-regional competitions over the regional chieftainship in which the preexisting chieftain's lineage was defeated and a new one became connected with the paramount and the KCR elite or the paramount and the KCR elite's own move to replace the preexisting regional chief with a new one. In actuality, both the events

could have occurred. The power and authority of the paramount residing in the KCR, as revealed by the gap in mound size between the KCR tumuli and those in other regions, became such that the paramount chieftain might have, at times, been able to intervene in the succession to the regional chieftainship.

It should be noted that many of the tumuli clusters which emerged during the Late Kofun period in the Kanto region consist of more than two keyhole tumuli sequences (see e.g. Ishino 1995, 150–157). The Dairizuka cluster in the present-day Chiba prefecture was comprised of a sequence of the largest tumuli of individual phases and a sequence of smaller tumuli (see Ishino 1995, 156, Hirose 2009). The cluster, as a whole, can be understood to have represented an alliance of a number of hierarchised local communities from which the paramount chieftain was chosen in individual phases. This was merely the continuation of what occurred elsewhere in the Middle Kofun. One problematic finding, however, is that many clusters of this type emerged in the Kanto region during the Late Kofun, long after this type of cluster formation had disappeared elsewhere (for instance, compare Ishino 1995, 150–157, with the other regions immediately surrounding the KCR featured in the same volume). The phenomenon suggests that many of the probably 'chiefdom-like' communities of the region enjoyed the same degree of autonomy as that enjoyed by western Japan during the Middle Kofun period. Further, examples like the Dairizuka cluster suggest that alliances between chieftains could still be formed and the hierarchisation of inter-chieftain relations was still in progress at this time. In short, it was still possible for chiefdom-like regional units of integration to develop and integrate into larger units in the Kanto region. In addition, we can infer that such keyhole tumuli clusters would have still continued to function as locales for the manifestation of communal well-being embodied by the dead chiefs buried there.[7]

7 The phenomenon effectively shows that eastern Japan remained occupied by autonomous chiefdom-like polities in each of which inter-clan alliances and competitions played important roles in the integration of the polity, whereas western Japan individual regional chiefdom-like polities increasingly came under the control of the KCR elite through their forging asymmetrical ties with clan heads, previously subordinate to the chief of a regional polity.

From the second half of the sixth century on-wards, there were greater numbers of large PTCs in those regions, and many of them, like their equivalents in the KCR and the surrounding regions, had small keyhole tumuli within the clusters or near them (Shiraishi 1999; Sasaki 2007; Hirose 2009). Those observations suggest that there were two different types of connections in operation between those regions and the KCR: one was the traditional type of connection between the regional elite, as representatives of the communal well-being, and the KCR elite (e.g. as represented by the formation process of the Dairizuka cluster), while the other was a new type of connection between KCR elite and the newly emerged elite who were leaders of kin-based communities, often involved in specialised production activities.

This can be characterised as a situation during the *transitional* phase in the process of 'state-formation': on one hand, the elite and the paramount chieftain of the KCR still needed to be connected with regional chieftains as *allies*; on the other hand, the former began incorporating clan-like kin-based groupings, which would have formerly been under the control of the regional elite, into their direct control by entrusting them with specialised production activities and treating their leaders as primitive bureaucrats.

In that case, it is most likely that the *traditional* type of connections continued to be strongly maintained between the paramount and the KCR elite and the regional chiefs of the Kanto region, whereas the new type of connection became most widespread between the KCR and the regions immediately surrounding it. In the Kyushu, Chugoku, Shikoku, Tokai and Hokuriku regions, both types of connections coexisted for a while, because the authority of the traditional elite would have succeeded in resisting the increasing interventions from the paramount chieftain and the KCR elite.

5. SETTLEMENT, PRODUCTION AND CIRCULATION

5.1. A New Settlement-Scape

The villages of this time still commonly consisted of several residential units, but each of them was segmented into blocks by now (Figure 10.8) (e.g.

Tsude 1989, chap. 3). Each of these blocks comprised one or two pit houses and probably some storage facilities (Figure 10.8). Such blocks were sometimes enclosed by a shallow ditch, and possibly by stake fences. In the case of unenclosed blocks, the blocks can still be identified from either the traces of successive (re)constructions of pit dwellings and storage facilities in the same spots or empty spaces left between clusters of such features (ibid.).

This clearly shows the emergence of a new village-scape. Residential units constituting individual villages, before the Late Kofun, tended to be the smallest units with certain stability; while dwellings could be added to or removed from units due to the relocation of their positions, the unit itself often continued as long as the village continued. I have already suggested that such a residential unit must have represented a lineage-like grouping, belonging to a larger, clan-like communal unit cross-cutting a number of villages (see relevant descriptions in Chapters 6 through 9). If we accept this inference, the above picture would represent the segmentation of individual lineages into smaller units, probably household-scale (or extended-family-scale) groupings (Tanaka 1995).

Individual villages would have still been a coherent unit of collaborative labour; it is rare to see a village consisting of a single residential unit, which suggests that the maintenance of paddies and so on was still undertaken by means of collaboration between a number of lineage-scale groupings. It would also have been the case that a lineage-scale grouping would continue to act as a coherent collaborative unit fulfilling certain social functions. However, in this period, it was constituted by segments, and they appear to have acted in a 'selfish' manner, to some extent. Blocks constituting a residential unit often show differences in their contents and scales: some occupied more space than the others in the residential unit, while some had more storage facilities than the others (Figure 10.8; Tsude 1989, chap. 3). It is also interesting to note that, when there were more than two dwellings per block, their sizes were also, at times, quite different. This suggests that the individual households themselves may well have been segmented into smaller units.

This last point shares a significant resonance with the osteo-archaeological finding that the phase saw the emergence of the unilinear descent system (Tanaka 1995, 281–285). As we saw earlier, the inheritance of wealth and rights appears to have descended through the lineage, and those who were dropped from the lineage inevitably became subordinates. The smaller blocks in a residential unit, as well as the smaller dwellings in a block, may well have been the houses of the people who were dropped from the main line of inheritance of wealth and various social rights.

As mentioned in our investigation of the mortuary discourse of the period, the relationship between the units of collaborative labour and inheritance would have had elements of mutual competition. The units would have tried to outdo others on various occasions, including the construction of small tumuli and the funeral of their members. From the perspective of the dominant groups, this competition would have generated a new opportunity for enhancing their authority and dominance. If they manipulated this competition by awarding favours to those who served them more than to others, it would have encouraged voluntary subordination among the commoners.

There are two schools of thought explaining the emergence of the PTC as mentioned. One suggests that the commoners, who were previously forbidden to bury the dead in tumuli, were sanctioned by the elite to do so (e.g. Nishijima 1961), while the other posits that the commoners, who were increasingly able to accumulate wealth and labour force due to various technological developments, began emulating the elite custom of burying the dead in tumuli (e.g. Kondo 1952). The fact that these tumuli are rarely keyhole-shaped suggests that some sort of restrictions were imposed on the manner in which the dead were buried, which probably supports the former theory. However, with regard to the latter consideration, there does seem to be an element of competitive emulation that cannot be ignored. The reality would have been that the segmentation of communal groupings into smaller, mutually competing units and the strengthening of the system of dominance would have progressed concurrently with the unilinearisation of the descent system, resulting in the emergence of the new village-scape and the PTC.

The scenario in Kanto (see pp. 312–313) shows that the two emergent layers of the KCR-centred horizon of production and circulation did not completely cover the horizon of the Kofun tumuli,

which had spread from Kyushu to the western reaches of eastern Japan and eastward as far as the riverine plain of the Kitakami settlement in the present-day Iwate prefecture. It appears that the Kanto region constituted a semi-autonomous, peripheral region: the KCR elite attempted to expand their control across the region by means of direct interventions in the region, at times, and by maintaining and reinforcing alliances with the local elite at other times. The Kanto elite, in their turn, sought to enhance their standing among their peers by trying to outdo the others by both constructing large tumuli and forging and/or consolidating their ties with the KCR elite.

5.2. Production and Circulation

Iron production, by this time, had technically matured to such an extent that traces of iron smelting began to appear across western Japan (Murakami 1998, chap. 3). The production of iron agricultural implements and 'lower-ranked' weapons such as arrowheads came to be undertaken locally: according to Motoki Onoue (1993), the arrowheads of this period found in the regions around the Inland Sea area can be classified into a number of regional styles. Other types of lower-ranked iron implements, such as minor equestrian-gear items like horse bits, would also have been produced locally.

In contrast, the 'higher-ranked' implements, such as long swords with decorated hilts, gilded iron-framed saddles and so on, appear to have only been produced in the KCR. Items with identical stylistic and technical characteristics show extremely large horizons with some regions of high concentration (e.g. Niiro 1983). These centrally produced items are found not only in the large keyhole tumuli but also in the nontraditional small keyhole tumuli and, in rare cases, in the round tumuli constituting the PTC. It is likely that these items were strategically presented by the KCR elite to local elite figures of various standings. In rare cases, the items were further presented by those local elite to their subordinates. Some scholars content that the items were situated in a system of ranking. However, considering the ad hoc manner in which they were presented, the system does not appear to have been rigidly imposed, and the recipients of the items would not

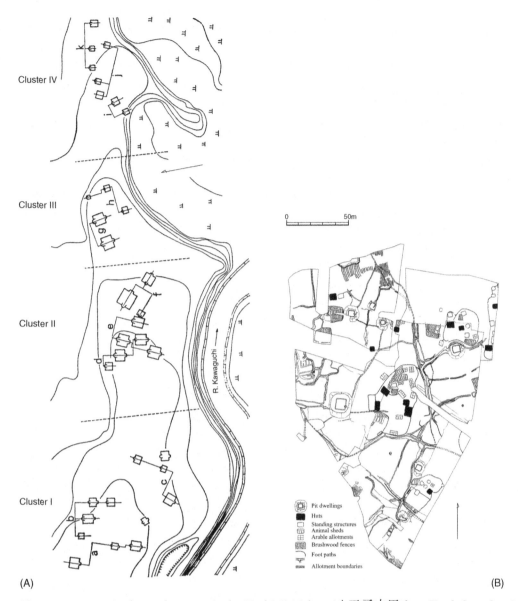

Figure 10.8. Late Kofun settlements. A: the Hachioji-Nakata (八王子中田 from Tsude [1989], original Hachioji-Nakata iseki chosa-iinkai 1966–1968, with additions). B: Kuroimine (黒井峯; from Sugii [2010], original Ishii [1991]). With kind permission from Iwanami Shoten Publishing Co. and Yoshikawakobunkan Publishing Co.

have clearly known which stratum they occupied in the system. It is more likely that the elite drew on certain remnants of the conception of reciprocity in forging and maintaining these asymmetrical relations of service and reward. The fact that many of the items show a high concentration of distribution in northern Kyushu and Kanto would support this thesis (ibid.). The *Nihonshoki* chronicle mentions that many northern Kyushu clans were involved in militaristic interventions in the interpolity conflicts in the Korean peninsula. These interventions were either instigated by the KCR or initiated by northern Kyushu clans through the ties they forged with the groups in the penin-

sula. However, clans located far way from northern Kyushu are also known to have been involved in them. The militaristic interventions would have brought in wealth, new technology and prestige and thereby motivated the elite of those communities. The KCR polity, which, by this time, was run by a group of elite clans, would have taken advantage of its mediating position and consolidated its domination by materialising the asymmetrical relationship, probably still perceived as based upon the principle of reciprocity, by means of strategic gift-giving of high-tech, high-ranked items in return for services provided by the regional elite.

In consequence, two levels of production and circulation systems were established – one centralised and the other local. The production and circulation of goods required for the sustenance of daily life (e.g. agricultural tools and arrowheads) became increasingly specialised and locally organised. Meanwhile, the production of certain items (e.g. long swords with gilt hilts, gilded-framed arrow containers and gilded-framed horse saddles) which were strategically presented to local chiefs of various standings, and at times to commoners, as rewards for their services became highly centralised as well as specialised. While the latter drew on remnants of the concept of reciprocity, the items presented increasingly became indicators of the recipients' specific subordinate positions to the giver, i.e., the KCR elite. This would have made the forged and/or confirmed relations of domination and subordination increasingly *personal* in nature, and consequently made the recipients, i.e., the local chiefs of various standings, who were mostly buried in either nontraditional keyhole tumuli or larger round tumuli, local *bureaucratic* figures who now increasingly controlled the circulation of localised products on behalf of the KCR elite. This, together with the segmentation of individual kin-based communal groupings into household-scale units, would have eroded the norm of communal labour, which would also have been a severe blow to the already fatally weakened norm of communal togetherness. The emergence of tax-like tributes from individual household-scale units was now only a step away.

A slightly different scenario existed in the Kanto region. Studies have revealed that there were movements of goods between elite groups across significant distances. The *Haniwa* vessels produced in the northern Kanto Plain, for instance, were brought into the middle Boso peninsula (coinciding with Chiba prefecture) when some keyhole tumuli were built there (Figure 10.9; Takahashi 1994). Keeping in mind the symbolic meaning content attached to the *Haniwa*, although it did become less significant during the Late Kofun period, it is likely that alliance-like ties were either reconfirmed or newly forged through the exchange of certain goods during the mortuary occasions in which, as I have often mentioned, various social relations were reproduced. This suggests that inter-regional elite connections

were as significant as, or on some occasions even more important than, connections with the KCR elite. The latter half of the Late Kofun period in the Kanto region saw the ongoing construction of traditional keyhole tumuli constituting tumuli clusters. I have already argued that they indicated the continuous autonomy of the elite of those communities which continued to construct the traditional monuments and locales, and the inter-regional ties indicated by the movements of the goods suggest the elite forged new ties between each other and competed for domination over the neighbouring communities by utilising these semi-long-distance (i.e. within the Kanto region) ties.

6. CONCLUSION

The emergence of the PTC symbolised the change witnessed by the entire phase. It appears that the ongoing segmentation of corporate groupings reached a point where the lineages became segmented into households. Following this, households began to function as basic units of production and ownership and competed among each other for the favours awarded by the elite of individual clans; these clans, moreover, had almost lost their erstwhile characteristics of corporate groups and were now merely functioning as units of domination and control.

Some clans, if individual PTCs (and individual L-scale groups comprising a large PTC) can indeed be said to represent clan groupings, appear to have become specialised in such skilled tasks as salt and iron production. The households which did some distinguished service for the elite were rewarded in the form of prestigious goods such as long swords with gilded hilts or gilded-framed arrow containers (see Figures 10.5 and 10.6), which were produced in workshops attached to the paramount chieftain or the KCR elite groups. Descriptions in the *Kojiki* and *Nihonshoki* chronicles record the existence of pseudo-kin groupings called *uji* (氏), which connected local communities with the KCR clans. One of the functions of the *uji* groupings, as revealed by the relevant depictions in the chronicles, was that the elite of individual *uji* groupings residing in the KCR entrusted the local communities with certain tasks and received their material outcomes as tributes. This custom can be described as a form of 'primitive taxation'

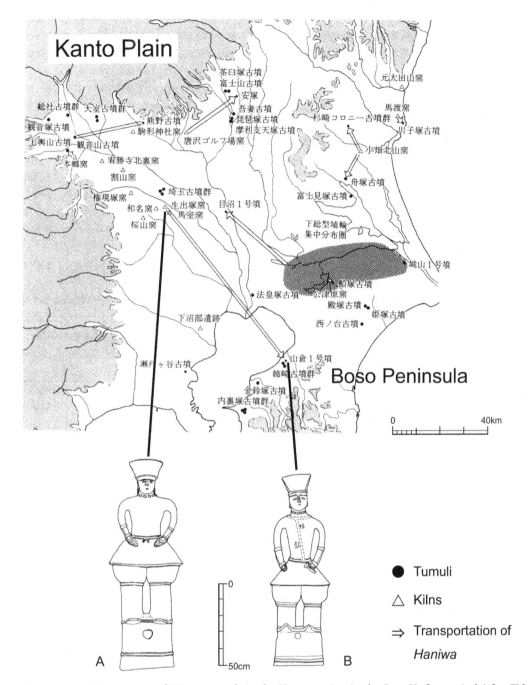

Figure 10.9. Movements of *Haniwa* vessels in the Kanto region in the Late Kofun period (after Takahashi [1994, figs. 4 and 5], with additions). **A**: Oinezuka Kiln (Saitama prefecture). **B**: Yamakura No. 1 Tumulus (Chiba prefecture). Note that *Haniwa* vessels were transported across significant distances between the kilns and tumuli, marked by arrows.

disguised as communal obligation. At times, some PTCs are extremely large, and it is possible that they were cemeteries for *uji* groupings (see Shiraishi 1966). The fact that communities belonging to such a pseudo-corporate grouping brought their dead across a certain distance to bury them in this communal resting place suggests that it was still necessary to maintain the ethos of communal togetherness. Internally, however, it was almost destroyed, and a primitive-taxation-like collection of products and tributes was in place. In that sense, the communal ethos of the time served as an 'ideology' disguising the demise of communal groupings and maintaining large-scale units of control, which were increasingly turning into a form of 'governance'.

CHAPTER 11

AN ARCHAEOLOGY OF GOVERNANCE: THE ESTABLISHMENT OF THE *TEN'NO* EMPEROR (AD 600–700)

1. INTRODUCTION

The end of the sixth century marked the cessation of the construction of keyhole tumuli, except in parts of the Kanto region. As we have seen, by this time, most of the original characteristics of the tumuli as locales for the reproduction of the order and well-being of communities had disappeared. In their place, the dead were now buried as individuals with different biographies, and I have already suggested in the previous chapters that the hierarchical order of the world of the living was also considered to exist in the world of the dead. This order would have finally differentiated the realm of the transcendental(s) from that of the elite ancestors/the dead chief. It is possible to speculate that this was the point when the myth explaining the origin of the rule of the *Ten'no* (天皇) emperor, which features in the *Kojiki* and *Nihonshoki* chronicles, became formalised. This was also the point when individual 'gods', who were differently ranked and assigned different roles in the creation, development and rule of the land of *Toyoashihara-mizuho-no-kuni* (see Chapter 1), came to be differentiated and associated with individual elite clans as their 'ancestors' (see e.g. Matsuki 2006).

A similar change occurred in the case of the commoners, who were now able to bury their dead in small round tumuli, forming the packed tumuli cluster (*Gunshu-fun*, 群集墳; PTC). The formation process and structure of the PTC reflected the emerging differentiation of commoner groupings which were often smaller than lineages, probably the size of households (see Chapter 10.2); the characteristic grave goods in these PTCs, such as various working tools including those for ironworking, which were sometimes placed in the gallery burial chamber, suggest that such groupings had now become a unit of production, consumption and control. The frequent presence of weapons and equestrian gear also suggests that the elite controlled the commoners by organising them into groups such as farmers/artisan-soldiers. Such groupings, still included in the larger clan-type corporate groupings, which were, in their turn, represented by sub-groups (L-scale group; see Chapter 10.2) of individual large- or small-scale PTCs, appear to have had connections with local chiefs, who further had connections with the KCR elite (for the definition of the KCR ['Kinki-core region'], see p. 199 in this volume). In addition, as suggested in the previous chapter, items denoting a high status, which could only be produced in the KCR workshops – such as swords with gilded hilts, gilded horse saddles and so on (see Figures 10.5 and 10.6) – were given to members of household-scale groupings, probably for providing some outstanding service to the elite.

On the whole, an individual came to be perceived as an individual with a distinct biography, including a list of achievements which were, at times, rewarded by the elite; however, that individual was still situated in several layers of *communal* groupings, that is, a household/sub-lineage, a lineage and a clan. This would imply, however, that if those layers of communal groupings were to be incorporated into a system of governance/control and organised as its units, and if the individual were to be 'registered' in one way or another as the subject of such control, the result would have been a governing entity which could well be described as an 'inchoate state'. This is roughly what happened during the late sixth and seventh centuries. The keyhole tumulus as the monumental material embodiment of communality had disappeared by this time. Small round mounds, which embodied the aforementioned duality of the individual – constituted by the individual's existence as an entity with a distinct biography as well as a member of a community – were also being phased out. At the same time, the spatial structure of the residence of the paramount chief became increasingly formalised and gradually assumed the form of a palace (*Miya*, 宮). All these transformations progressed concurrently with (a) the acceleration of interventions in overseas affairs under the leadership of the KCR elite, (b) the technological development significantly stimulated by these interventions, (c) the further development of production and distribution systems stimulated by the technological development and (d) an exponential increase in the range of contingencies experienced by the elite (and probably to a lesser extent by the commoners) in their (social) lives.

In the following sections, I chart the final phase of the formation process of the ancient state by examining these changes as well as the material items that mediated and resulted from the reactions to those changes, which finally paved the way for the establishment of the ancient state.

2. THE END OF THE KEYHOLE-TUMULUS CONSTRUCTION AND THE ESTABLISHMENT OF THE PALACE

2.1. The Last of the Gigantic Keyhole Tumuli

The construction of the gigantic tumuli mounds would have embodied and evoked the notion that the contingencies of the world were solved by and for the sake of the communities involved in the construction. Based on this notion, the elite not only were perceived but also worked as representatives of the communal interests. As we have seen, ever since the emergence of stable hierarchical social relations in the Late Yayoi, this type of communal ideology was slowly moving along the path to erosion and decline. The elite were becoming the *rulers*, and the segmentation of communities into increasingly smaller units accelerated this process. The cessation of the construction of keyhole tumuli, in that sense, marked the completion of the process: the elite now regarded themselves as the rulers and the commoners as their subjects, and it became redundant to involve the commoners in the construction of gigantic tumuli as a communal act for ensuring the community's well-being.

This would also have marked the final establishment of the KCR elite's dominance over their equivalents in other regions. As we have seen in Chapters 9 and 10, the construction of keyhole tumuli and the performance of formalised mortuary practices in, on and around the tumuli were characterised by ritual-political-ceremonial elements which served to reconfirm and reproduce the relations between the KCR elite and those of other polities in order to ensure the constant flow of various resources and information. By now, the preceding relationship had become firmly hierarchised and the KCR elite had managed to centralise and control the flow of resources and information. Accordingly, the material means, symbols and embodiments of inter-polity collaboration for the sustenance of this flow became redundant.

The Mise-Maruyama (見瀬丸山) keyhole tumulus (see Figure 9.13 for the location), the last gigantic tumulus (approximately 318 metres long), stands witness to the above-mentioned change. Considering the size difference between this tumulus and its contemporary second-largest – around 100 metres – the gap now became truly great. As Yoshiro Kondo (1983, 370–374) points out, it is as if all the construction effort was focused on making the *scale* of the mound and its chamber as spectacular as possible. The mound neither was covered with stones nor had cylindrical *Haniwa* vessels placed on it (ibid.). The chamber – which has a total length of 24.80 metres, with the main chamber being 8.30 metres long – was built of large, roughly worked rectangular stone slabs and is the largest among the tumuli chambers excavated/researched so far (e.g. Inokuma 1992). The fact that the mound was not encircled with cylindrical *Haniwas* suggests the disappearance of the last remnants of the material media representing the role of the keyhole tumulus as a locale for offering prayers for communal well-being; these *Haniwas* symbolised food offerings made by the commoners to the dead chief (Kondo 1983, 195), and this symbolic element appears to have continued in the form of occasional pictorial representations on them which symbolised the fertility of rice until at least the first half of the Late Kofun period (see Chapter 10.3). The ultimate disappearance of the cylindrical *Haniwas* suggests that those who were involved in the tumuli construction would have literally been *mobilised* for the purpose, and the spectacular scale of the mobilisation, without the implication of any communal rituals, might have been designed to make a highly political statement declaring the undisputable supremacy and power of the paramount.

The disappearance of the keyhole tumulus coincided with the emergence of a centralised hierarchy, indicated by subtle differences in certain material items. Izumi Niiro (1983) has shown that the formation of a pyramidal hierarchy can be clearly recognised by the differences between (a) those who were buried with a sword, often with a gilded, decorated hilt; (b) those buried with equestrian gear and/or a sword without a decorated hilt; (c) those buried with arrowheads; and (d) those buried without grave goods. These differences, and particularly the differences between (a) and (b), clearly show the increasingly *fixed* nature of the hierarchical relationship between the giver and the receiver of such items. The preceding phenomenon actually represents the diminishing significance of generosity in strategic gift-giving by the elite in order to reproduce their relationship with the subordinates. In contrast, the authority confirmed the receivers' fixed positions in an established system and marked it by gifting increasingly fixed and formalised sets of status items. The sense of mutuality and reciprocity was dying.

It has also been suggested that the period saw the KCR elite's establishment of production systems of formerly redistributed high-tech items such as *Sue* wares in individual regions (Hishida 2007, 102–155). From the second half of the Late Kofun period onwards, new *Sue*-ware kilns were set up in many regions. At the same time, iron and salt production units were established in regions such as the Kibi and Tsukushi provinces, which were strategically important regions for the KCR with regard to its continuing interventions in the peninsula (ibid.). It is possible that those regions were specifically assigned the task of producing strategically important resources such as salt for horse rearing and iron for the manufacture of weapons.

With regard to the fact that a number of PTCs continued to be built in the seventh century, well after the cessation of keyhole-tumuli construction in the respective regions, the increasingly strategically organised production activities were assigned to various regions through pre-existing communally segmented groupings represented by the internal spatio-temporal configuration of the PTC. However, the character of the PTC was transformed in the course of the seventh century: only one deceased person was now buried in the individual, very small round tumuli, which were even smaller than the majority of those constituting the PTC of the late sixth and early seventh centuries (e.g. Tamura 1999). Moreover, these tumuli disappeared towards the end of the century. The deceased persons who were singly buried in those very small tumuli are most likely to have been the leaders of individual groupings assigned production tasks, and would have been, at times, responsible for meeting the assigned production targets. The other members of the group were no longer buried in these tumuli, indicating that the sense of communality had lost its material expression in the sphere of burying the dead. Instead, the representation of communality had become abstract, nonmaterial and formalised. This trend was embodied, at the highest echelon of the developing hierarchy, by the transformation of the structure of the paramount's residence in the KCR.

2.2. The Rise of the Palace

As mentioned earlier, the elite precincts of the Kofun period constituted a complex with an elite residential sector, some sectors for various ritual acts, ones for production and storage, and probably a number of sectors for the subordinate fellow clan members (see Figure 9.15). These facilities were often not all compounded into a single precinct but distributed over a wider area whose structure, as I have argued earlier, represented a conical structure with hierarchically positioned kin groups undertaking their own specialised or other production activities (see Chapter 9.3; Ban 2008). Such precincts, particularly that housing the KCR's paramount, appear to have increased in scale from the end of the Middle Kofun period onwards, but their basic structure seems to have remained unchanged throughout the Late Kofun period. This suggests that the elite were still predominantly responsible for mediating a wide range of intra- and inter-communal relations by partly controlling the production and distribution of goods and also mediating the community's relationship with the transcendental(s) so as to deal with the contingencies endangering the coherence and reproduction of the community. In other words, the political and ritual functions were undifferentiated in the elite's duties.[1]

A significant change, as suggested by the outcome of historical researches into the *Nihonshoki* chronicle, occurred at some point of time in the beginning of the seventh century, immediately after the construction of the keyhole tumuli was discontinued. The Oharida palace (小墾田宮) – the palace of the paramount Suiko (推古, the female paramount who reigned between AD 593 and 628) – was completed in AD 603 in Asuka (飛鳥) area (the present-day Asuka village, 明日香村), Nara prefecture; as reconstructed from the depiction in the *Nihonshoki* chronicle, it was divided into at least two sectors separated by walls and gates, and the frontal sector was an open space sandwiched between two buildings meant for seating the assembled elite. The other sector, separated from the former by a wall and a gate, contained the main hall where the paramount herself was seated (Kumagai 2001, 231–233; Nito 2008, 49–53). Considering the structure of the subsequent palaces, it is thought that the main hall was situated in the residential compound of the paramount. This suggests the following: first, the field of political communication and decision making came to be divided into two hierarchical layers – that of the elite and that between the elite and the paramount; second, this differentiation would have divided the elite into those who could directly contact the paramount and those who could not. This implies that the differentiation resulted in a division between those whose opinions were only heard by the paramount in the form of collective decisions taken in the frontal sector of the palace and those who could personally meet and discuss matters with the paramount at the paramount's residence.

The second inference needs further explanation. The spatial differentiation of the locale for the discussion and decision making of the elite meant the establishment of a formal public domain for political decision making. The emergence of this formal public domain must have been a considerable change from the former informal private domain for decision making. This does not imply that an informal private domain for decision making did not previously exist. The change, I would argue, would have rather constituted an increasing sophistication/centralisation of the decision-making process. This statement also needs to be further explained. The opening up of the informal private domain meant that decisions could actually be taken by those who had access to the domain. Thereafter, the decision which was covertly taken in that private domain could be disseminated among those who did not have this access, after which the decision could have again been taken, as if for the first time, and reported (reported back, in actuality) to the paramount, who would then give the decision authority and legitimacy. In this way, the decision-making process would have been accelerated and its obedience, reinforced. On the whole, the authority of the paramount – which was previously based upon the collective will of the elite of the keyhole tumuli horizon, or the KCR elite, in actual terms – became, in terms of its representation, *detached from and independent of the collective will*. This would have been of vital importance for coping with the increasing complexity of the issues that were collectively addressed by the KCR elite, including formal contacts with the unified Chinese empire of Sui (隋; AD 581~618) and dealing with the increasingly complicated relations with the three kingdoms of the peninsula, caused by the establishment of the Sui empire (see Chapter 4.3).

The process set in motion by the construction of the Oharida palace progressed as follows (e.g. Yamanaka 1986, 260–278):

(a) The frontal sector of the palace grew larger and more buildings were constructed (the number was eventually fixed at twelve) to seat the assembled elite so that they could discuss matters.

---

1 Different specialised production activities, such as those involving the production of armour, equestrian gear, special weapons such as swords with decorated hilts and so on, appear to have been assigned to different elite groups, that is, *uji* groupings mentioned in Chapter 10.6.

(b) The main hall of the palace (which eventually came to be called the *Daigokuden* [大極殿] hall) was detached from the residence of the paramount.

The process described in (a) progressed with the accompanying increase in the scale and coverage of administrative governance, leading to the segmentation and specialisation of various administrative tasks and an increase in the number of those who undertook them. The process described in (b) implies that the paramount came to be perceived and portrayed as the ultimate authority; the paramount chiefs presented themselves as detached not only from the elite gathered for decision making but also from their own private domain, where covert decisions were taken after covert consultations with the powerful and influential elite members (see the preceding discussion). In other words, the paramount chiefs now transcended the difference between the public and the private in terms of worldly matters. In that sense, the process can be understood as that through which the paramount chiefs increasingly established themselves as the ultimate, despotic rulers under the sky, the *Ten* ([descended from] heaven, 天) – *no* (king, 皇), 天皇; in other words, *the living paramounts themselves now became transcendental beings*. The abovementioned processes were completely implemented by the time of the construction of the Fujiwara (藤原) palace, officially the capital between AD 694 and 710 (Figure 11.1).

The preceding process, which can be traced through relevant archaeological evidence, paralleled the emergence and development of regional administrative complexes (e.g. Yamanaka 1986, 278–286). Before the mid-seventh century, there was no fixed configuration for buildings, which consisted of various types of structures including raised-floor buildings for storage and pit dwellings: the building structures were virtually identical to the elite precincts of the Kofun period, though they now were rarely enclosed by ditches. However, as the above-mentioned processes, (a) and (b), progressed, buildings began to be built in the form of square enclosures, with a main hall and some buildings – mostly two of them, for seating the regional administrative elite – placed in an identical configuration to that of the paramount's palace. The notable differences in this

structure are that the main hall was not separated from the area reserved for public decision making and that the residential area of the region's top administrator (Hyo-toku/Kohri-no-kami [評督]; thought to have included the former regional chiefs of the Kofun period; e.g. Yamanaka 1986, 282) was situated somewhere nearby, though not attached to the square enclosure. This would have implied the beginning of differentiation between the *public* and the *private* in the governance-administration of individual regions and suggested that the region's top administrator had become the *proxy* of the KCR paramount; due to this, the private life of the region's top administrator did not need to be treated as relevant to his/her public duty/undertaking. By now, the local communities were perceived as parts of the whole, i.e., the *ancient state* – they were no longer units filled with a sense of communal togetherness, communal ownership and shared well-being.

This was made possible by the widespread perception, at least shared among the KCR elite, that the commoners could be and had to be administered *individually*, which would have required the implementation of a range of devices to replace the communal, collective ideology embodied by the keyhole tumulus. Buddhism and the related media fulfilled this requirement. Let us now discuss this aspect of the ancient state.

3. BUDDHISM

The aforementioned dissolution of the communal ideology, I would argue, holds a key to our understanding of the implications of Buddhism's introduction in the Japanese archipelago (recorded as introduced from the Paekche (百済) kingdom; see Footnote 3 to Chapter 10 for the date of the introduction and the debate concerning it).

By the end of the sixth century, the elite became increasingly detached from being concerned with the well-being of their respective communities and instead focused on more diverse and specialised matters; the individual elite were now assigned increasingly specific tasks by the paramount. According to the historical research, by the end of the sixth and early seventh centuries, the elite of different clans in the KCR were assigned specialised roles in governance and the running of the court (e.g. Kumagai 2001, 183–189).

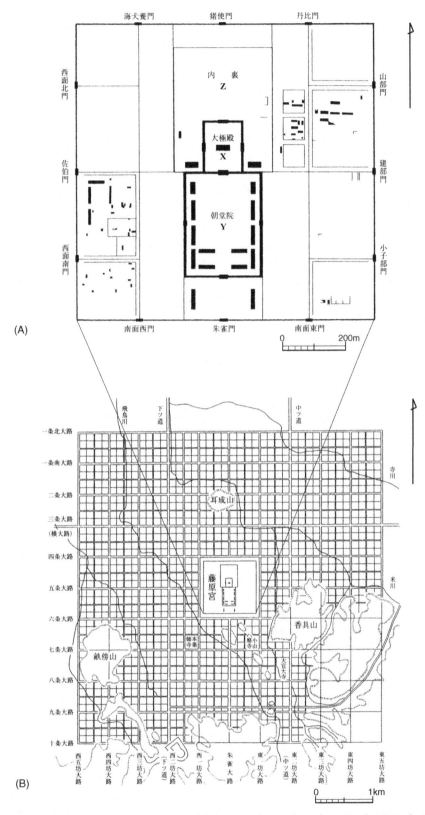

Figure 11.1. The Fujiwara palace and the capital. **A**: The palace. X: the *Daigokuden* hall, Y: the *Chodoin* (朝堂院) frontal sector compound, Z: the *Dairi* (内裏) residential compound. Note that the compounds surrounding the *Daigokuden*, *Chodoin* and *Dairi* compounds were various administrative office compounds, which have not been fully excavated. **B**: the capital. Note that the grid-patterned streets define residential units and blocks, which were not necessarily completely occupied, according to excavation results (after Ozawa [2003, figs. 20 and 23], with additions). With kind permission from Aoki Shoten Publishing Co.

Although they were still responsible for the well-being of the members of their respective clans (fictive kin relations-based clans called *uji* [氏]; see Matsuki 2006), their worldly concerns were increasingly focused not only on their own survival, which required the successful completion of their assigned roles amid the ever-intensifying power struggles in the court, but also on the running of the emergent state under their governance. These domains straightaway presented the elite with a range of contingencies and complex decisions that required their attention. They were required to confront several worldly concerns, that is, their positioning in the inner circle of power, which they could not mediate solely by virtue of being members of their respective corporate communities. These circumstances would have slowly but surely compelled them to appreciate the contingencies immediately surrounding them and hence influencing their positions with respect to the world.

The introduction of Buddhism in the archipelago is widely recognised to have resulted from the emergent governing class's desire to emulate the world religion pursued by the Shui (隋) dynasty of China and the Koguryo (高句麗) and Shilla (新羅) kingdoms of the peninsula, who were rivals of the Wa polity on the periphery of the sphere of Chinese intervention and influence (e.g. Inoue 1974, chap. 5). This inference has been largely verified. In addition, competition with and attempts to gain control over those peninsula polities would have required the authorities to evaluate (and discredit) their deeds by referring to a unified and universal value system. Buddhism would have functioned as a universal system of reference for this kind of value judgement. However, we cannot ignore the fact that the essentials of Buddhist teaching were also in accordance with the rising need for the elite to forge connections and deal with a world of contingencies that had become much wider than their former parochial communal concerns. In other words, Buddhism would have taught the individual elite how to act as individuals living individual lives in the world.

The oldest Buddhist temple with a fully excavated central complex is the Asuka-dera (飛鳥寺; or Hoko-ji, 法興寺) temple, built between the end of the sixth century and the beginning of the seventh century AD (Kumagai 2001, 207–211). The tower of this temple, which supposedly contains the bones (called *Shari*, 舎利) of the Buddha in its foundation platform, was surrounded by three *Kon-do* (金堂, golden halls) installed with Buddhist images. The halls' roofs were tiled, and the halls were enclosed within corridored walls, also with tiled roofs, with their main gate opening to the south. The *Ko-do* (講堂, lecture hall) was situated right outside the enclosure to the north (ibid.). The configuration of the buildings and the style of the roof tiles can be traced back to the peninsular polity of Koguryo (ibid.). Based on the line of interpretation followed in the current chapter, it is important to note the positioning of the tower. The tower is clearly positioned in the centre of the complex; hence, it is awarded the highest significance. The tower was designed to symbolise the once-physical existence of the Buddha and embody his personal enlightenment, which is why it contains his physical remains. The remains, the *Shari*, at the Asuka-dera were a combination of coloured glass and crystal beads, deposited with other types of personal accessories, weapons and pieces of armour, which gave the excavators the impression that they were excavating a gallery mortuary chamber of the Late Kofun period (ibid.). Kimio Kumagai compares the significance attributed to the tower with the Kofun mortuary practices and suggests that the preexisting custom of worshipping the ancestral spirits, which was widespread in the Late Kofun period, characterised the way in which Buddhism was introduced in the archipelago (ibid.). I find this thesis persuasive. However, what appears to be even more important is the fact that the tower's significance gradually came to equal that of the *Kon-do* and the *Ko-do* in the configuration of the temples built subsequently; the Asuka-dera type of configuration was followed by the Shiten'no-ji (四天王寺) type, further followed by the Horyu-ji (法隆寺), Hoki-ji (法起寺) and Yakushi-ji (薬師寺) types of temples, and the changing trends included shifting the positioning of the tower to the building of two towers, as if they were decorative additions to the main *Kon-do* in the Yakushi-ji type, built at the turn of the seventh century (Uehara 1986). In addition, the *Ko-do* became incorporated into the enclosure. The process suggests that the significant spot of the temple shifted from the physical remains of the Buddha to the contents of his teaching, embodied by the configuration of Buddhist images inside the *Kon-do* and the lectures conducted in the *Ko-do*. During the course of the seventh century, it became increasingly important to gain an understanding of the way in which individuals could achieve enlightenment. This suggests that it might be unwise to emphasise too strongly that the introduction of Buddhism in the archipelago was merely the result of both the continuation of the ancestor-worship ideology and the political fallout of the international situation.

The cessation of keyhole tumulus construction, in that sense, marked the end of the communal-ancestral-ideology-based technology of social reproduction, at least within the lifeworld of the elite.

4. CONCLUSION: FROM THE PARAMOUNT CHIEF TO THE *TEN'NO* EMPEROR

We have come a long way since the fixation of certain tasks to certain categories of people in individual communities began to generate permanent hierarchies in the community, mainly due to the introduction of the rice paddy field agricultural technology package and its related sociocultural complex. The hierarchisation inevitably led to the erosion of the preexisting communal, egalitarian ethos and the segmentation of communal groupings into ever-smaller units. However, until the end of the later Kofun period, i.e., the sixth century AD, it had seemed to be necessary to maintain the communal, egalitarian ethos, even if its nature had changed from a way of life to an ideological code.

By the end of this period, however, this disguise of reality became finally redundant. Under the *Ritsuryo* (律令) law-code (the first of its kind, the Taiho-ritsuryo [大宝律令] law-code, was implemented in the year 701; also see Footnote 2 to Chapter 3), the KCR elite were organised into a formal bureaucratic structure, and local populations were no longer controlled through pseudo-communal groupings; from now onwards, individual households were registered not on the basis of their communal affiliations but by their places of residence (*Kogonenjaku*, 庚午年籍; this compilation began in AD 670), and they were registered as subjects of the paramount chief. They now had to pay tax and perform obligatory services for their paramount. The regional chieftains and other elite were also transformed into regional bureaucrats attached to the local administrative offices; they were entrusted with managing taxation and public works on behalf of the paramount chiefs, who now began to call themselves the *Ten'no* (天皇) emperors.

Henceforth, the reproduction of everyone's lifeworld, at least in perception, relied on a figure who was remote from everyone else, but everyone was attached to this figure directly for all their life. This marked the virtual completion of the *abstraction* of the authority figure. As if to symbolise this situation, the resting place of the *Ten'no* emperors became either octagonal mounds (八角形墳; Figure 9.1.H) or composite mounds with square bases and round tops (上円下方墳; e.g. Shiraishi 1999, 191–196). Taichiro Shiraishi argues that these mound shapes were influenced by Chinese political philosophy (ibid.). He is probably right, but I would also like to suggest that the symbolism of the mound shapes, probably embodying the conceptual shape of the world, was as important as the contents of the philosophy; henceforth, the deceased and the successive emperors were the centre of the world and embodied the world. There was no need of material mediation for representing the authority of the emperor; the emperor was the world and, hence, omnipresent.

CHAPTER 12

CONCLUSION

1. THE LONG-TERM TRAJECTORY

What we have seen so far in this volume can be described as the long-term process of co-transformation between different fields of social life or communication. Each of these fields underwent its own unique process of transformation, and each also reacted to the changes which occurred in other fields. Perhaps it was only natural, in that case, for many of the changes to take place simultaneously, and they punctuated the trajectories of change in the feelings, thoughts and deeds of people. The internal structure of each of those fields became increasingly complex, and the spatial extension of some of them became extremely large. The reproduction of those fields, or in other words, the maintenance of sociality was challenged by an accumulation of new problems, and each of the above fields had to cope with these problems in its own unique way. This required the constant invention of new media for communication, which in turn led to changes in the identities and self-images of people.

The sociality between residential communities was reproduced by kin-based sodalities such as clans: it was reflected by the common spatial structure of the Yayoi settlement (i.e., village), consisting of a number of residential units (i.e., hamlets), each of which would have been a segment of a clan-type sodality spreading across a number of settlements (Chapters 5 and 6; see e.g. Figure 6.6). The sodalities would have been reproduced through the fulfilment of various social, basically reciprocal, obligations – often related to birth, death and marriage – involving the exchange of goods, information and people.

As the network comprising sodalities and other channels of exchange developed, the residential communities located at the nodal positions in the network came to attract a greater flow of goods, people and information than before because of their topological positions and the high centrality generated by them (Chapter 6, esp. see pp. 125–135). As their population increased, these communities must have witnessed more deaths, marriages and births than did their smaller counterparts, thus giving rise to the need to fulfil more obligations, conduct more negotiations and settle more disputes. The necessity of mediating and controlling the flow of goods, people and information became much more intense in these residential communities than in their smaller counterparts. Accordingly, the former began to acquire the characteristics of the *central place*: the loop of 'positive feed-back' between the increasing flow of goods, people and information and the mechanism of organising them and maintaining order further accelerated the trend (Chapter 6.4.2). The intensity of rituals, as occasions on which the activities of mediating and controlling the flow of goods, people and information were acted out in the form of the fulfilment of obligations to the ancestors and/or the transcendental(s), became more important in such central places than in their smaller counterparts, and those who lived in these central places and were involved in such mediation and control increasingly acquired privileges as well as obligations in a cumulative manner. This is well attested by the fact that elite burial grounds emerged and developed only in those regional centres. This process progressed faster from the end of the Yayoi I onwards, and it led the gradual development of inter- and intra-communal hierarchy.

We have seen a range of strategies implemented, both consciously and subconsciously, to cope with this development in the field of ritual communication. In the field of mortuary communication, we have discussed the society's transformation from a mode emphasising communal togetherness to that emphasising genealogical continuity, which was materially expressed by the spatio-temporal configuration of burials in northern Kyushu, for instance (Chapter 6.6.1); the initial difficulty of maintaining intra- and inter-communal order was addressed by placing emphasis on communality, and the differentiation of the elite as mediators of the mounting difficulties was represented by the formation of genealogical burial sequences. The emergence of intra- and inter-communal hierarchy and the segmentation of lineage-type communal units resulted in the development of rituals characterised by the deposition of bronze implements and weapons in regions around northern Kyushu and bronze bells in areas around the Kinki region from the Yayoi IV onwards (Chapter 6.7 and Chapter 7). The emphasis upon communal togetherness and communal well-being in those rituals would have prevented the further fragmentation of intra- and inter-communal ties, already corroded by the increasing differentiation between the central places and their satellites and the hierarchisation of their relations. The sense of shared destiny, enhanced by the shared conception of the transformative interdependence between the death and regeneration of human beings and that of rice, that appears to have been reproduced through the jar burial mortuary practice of northern Kyushu (Chapters 5 and 6) and embodied by a 'myth' represented by the pictorial representations on some *Dotaku* bronze bells (Chapter 6.7.2), would have contributed to the maintenance of the sense of communality. Clan-type sodalities played a vital role in maintaining the network of the flow of goods, people and information, the scale of which continued to increase, and the recognition of kin ties (increasingly becoming pseudo/fictive kin ties as the spatial extension of sodalities increased) and the mutual help and obligations they entailed would have been of vital importance for their reproduction.

The emergence of the keyhole tumulus (Chapters 8 and 9) was a natural consequence of this ongoing process. The networks of flow of goods, people and information had gradually covered almost the whole of Kyushu, western Japan and the western part of eastern Japan by the end of the Yayoi V (Chapter 8.2–3). In order for them to function without generating too much of conflict, which would only result in their self-destruction, it was crucial to develop and establish proper protocols, codes and media to reduce potential tensions and stress resulting from the actual occasions of negotiation and fulfilment of obligations both mediating and mediated by the exchange of goods, people and information. Initially, this requirement was addressed by the development of both (a) rituals for the successful reproduction of daily life, including agricultural cycles, and (b) rituals pertaining to the dead and the ancestors, probably fulfilling the same purpose. The rituals involving the deposition of bronze spearheads in northern Kyushu and the regions beyond, and that of bronze bells around the Kinki and Tokai regions, were examples of the former (Chapter 7.2.2), and the development of the custom of burying the elite in uniquely shaped tumuli with distinct paraphernalia in the Kibi province and the San'in region were the examples of the latter (Chapter 7.3.2). The latter strategy was eventually 'selected', through accumulated experiences of success and failure in various social negotiations, to cope with the problems. It can be inferred that the rituals pertaining to the dead and the ancestors were more effective for maintaining the networks, because the forging of kin ties would have obliged those involved in necessary negotiations in the exchange of goods, people and information to remain friendly and cordial as *relatives* (Sahlins [1974] 2004).

Many communities came to share the custom of conducting burial rituals on tumuli of various shapes, which had become widespread by the end of the Yayoi V. The first half of the Shonai pottery phase, that is, the Yayoi-Kofun transitional period, saw the spread of variously shaped keyhole mounds as locales for burial rituals across the horizon – together with the square mounds with four tails sticking out of their corners, which had originated in the San'in region, and the simple square mounds which had originated in northern Kinki (Chapter 7.3.2 and Chapter 8.3). The second half of the Yayoi-Kofun transitional phase saw the increasing adoption of keyhole mounds and the amalgamation of their various shapes into those with round or square rear mounds (Chapter 8.3). Moreover, the beginning of the Furu pottery phase saw the standardisation of the keyhole shape with a round rear mound; this shape began to spread widely across the archipelago, although tumuli with square rear mounds remained popular in eastern Japan and square tumuli continued to be built in parts of the San'in region, both until the end of the Early Kofun period (see Figure 8.5 and relevant descriptions). The process can be understood as a typical example of the evolution of a communication system and its media; the mounting difficulties in maintaining a system prompts the emergence of a wide range of new modes and media of communication; they are selected under the pressure of ensuring the successful continuation of communication, and only those modes and media that are proved to successfully mediate communication remain.

This 'evolutionary' process[1] corresponded with the stabilisation of hierarchy in and between communities. In addition, the different topological potentiality determined by the structure of the system of individual 'nodes', such as northern Kyushu, San'in, Kibi, Awa-Sanuki, Kinki-core, northern Kinki, Hokuriku, Tokai and Kanto, gave rise to the centralisation and hierarchisation of the system of which the Kinki-core region (the KCR) formed the centre: the centralisation and hierarchisation were not necessarily caused by the different abilities or material potentials that emerged between communities; rather, they resulted from the *topological* positions that these nodes assumed, with quite fateful implications, in the emergent network of flow of goods, people and information (Chapter 8.3). The weakening of the late Han dynasty of China led to certain chronic fluctuations in the policy of control and governance of the peripheries of the domain; this dynasty was even-

tually toppled by the Wei, which made it vitally important to acquire prestigious items maintaining the exchange network and the authority of the elite of the archipelago, and this, in turn, would have accelerated the progression of the above-mentioned process (Chapter 4.3). A cooling of the climate, associated with climatic deterioration and probably leading to the deterioration of agricultural production (Chapter 4.2), would also have contributed to the acceleration of the process.

The authority of the elite of the Earlier Kofun period was based on their ability to *mediate* intra- and inter-communal matters; the production, distribution and circulation of goods; and relations with the transcendental(s) in order to cope with the contingencies that could endanger the well-being of the community (Chapter 9). The keyhole and other types of tumuli served as locales for these undertakings of the elite to be acted out in a ritualistically formalised and symbolic manner, and the whole range of relevant paraphernalia were invented and/or developed as material media for them (Chapter 9.2). The sense of communal togetherness continued to underlie most of the fields of social life, although it became increasingly corrupted by the ever-increasing complexity of matters which the elite had to deal with, including, from the fourth century onwards, interventions in inter-communal conflicts in the Korean peninsula and the related negotiations. The structure of the daily life of the elite and the commoners was materially represented by a conical spatial configuration comprised of the elite residential compound, facilities for rituals conducted by the elite, various workshops, storage facilities under the control of the elite and the residential units of commoners in the regional settlement complexes (Chapter 9.3).

The paramount chieftainship of the KCR and certain developing regional polities such as the Tsukushi and Kibi provinces appear to have been the subject of competition during the Earlier Kofun period: the construction of individual gigantic keyhole tumuli seems to have become an occasion for displaying, in a truly spectacular manner, the will and mustering power of those who buried their elite dead and succeeded to the paramount status; the size and the location of the largest keyhole tumulus of individual phases fluctuated

---

1 Note that the word *evolutionary* is used to characterise the process through which (1) a range of variants were generated to react to a new social/natural environment, (2) the concerned community underwent the process of accumulated successes and failures in coping with the new environment by using the new variants as medium, and (3) the most successful variant used in coping with it became stabilised and established as a new category of material medium.

and changed accordingly (Chapter 9, pp. 272–281). The construction of these gigantic keyhole tumuli itself would have enabled the reproduction of a very large-scale network of flow of goods, people and information by inscribing a sense of (pseudo-) communal togetherness on the minds and bodies of those who participated in their construction. However, this began to cease in the Late Kofun period (Chapter 10). Towards the end of the Earlier Kofun period, the formation of many of the tumuli sequences of local paramounts was either terminated or drastically reduced in terms of the scale of the tumuli constituting them, which suggests that the pseudo/fictive-kin ties which had previously maintained mutuality between the KCR and regional elites were transformed gradually into relations of domination and subordination. A combination of the increasing dependence of the regional elite upon the increasingly monopolised supply of 'high-tech' goods by the KCR and the accumulation of militaristic power by the KCR through the large-scale production of iron weapons, among other factors, even accelerated this trend.

The deterioration of the sense of communality in the relationship between the KCR and the regional elite was accompanied by the internal fragmentation of the commoners' communities. The emergence and spread of the packed tumuli clusters (PTCs) shows that a unit smaller than the lineage was becoming the unit of production, consumption and ownership (Chapter 10.2). Further, this phenomenon was associated with the emergence of the perception that a person's individuality, including his or her social status, continued in the afterlife, along with the new conception of an individual's biography in the form of achievements rewarded by the elite for providing outstanding services to them. These phenomena appear to have impacted both the elite and the commoners and would have led to the shift in the mode of social control from the *mediation* of communal interests to *governance* by utilising levels of communal units as the units of control. The small round tumuli constituting the individual PTCs were also situated in individual sub-groupings of such tumuli. This suggests that a sub-group, if comprised of a large number of tumuli, would have represented a clan-scale grouping (L-scale groups; Chapter 10.2), and if these amounted to three/four or so tumuli,

they would have represented lineage/household-scale groupings (S-scale groups; ibid.). In the case of the former, individual micro-groupings in the sub-group would have represented a lineage, and in the case of the latter, a household. In the case of the former, a PTC consisting of such sub-groups would have represented a tribal-scale grouping, and in the case of the latter, a clan-scale grouping. In any case, layers of communal groupings were still in place. However, groupings smaller than clans were now associated with the KCR elite through the mediation of the local elite, at times represented by the keyhole tumuli constructed in or near individual PTCs. This can be proved by the presence of grave goods such as swords with gilded hilts buried in the small tumuli, which could only have been produced in workshops in the KCR.

This fragmentation of communities would have taken place as a reaction to the increasing assignment of specialised production tasks, the development of agricultural technology, which gradually released individual households from communal burdens, and so on. There was another important, fundamental implication of the trend: if layers of communal groupings could be incorporated into the hierarchical system of control and governance (i.e., registration by the place of residence, taxation and mobilisation for public and military duties), the system would give rise to an entity which could be described as a 'state'.

This is exactly what happened during the course of the seventh century, along with corresponding changes in many other fields of social life, notably the fields of ritual practices, elite decision making and regional governance (Chapter 11). First, the practice of building keyhole tumuli disappeared towards the end of the sixth century. This marked the end of the physical manifestation of the importance of communality for the reproduction of sociality and a hierarchical social order. This was replaced by the formalised discussion of matters and decision making by the elite, both of which took place in the paramount chieftain's palace. The operation of power no longer needed to be manifested and mediated by voluntary gatherings on a monumental scale. Now, communication about matters concerning control over the flow of goods, people and information was conducted on the basis of rules and formal protocols materially structured by the physical-architectural structure of the palace. The differentiation between the public and private domains of political communication, marked by this structure, made for efficient decision making at the highest level (Chapter 11, pp. 320–322). Moreover, once the paramount came to be portrayed as transcending the public-private division, the paramount himself or herself became the living god, who, together with the other deities, governed the land. This transformation also corresponded with the spread of local administrative complexes built in a simplified version of the palace of the *Ten'no*. Now, the will of God could spread to the every corner of the land. Under the rule of the *Ten'no*, people were individually registered as 'subejcts' of the state; they had to pay tax and fulfil their assigned public duties as stipulated by the law of the land, the *Ritsuryo*, adopted from the Tang dynasty of China.

2. BEING AND TIME

The trajectory explained above completely transformed the people's mode of being, i.e., the way in which people recognised who and what they were and the way they formed connections with other people, the society and the world.

During the Early and Middle Yayoi periods (Chapters 5 and 6), people learnt to situate themselves in various layers of communal units, the scale of which was basically increasing with occasional ups and downs. This trend created differences between those who lived in central-place-type settlements and those who lived in smaller settlements. The former were exposed to a larger flow of goods, people and information, and some of them were entrusted with mediating the problems and tensions generated by the negotiations involved in their exchange. These persons would have had increasing contacts with other societies and partners who felt obliged to send them things as well as people in return for their generosity and services. In this way, some of these people involved in the exchange accumulated prestige, began to be treated as leaders and had their identities marked, commemorated and internalised by those who attended the occasions of their burials. Asymmetrical social relations were first generated between residential communities, which

then would have spread to the intra-communal relations.

Once these asymmetrical social relationships were established, however, those who attained an authoritative and privileged position appear to have begun to accumulate social and material wealth. On one hand, this encouraged the development of the desire for inheritance, leading to the emergence of the primitive conception of genealogy, marked in the ground, for instance, in the form of jar burial micro-sequences in northern Kyushu (e.g., Chapter 6, pp. 149–154). On the other hand, this rise of the elite class could endanger the sense of communal togetherness, which was of vital importance to the maintenance of stable exchange networks mediated by (often pseudo-)communal ties; this led to the development of communal rituals involving the deposition of bronze items (e.g., Chapter 6.7). The former would have generated the sense of a linear temporal sequence, or the sense of the *history* of individual communal units, while the latter would have drawn upon the *cyclic* sense of time, metaphorically connected with the annual cycle of paddy field farming and the other tasks scheduled in relation to it.

In a way, the co-presence of these two different modes of marking and conceptualising time presented a contradiction. The former was related to the trend, that is, hierarchisation, which could endanger the cohesion of layers of communal togetherness, while the latter was related to the very essence of communality, that is, communal labour involved in the annual cycle of farming and other subsistence activities. Therefore, combining the cyclic regeneration of rice grains and the dead, in metaphorical terms (the 'Yayoi structuring principle'; see relevant discussions in Chapters 5 and 6), would have been an excellent way to solve this serious contradiction in people's perception of world order. The burial jar of northern Kyushu developed from the globular jar shape-type of the Initial Yayoi and Yayoi I periods; the shape-type was originally used to store rice grains. This globular jar shape-type was often painted red, symbolising the rice grains' potential of regeneration. Its former version – when its use as a burial container had been established – was painted red on the inside and black on the outside (Chapter 5.5 and Chapter 6; Figure 5.13).

The notion of death and the regeneration of life, mediated by the notion of cyclic time, continued throughout the Middle Yayoi and possibly through the Yayoi V into the Kofun period (see Chapter 9.2.2–3); the use of red pigments around the dead body continued into the Kofun period, probably echoing the metaphorical connection between the regeneration of grains and that of life. This suggests that as long as the dead body of the elite was associated with the notion of the regeneration of life, a typical cyclic notion of temporality, the dead elite could also be perceived as metaphorical representatives of communal interests, including the good growth and harvest of grain.

The keyhole tumulus, in that sense, was a locale where the *linear* as well as *cyclic* senses of time, *hierarchy* and *communality* were symbolically signified, acted out through ritual practices and materialised in a monumental form. As argued earlier, the construction of a tumulus represented the *beginning of the world* (Chapter 8.4), and the contents and configuration of the tumuli paraphernalia embodied the cyclic stability of that world's order in the form of the complex of various *Haniwa* vessels and grave goods signifying the eternal existence of the dead chief representing communal interests and well-being. At the same time, the tumuli were often situated to signify genealogical continuity. For instance, at the Saki cluster of gigantic keyhole tumuli, the tumuli were constructed one by one from the west to the east (cf. Chapter 9, pp. 283–284). In that sense, the keyhole tumulus embodied the genealogical continuation of the elite while it simultaneously represented the timeless well-being of the egalitarian community.

The elements embodying communality, such as *Haniwa*, declined during the course of the Late Kofun period and eventually disappeared just before the construction of the keyhole tumuli ended. This coincided with the development of the packed tumuli clusters (PTC), which embodied the fragmentation of the commoners' communities and the corruption of the sense of communal togetherness (Chapter 10.2). By this time, the individual was treated as one with a *personal biography*, and the status of the living individual appears to have been perceived to continue into the afterlife. Therefore, individuals, in both elite and commoner populations, now had to identify themselves on the basis of what they did to distinguish themselves, not on the basis of their reciprocal behaviour with fellow members of the community. This would have generated a sense of *causality* in social occurrences, personal biographies and, ultimately, *history*. In that sense, it is particularly interesting to note that according to historical research, the chronicles which preceded the *Kojiki* and the *Nihonshoki*, called the *Teiki* (帝記) and *Kyuji* (旧辞) chronicles, began to be compiled at some time towards the end of the sixth and beginning of the seventh centuries AD: indeed, *history began when the individual became the individual* (Chapter 11).

The technologies for the governance and control of an entity which could be described as a 'state' were developed by drawing upon this emergence of the individual and the conception of a personal biography and history. The status designated to an individual by law, the registration of that individual under the state based on his/her place of residence, not his/her kin affiliation, and the elite's decision-making based on past decisions taken by the authority – all would have been impossible without those technologies. Hence, *the state required a certain presence with regard to a certain conception of time*.

3. CONCLUSION: THERE WAS NO *ONE BEGINNING* BUT A NUMBER OF *BECOMINGS*

It would be interesting to conclude the volume by asking the following question: what would have happened if the Japanese archipelago had been situated in the middle of nowhere? Would we have witnessed the same kind of trajectory unfold in that case? The answer – after going through this volume's examination of the transformation of the archipelago society from the end of the Jomon period to the establishment of the ancient state – is, probably, no.

Jomon communities developed clan-type sodalities and nodes in the form of circular settlements with a segmentary spatial structure, typically seen in the Tohoku, Kanto and Chubu regions in the Middle Jomon period (Chapter 5). Each of these segmented units consisting of pit dwellings and burials would have represented a clan segment or a lineage. However, those communal units still relocated quite often, for example, in the form of seasonal forays for procuring different types of resources. Therefore, the differences between central-place-type settlements and the smaller satellite-type settlements were neither fixed nor gave rise to hierarchisation within and between individual communities. However, these very aspects were introduced in the Yayoi period, and this would not have happened if the socio-technological complex based on rice paddy field agriculture had not been introduced to the archipelago from the southern coastal region of the Korean peninsula. The introduction eventually led to the budding off of small (hamlet-scaled) residential communities from the preexisting settlements (villages), which took place across northern Kyushu and western Japan in the final Yayoi I and Yayoi II periods, and it gave rise to the formation of central-place-type and satellite-type settlements with clan-type sodalities cross-cutting them and mediating the flow of goods, people and information through them. It has already been mentioned that the differentiation between central places and their satellites had ignited the process of intra- and inter-communal hierarchisation (Chapters 6 and 7).

When the centralisation and hierarchisation of inter-regional relations began in the Yayoi–Kofun transitional period, increasingly greater quantities of goods, people and information, including prestigious goods and high technology imported from overseas, began to be circulated through the (pseudo/fictive-)kin-tie-based network covering northern Kyushu, western Japan and the western part of eastern Japan (Chapter 8). Different centrality potentials determined by different positions in the network occupied by the developing regional polities gave rise to a hierarchisation and centralisation in which the KCR assumed a dominant position. The large-scale network mentioned earlier was formed from a mixture of the establishment of a chiefly lineage in individual clans and the rising necessity of circulating prestigious goods and high technology imported from the Chinese dynasty of Wei, which was needed for maintaining the authority of the chiefs. Contacts with a Chinese dynasty, or the expansion of the domain of its political interventions as seen from the perception of the dynasty, played as

significant a role as the development of intra-communal hierarchy in the development of centralisation and hierarchisation in the inter-regional relations.

The shift in the image of the elite leader from the representative of communal interests and well-being to the commander-executor of communal will was significantly stimulated by the elite's interventions in the inter-polity conflicts of the Korean peninsula (see Chapter 4.3 and Chapters 9 and 10), and the segmentation of ever-smaller communal units as units of production, ownership and control was also accelerated by the inflow of know-how regarding high-tech goods and engineering brought by migrants from the peninsula (Chapters 9 and 10).

When the ancient state eventually came into being, its most significant material expression, the palace and the capital, was constructed by emulating the Chinese ideology (Chapter 11).

On the whole, the long-term trajectory of the transformation of communities in the Japanese archipelago leading to the emergence of the ancient state was significantly constituted by interactions with other polities and communities in the north-eastern part of the Eurasian continent. The archipelago's proximity to the north-eastern fringe of the Eurasian continent significantly influenced this trajectory. However, what actually occurred in the archipelago was the *becoming* of a society, or rather a sequence of *becomings* that took place in various fields of social life. These fields were reproduced through the recursive acts of people, drawing upon their thoughts, feelings and memories. These thoughts, feelings and memories, in turn, would have been transformed through their acts, which would also have transformed the range of media relating to those acts, both material and immaterial. The media, thoughts, feelings and memories would also have been changed through their encounters with things that had not existed before in the fields of social life, including news, knowledge, technologies, customs, rules, goods and people from the outside world.

In that sense, there was no fixable/definite *Japanese beginning*, ignited either by outside stimuli or by great autonomous inventions/inventiveness. Nor did there ever exist a *completely closed, totally autonomous entity* that was to eventually become the ancient state of Japan. What did exist, however, that eventually became the ancient state of Japan was the *nexus* of deeds, thoughts, feelings, memories and their material and immaterial media that were interconnected, interdependent and ever-transforming one another while simultaneously generating a new set of problems as well as a new set of solutions that could be used to cope with the problems. After all, is this not what living in the world is all about?

REFERENCES

The treatment of the editorship/authorship of those Board of Education–published excavation reports needs to be mentioned here. In many cases, the individual editorship of those publications is not credited for the reason that the editing as well as writing are often undertaken in collaboration and that the editorial responsibility is difficult to specify. For that reason, most of the Board of Education–published excavation reports listed here are credited as edited by the respective bodies using the following conventions: the Board of Education (*Kyoiku-iinkai*, 教育委員会), the publication body of many of the excavation reports in Japan, is abbreviated BOE. In the case of the Municipal Board of Education, MBE is used; for the Prefectural Board of Education, PBE; and for the Town Board of Education, TBE.

Adachi, Katsumi. 2011. *Nihon no iseki, Vol. 44: Kojindani-iseki* (Archaeological sites of Japan, Vol. 44: Kojindani site). Tokyo: Doseisha.

Aihara, Koji. 1985. Iwate-ken Nishida-iseki (The Nishida site, Iwate prefecture). In *Tanbo Jomon no iseki, Higashi-Nihon hen* (Visiting important sites of the Jomon period, Eastern Japan volume), edited by M. Tozawa, 88–94. Tokyo: Yuhikaku.

Akiyama, Kozo. 2007. *Yayoi-jidai ogata noko-shuraku no kenkyu* (An archaeological study of large-scale settlements of the Yayoi period). Tokyo: Aoki Shoten.

Amagaski MBE. 1982. *Amagasaki-shi bunkazai chosa-hokoku-sho, Vol. 15: Tano-iseki hakkutsu-chosa hokokusho* (Amagaski city cultural properties research report, Vol. 15: The excavation report of the Tano site). Amagaski, Japan: Amagasaki MBE.

Amino, Yoshihiko. 2000. *Nihon no rekishi Volume 0: Nihon toha nanika* (A history of Japan, Vol. 0: What is "Japan"). Tokyo: Kodansha.

Anazawa, Wako. 1994. Kobayashi Yukio hakase no kiseki (The carrier trajectory of Dr. Yukio Kobayashi). In *Kokogaku Kyoto-gakuha (The Kyoto school of archaeology)*, edited by B. Tsunoda, 178–210. Tokyo: Yusankaku.

Anderson, Benedict. 2006. *Imagined communities: reflections on the origin and spread of nationalism.* Rev. ed. London: Verso.

Ando, Hiromichi. 2003. Yayoi-jidai shuraku-gun no chiiki-tan'i to sono kozo (The regional unit of Yayoi settlements and its structure). *Kokogaku kenkyu (Quarterly of Archaeological Studies)*, 50(1):77–97.

————. 2008. Ijyu ido to shakai no henka (Migrations, population movements and social change). In *Yayoi-jidai no kokogaku, Vol. 8: Shuraku kara yomu Yayoi-jidai* (The archaeology of the Yayoi period, Vol. 8: The Yayoi period as seen from the settlements), edited by T. Matsugi, S. Fujio, and H. Shitara, 148–162. Tokyo: Doseisha.

Aoyagi, Tanenobu. 1976. *Ryuen koki-ryaku-ko.* Tokyo: Bunken Shuppan.

Aston, William G. 1990. *Nihongi: Chronicles of Japan from the earliest times to A.D. 697.* Tokyo: Charles E. Tuttle.

Baba, Shin'ichiro. 2008. Nagano bonchi: Matsubara-iseki (The Matsubara site, the Nagano plain). In *Yayoi-jidai no kokogaku, Vol. 8: Shuraku kara yomu Yayoi-jidai* (The archaeology of the Yayoi period, Vol. 8: The Yayoi period as seen from the settlements), edited by T. Matsugi, S. Fujio, and H. Shitara, 148–162. Tokyo: Doseisha.

Ban, Yasushi. 2008. Nara bonchi no Kofun-jidai shuraku to kyokan (Analysis of settlements and chiefly residences in the Nara Basin in the Kofun period). *Kokogaku kenkyu (Quarterly of Archaeological Studies)*, 55(2):29–44.

Barnes, Gina. 2007. *State formation in Japan: Emergence of a 4th-century ruling elite.* London: Routledge.

Barrett, John C. 1993. *Fragments from antiquity: Archaeology of social life in Britain, 2900–1200 BC.* Oxford, UK: Blackwell.

Borgatti, Stephen P., Martin G. Everett, and Linton C. Freeman. 2002. *UCINET for Windows: Software for Social Network Analysis.* Harvard, MA: Analytic Technology.

Bourdieu, Pierre. 1990. *The logic of practice.* Cambridge, UK: Polity.

Bradley, Richard. 2002. *The past in prehistoric societies.* London: Routledge.

Brumfiel, Elizabeth, and John W. Fox, eds. 1994. *Factional competition and political development in the New World.* Cambridge: Cambridge University Press.

Burroughs, William J. 2005. *Climate change in prehistory.* Cambridge: Cambridge University Press.

Busan National University Museum, ed. 1995. *Geomdan-ri village site.* Busan, South Korea: Busan National Museum.

Carrington, Peter J., John Scott, and Stanley Wasserman, ed. 2005. *Models and Methods in Social Network Analysis.* Cambridge: Cambridge University Press.

Carsten, Janer, and Stephen Hugh-Jones. 1995. *About the house: Levi-Strauss and beyond.* Cambridge: Cambridge University Press.

Chiga, Hisashi, ed. 2005. *Shuu-ki tokubetu-ten kyodai Haniwa to Iware no O-bo* (Extraordinary large Haniwas and the kingly tombs of the Iware area: Autumn special exhibition). Kashihara, Japan: Museum of Nara Prefectural Kashihara Archaeological Research Institute.

Chikushino City Committee for the Compilation of the History of the City, ed. 1999. *Chikushino shi-shi, Vol. 1* (The history of Chikushino city, Vol. 1). Chikushino, Japan: Chikushino City.

Chikushino MBE, ed. 1981. *Chikushino-shi bunkazai chosa hokoku-sho, Vol. 6: Nagaoka-iseki* (Chikushino city buried cultural properties research reports, Vol. 6: Nagaoka site). Chikushino, Japan: Chikushino MBE.

————. 1990. *Chikushino-shi bunkazai chosa hokoku-sho, Vol. 26: Nagaoka-iseki II* (Chikushino city cultural properties research reports, Vol. 26: Nagaoka site II). Chikushino, Japan: Chikushino MBE.

————. 1993. *Chikushino-shi bunkazai chosa hokoku-sho, Vol. 38: Kuma-Nishioda chiku iseki-gun* (Chikushino city cultural properties research reports, Vol. 38: Kuma-Nishioda site cluster). Chikushino, Japan: Chikushino MBE.

Childe, Vere Gordon. 1950. The urban revolution. *Town Planning Review*, 21:3–17.

Christaller, Walter. 1933. *Die zentralen Orte in Süddeutschland*. Jena, Germany: Gustav Fischer.

Clarke, David. 1978. *Analytical archaeology. 2nd ed.* New York: Columbia University Press.

Clastre, Pierre. 1999. *Society against the State*. New York: Zone.

Committee for the Investigation of the Tateiwa Site, ed. 1977. *Tateiwa-iseki* (Tateiwa site). Tokyo: Kawade-shobo-shinsha.

Dehara, Keizo. 1999. Minami-Shikoku ni okeru Yayoi-jidai Chu Ko-ki shuraku no shocho (Settlement pattern in the southern Shikoku district during the Middle and Late Yayoi periods). In *Yayoi-jidai no shuraku: Chu Ko-ki wo chushin to shite* (The settlements of the Yayoi period: The examination of examples from the Middle and Late Yayoi), edited by Buried Cultural Properties Research Group, 73–81. Fukuoka, Japan: Buried Cultural Properties Research Group.

Díaz-Andreu, Margarita. 2007. *A world history of Nineteenth-century archaeology: Nationalism, colonialism, and the past*. Oxford, UK: Oxford University Press.

Díaz-Andreu, Margarita, and Timothy Champion, eds. 1996. *Nationalism and archaeology in Europe*. London: UCL press.

Dobres, Marcia-Ann, and John Robb. 2000. Agency in archaeology: paradigm or platitude? In *Agency in Archaeology*, edited by M. A. Dobres and J. Robb, 3–17. London: Routledge.

Durkheim, Émile. [1893] 1997. *De la division du travail social* (The division of labour in society). New York: Free Press.

Edwards, Walter. 1998. Miyazaki-shi shozai 'Hakko ichiu no to' ni tsuite (On the Hakko ichiu Tower in Miyazaki). *Tenri University Journal*, 187:143–155.

Egami, Namio. 1967. *Kiba-minzoku kokka* (The nation of horse riders: An approach to Japanese ancient history). Tokyo: Chuokoron-sha.

Feinman, G. 1998. Scale and social organization: perspectives on the archaic state. In *Archaic State*, edited by G. Feinman and J. Marcus, 95–133. Santa Fe, NM: School of American Research Press.

Friedman, Jonathan, and Michael J. Rowlands. 1977. Notes towards an epigenetic model of the evolution of 'civilisation'. In *The Evolution of Social Systems*, edited by J. Friedman and M.J. Rowlands, 201–276. London: Duckworth.

Fujimoto, Tsuyoshi. 1988. *Mou futatsu no Nihon-bunka: Hokkaido to Nanto no bunka* (The other two Japanese cultures: The cultures of the Hokkaido and Nanto Islands). Tokyo: Tokyo University Press.

Fujio, Shin'ichiro. 2003. Kinki ni okeru Ongagawa-kei kame no seiritsu-katei (The emergence of the Ongagawa-style-derived cooking jar shape-types in the Kinki region). *Kokuritsu rekishi-minzoku hakubutsukan kenkyu hokoku* (*Bulletin of the National Museum of Japanese History*), 108:45–66.

Fujisawa, Atsushi. 2004a. Soshutsu sareta kyokai: Wajin to Emishi wo wakatsu mono (Creating a frontier: The division between the Wa and the Emishi). In *Kokogaku kenkyu-kai 50-shunen kinen ronbun-shu: Bunka no tayosei to hikaku-kokogaku* (The society of archaeological studies 50th anniversary volume: Cultural diversities and comparative archaeology), edited by Society of Archaeological Studies, 261–268. Okayama, Japan: Society of Archaeological Studies.

————. 2004b. Zenpo-koho-fun no henshitsu (The transformation of the keyhole tumulus with a square rear mound). In *Kofun-jidai no seiji-kozo: Zenpo-koen-fun karano apuroochi* (The political structure of the Kofun period: As seen from the keyhole tumulus), edited by K. Hirose, M. Kishimoto, T. Ugaki, T. Okubo, M. Nakai, and A. Fujisawa, 216–234. Tokyo: Aoki Shoten.

Fujisawa, Choji. 1966. Kofun-jidai kenkyu no ayumi (The history of the study of the Kofun period). In *Nihon no Kokogaku, Vol. 4: Kofun-jidai* (The archaeology of Japan, Vol. 4: The Kofun period), edited by Y. Kondo and C. Fujisawa, 26–38. Tokyo: Kawade-shobo-shinsha.

Fujita, Hitoshi. 1994. *Yayoi-jidai garasu no kenkyu: Kokogaku teki kenkyu* (The study of the glass implements of the Yayoi period: The archaeological approach). Tokyo: Meicho Shuppan.

Fujita, Kenji. 1982. Chubu Setouchi no zenki Yayoi-doki no yoso (The Early Yayoi pottery of the central Seto Inland Sea region). *Kurashiki koko-kan kenkyu-shuho* (*Bulletin of the Kurashiki Archaeological Museum*), 17:54–132.

Fujita, Saburo. 2006. Kaiga-doki no mikata (How to examine potsherds with pictorial representations). In *Genshi-kaiga no kenkyu* (A study of pictorial representations in Ancient Japan), edited by H. Shitara, 73–84. Tokyo: Rokuichi Shobo.

Fujitani, Tadashi. 1994. *Ten'no no pe'ejento* (The pageantry of the Japanese modern emperor). Tokyo: Nippon-hoso shuppan kyokai.

Fujiwara, Satoshi. 2004. Yayoi-jidai no sento-gijutsu (Combat techniques of the Yayoi period). *Nihon kokogaku* (*Journal of the Japanese Archaeological Association*), 18:37–52.

Fukasawa, Yoshiki. 1986. Yayoi-jidai no Kinki (The Kinki district in the Yayoi period). In *Iwanami-koza Nihon Kokogaku, Vol. 5: Bunka to chiiki-sei* (Iwanami seminars in Japanese archaeology, Vol. 5: The culture and regional characteristics), edited by Y. Kondo and K. Yokoyama, 157–186. Tokyo: Iwanami Shoten.

———. 2011. Yayoi-doki no seisaku-gijutsu to chi'iki-kan koryu (The production technique of the Yayoi pottery and inter-communal connections). In *Koza Nihon no kokogaku, Vol. 5: Yayoi-jidai* (Seminars in Japanese archaeology, Vol. 5: The Yayoi period, part 1), edited by M. Komoto and K. Terasawa, 589–617. Tokyo: Aoki Shoten.

Fukunaga, Shin'ya. 1989. Kofun-jidai no kyodo bochi: misshu-gata doko-bo no hyoka ni tsuite (Communal cemeteries of the Kofun period: A consideration of the densely clustered pit burials). *Machikaneyama ronso*, 23:83–103.

———. 1998. Dotaku kara dokyo he (From bronze bells to bronze mirrors). In *Kodai-kokka ha koshite umareta* (How the ancient state of Japan emerged), edited by H. Tsude, 217–275. Tokyo: Kadokawa Shoten.

———. 1999. Kofun no shutsugen to girei kanri (The emergence of the Kofun tumulus and the control of allied rituals). *Kokogaku kenkyu* (*Quarterly of Archaeological Studies*), 46(2):53–72.

———. 2001. *Yamatai-koku kara Yamato-seiken he* (From the Yamataikoku polity to the Yamato polity). Toyonaka, Japan: Osaka University.

Fukunaga, Shin'ya, Hidenori Okamura, Naofumi Kishimoto, Masahiko Kurumazaki, Koichi Koyamada, and Shoji Morishita. 2003. *Shinpojiumu Sankakuen-shinju-kyo* (Triangular-Rimed Bronze Mirrors with deity-beast motifs Symposium). Tokyo: Gakuseisha.

Fukunaga, Shin'ya, and Ken Sugii, eds. 1996. *Yukinoyama kofun no kenkyu* (Studies of the Yukinoyama tumulus). Toyonaka, Japan: Research Team for the Yukinoyama Excavations.

Fukuoka MBE (Fukuoka-shi kyoiku-iinkai), ed. 1970. *Takaradai-iseki (Takaradai site): Fukuoka-shi Kaminagao shozai Yayoi-jidai shuraku-iseki chosa-hokoku* (An excavation report of a Yayoi-period settlement site in Kaminagao, Fukuoka city). Fukuoka, Japan: Nihon Jutaku-kodan Fukuoka-shisho.

———. 1979. *Fukuoka-shi maizo-bunkazai chosa-hokoku-sho, Vol. 49: Itazuke-iseki chosa-gaiho* (Fukuoka city buried cultural properties research reports, Vol. 49: Preliminary report on the excavations of Itazuke site, 1977–1978). Fukuoka, Japan: Fukuoka MBE.

———. 1981. *Fukuoka-shi maizo-bunkazai chosa-hokoku-sho, Vol. 75: Imayama-Imajyuku iseki* (Fukuoka city buried cultural properties research reports, Vol. 75: Imayama and Imajuku sites). Fukuoka, Japan: Fukuoka MBE.

———. 1982. *Fukuoka-shi maizo-bunkazai chosa-hokoku-sho, Vol.79: Nishijin-machi iseki* (Fukuoka city buried cultural properties research report, Vol. 79: Nishijin-machi site). Fukuoka, Japan: Fukuoka MBE.

———. 1987a. *Fukuoka-shi maizo-bunka-zai chosa-hokoku-sho, Vol. 163: Naka-Kyuhira iseki II* (Fukuoka city buried cultural properties research reports, Vol. 163: Naka-Kyuhira site II). Fukuoka, Japan: Fukuoka MBE.

———. 1987b. *Fukuoka-shi maizo-bunka-zai chosa-hokoku-sho, Vol. 169: Aoki-iseki* (Fukuoka city buried cultural properties research reports, Vol. 169: Aoki site). Fukuoka, Japan: Fukuoka MBE.

———. 1989. *Fukuoka-shi maizo-bunkazai chosa-hokoku-sho, Vol. 209: Roji kofun* (Fukuoka city buried cultural properties research reports, Vol. 209: The Roji tumulus). Fukuoka, Japan: Fukuoka MBE.

———. 1993. *Fukuoka-shi maizo-bunka-zai chosa-hokoku-sho, Vol. 350: Aoki-iseki* (Fukuoka city buried cultural properties research reports, Vol. 350: Aoki site). Fukuoka, Japan: Fukuoka MBE.

———. 1994. *Fukuoka-shi maizo-bunka-zai chosa-hokoku-sho, Vol. 366: Naka 11: Niju-kango-shuraku no chosa* (Fukuoka city buried cultural properties research reports, Vol. 366: Naka 11: The excavation of a double-ditched settlement). Fukuoka, Japan: Fukuoka MBE.

———. 1996a. *Fukuoka-shi maizo-bunka-zai chosa-hokoku-sho, Vol. 457: Shimotsukiguma-Tenjin'nomori-iseki III* (Fukuoka city buried cultural properties research report, Vol. 457: Shimo-Tsukiguma-Tenjin'nomori-iseki III). Fukuoka, Japan: Fukuoka MBE.

———. 1996b. *Fukuoka-shi maizo-bunkazai chosa hokokusyo, Vol. 451: Hie iseki-gun XX* (Fukuoka city buried cultural properties research reports, Vol. 451: Hie site cluster XX). Fukuoka, Japan: Fukuoka MBE.

———. 1996c. *Fukuoka-shi maizo-bunkazai chosa-hokoku-sho, Vol. 461: Yoshitake-iseki-gun VIII* (Fukuoka city buried cultural properties research reports, Vol. 461: The Yoshitake site cluster VIII). Fukuoka, Japan: Fukuoka MBE.

———. 2003a. *Fukuoka-shi maizo-bunkazai chosa-hokoku-sho, Vol. 746: Sasai VII* (Fukuoka city buried cultural properties research reports, Vol. 746: The Sasai site VII). Fukuoka, Japan: Fukuoka MBE.

———. 2003b. *Fukuoka-shi maizo-bunkazai chosa-hokoku-sho, Vol. 744: Motooka-Kuwabara-iseki-gun 2* (Fukuoka city buried cultural properties research reports, Vol. 744: The Motooka-Kuwabara site cluster 2). Fukuoka, Japan: Fukuoka MBE.

———. 2005a. *Fukuoka-shi maizo-bunkazai chosa-hokoku-sho, Vol. 868: Zasshonokuma 5* (Fukuoka city buried cultural properties research reports, Vol. 868: The 14th and 15th excavation of the Zasshonokuma site 5). Fukuoka, Japan: Fukuoka MBE.

———. 2005b. *Fukuoka-shi maizo-bunkazai chosa-hokoku-sho Vol. 835: Imayama-iseki dai 8ji chosa* (Fukuoka city buried cultural properties research reports, Vol. 835: The 8th excavation of the Imayama site). Fukuoka, Japan: Fukuoka MBE.

———. 2010. *Fukuoka-shi maizo-bunkazai chosa-hokoku-sho, Vol. 1069: Itazuke 10* (Fukuoka city buried cultural properties research reports, Vol. 1069: Itazuke 10). Fukuoka, Japan: Fukuoka MBE.

Fukuoka PBE (Fukuoka-ken kyoiku-iinkai), ed. 1976. *Chikushino-shi shozai Nagaoka kamekan-iseki, Figures and photographs: Fukuoka minami baipasu kankei maizo bunkazai chosa hokoku Vol. 4* (Nagaoka jar burial site of Chikushino city, figures and photographs: Research reports on the buried cultural properties excavated prior to the construction of Fukuoka minami bypass, Vol. 4). Fukuoka, Japan: Fukuoka PBE.

————. 1977. *Chikushino-shi shozai Nagaoka kamekan-iseki, Descriptions: Fukuoka minami baipasu kankei maizo bunkazai chosa hokoku Vol. 5* (Nagaoka jar burial site of Chikushino city: Research reports on the buried cultural properties excavated prior to the construction of Fukuoka minami bypass, Vol. 5). Fukuoka, Japan: Fukuoka PBE.

————. 1980. *Fukuoka-ken bunkazai-chosa-hokokusho, Vol. 58: Mikumo-iseki I* (Fukuoka prefecture cultural properties research reports, Vol. 58: The Mikumo site I). Fukuoka, Japan: Fukuoka PBE.

————. 1983a. *Imajuku-baipasu kankei maizo-bunkazai chosa-hokokusho, Vol.8: Ishigasaki-Magarita-iseki I* (Rescue excavation reports of the Imajuku bypass, Vol. 8: Ishigasaki-Magarita site I). Fukuoka, Japan: Fukuoka PBE.

————. 1983b. *Fukuoka-ken bunkazai-chosa-hokokusho, Vol. 65: Mikumo-iseki, Vol. 4* (Fukuoka prefecture cultural properties research reports, Vol. 4: The Mikumo site IV). Fukuoka, Japan: Fukuoka PBE.

————. 1984. *Imajuku-baipasu kankei maizo-bunkazai chosa-hokokusho, Vol.9: Ishigasaki-Magarita-iseki II* (Rescue excavation reports of the Imajuku bypass, Vol. 9: Ishigasaki-Magarita site II). Fukuoka, Japan: Fukuoka PBE.

————. 1985a. *Imajuku-baipasu kankei maizo-bunkazai chosa-hokokusho, Vol. 11: Ishigasaki-Magarita-iseki III* (Rescue excavation reports of the Imajuku bypass, Vol. 11: Ishigasaki-Magarita site III). Fukuoka, Japan: Fukuoka PBE.

————. 1985b. *Fukuoka-ken bunkazai-chosa-hokokusho, Vol. 69: Mikumo-iseki (Minamishoji-chiku hen)* (Fukuoka prefecture cultural properties research reports, Vol. 69: The Mikumo site: Loc. Minamishoji). Fukuoka, Japan: Fukuoka PBE.

————. 2000. *Fukuoka-ken bunkazai-chosa-hokokusho, Vol. 154: Nishijinmachi-iseki Vol. 2* (Fukuoka prefecture cultural properties research reports, Vol. 154: Nishijinmachi site, Vol. 2). Fukuoka, Japan: Fukuoka PBE.

————. 2003. *Fukuoka-ken bunkazai-chosa-hokokusho, Vol. 178: Nishijinmachi-iseki Vol. 5* (Fukuoka prefecture cultural properties research reports, Vol. 178: Nhshijinmachi site, Vol. 5). Fukuoka, Japan: Fukuoka PBE.

————. 2009. *Fukuoka-ken bunkazai-chosa-hokokusho, Vol. 221: Nishijinmachi-iseki, Vol. 9* (Fukuoka prefecture cultural properties research reports, Vol. 221: Nhshijinmachi site, Vol. 9). Fukuoka, Japan: Fukuoka PBE.

Funahashi, Kyoko. 2010. *Basshi to shakai-shudan: Retto senshi-shakai wo chushin to shite* (Tooth extraction and social groupings: Mainly as seen from prehistoric Japanese archipelago). Tokyo: Suiren-sha.

Furukawa, Noboru, ed. 2010. *Obayama funbo-gun no kenkyu: Koshi-chiho ni okeru Yayoi-jidai funkyu-bo no kenkyu* (A study of the Obayama tumuli cluster: A study of the tumuli of the Yayoi period in the ancient province of Koshi). Shimizu, Japan: Shimizu TBE.

Furukawa, Noboru, Sadayoshi Mitake, Naohiro Toyoshima, Tomohiro Tanabe, Kunihiko Shimizu, Yoshiharu Asano and Takai Yoshimi. 2010. Koshi-chiho ni okeru funkyu-bo wo chushin to shita Yayoi-jidai maiso-iko kankei jissoku-zu shusei (A corpus of Yayoi period burial facilities and allied features mainly from the tumuli of the ancient province of Koshi). In *Obayama funbo-gun no kenkyu: Koshi-chiho ni okeru Yayoi-jidai funkyu-bo no kenkyu* (A study of the Obayama tumuli cluster: A study of the tumuli of the Yayoi period in the ancient province of Koshi), ed. by N. Furukawa, 55–148. Fukui, Japan: Fukui Municipal Museum of Local History.

Furuya, Noriyuki. 2007. *Kofun no seiritsu to soso-saishi* (The genesis of the Kofun tumulus and mortuary ritual). Tokyo: Yusankaku.

Geertz, Clifford. 1973. *The interpretation of cultures*. New York: Basic Books.

Gellner, Ernest. 2006. *Nations and nationalism* 2nd ed. Ithaca, NY: Cornell University Press.

Giddens, Anthony. 1981. *A Contemporary Critique of Historical Materialism. Vol. 1. Power, Property and the State*. London: Macmillan.

————. 1984. *The Constitution of Society: Outline of the Theory of Structuration*. Cambridge, UK: Polity.

Gobo MBE, ed. 2002. *Katada-iseki* (Katada site). Gobo, Japan: Gobo MBE.

Goto, Shuichi. 1939. Joko-jidai tetsuzoku no nendai kenkyu (Iron arrow-heads of the ancient burial mound period [original English title]). *Jinruigaku-zasshi* (*Journal of Anthropological Society of Nippon*), (54)4:1–29.

————. 1947. *Nihon kodai-shi no Kokogaku-teki kento* (An archaeological examination of the Japanese ancient history). Tokyo: Yamaoka Shoten.

Goto, Tadashi. 1980. Chosen-nanbu no ninuri-maken tsubo (The red-painted and burnished globular jars of the southern Korean peninsula). In *Kagamiyama Takeshi sensei koki-kinen kobunka ronko* (Papers in antiquity for the celebration of Professor Takeshi Kagamiyama's 70th birthday), edited by the Committee for the Celebration of Professor Takeshi Kagamiyama's 70th Birthday, 269–309. Fukuoka, Japan: The committee for the celebration of Professor Takeshi Kagamiyama's 70th birthday.

Gunma PBE. 1988. *Joetsu shinkansen-kankei maizo bunkazai chosa-hokoku-sho, Vol. 8: Mitsudera 1 iseki* (Excavation reports concerning the construction of the Joetsu high-speed railway lines, Vol. 8: Mitsudera 1 site). Maebashi, Japan: Gunma PBE.

————. 1991. *Gunma PBE excavation reports, Vol. 93: Mitsudera 2 iseki* (Mitsudera 2 site). Maebashi, Japan: Gunma PBE.

Gyeongnam Archaeological Research Institute, ed. 2003. Sacheon Lgeum-dong yujeok (The Lgeum-dong site, Sacheon). Jinju, South Korea: Gyeongnam Archaeological Research Institute.

Gyeongsang University. 2001. *Jinju Teppyong'ni Yubang Loc. 3*. Jinju, South Korea: Gyeongsang National University Museum.

Habu, Junko. 2004. *Ancient Jomon of Japan*. Cambridge: Cambridge University Press.

Hachioji-Nakata iseki chosa-iinkai (Committee for the Excavation of the Hachioji-Nakata Site), ed. 1966–1968. *Hachioji-Nakata iseki: Shiryo-hen, Vols. 1–3* (Hachioji-Nakata site: Data, Vols. 1–3). Hachioji, Japan: Hachioji Bunka Kyokai.

Hamada, Tatsuhiko. 2006. Hoki-chiiki ni okeru Yayoi-jidai chuki kara Kofun-jidai zenki no shuraku-kozo (The intra-settlement structure of the Hoki region from the Middle Yayoi to the Early Kofun period). In *Yayoi no ogata-tatemono to sono tenkai* (The nature and the development of the large architectural structures of the Yayoi period), edited by K. Hirose and I. Iba, 29–53. Hikone, Japan: Sunrise Shuppan.

———. 2009. San'in-chiho no Yayoi-shuraku-zo (The image of the Yayoi settlement in San'in). *Kokuritsu rekishi-minzoku hakubutsukan kenkyu hokoku (Bulletin of the National Museum of Japanese History)*, 149:233–311.

Hanneman, Robert A., and Mark Riddle. 2005. *Introduction to Social Network Methods*. Riverside: University of California. http://faculty.ucr.edu/~hanneman/.

Harunari, Hideji. 1982. Dotaku no jidai (The age of the Dotaku bronze bell). *Kokuritsu rekishi-minzoku hakubutsukan kenkyu hokoku (Bulletin of the National Museum of Japanese History)*, 1:1–48.

———. 1985. Yayoi-jidai Kinai no shinzoku-kozo (The kinship structure of the Kinki region in the Yayoi period). *Kokuritsu rekishi-minzoku hakubutsukan kenkyu hokoku (Bulletin of the National Museum of Japanese History)*, 5:1–47.

———. 1991. Kaiga kara kigo he (From pictorial representations to signs): Yayoi-jidai ni okeru noko-girei no seisui (Changes in farming-related rituals in the Yayoi period). *Kokuritsu rekishi-minzoku hakubutsukan kenkyu hokoku (Bulletin of the National Museum of Japanese History)*, 35:3–65.

———. 1992. Dotaku no seisaku-kojin (Specialist groups of the bronze bell [Dotaku] production). *Kokogaku kenkyu (Quarterly of Archaeological Studies)*, 39(2):9–44.

———. 1993. Yayoi-jidai no saiso-sei (The custom of reburial in the Yayoi period). *Kokuritsu rekishi-minzoku hakubutsukan kenkyu hokoku (Bulletin of the National Museum of Japanese History)*, 49:47–91.

Hashiguchi, Tatsuya. 1979. Kame-kan no hen'nen-teki kenkyu (A chronological study of the Yayoi burial jar of northern Kyushu). In *Kyushu jukan jidosha-do kankei maizoubunkazai chosa hokoku-sho, Vol. 31–2* (A report on the excavations prior to the construction of the Kyushu expressway, Vol. 31–2), edited by Fukuoka PBE, 133–203. Fukuoka, Japan: Fukuoka PBE.

———. 1999. Kamekan-bo no seiritsu (The emergence of the jar burial of Yayoi period northern Kyushu). *Kikan kokogaku (Archaeology Quarterly)*, 67:34–38.

———. 2005. Meiki-doka ko (A study of the bronze halberds specifically made as grave goods). *Kyushu rekishi-shiryo-kan kenkyu-hokoku (Bulletin of the Kyushu Historical Museum)*, 30:1–19.

Hashimoto, Tatsuya, Daisuke Fujii, and Kota Kai, eds. 2008. *Osumi Kushira Okazaki kofun-gun no kenkyu* (Studies on Osumi Kushira Okazaki tumuli). Kagoshima, Japan: Kagoshima University Museum.

Hashino, Shimpei. 2003. Shiseki-bo denpa no purosesu (The diffusion process of dolmens in southern Korea and northern Kyushu). *Nihon kokogaku (Journal of the Japanese Archaeological Association)*, 16:1–25.

Hashino, Shimpei, Tomoko Ishida, Yoshihisa Watanabe, and Masato Okuno. 2006. Kan-hanto nanbu no Shogikuri-gata jukyo, hottatebashira-tatemono to shuraku-kozo (The Shogikuri-style pit dwellings, pillared buildings and the settlement structure of the southern Korean peninsula in the Middle Mumun period). In *The proceedings of the 55th meeting of the buried cultural properties study group*, edited by Local Organising Committee, 427–447. Fukuoka, Japan: Local Organising Committee.

Hayashi, Kensaku. 1986. Kamegaoka to Ongagawa (The Kamegaoka and the Ongagawa cultural complexes). In *Iwanami-koza Nihon-kokogaku, Vol. 5: Bunka to Chiiki-sei* (Iwanimi seminars in Japanese archaeology, Vol. 5: Local culture and local characteristics), edited by Y. Kondo and K. Yokoyama, 93–124. Tokyo: Iwanami Shoten.

Hayden, Brian. 1995. Pathways to power: principles for creating socioeconomic inequities. In *Foundations of social inequality*, edited by T. D. Price and G. Feinman, 15–85. New York: Plenum Press.

Higashi, Kazuyuki. 2011. Kyushu-nanbu-chiho (The southern Kyushu region). In *Koza Nihon no kokogaku, Vol. 5: Yayoi-jidai part I* (Seminars in Japanese archaeology, Vol. 5: The Yayoi period, part 1), edited by M. Komoto and K. Terasawa, 146–164. Tokyo: Aoki Shoten.

Higashikage, Yu, ed. 2011. *Higashi-Ajia ni okeru shoki-kyuto oyobi obo no kokogaku-teki kenkyu* (The archaeological investigation of the early palaces and kingly tumuli of East Asia). Kashihara, Japan: Nara prefectural Kashihara institute for archaeological research.

Hirata, Sadayuki. 2003. Nakoku iseki-gun (The site cluster representing the ancient polity of "Na"). In *Kasuga-shi bunkazai chosa hokoku-sho, Vol. 35: Hakugensha-iseki* (Kasuga city cultural properties research reports, Vol. 35: Hakugensha site), edited by Y. Yanagida, 175–181. Kasuga, Japan: Kasuga MBE.

Hirosaki MBE, ed. 1991. *Sunazawa-iseki* (Sunazawa site). Hirosaki, Japan: Hirosaki-shi kyoiku-iinkai.

Hirose, Kazuo. 1987. Daio-bo no keifu to sono tokushitsu (1) (The genealogy of royal tombs and its characteristics[1]). *Kokogaku kenkyu (Quarterly of Archaeological Studies)*, 34(3):23–46.

———. 1988. Daio-bo no keifu to sono tokushitsu (2) (The genealogy of royal tombs and its characteristics[2]). *Kokogaku kenkyu (Quarterly of Archaeological Studies)*, 34(4):68–84.

———. 1997a. *Jomon kara Yayoi heno shin-rekishi-zo* (A new historical model of the Jomon and the Yayoi periods). Tokyo: Kadokawa Shoten.

———. 1997b. Seki to suiro (Dams and irrigation canals). In *Yayoi-bunka no kenkyu, Vol. 2: Seigyo* (The study of the Yayoi culture, Vol. 2: Subsistence), edited by H. Kanaseki and M. Sahara, 39–53. Tokyo: Yusankaku.

———. 2003. *Zenpo-koen-fun kokka* (The Keyhole-shaped tumulus state). Tokyo: Kadokawa Shoten.

———. 2009. Kofun-jidai-zo sai-kochiku no tameno kosatsu (A consideration for the re-construction of the image of the Kofun period). *Kokuritsu rekishi-minzoku hakubutsukan kenkyu hokoku (Bulletin of the National Museum of Japanese History)*, 150:33–147.

Hirose, Kazuo, and Isao Iba, eds. 2006. *Yayoi no ogata-tatemono to sono tenkai* (The nature and the development of the large architectural structures of the Yayoi period). Hikone, Japan: Sunrise Shuppan.

Hirose, Satoru. 2008. Mesuriyama-kofun shutsudo *Haniwa* no sai-kento (A re-analysis of the Haniwa cylindrical vessels from the Mesuriyama tumulus). In *Osaka shiritsu daigaku kokogaku kenkyu hokoku, Vol. 3: Mesuriyama-kofun no kenkyu* (Osaka City University archaeological research report, Vol. 3: A study of the Mesuriyama tumulus), edited by N. Kishimoto and A. Tokoro, 90–102. Osaka, Japan: Osaka City University.

Hiroshima PBE and Hiroshima Prefectural Buried Cultural Properties Research Centre, eds. 1981. *Matsugasako-iseki-gun hakkutsu-chosa hokoku* (An excavation report of the Matsugasako site cluster). Hiroshima, Japan: Hiroshima PBE and Hiroshima Prefectural Buried Cultural Properties Research Centre.

Hishida, Tetsuo. 2007. *Kodai Nihon: Kokka-keisei no kokogaku* (Ancient Japan: The archaeology of state formation). Kyoto, Japan: Kyoto University Press.

Hodder, Ian, 1987. The meaning of discard: Ash and domestic space in Baringo. In *Method and theory for activity area research: An ethnoarchaeological approach*, edited by S. Kent, 424–448. New York: Columbia University Press.

Hojo, Yoshitaka. 1986. Funkyu ni hyoji sareta Zenpo-koen-fun no teishiki to sono hyoka (The design of the keyhole type tumuli in the early Kofun period). *Kokogaku kenkyu (Quarterly of Archaeological Studies)*, 32(4):42–66.

———. 1996. Yukinoyama kofun no sekisei-hin (Stone implements from the Yukinoyama tumulus). In *Yukinoyama kofun no kenkyu* (Studies of the Yukinoyama tumulus), edited by S. Fukunaga and K. Sugii, 309–350. Toyonaka, Japan: Research team for the Yukinoyama excavations.

———. 1999a. Kofun-jidai zenki no sekiseihin kenkyu wo megutte (On the study of the stone accessories and stone ritual implements of the Early Kofun period). *Kokogaku janaru (Archaeological Journal)*, 453:2–5.

———. 1999b. Sanuki-gata zenpo-koen-fun no teisho (Proposing the Sanuki-type keyhole tumuli as a new category). In *Kokka-keisei-ki no kokogaku: Osaka daigaku kokogaku-kenkyu-shitsu 10-shunen kinen ronshu* (Archaeological studies of the state formation period: Papers in celebration of 10th anniversary of the foundation of the archaeological laboratory of Osaka university), edited by the Laboratory, 205–229. Toyonaka, Japan: Osaka University Archaeological Laboratory.

———. 2000. Zenpo-koen-fun to Wa-oken (The keyhole tumulus and the Wa kingship). In *Kofun-jidai-zo wo minaosu* (Social structure and social change in the formative phase of the mounded-tomb period of Japan: A new perspective), edited by Y. Hojo, K. Mizoguchi, and Y. Murakami, 77–135. Tokyo: Aoki Shoten.

Hojo, Yoshitaka, Koji Mizoguchi, and Yasuyuki Murakami, eds. 2000. *Kofun-jidai-zo wo minaosu* (Social structure and social change in the formative phase of the mounded-tomb period of Japan: A new perspective). Tokyo: Aoki Shoten.

Honami TBE, ed. 1992. *Honami-machi bunkazai chosa hokoku-sho, Vol. 7: Honami-chiku iseki-gun Vol. 4* (Research reports on the cultural properties of Honami township, Vol. 7: Honami area site cluster, Vol. 4). Honami, Japan: Honami TBE.

Hori, Daisuke. 2011. Hokuriku-chiiki (The Hokuriku district). In *Koza Nihon no kokogaku, Vol. 5: Yayoi-jidai Part I* (Seminars in Japanese archaeology, Vol. 5: The Yayoi period, part 1), edited by M. Komoto and K. Terasawa, 331–352. Tokyo: Aoki Shoten.

Horikawa, Yoshihide. 1982. Tajima-iseki (Tajima site). In *Matsura-koku* (The ancient polity of Matsura), edited

by Committee for the Investigation of the Circum-Karatsu-Bay Area, 217–221. Tokyo: Rokko Shuppan.

Hozumi, Yasumasa. 2007. Fujikomeru chikara (The force to enclose the evil spirit). In *Doshisha daigaku Kokogaku shirizu, Vol. 8: Mori Koichi-sensei sanju-kinen kentei-ronshu* (Doshisha university archaeology series, Vol. 8: Papers dedicated to Prof. Koichi Mori on his 80th birthday), edited by K. Matsufuji, 335–348. Kyoto, Japan: Doshisha University Archaeology Series Publication Committee.

Hyogo PBE, ed. 1995. *Higashi-Muko iseki* (Higashi-Muko site). Kobe, Japan: Hyogo PBE.

Ikefuchi, Shun'ichi. 1997. Ogata ho-fun ha nani wo imi suru ka (What do the large square-shaped Kofun tumuli of the Izumo province mean?). In *Kodai Izumo bunka-ten* (The catalogue of the exhibition of the ancient Izumo culture), edited by Shimane PBE and Ashahi Shinbun Co., 90–93. Matsue, Japan: Shimane PBE and Asahi Shinbun Co.

———. 2000. Kanbara-jinja kofun shutsudo Nomigashira-shiki tetsuzoku ni kansuru shiron (A tentative consideration of the Nomigashira-type iron arrowheads from the Kanbara-jinja tumulus). In *Kanbara-jinja kofun* (The Kanbara-jinja tumulus), edited by Kamo TBE, 212–242. Kamo, Japan: Kamo TBE.

Imamura, Keiji. 1996. *Prehistoric Japan: New Perspectives on Insular East Asia*. London: University College London Press.

———. 1999. *Jomon no jitsuzo wo motomete* (Seeking the realistic image of the Jomon period). Tokyo: Yoshi-kawakobunkan.

Inokuma, Kanekatsu, ed. 1992. *Mise-Maruyama kofun to tenno-ryo* (Mise-Maruyama tumulus and the imperial mausolea). Tokyo: Yusankaku.

Inoue, Mitsusada. 1960. *Nihon-kokka no kigen* (The origin of the ancient Japanese state). Tokyo: Iwanami Shoten.

———. 1965. *Nihon kodai-koka no kenkyu* (A study of Japanese ancient state). Tokyo: Iwanami Shoten.

———. 1974. *Nihon no rekishi, Vol. 3: Asuka no chotei* (Japanese history, Vol. 3: The Asuka court). Tokyo: Shogakkan.

Inoue, Tomohiro. 2005. Shoyo-jyurin-tai, kaigan-heiya no suiden (2): Setouchi, Kinki, Tokai-seibu (The emergence and development of rice paddy field technology). *Kokogaku jyanaru (Archaeological Journal)*, 518: 8–12.

Inoue, Yasuhiro. 2008. *Hokubu-Kyushu Yayoi-Kofun-shakai no tennkai* (The trajectory of the Yayoi and Kofun social development of northern Kyushu). Fukuoka, Japan: Azusa Shoin.

Inoue, Yoshiya. 2009. Sugu-iseki-gun no shuraku-kozo (The structure of the Sugu site cluster). In *Yayoi-jidai koki no shakai-henka* (The social transformation of the Late Yayoi period), edited by Committee for the 58th meeting of the Buried Cultural Properties Research Group, 121–138. Harima, Japan: Committee for the 58th Meeting of the Buried Cultural Properties Research Group.

Inoue, Yuichi. 2010. Kotai-seki no kozo-bunseki (A structural analysis of the Kotaiseki stone). In *Hikaku-kokogaku no shin-chihei* (A new horizon of comparative archaeologies), edited by T. Kikuchi, 234–244. Tokyo: Doseisha.

IntCal09. 2009. IntCal09 Calibration Issue. *Radiocarbon*, 51(4).

Iseki, Hirotaro. 1983. *Chuseki-heiya* (Alluvial plain). Tokyo: Tokyo University Press.

Ishida, Tomoko. 2010. Sugu-shiki doki ni okeru sekisai-doki no igi (The significance of the red-painted vessels of the Sugu style pottery of the Middle Yayoi period of northern Kyushu, Japan). *Kyushu kokogaku (Journal of the Archaeological Society of Kyushu)*, 85: 21–47.

———. n.d. Hokubu-Kyushu Yayoi-jidai chuki ni okeru chiiki-sei (The rocal valiability of the pottery of the Middle Yayoi period in northern Kyushu). *Kyushu kokogaku-kai Heisei 20-nendo sokai shiryo-shu* (The Archaeological Society of Kyushu 2008 general meeting abstract book). Fukuoka, Japan: Kyushu kokogaku-kai.

Ishiguro, Tatsuhito. 2003. Chubu-chiho no doki (The pottery of the Chubu district). In *Koko-shiryo taikan, Vol. 1: Yayoi, Kofun-jidai doki No. 1* (The compendium of archaeological materials, Vol. 1: The pottery of the Yayoi and Kofun periods, No.1), edited by J. Takesue and H. Ishikawa, 253–316. Tokyo: Shogakkan.

———. 2011. Tokai Chubu-kochi-nan'bu (The Tokai and southern Chubu Highland districts). In *Koza Nihon no kokogaku, Vol. 5: Yayoi-jidai Part I* (Seminars in Japanese archaeology, Vol. 5: The Yayoi period, part 1), edited by M. Komoto and K. Terasawa, 353–396. Tokyo: Aoki Shoten.

Ishii, Katsumi, ed. 1991. *Kuroimine-iseki hakkutsu-chosa hokoku-sho* (The excavation report of the Kuroimine site). Komochi, Japan: Komochi Village Board of Education.

Ishikawa, Hideshi. 2000. Tohoku-Nihon no hitobito no kurashi (The life of the people of north-eastern Japan). In *Wa-jin wo torimaku sekai* (The worlds surrounding the domain of the Wa people), edited by National Museum of Japanese History, 68–86. Tokyo: Yamakawa Shuppan.

———. 2003. Kanto, Tohoku-chiho no doki (The pottery of the Kanto district). In *Koko-shiryo taikan, Vol.1: Yayoi, Kofun-jidai doki No. 1* (The compendium of archaeological materials, Vol. 1: The pottery of the Yayoi and Kofun periods, No.1), edited by J. Takesue and H. Ishikawa, 317–368. Tokyo: Shogakkan.

———. 2008. 'Yayoi-jidai' no hakken (The discovery of the Yayoi period). Tokyo: Shinsensha.

———. 2011a. Kanto-chiho ni okeru kyodai noko-shuraku no shutsugen to sono haikei (The emergence of extremely large agrarian villages in the Kanto region and its backgrounds). In *Yayoi-jidai no kenkyu, Vol. 3: Tayo-ka suru Yayoi-jidai* (Studies in the Yayoi period, Vol. 3: The Yayoi culture diverging), edited by H. Shitara, S. Fujio and T. Matsugi, 102–113. Tokyo: Doseisha.

———. 2011b. Kanto-chiiki. In *Koza Nihon no kokogaku, Vol. 5: Yayoi-jidai Part I* (Seminars in Japanese archaeology, Vol. 5: The Yayoi period, part 1), edited by M. Komoto and K. Terasawa, 397–429. Tokyo: Aoki Shoten.

Ishino, Hironobu, ed. 1995. *Zenkoku kofun hen'nen-shusei* (The compendium of the regional chronology of the Kofun tumuli of Japan). Tokyo: Yusankaku.

———. 2005. *Kofun-jidai-shi (Zo-ho-kaitei-ban)* (The history of the Kofun period), rev. ed. Tokyo: Yusankaku.

Itakura, Yudai. 2006. Masei-sekifu kara mita Kyushu Jomon-jidai zenki iko no seigyo kyoju-keitai (Transformation of subsistence-settlement system through the latter half of the Jomon period in the Kyushu region: As seen from the analysis of polished stone axes and adzes). *Nihon kokogaku (Journal of the Japanese Archaeological Association)*, 21:1–19.

Iwanaga, Shozo. 1980. Yayoi-jidai seido-ki keishiki-bunrui hen'nen saiko (A reconsideration of the typo-chronology of the bronze implements of the Yayoi period): ken, hoko, ka wo chushin ni (focussing on the dagger, spearhead and halberd). *Kyushu kokogaku (Journal of the Archaeological Society of Kyushu)*, 55:1–22.

———. 1986. Hoko-gata saiki (The bronze spearhead-shaped ritual implement). In *Yayoi-bunka no kenkyu, Vol. 6: Dogu to gijutsu part 2* (The study of the Yayoi culture, Vol. 6: Tools and technology, part 2), edited by H. Kanaseki and M. Sahara, 113–118. Tokyo: Yusankaku.

———. 1987. Dense ko (On the phenomenon of the long-term inheritance of material items). In *Higashi-Ajia no koko to rekishi, Vol. 2* (Archaeology and history in East Asia, Vol. 2), edited by The Committee for the Celebration of the Retirement of Professor Takashi Okazaki, 457–478. Kyoto, Japan: Dohosha.

———. 1994. Nihon-retto san seido buki-rui shutsugen no kokogaku teki igi (The emergence of indigenous weapon-shaped bronze ritual implements: Its archaeological context and significance). *Kobunka Danso (Journal of the Society of Kyushu Prehistoric and Ancient Cultural Studies)*, 33:37–60.

———. 1997. *Rekishi-hakkutsu, Vol. 7: Kinzokki-tojo* (Excavating history, Vol. 7: The emergence of the metal implements). Tokyo: Kodansha.

Iwata, Keiji. 1970. *Sekai no shukyo, Vol. 10: Kami no tanjo* (Religions of the world, Vol. 10: The birth of the gods). Tokyo: Tankosha.

Iwate PBE. 1980. *Tohoku shinkansen kankei maizo-bunkazai chosa-hokoku-sho, Vol. 7: Nishida iseki* (Reports on the excavations prior to the construction of the Tohoku shinkansen bullet train network, Vol. 7: Nishida site). Morioka, Japan: Iwate PBE.

Izumi MBE, ed. 2004. *Shiseki Ikegami-Sone 99* (Designated national cultural asset Ikegami-Sone site 1999). Izumi, Japan: Izumi MBE.

Izumi, Takura. 1989. Nishi-nihon maken-doki-yoshiki (The western Japan burnished pottery style). In *Jomon-doki taikan, Vol. 4: Ko-ki, ban-ki, zoku-jomon* (The outline of the Jomon pottery, Vol. 4: The late, final and the epi-Jomon periods) edited by T. Kobayashi, 311–314. Tokyo: Kodansha.

Izumo MBE. 2000. *Nishitani funbo-gun: Heisei 10-nendo hakkutsu-chosa hokoku-sho* (The Nishitani tumuli cluster: The report of the excavation undertaken in the 10th year of the Heisei era). Izumo, Japan: Izumo MBE.

Jansen, Marius B, ed. 1989. *The Cambridge History of Japan, Vol. 5: The nineteenth century*. Cambridge: Cambridge University Press.

Japanese Archaeological Association, ed. 2003. *Zen-chuki kyuseki-mondai no kento* (The investigation into the forgery of "lower" and "middle" Palaeolithic sites). Tokyo: Japanese Archaeological Association.

Johnson, Allen and Timothy Earle. 2000. *The evolution of social systems: From foraging groups to agrarian state.* Stanford, CA: Stanford University Press.

Kaku, Takayo. 1997. Dotaku no tori: Tsuru mo irushi Sagi mo iru (Bird motifs depicted on ritual bronze bells of Yayoi period Japan). *Kokogaku kenkyu (Quarterly of Archaeological Studies)*, 44(1):93–105.

Kaneko, Hiromasa. 1997. Shuryo (Hunting). In *Yayoi-bunka no kenkyu, Vol. 2: Seigyo* (The study of the Yayoi culture, Vol. 2: Subsistence), edited by H. Kanaseki and M. Sahara, 141–152. Tokyo: Yusankaku.

Kaner, Simon, ed. 2009. *The power of Dogu: Ceramic figurines from ancient Japan.* London: British Museum Press.

Kano, Shunsuke, and Tatsuhito Ishiguro, eds. 2002. *Yayoi-doki no yoshiki to hen'nen: Tokai-hen* (The styles and chronologies of the Yayoi pottery: The Tokai region). Tokyo: Mokujisha.

Karatsu MBE. 1982. *Nabatake.* Karatsu, Japan: Karatsu MBE.

Kasuga MBE, ed. 1994. *Nakoku no shuto Sugu-Okamoto iseki* (The capital of the polity of Na, Sugu-Okamoto site). Tokyo: Yoshikawakobunkan.

———. 2004. *Kasuga-shi bunkazai chosa hokoku-sho, Vol. 37: Nioute-iseki A-chiten* (Kasuga city cultural properties research reports, Vol. 37: Niote site Location A). Kasuga, Japan: Kasuga MBE.

———. 2010. *Kasuga-shi bunkazai chosa hokoku-sho, Vol. 58: Sugu Okmamoto iseki, Vol. 3* (Kasuga city cultural properties research reports, Vol. 58: Sugu Okamoto site, Vol. 3) Kasuga, Japan: Kasuga MBE.

———. 2011. *Kasuga-shi bunkazai chosa hokoku-sho, Vol. 61: Sugu Okmamoto iseki, Vol. 4* (Kasuga city cultural properties research reports, Vol. 61: Sugu Okamoto site, Vol. 4). Kasuga, Japan: Kasuga MBE.

Kasuya TBE, ed. 2002. *Kasuya-machi bunkazai chosa-houkoku-sho, Vol. 19: Etsuji-iseki dai-go chiten* (The research report of the cultural properties of Kasuya Town, Vol. 19: The Etsuji site Loc. 5). Kasuya, Japan: Kasuya TBE.

———. 2009. *Kasuya-machi bunkazai chosa-hokoku-sho, Vol. 28: Etsuji-iseki dai-hachi chiten* (The research report of the cultural properties of Kasuya Town, Vol. 28: The Etsuji site Loc. 8). Kasuya, Japan: Kasuya TBE.

Kataoka, Koji. 1999. *Yayoi-jidai torai-jin to doki, seido-ki* (The pottery, bronze artefacts and migrants from Korean peninsula in the Yayoi period). Tokyo: Yusankaku.

———. 2003. Suiden inasaku noko no teichaku to ten-kai (The adoption and development of rice paddy field agriculture). In *Ogori-shi bunkazai chosa hokoku-sho, Vol. 181: Mitsusawa Kitanakao 1 chiten* (Ogori city cultural properties research report, Vol. 181: Mitsusawa Kitana-kao site, Location 1), edited by Ogori MBE, 117–176. Ogori, Japan: Ogori MBE.

Katata, Sunao. 1964. *Ikeda Chausuyama kofun no ken-kyu* (A study of the Ikeda Chausuyama tumulus). Nara, Japan: Laboratory of Archaeology, Tezukayama University.

Kawai, Osamu. 2009. *Sima-machi bunkazai chosa-hokoku-sho, Vol. 30: Ichinomachi-iseki* (Shima town cultural properties research reports, Vol. 30: Ichinomachi site). Shima, Japan: Shima TBE.

Kawai, Shinobu. 2003. Yayoi-jidai koki-shoto ni okeru doki-yoshiki no henkaku to chiikikan-kankei (The stylistic transformation of the pottery assemblage of the beginning of the Late Yayoi period as seen from the inter-regional relationships). In *Toyama daigaku kokogaku kenkyu-shitsu ronshu: Akiyama Shingo sensei koki-kinen* (Papers from the laboratory of archaeology, Toyama University: In celebration of Professor Shingo Akiyama's 70th birthday), edited by Committee for the Celeb-ration of Professor Shingo Akiyama's 70th birthday, 85–121. Tokyo: Rokuichi Shobo.

Kawamura, Yoshimitsu. 2010. *Wa no gyokki: Tamatsukuri to Wa-koku no jidai* (Stone accessory production and the age of the Wa polity). Tokyo: Aoki Shoten.

Kawano, Kazutaka, and Toshikatsu Nishikawa, eds. 2003. *Kokogaku to reki-nendai* (Archaeology and absolute dates). Tokyo: Mineruba Shobo.

Keesing, Roger M. 1975. *Kin Groups and Social Structure.* Fort Worth, TX: Harcourt College.

Kimoto, Mamoru. 2008. Kinai-seiken to shuhen chiiki no gunshu-fun (Packed tumuli clusters in the core and periphery of the Kinai polity). *Nihon kokogaku (Journal of the Japanese Archaeological Association)*, 26:23–40.

Kinoshita, Naoko. 1996. *Nankai kai-bunka no kenkyu: Kai no michi no kokogaku* (The archaeology of the shell route: A study of the shell culture of the southern maritime region of the Japanese archipelago). Tokyo: Hosei University Press.

Kishimoto, Naofumi, ed. 2005. *Zenpo-koen-fun no chikuzo-kikaku kara mita Kofun-jidai no seiji-hendo no kenkyu* (A study of the political changes of the Kofun period as seen from the reconstructed construction plans of the keyhole tumuli). Osaka, Japan: Osaka City University.

Kita, Sadakichi. 1979 (original published in 1914). *Kofunbo nendai no kenkyu: Kita Sadakichi chosaku-shu, Vol. 2* (A study of the dating of ancient tumuli: Works by Sadakichi Kita, Vol. 2), edited by Y. Kobayashi. Tokyo: Heibonsha.

Kitakyushu-shi kyoiku-bunka-jigyo-dan, ed. 1999. *Shigetome-iseki dai 2 chiten* (Location 2 of the Shi-getome site). Kitakyushu, Japan: Kitakyushu-shi kyoiku-bunka-jigyo-dan.

Kiyama Town Site Excavation Team, ed. 1978. *Sendoyama iseki* (Sendoyama site). Kiyama, Japan: Kiyama Town Site Excavation Team.

Kobayashi, Masashi. 2011. *Doki shiyokon kenkyu: Susu, koge kara mita Yayoi-doki, Hajiki niyoru chori hoho no fukugen* (A study of the use trace of pottery: The reconstruction of the cooking methods with the Yayoi pottery and Haji ware as seen from soot and burnt adherents). Kanazawa, Japan: Kobayashi Masashi.

Kobayashi, Yukio. 1937. Zenpo-koen-fun (The keyhole tumulus). *Kokogaku (Archaeology)*, 8(1):1–14.

———. 1959. Kofun ga tsukurareta jidai (The age when the Kofun tumuli were built). In *Sekai kokogaku-taikei, Vol. 3: Nihon III* (The compendium of world archae-ology, Vol. 3: Japan III), edited by Y. Kobayashi, 1–10. Tokyo: Heibonsha.

———. 1961. *Kofun-jidai no kenkyu* (Studies in the Kofun period). Tokyo: Aoki Shoten.

————. 1967. *Kokumin no rekishi, Vol. 1: Jo'oh-koku no shutsugen* (The history of the Japanese nation, Vol. 1: The emergence of the queendom). Tokyo: Bun'eido.

————. [1949] 1976. Yomotsuhegui. In *Kofun-bunka ronko* (Studies in the Kofun culture [collected papers by Y. Kobayashi]), 263–281. Tokyo: Heibonsha.

Kobayashi, Yukio, and Yoshiro Kondo. 1959. Kofun no hensen (The transformation of the Kofun tumuli). In *Sekai kokogaku-taikei, Vol. 3: Nihon III* (The compendium of world archaeology, Vol. 3: Japan III), edited by Y. Kobayashi, 11–50. Tokyo: Heibonsha.

Kobe MBE, ed. 1993. *Daikai iseki hakkutsu-chosa hokoku-sho* (The excavation report of Daikai site). Kobe, Japan: Kobe MBE.

————. 2008. *Shiramizu Hisagozuka kofun: Hakkutsu-chosa hokoku-sho (The Shiramizu Hisagozuka tumulus: An excavation report).* Kobe, Japan: Kobe MBE.

Kohama, Sei. 2008. Kofun ni okeru girei-no-ba no hensen-katei to Wa-oken (The transformation of the ritual locale of the Kofun tumulus and the Wa-kingship). In *Haniwa-gunzo no kokogaku* (Archaeologies of the Haniwa vessels), edited by Osaka Prefectural Chikatsu Asuka Museum, 171–198. Tokyo: Aoki Shoten.

Kohl, Philip, and Clare Fawcett, eds. 1996. *Nationalism, politics and the practice of archaeology.* Cambridge: Cambridge University Press.

Koide, Yoshiharu. 1966. Saishi (Ritual). In *Nihon no Kokogaku, Vol. 4: Kofun-jidai 2* (The archaeology of Japan, Vol. 4: The Kofun period 2), edited by Y. Kondo and C. Fujiswa, 276–314. Tokyo: Kawade-shobo-shinsha.

Kojima, Takato. 1977. Chosa-kenkyu no ayumi. In *Tateiwa iseki* (Archaeological research at Tate'iwa 1963 and 1965), edited by Archaeological Research Commission for Tate'iwa, 26–30. Tokyo: Kawade Shobo.

Komori, Yoichi. 2001. *Posutokoroniaru* (Postcolonial). Tokyo: Iwanami Shoten.

Komoto, Masayuki, ed. 2007. *Sakyu-keisei to kanreika gensho* (The formation of sand dunes and climatic deterioration). Kumamoto, Japan: Kumamoto University Faculty of Literature.

Komura, Hiroshi. 1983. *Yayoi-jidai seiritsu no kenkyu* (A study of the beginning of the Yayoi era). Nagoya, Japan: Komura Hiroshi.

Kondo, Hiroshi. 2006. Omi-nanbu ni okeru Yayoi-shuraku to ogata-tatemono (The Yayoi settlement and the large architectural structures in the southern Omi region). In *Yayoi no ogata-tatemono to sono tenkai* (The nature and the development of the large architectural structures of the Yayoi period), edited by K. Hirose and I. Iba, 11–27. Hikone, Japan: Sunrise Shuppan.

Kondo, Yoshiro. 1952. *Sarayama kofun-gun no kenkyu* (A study of the Sarayama clustered tumuli). Tsuyama, Japan: Tsuyama MBE.

————. 1959. Kyodotai to tan'i-shudan (The corporate grouping and the basic residential unit). *Kokogaku kenkyu (Quarterly of Archaeological Studies)*, 6(1):13–20.

————. 1983. *Zenpo-koen-fun no jidai* (The age of the keyhole tumulus). Tokyo: Iwanami Shoten.

————, ed. 1992. *Zenpo-koen-fun shusei: Kinki-hen* (The corpus of the keyhole tumuli: Volume the Kinki district). Tokyo: Yamakawa Shuppan.

————, ed. 2002. *Tatetsuki Yayoi funkyu-bo (Tatetsuki Yayoi tumulus).* Okayama, Japan: Kibito Shuppan.

Kondo, Yoshiro, and Hideji Harunari. 1967. Haniwa no kigen (The origin of the cylindrical Haniwa vessel). *Kokogaku kenkyu (Quarterly of Archaeological Studies)*, 13(3):13–35.

Koryo TBE, ed. 2005. *Suyama-kofun chosa gaiho* (Preliminary report of an excavation of the Suyama tumulus). Tokyo: Gakuseisha.

Kosugi, Yasushi. 2002. Shinzo ga kaiki suru shakai (Society in which the image of the gods returns). In *Jomon shakai-ron* (The study of the Jomon society), edited by M. Anzai, 133–180. Tokyo: Doseisha.

Kosugi, Yasushi, Yasuhiro Taniguchi, Yasutami Nishida, Kazutomo Mizunoe, and Ken'ichi Yano, eds. 2007a. *Jomon-jidai no Kokogaku, Vol. 11: Shukyo-kan'nen to shakai-chitsujo* (The archaeology of the Jomon period, Vol. 11: Religious concepts and social order). Tokyo: Doseisha.

————, eds. 2007b. *Jomon-jidai no Kokogaku, Vol. 9: Shi to tomurai* (The archaeology of the Jomon period, Vol. 9: Death and mourning). Tokyo: Doseisha.

Kumagai, Kimio. 2001. *Nihon no rekishi, Vol. 3: Daio kara Ten'no he* (History of Japan, Vol. 3: From the paramount chief to the Ten'no emperor). Tokyo: Kodansha.

Kume, Kunitake. 1891a. Shinto ha sai-ten no kozoku (Shintoism as an ancient custom of the ritual of the heaven). *Shigakukai-zasshi (Journal of the Historical Society of Japan)*, 23:1–23.

————. 1891b. Shinto ha sai-ten no kozoku (Shintoism as an ancient custom of the ritual of the heaven). *Shigakukai-zasshi (Journal of the Historical Society of Japan)*, 24:25–40.

————. 1891c. Shinto ha sai-ten no kozoku (Shintoism as an ancient custom of the ritual of the heaven). *Shigakukai-zasshi (Journal of the Historical Society of Japan)*, 25:12–24.

Kurosaki, Sunao. 1985. Kuwa to suki (Wooden picks and shovels). In *Yayoi-bunka no kenkyu Vol. 5* (The study of the Yayoi culture, Vol. 5), edited by H. Kanaseki and M. Sahara, 77–84. Tokyo: Yusankaku.

Kusano, Takanori. 2010. Jomon kara Yayoi he (From the Jomon to the Yayoi): Okayama heiya no keesu kara (A case study on the Okayama plain). *Kokogaku kenkyu (Quarterly of Archaeological Studies)*, 57(3):82–100.

Kusumi, Takeo. 1999. Hokubu-Kyushu ni okeru Shonai-shiki heiko-ki no doki-yoso (The pottery assemblage of the northern Kyushu region in the Shonai stylistic phase). *Shonai-shiki doki kenkyu (Studies in the Shonai Style Pottery)*, 19:62–143.

————. 2006. Hokubu-kyushu ni okeru tokutei-kango-kukaku to ogata-tatemono no tenkai (The segregated enclosures and large buildings of the northern Kyushu region). In *Yayoi no ogata-tatemono to sono tenkai* (The formation and transformation of the extraordinary large buildings of the Yayoi period), edited by K. Hirose and I. Iba, 145–190. Hikone, Japan: Sanraizu Shuppan.

————. 2007. 'Hakata-wan boeki' no seiritsu to kaitai (The emergence and cessation of the 'Hakata bay tradesphere'). *Kokogaku kenkyu (Quarterly of Archaeological Studies)*, 53(4):20–36.

————. 2008. Fukuoka-heiya Hie-Naka iseki-gun (The Hie-Naka site cluster of the Fukuoka plain): retto ni okeru saiko no 'toshi' (The oldest 'town' in the archipelago). In *Yayoi-jidai no kokogaku, Vol. 8: Shuraku kara yomu Yayoi-shakai* (The archaeology of the Yayoi period, Vol. 8: The Yayoi society as seen from the settlement), edited by T. Matsugi, S. Fujio, and H. Shitara), 240–263. Tokyo: Doseisha.

Kuze, Tatsuo. 2001. *Shuraku-iko kara mita Minami Kanto no Yayoi-shakai* (The organization of the Yayoi society as seen from the settlement evidence of the southern Kanto region). Tokyo: Rokuichi Shobo.

Kyoto National Museum, ed. 1982. *Tomio Maruyama kofun Nishimiyayama kofun shutsudo ibutsu* (The Kyoto National Museum collection of burial objects from Tomio Maruyama and Nishimiyayama tumuli). Kyoto, Japan: Kyoto National Museum.

Kyoto PBE, ed. 1955. *Kyoto-fu bunkazai chosa-hokoku* (Kyoto prefectural cultural properties research report), Vol. 21. Kyoto, Japan: Kyoto PBE.

Kyoto Prefectural Research Centre of Buried Cultural Properties, ed. 2001. *Kyoto-fu iseki chosa gaiho, Vol. 100: Akasaka-Imai funkyu-bo* (Kyoto prefectural board of education preliminary excavation reports, Vol. 100: Akasaka-Imai tumulus). Kyoto, Japan: Kyoto Prefectural Research Centre of Buried Cultural Properties.

Lévi-Strauss, Claude. 1963. *Structural anthropology*. New York: Doubleday Anchor Books.

————. 1966. *The savage mind*. Chicago: University of Chicago Press.

————. 1970. *The raw and the cooked*. New York: Harper & Row.

Local Organising Committee of the Proceedings of the 55th Meeting of the Buried Cultural Properties Study Group, ed. 2006. *The proceedings of the 55th meeting of the Buried Cultural Properties Study Group*. Fukuoka, Japan: Local Organising Committee.

Luhmann, Niklas. 1994. *Social systems*. Palo Alto, CA: Stanford University Press.

Mabuchi, Hisao, and Yoshimitsu Hirao. 1982. Namari-doitai-hi kara mita Dotaku no genryo (The source material of the Dotaku bronze bells as seen from lead isotope analysis). *Kokogaku-zasshi* (*Journal of Archaeology*), 68(1):42–62.

Machida, Katsunori. 2010. Chubu Nihon (The Chubu district of Japan). *Kikan kokogaku* (*Archaeology Quarterly*), 111:79–84.

Maeda, Kiyohiko, and Toyoe Suzuki. 2002. Mikawa-chiiki (The Mikawa region). In *Yayoi-doki no yoshiki to hen'nen: Tokai hen* (The styles and chronology of the Yayoi pottery: The Tokai district), edited by S. Kano and T. Ishiguro, 419–516. Tokyo: Mokujisha.

Malinowski, Bronislaw. [1922] 1984. *Argonauts of the western Pacific: An account of native enterprise and adventure in the archipelagoes of Melanesian New Guinea*. Prospect Heights, IL: Waveland Press.

Mametani, Kazuyuki. 2008. Nara-bonchi, Karako-Kagi-iseki (Karako-Kagi-iseki of the Nara Basin). In *Yayoi-jidai no kokogaku, Vol. 8: Shuraku kara yomu Yayoi-shakai* (The archaeology of the Yayoi period, Vol. 8: The Yayoi society as seen from the settlement), edited by T. Matsugi, S. Fujio, and H. Shitara, 208–223. Tokyo: Doseisha.

Marsh, Nigel D., and Henrik Svensmark. 2003. Galactic cosmic ray and El Niño-southern oscillation trends in International Satellite Cloud Climatology Project D2 low-cloud properties, *Journal of Geophysical Research* (*Atmospheres*), 108(D6):1–11.

Masaoka, Mutsuo. 1992. Bizen chiiki (The Bizen area). In *Yayoi-doki no yoshiki to hen'nen: Chugoku Shikoku-hen* (The styles and chronologies of the Yayoi pottery: The Chugoku and Shikoku regions), edited by M. Masaoka and I. Matsumoto, 3–78. Tokyo: Mokujisha.

Matsugi, Takehiko. 1996. Zenki-kofun fukuso zoku-gun no seiritsu-katei to kosei (The emergence and contents of the arrowhead assemblage of the Early Kofun period). In *Yukinoyama kofun no kenkyu* (Studies of the Yukinoyama tumulus), edited by S. Fukunaga and K. Sugii, 351–384. Toyonaka, Japan: Research Team for the Yukinoyama Excavations.

————. 1998. "Tatakai" kara "senso" he (From the battle to the warfare). In *Kodai-kokka ha koshite umareta* (How the ancient state emerged), edited by H. Tsude, 163–216. Tokyo: Kadokawa Shoten.

————. 2001. Kibi no Yayoi-shuraku to shakai (The settlement and society of the Kibi region in the Yayoi period). In *Yayoi-jidai no shuraku* (The settlement of the Yayoi period), edited by Osaka Prefectural Museum of Yayoi Culture, 118–128. Tokyo: Gakuseisha.

————. 2007. *Nihon-retto no senso to shoki-kokka kei-sei* (Warfare and the state formation of the Japanese archipelago). Tokyo: Tokyo University Press.

Matsui, Kazuaki. 2001. Tozai-Nihon Yayoi-shuraku no kosaten: Tokai no Yayoi-shuraku (The crossroad of the East and the West in Yayoi period settlement formation: settlements of the Tokai region). In *Yayoi-jidai no shuraku* (The settlement of the Yayoi period), edited by Osaka Prefectural Museum of Yayoi Culture, 196–210. Tokyo: Gakuseisha.

————. 2004. Sho-Dotaku to Dotaku saishi (Sho-Dotaku-type small Dotaku bells and their ritual). *Kikan kokogaku* (*Archaeology Quarterly*), 86:67–71.

Matsuki, Toshiaki. 2006. *Gensetsu-kukan to site no Yamato-seiken: Nihon-kodai no densho to kenryoku* (The Yamato government as a discursive space: Tradition and power in ancient Japan). Tokyo: Yamakawa shuppan.

Matsumoto, Iwao, ed. 2003. *Miyayama kofun-gun no kenkyu* (A study of the Miyayama tumuli cluster). Izumo, Japan: Shimane Prefectural Ancient Cultural Research Centre.

Migishima, Kazuo. 2009. Gunshu-fun kenkyu no genjo to kadai (The current state and issues in the study of the packed tumuli cluster). *Kikan kokogaku* (*Archaeology Quarterly*), 106:37–541.

Miller, Daniel. 1985. *Artefacts as categories: A study of Ceramic Variability in Central India*. Cambridge: Cambridge University Press.

Miller, Daniel, and Christopher Tilley. 1984. Ideology, power and prehistory: An introduction. In *Ideology, power and prehistory*, edited by D. Miller and C. Tilley, 1–15. Cambridge: Cambridge University Press.

Misaka, Kazunori. nd. Doki seisaku-gijutsu kara mita bunka-hen'yo katei: Yayoi jidai kaishi zengo no hok-ubu Kyushu wo taisyo to shite (The process of acculturation as seen from pottery-making technology: The case of the beginning of the Yayoi period in northern Kyushu). In *The proceedings of the archaeology section of the Kyushu historical society annual meeting 2009.* Fukuoka, Japan: Kyushu University Laboratory of Archaeology.

Miyamoto, Kazuo. 2009. *Noko no kigen wo saguru: Ine no kita michi* (Investigating the origin of agriculture: The route through which rice reached the Japanese archipelago). Tokyo: Yoshikawakobunkan.

Mizoguchi, Koji. 1987. Doki ni okeru chiiki shoku: Yayoi jidai chuki no Chubu-Setouchi, Kinki wo sozai to shite (The local characteristics of the pottery: The case of the central Setouchi and Kinki regions in the Middle Yayoi period). *Kobunka Danso* (*Journal of the Society of Kyushu Prehistoric and Ancient Cultural Studies*), 17:137–158.

———. 1988. Kofun shutsugen zengo no doki-so: Chikuzen-chiho wo chushin to shite (Pottery before and after the emergence of the Kofun tumulus in the Chikuzen region). *Kokogaku kenkyu* (*Quarterly of Archaeological Studies*), 35(2):90–117.

———. 1995a. Fukuoka ken Chikushino shi Nagaoka-iseki no kenkyu: Iwayuru "niretsu maiso bochi" no ichirei no Shaki-kogaku teki saikento (A study of Yayoi period jar coffin cemetery of Nagaoka: A social archaeology of a linear-aligned cemetery with two rows of burials). *Kobunka Danso* (*Journal of the Society of Kyushu Prehistoric and Ancient Cultural Studies*), 34:159–192.

———. 1995b. Fukuoka-ken Amagi-shi Kuriyama-iseki C-gun boiki no kenkyu (A study of burial cluster C at the cemetery site of Kuriyama, Amagi city, Fukuoka prefecture: social archaeology of a jar burial site of the Middle Yayoi period in northern Kyushu). *Nihon kokogaku* (*Journal of the Japanese Archaeological Association*), 2:69–94.

———. 1997a. The reproduction of archaeological discourse: The case of Japan. *Journal of European Archaeology*, 5(2):149–165.

———. 1997b. Niretsu maiso bochi no shuen: Hokubu-Kyushu ni okeru bochi kuukan kosei-genri no hen'yo no shakai-kogaku teki kenkyu (Of the end of linear cemeteries in early Middle Yayoi period in northern Kyushu: The change in the remembrance of the ancestors in mortuary practices). *Kobunka Danso* (*Journal of the Society of Kyushu Prehistoric and Ancient Cultural Studies*), 38:1–40.

———. 1998. Bozen no matsuri (Rituals conducted in front of Yayoi period jar burials in northern Kyushu). In *Nihon no shinko-iseki* (Japanese archaeology of ritual and religion), edited by H. Kaneko, 53–74. Tokyo: Yusankaku.

———. 2000. Bochi to maiso-koi no hensen: Kofun-jidai no kaishi no shakai-teki haikei no rikai no tameni (The transformation of the cemeteries and mortuary practices during the Later Yayoi and the beginning of the Kofun period: For the understanding of the mechanism of the beginning of the Kofun period). In *Kofun-jidai-zo wo minaosu* (Social structure and social change in the formative phase of the mounded-tomb period of Japan: A new perspective), edited by Y. Hojo, K. Mizoguchi, and Y. Murakami, 201–273. Tokyo: Aoki Shoten.

———. 2001. Yayoi-jidai no shakai (The social structure of the Yayoi period). In *Gendai-no kokogaku, Vol. 6: Sonraku to shakai no kokogaku* (Contemporary archaeology, Vol. 6: Archaeologies of settlement and society), edited by R. Takahashi, 135–160. Tokyo: Asakura Shoten.

———. 2002. *An archaeological history of Japan, 30,000 B.C. to A.D. 700.* Philadelphia: University of Pennsylvania Press.

———. 2004. Kokogaku ha naniwo katarunoka (Why we have come to talk about/through archaeology in the way we do). In *The Society of Archaeological Studies 50th anniversary volume: Cultural diversities and comparative archaeology*, edited by Society of Archaeological Studies, 361–370. Okayama, Japan: Society of Archaeological Studies.

———. 2005. Genealogy in the ground: observations of jar burials of the Yayoi period, northern Kyushu, Japan. *Antiquity*, 79(304):316–326.

———. 2006a. *Archaeology, society and identity in modern Japan.* Cambridge: Cambridge University Press.

———. 2006b. Nishi kara no shiten (A view from the west). In *Sinpojiumu kiroku* (Symposium records), *No. 5*, edited by Kokogaku-kenkyu-kai reikai-iinkai, 29–58. Okayama, Japan: Society of Archaeological Studies.

———. 2007. The emergence of anthropomorphic representation in the Japanese archipelago: A social systemic perspective. In *Image and imagination: A global prehistory of figurative representation*, edited by C. Renfrew and I. Morley, 185–195. Cambridge, UK: McDonald Institute for Archaeological Research.

———. 2008. Yayoi-shakai no soshiki to kategori (The organisation and categories of the Yayoi society). In *Yayoi-jidai no kokogaku, Vol. 8: Shuraku kara yomu Yayoi-shakai* (The archaeology of the Yayoi period, Vol. 8: The Yayoi society as seen from the settlement), edited by T. Matsugi, S. Fujio, and H. Shitara, 74–95. Tokyo: Doseisha.

———. 2009. Nodes and edges: A network approach to hierarchisation and state formation in Japan. *Journal of Anthropological Archaeology*, 28:14–26.

———. 2010a. Yayoi-shakai no soshiki to seiso ka: Komyunikeishon, guhatsusei, nettwark (The organisation of the Yayoi society and its hierarchisation: Communication, contingency and networks). *Kokogaku kenkyu* (*Quarterly of Archaeological Studies*), 57(2):22–37.

———. 2010b. The colonial experience of the uncolonized and the colonized: The case of East Asia, mainly as seen from Japan. In *A handbook of post-colonial archaeologies*, edited by J. Lydon and U. Rizvi, 81–91. Walnut Creek, CA: Leftcoast Press.

Mizuno, Masayoshi. 1975. Gunshu-fun no kozo to seikaku (The structure and nature of the clustered tumuli). In *Kodaishi hakkutsu, Vol. 6: Kofun to kokka no naritachi* (Excavating ancient history, Vol. 6: The Kofun tumulus and the formation of the state), edited by T. Onoyama, 143–158. Tokyo: Kodansha.

Mizuno, Yu. 1954. *Nihon kodai ocho shiron josetsu* (A treatise on the dynastic history of ancient Japan). Tokyo: Komiyama Shoten.

Mori, Takanori. 2010a. Hokubu-Kyushu: Imayama-kei sekifu no ryutsu wo chusin ni (Northern Kyushu: As seen from the circulation of stone axes produced in and around the Imayama hill). *Kikan kokogaku* (*Archaeology Quarterly*), 111:55–59.

———. 2010b. Yayoi-jidai hokubu-Kyushu ni okeru sekifu-seisan (The stone axe production and distribution of the Yayoi period in the northern Kyushu region): Imayama-kei sekifu no seisaku-giho to kikakusei no kento (a study of basalt axes produced at the Imayama hill). *Kyushu kokogaku (Journal of the Archaeological Society of Kyushu)*, 85:1–19.

Mori, Teijiro, and Takashi Okazaki. 1961. Fukuoka-ken Itazuke-iseki (Itazuke site, Fukuoka prefecture). In *Nihon noko-bunka no seisei* (The genesis of the agrarian culture of Japan), edited by Japanese Archaeological Association, 37–77. Tokyo: Tokyo-do shuppan.

Morii, Sadao. 2001. Kinki-chiho no kango-shuraku (Ditch-enclosed settlements of the Kinki region). In *Yayoi-jidai no shuraku* (The settlement of the Yayoi period), edited by Osaka Prefectural Museum of Yayoi culture, 135–155. Tokyo: Gakuseisha.

Morioka, Hideto. 1985. Tottaimon-doki chiiki-shoku ni kansuru jakkan no kento (Some considerations on the regional characteristics of Middle Yayoi period pottery from the area characterized by the application of cordoned motifs on the neck of globular jars). In *Suenaga-sensei beiju-kinen kentei ronbun-shu, Vol. 1* (Papers in celebration of Professor Masao Suenaga's 88th birthday, 'Ken' [Vol. 1]), edited by Celebration Committee, 81–114. Kashihara, Japan: Celebration Committee.

———. 1989. Seido-ki no kokusanka to sono bunpu: Dokyo (The beginning of the domestic production of bronze implements and the distribution of the products: bronze mirrors). *Kikan kokogaku (Archaeology Quarterly)*, 43:47–52.

———. 2006. Tobu Setouchi to Yamato (The eastern Seto Inland Sea region and Yamato). In *Yamatai-koku jidai no Awa, Sanuki, Harima to Yamato* (Awa, Sanuki, Harima and Yamato in the Yamataikoku era), edited by Kashiba Municipal Nijosan Museum, 1–18. Kashiba, Japan: Kashiba Municipal Nijosan Museum.

———. 2010. Yayoi-kei seidoki kara mita kofun-shutsugen katei (The emergence of the Kofun tumulus as seen from the bronze items originated in the Yayoi period and continuing into the beginning of the Kofun period). In *Nihon kokogaku kyokai 2010-nendo Hyogo taikai kenkyu-happyo shiryo-shu* (The proceedings of the meeting of the Japanese Archaeological Association in 2010), edited by Organizing Committee, 131–152. Harima, Japan: Organizing Committee.

———. 2011. Kinki-chiiki. In *Koza Nihon no kokogaku, Vol. 5: Yayoi-jidai, part 1* (Seminars in Japanese archaeology, Vol. 5: The Yayoi period, part 1), edited by M. Komoto and K. Terasawa, 267–330. Tokyo: Aoki Shoten.

Morioka, Hideto, and Ayumu Nishimura, eds. 2006. *Koshiki-hajiki no nendai-gaku* (The chronological study of the early Haji ware). Osaka, Japan: Osaka Centre for Cultural Properties.

Morishita, Hiroyuki. 1986. Nihon ni okeru yokoana-shiki sekishitsu no shutsugen to sono keifu: Kinai-gata to Kyushu-gata (The emergence and the genealogy of the gallery mortuary chamber of Japan: The Kinai and Kyushu types). *Kodai-gaku kenkyu (The Study of the Ancient Era)*, 111:1–17.

Morita, Katsuyuki. 2008. Shin Haniwa geino-ron (The Haniwa anthropomorphic and zoomorphic vessels: A new consideration). In *Haniwa-gunzo no kokogaku* (Archaeologies of the Haniwa vessels), edited by Osaka Prefectural Chikatsu Asuka Museum, 27–66. Tokyo: Aoki Shoten.

Munakata MBE. 2004. *Munakata-shi bunkazai chosa-hokoku-sho, Vol. 57: Mitsuoka Nagao I* (Munakata city cultural properties research report Vol. 57: Mitsuoka Nagao site I). Munakata, Japan: Munakata MBE.

Murakami, Yasuyuki. 1998. *Wajin to tetsu no kokogaku* (The archaeology of the Wa population and iron). Tokyo: Aoki Shoten.

———. 2000. Tekki seisan ryutsu to syakai henkaku (Iron production and exchange and social transformation). In *Kofun-jidai-zo wo minaosu* (Social structure and social change in the formative phase of the mounded-tomb period of Japan: A new perspective), edited by Y. Hojo, K. Mizoguchi, and Y. Murakami, 137–200. Tokyo: Aoki Shoten.

Murdock, George P. 1967. *Ethnographic Atlas: A Summary*. Pittsburgh, PA: University of Pittsburgh Press.

Nagai, Masafumi. 1977. Shell bracelets. In *Tateiwa iseki* (Archaeological research at Tate'iwa 1963 and 1965), edited by Archaeological Research Commission for Tate'iwa, 267–283. Tokyo: Kawade Shobo.

Nagano Prefectural Buried Cultural Properties Research Centre (Nagano-ken-maizo-bunkazai-senta), ed. 1999. *Enokida-iseki* (Enokida site). Nagano, Japan: Nagano Prefectural Cultural Properties Research Centre.

Naka, Michiyo. 1888. Nihon joko nendai-ko (Investigating the ancient historical dates of Japan). *Bun*, 1(8):107–111.

Nakahashi, Takahiro. 1990. Nagaoka-iseki shutsudo no Yayoi-jidai jinkotsu (Yayoi skeletal remains from the Nagaoka site). In *Chikushino-shi bunkazai chosa hokoku-sho, Vol. 26: Nagaoka-iseki II* (Chikushino city cultural properties research reports, Vol. 26: Nagaoka site II), edited by Chikushino MBE, 183–204. Chikushino, Japan: Chikushino MBE.

Nakajima, Ei'ichi. 1995. Sekkan, Dokan. In *Jomon-bunka no kenkyu, Vol. 9: Jomon-jin no seishin-bunka* (Studies in the Jomon culture, Vol. 9: The spiritual culture of the Jomon people), edited by S. Kato, T. Kobayashi, and T. Fujimoto, 149–169. Tokyo: Yusankaku.

Nakama, Kenji. 1987. Shogikuri-gata jukyo (The Shogikuri-type pit-dwelling). In *Higashi-Ajia no koko to rekishi* (Archaeology and history in East Asia), Vol. 2, edited by the Committee for the Celebration of the Retirement of Professor Takashi Okazaki, 593–634. Kyoto, Japan: Dohosha.

Nakamura, Daisuke. 2006. Yayoi-jidai kaishiki ni okeru fukuso-shuzoku no juyo (The adoption of burial customs from the Korean peninsula in the beginning of the Yayoi period). *Nihon kokogaku (Journal of the Japanese Archaeological Association)*, 21:21–54.

———. 2007. Hokei-shuko-bo no keifu to sono shakai (The genealogical connections of the Hokei-shuko-bo rectangular mortuary compounds and their social backgrounds). In *Bosei kara Yayoi-shakai wo kangaeru* (The Yayoi society as seen from the mortuary practices), edited by Society of the Kinki Yayoi culture, 73–116. Tokyo: Rokuichi Shobo.

Nakamura, Yutaka. 2007. Jomon Yayoi iko-ki no ogata-sekibo saishi (Ritual practices involving large stone rods in the transitional period between the Jomon and the Yayoi). In *Jomon-jidai no Kokogaku, Vol. 11: Shukyo-kan'nen to shakai-chitsujo* (The archaeology of the Jomon period, Vol. 11: Religious concepts and social order), edited by Y. Kosugi, Y. Taniguchi, Y. Nishida, K. Mizunoe and K. Yano, 283–294. Tokyo: Doseisha.

Nakashima, Ei'ichi. 1995. Seki-kan, Do-kan (Stone crown- and pottery crown-shaped implements). In *Jomon-bunka no kenkyu, Vol. 9: Jomon-jin no seishin-bunka* (The study of the Jomon culture, Vol. 11: The spiritual culture of the Jomon people), edited by S. Kato, T. Kobayashi and T. Fujimoto, 149–169. Tokyo: Yusankaku.

Nakayama, Heijiro. 1917a. Kyushu hokubu ni okeru Senshi-Genshi ryo-jidai chukan-kikan no ibutsu ni tsuite (Relics belonging to the Intermediate Period between the Prehistoric and Protohistoric Ages in the Northern part of Kyushu [original English title]). *Kokogaku zasshi (Archaeological Journal)*, 7(10):1–38.

———. 1917b. Kyushu hokubu ni okeru Senshi-Genshi ryo-jidai chukan-kikan no ibutsu ni tsuite (Relics belonging to the Intermediate Period between the Prehistoric and Protohistoric Ages in the Northern part of Kyushu [original English title]). *Kokogaku zasshi (Archaeological Journal)*, 7(11):1–34.

———. 1918a. Kyushu hokubu ni okeru Senshi-Genshi ryo-jidai chukan-kikan no ibutsu ni tsuite (Relics belonging to the Intermediate Period between the Prehistoric and Protohistoric Ages in the Northern part of Kyushu [original English title]). *Kokogaku zasshi (Archaeological Journal)*, 8(1):16–41.

———. 1918b. Kyushu hokubu ni okeru Senshi-Genshi ryo-jidai chukan-kikan no ibutsu ni tsuite (Relics belonging to the Intermediate Period between the Prehistoric and Protohistoric Ages in the Northern part of Kyushu [original English title]). *Kokogaku zasshi (Archaeological Journal)*, 8(2):15–47.

———. 1920. Doki no umu misho naru Sekki-jidai iseki (Sites of the remains of the Stone Age with no pottery as yet found [original English title]). *Kokogaku zasshi (Archaeological Journal)*, 10(11):583–595.

———. 1922. Meiji 32-nen ni okeru Sugu-Okamoto hakkutsu-butsu no shutsudo-jotai (The condition of the archaeological finds excavated at Sugu, Chikuzen province). *Kokogaku zasshi (Archaeological Journal)*, 12(10):587–610.

———. 1927. Sugu-Okamoto no ibutsu (The artefacts excavated from the Sugu-Okamoto). *Kokogaku zasshi (Archaeological Journal)*, 17(8):509–534.

Nakazawa, Michihiko. 2009. Jomon noko-ron wo megutte (On the Jomon farming thesis): Saibai-shu syokubutsu-shushi no kensho wo chushin ni (with especial focus on the seed remains of domesticated plants). In *Yayoi-jidai no kokogaku, Vol. 5: Shokuryo no kakutoku to seisan* (The archaeology of the Yayoi period, Vol. 5: The procurement and production of foodstuff), edited by T. Matsugi, S. Fujio, and H. Shitara, 163–175. Tokyo: Doseisha.

Nakazono, Satoru. 1991. Funbo ni arawareta imi: tok-uni Yayoi-jidai chuki-kohan no kamekan-bo ni miru kaisosei ni tsuite (Meanings signified by the burial: The hierarchical order of jar burials in the Middle Yayoi period). *Kobunka Danso (Journal of the Society of Kyushu Prehistoric and Ancient Cultural Studies)*, 25: 51–92.

Nara Prefectural Kashihara Archaeological Research Institute, ed. 1984. *Ichio-Hakayama kofun* (The Ichio-Hakayama tumulus). Takatori, Japan: Takatori TBE.

———. 1987. *Yayoi-jin no shiki* (The four seasons of the Yayoi people). Tokyo: Rokko Shuppan.

———. 1988. *Kawai-cho bunkazai chosa-hokoku, Vol. 2: Otomeyama-kofun: with Takayama 2-go fun: Han'i-kakunin chosa hokoku-sho.* (Kawai town cultural properties research report, Vol. 2: The Otomeyama tumulus: Takayama No. 2 tumulus: A report on the survey). Kawai, Japan: Kawai TBE.

———. 1991. *Nara-ken bunkazai chosa-hokoku-sho, Vol. 62: Teraguchi-senzuka kofun-gun* (Nara prefecture cultural properties research reports, Vol. 62: Teraguchi-senzuka tumuli cluster). Kashihara, Japan: Nara Prefectural Kashihara Archaeological Research Institute.

———. 1997. *Shimanoyama kofun chosa gaiho* (A preliminary report of the excavation of the Shimanoyama tumulus). Kashihara, Japan: Nara Prefectural Kashihara Archaeological Research Institute.

———. 1999. *Kurozuka-kofun chosa gaiho* (Preliminary report on the excavation of the Kurozuka tumulus). Tokyo: Gakuseisha.

———. 2002. *Nara-ken bunkazai chosa-hokoku-sho, Vol. 89: Hashihaka-kofun syuhen no chosa* (Nara prefecture cultural properties research reports, Vol. 89: The excavation of the vicinity of the Hashihaka tumulus). Kashihara, Japan: Nara Prefectural Kashihara Archaeological Research Institute.

———. 2007. *Gokurakuji-Hibiki iseki* (Gokurakuji-Hibiki site). Nara, Japan: Nara Prefectural Kashihara Archaeological Institute.

———. 2009. *Sakurai-Chausuyama kofun* (Sakurai-Chausuyama tumulus) [pamphlet]. Kashihara, Japan: Nara Prefectural Kashihara Archaeological Research Institute.

Nara Prefectural Kashihara Archaeological Research Institute and Shinjo TBE, ed. 1988. *Teraguchi-Oshimi kofun-gun* (Teraguchi-Oshimi tumuli cluster). Shinjo, Japan: Shinjo TBE.

National Museum of Japanese History, ed. 1997. *Rekihaku-foramu: Dotaku no e wo yomitoku* (National Museum of Japanese History forum: Deciphering the pictorial representations appearing on the Dotaku bronze bell). Tokyo: Shogakkan.

———. 2004. *Jomon-jidai, Yayoi-jidai no ko-seido nendai taikei no kochiku* (The construction of the high-resolution dating system of the Jomon and Yayoi periods). Sakura: National Museum of Japanese History.

———. 2011. Kofun shutsugen-ki no tanso 14 nendai sokutei (AMS dating of materials from the beginning of the Kofun period). *Kokuritsu rekishi-minzoku hakubut-sukan kenkyu hokoku (Bulletin of the National Museum of Japanese History)*, 163:133–176.

National Museum of Korea, ed. 1990. *Report of the research of antiquities of the National Museum of Korea, Vol. XXII: Hyuam-ri site.* Seoul, South Korea: National Museum of Korea.

Needham, Rodney. 1979. *Symbolic classification.* Santa Monica, CA: Goodyear Publishing.

Negita, Yoshio. 1998. Sekki kara Tekki he (From stone to iron tools). In *Kodai-kokka ha koshite umareta* (How the ancient state emerged), edited by H. Tsude, 163–216. Tokyo: Kadokawa Shoten.

Nihonshi-kenkyu-kai and Kyoto-minka-rekishi-bukai, eds. 1995. *"Ryobo" kara mita Nihon-shi* (Japanese history as seen from the "imperial mousolea"). Tokyo: Aoki Shoten.

Niiro, Izumi. 1983. Soshoku-tsuki tachi to Kofun-jidai ko-ki no heisei (Ornamented swords and the military organization of the Late Kofun period). *Kokogaku kenkyu* (*Quarterly of Archaeological Studies*), 30(3):50–70.

Nishiguchi, Yoichi. 1987. Ishi, Kofun, Awaji (Stone, tombs and Awaji island). *Kokogaku kenkyu* (*Quarterly of Archaeological Studies*), 34(2):118–129.

Nishijima, Sadao. 1961. Kofun to Yamato-seiken (The Kofun tumulus and the Yamato polity). *Okayama Shigaku*, 10:154–207.

———. 1983. *Chugoku kodai-kokka to higashi-ajia sekai* (Chinese ancient states and the East Asian world). Tokyo: Tokyo University Press.

———. 1985. *Nihon-rekishi no kokusai kankyo* (The international settings of Japanese history). Tokyo: Tokyo University Press.

Nishikawa, Nagao, and Hideharu Matsumiya. 1995. *Bakumatsu-Meiji-ki no kokumin-kokka keisei to bunka hen'yo* (The formation of the Japanese nation state and cultural transformation during the final Edo and Meiji periods). Tokyo: Shin'yosha.

Nishitani, Shinji, and Yoshimasa Kamaki. 1959. *Kanakurayama kofun* (The Kanakurayama tumulus). Kurashiki, Japan: Kurashiki koko-kan.

Nito, Atsushi. 2008. 6, 7-seiki no miya to shihai-kankei (Palaces and ruling systems during the 6th and 7th centuries in ancient Japan). *Kokogaku kenkyu* (*Quarterly of Archaeological Studies*), 55(2):45–60.

Noi, Hideaki. 1991. Hie-iseki dai 24, 25-ji chosa niyotte erareta shiryo no kafun-bunseki (The pollen analysis of samples from the 24th and 25th excavations of the Hie site). In *Fukuoka-shi maizo-bunkazai chosa hokokusyo, Vol. 255: Hie iseki-gun, No. 10* (Research report of the buried cultural properties of the city of Fukuoka, Vol. 255: Hie site cluster No. 10), edited by Fukuoka MBE, 229–233. Fukuoka, Japan: Fukuoka MBE.

Oba, Shigenobu. 2001. Kami-iseki hokei-shuko-bo no soso-katei no fukugen (The reconstruction of the mortuary process of a rectangular burial compound of the Kami site). *Osaka-shi bunkazai-kyokai kenkyu-kiyo* (*Bulletin of the Osaka City Cultural Properties Association*), 4:27–38.

———. 2007. Nagahara-iseki Yayoi-jidai Chuki no sosaijo no fukugen (The reconstruction of the mortuary ritual site of the Nagahara site in the Middle Yayoi period). *Osaka rekishi hakubutsukan kenkyu-kiyo* (*Bulletin of the Osaka Historical Museum*), 6:63–78.

Ochiai TBE. 1978. *Ochiai-cho maizo-bunkazai hakkutsu-chosa hokoku-sho, Vol. 1: Nakayama-iseki* (Ochiai town buried cultural properties excavation report, Vol. 1: The Nakayama site). Ochiai, Japan: Ochiai TBE.

Oda, Fujio, ed. 1988. *Okinoshima to kodai-saishi* (The Okinoshima islet and the ancient ritual practice). Tokyo: Yoshikawakobunkan.

Oda, Fujio, and Ryuji Ueda, eds. 2004. *Fukuoka daigaku kokogaku-kenkyu-shitsu kenkyu-chosa hokoku, Vol. 3:*

Nagasaki-ken Keikaen-iseki no kenkyu (Fukuoka University Laboratory of Archaeology research report, Vol. 3: A study of the Keikaen site of Nagasaki prefecture). Fukuoka, Japan: Fukuoka University Laboratory of Archaeology.

Odawara MBE, ed. 2000. *Heisei 12-nendo Odawara-shi iseki chosa happyo-kai, Nakazato-iseki koen-kai* (Public hearing of the rescue excavations conducted during the fiscal year Heisei 12th, with especial focus on the Nakazato site). Odawara, Japan: Odawara MBE.

Oguma, Eiji. 2002. *"Minshu" to "aikoku"* (The "democratic" and the "patriotic"). Tokyo: Shin'yosha.

Ohnuki-Tierney, Emiko. 1993. *Rice as self: Japanese identities through time*. Princeton, NJ: Princeton University Press.

Okabayashi, Kosaku. 2002. Mokkaku, tateana-shiki sekishitsu (Composite wooden mortuary chambers and stone cists). In *Nihon kokogaku-kyokai 2002-nendo Kashihara taikai kenkyu-happyo shiryo-shu* (The proceedings of 2002 annual meeting of the Japanese Archaeological Association in Kashihara), edited by Committee for 2002 Annual Meeting of the Japanese Archaeological Association in Kashihara, 253–262. Kashihara, Japan: Committee for 2002 Annual Meeting of the Japanese Archaeological Association in Kashihara.

Okada, Hiroyuki. 2004. Kofun-jidai ko-ki no chiiki-hensei: Miyako-heiya, Munakata-chiiki ni okeru Kofun no bunpu-yoso kara (A regional organization in the later Kofu period: The distribution of Kofun in the Miyako plain and Munakata area). *Shien* (*Journal of History*), 141:117–136.

Okamura, Hidenori. 1984. Zen-Kan-kyo no hen'nen to yoshiki (The typo-chronology and stylistic changes of the early Han Chinese bronze mirrors). *Shirin*, 67(5):1–42.

———. 1993. Go-Kan-kyo no hen'nen (The chronology of later Han mirrors). *Kokuritsu rekishi-minzoku hakubutsukan kenkyu hokoku* (*Bulletin of the National Museum of Japanese History*), 55:39–83.

———. 1999. *Sankakubuchi-shinjukyo no jidai* (The age of triangular-rimed bronze mirrors with deity-beast motifs). Tokyo: Yoshikawakobunkan.

Okamura, Wataru. 2008. Seisei heiya: Toro-iseki (Toro site in the Seisei plain). In *Yayoi-jidai no kokogaku, Vol. 8: Shuraku kara yomu Yayoi-shakai* (The archaeology of the Yayoi period, Vol. 8: The Yayoi society as seen from the settlement), edited by T. Matsugi, S. Fujio and H. Shitara, 163–175. Tokyo: Doseisha.

Okayama MBE. 2005. *Minamikata (Saiseikai)-iseki: Mokki-hen* (Minamikata [Saiseikai] site: Wooden implements). Okayama, Japan: Okayama MBE.

Okayama PBE, ed. 1974. *Okayama-ken maizo-bunkazai hakkutsu-chosa-hokoku, Vol. 2: San'yo-shinkansen kensetsu ni tomonau chosa II* (Okayama PBE buried cultural properties research report, Vol. 2: Excavations prior to the construction of the San'yo highspeed railway system, II). Okayama, Japan: Okayama PBE.

———. 1980. *Okayama-ken maizo-bunkazai hakkutsu-chosa-hokoku, Vol. 39: Hyakkengawa Haraojima iseki* (Okayama PBE buried cultural properties research report, Vol. 39: Hyakkengawa Haraojima site). Okayama, Japan: Okayama PBE.

————. 1985. *Okayama-ken maizo-bunkazai hakkutsu-chosa-hokoku, Vol. 59: Hyakkengawa Sawada iseki 2, Hyakkengawa Nagatani iseki 2.* (Okayama PBE buried cultural properties research report, Vol. 59: hyakkengawa Sawada site 2, Hyakkengawa Nagatani site 2). Okayama, Japan: Okayama PBE.

————. 1993. *Okayama-ken maizo-bunkazai hakkutsu-chosa-hokoku, Vol. 84: Hyakkengawa Sawada iseki 3* (Okayama PBE buried cultural properties research report, Vol. 84: Hyakkengawa Sawada site 3). Okayama, Japan: Okayama PBE.

Okazaki, Takashi. 1977. Kagami to sono nendai (The bronze mirrors and their date). In *Tateiwa-iseki* (Tateiwa site), edited by Committee for the Investigation of the Tateiwa Site, 335–378. Tokyo: Kawade-shobo-shinsha.

Okubo, Tetsuya. 2004. Sanuki no Kofun-jidai seiji-chitsujo heno shiron (A tentative approach to the political order of the ancient province of Sanuki during the Kofun period). In *Kofun-jidai no seiji-kozo: Zenpo-koen-fun karano apuroochi* (The political structure of the Kofun period: As seen from the keyhole tumulus), edited by K. Hirose, M. Kishimoto, T. Ugaki, T. Okubo, M. Nakai and A. Fujisawa, 80–105. Tokyo: Aoki Shoten.

————. 2006. Sanuki no shuraku to shoki Kofun (Settlements and early Kofun tumuli of Sanuki). In *Yamatai-koku jidai no Awa, Sanuki, Harima to Yamato* (Awa, Sanuki, Harima and Yamato in the Yamataikoku era), edited by Kashiba Municipal Nijosan Museum, 97–120. Kashiba: Kashiba Municipal Nijosan Museum.

Omiya TBE, ed. 2001. *Kyoto-fu Omiya-machi bunkazai-chosa-hokoku, Vol. 20: Sasaka kofun (funbo) gun G-shigun* (Research reports on the cultural properties of Omiya Township, Kyoto Prefecture. Vol 20: Location G of the Sasaka tumuli cluster). Omiya, Japan: Omiya TBE.

Omura-shi bunkazai hogo-kyokai, ed. 1987. *Tominoharu* (Tominoharu site). Omura, Japan: Omura Municipal Association for the Protection of Cultural Properties.

Onoue, Motoki. 1993. Kofun-jidai tetsuzoku no chiikisei (Regional variations of the long-necked iron arrowheads of the Kofun period). *Kokogaku kenkyu* (Quarterly of Archaeological Studies), 40(1):61–85.

Onoyama, Takashi. 1970. 5 (go)-seiki ni okeru kofun no kisei (The regulation imposed on the Kofun tumuli during the 5th century). *Kokogaku kenkyu* (Quarterly of Archaeological Studies), 16(3):73–83.

————. 1975a. Kiba-minzoku seifuku-ocho setsu wo megutte (On the horse-rider-conquest dynasty theory). In *Kodaishi hakkutsu, Vol. 6: Kofun to kokka no naritachi* (Excavating ancient history, Vol. 6: The Kofun tumulus and the formation of the state), edited by T. Onoyama, 124–125. Tokyo: Kodansha.

————. 1975b. Obikanagu kara kanmuri he (From belt ornaments to metal crowns). In *Kodaishi hakkutsu, Vol. 6: Kofun to kokka no naritachi* (Excavating ancient history, Vol. 6: The Kofun tumulus and the formation of the state), edited by T. Onoyama, 112–123. Tokyo: Kodansha.

Organisation committee of the general meeting of the Japanese Archaeological Association 2002, ed. 2002. *Nihon Kokogaku-kyokai 2002-nendo Kashiwara-taikai kenkyu-happyo-kai shiryo-shu* (The proceedings of the general meeting of the Japanese Archaeological Association 2002). Kashiwara, Japan: Organisation Committee of the General Meeting of the Japanese Archaeological Association 2002.

Osaka prefectural Chikatsu Asuka museum, ed. 2008. *Haniwa-gunzo no kokogaku* (Archaeologies of the Haniwa vessels). Tokyo: Aoki Shoten.

Osaka university section of Japanese history, ed. 1964. *Kawachi ni okeru Kofun no chosa* (Excavations of some Kofun tumuli in the Kawachi region). Toyonaka, Japan: Osaka University Section of Japanese History.

Osaka-fu kyoiku iinkai (Osaka PBE). 1993. *Kawachi-heiya iseki-gun no dotai, Vol. 4* (The pattern and transformation of the sites of the Kawachi plain, Vol. 4). Higashiosaka, Japan: Osaka bunkazai senta (Osaka Buried Cultural Properties Research Centre).

Otani, Koji. 1995. Izumo Iwami (Izumo and Iwami provinces). In *Zenkoku kofun hen'nen-shusei* (The compendium of the regional chronology of the Kofun tumuli of Japan), edited by H. Ishino, 44–47. Tokyo: Yusankaku.

Ozawa, Tsuyoshi. 2003. *Nihon kodai tokyu no kozo* (The structure of the palaces and capitals of ancient Japan). Tokyo: Aoki Shoten.

Ozawa, Yoshinori. 2000. Yayoi-shuraku no dotai to kakki: Fukuoka-ken Kasuga kyuryo-iki wo taisho to shite (The development and changes of the Yayoi settlements: With especial focus on the Kasuga hill area of Fukuoka prefecture). *Kobunka Danso* (Journal of the Society of Kyushu Prehistoric and Ancient Cultural Studies), 44:1–37.

————. 2006. Genkainada engan chiiki no Yayoi-jidai zenhan-ki shuraku no yoso (The settlements of the first half of the Yayoi period in the circum-Genkainada sea area). In *Yayoi-shuraku no seiritsu to tenkai: dai 55-kai maizo-bunkazai kenkyu-shukai* (The emergence and development of the Yayoi settlement: The proceedings of the 55th meeting of the buried cultural properties study group), edited by Local Organizing Committee, 1–26. Fukuoka, Japan: Local Organising Committee.

Park, Chun-soo. 2007. *Kaya to Wa: Kan-hanto to Nihon-retto no kokogaku* (Gaya and Wa: The archaeology of the Korean peninsula and Japanese archipelago). Tokyo: Kodansha.

Polanyi, Karl. 1966. *Dahomey and the slave trade: An analysis of an archaic economy.* Seattle: University of Washington Press.

Renfrew, Colin, and Paul Barn. 2008. *Archaeology: Theories, methods and practice.* 5th ed. London: Thames and Hudson.

Rowlands, Michael J., and Mogens T. Larsen, eds. 1987. *Centre and periphery in the ancient world.* Cambridge: Cambridge University Press.

Saga PBE, ed. 1981. *Saga-ken bunkazai hokoku-sho, Vol. 61: Kawayoriyoshihara-iseki* (Saga prefectural cultural properties research report, Vol. 61: Kawayoriyoshihara site). Saga, Japan: Saga PBE.

————. 1994. *Yoshinogari.* Saga, Japan: Saga PBE.

————. 1997. *Yoshinogari-iseki: heisei 2-nendo~7-nendo no hakkutsu-chosa no gaiyo* (Yoshinogari site: The preliminary report of the excavations from 1989 to 1995). Saga, Japan: Saga PBE.

————. 2002. *Saga-ken bunkazai hokoku-sho, Vol. 152: Yoshinogari-dotaku* (Saga prefectural cultural properties research reports, Vol. 152: The Yoshinogari bronze bell). Saga, Japan: Saga PBE.

————. 2003. *Saga-ken bunkazai hokoku-sho, Vol. 155: Yubi-iseki-gun, No. 3: Yubihon'mura-iseki* (Saga prefectural cultural properties reseach reports, Vol. 155: Yubi site cluster, No. 3: Yubihon'mura site). Saga, Japan: Saga PBE.

Sahara, Makoto. 1960. Dotaku no chuzo (The production of the Dotaku bronze bell). In *Sekai kokogaku taikei, Vol. 2: Nihon* (The compendium of world archaeology, Vol. 2: Japan), edited by S. Sugihara, 92–104. Tokyo: Heibonsha.

————. 1982. 34 (sanju-yon) no kyanbasu: rensaku 4 (yon) Dotaku no kaiga no bunpo (34 canvases: successively produced 4 bronze bells and the pictorial representations on them). In *Kokogaku-ronko* (Papers in Archaeology): *Papers in the celebration of the retirement of Dr Yukio Kobayashi*, edited by Editorial Committee for the Collected Papers in the Celebration of the Retirement of Dr. Yukio Kobayashi, 245–280. Tokyo: Heibonsha.

————. 1987. *Taikei Nihon no rekishi, Vol.1: Nihon-jin no tanjo* (A compendium of Japanese history, Vol. 1: The birth of the "Japanese"). Tokyo: Shogakkan.

————. 2002. *Dotaku no kokogaku* (The archaeology of the Dotaku bronze bell). Tokyo: Tokyo University Press.

————, ed. 1983. *Yayoi doki* (The Yayoi pottery), Vol. 1. Tokyo: Nyu-Saiensu-sha.

Sahlins, Marshall. [1974] 2004. *Stone Age economics.* London: Tavistock.

————. 1985. *Islands of history.* Chicago: University of Chicago Press.

Saino, Hirohiko. 2005. Suiden-ato no kozo to rikai (A study of wet paddy-fields in the Yayoi period). *Kodai bunka* (*Cultura Antiqua*), 57(5):43–61.

————. 2011. Tohoku-chiiki (The Tohoku area). In *Koza Nihon no kokogaku, Vol. 5: Yayoi-jidai* (Seminars in Japanese archaeology, Vol. 5: The Yayoi period, part 1), edited by M. Komoto and K. Terasawa, 430–484. Tokyo: Aoki Shoten.

Saitama PBE, ed. 1980. *Sakitama Inariyama kofun* (Sakitama Inariyama tumulus). Urawa, Japan: Saitama PBE.

Sakaguchi, Yutaka. 1982. Climatic variability during the Holocene epoch in Japan and its causes. *Bulletin of the Department of Geography, University of Tokyo,* 14:1–27.

————. 1983. Warm and cold stages in the past 7600 years in Japan and their global correlation: Especially on climatic impacts to the global sea level changes and the ancient Japanese history. *Bulletin of the Department of Geography, University of Tokyo,* 15:1–31.

Sakai, Ryuichi. 1974. Ishi-bocho no seisan to shohi wo meguru futatsu no moderu (Two models for the production and consumption of stone reaping knives of the Yayoi period). *Kokogaku kenkyu* (*Quarterly of Archaeological Studies*), 21(2):23–36.

————. 1984. Yayoi-jidai chuki Kinai-shakai no kozo to setrumento-sisutemu (The structure and the settlement system of the society of the Kinai region in the Middle Yayoi period). *Bunkazai-gakuho* (*Studies in Cultural Properties*), 3:37–51.

Sakamoto, Yoshihiro. 1994. Umegame kara kamekan he: Kyushu-Jomon Umegame-ko (From Umegame to jar coffins: A study of Umegame [buried vessels containing human remains] in the Kyushu Jomon period). *Kobunka Danso* (*Journal of the Society of Kyushu Prehistoric and Ancient Cultural Studies*), 32:1–28.

Sameshima, Kazuhiro. 1996. Yayoi-cho no tsubo to kango-shuraku (The pottery from the Yayoi-cho site: its relation to the moated settlement). *Tokyo-daigaku kokogaku-kenkyu-shitsu kiyo* (*Bulletin of the Department of Archaeology, the University of Tokyo*), 14: 131–154.

Sasaki, Ken'ichi, ed. 2007. *Kanto no koki kofun-gun* (The tumuli clusters of the Kanto district in the Late Kofun period). Tokyo: Rokuichi Shobo.

Sato, Yukio. 1994. Ni-taki suru tsubo (Storage jars used for cooking). *Kokogaku kenkyu* (*Quarterly of Archaeological Studies*), 40(4):75–100.

Scott, John. 2000. *Social network analysis: A handbook.* London: Sage.

Seki, Akira. 1956. *Kika-jin* (The naturalised Japanese in ancient Japan). Tokyo: Shibundo.

Service, Elman. 1962. *Primitive social organization: An evolutionary perspective.* New York: Random House.

Shigematsu, Tatsuji. 2006. San'in-chiho ni okeru funkyu-bo shutsudo doki no kento (A study of the pottery excavated from mounded-burials in the San'in region). *Kodai-bunka kenkyu* (*Studies of the Ancient Culture*), 14: 1–24.

Shima TBE, ed. 1987. *Shima-machi bunkazai chosa-hokoku-sho, Vol.7: Shinmachi-iseki* (Shima town cultural properties research report, Vol. 7: Shinmachi site). Shima, Japan: Shima TBE.

Shimane PBE. 1996. *Izumo Kanba-Kojindani-iseki* (Kanba-Kojindani site of the ancient Izumo province). Matsue, Japan: Shimane PBE.

Shimane Prefectural Ancient Culture Research Centre, ed. 2007. *Yosumi-tossyutsu-gata funkyu-bo to Yayoi-bosei no kenkyu* (The study of the Yosumi-tossyutsu-gata tumulus and the mortuary practices of the Yayoi period). Matsue, Japan: Shimane Prefectural Ancient Culture Research Centre.

Shimogaki, Hitoshi. 2003. Kofun-jidai zenki Wa-sei kyo no ryutsu (The circulation of Wa-made bronze mirrors during the Early Kofun period). *Kobunka Danso* (*Journal of the Society of Kyushu Prehistoric and Ancient Cultural Studies*), 50:7–35.

Shimojo, Nobuyuki. 1975. Hokubu-Kyushu ni okeru Yayoi-jidai no sekki-seisan (The lithic production of the northern Kyushu region in the Yayoi period). *Kokogaku kenkyu* (*Quarterly of Archaeological Studies*), 22(1):7–21.

————. 1982. Dohoko-gata saiki no seisan to hakyu (The production and the diffusion of the bronze spearhead-shaped ritual implement). In *Mori Teijiro hakase koki kinen kobunka ronshu* (Papers on ancient history in celebration of Dr. Teijiro Mori's 70th birthday), edited by Editorial Committee, 595–623. Fukuoka, Japan: Committee for the Publication of the Volume.

————. 1984. Yayoi, Kofun-jidai no Kyushu-gata sekisui ni tsuite (The Kyushu-type stone net-sinkers). *Kyushu Bunka-shi kenkyusho kiyo* (*Bulletin of the Kyushu Institute of Culture History*), 29:71–103.

————. 1985. Bassai-sekifu (Tree-felling stone axes). In *Yayoi-bunka no kenkyu* (The study of the Yayoi culture), Vol. 5, edited by H. Kanaseki and M. Sahara, 43–47. Tokyo: Yusankaku.

————. 1986. Nihon inasaku juyoki no tairiku-kei masei-sekki no tenkai (The development of the Asian-mainland-originated lithics in the beginning of the Yayoi period). *Kyushu bunka-shi kenkyusho kiyo* (*Bulletin of the Institute of Kyushu Cultural History*), 31:103–140.

————. 1989. Mura to kobo (The villages and the workshops of the Yayoi period). In *Kodaishi fukugen, Vol. 4: Yayoi-noson no tanjo* (Reconstructing ancient history, Vol. 4: The genesis of the Yayoi agrarian village) edited by N. Shimojo, 113–124. Tokyo: Kodansha.

————. 1991. Hokubu-Kyushu Yayoi-chuki no kokka kan kozo to Tateiwa-iseki (The inter-polity relationship of northern Kyushu Middle Yayoi period and the Tateiwa site). In *Kojima Takato sensei kiju-kinen kobunka-ronso* (Papers in the celebration of the 77th birthday of Professor Takato Kojima), edited by Committee for the Celebration of the 77th Birthday of Professor Takato Kojima, 77–106. Iizuka, Japan: Committee for the Celebration of the 77th Birthday of Professor Takato Kojima.

————. 2002. Ine no denpa to nogyo-gijutsu no hattatsu (The diffusion of rice paddy-field agricultural technology and its development). In *Kodai wo kangaeru: Ine, kinzoku, senso* (Thinking the past: Rice, metal and warfare), edited by M. Sahara, 19–46. Tokyo: Yoshikawakobunkan.

Shinoda, Ken'ichi, and Takehiro Kunisada. 1994. Analysis of ancient Japanese society through mitochondrial DNA sequencing. *International Journal of Osteoarchaeology*, 4(4):291–297.

Shintaku, Nobuhisa. 1994. Etsuji-iseki no chosa (The excavation of the Etsuji site). In *Kyushu Kokogakkai-Reinan Kokogakkai dai-ikkai godo kokogakukai* (The 1st joint meeting of the Kyushu and Reinan archaeological societies), edited by Organising Committee, 118–135. Fukuoka, Japan: Organising Committee of the Joint Meeting of the Kyushu and Reinan Archaeological Societies.

Shiraishi, Taichiro. 1966. Kinai no ko-ki ogata gunshu-fun ni kansuru ichi shiron (A study of the large-scale clustered tumuli of the Kinai district in the Late Kofun period). *Kodai-gaku kenkyu* (*The Study of the Ancient Era*), 42–43:33–64.

————. 1985. Kokogaku sirizu, Vol. 19: Kofun no chishiki: funkyu to naibu-kozo (Archaeology series: What we know about the Kofun tumulus: The mound and the burial facility). Tokyo: Tokyo Bijutsu.

————. 1997. Seien (salt production). In *Yayoi bunka no kenkyu* (*Studies in the Yayoi culture*), Vol. 2, edited by H. Kanaseki and M. Sahara, 162–170. Tokyo: Yusankaku.

————. 1999. Kofun to Yamato seiken (The Kofun tumulus and the Yamato polity). Tokyo: Bungeishunjusha.

————. 2000. Kofun to kofun-gun no kenkyu (A study of the Kofun tumulus and tumuli clusters). Tokyo: Hanawa shobo.

Shitara, Hiromi. 2006. Yayoi-jidai kaitei nendai to kiko-hendo: Sakaguchi 1982 ronbun no sai-hyoka (Altered Yayoi absolute dates and climatic change: A reevaluation

of Sakaguchi 1982 article). *Komazawa shigaku*, 67:129–154.

————. 2007. Yayoi-jidai no danjo-zo: Nihon senshi-jidai ni okeru danjo no shakai-kankei to sono henka (The figurative representations of the sexes in the Yayoi period: The relationship between the sexes and its transformation in Japanese prehistory). *Kokogaku-zasshi* (*Journal of Archaeology*), 91(2):32–80.

————. 2008. *Yayoi saiso-bo to shakai* (The social meaning of the reburial system in the Yayoi period). Tokyo: Hanawa Shobo.

————. 2009. Dokuritsu munamochi-bashira tatemono to sorei-saishi (Yayoi buildings with freestanding *munamochibashira* pillars and ancestral rituals). *Kokuritsu rekishi-minzoku hakubutsukan kenkyu hokoku* (*Bulletin of the National Museum of Japanese History*), 149:5–89.

————. 2011. *Yayoi-chuki toiu jidai* (The age called the Middle Yayoi). In *Yayoi-jidai no kokogaku, Vol. 3: Tayo-ka suru Yayoi-bunka* (The archaeology of the Yayoi period, Vol. 3: The Yayoi culture diverging), edited by T. Matsugi, S. Fujio, and H. Shitara, 3–24. Tokyo: Doseisha.

Shitara, Hiromi, and Seiji Kobayashi. 2007. Iatazuke I-siki doki seiritsu ni okeru Kamegaoka-kei doki no kan'yo (Influences by the Kamegaoka style pottery over the emergence of the Itazuke I style pottery). In *Shin Yayoi-jidai no hajimari, Vol. 2: Jomon-jidai kara Yayoi-jidai he* (New approaches to the beginning of the Yayoi period, Vol. 2: From the Jomon to the Yayoi), edited by T. Nishimoto, 66–107. Tokyo: Yusankaku.

Shinpojiumu Minami-Kanto no Yayoi-doki jikko-iinkai, ed. 2005. *Minami-Kanto no Yayoi-doki* (The Yayoi pottery of the southern Kanto region). Tokyo: Rokuichi Shobo.

Smith, Anthony D. 2001. *Nationalism*. Cambridge, UK: Polity.

Social Studies/History Textbooks Discussion Committee. 2008. Shakai-ka rekishi-kyokasho wo kangaeru (Description of Palaeolithic and Jomon disappeared from the textbooks of elementary school). *Nihon kokogaku* (*Journal of the Japanese Archaeological Association*) 26:181–203.

Soja City Culture Promotion Agency, ed. 1996. *Iyobeyama funbo-gun* (Iyobeyama burial cluster). Soja, Japan: Soja City Culture Promotion Agency.

Sorensen, Marie-Louise S. 1996. The fall of a nation, the birth of a subject: The national use of archaeology in nineteenth-century Denmark. In *Nationalism and archaeology in Europe*, edited by M. Díaz-Andreu and T. Champion, 24–47. London: UCL press.

Suenaga, Masao, ed. [1943] 1976. *Kyoto teikoku-daigaku Bungaku-bu kokogaku kenkyu-hokoku, Vol. 16: Yamato Karako Yayoi-shiki iseki no kenkyu* (Kyoto Imperial University faculty of literature archaeology laboratory research reports, Vol. 16: A study of the Yayoi period site of Karako, Ancient Yamato province). Kyoto, Japan: Rinsen Shoten.

Suenaga, Masao. 1975. *Kofun no koku taikan* (The corpus of aerial photographs of Kofun tumuli). Tokyo: Gakuseisha.

Sugawara, Toshiyuki, ed. 1987. *Akita-shi Akita Shin-toshi kaihatsu-seibi jigyo kankei maizobunkazai hakkutsu-chosa hokoku-sho: Jizoden B iseki, Dai A iseki, Yunosawa A iseki, Yunosawa F iseki* (A report on the rescue excavations of the buried cultural properties prior to the development of the Akita new town: Jizoden B, Dai A, Yunosawa A and F sites). Akita, Japan: Akita MBE.

Sugawara, Yasuo. 2006. Awa no shuraku to shoki Kofun (Settlements and early Kofun tumuli of Awa). In *Yamatai-koku jidai no Awa, Sanuki, Harima to Yamato* (Awa, Sanuki, Harima and Yamato in the Yamataikoku era), edited by Kashiba Municipal Nijosan Museum, 121–173. Kashiba, Japan: Kashiba Municipal Nijosan Museum.

Sugihara, Sosuke. 1956. *Meiji daigaku Bungaku-bu kenkyu-hokoku, Vol.1: Gunma-ken Iwajuku hakken no sekki-bunka* (Research report of the Faculty of Letters, Meiji University, Vol. 1: The lithic assemblage discovered at Iwajuku, Gunma prefecture). Tokyo: Meiji University Faculty of Letters Research Institute.

Sugii, Ken. 2010. Shucho-kyokan to shuraku-seikatsu (The elite residential compounds, settlements of the commoners and their lives). In *Shiseki de yomu Nihon-rekishi, Vol. 2: Kofun no jidai* (Reading the Japanese history from historical sites, Vol. 2: The age of the Kofun tumuli), edited by N. Kishimoto, 181–211. Tokyo: Yoshikawakobunkan.

Sumi, Hiroyuki. 2006. Mikumo-Iwara Yayoi-shuraku no seiritsu to hensen (The emergence and the trasnformation of the Mikumo-Ihara Yayoi settlement). *Itokoku rekishi hakubutsukan kiyo* (Bulletin of the Itokoku Historical Museum), 1:15–24.

Tajiri, Yoshinori. 2001. Yayoi-jidai seido-ki seisan ni okeru seisan-taisei ron (The production system of bronze artefacts in the Yayoi period as seen from casting moulds from the northern Kyushu region). *Kyushu kokogaku* (Journal of the Archaeological Society of Kyushu), 76:11–33.

Takabatake, Tomonori. 1992. Bicchu chiiki (The Bicchu area). In *Yayoi-doki no yoshiki to hen'nen: Chugoku Shikoku-hen* (The styles and chronologies of the Yayoi pottery: The Chugoku and Shikoku regions), edited by M. Masaoka and I. Matsumoto, 79–153. Tokyo: Mokujisha.

Takagi, Hiroshi. 2010. *Ryobo to bunkazai no kindai* (The modernity of the imperial mausolea and related cultural properties). Tokyo: Yamakawa Shuppan.

Takahashi, Katsuhisa. 1994. Haniwa-seisan no tenkai (The development of the production system of the Haniwa vessels). *Kokogaku kenkyu* (Quarterly of Archaeological Studies), 41(2):27–48.

———. 1996. *Rekishi hakkutsu, Vol. 9: Haniwa no seiki* (Excavating history, Vol. 9: The centuries of the Haniwa vessles). Tokyo: Kodansha.

———. 2008. Oken to Haniwa seisan (The kingship and the Haniwa production). In *Haniwa-gunzo no kokogaku* (Archaeologies of the Haniwa vessels), edited by Osaka Prefectural Chikatsu Asuka Museum, 101–135. Tokyo: Aoki Shoten.

Takahashi, Koji. 2005. Hokuriku no Yayoi funbo kara Kofun he (From Yayoi burials to Kofun tumuli in the Hokuriku region). *Kikan kokogaku* (Archaeology Quarterly), 92:70–73.

Takahashi, Mamoru, Yoshimasa Kamaki, and Yoshiro Kondo, eds. 1987. Miyayama funbo-gun (the Miyayama burial cluster). In *Soja-shishi: Koko-shiryo-hen* (The history of Soja city: Archaeological data), edited by Editorial Committee of the Series, 61–70. Soja: Soja City.

Takahashi, Nobuo. 1991. Ezuriko kofun-gun (The Ezuriko tumuli cluster). In *Zusetsu Nihon no shiseki, Vol. 2, Gen-shi, part 2* (The registered historical remains in Japan, Vol. 2: Pre- and proto-history, part 2), edited by the Agency of Cultural Affairs, 28. Tokyo: Dohosha.

Takakura, Hiroaki. 1995. *Kin'in-kokka-gun no jidai* (The age of the polities issued golden seals by the Chinese empire). Tokyo: Aoki Shoten.

Takase, Katsunori. 2004. *Honshu-to hokubu no Yayoi-shakai-shi* (Sociography of the Yayoi period in the northeastern Honshu island). Tokyo: Rokuichi Shobo.

Takashima, Chuhei. 1980. Saga-ken Kawayoriyoshihara-iseki shutsudo no taku-gata doseihin no jinbutsu-kaiga (A human figuration on a Dotaku bronze bell-shaped clay implement from the Kawayoriyoshihara site, Saga Prefecture). *Kokogaku zasshi* (Journal of Archaeology), 66(1):45–48.

Takatsuki MBE, ed. 1977. *Takatsuki-shi bunkazai chosa-hokoku-sho, Vol. 10: Ama-iseki hakkutsu-chosa hokoku-sho, Dai 9 chiku no chosa* (Takatsuki city cultural properties research reports, Vol. 10: An excavation report of the Ama site, Loc. 9). Takatsuki, Japan: Takatsuki MBE.

Takatsuki Municipal Buried Cultural Properties Research Centre, ed. 1996. Kosobe-Shibatani iseki (Kosobe-Shibatani site). Takatsuki, Japan: Takatsuki Municipal Buried Cultural Properties Research Centre.

Takehiro, Fumiaki. 2010. Sanukaito no ryutsu (The circulation of Sanukitoid procured in the Kanayama mountain, Kagawa prefecture). *Kikan kokogaku* (Archaeology Quarterly), 111:40–43.

Takesue, Jun'ichi. 1982. Maino-dohoko ron (A study of deposited bronze spearheads of the Yayoi period). *Kobunka Danso* (Journal of the Society of Kyushu Prehistoric and Ancient Cultural Studies), 9:119–156.

———. 1985. Noko-shuraku no tenkai (The development of the agrarian settlement). In *Kitakyushu-shi-shi: So-ron, Senshi, Genshi* (The history of Kitakyushu city: The general description, the prehistory and the proto-history), edited by Editorial Committee, 374–428. Kitakyushu, Japan: Kitakyushu City.

———. 1990a. Haka no seido-ki, matsuri no seido-ki (The bronze implements deposited in the burial and in the ritual context). *Kobunka Danso* (Journal of the Society of Kyushu Prehistoric and Ancient Cultural Studies), 22:47–55.

———. 1990b. Hokubu-Kyushu no kango-shuraku (Ditch-enclosed villages of the Kyushu region in the Yayoi period). In *Otomasu Shigetaka sensei koki-kinen Kyushu jodai-bunka ronshu* (Papers in Kyushu ancient history in celebration of Professor Shigetaka Otomasu's 70th birthday), edited by Editorial Committee, 213–238. Kumamoto, Japan: Committee for the Celebration of Professor Shigetaka Otomasu's 70th Birthday.

———. 1999. Kuni no keisei (The formation of "Kuni" polities). In *Chikushino shi-shi* (The history of Chikushino city), *Vol. 1*, edited by Chikushino-shi-shi-hensan-iin-kai, 413–451. Chikushino, Japan: Chikushino City.

———. 2002. *Yayoi no mura* (The settlement of the Yayoi period). Tokyo: Yamakawa Shuppan.

Takesue, Jun'ichi. 2003. Kyushu-chiho no doki (The pottery of the Kyushu region). In *Koko-shiryo taikan: Yayoi Kofun jidai doki I, Vol. 1* (The compendium of archaeological materials: The pottery of the Yayoi and Kofun periods, Vol. 1), edited by J. Takesue and H. Ishikawa, 45–112. Tokyo: Shogakkan.

———. 2004. Yayoi-jidai no reki-nendai (The calendar years of the Yayoi period). In *Fukuoka-daigaku Kokogaku-ronshu: Oda Fujio sensei taishoku kinen* (Archaeological studies from Fukuoka University: The commemorative volume of the retirement of Professor Fujio Oda), edited by Committee for the Commemoration of the Retirement of Professor Fujio Oda, 129–156. Fukuoka, Japan: Committee for the Commemoration of the Retirement of Professor Fujio Oda.

Tamura, Satoru. 1999. Shumatsu-ki gunshu-fun no tenkai (The development of the packed tumuli clusters of the Final Kofun period). *Kobunka Danso (Journal of the Society of Kyushu Prehistoric and Ancient Cultural Studies)*, 43:41–79.

Tanabe, Shozo, and Makoto Sahara. 1966. Kinki (The Kinki region). In *Nihon no kokogaku, Vol. 3: Yayoi-jidai* (Japanese archaeology, Vol. 3: The Yayoi period), edited by S. Wajima, 108–140. Tokyo: Kawade-shobo-shinsha.

Tanaka, Migaku. 1970. Matsuri kara matsurigoto he (From rituals to politics). In *Kodai no Nihon, Vol. 5: Kinki* (Japan in the ancient period, Vol. 5: Kinki), edited by K. Tsuboi and T. Kishi, 44–59. Tokyo: Kadokawa Shoten.

Tanaka, Satoshi. 2004. Ezo to Hayato, Nan-to no shakai (The Ezo, Hayato and the society of the "Nanto" Islands). In *Nihonshi koza, Vol. 1: Higashi-Ajia ni okeru kokka no keisei* (Seminars in Japanese history, Vol. 1: State formations in East Asia), edited by Rekishigaku-kenkyu-kai and Nihon-shi-kenkyu-kai, 267–299. Tokyo: Tokyo University Press.

Tanaka, Shinji. 1984. Shutsugen ki kofun no rikai to tenbo: To goku Godo 5 go fun no chosa to kanren shite (An understanding and perspective of the tumuli of the initial Kofun period: As seen from the excavation of Godo No. 5 tumulus). *Kodai*, 77:1–53.

Tanaka, Yoshiaki, ed. 1988. *San'in-chiho ni okeru Yayoi funkyu-bo no kenkyu* (A study of Yayoi period tumuli of the San'in region). Matsue, Japan: Shimane University Laboratory of Archaeology.

Tanaka, Yoshiyuki. 1986. Jomon doki to Yayoi doki: Nishi Nihon (The Jomon and Yayoi potteries: Western Japan). In *Yayoi bunka no kenkyu, Vol. 3* (Studies in the Yayoi culture, Vol. 3), edited by H. Kanaseki and M. Sahara, 115–125. Tokyo: Yusankaku.

———. 1991. Iwayuru torai-setsu no sai-kento (A reconsideration of the "migration theory" in the explanation of the beginning of the Yayoi period). In *Yokoyama Koichi sensei taikan kinen ronbun-shu, Vol. II: Nihon ni okeru shoki noko-bunka no seiritsu* (Collected papers in the celebration of the retirement of Professor Koichi Yokoyama, Vol. II: The establishment of early agrarian culture in Japan), edited by H. Takakura, 482–505. Fukuoka, Japan: Committee for the Celebration of the Retirement of Professor Koichi Yokoyama.

———. 1995. *Kofun-jidai shinzoku-kozo no kenkyu* (A study of the kinship structure of the Kofun period). Tokyo: Kashiwa Shobo.

———. 1999. Doki ga kataru jomon-shakai (The Jomon society as seen from the pottery evidence). *Kitakyushu-shiritsu koko hakubutsukan kenkyu-kiyo (Bulletin of the Kitakyushu Municipal Museum of Archaeology)*, 6:1–22.

———. 2000. Bochi kara mita shinzoku-kazoku (Kin organizations and families as seen from mortuary practices). In *Kodaishi no ronten, Vol. 2: On'na to otoko, ie to mura* (Debates in ancient history, Vol. 2: Women and men, households and villages), edited by H. Tsude and M. Sahara, 131–152. Tokyo: Shogakkan.

———. 2002. Yayoi-jin (The Yayoi people). In *Kodai wo kangaeru: Ine, tetsu, senso* (Considering the ancient period: Rice, iron and war), edited by M. Sahara, 47–76. Tokyo: Yoshikawakobunkan.

Tanaka, Yoshiyuki, Koji Mizoguchi, and Shozo Iwanaga. 2004. Yayoi-jinkotsu wo mochiita AMS-nendai sokutei (A preliminary report on the AMS dating of Yayoi skeletal remains). In *Proceedings of the 6th joint conference of the Kyushu and Yong-nam Archaeological Societies*, 245–251. Pusan: Organising Committee for the 6th Joint Conference of the Kyushu and Yong-nam Archaeological Societies.

Taniguchi, Yasuhiro. 2002. Kanjo-shuraku to buzoku-shakai (The circular settlements and the tribal society of the Jomon period): Zen, Chu-ki no retto chuo-bu (The central area of the archipelago during the Early and Middle Jomon). In *Jomon-shakai ron* (Papers in the Jomon society), edited by M. Anzai, 1:19–65. Tokyo: Doseisha.

———. 2005. *Kanjo-shuraku to Jomon shakai-kozo* (Circular settlements and the Jomon social structure). Tokyo: Gakuseisha.

———. 2010. Jomon-jidai no tateana-kaoku ni miru kukan-bunsetsu to sinborizumu (Spatial segmentation and symbolic representations as seen in Jomon houses). *Bulletin of Kokugakuin University Centre for Traditional Cultural Research*, 2: 37–47.

Tasaki, Hiroyuki. 2006. Setouchi ni okeru Yayoi-shuraku: Ehimeken Bunkyo-iseki no misshu-gata daikibo shuraku, Hokubu-Kyushu tono hikaku (The Yayoi settlements of the Setouchi district: The densely occupied large settlement of the Bunkyo, Ehime prefecture and some comparisons with its northern Kyushu equivalents). In *Proceedings of the 2006 meeting of the Japanese Archaeological Association in Ehime*, edited by Ehime Organising Committee, 17–44. Matsuyama, Japan: Committee for the 2006 Meeting of the Japanese Archaeological Association in Ehime.

Tatetsuki kanko-kai, ed. 1992. *Tatetsuki Yayoi funkyu-bo no kenkyu* (A study of the Tatetsuki Yayoi tumulus). Okayama, Japan: Tatetsuki kanko-kai.

Tatsumi, Kazuhiro. 2006. Kofun-jidai no kyokan to Ogata tatemono (The chiefly residences and large buildings of the Kofun period). In *Yayoi no ogata-tatemono to sono tenkai* (The formation and transformation of the extraordinary large buildings of the Yayoi period), edited by K. Hirose and I. Iba, 193–214. Hikone, Japan: Sunrise Shuppan.

Tenri MBE. 2000. *Tenri-shi maizo-bunkazai chosa hokoku-sho, Vol. 7: Nishitonozuka-kofun, Higashitonozuka-kofun* (Tenri city buried cultural properties research report,

Vol. 7: Nishtonozuka and Higashitonozuka tumuli). Tenri, Japan: Tenri MBE.

Teramae, Naoto. 2006. Seisan to ryutsu kara mita Kinai Yayoi-shakai (The society of the Kinai district in the Yayoi period as seen from the production and circulation of goods). In *Sinpojiumu kiroku* (Symposium records), *No. 5*, edited by Kokogaku-kenkyu-kai-reikai-iinkai, 105–122. Okayama, Japan: Kokogaku kenkyukai.

Terasawa, Kaoru. 1990. Seido-ki no fukuso to obo no keisei (The deposition of bronze implements as burial goods and the emergence of kingly burials). *Kodai-gaku kenkyu (The Study of the Ancient Era)*, 121:1–35.

———. 2000. *Nihon no rekishi, Vol. 2: Oken tanjo* (History of Japan, Vol. 2: The genesis of the kingship). Tokyo: Kodansha.

———. 2010. *Seido-ki no matsuri to seiji-shakai* (The rituals conducted with bronze implements and the politics of the Yayoi period). Tokyo: Yoshikawakobunkan.

Teshigawara, Akira. 1995. *Nihon-kokogaku no ayumi* (The history of Japanese archaeology). Tokyo: Meicho Shuppan.

———. 2005. *Rekishi-kyokasyo ha rekishi wo do kaite kitaka* (How Japanese history has been described in school textbooks). Tokyo: Shin-Nihon Shuppan.

Tilley, Christopher. 1994. *A phenomenology of landscape: Places, paths and monuments*. Oxford, UK: Berg.

Tokushima Prefectural Buried Cultural Properties Research Centre, ed. 1993. *Yano Dotaku* (The Yano Dotaku bronze bell). Tokushima: Tokushima Prefectural Buried Cultural Properties Research Centre.

———. 1997. *Tokushima Prefectural Buried Cultural Properties Research Centre annual bulletin, Vol. 9*. Tokushima, Japan: Tokushima Prefectural Buried Cultural Properties Research Centre.

Tosu MBE. 1984. *Tosu-shi bunkazai chosa-hokoku-sho, Vol. 21: Okadera zenpo-koen-fun* (Tosu city buried cultural properties research reports, Vol. 21: The Okadara keyhole tumulus). Tosu, Japan: Tosu MBE.

Tsuboi, Shogoro. 1888. Ashikaga-kofun hakkutsu hokoku (The excavation report of the Ashikaga tumuli). *Tokyo Jinrui-gaku zasshi (Journal of the Anthropological Society of Tokyo)*, 30:330–380.

Tsuda, Sokichi. 1924. *Shindai-shi no kenkyu* (A study of the mythical era depicted in *Kojiki* and *Nihonshoki*). Tokyo: Iwanami Shoten.

Tsude, Hiroshi. 1984. Noko-shakai no keisei (The formation of the agrarian society). In *Koza Nihon rekishi, Vol. 1: Genshi-kodai 1* (Seminar in Japanese history, Vol. 1: The prehistoric and ancient eras, part 1), edited by Rekishi-gaku-kenkyu-kai and Nihon-shi-kenkyu-kai, 117–158. Tokyo: Tokyo University Press.

———. 1989. *Nihon noko-shakai no seiritsu-katei* (The formation process of agrarian society in Japan). Tokyo: Iwanami Shoten.

———. 1996. Kokka-keisei no sho-dankai (Stages in the state formation process): Shucho-sei, shoki-kokka, seijuku-kokka (chiefdoms, inchoate states, and mature state). *Rekishi-hyoron (Historical Review)*, 551:3–16.

———. 1998. Yayoi kara Kofun he (From the Yayoi to the Kofun period). In *Kodai-kokka ha koshite umareta* (How the Ancient State of Japan Emerged), edited by H. Tsude, 8–50. Tokyo: Kadokawa Shoten.

———. 2005. *Zenpo-koen-fun to shakai* (The keyhole-shaped tumulus and the society). Tokyo: Hanawa Shobo.

Tsugiyama, Jun. 2007. Kofun-jidai shoki no Setouchi ruto wo meguru doki to koryu (Pottery and interaction through the Seto Inland Sea route at the beginning of the Kofun period). *Kokogaku kenkyu (Quarterly of Archaeological Studies)*, 54(3):20–33.

Tsuji, Seiichiro. 1997. Shokubutsu to kiko (The plant and the climate). In *Yayoi-bunka no kenkyu Vol. 1: Yayoi-jin to sono kankyo* (Studies in the Yayoi period, Vol. 1: The Yayoi people and their environment), edited by H. Kanaseki and M. Sahara, 160–173. Tokyo: Yusankaku.

Tsujita, Jun'ichiro. 2007. *Kagami to shoki Yamato seiken* (Bronze mirrors and the early Yamato polity). Tokyo: Suirensha.

Tuzin, Donald. 2001. *Social complexity in the making: A case study among the Arapesh of New Guinea*. London: Routledge.

Ueda, Hironori. 1969. *Zenpo-koen-fun* (The keyhole tumulus). Tokyo: Gakuseisha.

Uehara, Mahito. 1986. Bukkyo (Buddhism). In *Iwanami-koza Nihon Kokogaku, Vol. 4: Shuraku to saishi* (Iwanami seminars in Japanese archaeology, Vol. 4: The settlement and ritual), edited by Y. Kondo and K. Yokoyama, 307–366. Tokyo: Iwanami Shoten.

Ugaki, Tadamasa. 2004. Hotategai-gata kofun no tokusei (The nature of the Hotategai [scallop]-shaped tumulus). In *Kofun-jidai no seiji-kozo: Zenpo-koen-fun karano apuroochi* (The political structure of the Kofun period: As seen from the keyhole tumulus), edited by K. Hirose, M. Kishimoto, T. Ugaki, T. Okubo, M. Nakai and A. Fujisawa, 235–245. Tokyo: Aoki Shoten.

Umehara, Sueji. 1923. Buzen Usa gun Akatsuka kofun chosa-hokoku (The report of the excavation of the Akatsuka tumulus of Usa county, Buzen province). *Kokogaku zasshi (Archaeological Journal)*, 14(3):7–20.

Umemiya, Shigeru and Kenji Otake, eds. 1986. *Ryozen Negoya-iseki no kenkyu (A study of the Ryozen Negoya-iseki): Fukushima-ken Ryozen-machi Negoya ni okeru saiso-bo-gun* (A group of processed bone burials at Negoya, Ryozen town, Fukushima prefecture). Ryozen, Japan: Ryozen TBE.

Uryudo-iseki chosa-kai, ed. 1982. *Uryudo-iseki* (Uryudo site), III. Osaka, Japan: Uryudo iseki chosa-kai.

Wada, Seigo. 1986. Kinzoku-ki no seisan to ryutsu (The production and distribution of bronze implements). In *Iwanami koza Nihon kokogaku, Vol. 3: Seisan to ryutsu* (Iwanami seminars in Japanese archaeology, Vol. 3: Production and distribution), edited by Y. Kondo and K. Yokoyama, 264–313. Tokyo: Iwanami Shoten.

———. 1987. Kofun-jidai no jiki-kubun wo megutte (On the chronological staging of the Kofun period). *Kokogaku kenkyu (Quarterly of Archaeological Studies)*, 34(2):44–55.

———. 2004. Kofun-bunka ron (The Kofun culture). In *Nihonshi koza, Vol. 1: Higashi-Ajia ni okeru kokka no keisei* (Seminars in Japanese history, Vol. 1: State formations in East Asia), edited by Rekishigaku-kenkyu-kai and Nihon-shi-kenkyu-kai, 167–200. Tokyo: Tokyo University Press.

_____. 2007. Kofun-gun no bunseki-shikaku to gunshu-fun (The methodology of the study of Kofun tumuli clusters and the gunshu-fun clustered tumuli). In *Kanto no koki kofun-gun* (The tumuli clusters of the late Kofun period in the Kanto district), edited by K. Sasaki, 7–32. Tokyo: Rokuichi Shobo.

_____. 2008. Yominokuni to yokoana-shiki sekishitu (The Yominokuni netherworld and the mortuary gallery chamber). In *Ware-ware no kokogaku* (Our archaeology), edited by Committee for the Publication of the Collected Papers for Professor Seigo Wada's 60th Birthday, 601–608. Kyoto: Committee for the Publication of the Collected Papers.

_____. 2009. Kofun no takai-kan (The image of the afterlife expressed in and through Kofun mortuary practices). *Kokuritsu rekishi-minzoku hakubutsukan kenkyu hokoku* (*Bulletin of the National Museum of Japanese History*), 152:247–272.

Wajima, Seiichi. 1966. Yayoi-jidai shakai no kozo (The structure of the Yayoi society). In *Nihon no kokogaku, Vol. 3: Yayoi-jidai* (Japanese archaeology, Vol. 3: The Yayoi period), edited by S. Wajima), 1–30. Tokyo: Kawade-shobo-shinsha.

Wakabayashi, Kunihiko. 2001. Yayoi-jidai daikibo shuraku no hyoka (The nature of large-scale Yayoi settlements: The case of the Middle Yayoi period of Osaka plain). *Nihon kokogaku* (*Journal of the Japanese Archaeological Association*), 12:35–53.

_____. 2003. Kinki-chiho no doki (The pottery of the Kinki region). In *Koko-shiryo taikan: Yayoi Kofun jidai doki I, Vol. 1* (The compendium of archaeological materials, I: The pottery of the Yayoi and Kofun periods, Vol. 1), edited by J. Tekesue and H. Ishikawa, 181–252. Tokyo: Shogakkan.

_____. 2006. Kyuryo-jo Yayoi-shuraku to fukugo-shakai no kakudai: Kinki-chiho no jirei kara (Yayoi hilltop settlements and the development of complex society: Some cases from the Kinki district). *Kodai bunka* (*Cultura Antiqua*), 58(2):96–105.

Wakasa, Toru. 2007. *Kofun-jidai no suiri-shakai kenkyu* (The study of the hydraulic control of the Kofun period). Tokyo: Gakuseisha.

Watabe, Yoshimichi. [1936] 1947. *Nihon kodai shakai* (The ancient society of Japan). Tokyo: Mikasa Shobo.

Watabe, Yoshimichi, Jiro Hayakawa, Kimio Izu, and Akira Misawa. 1936. *Nihon rekishi kyotei, Vol. 1: Genshi-shakai no hokai made* (The course in Japanese history, Vol. 1: To the collapse of ancient society). Tokyo: Hakuyosha.

Watanabe, Makoto. 1985. Seihoku-Kyushu no Jomon-jidai gyoro-bunka (The fishery culture of the northwestern Kyushu region of Japan in the Jomon period). *Retto no bunka-shi* (*The Cultural History of Japanese Archipelago*), 2:45–96.

Watanabe, Masahiro. 2001. Kanjo ni meguru Jomon no shuraku to bochi (Circular settlements and cemeteries of the Jomon period). In *Yayoi-jidai no shuraku* (The settlement of the Yayoi period), edited by Osaka Prefectural Museum of Yayoi Culture, 42–51. Tokyo: Gakuseisha.

Watanabe, Takashi. 2007. Toishi kara mita Yayoi-jidai tekki-ka heno shoyoso: Hie-Naka-iseki-gun shutsudo-shiryo yori (The introduction of iron implements to northern Kyushu Yayoi communities as seen from whetstones from Hie and Naka sites of Fukuoka city, Japan). *Kyushu kokogaku* (*Journal of the Archaeological Society of Kyushu*), 82:77–88.

Waters, Malcolm. 1999. General commentary: The meaning of modernity. In *Modernity: critical concepts*, edited by M. Waters, xi–xxiii. London: Routledge.

Wittfogel, Karl. 1957. *Oriental despotism: A comparative study of total power*. New Haven, CT: Yale University Press.

Yamada, Yasuhiro. 1995. Tasuu gasso-rei no igi (The meanings of the collective burials of the Jomon period in the Kanto region). *Kokogaku kenkyu* (*Quarterly of Archaeological Studies*), 42(2):52–67.

_____. 2000. San'in-chiho ni okeru retsu-jo haichi boiki no tenkai (The development of linear-aligned burial grounds in the San'in region). *Shimane-ken koko-gakkai shi* (*Journal of the Shimane Prefectural Archaeological Society*), 17:15–38.

Yamanaka, Toshifumi. 1986. Ritsuryo-kokka no seiritsu (The establishment of the Ritsuryo state). In *Iwanami-koza Nihon Kokogaku, Vol. 6: Henka to Kakki* (Iwanami semianrs in Japanese archaeology, Vol. 6: Changes and stages), edited by Y. Kondo and K. Yokoyama, 227–294. Tokyo: Iwanami Shoten.

Yamanouchi, Sugao. 1925. Sekki-jidai nimo ine ari (The evidence of rice cultivation in the Lithic age). *Jinruigaku-zasshi* (*Journal of Anthropological Society of Nippon*), 40(5): 181–184.

_____. 1967 [1932]. Nippon enko no bunka (Ancient cultures of Japan). In *Senshi-kokogaku ronbun-shu* (Papers in prehistoric archaeology), 1–44. Tokyo: Senshi-kokogaku-kai.

_____. 1937. Jomon doki no taibetsu to saibetsu (The establishment of the phases and regional sequences of the Jomon pottery). *Senshi kokogaku kenkyu* (*Studies in Prehistoric Archaeology*), 1(1):29–32.

Yamao, Yukihisa. 1977. *Nihon-kokka no keisei* (The formation of the Japanese state). Tokyo: Iwanami Shoten.

_____. 1986. *Shinpan Gishi-Wajin-den* (Gishi-Wajin-den chronicle). 2nd ed. Tokyo: Kodansha.

_____. 2003. *Kodai-oken no genzo* (The real image of the ancient Japanese kingship). Tokyo: Gakuseisha.

Yamasaki, Sumio. 1980. Yayoi-bunka seiritsu-ki ni okeru doki no hen'nen-teki kenkyu (A typo-chronological study of the pottery of the Incipient and the Early Yayoi period). In *Kagamiyama Takeshi sensei koki kinen kobunka ronko* (Papers on ancient history in celebration of Professor Takeshi Kagamiyama's 70th birthday), edited by Editorial Committee, 117–192. Fukuoka, Japan: Committee for the Publication of the Volume.

_____. 1987. Hokubu Kyushu ni okeru shoki-suiden (Remains of rice paddy fields of the Incipient and the Early Yayoi periods in northern Kyushu). *Kyushu bunka-shi kenkyusho kiyo* (*Bulletin of the Institute of Kyushu Culture History*), 32:127–186.

_____. 2007. Kyushu ni okeru akkon-shiryo to Jomon-noko (Examples of crop imprints on potsherds in Kyushu and the Jomon farming). In *Nihon Kokogaku-kyokai 2007-nendo Kumamoto taikai kenkyu-happyo shiryo-shu* (The proceedings of the Japanese archaeological association annual meeting in Kumamoto), edited by Local Organising Committee, 344–353. Kumamoto, Japan: Organising Committee.

———. 2008. *Saiko no noson: Itazuke iseki* (The oldest agrarian village: Itazuke site). Tokyo: Shinsensha.

Yanagida, Yasuo. 1983. Ito-koku no kokogaku (The archaeology of the Ito polity): taigai-kosho no haji-mari (the beginning of overseas diplomacy). In *Kyushu rekishi-shiryo kan kaikan 10-shunen kinen Dazaifu kobunka ronso* (Papers in ancient histories related to the Dazaifu ancient provincial capital in celebration of the 10th anniversary of the Kyushu Historical Museum), edited by Kyushu Historical Museum, 1–31. Tokyo: Yoshika-wakobunkan.

———. 1986a. Shudan-bochi kara obo he (From communal cemeteries to kingly burials). In *Hakkutsu ga kataru Nihon-shi* (Japanese history as seen from excavations), *Vol. 6*, edited by K. Yokoyama, 137–147. Tokyo: Shin-Jinbutsuoraisha.

———. 1986b. Seidoki no sosaku to shuen (The emergence and demise of Yayoi bronze implements). *Kyushu kokogaku* (*Journal of the Archaeological Society of Kyushu*), 60:21–40.

———. 2003. Masei-sekken (Polished stone daggers). In *Kasuga-shi bunkazai chosa-hokoku-sho, Vol. 35: Hakugensha-iseki* (Kasuga city buried cultural properties research reports, Vol. 35: Hakugensha site), edited by Y. Yanagida, 98–107. Kasuga, Japan: Kasuga MBE.

Yanagisawa, Kazuo. 1980. Higo-gata yokoana-shiki sekishitsu ko: Shoki yokoana-shiki sekishitsu no keifu (Of the Higo type gallery mortuary chamber: The genealogy of the earliest gallery mortuary chamber of the Japanese archipelago). In *Kagamiyama Takeshi sennsei koki kinen kobunka ronko* (Papers on ancient history in celebration of Professor Takeshi Kagamiyama's 70th birthday), edited by Editorial Committee, 465–497. Fukuoka, Japan: Committee for the Publication of the Volume.

———. 1982. Tateana-kei yokoana-shiki sekishits saiko: shoki yokoana-shiki sekishitsu no keifu (A re-examination of the cist-like morturay chamber with a short entrance). In *Mori Teijiro hakase koki kinen kobunka ronshu* (Papers on ancient history in celebration of Dr. Teijiro Mori's 70th birthday), edited by Editorial Committee, 1051–1109. Fukuoka, Japan: Committee for the Publication of the Volume.

Yane, Yoshimasa. 1984. Jomon-doki kara Yayoi-doki he (From the Jomon to the Yayoi pottery). In *Jomon kara Yayoi he* (From the Jomon to the Yayoi), edited by Tezukayama Institute of Archaeology, 49–91. Nara, Japan: Tezukayama Institute of Archaeology.

Yasu, Hideki. 2009. Hokuriku ni okeru Yayoi-jidai chu-ki ko-ki no shuraku (The settlements of the Middle and Late Yayoi periods of the Hokuriku district). *Kokuritsu rekishi-minzoku hakubutsukan kenkyu hokoku* (*Bulletin of the National Museum of Japanese History*), 149:349–371.

Yasu-cho-shi hensan-iinkai, ed. 1991. *Yasu-cho-shi* (The history of Yasu township). Yasu, Japan: Yasu Township.

Yasuda, Hiroshi. 1998. *Ten'no no seiji-shi* (Emperors in the modern political history of Japan). Tokyo: Aoki Shoten.

Yoffee, Norman. 2005. *Myths of the archaic state: Evolution of the earliest cities, states, and civilizations.* Cambridge: Cambridge University Press.

Yokoana-shiki-sekishitsu kenkyukai, ed. 2007. *Kenkyu-shukai Kinki no yokoana-shiki sekishitsu* (Study meeting on the gallery mortuary chamber of the Kinki district). Nishinomiya, Japan: Gallery Mortuary Chamber Study Group.

Yokohama-shi maizo-bunkazai chosa iinkai. 1980. *Orimotonishihara-iseki* (Orimotonishihara site). Yokohama: Yokohama City Committee for the Research of Buried Cultural Properties.

Yonetani, Tadashi. 2001. Kodai Higashi-Ajia-sekai to Ten'no-shinwa (Ancient East Asian world and the mythology of the emperor). In *Nihon no rekishi, Vol. 8: Kodai Ten'no-sei wo kangaeru* (History of Japan, Vol. 8: Considering the ancient emperor system), 289–341. Tokyo: Kodansha.

Yoshida, Akira. 1998. *Wa-oken no jidai* (The age of the Wa kingship). Tokyo: Shin'nihon Shuppan.

Yoshidome, Hidetoshi. 1992. Juryo ko (A study of the Kofun tumuli constructed before the death of the to-be-buried). In *Kyu-han: Maizo-bunkazai kenkyukai 15-shunen kinen ronbun-shu* (The 15th anniversary volume of the buried cultural properties study group), edited by Editorial Committee of the 15th Anniversary Volume of the Buried Cultural Properties Study Group, 213–222. Toyonaka, Japan: Editorial Committee.

———. 2005. Shoyo-jyurin-tai, kaigan-heiya no suiden (1): Hokubu-Kyushu (The emergence and development of rice paddy field technology). *Kokogaku jyanaru* (*Archaeological Journal*), 518:4–7.

Yoshimura, Kazuaki. 1988. Tanko keifu shiron: byodome-ho donyu igo wo chushin to shite (The geneaology of the iron body armour of the Kofun period). *Kashihara kokogaku kenkyu-sho kiyo* (*Bulletin of Nara Prefectural Kashihara Archaeological Institute*), 13:21–39.

INDEX

Note: Page numbers in *italics* indicate illustrations, figures, or tables.